Who's Who

On Television

A fully illustrated guide to 1000
best known faces on British television

Compiled and produced by ITV Books

ITV BOOKS
in association with Michael Joseph

Editors: Alan Curthoys, Jane Struthers, John Doyle
Designer: Jeremy Dixon

Published by

Independent Television Books Ltd
247 Tottenham Court Road
London W1P 0AU

In association with Michael Joseph Ltd

First published 1982

© Independent Television Books Ltd, 1982

Set in Helvetica 7/8pt by
The Yale Press
Norwood, London

Printed in Great Britain by
William Clowes (Beccles) Ltd
Beccles, Suffolk

Cased edition: 0 900727 96 9
Paperback edition: 0 900727 95 0

CONDITIONS OF SALE

Following a year of preparation and a seemingly endless stream of telephone calls and questionnaires, the New and Revised Edition of Who's Who On Television is ready.

Not everyone we would have wished is in the book: some did not want to be included, others we simply could not contact. To those who are in (almost half the entries are new to this edition), to the Press Offices of the BBC and ITV companies, the agents and all those who have patiently helped in the preparation of this book, we extend our grateful thanks. Our aim has been to make the book the most up-to-date available: without their help this would not have been possible.

We hope you will find this New and Revised Edition of Who's Who On Television as interesting and informative as we have while nursing it through its long gestation period. In most cases throughout the book, we have reported any comments in the words of the entries themselves.

A

West's gardening expert since 1971, his gardening programme being televised from his own garden and woodland just outside Bristol. Holds RHS Senior General Certificate and RHS Teacher's Certificate and in 1978 was made an Associate of Honour by the RHS, a rare honour awarded for distinguished services to his profession. Education: school and technical college, Hackney. m Diana, 1 s Michael. Address: c/o HTV, Bristol. Starsign: Gemini. Hobby: gardening. Person he would most like to meet: 'Twiggy, because she is so typically Cockney and a delight to see.'

manager/ producer rep companies 1954-60. TV: Skyport; Knight Errant; Len Fairclough in Coronation Street since 1961. Several stage tours. Education: elementary schools. m Jean, 2 s Michael, Greig. Address: c/o Granada TV, Manchester. Starsign: Aquarius. Hobbies: swimming, cooking, writing, social work. Person he would most like to have met: 'Aldous Huxley, who so inspired me as a schoolboy, I decided to create a brave new world for myself, which I did at the age of 19.'

ADAMS, Tony
Actor b 11.12.40 Anglesey, North Wales. Trained at the Italia Conti School. TV incl: Kiss Me, Kate (one of BBC 2's opening programmes); The Two Ronnies; Crossroads; For Your Eyes Only; Doctor Who; Court Martial; Crown Court; Bristol 600; General Hospital. Education: Hillgrove, Bangor, North Wales. Address: c/o Michael Ladkin, London WC2. Starsign: Sagittarius. Hobby: sailing. Person he would most like to meet: 'The right person.'

ADAMSON, Peter
Actor b 16.2.30 Liverpool. Started as an amateur, trained at LAMDA, with Fortescue Players, Bury, Lancs 1949-54. Actor/

ABRAMS, John
Horticulturist b 11.6.05 London. Trained in private gardens in the Isle of Wight and Buckinghamshire and did advisory work before becoming Horticultural Officer for Bristol Corporation, a position he held for 18 years until retirement in 1970. HTV

ADDICOTT, Graham
Reporter b 13.10.50 Cardiff, South Wales. Brought up in India and South Africa and started as a reporter on the Johannesburg Sunday Times. Returned to England in 1972 and worked on the Hertfordshire Evening Echo as a reporter before going to Independent Radio News (1973) and HTV Wales (1974). Joined Thames TV as chief reporter Thames News 1975. Is now on Reporting London. Education: St George's, Calcutta, India; Northgate Grammar,

Ipswich; Kempton, Johannesburg, South Africa. Address: c/o Thames TV, London NW1. Starsign: Libra. Hobbies: politics, food, drink. Person he would most like to meet: 'James Cameron – to journalists of my generation he is always the journalistic idol.'

AIRD, Holly
Child actress b 18.5.69 Aldershot, Hants. Still attending ballet school. First part when she was 10 as the young Miss Polly in The History of Mr Polly, followed in 1981 by The Flame Trees of Thika, for which she spent three months in Kenya; The Tales of Beatrix Potter. Education: Bush Davies Ballet School. Address: Danehill, Sussex. Starsign: Taurus. Hobbies: dancing, skiing, sailing, music. Person she would most like to meet: 'Elizabeth Taylor, because she is the best actress in the world.'

ALAN, Ray
Ventriloquist b 18th September, Greenwich, London. At 13 was call boy/lime boy at Lewisham

Hippodrome then started entertaining as magician/impressionist. Added ventriloquism which soon became main attraction to agents and bookers. Famous for his Lord Charles creation which was first tried out at a charity show at Wormwood Scrubs prison. His many TV appearances incl: The Good Old Days; Ice Cabaret; Starburst; Where in the World. Co-presenter of HTV's 3 Little Words with his wife. Education: Morden Terrace School, Lewisham, London. m Barbie. Address: c/o Peter Prichard, London SW1. Starsign: Virgo. Hobbies: model railways, old films. Person he would most like to meet: 'George Burns – I love his sense of humour and delivery.'

ALDA, Alan
Actor b 28.1.36 New York City. Nurse-chasing hero Hawkeye in TV series M*A*S*H. Wanted to be a nightclub comic and though he grew up in Hollywood and was stage trained, his father, actor Robert Alda, tried to persuade him to become a doctor. Professional debut at 16, serving as a theatrical apprentice. Broadway appearance in The Owl and the Pussycat marked the turning point in his career. Films incl: Paper Lion; The Mephisto Waltz; To Kill a Clown; Same Time Next Year; California Suite; The Seduction of Joe Tynan; The Four Seasons; The Glass House. Education: high

school; Fordham University, New York. m clarinetist Arlene, 3 d Eve, Beatrice, Elizabeth. Address: Leonia, New Jersey. Starsign: Aquarius.

ALEXANDER, Terence
Actor b 11.3.23 London. Started with the White Rose Players, Harrogate, when he was 16, followed by wide rep experience before coming to London. Has appeared in many plays incl: Move Over Mrs Markham; Two and Two Make Sex; There Goes the Bride; Fringe Benefits. Films incl: League of Gentlemen; Magic Christian; Waterloo; Run a Crooked Mile; The Day of the Jackal; Internecine Affair. Radio incl: several plays as well as Law and Disorder and two series of The Toff. TV incl: Codename; Forsyte Saga; The Pallisers; Churchill and the Generals; Les Dawson; Dick Emery; Devenish; Unity; Just Liz; Terry and June; Bergerac; Crown Court. Education: Ratcliffe College. m (1st) Juno, (2nd) actress Jane Downs, 2 s Nicholas, Marcus (from 1st m). Address: Fulham, London. Starsign: Pisces. Hobby: searching for drinkable wine at a reasonable price. Person he would most like to meet: 'The owner of Chateau Mouton Rothschild to help him drink some of it.'

ALLEN, Patrick
Actor b 17.3.27 Malawi. Came to England as a child

and was evacuated to Canada during the war. Returned to England in 1953 after local radio station experience. Has worked with the Royal Shakespeare Company. Films incl: Dial M for Murder; High Tide at Noon; I Was Monty's Double; Dunkirk; The Night of the Generals; The Troubleshooters; The Gold Robbers; Codename; Puppet on a Chain; The Wilby Conspiracy; Murder Is Easy; Winds of War; Who Dares Wins. TV incl: Crane; Brett; Hard Times; Kidnapped; The Trial of Lady Chatterley; A Spy At Evening; The Brack Report. The voice behind countless TV commercials and has big business interests. Education: McGill University, Montreal. m actress Sarah Lawson, 2 s Stephen, Stuart. Address: c/o ICM, London W1. Starsign: Pisces. Hobby: fishing.

ALLSOP, Malcolm
Political editor b 9.9.50 London. Experience on newspapers, BBC local radio and BBC TV before joining Anglia TV. Presenter and editor of weekly current affairs programme Anglia Reports and political magazine Members Only. Producer of network documentaries In Troubled Waters and More British Than the British. Education: Highbury Grammar School, London. m Elaine, 1 s Timothy. Address: c/o Anglia TV. Starsign: Virgo. Person he would most like to have met: 'Lloyd George, because my father didn't know him!'

ANDREWS, Anthony
Actor b 12.1.48 London. Started stage career at Chichester Festival Theatre. TV play A Beast With Two Backs led to a long line of TV appearances incl: Doomwatch; Dixon of Dock Green; Follyfoot; The Fortunes of Nigel; The Pallisers; David Copperfield; Upstairs, Downstairs; The Duchess of Duke Street; French Without Tears; London Assurance; The Country Wife; A Superstition; Romeo and Juliet; Danger UXB; Brideshead Revisited (for which he won the BAFTA Award for Best TV Actor 1981); The Love Boat; The Black Bayu; La Ronde; Ivanhoe. Recent stage appearances incl: The Dragon Variation. Films incl: War of The Children; Operation Daybreak. Education: Royal Masonic School, Herts. m former actress Georgina, 1 d Jessica, 1 s Joshua. Address: c/o ICM, London W1. Starsign: Capricorn. Hobby: riding.

ANDREWS, Eamonn CBE (Hon)
Commentator/interviewer/presenter b 19.12.22 Dublin. Started as a boxing commentator on radio 1939, Radio Eireann 1941-50, BBC radio 1950, BBC TV 1951. TV incl: What's My Line?; Crackerjack; World of Sport; This is Your Life; Today; Time For Business; The Eamonn Andrews Show; Top of the World. Extensive business interests. Former All-Ireland Amateur Junior Boxing Champion (middle weight). Books: This is My Life; Surprise of Your Life. Education: the Irish Christian Brothers, Synge St, Dublin. m Grainne, 2 d Emma, Niamh, 1 s Fergal (all adopted). Address: c/o Thames TV, London NW1. Starsign: Sagittarius. Hobbies: walking and talking. Person he would most like to have met: 'William Shakespeare, so that I could ask him where he got all the energy from.'

ANGEL, Barry
Actor b 9.2.62 Manchester.

No formal acting training. First TV role was in Agony as the troubled office boy. Other TV incl: The Professionals; Codename Icarus; The London Programme. Education: Bury Grammar School, Lancs. Address: c/o Barry Brown Management, London SE11. Starsign: Aquarius. Hobbies: sport, music, fast cars. Person he would most like to meet: Barbra Streisand.

ANNIS, Francesca
Actress b 14.5.44 London. Trained for ballet at the Corona Academy but switched to drama after appearing in an Armchair Theatre play. Since been in rep at Richmond, Oxford and Leicester and with the RSC. Stage incl: The Sun and the Wind; Ophelia to Nicol Williamson's Hamlet in America; A Month in the Country (National Theatre). Films incl: Cleopatra; Run With the Wind; The Walking Stick; Macbeth; Coming Out of the Ice; Krull. TV incl: The Human Jungle; Heritage; Danger Man; Dr Finlay's Casebook; Great Expectations; View from the Bridge; The Family is a Vicious Circle; Edward the Seventh; Lillie (TV Times Best Actress on TV 1978-79); Why Didn't They Ask Evans?; Partners in Crime.
1 d Charlotte.
Address: c/o ICM London W1. Starsign: Taurus. Hobby: travel.

ANTHONY, Patrick
Presenter/journalist/announcer/actor b 20.4.45 Dublin. Trained in restaurant management before joining Chesterfield rep for the 1970-71 season. Station announcer for HTV 1973-76, then moved to Anglia TV. Stage incl: Old Time Music Hall chairman; plays with Chesterfield and Shanklin reps; dolphin presenter/compère at London Dolphinarium. Radio: school plays for Radio 4. TV incl: presenter for Anglia's The Next Week Show; About Anglia; Patrick's Pantry (weekly cookery item now in its 4th year); Jobline (series of programmes for the unemployed); World Freestyle Dancing Championships 1981 regional final. Vocal characterisation Tales of the Unexpected, Bygones, etc. Books: Patrick's Pantry; The Drinker's Companion (with Derek Nimmo). Education: De La Salle College, Dublin. m Vanessa, 1 d Francesca, 1 s Laurence. Address: c/o Anglia TV, Norwich. Starsign: Aries. Hobbies: TV, theatre books, haute cuisine. Person he would most like to have met: 'Mrs Beeton, to ask her for her favourite recipe.'

APANOWICZ, Kathryn
Actress b 3.6.60 Horsforth, Leeds. Started in Yorkshire TV's Junior Showtime, was in the film Bugsie Malone and has since presented Calendar Kids. TV incl:

Rooms; Black Stuff; Happy Since I Met You; Angels. Education: St Joseph's College, Leeds. Address: c/o Hamper-Neafsey Assocs, London W1. Starsign: Gemini. Hobbies: taking bad photographs, going to the cinema. Person she would most like to meet: 'Terry Wogan, because he always has something different to say.'

ARCHER, Geoffrey
ITN defence and science correspondent b 21.5.44 London. Formerly a solicitor's articled clerk. Worked as researcher, reporter and producer for Southern TV 1964, Anglia TV 1965, and Tyne Tees TV before joining ITN in 1970, for which he has reported widely in Europe, Africa, the Middle East and Britain. Education: Highgate School, London. m Eva, 1 d Alison, 1 s James. Address: c/o ITN, London W1. Starsign: Taurus/Gemini. Hobbies: gardening, cooking and eating, sailing.

ARNESS, James
Actor b 26.5.23 Minneapolis, USA. Started in

school plays and operettas. Served in Italian campaign in Second World War and was injured on the Anzio beach-head. Discharged in 1945, tried radio announcing; radio dramatic roles made him decide to make acting his career. To Hollywood and his first role in The Farmer's Daughter, then Battleground and 20 films in next three years. Other films incl: Island in the Sky; Hondo; Her Twelve Men; Many Rivers to Cross; Them; The Sea Chase; Hellgate. (Hellgate led to his part as Marshal Matt Dillon in Gun Law, perhaps his most famous role, which he played for 20 years, and which he first turned down.) Then took role of Zeb Macachan in How the West Was Won and more recently McClain's Law. Education: Beloit College, Wisconsin. m (1st) actress Virginia Chapman (dis), (2nd) actress Janet Surtees, 1 d Jenny (dec) (from 1st m), 2 s Craig, Rolf (from 1st m). Starsign: Gemini.

ARTHUR, Toni
Singer/actress b 26.12.41 Oxford. Originally trained as a nurse but went into show business, touring the world with her husband as a folk music duo in the early 1960s. Never happier than when entertaining children and between TV appearances devotes a lot of her time to voluntary work with young people. Her stage show, Toni Arthur's Music Box, designed to develop children's appreciation of music, was designed by her husband, an authority on British folklore. TV incl: Play School; Playaway; Take a Ticket To . . .; Seeing and Doing; What Do You Watch?; Watch This Space. Records incl: Play-A-Way; Bang on a Drum; Sing a Story; and songs from Seeing and Doing. Book: All the Year Round. Education: Mary Datchelor's Girls' School, Camberwell; Royal Academy of Music. m Dave Arthur, 2 s Jonathan, Timothy. Address: c/o Mason Joseph, London NW3. Starsign: Capricorn. Hobbies: studying women's lore, making cosmetics, learning any new strange musical instrument that comes along (she owns 14 musical instruments and can play every one), collecting folk tales. Person she would most like to meet: 'Diana Dors – I think she is the epitome of everything women should stand for, but don't, because they shout too much!'

ASHCROFT, Dame Peggy
Actress b 22.12.07 Croydon. Studied for the stage at the Central School of Dramatic Art under Elsie Fogerty and gained the Diploma of Dramatic Art awarded by London University. First stage appearance in Birmingham in 1926 and London debut the following year. In the course of a distinguished theatrical career of almost 60 years she has become the First Lady of Shakespearian Theatre, having played all the great Shakespearian heroines as well as parts in classical and contemporary plays. Played leading roles at the Old Vic and Sadlers Wells before the war, joined John Gielgud's company for his London season 1937-38 and was in Shakespearian seasons at Stratford-upon-Avon in 1953, 1957 and 1960, becoming a long-term contract player with the company in 1961 (when it was re-named the Royal Shakespeare Company), and a director of the company in 1968. In 1963 played Margaret of Anjou in The Wars of the Roses trilogy at Stratford and London. Joined the National Theatre at the Old Vic in 1975 and appeared as Lilian Bayliss in the National Theatre's farewell to the Old Vic 1976. In Nov 1962 she spoke the prologue at the opening of the Ashcroft Theatre, Croydon, so-named in her honour. First TV appearance in Shadow of Heroes, 1956. Other TV incl: The Cherry Orchard; The Wars of the Roses; Days in the Trees; Edward and Mrs Simpson; Caught on a Train; Cream in My Coffee; The Jewel in the Crown. Awarded CBE in Birthday Honours 1951; created DBE in Birthday Honours 1956. Many honorary degrees. BAFTA Award for Best TV Actress 1980. Education: Woodford School, Croydon. m (1st) Rupert Hart-Davis (dis), (2nd) Theodore Komisarjevsky (dis), (3rd) Jeremy Nicholas

Hutchinson (dis), 1 d Eliza, 1 s Nicholas. Address: c/o ICM, London W1. Starsign: Capricorn.

ASHLEY, Caroline
Actress/presenter b 4.3.58 Lancashire. Trained at the Scottish Royal Academy of Music, Glasgow and Queen Margaret Drama School, Edinburgh. Taught drama for a short time before joining the cast of Take the High Road in 1980. Education: Coatbridge High School. Address: c/o PVA Management Ltd, London W1. Starsign: Pisces. Hobbies: horse-riding, theatre-going, badminton. People she would most like to meet: 'Andrew Lloyd Webber and Tim Rice, so they could write me a hit musical.'

ASKEY, Arthur CBE
Comedian/entertainer b 6.6.1900 Liverpool. On leaving school became a Liverpool Corporation clerk. Started professional career 1924 with a touring concert party. Summer seasons; after-dinner entertainer in London; Palladium; revues; musical comedies; comedies; Royal Command Performances. Radio from 1938: Band Wagon; Forever Arthur; Big Time; Arthur's Inn; Hello Playmates. Films: Band Wagon; Charlie's Aunt; The Ghost Train; I Thank You; King Arthur Was a Gentleman; Miss London Ltd; Ramsbottom Rides Again. Stage: The Love Racket; Follow the Girls; The Kid from Stratford. TV: started in the early days of TV and has since appeared in almost every major programme, incl reading the lesson in the Epilogue; Before Your Very Eyes; Living It Up; The A A Show; Raise Your Glasses; Comedy Bandbox; Jokers Wild; The Blackpool Show. Education: Liverpool Institute. m Elizabeth (dec), 1 d actress Anthea. Address: Kensington, London. Starsign: Gemini. Hobbies: reading biographies, watching sport live and on TV; walking. Person he would most like to have met: Sir Winston Churchill.

ASNER, Edward
Actor b 15.11.26 Kansas City. Started acting career in school production of Richard II as Duke of York. Worked as delivery boy, cab driver, post office worker and shoe salesman after discharge from the army in 1953. Appeared in several off-Broadway productions until 1960 when he played opposite Jack Lemmon in Face of a Hero. This led to the part of Det Lt Burti in TV series Naked City. Moved to Hollywood in 1961. Comedy part as Mary Tyler Moore's boss in the Mary Tyler Moore Show led to his role in the award-winning Lou Grant in 1972. Films incl: Peter Gunn; The Slender Thread; The Satan Bug; Kid Galahad; Fort Apache, The Bronx; O'Hara's Wife. TV incl: Rich Man, Poor Man; Holocaust; The Gathering; Roots. Education: University of Chicago. m Nancy, 1 d Katherine, twins Liza, Matthew. Starsign: Scorpio.

ASPEL, Michael
Broadcaster/writer b 12.1.33 London. After a brief business career became a radio actor with BBC rep company in Cardiff 1954. BBC TV announcer and newsreader in London 1957-68 when he switched to freelancing, both on radio and TV. Radio incl: Today; Family Favourites; daily programme on Capital Radio. TV incl: Ask Aspel; Crackerjack; Aspel and Company; Give Us a Clue. Book: Polly Wants a Zebra. Education: Emanuel School, London. m actress Elizabeth Power. Address: c/o Bagenal Harvey Organisation, London W1. Starsign: Capricorn. Hobbies: cinema, travel, letter-writing. Person he would most like to meet: 'Too late, I've done it.'

ASTLEY, Gordon
Presenter b 1.12.48 Lytham St Annes, Lancs. Experience with BBC local radio (Radio

Stoke and Mercia Sound) before going into BBC Schools TV. Former presenter of We're Going Places and Cheggers Plays Pop and, since Sept 1981, with Tiswas. Education: Bromsgrove High School. m, 1 d, 1 s. Address: c/o London Management, London W1. Starsign: Sagittarius. Hobbies: comedy, music hall. Person he would most like to meet: 'Woody Allen – my hobby is comedy and he is the ultimate in stand-up comedy.'

ATKINSON, Rowan
Actor/writer b 6.1.55 Newcastle-upon-Tyne. Trained as an electrical engineer but decided on a show business career while at university. First came to viewers' notice in Canned Laughter in 1979. Has made numerous guest appearances in various programmes incl: The Innes Book of Records; The Lena Zavaroni Show; The Peter Cook Show; The Secret Policeman's Ball, but first came into prominence in Not the Nine O'Clock News (1980). Variety Club Award

Best BBC Personality of the Year 1980. Education: St Bee's School, Cumbria; Newcastle University; The Queen's College, Oxford (BSc, MSc Oxon). Address: c/o Noel Gay Ltd, London WC2. Starsign: Capricorn. Hobbies: all good music, electronics, truck driving.

ATTENBOROUGH, David CBE
Broadcaster and traveller b 8.5.26 London. After service in the Royal Navy, worked for a firm of educational book publishers. Joined BBC TV as trainee producer 1952. Two years later he made the first of his famous Zoo Quest programmes. Is now an acknowledged expert on the world's wildlife and his TV has incl: The Tribal Eye; Wildlife on One; Eastward with Attenborough and the mammoth 13-part series, Life on Earth. For that series he and his team travelled a million and a half miles, visited more than 30 countries and shot one and a quarter million feet of film. Controller of BBC 2 1965-68 and as such saw the channel into colour. Director of BBC TV programmes 1969-72, resigning from that post to return to programme making. Many awards and honours incl: Hon DLitt, Leicester; Hon DSc Liverpool; Hon LLD Bristol; Hon Fellow Manchester Polytechnic; Special Award, Society of Film and TV Arts (1961);

Silver Medal, Zoological Society of London (1966); Silver Medal, Royal Television Society (1966); Desmond Davies Award, Society of Film and TV Arts (1970); Cherry Kearton Medal and Award, RGS (1972). Books incl: Zoo Quest to Guiana; Zoo Quest for a Dragon; Zoo Quest in Paraguay; Quest in Paradise; Zoo Quest in Madagascar; Quest Under Capricorn; Tribal Eye; Life on Earth. Education: Wyggeston Grammar, Leicester; Clare College, Cambridge (Hons Degree Natural Sciences). m Jane, 1 d Susan, 1 s Robert. Address: c/o BBC, London W12. Starsign: Taurus. Hobby: collecting almost anything.

AVILA, Kay
TV reporter b 5.2.46 Whitstable, Kent. Research in newspapers, House of Commons, radio and TV incl: Westward and Thames TV where she is working on After Noon Plus. Education: Winchester County High; Surrey University (BSc Human Relations). m Adam Hoee. Address: c/o Thames TV, London NW1. Starsign: Aquarius. Hobbies: cooking, gardening, painting, playing piano. Person she would most like to have met: 'F Scott Fitzgerald, because he was so outrageous and such a good writer.'

AYRES, Rosalind
Actress b 7.12.46
Birmingham. Three-year
teacher-training course
specialising in drama at
Loughborough College of
Education, before becoming
an actress. TV incl: Nearest
and Dearest; Coronation
Street; The Lovers; Home
And Away; Suspicion;
General Hospital; Country
Matters; Father Brown;
Hindle Wakes; Affairs of the
Heart; Within These Walls;
The Limbo Connection;
Holding On; Public Eye;
Warship; Two's Company;
Dick Emery Show; Rings On
Their Fingers; Agony; The
Gentle Touch; Jackanory;
Psywarriors; The Bounder;
many plays. Appeared at
Windsor and Nottingham and
in London's West End
(I Claudius; Dracula). Films
incl: That'll Be The Day;
Stardust; Little Malcolm; The
Slipper and the Rose. Radio
incl: Evan Harrington;
Pickwick Papers; The Circle;
Room With a View; As You
Like It. Education: George
Dixon Grammar School for
Girls, Birmingham. m actor
Martin Jarvis. Address: c/o
Plant & Froggatt, London W1.
Starsign: Sagittarius.
Hobbies: interior decorating,
sewing.

AZIZ, Khalid
Broadcaster b 9.8.53
Lahore, Pakistan. Came to
this country when he was 10
months old and was brought
up in the West Country and
London. First broadcast for
BBC Plymouth when he was
16 and a year later made his
first TV report for Spotlight
South West. Spent a year
working for Radio 4 followed
by a year in the family
restaurant business. Then
moved to the East Midlands
as a freelance local radio
reporter and became
producer at Radio Leicester
when he was 21. Specialising
in community relations, made
the documentary Daughters
of Tradition for BBC
Midlands, on the plight of
Asian girls trapped between
two cultures, and secured the
first interview with an illegal
immigrant. Went to Leeds in
1977 as reporter on Look
North and became the
programme's presenter in
1979. Other TV incl: What Am
I Bid?; The Object in
Question; Lifelines;
Multi-coloured Swop Shop;
Mainstream; Close-Up North.
Has presented current affairs
programme Coast to Coast
for TVS since Jan 1982.
Education: Dulwich College
Preparatory School;
Aitcheson College, Lahore;
Westminster City School.
m Barbara, 2 d Nadira,
Fleur. Address: c/o PVA
Management Ltd, London
W1. Starsign: Leo. Hobbies:
squash, riding, flying
(aeroplanes and autogyros),
shooting, fishing. Person he
would most like to meet: 'The
Dalai Lama, to learn about a
really alternative way of
living.'

B

BACON, John
Newsreader/announcer
b 12.4.35 Norwich. Started
with BBC late 1959 and
joined Anglia TV early 1964.
Education: King Edward VI
School, Norwich. Address:
c/o Anglia TV, Norwich.
Starsign: Aries. Hobbies:
musical instruments, music,
books. Person he would most
like to meet: Sammy Davis
Jnr.

BACON, Jim
Weatherman b 22.6.50
Newmarket. Has been a
meteorologist since leaving
school in 1968. After serving
at various weather stations,
incl the Bracknell
headquarters, he joined the
London Weather Centre in
July 1978 and has been a
regular BBC weatherman
since Feb 1979. Education:
Thetford Grammar School;
Reading University (BSc
Met). m Marie-Louise.
Address: c/o London
Weather Centre, London
WC1. Starsign: Cancer.
Hobby: amateur radio.

BAILEY, Robin
Actor b. 5.10.19 Hucknall,
Nottingham. Began his
working life in the Post Office,
then moved to the War Office
and became interested in
amateur dramatics. Joined
Nottingham Theatre Royal as
an actor in 1938. Also in rep at
Newcastle-upon-Tyne,
Birmingham, Worthing
before coming to London.
Appeared in many plays
since. Films incl: Private
Angelo; Catch Us If You Can;
Blind Terror. Served during
the war in the RASC.
Appeared in many TV
programmes, incl:
compèring The 64,000
Challenge. Recent TV incl:
The Pallisers; Upstairs,
Downstairs; North and South;

Punch Revue; A Legacy;
I Didn't Know You Cared; For
Services Rendered; If You Go
Down In The Woods; Cupid's
Dart; Sorry, I'm A Stranger
Here Myself; Jane.
Education: Henry Mellish
School, Nottingham.
m Patricia, 3 s Nicolas,
Simon, Justin. Address: c/o
Derek Glynne Ltd, London
SW1. Starsign: Libra.
Hobbies: gardening, cricket.
Person he would most like to
meet: 'Vaclav Havel, the
dissident Czech playwright. I
did one of his plays last year.
He is in prison in
Czechoslovakia and if I were
able to meet him, it would
mean he is free.'

BAKER, Colin
News and current affairs
presenter/reporter b 11.4.48
Bilston, Staffs. Journalistic
experience incl news agency
and Daily Sketch, before
joining Ulster TV in 1973 and
moving to BBC in 1977.
Thames TV since 1979.
Education: Bilston Grammar.
m Edna, 2 s Colin, Richard.
Address: c/o Thames TV,
London NW1. Starsign: Aries.
Hobbies: golf, collecting
airline sick-bags and menus.
Person he would most like to
have met: Gershwin or Cole
Porter.

BAKER, George
Actor/writer/director
b 1.4.31 Bulgaria. Always
wanted to be an actor and
after several jobs and
National Service, worked in
almost every rep in the
country. Has since been in 20

13

plays in London's West End and seasons with the Old Vic and Royal Shakespeare Company. Recently directed The Lady's Not For Burning at the Old Vic. More than 40 appearances in films incl: The Dambusters; The Ship That Died of Shame; The Moonraker; A Hill in Korea; Goodbye Mr Chips; On Her Majesty's Secret Service; The Thirty Nine Steps; Hopscotch. On TV he has been in more than 100 plays and also starred in his own series, Bowler, a spin-off from the character he played in The Fenn Street Gang. Other TV incl: Death of a Salesman; Medea; Candida; Rupert of Hentzau; I Claudius (as Tiberius); and more recently Goodbye Darling; Triangle. Is the author of the award-winning TV play, The Fatal Spring. Education: Lancing College. m actress Sally Home, 1 d Sarah. Four other daughters by previous marriage. Address: c/o ICM, London W1. Starsign: Aries.

BAKER, Richard OBE
Newsreader/presenter
b 15.6.25 Willesden, London. Cambridge ADC and Footlights; actor 1948-49; joined BBC 1950; radio announcer 1951-54. TV since 1954, newsreader on BBC 1 and 2, commentator on major events, particularly royal visits and concerts such as The Proms, panelist on BBC 2's Face The Music. Hon LL D, Strathclyde University. Book: Mozart. Education: Kilburn Grammar; Peterhouse; Cambridge University (MA). m Margaret Martin, 2 s Andrew, James. Address: c/o BBC London. Starsign: Gemini. Hobbies: music, sailing. Person he would most like to meet: 'The Pope. I profoundly admire the way he lives out his beliefs with courage and compassion.'

BAKEWELL, Joan
Interviewer b 16th April Stockport, Cheshire. Started as studio manager for BBC radio. Many radio programmes incl: PM on Radio 4; Newsquiz. TV incl: Sunday Break; Home at 4.30; Meeting Point; Late Night Line-Up; Holiday 75,76,77; The Brontë Business; The Shakespeare Business; Reports Action; BBC TV Arts Correspondent since 1981. Books: The New Priesthood; British Television Today; A Fine and Private Place; The Complete Traveller. Education: Stockport High for Girls; Cambridge University (Economics, History). m (1st) TV director Michael Bakewell, (2nd) Jack Emery, 1 d Harriet, 1 s Matthew (both from 1st m). Address:

c/o A D Peters, London WC2. Starsign: Aries. Hobbies: travel, theatre.

BALL, Bobby
Comedian b 28.1.44 Oldham. Half of the comedy partnership, Cannon and Ball. Former workmates in a Lancashire engineering factory by day and a singing duo, The Harper Brothers, at night. Changed names to Cannon and Ball nine years ago and are now major club and theatre attractions. Voted clubland's top comedy duo 1975. Summer seasons in Bournemouth, Jersey, Cleethorpes and Great Yarmouth and pantomine in Bradford, Leeds, Stockport and Liverpool. TV incl: Wheeltappers and Shunters' Social Club; Bruce Forsyth's Big Night; and their own series, Cannon and Ball. Education: High Crompton Secondary, Shaw, Oldham. m Yvonne, 1 d Joanne, 2 s Darren, Robert. Address: c/o Stuart Littlewood Assocs, Oldham, Lancs. Starsign: Aquarius. Hobby: fishing. Person he would most like to meet: 'Max Wall, because I think he is a genius.'

BALL, Johnny
Writer/presenter b 23.5.38 Bristol. National Service, Butlin's Redcoat, Northern club and cabaret before going into TV. Apart from numerous appearances on radio and TV variety shows, has concentrated on children's TV since 1967, incl

Play School, Playaway and Star Turn. Created Cabbages and Kings and such entertaining maths and science programmes as the Think programmes – Think of a Number; Think Again; Think Backwards and Think This Way, the latest in the series. Education: Bolton County Grammar School, Lancs. m Dianne, 1 d Zoe, 2 s Nicholas, Daniel. Address: c/o Roger Hancock Ltd, London SW1. Starsign: Gemini. Hobbies: recreational maths and games, furniture making, supporting Liverpool FC. Person he would most like to meet: 'Martin Gardner, the mathematical games editor for Scientific American, to thank him for his inspiration and pick up some more.'

BARKER, Ronnie OBE
Actor/comedian b 25.9.29 Bedford. Started as an amateur; Aylesbury Rep 1948, then Manchester and Oxford. Films incl: Futtocks End; Home of Your Own; Robin and Marian; Porridge. Radio incl: Floggitts; The Navy Lark. TV incl: I'm Not Bothered; Frost Report;

Foreign Affairs; The Ronnie Barker Playhouse; Frost On Sunday; Hark at Barker; 6 Dates With Barker; His Lordship Entertains; A Midsummer Night's Dream; Seven of One; The Picnic; The Two Ronnies; Porridge; Open All Hours; Going Straight. Education: City of Oxford High School. m Joy Tubb, 1 d Charlotte, 2 s Larry, Adam. Address: c/o Peter Eade Ltd, London W1. Starsign: Libra. Hobby: collecting Victoriana (postcards, books and prints). Person he would most like to have met: 'John Logie Baird, just to thank him, on behalf of us all.'

BARKWORTH, Peter
Actor b 14.1.29 Margate. Trained at RADA and, after rep at Folkestone, was called up for the army. Returned to more rep at Folkestone and Sheffield. West End successes incl: Roar Like A Dove; Crown Matrimonial (and on TV); Donkey's Years; Can You Hear Me at the Back?; A Coat of Varnish. Directed Sisterly Feelings (Theatre Royal, Brighton). TV incl: The Power Game; Manhunt; A Death in the Family; Rasputin; The Passenger; The Rivals of Sherlock Holmes; The Company Man; Intent to Murder; Melissa; The Country Party; The Saturday Party; Professional Foul; Secret Army; Telford's Change; Winston Churchill The Wilderness Years. Book: About Acting. Education:

Stockport. Address: c/o London Management, London W1. Starsign: Capricorn. Hobbies: looking at the countryside, and at paintings, listening to music, walking, gardening, entertaining. Person he would most like to meet: 'Myself at 20: I could tell him a thing or two.'

BARLOW, Thelma
Actress b 19th June Middlesbrough, Yorks. Secretary in Huddersfield before joining Joan Littlewood's Theatre Workshop in East London. Then in rep before joining Coronation Street as Mavis in 1974. Education: in Huddersfield. m drama lecturer Graham Barlow, 2 s Clive, James. Address: c/o Granada TV, Manchester Starsign: Gemini. Hobbies: yoga, cookery, growing herbs, wine-making, making her own clothes. Person she would most like to have met: 'My father, who died six weeks before I was born.'

BARNES, Bobby
Professional wrestler b 27.8.39 Lewisham,

London. Spent three years as an amateur before turning professional. Has since wrestled in Spain, France, Germany, Holland and Belgium as well as Britain. Education: Brockley County Grammar School. m Jeanette, 1 d Bobbie-Jean, 2 s Steven, Antony. Address: c/o Dale Martin Promotions, London SW9. Starsign: Virgo. Hobbies: swimming, cycling, collecting video films. Person he would most like to meet: 'Muhammad Ali, the world's greatest sportsman and showman.'

BARNES, Carol
TV journalist b 13.9.44 Norwich. One-time public relations officer at London's Royal Court Theatre. Before joining ITN was in radio (BBC and LBC) where she was also a reporter, and production manager on Time Out magazine. Education: St Martin in the Fields High School; South West London College; Sheffield University (BA Languages and teaching diploma). m Nigel Thomson, 1 d Clare, 1 s. Address: c/o ITN, London W1. Starsign: Virgo. Hobbies: skiing, good food.

BARNES, Paul
Presenter/reporter b 31.7.39 Coventry. Many years in the advertising and documentary film business, ultimately as a director (Black Five; King George V; Tanker) before becoming contributor and presenter for numerous radio and TV programmes

which incl: Today; World at One; Woman's Hour; In Vision; Parents and Children; The Winners; The Book Programme; Six-O-One (Granada); ATV Today; Write Now; About Anglia; and two series of Portrait of a Village. Education: Leamington College; Coventry College of Art. m Jean, 2 s Matt, Dan. Address: Hatfield, Herts. Starsign: Leo. Hobbies: early transport (railways in particular), preserving old vehicles (he owns a steam-roller and a single-deck bus), jazz (especially big bands), riding. Person he would most like to meet: 'Too numerous to mention.'

BARON, Lynda
Actress b 24th March Manchester. Ballet-trained at the Royal Academy of Dancing. Appeared in all kinds of entertainment from cabaret, Principal Boy in pantomime and films to plays in London's West End and TV. Her stage appearances incl: Living For Pleasure; The Bedwinner; Real Inspector Hound; One Over the Eight; Bedful of Foreigners; After

Magrit; Talk of the Town. Has also been in Move Over Mrs Markham; Not Now, Darling; Goodbye Charlie; Butterflies Are Free; Abigail's Party. First caught the eye of viewers in That Was The Week That Was. Apart from being a guest on dozens of TV programmes, TV incl: Play of the Month; Don't Forget to Write; Heartlands; Grundy; Open All Hours. Education: Flixton Girls' School. m John M Lee, 1 d Sarah, 1 s Morgan. Address: c/o Peter Charlesworth Ltd, London SW7. Starsign: Aries. Hobbies: writing, wine-making, squash. Person she would most like to have met: 'My great-great-grandmother. Being fascinated by the past I could hear of it first-hand.'

BARRACLOUGH, Roy
Actor b 12.7.35 Preston, Lancs. No formal training; entered the profession from an engineering works when he was 28, has since appeared in many TV comedy shows and is probably best known for his Les Dawson partnership in the Les Dawson shows. Starred in his own children's series, Pardon My Genie, and claims the record, with George Waring, for appearing as the most characters in Coronation Street. Education: local grammar school. Address: c/o Norman Murray and Anne Chudleigh Ltd, London W1. Starsign: Cancer. Hobbies: good food, music.

BARRON, George
Gardener b 8.3.14
Aberdeen. Co-presenter,
with Jim McColl, of BBC
Scotland's gardening
programme, Beechgrove
Garden. Started as
apprentice at Monymusk
House gardens and after four
years went to the Botanic
Gardens, Aberdeen. After a
further four years there he
went to Mount Blary House,
near Turriff, where he stayed
for nine years, five of them as
head gardener. In 1948 he
went to work at Pitmedden
House (now National Trust),
where he remained for 30
years until his retirement in
1978. For his services to
horticulture in Scotland he
was awarded the Royal
Caledonian Horticultural
Society's medal in 1977.
Education: public school at
Pitmedden. m Mima,
1 d Aileen. Address: c/o
BBC, Aberdeen. Starsign:
Pisces. Hobby: woodwork.
Person he would most like to
meet: 'Jim Davidson – an
excellent comedian.'

BARRON, John
Actor b 24.12.20
Marylebone, London.

Trained at RADA, then rep at
Croydon, Leicester and
Brighton. Apart from war
service in Royal Navy, has
been an actor all his working
life. Films incl: Jigsaw; The
Great Question. TV incl: Fly
Away Peter; Emergency –
Ward 10; Softly, Softly; All
Gas and Gaiters;
Doomwatch; Crown Court;
Timeslip; Ace of Wands; The
Fall and Rise of Reginald
Perrin; The Foundation;
Potter; Bernie; Spooner's
Patch; Shelley; The Glums;
The Wizard of Crumm; Yes,
Minister; To The Manor Born;
The Gentle Touch; The
Taming of the Shrew; Othello;
Cowboys; Whoops
Apocalypse. Education:
Portsmouth Grammar.
m actress Joan Peart,
1 step-d. Address: c/o Green
and Underwood, London W3.
Starsign: Capricorn. Hobby:
collecting wine. Person he
would most like to meet:
'Admiral of the Fleet Earl
Beatty – the last naval hero.'

BARRON, Keith
Actor b 8.8.34 Mexborough,
Yorks. After working in the
family wholesale provision
business, started acting
career with Sheffield Rep.
Small parts on TV and
appearances at Bristol Old
Vic led to The Odd Man and
Lucky Jim series. Other TV
incl: My Good Woman; A
Family at War; Let's Get Away
From It All; Nigel Barton;
Telford's Change; Prince
Regent; Watching Me,
Watching You; West Country
Tales. Education:

Mexborough Technical
College. m stage designer
Mary Pickard, 1 s Jamie.
Address: c/o Duncan Heath
Assocs, London SW10.
Starsign: Leo. Hobby:
recovering from visits to the
dentist. Person he would
most like to have met: Lord
Byron.

BASTABLE, Tony
Presenter/writer b 15.10.44
Hexham, Northumberland.
Former schoolmaster and
reporter before breaking into
TV with Southern TV's Three
Go Round. Has since worked
on numerous TV series incl:
Magpie; Drive-in;
Money-Go-Round.
Education: University
College School, Hampstead.
m Jacqueline Colkett,
1 d Kate. Address: c/o
Thames TV, London NW1.
Starsign: Libra. Hobbies:
cricket, reading history.
Person he would most like to
have met: Isambard
Kingdom Brunel, the
Victorian engineer.

BATEY, Derek
Compère/presenter b 8.8.28
Brampton, Cumberland.
Trained as accountant before

going into broadcasting, first with BBC. Joined Border TV when it began in 1961 and now Assistant Controller of Programmes. Presented and produced hundreds of current affairs, sports and light entertainment programmes for Border. Regular appearances on Celebrity Squares; Family Fortunes; 3-2-1; Sale of the Century; producer and host of Mr & Mrs and Look Who's Talking, and presenter of Yorkshire TV's Your Hundred Best Hymns. Education: White House, Brampton. m Edith, 1 d Diane. Address: c/o Border TV, Carlisle. Starsign: Leo. Hobbies: golf, tennis, family, travel. People he would most like to meet: 'The Prince and Princess of Wales, preferably on Mr & Mrs.'

BAXTER, Stanley
Actor b 24.5.28 Glasgow. Revues and pantomimes in Scotland after three and a half years with Glasgow Citizens' Theatre. Moved to London 1959. TV revues for BBC then London Weekend TV. West End shows incl: The Amorous Prawn; On the Brighter Side; What the Butler Saw; Phil the Fluter. TV incl: The Stanley Baxter Picture Show (Parts I – III); Stanley Baxter's Christmas Box (1976); Merrie Old Christmas (1977); Stanley Baxter on Television (1979); The Stanley Baxter Series (1981). Education: Hillhead High School, Glasgow; CSE Singapore. m Moira.

Address: c/o David White Assocs, London W1. Starsign: Gemini. Hobbies: swimming, cycling, reading. Person he would most like to have met: 'Lytton Strachey, to thank him for the intense pleasure his prose has given me. Elegant and wildly funny – a rare combination.'

BAYLDON, Geoffrey
Actor b 7.1.24 Leeds. Amateur theatricals before training at Old Vic Theatre School. First professional appearance in Cochrane's Tough at the Top. Shakespeare Memorial Theatre; Birmingham Rep and Glasgow Citizens'. Films incl: Casino Royale; A Night to Remember; To Sir With Love; King Rat; Dandy in Aspic; 55 Days in Peking; Otley; The Slipper and the Rose; The Pink Panther Strikes Again. Extensive radio and TV. TV incl: An Age of Kings; The Massingham Affair; The Victorians; Nicholas Nickleby; Under Western Eyes; The Wood Demon; Catweazle (title role); The Avengers; The Saint; Devenish; Alice Through The Looking Glass; Abide with Me; Edward the Seventh; The Venlo Incident; Worzel Gummidge; All Creatures Great and Small; Bergerac; Juliet Bravo. Education: Bridlington School; Hull College of Architecture. Address: c/o Joy Jameson Ltd, London SW1. Starsign: Capricorn. Hobbies: gardening, walking, painting. People he would most like to

have met; 'My paternal grandmother or grandfather, because I missed them.'

BEADLE, Jeremy
Writer/broadcaster/'curator of oddities' b 12th April London. Numerous factory and driving jobs before going into radio and TV, both as contributor and as a performer. Has contributed to Kenny Everett's Show on Capital Radio and on TV to Lucky Numbers; Celebrity Squares; You Must Be Joking; Under Manning; Jigsaw; Magic London (for American TV); April Fool. Also has his own phone-in programme on LBC. On TV he has made guest appearances on numerous chat and magazine programmes, as well as Fun Factory; The Deceivers (of which he was also co-writer) and Game For a Laugh. Books: Today's the Day (British and US editions); own cartoon strip, Today's the Day; biggest contributor to Book of Lists 1 and 2; London editor The People's Almanac Book of Predictions; co-editor Time Out. Education: Orpington Secondary Modern (expelled). Address: c/o Noel Gay Artists, London W1. Hobbies: 'Who's got time for hobbies?' he asks. Person he would most like to have met: 'The explorer Sir Richard Burton – no man has more exotic, erotic secret gossip to relate.'

BEATTIE, Johnny
Entertainer b 9th November Glasgow. Has been in every kind of show and claims to have worked every theatre in Scotland. On TV he has done five series of Welcome to the Ceilidh and three series of Now You See It. Education: St Constantine's, St Gerrard's, Glasgow. m Kitty Lamonte, 2 d Maureen, Louise, 2 s Paul, Mark. Address: c/o STV, Glasgow. Starsign: Scorpio. Hobbies: walking, reading, golf. Person he would most like to meet: 'Pope John Paul II – in spite of high office, a most happy fella!'

BEENY, Christopher
Actor b 7.7.41 Bristol. Wanted to be a dancer. Joined Ballet Rambert 1949 while attending stage school. First acting appearance was Peter Pan 1951. First TV series, The Grove Family, when he was 12; appeared regularly on TV in Dixon of Dock Green; Emergency – Ward 10; The Plane Makers; Armchair Theatre. Then took a course at RADA, but quit acting because of lack of work and started a building

firm. An episode of Softly, Softly in 1970 brought him back to acting – Upstairs, Downstairs; Miss Jones and Son; The Rag Trade; In Loving Memory. Education: XIV School, Bristol. m (1st) (dis), (2nd) singer Diana Kirkwood, 1 d Joanne, 1 s Richard. Address: c/o London Management, London W1. Starsign: Cancer. Hobbies: photography, swimming, relaxing in the sun, water skiing. Person he would most like to have met: Sir Winston Churchill.

BEL GEDDES, Barbara
Actress b 31.10.22 New York City. Stage debut walking-on in The School for Scandal at Clinton Playhouse, Connecticut, 1940 and New York debut in Out of the Frying Pan the following year. Toured army camps for USA 1942 in Junior Miss. Has since played many leading roles in a variety of plays incl: The Moon is Blue; The Living Room; Cat on a Hot Tin Roof; Ah, Wilderness!; The Voice of the Turtle; Born Yesterday; Mary, Mary; Everything in the Garden. Entered films in The Long Night. Other films incl: I Remember Mamma; Blood on the Moon; Panic in the Streets; Five Branded Women; By Love Possessed; Summertree; The Todd Killings. On TV she has appeared in many dramatic parts, the latest being Ellie in Dallas. Education: Buxton County School; Putney

School; Andrebrook. Address: c/o Actors Equity Assoc, New York. Starsign: Scorpio. Hobbies: painting, music.

BELL, Ann
Actress b 29.4.40 Wallasey, Cheshire. After training for the stage at RADA went to Nottingham Rep and then the Old Vic Company and has since played in many theatres in London and America. Films incl: To Sir With Love; The Reckoning; The Statue. Many TV credits incl: Jane Eyre; Company of Five; Uncle Vanya; The Lost Boys; Very Like a Whale; Three Sisters; Ghost Sonata; Macbeth; Way of the World; War and Peace; For Whom the Bell Tolls; Resurrection; Tenko. Education: Birkenhead High School (GPDST). m actor Robert Lang, 1 d Rebecca, 1 s John. Address: c/o Leading Artists, London SW1. Starsign: Taurus. Hobbies: reading, swimming. Person she would most like to meet:' The Pope, because of his great personality.'

BELL, Martin
BBC TV News North America Correspondent b 31.8.38 Redisham, Suffolk. News assistant to BBC Norwich 1962 and joined BBC TV News, London two years later. BBC TV News North America Correspondent since 1977. Royal Television Society's award as Reporter of the Year 1977. Education:

The Leys School; King's College, Cambridge. m Nelly Luciene Gourdon, 2 d Melissa, Catherine. Address: c/o BBC, Washington DC 20036. Starsign: Virgo. Hobbies: 'No time for any.'

BELLAMY, David
Botanist/ writer/ broadcaster b 18.1.33 London. Had several jobs when he left school because he had no idea what he wanted to do until he became a lab assistant at Ewell County Technical College, Surrey. Within five years (in 1960) he was a lecturer and then senior lecturer in Botany at Durham University. Now Professor of Adult and Continuing Education. 'Discovered' by radio and TV in 1967 through his views on pollution at the time of the Torrey Canyon oil tanker disaster. Popularised wildlife in TV programmes for adults and children on both BBC and ITV. TV incl: Life In Our Sea; Bellamy on Botany; Bellamy's Britain; Animal Game; What on Earth Are We Doing?; Bellamy's Europe; Don't Ask Me; It's Life; It's

More Life; Botanic Man (three times round the world to collect material); Looks Natural; Bellamy on Heathland; Up a Gum Tree; The Great Seasons; Backyard Safari. Books incl: Bellamy on Botany; World of Plants; Bellamy's Britain; It's Life; Bellamy's Europe; Life-giving Sea; Botanic Man; Botanic Action; Half of Paradise; The Great Seasons; Backyard Safari. Awards: Duke of Edinburgh Prize for Underwater Research 1969; British Association Certificate of Merit (for Deep in the Mire) 1973; Karl-Foerster-Stiftung Award (for Bellamy on Botany) 1973; BSAC Diver of the Year 1974; BISFA Bronze Medal 1978; Golden Ear Award at Berlin Agricultural Film Festival (for Bellamy on Heathland) 1978; Richard Dimbleby (BAFTA) Award 1978; Radio Industries Club Award (best science-based programme) 1978; TVTimes Special Award (for Botanic Man) 1978-79; Multi-coloured Swop Shop Awards 1979-80, 1980-81. Education: London University; Chelsea College of Science and Technology (BSc); Bedford College (PhD). m marine biologist Rosemary, 3 d Henrietta, Brighid, Iseabal, 2 s Rufus, Eoghain (all adopted). Address: c/o BBC, London W12. Starsign: Capricorn. Hobbies: children, ballet. Person he would most like to have met: Alfred Russel Wallace, the natural historian and explorer.

BELLIN, David
Reporter/newscaster b 7.2.51 Gwent. Trained on newspapers (Western Mail, South Wales Argus) before working at HTV Wales 1974-81, when he joined Thames News as a reporter. Education: Croes y Ceiliog, Gwent. m Liz, 1 s James.

Address: c/o Thames TV, London W1. Starsign: Aquarius.

BELLINI, James
Writer/broadcaster b 13th October. Former lecturer in international politics, Birmingham University. Became head of political studies at the Hudson Institute in Paris in 1972 and since 1976 has been associated with the Henley Centre for Forecasting. On TV his programmes incl: Argentina – Land of Millionaires: Brazil the Last Frontier; Killing – Not Murder. He also presented the BBC's Money Programme from 1975-78, was reporter and presenter for Tonight and Panorama 1978-79 when he presented Rule Britannia, adapted from his book of the same name, for ATV. He has also presented Left, Right and Centre for ATV and various documentaries for other ITV companies. Is a director of Playfair Productions, one of their first major productions being a documentary on India for Channel 4. Books incl: The UK in 1980; Britain 2002;

Regeneration of British Industry; Rule Britannia. Education: St John's College, Cambridge (BA History and Politics); London School of Economics. Address: c/o PVA Management Ltd, London W1. Starsign: Libra. Hobbies: photography, cooking, fencing, squash, new restaurants. Person he would most like to have met: George Orwell.

BENJAMIN, Christopher
Actor b 27.12.34 Trowbridge, Wilts. Trained at RADA and rep seasons at Salisbury and Bristol Old Vic. West End stage incl: A Severed Head; Maigret and the Lady; Artuo Ui; John Bull's Other Island; Nicholas Nickleby. Films incl: Brief Encounter. TV incl: Churchill's People; Private Affairs; Dick Turpin; Donkey's Years; Therese Racquin; We the Accused; It Takes a Worried Man; Holding the Fort; Nicholas Nickleby. Education: Warminster School. m actress Anna Fox, 2 d Kate, Emilia, 1 s Sebastian. Address: c/o Scott Marshall, London W3. Starsign: Capricorn. Hobbies: music, cricket, gardening. Person he would most like to have met: 'William Shakespeare – I have a few questions to put to him!'

BENNETT, Dave Holgate
Announcer/newsreader/presenter b 18.2.53 Leeds. Trained with Nancy Day, LGSM, Jonathan Tremayne and Patients Broadcasting

Service, LGI. Experience with BBC Radio Leeds, Anglia TV, BBC 1, BBC 2, ATV, HTV and commercial voice-over work before joining Grampian TV. Contributions, in various capacities, to Electric Theatre Show; About Britain; By Appointment; Cuir Car; schools' series Mathman; Thinkin' An' Talkin'. Education: Agnes Stewart School and Park Lane College, Leeds. Address: c/o Grampian TV, Aberdeen. Starsign: Aquarius. Hobbies: music and the arts, travel, exercise, letter-writing, hospital radio, gourmet dining, people, pubs with atmosphere. Person he would most like to have met: 'Oscar Wilde, because he wore a green carnation.'

BENNETT, Hywell
Actor b 8.4.44 Garnant, South Wales. Family moved to London when he was five. Spent five years with the National Youth Theatre which he joined at the age of 14 to play Ophelia. Went to RADA on a scholarship and was in plays in London's West End, Edinburgh Festival and TV before big break in his first

film, The Family Way, with Hayley Mills. Other films incl: Twisted Nerve; The Virgin Soldiers; Loot; Percy; Endless Night; It's a 2 ft 6 in Above the Ground World; The Buttercup-Chain. Stage incl: Night Must Fall; Otherwise Engaged; Julius Caesar (Young Vic). TV incl: Redcap; The Sweeney; Pennies from Heaven; Strangers; Malice Aforethought; Tinker, Tailor, Soldier, Spy; Shelley; Artemis 81; The Critic. Education: grammar school, Clapham. m former TV personality girl Cathy McGowan (dis), 1 d Emma. Address: c/o Fraser and Dunlop, London W1. Starsign: Aries.

BENNETT, Lennie
Comedian b 26.9.38 Blackpool. A former journalist with the West Lancs Evening Gazette, he became a professional entertainer in 1965. First TV was in The Good Old Days in 1966, and is now associated with Punchlines. Other TV incl: International Cabaret; Lennie and Jerry Show; London Night Out; Rising Stars; Starburst. Education: Palatine Secondary School, Blackpool. m Margaret, 1 s Tony. Address: c/o Mockingbird Management, London W1. Starsign: Libra. Hobbies: running, squash. Person he would most like to meet: 'Lester Piggott – the greatest horseman who has ever lived.'

BENTINE, Michael
Writer/actor/ comedian
b 26.1.22 Watford, Herts.
Show business career
started in Cardiff 1940
playing juvenile lead in Sweet
Lavender; then with Robert
Atkins's Shakespearian
company in Regent's Park,
London. Volunteered for
service in the RAF. After the
war Windmill Theatre, revues
(Starlight Roof) and variety.
Founder member of The
Goons. Two years in Australia
(1954-55) after TV in
America. Radio incl: Round
the Bend. Films incl: The
Sandwich Man: Bachelor of
Arts. TV incl: Quick On the
Draw; The Bumblies; The
Cathode Ray Tube Show; It's
A Square World; Potty Time;
Celebrity Squares. Books:
The Long Banana Skin; The
Door Marked Summer
(autobiographies).
Education: Eton. m (1st)
(dis), (2nd) ex-ballet dancer
Clementina Stuart,
3 d Elaine (from 1st m),
Fusty, Suki (from 2nd m),
1 s Peski (from 2nd m).
Address: c/o Spotlight,
London WC2. Starsign:
Aquarius. Hobbies: sailing,
fencing, archery, guns,
Egyptology. Person he would
most like to meet: 'Albert
Einstein – it would prove
survival, once and for all'.

BERRY, Mary
Cookery presenter b 24.3.35
Bath. Cookery expert on After
Noon Plus since 1974.
Trained at Bath College of
Domestic Science and Paris
Cordon Bleu. Teacher of

cookery, caterer and cookery
editor and consultant of
national magazines. Also
presenter of new products
and author of 12 books with a
two million sale. Education:
Bath High School. m Paul
Hunnings, 1 d Annabel,
2 s Thomas, William.
Address: c/o Thames TV,
London NW1. Starsign: Aries.
Hobbies: skiing, cooking,
antiques, gardening,
arranging flowers – without
fuss. Person she would most
like to meet: 'Barbara
Woodhouse, because our
smashing new puppy needs
training and I think she is
marvellous.'

BEWES, Rodney
Actor b 27.11.38 Bingley,
Yorks. First became
interested in acting (at 12
years old) when BBC
advertised for boys for a
production of Billy Bunter.
Rodney didn't get the part but
was put into two other plays
and recommended for
PARADA, a preparatory to
RADA. After a year at RADA
went into RAF for National
Service for two years.
Returned to RADA, was
expelled after one term, then

went into rep at Stockton-
on-Tees, Hull, York, Watford,
Eastbourne, Morecambe and
Hastings. First break in the
1960s in Harold Pinter's A
Night Out. Decided to
concentrate on TV (both BBC
and ITV), which led to the
successful series The Likely
Lads; Whatever Happened to
the Likely Lads?, and the
series he wrote and
produced, Dear Mother . . .
Love Albert. Other TV incl:
Love Story; Z Cars; Albert;
Jonah and the Whale; Just
Liz. Stage incl: The Loudest
Tears in Town; Middle-Age
Spread. Films incl: Billy Liar;
Decline and Fall; Spring and
Port Wine; Dance to Your
Daddy; Whatever Happened
to the Likely Lads?
Education: nil. m fashion
designer Daphne Black,
1 d Daisy, 3 s Joe, Tom,
Billy (triplets). Address: c/o
ICM, London W1. Starsign:
Sagittarius. Hobbies:
antiques, children. Person he
would most like to meet: 'The
Queen at Buckingham
Palace when she's giving me
a well-deserved knighthood.'

BIG DADDY
(Shirley Crabtree)
Wrestler b 14.11.36 Halifax;
Yorks. One of the three
brothers who are all in
wrestling (one, Brian
Crabtree, is a referee).
Trained at gyms and YMCAs
all over the country. Taught
wrestling at University of
Vienna in 1972. Weighs 24st
2lb. Education: secondary
modern. m Eunice,
1 d Jane, 1 step-s Paul.

Address: c/o Joint Promotions Ltd, Leeds. Starsign: Scorpio. Hobbies: reading, music, walking, training, everything appertaining to sport. Person he would most like to have met: 'Sir Winston Churchill, a man of character and strength.'

BIGGINS, Christopher
Actor b 16.12.48 Oldham, Lancs. Trained at the Bristol Old Vic Theatre School, then rep at Salisbury, Derby, Royal Shakespeare Company. Other stage incl: Winnie the Pooh; Beyond the Fringe; Touch of Spring; Side By Side By Sondheim. Has also directed at the Open Air Theatre at London's Regent's Park. Films incl: Eskimo Nell; Applause; The Rocky Horror Picture Show; The Tempest; Massada. TV incl: Paul Temple; The Likely Lads; Porridge; Man of Straw; Upstairs, Downstairs; Some Mothers Do 'Ave 'Em; Kidnapped; Brontë Connection; Dancing Princess; Jackanory; Rentaghost; Watch This Space; Give Us a Clue; Blankety Blank; Punchlines; Brendan Chase; Shoestring; I Claudius; Poldark; On Safari. Education: St Probus School, Salisbury, Wilts. Address: c/o Marina Martin, London W1. Starsign: Sagittarius. Hobbies: eating, going to the cinema and theatre, travelling, staying in luxury hotels, cooking, badminton, swimming. Person he would most like to meet: 'The

Queen of England.'

BILBOW, Tony
Writer/broadcaster b 17th April Burnham, Bucks. TV anchorman for many shows on BBC and ITV. TV writing incl: Mind Your Own Business (with Mike Fentiman); seven episodes of Please Sir! and The Fenn Street Gang; sketches for Nuts; Took and Co; The Rockers. TV appearances incl: Late Night Line Up; Film Night; Play It Again; Pebble Mill at One. Shared in the Writers Guild 1972 Award for the Best British Radio Comedy Series (for Lines From My Grandfather's Forehead). Also wrote The World of Melanie Parker, a satirical soap opera for LBC. Education: he says 'none'. m (dis), 1 d Susan, 2 s Timothy, Sean. Address: c/o Harvey Unna and Stephen Durbridge Ltd, London W1. Starsign: Aries. Hobby: hang-gliding. People he would most like to meet: playwright Nevil Smith and director Tom Corcoran.

BIRD, John
Writer/actor/director b 22.11.36 Nottingham. No formal acting training but after appearing in and directing plays while at Cambridge University, joined the Royal Court, London as assistant to the director George Devine and later as associate artistic director. First appearance in London's West End was in 1973 in Habeas Corpus Has

appeared on and written for TV frequently incl: Not So Much a Programme, More a Way of Life; BBC3; Last Laugh; The Late Show; My Father Knew Lloyd George; A Series of Birds; With Bird Will Travel; If It Moves File It; Well, Anyway; In the Looking Glass; Full House/Second House; Second City Reports; John Bird/John Wells; Blue Remembered Hills; A Walk in the Forest; High Tide; Graham Greene series; The Combination; The Taming of the Shrew; Timon of Athens; King Lear. Films incl: Take a Girl Like You; The Seven Per Cent Solution. Address: c/o Chatto and Linnit, London W1. Starsign: Scorpio. Hobbies: photography, music, reading, cricket, graphic design. Person he would most like to meet: 'Ivan Illych, to ask how one should live one's life (and laugh).'

BIXBY, Bill
Actor b 22nd January San Francisco. Dr David Barber in The Incredible Hulk. After army service went to Hollywood to pursue an acting career, but his first job was as a hotel clerk, later

23

becoming lifeguard at the pool. While there he was approached to make industrial films – in Detroit. Shortly after returned to Hollywood to appear in such films as Lonely Are the Brave; Irma La Duce; The Apple Dumpling Gang. TV incl: The Danny Williams Show; The Andy Griffith Show; The Joey Bishop Show; My Favourite Martian (1963); Courtship of Eddie's Father; The Magician; Agatha Christie's Murder Is Easy. Education: San Francisco City College; Berkeley. m actress Brenda Benet, 1 s Christopher. Address: Brentwood and Malibu, California. Starsign: Aquarius.

BLAIR, Isla
Actress b 29.9.44 India. Trained at RADA, went straight into West End production of A Funny Thing Happened On the Way to the Forum. Much stage and TV. Stage incl: The Rivals; Popkiss; Man of Mode; Subject to Fits; King Lear; What The Butler Saw; Niece in her Teens; Othello; Jumpers; Vivat Regina; Hobson's Choice; The Cherry Orchard; Abelard and Heloise; Kiss Me, Kate; Hay Fever; Design For Living; Private Lives; Mrs Warren's Profession. Films incl: The Blood of Dracula; The Battle of Britain. TV incl: The Dickie Henderson Show; The Doctors; The Regiment; The Crezz; When the Boat Comes In; Forgotten Love Songs; Wilde Alliance; The History

Man; Alexa; The Bounder. Education: private boarding school, Sussex. m actor Julian Glover, 1 s Jamie. Address: c/o London Management, London W1. Starsign: Libra. Hobby: tennis. Person she would most like to meet: 'Katharine Hepburn – I have always admired her, not only for her acting, but also for the way she has kept her private life private.'

BLAIR, Lionel
Actor/director b 12.12.32 Montreal, Canada. Started as a boy actor and made his first stage appearance in 1942 in The Wizard of Oz in Croydon. With no professional training and by sheer hard work, he has acted, danced, sung, choreographed and directed numerous plays, musicals and revues and appeared in several Royal Command Performances. As he says, 'You name it, I've done it'. Many TV appearances in variety. The men's team captain in Give Us a Clue. Education: Egerton Road School, Stamford Hill. m Susan, 1 d Lucy, 1 s Daniel. Address: c/o Peter Charlesworth, London WC2. Starsign: Sagittarius. Hobby: work. Person he would most like to meet; 'Fred Astaire – he's the best.'

BLAKE, Christopher
Actor b 23.8.49 London. Trained for three years at Central School of Speech and Drama. Then played juvenile lead in BBC

children's series Anna of Avonlea; Yorkshire TV's Death or Glory Boy; The Trials of Oscar Wilde; at Oxford; the film Aces High. Recent TV incl: Love For Lydia; Mixed Blessings; Mill on the Floss; The Lost Boys; That's My Boy; Alexa. Education: Fitzherbert Secondary Modern, Brighton, Sussex. m Wendy, 2 d Charlotte, Louise, 1 s Sean. Address: c/o ICM, London W1. Starsign: Virgo. Hobbies: cricket, photography. Person he would most like to have met: 'John Lennon, the most influential figure in my life since the age of 14. I had the good fortune to see him perform several times but I would love to have met him.'

BLANCH, Dennis
Actor b 4.2.47 Barnet, Herts. Rep experience at Exeter, Billingham and Newcastle before going into TV and films. Films incl: Permission to Kill; International Velvet. Many TV credits incl: The XYY Man; Strangers; Thriller; Villains; New Scotland Yard; Warship; The Sweeney; No Honestly; General Hospital. Education: secondary

modern. m Carol,
1 s David. Address: c/o
Essanay Ltd, London W14.
Starsign: Aquarius. Hobbies:
cricket, football. Person he
would most like to meet:
'Geoff Boycott – to teach me
how to bat properly.'

BLOOM, Claire
Actress b 15.2.31 London.
Won a scholarship to the
Guildhall School of Music and
Drama, studied under Eileen
Thorndike and then at the
Central School of Speech
Training. First stage
appearance at Oxford Rep in
1946; first appearance in
London's West End the
following year. Was at the
Stratford-upon-Avon
Memorial Theatre for the
1948 season; Old Vic
1952-54 and went to America
and Canada with that
company 1956-57. Since
then her stage work has been
divided between London and
America, in such plays as The
Trojan Women (as
Andromache); Ivanov (as
Sacha); A Doll's House (as
Nora); the title role in Hedda
Gabler; Vivat! Vivat! Regina!
(as Mary Queen of Scots); A
Streetcar Named Desire (as
Blanche du Bois); The
Innocents (as Miss Giddens).
Films incl: The Blind
Goddess; Look Back In
Anger; Richard III; The Spy
Who Came In From The Cold;
Limelight. TV appearances
incl: Juliet, in the Old Vic
production of Romeo and
Juliet; the title role in Anna
Karenina; and more recently,
The Legacy; Wessex Tales;

In Praise of Love; Henry VIII;
Hamlet; Brideshead
Revisited; Cymbeline. Book:
Limelight and After
(autobiography). Education:
Badminton School, Bristol;
Fern Hill Manor, New Milton.
m (1st) actor Rod Steiger
(dis), (2nd) producer Hillard
Elkins, 1 d Anna-Justine
(from 1st m). Address: c/o
Chatto and Linnit, London
W1. Starsign: Aquarius.
Hobbies: ballet, reading.

BLY, John
Antiques expert b 27.5.39
Tring, Herts. Born in an
antique shop, he trained at
Sotheby's for four years
before joining the family
business. Dealer, author and
lecturer in England and
America, is a regular
contributor to BBC Radio and
TV programmes and is
resident presenter of Anglia
TV's Heirloom series. Fellow
of the Royal Society of Arts
and a Freeman of the
Worshipful Company of
Goldsmiths. Education:
Berkhamsted Public Shool.
m Virginia, 2 s Julian,
James. Address: c/o Anglia
TV. Starsign: Gemini.
Hobbies: jazz, most ball
games. Person he would
most like to meet: 'Frank
Sinatra – justly a legend in his
own time.'

BOARDMAN, Stan
Comedian b 7th December
Liverpool. Ran his own
haulage business before
winning a holiday camp
competition which set him on
the showbiz road. TV incl:

Opportunity Knocks;
Celebrity Squares; Seaside
Special; Runaround; The
Comedians; The Video
Entertainers; Success.
Summer season 1982 in
Lowestoft. Aladdin
pantomime 1982. m Vivien,
1 d Andrea, 1 s Paul.
Address: c/o Bernard Lee
Management, Warlingham,
Surrey. Starsign: Sagittarius.
Hobbies: football, all sports.

BOUGH, Frank
Sports commentator
b 15.1.33 Fenton,
Stoke-on-Trent. Started with
ICI, in organisation and
methods. TV incl: BBC
Newcastle 1962 on Look
North news magazine; BBC
London 1964 in Sportsview.
Presenter of Grandstand
since 1970, and of Olympic
Games, Tokyo, Mexico,
Munich, Montreal and
Moscow. Also World Cups
and Commonwealth Games.
Presenter of Nationwide
since 1972. Richard
Dimbleby Award (BAFTA) for
outstanding contribution to
factual television 1977. Book:
Cue Frank. Education:
Oswestry Boys' High; Merton
College, Oxford (Soccer Blue

and degree in History).
m Nesta, 3 s David,
Stephen, Andrew. Address:
c/o BBC TV, London W12.
Starsign: Capricorn.
Hobbies: music, gardening,
the river. Person he would
most like to have met: 'My
father, who died
unreasonably early.'

BOWEN, Jim
Entertainer b 20.8.37
Heswall, Cheshire. Originally
a teacher working in several
schools in Lancashire incl
Caton Primary School, near
Lancaster, where he was
Deputy Head. An entertainer
in his spare time, he was
'discovered' in The
Comedians and eventually
had to choose between
continuing his career as a
teacher or becoming a
full-time entertainer. He
chose the latter and in
addition to his club and
cabaret appearances, TV
incl: Starburst; Up for the
Cup; Take Two; Bullseye;
Muck and Brass. Education:
Accrington Grammar School;
Chester Teachers' Training
College. m Phyllis,
1 d Susan, 1 s Peter.
Address: c/o Ray Donn,
Valley Club, Charlton.
Starsign: Leo. Hobby: horses
– especially hacking. Person
he would most like to meet:
'George Burns – to make an
attempt to steal his
experience and timing, which
is the best in the business.'

BOWERS, Lally
Actress b 21.1.17 Oldham,
Lancs. Was a secretary

before walking-on and
understudying at the
Shakespeare Memorial
Theatre, Stratford-upon-
Avon. Has since been in
hundreds of stage
productions, films, and TV
programmes and in rep at
Manchester, Sheffield,
Southport, Guildford,
Liverpool, Birmingham and
Bristol Old Vic. Her London
debut was in 1944 and her
many West End successes
since incl: Dinner With The
Family (Clarence Derwent
Award 1957); Difference of
Opinion; The Killing of Sister
George; Dear Octopus; The
Beastly Beatitudes of
Balthazar B. Recent films incl:
The Slipper and the Rose. TV
incl: The Duchess of Duke
Street; Mr Axelford's Angel;
My Name is Harry Worth; The
Life and Death of Penelope;
The Importance of Being
Earnest; Pygmalion; Fallen
Angels; John McNab; You're
Only Young Twice; Tales of
the Unexpected; Trelawny of
the Wells; Rasputin; Room
with a View. Education:
Hulme Grammar School,
Oldham. Address: c/o Larry
Dalzell Assocs, London WC2.
Starsign: Aquarius. Hobby:
counting the calories. Person
she would most like to meet:
'Jonathan Miller, a most
interesting, amusing and
attractive TV personality.'

BOWLES, Peter
Actor b 16.10.36 London.
Trained at RADA and by the
age of 18 was a professional
actor. Went to Old Vic for a
year, then into rep. His break

came with his part in Happy
Haven at Bristol Old Vic,
which he repeated in London
1960. Is in constant work on
stage, films, and TV. Stage
incl: Absent Friends; Dirty
Linen; Born in the Gardens.
Films incl: Charge of the Light
Brigade; The Informer; Live
Now, Pay Later; Yellow Rolls
Royce; Blow Up; Joe Egg. TV
incl: The Avengers; The Saint;
The Prisoner; Isadora; A
Thinking Man As Hero;
Napoleon and Love; The
Survivors; Churchill's People;
Only on Sunday; The Crezz;
Vice Versa; Rumpole of the
Bailey; To the Manor Born;
Only When I Laugh; The
Bounder; Experiences of an
Irish RM. Education:
Nottingham High Pavement
Grammar School. m Susan,
1 d Sasha, 2 s Guy, Adam.
Address: c/o Leading Artists,
London SW1. Starsign: Libra.
Hobby: modern British art.
Person he would most like to
meet: 'Neil Innes, the most
innovative man working in
comedy today.'

BOWNS, Roger
Journalist b 25.12.35
Alderbury, Wilts. Trained on
newspapers before joining

Channel TV early in 1966. Education: privately in Salisbury. 1 d Anna-Martine. Address: c/o Channel TV, Guernsey. Starsign: Capricorn. Hobbies: outdoor life, cinema, photography, crosswords, reading. Person he would most like to meet: 'James Cameron – the journalist I most admire.'

BOYLE, Ed
Political correspondent/interviewer b 7.2.48 London. Journalistic experience on local and provincial newspapers as well as London Evening News and Evening Standard before going into radio 1965. Reporting for BBC Radio's Today and World at One programmes, and Independent Radio News. Joined Thames News 1979. Education: Stoneyhurst College, Lancs. Address: c/o Thames News, London NW1. Starsign: Aquarius. Hobby: the quiet life. Person he would most like to have met: 'Sir Thomas More – for his courage in silence.'

BRADY, Terence
Playwright/actor b 13.3.39 London. Experienced in all fields of entertainment, but is probably better known as a writer with his wife, Charlotte Bingham. They have written scripts for TV series incl: Upstairs, Downstairs; No, Honestly; Yes, Honestly; Play for Today; Thomas and Sarah; Plays of Marriage;

Take Three Girls; Pig in the Middle; Nanny. He also appeared in the last three series as well as Dig This Rhubarb; First Impressions; Broad and Narrow; Boy Meets Girl; Love Story; Three Resounding Tinkles. As a stage actor he took over from Peter Cook in Beyond the Fringe and was also in In the Picture and Present From the Corporation. His films incl: Baby Love; Foreign Exchange. Education: Merchant Taylors, Northwood; Trinity College, Dublin (BA Moderatorship). m Charlotte Bingham, 1 d Candida, 1 s Matthew. Address: c/o AD Peters, London WC1. Starsign: Pisces. Hobbies: music (piano), painting, horse-riding and racing, gardening, playing the drums, avoiding parties. Person he would most like to meet: 'I married her.'

BRAGG, Melvyn
Writer/presenter/editor b 6.10.39 Carlisle, Cumbria. BBC Radio and TV producer 1961-67; Monitor 1962-65; presenter 2nd House 1973-77; Read All About It

(also editor) 1976-77; editor of The South Bank Show since 1978. Scripts for documentaries incl: Barbirolli; Debussy; John le Carré; Tennessee Williams. Plays written incl: Mardi Gras; Prince of Wales (musical); Orion. Filmscripts incl: Isadora; Jesus Christ Superstar (with Ken Russell); Clouds of Glory. Books incl: For Want of a Nail; The Second Inheritance; Without a City Wall; The Hired Man; A Place in England; The Nerve; Josh Lawton; The Silken Net; Speak for England; A Christmas Child; Autumn Manoeuvres; Kingdom Come. Education: Nelson-Thomlinson Grammar School, Wigton; Wadham College, Oxford (MA Hons Modern History). Fellow of the Royal Society of Literature. In 1982 received a BAFTA nomination for Best Programme for The South Bank Show. m (1st) Marie-Elisabeth (dec), (2nd) Catherine, 2 d Marie Elsa (from 1st m), Alice Mary, 1 s Tom (both from 2nd m). Address: c/o LWT, London SE1. Starsign: Libra. Hobbies: walking, books.

BRANDON, Tony
Entertainer b 12.12.33 Portland, Dorset. Background of concert party, variety and clubs as well as radio and considerable TV experience. TV incl: Who Do You Do?; 2 G's and the Pop People; He Said, She Said; Jokers Wild; Morecambe and Wise Show; Not in Front of the

Children; Brandon Exchange; Definition; Learning Tree; Secombe With Music. Education: Portsmouth Grammar School. m Jill. Address: c/o Noel Gay Artists Ltd, London WC2. Starsign: Sagittarius. Hobbies: gardening, backgammon, restoring old cars. Person he would most like to have met: 'Alastair Sim – one of the finest comedy actors in the history of the British cinema.'

BREACH, Ian
Current affairs presenter b 30.9.40 Gatley, Cheshire. Former technical journalist (The Guardian), he was with the United Nations and with the BBC news and current affairs and BBC community programmes unit before joining Tyne Tees TV in Sept 1981 to present the station's Briefing programme. In 1981 he won the Shell/BAFTA Award for his documentary, Mr Bull's Battle, and in 1982 received a BAFTA nomination for his Briefing programme on ship repairing. Education: grammar school and technical college, where he served a marine engineering apprenticeship. m Jacky, 1 d Emma. Address: c/o Tyne Tees TV, Newcastle. Starsign: Libra. Hobby: rebuilding derelict cottages while still living in them. Person he would most like to meet again: 'My father, who died in 1968. We'd have a lot to talk about.'

BREAKS, Jim
Wrestler b 25.3.40 Bradford. Started as amateur and was British amateur champion, Northern Counties champion, Yorkshire champion, British lightweight champion. Education: secondary school in Bradford. m Carole, 2 d Karen, Stacey, 1 s Gary. Address: c/o ATS, Leeds. Starsign: Aries. Hobbies: football, running a pub. Person he would most like to meet: 'Kevin Keegan, because he is small and made it, and I am small and nearly made it.'

BRETT, Jeremy
Actor b 3.11.38 Berkswell, Nr Coventry. Studied for the stage at Central School of Speech and Drama and began his acting career at the Library Theatre, Manchester. Came to London and joined the Old Vic 1956. Has since appeared in many London theatres and in America and Canada and was with the National Theatre at the Old Vic for the 1967 season. Appeared as Hamlet at the Royal Court 1961. More recent stage incl: Hedda Gabler; A Voyage Round My Father; Traveller Without Baggage; Rosmersholm; Design For Living; The Way of the World. Recent TV incl: Rebecca; The Good Soldier; The Last Visitor; William Pitt the Younger. Education: Eton. m (1st) actress Anna Massey (dis), (2nd) Joan, 1 d Rebekah, 2 s David, Caleb. Address: c/o William Morris Agency, London W1. Starsign: Scorpio. Hobbies: archery, riding. People he would most like to meet again: 'My late mother and father. I miss them.'

BRIDGES, Wayne
Professional wrestler b 7th July, Gillingham, Kent. World Heavyweight Champion. Started as an amateur with Ashdown. Turned professional in 1965 under the late Mike Marino. Has held the World Heavyweight title twice. He lost it to John Quinn and regained it in 1981. The title became vacant when Quinn failed to accept Wayne's challenge within the prescribed time limits. Education: Hornsey Road Secondary Modern, North London. m Sheila, 1 d Joann, 1 s Dean. Address: c/o Dale Martin Promotions Ltd, London SW9. Starsign: Cancer. Hobbies: swimming, reading (especially about the Second World War). Person he would most like to meet: 'Boxer Alan Minter – I admire him for his dedication.'

BRIERS, Richard
Actor b 14.1.34 Merton, Surrey. Started as a clerk, RADA 1954-56. Rep at Liverpool, Leatherhead, Coventry. London debut 1959. Plays incl: Present Laughter; Arsenic and Old Lace; Cat Among the Pigeons; Butley; Absurd Person Singular; Absent Friends; The Wild Duck; Middle-Age Spread; Arms and the Man. Films incl: Fathom; All The Way Up. Radio series incl: Brothers in Law; Doctor in the House; Marriage Lines. TV plays and series incl: Brothers in Law; Marriage Lines; Ben Travers farces; Norman Conquests; The Good Life; The Other One; Goodbye Mr Kent; PQ17. Education: Wimbledon. m actress Ann Davies, 2 d Katy, Lucy. Address: c/o International Famous Agency, London W1. Starsign: Capricorn. Hobby: theatre history. Person he would most like to have met: 'Henry Irving, of course, because I could learn so much about the magic of the Victorian theatre.'

BRIGGS, Johnny
Actor b 5.9.35 London. Italia Conti Stage School pupil 1947-53. Films incl: Cosh Boy; Hue and Cry; Perfect Friday; Best Pair of Legs in the Business. TV incl: No Hiding Place; The Young Generation; The Saint; The Avengers; Crime of Passion; Danger Man; The Persuaders; Softly, Softly;

Mike Baldwin in Coronation Street and many more too numerous to mention. Education: Schools' Certificate standard. m (1st) Carole, (2nd) Christine, 2 d Karen, Jennifer, 1 s Mark. Address: c/o Marina Martin Management, London W1. Starsign: Virgo. Hobbies: golf, squash, snooker. Person he would most like to meet: 'Quin Martin – I may be able to talk him into putting me into one of his American TV series.'

BRITTON, Fern
Presenter b 17.7.57 Ealing, West London. Trained in stage management at Central School of Speech and Drama and worked with Cambridge Theatre Company, a touring company, until she joined Westward TV as a continuity announcer 1980. Joined BBC in Plymouth 1981 as co-presenter of Spotlight, the South West's segment of Nationwide. Education: Dr Challoner's High School for Girls, Little Chalfont, Bucks. Address: c/o BBC, Plymouth. Starsign: Cancer. Hobbies: reading, eating, wasting time.

Person she would most like to meet: 'Prince Charles – because I think he's wonderful.'

BRITTON, Tony
Actor b 9.6.24 Birmingham. First worked in estate agents and aircraft factory at Weston-super-Mare. Joined amateur dramatic group. First professional appearance in Weston-super-Mare. After war service in army, rep in Manchester, two seasons at Stratford-upon-Avon, Old Vic, toured 1964-66 in My Fair Lady. Wide stage, film, radio and TV experience. Stage incl: Move Over Mrs Markham; No, No, Nanette; The Dame of Sark; My Fair Lady (London and on tour) 1978-82. Films incl: Sunday, Bloody Sunday; There's a Girl In My Soup; The Day Of The Jackal. TV incl: Romeo and Juliet; The Six Proud Walkers; Melissa; The Nearly Man; Father, Dear Father; Robin's Nest. Education: Edgbaston Collegiate, Birmingham; Thornbury Grammar, Glos. m (1st) Ruth (dis), (2nd) Danish sculptress Eve Birkefeldt, 2 d Cherry, Fern (both from 1st m), 1 s Jasper (from 2nd m). Address: c/o International Creative Management Ltd, London W1. Starsign: Gemini. Hobbies; golf, cricket, gardening, photography, wine, food, flying (holds private pilot's licence). Person he would most like to have met: 'William Shakespeare, the greatest

playwright. He said everything more beautifully and briefly than all others.'

BROCKLEBANK, Ted
Broadcaster b 24.9.42 St Andrews, Fife. Training on local newspapers and in Fleet Street. With Scottish TV before joining Grampian TV where he is now Head of News and Current Affairs. TV: presenter and producer of news, current affairs and political programmes and network documentaries incl: What Price Oil? (presenter); Highland One; Black Water – Bright Hope; Cinderella from the Sea (producer); A Tale of Two Cities (producer/presenter); Eagle (producer). Education: Madras College, St Andrews. 2 s Andrew, Jonathan. Address: c/o Grampian TV, Aberdeen. Starsign: Libra. Hobbies: making television programmes, reading, music, sketching. Person he would most like to meet: 'The man from Littlewoods, telling me I have won the Pools.'

BRODIE, Anne
Announcer b 4.8.50 Aberdeen. Joined Grampian TV in 1971 and trained there. Freelance announcer Scottish TV 1975-78 and returned to Grampian as freelance 1980. Education: Convent of the Sacred Heart, Aberdeen; Aberdeen Academy; School of Radio Diagnosis, Forest Hill

Hospital, Aberdeen (MSR); Strathclyde University, Glasgow (ABPI). 1 d Dorothy, 1 s Donald. Address: c/o Grampian TV, Aberdeen. Starsign: Leo. Hobbies: jogging, gardening, knitting, bridge, running a youth club. Person she would most like to meet: 'Jim Davidson – he seems to have my sense of humour.'

BROOKE-TAYLOR, Tim
Actor-scriptwriter b 17.7.40 Buxton, Derbyshire. Has a law degree, but started his career in Cambridge Footlights Revue, followed by the successful Cambridge Circus revue in London and Broadway. Then came the radio show, I'm Sorry I'll Read That Again followed by At Last The 1948 Show; Marty; Broaden Your Mind and The Goodies, all on TV. Other TV incl: On The Braden Beat; His and Hers; Hello Cheeky (and radio); The Rough With The Smooth; Shades of Greene; Does The Team Think? Theatre incl: The Unvarnished Truth. Films incl: Twelve Plus One; The Statue. Records incl: Funky Gibbon; The Least Worst of Hello

Cheeky; The Seedy Sounds of Hello Cheeky; The New Goodies LP; The Goodies' Beastly Record. Education: Winchester College; Pembroke College, Cambridge. Rector of St Andrews University and a director of Derby County Football Club. m Christine, 2 s Ben, Edward. Address: c/o Jill Foster, London SW3. Starsign: Cancer. Hobbies: travel, skiing, golf, watching all sport, films and TV. Person he would most like to meet: Jack Nicklaus.

BROOKS, David
Anglia weatherman b 7.2.39 Darlington. Obtained a BSc degree at Durham University and was then commissioned in the Royal Navy in which he served for 12 years. His service included two and a half years in Malta where he was a weather forecaster for NATO. His last naval appointment before joining Anglia TV in 1972 was at the Royal Naval Air Station at Lossiemouth. m Sylvia, 2 d Jennie, Helen. Address: c/o Anglia TV, Norwich. Starsign: Aquarius. Hobbies: golf, soccer, good food and wine, good beer. Person he would most like to meet: 'Jack Nicklaus, my favourite golfer on and off the course.'

BROWN, Duggie
Actor/comedian b 7.8.40 Rotherham, Yorks. One of the highest paid club and cabaret performers. Played guitar with The Four Imps for

12 years and appeared on Six-Five Special. His patter while with the group got him noticed and chosen for The Good Old Days and The Comedians series. Further light entertainment on TV incl: The Wheeltappers and Shunters Club; 3-2-1; Square One; Pro Celebrity Snooker. A part in the film Kes, led to further straight acting roles and situation comedy incl: The House That Jack Built; Days of Hope; The Price of Coal; Leeds United; Say Goodnight to Grandma; Crown Court; The Combination; The Enigma Files; The Mersey Pirates; Take My Wife; The Glamour Girls; The Cuckoo Waltz. Education: secondary modern and technical college. Address: c/o Richard Stone, London WC2. Starsign: Leo. Hobbies: golf, darts, snooker, racing. Person he would most like to meet: 'George Burns, because I would like to find out how you can keep working at his age.'

BROWN, Faith
Singer/impressionist
b 28.5.44 Liverpool. At one

time was a sales demonstrator at a Liverpool store. Entered show business through local talent contests and started singing with a Liverpool-based band when she was 16, before forming a vocal group with three of her four brothers. Turning professional they made their debut at Blackpool and appeared on various TV shows. When the group split up she went solo, put some impressions into her act and has since toured world-wide as well as cabaret and concert engagements. Her TV credits incl: Who Do You Do?; For My Next Trick; Celebrity Squares; The Faith Brown Awards; Blankety Blank; The Faith Brown Chat Show; Golden Gala; Starburst; as well as guest artist on many TV programmes. Voted Speciality Act of the Year 1980; TV Times Award for Funniest Woman on TV 1980; COPS (Californian Organisation of Police and Sheriffs) Award 1981 for services to charities in America. Education: St Francis de Sales, Walton, Liverpool. m musician/manager Leonard Wady, 1 d Danielle. Address: c/o Million Dollar Music, London W2. Starsign: Gemini. Hobbies: fishing, swimming, cooking.

BROWN, Janet
Comedienne b Glasgow. Began doing impersonations while still a teenager. After serving with the ATS during

the war, went to London and worked on a radio show which led to a summer show in Scarborough, in which she met her husband. More radio and TV, followed by a stage play with Alastair Sim, Mr Gillie. TV incl: Rainbow Room; Where Shall We Go?; Friends and Neighbours; Who Do You Do?; Mike Yarwood in Persons; Janet and Co (1981 and 1982). Education: Rutherglen Academy. m comedian Peter Butterworth (dec),
1 d Emma, 1 s Tyler. Address: c/o Bernard Lee Management, Caterham,. Surrey. Hobbies: collecting antiques, cooking, sitting in the sun by the sea. Person she would most like to meet: 'Bette Midler. I think she is marvellous and I would love to impersonate her.'

BROWN, Joe
Entertainer/musician
b 13.5.41 Swarby, Lincs. Brought up in London and was barrow boy, electrician's apprentice, railway fireman and a member of a skiffle group before music took over. A self-taught guitarist, he was spotted by Jack Good to appear in Boy Meets Girls on TV. Since then he has made hit records, toured, appeared in cabaret and in such stage shows as Charley Girl. He has also been in many pantomimes and his TV credits incl: Set 'Em Up, Joe; the revival of Oh Boy!; Square One; and guest on many programmes. His hit records incl: A Picture of You; It Took

Only a Minute; That's What Love Will Do; 'Enery the Eighth; All Things Bright and Beautiful (with his wife). Education: Plaistow Grammar School; Pretoria Road School, Plaistow. m Vicki, 1 d Samantha, 1 s Peter. Address: c/o Derek Block, London W1. Starsign: Taurus. Hobbies: snooker, skin-diving, wind-skiing, wind-surfing. Person he would most like to have met: 'Sir Winston Churchill, because he was a great Englishman.'

industrial, agricultural and political matters and BBC West's Industrial Correspondent since 1965. Education: Lord Wandsworth College, Hants. m Heather, 2 d Victoria, Catherine, 2 s William, James. Address: c/o BBC, Bristol. Starsign: Cancer. Hobby: walking. Person he would most like to meet: 'Katharine Hepburn – it's the voice and the walk. Still!'

BROWN, Paul
Journalist b 29.3.50 North Wales. Journalistic training on local newspapers in Jersey before joining Channel TV in 1970. TV incl: Report at 6; Channel Report (both current affairs magazines); Brown Study (arts programme); All That Jazz (music series). Education Clwyd Street Primary, Rhyl; Rhyl Grammar; Hauliet School, Jersey. Address: c/o Channel TV, Jersey. Starsign: Aries. Hobbies: bridge, chess, fencing, jazz, The Times crossword, claret, cognac, women. Person he would most like to have met: 'John Logie Baird – to tell him it was all a mistake!'

BROWN, Peter
Industrial correspondent, BBC West b 8.7.27 Longhope, Glos. Started as a freelance broadcaster on radio and TV for both BBC and ATV. Experienced in

BRUNSON, Michael
Journalist b 12.8.40 Norwich. Formerly with BBC Radio and TV, joined ITN 1968. US Correspondent 1973-77, covering Watergate, US Bicentennial and US Presidential election. Has since been reporter/ newscaster and was with Mrs Thatcher throughout her 1979 election campaign. Now ITN's Diplomatic Editor. Education: Bedford School; Queen's College, Oxford. m Susan, 2 s Jonathan, Robin. Address: c/o ITN, London W1. Starsign: Leo. Hobbies: 'Don't have time.' Person he would most like to meet: 'Peter Ustinov – he's one of the world's great wits,

and I've met all the politicians, anyway!'

BUCKMAN, Dr Robert
Presenter/comedian/writer b 22.8.48 London. Trained as a doctor but appearances with Cambridge University Footlights gave him a taste for entertainment. Radio incl: Start The Week; Marks In His Diary; Kaleidoscope; Get The Most Out Of Your Body. TV incl: Don't Ask Me; Don't Just Sit There; The Pink Medicine Show; Where There's Life; Your Own Worst Enemy. Contributes to various magazines incl Honey, Punch, The Lancet. Books: Out of Practice; Jogging From Memory. Education: University College School; Cambridge University; University College Hospital Medical School. Secretary of cancer charity Oncology Club Fund, London SW3. m Dr Joan-Ida Van Dem Ende, 2 d Joanna, Susan. Address: c/o Fraser and Dunlop, London W1. Starsign: Leo/Virgo (and Aston Villa according to some). Hobbies: collecting books, inventing filing systems, avoiding astrologers. Person he would most like to meet: 'My first great-great-great- grandchild.'

BUNNAGE, Avis
Actress b 22nd April Manchester. Formerly a telephonist and nursery teacher. Gained stage experience in rep and made her first professional

appearance at Chorlton Rep Theatre, Manchester in 1947 and her first London appearance was with Theatre Workshop Company in 1952. Has since returned to that company many times in addition to other productions in London, Zurich, Moscow and America. Plays incl: An Enemy of the People; The Good Soldier Schweik; Mother Courage; The Italian Straw Hat; Captain Brassbound's Conversion; The Playboy of the Western World; A Taste of Honey; The Hostage; Ned Kelly; Fings Ain't Wot They Used T'Be; Oh What a Lovely War; Henry IV; The Marie Lloyd Story (title role); Fiddler on the Roof; Sweeney Todd; The Rivals; Billy. Films incl: The Loneliness of the Long Distance Runner; Sparrers Can't Sing; Tom Jones; The Whisperers. TV incl: Love on the Dole; My Lords, Ladies and Gentlemen; Eugenie Grandet; and more recently Spoils of War; In Loving Memory; Jessie. Education: Manley Park Municipal School and Chorlton Central School, Manchester. m Derek Orchard. Address: c/o NEMS Management, London SW3. Starsign: Taurus. Hobbies: playing Scrabble, gardening, reading, easy crosswords, embroidery. Person she would most like to meet: 'Deanna Durbin – I used to see all her films and buy all her music.'

BURKE, Alfred
Actor b 28.2.18 Peckham, London. Trained at RADA and started his career at the Barn Theatre, Shere, Surrey in 1939. Appeared at many reps incl Birmingham (where he spent three years), Leeds and Manchester. First appearance in London's West End was in Desire Caught by the Tail; he was also in Sailor Beware in London. Films incl: The Angry Silence; Yangtse Incident; Interpol; Bitter Victory; The House in Garibaldi Street; One Day in the Life of Ivan Denisovich. Many TV appearances, notably as Frank Marker in Public Eye; The Exiles; The Brontës; The Tip; Tales of the Unexpected; Treasure Island; Enemy at the Door; Mary Blandy; The Rod of Iron; No 10 (Pitt the Elder). Education: Leo St Boys' School; Walworth Central. m Barbara, former stage manager, two sets of twins: Jacob and Harriet, Kelly and Louisa. Address: c/o Joy Jameson Ltd, London SW1. Starsign: Pisces. Hobbies: football, music, historic houses.

BURNET, Alastair
Newscaster b 12.7.28 Sheffield. Worked on The Glasgow Herald and The Economist before joining ITN (1963). Anchorman for General Elections 1964, 1966, 1970 and 1979, and associated with This Week and News at Ten, of which he was one of the original newscasters. Editor of The

Economist 1965, won Richard Dimbleby Award for work in TV 1966, 1970 and 1979. With BBC 1972-74 as presenter of Panorama and anchorman for both General Elections 1974. Editor Daily Express 1974, returned to ITN 1976 to present News at 5.45 and then News at Ten. TV Times Editor's Award 1981-82 for coverage of Prince Charles' wedding. Education: Leys, Cambridge; Worcester College, Oxford. m Maureen Sinclair. Address: c/o ITN, London W1. Starsign: Cancer. Person he would most like to meet: 'The next Derby winner (before the race).'

BURNS, Gordon
Producer/presenter b 10.6.42 Belfast. Reporter East Antrim Times and Belfast Telegraph. Sports department of BBC Radio. TV: Ulster – UTV Reports; Gordon Burns Hour; Granada – Reports Politics; Granada Reports; The Krypton Factor; World in Action. Commentator at political party conferences, Blackpool. Education: Dulwich College, London;

Campbell College, Belfast. m Sheelagh, 1 d Anna, 1 s Tristun. Address: c/o David Anthony Promotions, Warrington. Starsign: Gemini. Hobby: watching Liverpool FC win everything! Person he would most like to meet: 'So far nameless – the man (or woman) who solves the Irish question and brings a genuine and lasting peace to the troubled province of Ulster. I hope he (or she) is alive right now.'

BURT, Andrew
Actor b 23.5.45 Wakefield, Yorks. Trained at Rose Bruford College of Drama and then went into rep incl Perth and Cheltenham. Recent TV incl: Warship; The Legend of King Arthur; The Voyage of Charles Darwin; Lilliput, in which he played Gulliver. Education: Silcoates School, Wakefield; University of Kent (BA Hons). Address: c/o Green and Underwood Ltd, London W3. Starsign: Gemini. Hobby: acting.

BURTON, David
Sports reporter/presenter b 29.9.49 Dulwich, London. BA Hons in Law, graduate

trainee for Tyne Tees (1974). TV: reporter/presenter on weekly sports magazine Sportstime and daily news magazine Northern Life. Co-presenter of weekend football programme Shoot. Presenter/commentator of numerous sporting outside broadcasts incl cricket, golf, speedway, showjumping, squash. Education: Cheltenham College, Gloucestershire; St John's College, Cambridge. m Northern Life reporter, Anne Avery. Address: c/o Tyne Tees TV, Newcastle. Starsign: Libra. Hobbies: all sports, particularly golf (Cambridge Blue, 1972) and squash (Northumberland County Champion, 1976, 1978-79), current affairs, music, theatre, crosswords, good food and social drinking. Person he would most like to meet: 'Jack Nicklaus – he might inspire me to hit the fairway more often.'

BURTON, Humphrey
Presenter/producer/executive b 25.3.31 Trowbridge, Wilts. Began as radio effects boy with BBC Radio, then studio manager and music producer. BBC TV 1958-67, then he joined London Weekend TV as founder member. Edited and introduced Aquarius 1970-75 then he returned to BBC as Head of Music and Arts and introduced Omnibus. In 1981 he returned to production and direction for the BBC in the field of the performing

arts. He has also worked freelance on programmes in Austria, Germany and America. Other TV incl: In Performance; Opera Month: Young Musician of the Year 1982. Education: Long Dene, Chiddingstone; The Judd School, Trowbridge; Fitzwilliam House, Cambridge University (BA). m (1st) Gretel (dis), (2nd) photographer Christina, 2 d Clare (from 1st m), Helena (from 2nd m), 2 s Matthew (from 1st m), Lukas (from 2nd m). Address: c/o BBC TV, London W12. Starsign: Aries. Hobbies: tennis, ping-pong, playing duets, travel.

BYGRAVES, Max
Singer/actor/entertainer b 16.10.22 Rotherhithe, London. Won a talent contest at 13. West End debut at London Palladium 1949 after service in the RAF. Countless stage and TV shows and hit records. Films incl: Charlie Moon; A Cry From The Streets; Spare the Rod. Radio incl: Educating Archie. TV incl: Max Bygraves; Max; Singalongamax; Lingalongamax; Max Rolls On; Side by Side. More Royal Variety Performances than any other artist. Has three platinum, 29 gold and 15 silver discs, all from his Singalong LPs, which represent sales in excess of six million. Books: I Wanna Tell You A Story (autobiography); The Milkman's On His Way (novel). Education: St

Joseph, Paradise Street,
Rotherhithe. m Gladys
(Blossom), 2 d Christine,
. Maxine, 1 s Anthony.
Address. London SW1.
Starsign: Libra. Hobbies:
golf, vintage cars.

BYRNE, Peter
Actor/director b 29.1.28
London. Trained at Italia
Conti Stage School. Stage
incl: Double Edge; Boeing –
Boeing; There's a Girl in My
Soup; Underground; There's
a Small Hotel; Move Over Mrs
Markham (Toronto); Mother
Goose pantomime; Murder
Among Friends (tour). Films
incl: Large Rope; Reach for
the Sky; Carry on Cabby. TV
incl: hundreds of
appearances in Dixon of
Dock Green as well as Mutiny
at Spithead; The New
Canadians; Whodunnit?;
Looks Familiar; Blake's
Seven. Education: Finchley
Grammar. Address: c/o
Susan James Personal
Management, London W2.
Starsign: Aquarius. Hobbies:
squash, swimming, riding,
golf, cars.

languages and planned to
take a degree, but gave it up
in favour of acting and won a
scholarship to the Old Vic
Theatre School. It was
wartime and she was called
up to work as a censor for the
Ministry of Information. After
the war came her acclaimed
part of a mad nun in the film
Black Narcissus. Other films
incl: A Matter of Life and
Death; Small Back Room;
Prelude to Fame; Madness of
the Heart; Elephant Man;
From a Far Country. Came
into TV 1957, incl: Emergency
– Ward 10; The Avengers;
Who Is Sylvia?;
Countercrime; That Woman is
Wrecking Our Marriage;
Emmerdale Farm; The
Golden Bowl; Portrait of a
Lady; Moonstone; Heidi;
Tales of the Supernatural;
The Professionals; Minder;
General Hospital; Hedda
Gabler; Together (series);
Unity; Nancy Astor; Angels.
m writer Alaric Jacob,
1 d Harriet, 1 s Jasper.
Address: c/o RMK Ltd,
London W1. Hobbies:
pottery, gardening. Person
she would most like to meet:
'Anthony Wedgwood Benn,
because he seems to be so
misrepresented in the
media.'

BYRON, Kathleen
Actress b London. Studied

C

CAINE, Marti
Comedienne/vocalist
b 26.1.45 Sheffield. Wanted to be a singer but gradually built up the comedy in local working men's clubs. First big show business break in New Faces in 1975. Since then she has appeared at the London Palladium; three series for ATV; four series for BBC; numerous TV specials; Las Vegas. m manager Malcolm Stringer (dis), 2 s Lee, Max. Address: c/o Johnnie Peller Enterprises, Sheffield. Starsign: Aquarius. Hobbies: housework, photography, listening to records. Person she would most like to meet: Robert Redford.

CADELL, Simon
Actor b 19.7.50 London. Trained at Bristol Old Vic Theatre School, then joined the Bristol Old Vic Company. Many theatre appearances. TV incl: Hadleigh; Hine; Love Story; A Man from Haven; Love School; Glittering Prizes; Wings; She Fell Among Thieves; Play For Today; Enemy at the Door; Edward and Mrs Simpson; Hi-De-Hi; and many radio appearances. Education: Bedale's, Petersfield, Hants. Address: c/o MLR Ltd, London SW5. Starsign: Cancer. Hobby: travelling. Person he would most like to have met: Galileo.

CALDICOT, Richard
Actor b 7.10.08 London. Trained for the stage at RADA and made his first professional appearance in Huddersfield in 1928, since when he has appeared in parts that range from the classics to comedy with spells of variety, revue, rep, musicals and farce in between. From June 1971 to Feb 1976 he played Mr Bromhead in No Sex Please, We're British. Films incl: The VIPs; The Spy Who Came in from the Cold. On TV he has made numerous appearances, incl plays and series, most recently in Let There Be Love; The Other Side of Me; Crown Court; Fawlty Towers; Sharp Intake of Breath; Morecambe and Wise Show; Coronation Street; The Two Ronnies; etc. Education: Dulwich College. m Judith, 1 s Jonathan. Address: c/o Essanay Ltd, London W14. Starsign: Libra. Hobbies: golf, stamps. Person he would most like to meet: 'Jane Fonda – a lovely lady.'

CAMPBELL, Angus Peter
TV journalist b 29.4.54 Isle of South Uist. Newspaper journalistic experience with West Highland Free Press before joining BBC Radio Highland as a reporter. Freelance work before becoming TV reporter with Grampian TV 1979. Education: in South Uist; Edinburgh University (MA Hons Politics and Modern History). m Jane. Address: c/o Grampian TV, Aberdeen. Starsign: Taurus. Hobbies: writing, reading, football, Gaelic, watching growth of CND. Person he would most like to meet: 'Have already met him – Sorley MacLean, the Gaelic poet.'

CANNON, Tommy
Comedian b 27.6.38 Oldham. The other half of the comedy partnership, Cannon and Ball. Former workmates in a Lancashire engineering

factory by day and a singing duo, The Harper Brothers, at night. Changed names to Cannon and Ball nine years ago and are now major club and theatre attractions. Voted clubland's top comedy duo 1975. Summer seasons in Bournemouth, Jersey and Cleethorpes, and broke all box-office records in Blackpool and Great Yarmouth, and pantomime in Bradford, Leeds, Stockport and Liverpool. TV incl: Wheeltappers and Shunters' Social Club; Bruce Forsyth's Big Night and their own series, Cannon and Ball. Education: Henshaw Secondary, Oldham. m Margaret, 2 d Janette, Julie. Address: c/o Stuart Littlewood Assocs, Oldham, Lancs. Starsign: Cancer. Hobby: golf. People he would most like to have met: 'Laurel and Hardy because they were a great comedy double act.'

CARBY, Fanny
Actress b 2nd February Sutton Coldfield, Warwicks. Originally wanted to be a dancer but gave it up for acting, spent eight years with

Joan Littlewood at Theatre Workshop where she was in such productions as Ned Kelly, Sparrers Can't Sing and Oh What A Lovely War (also in Paris and New York). Also in rep at Watford and Sheffield. Other stage work incl: Look After Lulu; The Threepenny Opera; Billy (as Billy's mum); and plays at Hampstead Theatre Club, Soho Poly and Royal Exchange, Manchester. Vast amount of TV incl: The History of Mr Polly; The Good Companions; Forgive Our Foolish Ways; Crossroads: three series with Spike Milligan; Angels; The Cost of Loving; and many TV plays. Films incl: The Elephant Man; Loophole. Education: private school and ballet school. Address: c/o Brian Wheeler, London W4. Starsign: Aquarius. Hobbies: gardening, antiques. Person she would most like to have met: 'Lottie Lenya, because she embodied completely the actress-singer and was so evocative of the Brecht-Weil success. I have been lucky enough to play her part in the musical Cabaret and also The Threepenny Opera.'

CARNE, Judy
Actress b 27.4.39 Northampton. Trained at the Bush-Davis Theatrical Boarding School. Equally well-known in her native country as in America where she made a name in the Laugh-In TV series. First went to America in 1961 where she

has since been in Fair Exchange; Love on a Rooftop; The Andy Williams Show; The Dean Martin Show; The Jerry Lewis Show; Ironside; Alias Smith and Jones; The Big Valley. On stage in America she has toured in Absurd Person Singular; The Owl and the Pussycat; Mary, Mary; Cabaret; Dames at Sea; the Broadway revival of The Boy Friend and her nightclub act at Caesar's Palace, Las Vegas. Before going to America she had been in various TV variety shows as well as The Rag Trade; Juke Box Jury; and on stage in For Amusement Only; On the Bright Side; Chrysanthemum. Since returning to England a couple of years ago, she has toured in Blithe Spirit and Happy Birthday, been in pantomime at Bath and Coventry and her many TV appearances incl: Give Us a Clue; Blankety Blank; The Basil Brush Show; On the Line; Saturday Night at the Mill; Starburst. Address: c/o Jo Peters, London W14. Starsign: Taurus. Hobbies: cooking, designing clothes. Person she would most like to meet: 'Mel Brooks, the funniest man in the business.'

CAROLGEES, Bob
Comedy entertainer/ puppeteer b 12.5.48 Birmingham. Considerable experience in cabaret and theatre and on TV incl: Tiswas; OTT; 3-2-1; Russell Harty; Square One.

Education: grammar school and college. Address: c/o Tony West Entertainments, Crosby, Liverpool. Starsign: Taurus. Hobbies: squash, swimming, remote control cars. Person he would most like to meet: 'Prince Charles, because I think he will make a great king.'

CARPENTER, Harry
Sports commentator b 17.10.25 London. Former Fleet Street sports journalist. Presenter of BBC's weekly Sportsnight programme and former Grandstand linkman. Commentator at world heavyweight title fights since 1955 and every Olympic Games since 1956. Joined BBC full-time in 1962. Also presenter of Wimbledon Lawn Tennis and Open Golf Championships. Other sports he has covered incl: greyhound racing and the Oxford-Cambridge boat race. Author of three books on boxing. Education: Selhurst Grammar, Croydon. m Phyllis, 1 s Clive. Address: c/o BBC TV Centre, London W12. Starsign: Libra. Hobbies: golf, classical music. Person he would most like to meet: 'The golf professional who can improve my game.'

CARROTT, Jasper
Comedian b 14.3.45 Birmingham. Before turning professional (1969) had a variety of jobs incl: trainee buyer in a paint store; carpet and car seat cover salesman; window cleaner; clerk;

builder's labourer; tote operator; barrow-boy; kitchen porter. Started in a club where he was host and compère, also in 1969. Became an all-round entertainer in clubs, universities and at concerts. Had own show, Folk Club (1972). TV debut in The Golden Game. Also, for BBC Midlands (1975), An Audience with Jasper Carrott. Other TV incl: Half Hour With Jasper Carrott; The Unrecorded Jasper Carrott; Carrott Gets Rowdy; Carrott de Sol. His records have earned him three gold and three silver discs. Education: Acock's Green Primary; Moseley Grammar. m Hazel, 3 d Lucy, Jennifer, Hannah, 1 s Jake. Address: c/o DJM Records, London WC1. Starsign: Pisces. Hobbies: football, squash, socialising with his best friends.

CARSON, Frank
Comedian b 6.11.26 Belfast. Was a TV favourite in Ireland before coming to England to try his luck in clubland. After The Good Old Days, Opportunity Knocks, and The Comedians, he has become

one of this country's leading performers who is much in demand and much televised. Other TV incl: The Melting Pot; Celebrity Squares; The Ballyskillen Opera House; a regular on Tiswas. Education: St Patrick's Elementary, Belfast. m Ruth, 1 d Majella, 2 s Tony, Aiadan. Address: Blackpool. Starsign: Scorpio. Hobbies: golf, collecting money. Person he would most like to meet: President Ronald Reagan.

CARSON, John
Actor b 28.2.27 Colombo, Sri Lanka. After gaining a law degree at Oxford and service in the Royal Artillery, experience with the New Zealand Broadcasting Service drama dept both as actor and producer. Came to England 1955 and after some time in rep got his first break in Emergency – Ward 10. Has since had vast experience on TV and his is a familiar voice on commercials. Stage incl: A Man For All Seasons; A Day In The Death Of Joe Egg (London and New York). Films incl: Capt Kronos; The Plague of the Zombies; The Man Who Haunted Himself. Recent TV incl: The Lie; Dombey and Son; Emma; Shades of Green; Raffles; The Troubleshooters; The Flaxborough Chronicles; Children of the New Forest; Send in the Girls; Secret Army; 1990; Kidnapped; The Professionals; Telford's Change; After Julius; Antonia White Quartet; Delacroix. Education: mainly in West

Australia but prep school in England and Oxford University (holds MA). m Luanshya Greer, 2 d Kate, Suzanna, 4 s Richard, Christopher (twins), Harry, Ben. Address: c/o Chatto & Linnit, London W1. Starsign: Pisces. Hobbies: fishing, riding, golf. Person he would most like to meet: 'Bernard Dunstan, the most articulate artist of our time, except for Feliks Topolski, the great chronicler.'

CARSON, Johnny
TV chat show host
b 23.10.25 Corning, Iowa. Service in US Navy, then radio and TV work and announcer 1950. His own programme, Carson's Cellar, and quizmaster 1954. Wrote for Red Skelton and star of the Johnny Carson Show. Took over the Tonight show from Jack Paar in 1962. Since then has become a TV legend in America and the highest paid TV performer, while the programme has become USA's most popular chat show. Education: University of Nebraska. Reticent about his private life but is now married to his third wife and lives in Beverly Hills, Los Angeles. Starsign: Libra.

CARSON, Violet OBE
Actress b 1.9.05 Manchester. Can't remember when she actually started in showbusiness, but played piano for silent films. Also concerts, private

engagements and broadcasts as singer and pianist. Introduced Northern edition of Woman's Hour for BBC and was pianist for Have a Go. Appeared in many TV plays before taking up residence in Coronation Street as Ena Sharples in 1960. Also many appearances as singer in Stars on Sunday. Education: 'Ordinary elementary – and very good too!' m George Peploe (dec). Address: c/o Granada TV, Manchester. Starsign: Virgo.

CARTER, Jilly
TV/radio presenter b 28.7.53 Widnes, Cheshire. Was a teacher in Paris, Lisbon and Rome where she started part-time work with the English language station Radio Daily American. Joined BBC Radio 4 as presenter and went to Bournemouth's Two Counties Radio 1981 presenting phone-in, chat, music and specialist programmes. Joined TSW March 1982. Education: Huyton College; University of London (BA English, French and Art History). Address: c/o TSW, Plymouth. Starsign:

Leo. Hobbies: theatre, good food and wine, books, cycling, dancing. Person she would most like to meet: 'Mr De Beers – diamonds are forever.'

CARTER, Rita
Broadcaster b 15.7.49 Southend-on-Sea, Essex. Trained in journalism on local paper before freelancing for newspapers and magazines. Spent a year freelancing in Singapore, then returned to England and became a researcher for the BBC. Presenter LBC Reports; Nightline; AM and a reporter for IRN/LBC 1976-78, when she joined Thames News. Education: Westcliff High School, Essex. Address: c/o Thames TV, London NW1. Starsign: Cancer. Hobbies: chess, astronomy. Person she would most like to have met: Rasputin.

CARTHEW, Anthony
ITN reporter specialising in coverage of the Royal Family b 2.4.27 London. Started in journalism as a graduate trainee reporter on the Sheffield Telegraph. Was on

the Daily Herald and the Sun before joining the Daily Mail as a foreign reporter. Also wrote for New York Times. Reporter of the Year 1965, 1968. Moved to ITN in 1971. Education: Birmingham University (BA Hons French and Italian). m Olwen, 2 d Rachel, Henrietta. Address: c/o ITN, London W1. Starsign: Aries. Hobbies: cooking, cricket. Person he would most like to have met: 'Mozart, to find out how anyone can write like that.'

CARTNER, Allan
Announcer b 13.12.33 Carlisle. National Service Officer in Royal Artillery, BBC TV outside broadcast cameraman 1957-61. Film commentator and voice-over for commercials. Senior announcer, Border TV since 1962. Education: Carlisle Grammar; University of Durham (BA). m Terri, 1 d Emma, 1 s Kimble. Address: c/o Border TV, Carlisle. Starsign: Sagittarius. Hobbies: wildlife photography, sound recording, fell-walking. Person he would most like to meet: 'Bob Hope – I appreciate his American humour.'

CARVER, Peter
Journalist/broadcaster b 14.7.42 Redhill, Surrey. Journalistic training on Croydon Advertiser, Sheffield Telegraph, and Central Press Features and wide local radio experience

with BRMB Birmingham. Lobby correspondent at Westminster since 1965. Political correspondent for HTV West in 1979, since when he has reported for Report West; Report Extra; West of Westminster; West Country Farming. Education: primary school, Redhill; secondary modern, Croydon. m Jane, 2 d Emily, Megan, 1 s Bethan. Address: c/o HTV West, Bristol. Starsign: Cancer. Hobbies: history, politics, walking, talking, cribbage. Person he would most like to have met: King John.

CASTLE, Roy
Entertainer/actor b 31.8.32 Scholes, near Huddersfield. Started in amateur concert party. Turned pro 1953. Stooge for Jimmy James and Jimmy Clitheroe. Learned to dance and can play any musical instrument. Breakthrough came on Dickie Valentine Show on TV. Other TV incl: New Look; The Roy Castle Show; Roy Castle Beats Time; The Record Breakers; Show Castle; guests spots on most variety

shows; 32 TV shows in America. Radio incl: Castle's on the Air. Stage incl: Pickwick (in America). Films incl: Dr Terror's House of Horrors; Doctor Who and the Daleks; Carry on Up the Khyber; The Plank; The Intrepid Mr Twigg. Education: Scholes Council School; Honley Grammar School. m Fiona, 2 d Julia, Antonia, 2 s Daniel, Benjamin. Address: c/o London Management. Starsign: Virgo. Hobbies: gardening, squash, golf, charity cricket, sleep. Person he would most like to meet: 'Terry Wogan at his day job.'

CAUNTER, Tony
Actor b 22.9.37 Southampton. Formerly a regular in the Royal Air Force. Trained at LAMDA. Stage incl: Chips With Everything (London and New York). Films incl: The Hill; Ipcress File; Cromwell; SOS Titanic. TV incl: Stockers Copper; Hunchback of Notre Dame; Pennies From Heaven; Sporting Club Dinner; Willy; Beryl's Lot; The Sweeney; The Professionals; The Vanishing Army; Waterloo Sunset; Rumpole of the Bailey; Speedking; Shoestring; Private Schultz; The Cause; PQ17; Boxwalling; Juliet Bravo. Education: Worthing High; Westcliff High School. m schoolteacher Frances, 1 d Sarah, 3 s Nicholas, William and James (twins). Address: c/o CCA, London SW6. Starsign: Virgo.

Hobbies: watching old movies, reading biographies, making home movies, cruising on the inland waterways of Great Britain. Person he would most like to have met: 'Sir Winston Churchill – in my opinion, the greatest Englishman of the 20th century.'

CAZENOVE, Christopher
Actor b 17.12.45 Winchester. Always wanted to be a film star, though his father wanted him to be an officer in the Coldstream Guards. Ironically, it was his role in The Regiment on TV that made his name. Trained at Bristol Old Vic Theatre School and rep in Leicester, Leatherhead, Windsor and Pitlochry before arriving in London's West End. Stage incl: Darling Daisy; The Lionel Touch; The Winslow Boy; Joking Apart. Starred in Goodbye Fidel on Broadway. Films incl: East of Elephant Rock; The Girl in Blue Velvet; Zulu Dawn. Latest films: The Eye of the Needle; From A Far Country; The Letter; Heat and Dust. In addition to The Regiment, TV incl: The Freewheelers; Rivals of Sherlock Holmes; The British Hero; Affairs of the Heart; Jennie, Lady Randolph Churchill; The Duchess of Duke Street; East Lynne. Education: Eton. m actress Angharad Rees, 2 s Linford, Rhys William. Address: c/o Chatto and Linnit, London W1. Starsign: Sagittarius.

CHADWICK, Philip
Reporter b 29.9.48 Nobut, Uttoxeter, Staffs. Newspaper training for four years on Midland weeklies and eight years freelancing for Fleet Street and radio and TV before joining Southern TV March 1980 where he spent two years script-writing. Moved to TSW Jan 1982. Education: Ipstones Primary and Leek High School, Staffs. m Alison. Address: c/o TSW, Plymouth. Starsign: Libra. Hobbies: gardening, walking, reading. Person he would most like to meet: 'The traffic warden who made my life hell in Portsmouth'.

CHALMERS, Judith
Presenter b 10th October Manchester. Always wanted to be a broadcaster and asked BBC Manchester for an audition when she was 13. Started on Northern Children's Hour, had her own radio programme at 17; first TV appearance was Northern TV announcer. Now one of TV's busiest women, introducing After Noon Plus and Wish You Were Here. Commentates for ITV on Royal Film Performance, Derby, beauty championships (incl Miss World, Miss UK, etc) and coverage of Royal and State occasions for ITV incl wedding of Prince Charles. Radio incl: regularly chairing Radio 4's Tuesday Call phone-in. Also commentates on special events for BBC radio OBs, incl: Grand National; Ascot and Royal occasions (Princess Anne's wedding; Silver Jubilee; State Opening of Parliament). Education: Withington Girls', Manchester; Miss Wilkinson's Secretarial School. m commentator Neil Durden-Smith, 1 d Emma, 1 s Mark. Address: c/o Thames TV, London NW1. Starsign: Libra. Hobbies: photography, cooking, gardening, watching cricket. Person she would most like to meet: 'Gene Kelly, if he would take me dancing in the rain.'

CHAMPNEY, Clive
Announcer/newsreader b 12.4.29 Wokingham, Berks. Entered broadcasting in Australia in 1949. Radio/TV incl: commercials and documentary voice-overs; recording Talking Books for the blind and language laboratory tapes; plays for BBC and ITV; writer/presenter (with his wife) of a daily radio serial for children (400 episodes). Announcer/newsreader with Border TV since 1963. Education: Ranelagh School, Berks. m Jo, 1 d Julia, 5 s Gerard, Jonothan, Adrian, Edmund, Matthew.

Address: c/o Border TV, Carlisle. Starsign: Aries. Hobbies: music, crosswords, cats. Person he would most like to meet: 'Artur Rubinstein: not only a supreme pianist – the experience of his 95 years and his joy of living make him a fascinating raconteur.'

CHAPMAN, Constance
Actress b 29.3.12 Weston-super-Mare. Trained at drama school in Bristol and spent many years acting at Bristol's Little Theatre and on radio. From Bristol she came to London to appear in The Celebration and The Contractor, two plays, she claims, which put her on the dramatic map, and she has scarcely stopped working since. She has also appeared at Bristol Old Vic and for the Royal Shakespeare Company, with whom she did a world tour in Hedda Gabler. Her first big parts on TV were in the Peter Nicholls play The Gorge, followed by Mummy and Daddy, and Hearts and Flowers – all Plays For Today. Other TV incl: Born and Bred; Angels; All Creatures Great and Small; A Kind of Loving; Winnie. Education: Redland High School, Bristol. m Travers Cousins (dis), 2 s Mark, Timothy. Address: c/o William Morris Agency Ltd, London W1. Starsign: Aries. Hobby: gardening. Person she would most like to meet: 'Ian Botham – to thank him for all the excitement he gave viewers on television.'

CHARLTON, Jack OBE
TV football commentator/ manager Sheffield Wednesday FC b 8.5.36 Ashington, Northumberland. Started playing with Leeds United as an amateur 1950; joined them as a professional two years later. England International player, being capped 35 times 1965-70 and a member of the World Cup winning team 1966. Manager of Middlesbrough FC 1974; joined Sheffield Wednesday FC in same capacity 1977. Football commentator on TV since 1974 World Cup. Introduces BBC angling programme, Hooked! Education: Hirst Park Modern School, Ashington. m Patricia, 1 d Debra, 2 s John, Peter. Address: Worsborough, Barnsley. Starsign: Taurus. Hobbies: shooting, fishing, gardening.

CHASE, Lorraine
Actress b 16.7.51 South London. Former model who became better known as the girl in the Campari commercials. TV appearances in Max Bygraves Show; Blankety

Blank; Pygmalion; The Other 'Arf (series); Give Us a Clue. Address: c/o Peter Charlesworth Ltd, London SW7. Starsign: Cancer.

CHEGWIN, Keith
Presenter b 17.1.57 Liverpool. Attended a London stage school for six years, but from the age of 11 sang in working men's clubs in the north as a member of a family trio. Stage shows incl: The Good Old Bad Old Days; Tom Brown's Schooldays. Films: Polanski's Macbeth; and, for the Children's Film Foundation, Eggheads Robot; Elspeth's Double; Robin Hood Junior. TV incl: Swop Shop; Cheggers Plays Pop; Ronnie Barker Show; Liver Birds; The Chester Mystery Plays; Wackers; My Old Man; Black Beauty; Armchair Theatre; Village Hall; Celebrity Squares; It's a Knockout; Star Turn; All Star Record Breakers. Radio: presents a regular Sunday morning show on Radio Liverpool and contributes to Radio 1. Used to sing with the Kenny pop group. Address: c/o BBC TV, London W12. Starsign: Capricorn. Hobbies: horse-riding, reading, skating, playing piano and guitar. Person he would most like to meet: 'James Cagney – I've always fancied myself as a tough guy in a gangster film.'

CHILD, Jeremy
Actor b 20.9.44 Woking, Surrey. Trained for the stage at Bristol Old Vic Theatre

and Clark Kent, one of my heroes as a child.'

School and has been in rep at Windsor, Guildford, Colchester, Canterbury, Greenwich and Bromley. Plays in which he has appeared in London incl: Conduct Unbecoming; Oh Kay; Crete and Sergeant Pepper; Misalliance; Donkey's Years. Films incl: Privilege; Peace Game; Breaking of Bumbo; Oh What a Lovely War; Play Dirty; Emily; The Stud; Chanel Solitaire. TV incl: Take Three Girls; Coronation Street; Father, Dear Father; Glittering Prizes; Backs to the Land; Upchat Line; The Sweeney; Edward and Mrs Simpson; Wings; Robin's Nest; Winston Churchill The Wilderness Years; Sapphire and Steel; Vice Versa; 'T'is Pity She's A Whore; When the Boat Comes In; BBC's Play of the Month and Play for Tomorrow; Bird of Prey. Education: Eton; University of Poitiers. m Jan, 1 d Leonora. Address: c/o Michael Ladkin Ltd, London W1. Starsign: Virgo. Hobbies: flying, squash, laughing. Person he would most like to meet: 'Sir Ralph Richardson, because he's the greatest actor in the world.'

CHRISTIAN, Glynn

Presenter/writer b 1.1.42 Auckland, New Zealand. Self-taught cook, presenter of cookery programmes on TV and biographer of his ancestor Fletcher Christian of Mutiny on the Bounty fame. From the age 10 wanted to be either in films or on TV and was one of the first full-time writers for TV in New Zealand. In Dec 1965 came to England to break into British TV and do research on Fletcher Christian. This has resulted in the first Fletcher Christian biography, Fragile Paradise, and appearances on Pebble Mill at One in cookery series. His interest in cookery stems from his travels in connection with his production of a travel brochure for Clarksons, which set the style for today's brochures. Was food adviser for Thames TV's Magpie programmes, has been food correspondent for LBC since 1977 and contributes occasional cookery items in Gloria Hunniford's Radio 2 programme. Owns two delicatessen shops and has written seven books as well as two TV series for slow-to-learn children, Stop, Look, Listen and Up in the Attic, and scripted a cartoon series, The Flower Stories. Also wrote the script for the film Her Private Hell. Books: The No-cook Cook Book; Cheese and Cheese-making; Bread and Yeast Cookery; LBC News Radio Cookbook; Fragile Paradise; Guide to Delicatessen Food; Get Fresh with Glynn Christian. Address: c/o Joe Gurnett, London SW7. Starsign: Capricorn. Hobbies: cooking, campaigning to save Pitcairn Island. People he would most like to meet: 'Fletcher Christian, to have a damned good talk because he caused so much trouble,

CHURCHILL, Donald

Writer/actor b 6.11.30 Southall, Middx. Entered films and TV 1956, since when his output, both as actor and playwright, has been impressive, incl some 40 plays for TV alone. His TV credits incl: Head Full of Crocodiles; The Ship That Couldn't Stop; The Referees; Bulldog Breed (own series); Always Something Hot; Comrades in Arms; Sharp at Four; The Cherry on the Top; The Paraffin Season; The Hot House; Man Without a Mortgage; It's Not Me, It's Them; The Floating Population; The Happy Sacking; Never a Cross Word (series); The Return Match; Feeling the Pinch; The Party Piece; A Room in Town; The Loving Lesson; A Fluid Arrangement; You Don't Know Me, But; Leftovers; Hearts and Flowers; Knightsbridge; Tonight We Meet Arthur Pendleton; A Bit of a Lift; Moody and Peg (with Julia Jones); Feeling His Way; The £5 Orange; Pig in the Sky; The Sun Trap; Heartland; Spooner's Patch; Jack's Trade; Good Night – God Bless (with Joe McGrath). Films incl: Victim; The Wild Affair; Zepplin; My Family and Other Animals. Theatre incl: Under My Skin; Fringe Benefits (with Peter Yeldham). Education: 'Not much,' he says. 'I went to 13 schools and left with ignorance intact at 14.'

m actress Pauline Yates,
2 d Jemma, Polly. Address:
London NW1. Starsign:
Scorpio. Hobby: fantasizing
about learning French.
Person he would most like to
meet: 'There is no one I would
most like to meet that I haven't
met already.'

CLARKE, Jacqueline
Character actress b 13.2.42
Bucks. Trained at RADA and
rep experience at York,
Harrogate and Bournemouth.
Has been in most light
entertainment shows on TV
incl: Dave Allen at Large (for
seven years), and with Mike
Yarwood, Mike Reid, Les
Dawson, Kelly Monteith,
Terry Scott, Harry Worth;
Sharp Intake of Breath for
nearly five years; Sheridan's
Restoration comedy The
Critic for BBC. Radio incl: Roy
Castle's radio show Castles
on the Air from 1976. Stage
incl: The Boy Friend.
Education: St Mary's Primary;
Wimbledon County Grammar
School for Girls. m actor
Peter Cartwright (dis),
1 d Catherine. Address: c/o
Barry Burnett Organisation,
London W1. Starsign:
Aquarius. Hobbies: interior
decorating, walking. Person
she would most like to meet:
'Ingrid Bergman – a complete
actress, a complete person.'

CLEALL, Peter
Actor b 16.3.44 Finchley,
Middx. After acting school,
first big TV hit was in Please
Sir! followed by The Fenn St
Gang. Other TV incl: Mr Big;
The Losers; Tale of Two

Cities; Spooner's Patch. Wide
rep experience incl: Regent's
Park Open Air Theatre,
London, and at Watford,
Westcliff, Northampton,
Chester, Worthing, Coventry,
Plymouth. Ran his own
touring company and at
present runs fringe theatre
company in Brighton
currently presenting local
new plays. m (dis),
2 s Miles, Damian. Address:
c/o John Mahoney
Management, London NW1.
Starsign: Pisces. Hobbies:
squash, writing. Person he
would most like to have met:
Humphrey Bogart.

CLEESE, John
Actor/writer b 27.10.39
Weston-super-Mare. Started
in the Cambridge Footlights
Revue. Went to America with
it and stayed on to play in Half
a Sixpence. Returned to
make Frost Report; I'm Sorry,
I'll Read That Again; At Last
the 1948 Show; Monty
Python's Flying Circus;
Fawlty Towers, for which he
won TVTimes Award as
Funniest Man on TV
(1978-79). Education: Clifton;
Cambridge (studying Law).
m (1st) actress Connie Booth

(dis), (2nd) film director
Barbara Trentham,
1 d Cynthia. Address: c/o
Roger Hancock Ltd, London
SW1. Starsign: Scorpio.
Hobby: filling in
questionnaires. Person he
would most like to meet: The
Editor of TVTimes.

CLIVE, John
Actor/author b 6.1.38
London. Started as a child
actor. While working as a
page boy at the Shakespeare
Theatre in Liverpool he got a
part in the famous children's
stage show Casey's Court.
After National Service in the
RAF, went into rep and revue
in London. Other stage work
incl: Absurd Person Singular;
The Real Inspector Hound
(for the Young Vic); Wizard of
Oz. Films incl: Smashing
Time; The Italian Job; Yellow
Submarine (Lennon's voice);
Clockwork Orange; Carry On
Abroad; Great Expectations.
TV incl: Perils of Pendragon;
Robert's Robots; How Green
Was My Valley; The History of
Mr Polly; The Government
Inspector; The Nesbitts Are
Coming; The Sweeney;
Rising Damp; The Dick
Emery Show; Tropic. Also
produced documentary,
Some Of Our Airmen Are No
Longer Missing. Books:
KG 200 (first novel and
international best-seller); The
Last Liberator; Barossa;
Broken Wings. Education:
schools in London, Wales,
Liverpool. m Carole,
1 d Hannah, 1 s Alexander.
Address: Delgany, Co

Wicklow, Ireland. Starsign: Capricorn. Hobbies: cinema, television, football. Person he would most like to have met: 'Errol Flynn, just to talk, chew the fat and ask him why.'

CLYDE, Jeremy
Actor b 22.3.41 Dorney, Bucks. Trained at Central School of Speech and Drama. Part of partnership, Chad and Jeremy, with several hits in the 1960s before big acting break on stage in Conduct Unbecoming. TV incl: The Pallisers; The Darkwater Hall Mystery; Strife; How Green Was My Valley; The Marrying Kind; Sexton Blake and the Demon God; Disraeli; Flight Fund; Prometheus; Vienna 1990; Dial M For Murder; David Garrick and Mrs Woffington; Magnesia Blossom; Chronicle. Films incl: The Silver Bears; Esther, Ruth and Jennifer. Education: Ludgrove; Eton. m Vanessa, 1 d Lucy, 2 s James, Matthew. Address: c/o Joy Jameson, London SW1. Starsign: Aries.

COIA, Paul
TV presenter b 19.6.55 Glasgow. Three years in local radio (Radio Clyde) before becoming a continuity announcer for STV, 1980. Co-presented STV's Hi-Summer Extra that year. In Feb 1981, hosted a UNICEF concert in the presence of Princess Anne on STV and now presents own chat show series, Meet Paul Coia (also

on STV). Education: St Aloysius College, Glasgow; Glasgow University; Paisley College of Technology. Address: c/o Tony Meehan Assocs, Glasgow. Starsign: Gemini. Hobbies: reading, golf, squash, surviving. Person he would most like to meet: 'My tax inspector, to see who I've been supporting all these years.'

COLDWELL, Pattie
TV reporter b 14.5.52 Preston, Lancs. Originally a secretary but joined Granada TV as reporter/presenter 1976. Joined Nationwide as reporter 1979 and since 1982 reporting for Watchdog section of the programme. Education: Clitheroe Royal Grammar School for Girls. Address: c/o BBC, London W12. Starsign: Taurus. Hobbies: music, films, theatre, food and wine, sport, people, TV. Person she would most like to meet: 'Bette Midler – she's so confident, doesn't mind what other people think and has a tremendous sense of humour.'

COLE, George
Actor b 22.4.25 London. Discovered in 1940 by Alastair Sim to play a Cockney evacuee in the West End play, Cottage to Let, and became a star overnight; also appeared in the film version. After three years' service in the RAF he was in such films as My Brother's Keeper; Quartet; Morning Departure; Lady Godiva Rides Again; Laughter in Paradise. Other films incl: Top Secret; Will Any Gentleman; The Belles of St Trinians; The Green Man; Blue Murder at St Trinians; The Great St Trinians Train Robbery; One Way Pendulum. Stage incl: Flare Path; Mr Bolfy; Dr Angelus; The Anatomist; Too True to be Good; The Three Sisters; The Philanthropist; Banana Ridge; Deja Revue; Brimstone and Treacle; The Pirates of Penzance. On radio he was a household name in a Life of Bliss, for 15 years. On TV he had another success in Man Of Our Times. Recent TV incl: Out of the Unknown; The Gold Robbers; Sex Game; Murder; The Good Humoured Man; Don't Forget To Write; Minder (three series); The Bounder, and many plays. Education: Morden Council Secondary. m former actress Penny Morrell, 1 d Tara, 1 s Toby. Address: c/o Joy Jameson Ltd, London SW1. Starsign: Taurus. Person he would most like to meet: Brigitte Bardot.

COLEMAN, David
Reporter/interviewer
b 26.4.26 Alderley Edge,
Cheshire. Started as
newspaper journalist, Editor
of Cheshire County Express
at 23. Freelance radio
contributor before joining
BBC in Birmingham and later
in London. TV incl: Match of
the Day; Grandstand;
Sportsnight with Coleman; A
Question of Sport.
m Barbara, 3 d Anne,
Mandy, Samantha,
3 s David and Dean (twins),
Michael. Address: c/o
Bagenal Harvey, London W1.
Starsign: Taurus. Hobby:
golf.

COLERIDGE, Kate
Actress b. 22.9.43 Inverness,
Scotland. Trained at RADA
then rep incl: Farnham,
Chesterfield, Leicester. Also
worked for Mermaid Theatre,
Young Vic and National
Theatre, Prospect Company
and Ludlow Festival. Much
radio incl: Book at Bedtime,
and TV incl: Oil Strike North;

Upstairs, Downstairs; Blake's
Seven; The Cedar Tree;
Heartland; The Dancing
Years; Armchair Thriller –
Dying Day; Stay With Me Till
Morning; Number On End;
Reunion. Education: Pax Hill,
Bentley, Hants, and self
taught. m writer/ stunt
co-ordinator Frank Maher.
Address: c/o John Mahoney,
London NW1. Starsign:
Virgo/Libra cusp. Hobby:
'Having Sunday lunch and
witty conversation with my
friends in a good restaurant
from 2 till 7.' Person she
would most like to have met:
'Whoever sculpted the four
horses on St Marks Basilica in
Venice. You only have to see
them close up to know why.'

COLLINS, Lewis
Actor b 27.5.46 Birkenhead.
Started as a ladies'
hairdresser, then played
drums and guitar in pop
groups and had a number of
jobs before deciding to
become an actor. Also taught
deaf children in America and
Canada. Trained at the
London Academy of Music
and Dramatic Art followed by
rep at Chesterfield and
Glasgow, touring with
Prospect Theatre Company
and London's West End.
Stage incl: City Sugar; The
Threepenny Opera;
Tamburlaine The Great. TV
incl: Warship; The New
Avengers; The Cuckoo Waltz;

The Professionals; Must Wear
Tights. Films incl: Who Dares
Wins. Expert rifle and pistol
shot and driver of slow cars
and fast motor-cycles; Black
Belt in ju-jitsu. Education:
Bidston Primary and Grange
School, Birkenhead.
Address: Hampstead,
London. Starsign: Gemini.
Hobbies: running, tennis,
weight training, swimming,
target shooting, ju-jitsu,
writing stories, film-making,
research, circuit-training his
1200cc Harris Magnum.
Person he would most like to
have met: Buster Keaton.

COLLINS, Joan
Actress b 23.5.36 London.
Once described as 'one of
England's most beautiful
exports to Hollywood', and
well-known for her Cinzano
TV commercials (with
Leonard Rossiter) and her
many screen siren roles. Her
latest is that of a female JR
Ewing in Dynasty. Her first
taste of acting was at the age
of three in a school play.
Always dreamed of being an
actress and studied at RADA.
While there she was
photographed for women's
magazine illustrations and as
a result was offered a screen
test and given a five-year film
contract. Film debut in Lady
Godiva Rides Again, 1951.
Other films incl: The Square
Ring; Turn the Key Softly;
Cosh Boy; Our Girl Friday;

Land of the Pharohs (first
Hollywood film); The Virgin
Queen; The Girl on the Red
Velvet Swing; The Opposite
Sex; Sea Wife; Island in the
Sun; The Wayward Bus; The
Bravados; Rally Round the
Flag, Boys; The Road to Hong
Kong (the last 'Road' picture
which was made in England);
Seven Thieves; Esther and
the King; Subterfuge,
Heironymous Merkin; Up in
the Cellar; Quest; Revenge;
Tales from the Crypt; Fear in
the Night; I Don't Want to be
Born; Witness Madness; Dark
Places; The Call of the Wolf;
Empire of the Ants; The Big
Sleep; The Day of the Fox;
The Stud; Zero to 60; Game
for Vultures; Sunburn; The
Bitch; Innocents Abroad;
Nutcracker. TV incl: The
Persuaders; The Man from
UNCLE; The Virginian; Fallen
Angels; Mission Impossible;
Space 1999; Celebrity
Squares; Police Woman;
Starsky and Hutch; Tales of
the Unexpected (Neck;
Georgy Porgy); A Girl Can't
Always Have Everything;
Dynasty. In 1980 she
appeared on stage at the
Chichester Festival in The
Last of Mrs Cheyney which
transferred to London's West
End. Voted the screen's top
sex symbol 1979. Books: My
Search for Love; Past
Imperfect; Joan Collins
Beauty Book; Katy.
Education: evacuated during
the war and attended 13
schools before Francis
Holland School for Girls,
London. m (1st) actor
Maxwell Reed (dis), (2nd)
actor Anthony Newley (dis),
(3rd) film producer Ron Kass,
3 d Tara, Sacha (from 2nd
m), Katyana (from 3rd m), 3
step-s David, Robert,
Johnathan. Address: c/o
ICM, London W1. Hobbies:
photography, collecting
antiques, giving parties.

CONN, Didi
Actress b Brooklyn, New
York. Benson's new
secretary, Denise, who has
been described as 'the perky
actress with the cartoon
voice'. Began her acting
career when she was 19 while
still studying drama. She
toured with the National
Theatre Company's Mimika
troupe, who perform in mime,
for a year and a half and then
decided to try the
commercial field. Her
unusual voice ('I was born
with it', she says) got her into
TV commercials and she
appeared in more than 50 of
them in 1973. In 1974 she
went to Hollywood to try and
break into TV. She appeared
in Happy Days; The Rookies;
Keep on Trucking; The
Practice; Benson. On stage
she has been in a production
of Room Service with Happy
Days star Henry Winkler, and
was the voice of Raggedy
Ann in a musical film rendition
of Raggedy Ann and Andy at
Radio City Music Hall.
Education: American Musical
Academy, New York.

CONNELL, Brian
Commentator and
programme consultant
b 12.4.16 London. Started
as a foreign exchange broker
in London in 1937. Went to
Hong Kong in 1939 as
manufacturers' agent and
then worked for Reuters and
was captured in Indo-China

by the Japanese on day of
Pearl Harbour. Served in the
RNVR from 1943-46, when he
became Daily Mail bureau
chief in Germany and roving
foreign correspondent. In
1950 moved to News
Chronicle as head of current
affairs bureau and roving
foreign correspondent. From
1954-55, TV commentator for
BBC on current affairs
programmes. Retained by
ITN 1955-60 as foreign affairs
commentator, regular
newscaster, diplomatic
correspondent, principle
foreign correspondent and
special events commentator.
Devised and presented first
transatlantic newscast via
Telstar (which won Producers
Guild Award for ITN). TV
programmes organised as
special events commentator
incl: coronation of Pope John;
Princess Margaret's
wedding; American
inauguration of President
Kennedy; wedding of
Princess Alexandra;
wedding of Duke of Kent;
death of Pope John; funeral of
President Kennedy; State
funeral of Sir Winston
Churchill; funeral of Senator
Robert Kennedy; interview
with Prince of Wales and his
investiture at Caernarvon.
From 1960-63 he was
chairman and principal
commentator of This Week
and since 1967 has given an
annual series of 13 half-hour
Brian Connell Interviews for
ITV. Since 1946 he has been
political commentator in

German, French and Spanish Overseas Service of BBC Radio. Is founder-editor of European Review, a regular contributor to various publications and newspapers and since 1950 has written 14 books and edited/translated five others. Education: Brighton Grammar School, studied Madrid (1933-36) and Berlin (1936-37) on travelling scholarships. m Esmée. Address: c/o Connell Editors, London EC2. Starsign: Aries. Hobbies: skiing, skin-diving, cooking. People he would most like to have met: 'The first Duke of Wellington and Lord Palmerston – more fascinating than anyone alive today'.

written two plays An' Me Wi A Bad Leg Tae, and When The Hair Was Long And Time Was Short. Films incl: Absolution. On radio he has appeared on Open House; Desert Island Discs, Start the Week. TV incl: The Elephant's Graveyard (Play for Today); The Kenny Everett Video Show; The Kenny Everett Television Show; Not the Nine O'Clock News; Swop Shop; Songs of Praise; The Book Programme; Parkinson. His six LPs have earned him four gold and two silver discs. Education: St Peter's Primary and St Gerard's Senior Secondary Schools, Glasgow. Address: c/o AMP Ltd, London W1. Starsign: Sagittarius. Hobbies: fishing, cooking, reading.

which was seen in 70 countries and won him the Golden Globe Award of the Hollywood Foreign Press Association, the Barcelona International Television Festival Award as Best Actor and four Emmy nominations as Best Actor in a Dramatic Series. He is now working on a new series in which he heads a team of young special agents, Today's FBI. Education: Fresno High School, where he was an athlete of considerable prowess excelling in football, baseball, basketball and track events. m college sweetheart Mary Lou Wiley, 1 d Dana Lee, 1 s Matthew Gunnar. Hobbies: classic cars, golf, tennis, water-skiing. Starsign: Leo.

CONNOLLY, Billy
Comedian b 24.11.42 Glasgow. Apprentice welder on the Clyde, paratrooper in the TA, oil rig welder in Biafra, busker and a member of the Humblebums group before becoming a successful solo comedian, first in Scotland, then the rest of Britain and now the world. On 14th April 1977 started out on the largest concert tour ever undertaken by an entertainer at that time – 51 dates. In 1980 his On Your Bike tour of Britain was even bigger – took in 86 dates and developed into the Bite Your Bum world tour. Apart from stage concerts, has also appeared with the Scottish Opera Company as the jailer in Die Fledermaus and the play Red Runner. Has also

CONNORS, Mike
Actor b 15.8.25 Fresno, California. After serving three years in the Air Force during World War II, he enrolled at the University of California, Los Angeles, to study law. While playing a game of basketball he was spotted by a film director and he was still at university when he signed for his first film – Sudden Fear with Joan Crawford. There were other minor roles before Sky Commando; Flesh is the Spur; Harlow; Panic Button; Stagecoach; Where Love Has Gone; Kiss the Girls and Make Them Cry. TV appearances in Cheyenne, Maverick and Wagon Train before he starred as Nick Stone in the Tightrope series. Then, in 1971 came Mannix,

CONRAD, Robert
Actor b 1.3.35 Chicago. Started as a singer and still has a night club act. Had jobs as deck-hand and milkman, but always wanted to be an actor. After small parts, he was given more substantial roles in Lawman; Maverick; 77 Sunset Strip; and a star part in Hawaiian Eye. Other TV incl: Wild West; Centennial. Education: public schools; Northwestern University in Chicago where he studied drama. m Joan, 2 d Joan, Nancy. Address: Hollywood. Starsign: Pisces. Hobbies: boxing, music, Spanish ballet, studying Spanish.

COOK, Sue
Presenter b 30.3.49 Ruislip, Middx. Spent nine years in radio and TV journalism – Capital Radio, BBC Radios 1 and 4, BBC TV and Thames TV. Since 1979 has been a presenter on Nationwide. Education: Vyner's Grammar School; Leicester University (BA Hons II Psychology, Archaeology and English). m John Wiliams. Address: c/o Bagenal Harvey Organisation, London W1. Starsign: Aries. Hobbies: singing (classical and popular), learning piano, psychology, driving. Person she would most like to meet: 'Graham Greene, my favourite author.'

COOMBS, Pat
Actress b 27th August London. First job was teaching at a kindergarten. Scholarship to LAMDA and after training stayed on to teach. Then rep at Scunthorpe and with companies all over England. First came to fore as Nola (with Irene Handl in Hello Playmates on radio). In constant demand for TV series – Lollipop Loves Mr

Mole; Beggar My Neighbour and other Reg Varney shows; Dick Emery's series; Don't Drink The Water; Celebrity Squares; fourth series of You're Only Young Twice; Blankety Blank; Punchlines; 3-2-1; This Is Your Life (as a victim). Recent films incl: Oooh . . .You Are Awful; Adolf Hitler – My Part In His Downfall. Education: County School for Girls, Beckenham, Kent. Address: Harrow-on-the-Hill, Middx. Starsign: Virgo. Hobbies: writing letters, driving, reading, puss-cats! Person she would most like to meet: 'The daughter of the late Violette Szabo GC to salute the courage of her parents and to give thanks for their poem The Life That I Have.'

COOPER, Syd (Cyanide)
Wrestler b 4.4.45 Queensbury, Yorks. Trained by British champion Eric Taylor. Has wrestled in Africa, Marubi, Zambia, Lagos, Kuwait, Belgium, France, Norway. Very experienced tag match wrestler having tagged with Giant Haystacks, John Quinn, Mick McManus, Steve Logan, Alan Dennison, Big Jim Harris and others. Finalist in November 1981 for the Mike Marino Memorial Trophy, losing to Superstar Sanders. Education: Secondary Modern School, Queensbury. m Sharon. Address: c/o Dale Martin Promotions Ltd, London SW9. Starsign: Aries. Hobby: football (a Leeds United

supporter). Person he would most like to meet: Charles Bronson.

COOPER, Tommy
Comedian b 19.3.22 Caerphilly. Childhood spent in Exeter and Southampton where he joined the army, serving in the Horse Guards for seven years. Became an entertainer on leaving the army 1947. Cabaret, music hall, revue, TV, Windmill Theatre London, summer seasons, pantomime London Palladium, own shows, appearances before royalty, Royal Variety Shows, visits to USA – he's done them all and is now one of the country's highest paid entertainers. Specialises in tricks that go wrong, but in fact is a fine straight magician and a member of the Inner Magic Circle. His TV shows have been screened in America, Europe and Australia, where he is extremely popular. Education: Mount Radford School, Exeter. m Gwen, 1 d Vicky, 1 s Thomas. Address: c/o Miff Ferrie, London SW1. Starsign: Pisces. Hobbies: boxing, judo, swimming, show business and magic. Person he would most like to meet: Jacques Tati.

COPLEY, Peter
Actor b 20.5.15 Bushey, Herts. Wanted to go into the Royal Navy when he left school, but became interested in the theatre through his housemaster.

Trained at the Old Vic School and later joined the Old Vic Company. Rep at Bexhill, Leeds and Dublin. First London appearance was as a footman in Viceroy Sarah 1935; Old Vic at New Theatre, London 1945-50; National Theatre 1979-80. Films incl: Jane Eyre; Troopship; King and Country; Shout At The Devil; Little Lord Fauntleroy. TV incl: The Gold Robbers; Hadleigh; Big Brother; Forsyte Saga; The Regiment; Manhunt; Father Brown; Survivors; Sutherland's Law; Bill Brand; Bless This House; The Foundation; Churchill and the Generals; The Gentle Touch; United Kingdom; Bless Me Father; Rabbit Pie Day; Tales of the Unexpected. Education: Westminster. m (1st) actress Pamela Brown, (2nd) actress Ninka, (3rd) writer Margaret Tabor, 2 d Fanny, Emma (step d), 1 step-s Gideon. Address: c/o St James Management, London SW1. Starsign: Taurus. Hobby: reading law (called to the Bar at Middle Temple 1963).

CORBETT, Matthew
Entertainer b 28.3.48

Yorkshire. Trained as an actor at Central School of Speech and Drama, and in rep at Bristol, York, Chelmsford, Dundee and Richmond. TV incl: Magpie; Rainbow; Matt and Gerry Ltd; and The Sooty Show which he took over following his father's (Harry) heart attack. Education: Woodhouse Grove Public School, Bradford, Yorks. m Sallie, 1 d Tamsin, 2 s Benjamin, Joe. Address: c/o Vincent Shaw Assocs, London W1. Starsign: Aries. Hobbies: music (writing and recording), photography, squash, poultry keeping. Person he would most like to meet: 'Paul McCartney, because I like and admire his music.'

CORBETT, Ronnie OBE
Actor/comedian b 4.12.30. Edinburgh. Started amateur dramatics at 16. Many TV shows incl: Crackerjack; Dickie Henderson Show. Spotted in Danny La Rue's nightclub by David Frost, then Frost Report; No – That's Me Over Here; Frost on Sunday; The Corbett Follies; The Two Ronnies; Sorry! m Anne Hart, 2 d Emma, Sophie. Address: c/o Kavanagh Entertainments, London W1. Starsign: Sagittarius. Hobbies: football, golf, horse-racing. Person he would most like to meet: Frank Sinatra.

CORBIN, Jane
TV reporter/presenter

b 16.7.54 Exeter, Devon. Started in TV as political researcher for Granada's State of the Nation series. Joined Thames TV as writer/researcher on This Week. Also investigative reporter on Thames Report, Inside Business and Thames News. Technology Writer of 1980 for articles in The New Statesman and Sunday Times. Education: London University (Hons Lit). Address: c/o Thames TV, London NW1. Starsign: Cancer. Hobbies: travelling, learning to fly. Person she would most like to meet. 'Indira Gandhi, because she is one of the greatest politicians of our time.'

CORNWELL, Judy
Actress b 22.2.42 London. Trained as a dancer and singer, was initially a student dancing teacher. Untrained as an actress except for a period of coaching by Sybil Wise. First stage appearance in pantomime at Brighton when 15; London debut in Oh What a Lovely War. Stage also incl; Mr Whatnot; Don't Let Summer Come; Old Flames and 1972 season with

RSC at Stratford. Films incl: Every Home Should Have One; Wuthering Heights. TV incl: Younger Generation series; Feydeau farces; Call Me Daddy (Emmy Award 1967); Relatively Speaking; Cork Moustache; Man of Straw; The Chinese Prime Minister; Night of the Tanks; Moody and Peg; London Assurance; Cranford (musical); Bonos; Mill on the Floss; Good Companions; Brothers Grimm (Omnibus); A Case of Spirits. Also children's programmes, story reading, panel games, plays and light entertainment shows. Education: Inglethorpe Prep, Norfolk; Convent of Mercy, Australia; Lewes Grammar for Girls, Sussex. m John Parry, 1 s Edward. Address: c/o Larry Dalzell, London WC2. Starsign: Pisces. Hobbies: writing, cooking, community involvement, psychology, gardening. Person she would most like to have met: 'Carl Jung – wouldn't you?'

COURTENAY, Margaret
Actress b 14.11.23 Cardiff. Was broadcasting when she was 14. Trained at LAMDA and rep, incl: Stratford, Bristol Old Vic, Oxford, Regent's Park, Welsh National Theatre, Chichester and tours of Europe, Canada and Australia. Theatre work in London's West End incl: Ring Round the Moon; Alfie; The Killing of Sister George; Hadrian VII; Mame; 13 Rue de l'Amour (for which she received the Society of West

End Managers Award for best supporting performance, 1976); Separate Tables; Murder Among Friends; The Rivals; The Beggar's Opera; What the Butler Saw; The Knight of the Burning Pestle; The Importance of Being Earnest; Cards on the Table. Films incl: Isadora; Under Milk Wood; Royal Flash; Sarah; Oh Heavenly Dog; The Mirror Crack'd. TV incl: Billy Liar; It Ain't Half Hot Mum; The Squirrels; Howerd Confessions; London Belongs to Me; Best of Friends; The Up-Chat Line; A Sharp Intake of Breath; Mind Your Language; Out; Fearless Frank; Rings on Their Fingers; The Old Curiosity Shop; Goodbye Darling; Good Companions; Winston Churchill The Wilderness Years; Only When I Laugh; The Kelly Monteith Show; Tom, Dick and Harriet. Education: grammar school. m (dis), 1 s Julian. Address: c/o Peter Browne Management, London SW9. Starsign: Scorpio. Hobbies: painting, gardening, mini-exploring, talking. Person she would most like to meet: 'Yehudi Menuhin – a great man of his time and a consumate artist.'

COWIE, Alan
Reporter/presenter
b 28.4.48 Aberdeen. Trained at Central School of Speech and Drama; Jordanhill College of Education; BBC and Grampian TV. Presenter 12

Noon and Northbeat 1972-75 on Radio 4 Scotland. Presenter/reporter Grampian TV since 1975, also commentator for Grampian documentaries Blowout at Bravo, and Cinderella from the Sea. Education: Aberdeen Grammar School. m Evelyn, 1 d Fiona. Address: c/o Grampian TV, Aberdeen. Starsign: Taurus. Hobbies: gardening, fishing.

COYNE, Tom
Presenter/interviewer
b 15.4.35 South Shields. Worked for Tyne Tees from 1959-64, appearing in the station's first programme. Link man on the nightly news magazine North East Roundabout; presenter of Spotlight; commentator at Duke of Kent's wedding. Joined BBC 1964; link man on nightly news magazine Midlands Today and Nationwide. Other BBC TV incl: Top Gear; Dance Date; Songs of Praise; Know How. Radio incl: The Archers. In 1980 left Midlands Today to become the main presenter and link man on Tyne Tees and presenter of the networked book programme A Better Read. Director of TV facilities company with its own TV studio. Education: Corby Hall, Sunderland. m Patricia, 1 d Elizabeth, 1 s Michael. Address: c/o Tyne Tees TV, Newcastle. Starsign: Aries. Hobby: writing. Person he would most like to have met: 'William Shakespeare – I would like his comments on all the

royalties he has been missing.'

CRAIG, Andy
Announcer b. 5.12.54 Cumbria. Always wanted to work in some branch of entertainment and began as freelance in commercial radio. Joined Metro Radio 1977 and Tyne Tees TV 1978. Also hosted show with BBC Radio Newcastle and wrote and broadcast series of 10 situation comedies for radio. Cut his first disc, Bad Dream, in 1978 and about to record again. Education: The Grammar School for Boys, Barrow in Furness; Newcastle University (Hons degree Agriculture). Address: c/o Tyne Tees TV, Newcastle. Starsign: Sagittarius. Hobbies: music, art, motor vehicles. Person he would most like to meet: 'Stanley Baxter – his impressions never cease to amaze me. A superb comic.'

CRAIG, Michael
Actor b 27.1.29 Poona, India. Served in the Merchant Navy 1944-49 when he started acting at the Castle Theatre, Farnham. Rep at

York, Windsor and Oxford when he was given a film contract with the Rank Organisation 1954-61. Appeared in about 50 films incl: Passage Home; House of Secrets; Yield to the Night; The Angry Silence (also the writer); Doctor in Love; Life at the Top; Star!; The Royal Hunt of the Sun; The Killing in Angel Street. Stage incl: season at Stratford 1963-64; A Whistle in the Dark; Funny Girl; The Homecoming (in New York). On TV has appeared in 49 plays and series, incl: Tiger Trap (also the writer); The Talking Head; Husbands and Lovers; Second Time Around; Saint Joan; The Foundation; The Danedyke Mystery; Triangle. Educated in Canada. m Susan, 1 d Jessica, 2 s Stephen, Michael. Address: c/o ICM, London W1. Starsign: Aquarius. Hobbies: sport, golf, snooker, reading. Person he would most like to have met: 'Voltaire, who did more than anyone to bring the human race out of the Middle Ages without killing anyone.'

CRAIG, Wendy
Actress b 20.6.34 Sacriston, Co Durham. Won first acting award at the age of three. Later trained at London's Central School of Dramatic Art before going to Ipswich Rep. Chosen by J B Priestley for the role of Monica Twigg in Mr Kettle and Mrs Moon. Leading stage appearances since, incl: George Dillon; The Sport of My Mad Mother;

Ride A Cock Horse; I Love You Mrs Patterson; Peter Pan. Films incl: Room at the Top; The Mindbenders; The Nanny; I'll Never Forget What's His Name; Joseph Andrews; The Servant. TV incl: Candida; Wings of a Dove; Not in Front of the Children; And Mother Makes Three; And Mother Makes Five; Butterflies; Nanny. Voted Funniest Woman on Television 1972/73/74 by TVTimes readers. TV Actress of the Year (Drama) BAFTA 1968. Variety Club TV Personality of the Year BBC 1969, ITV 1973. Education: Durham and Darlington High Schools; Yarm Grammar. m musician and writer Jack Bentley, 2 s Alaster, Ross. Address: c/o Hatton-Baker Agency, London W1. Starsign: Gemini. Hobbies: music, horticulture. Person she would most like to have met: 'Erik Satie – a musical genius and humourist.'

CRAMPTON, Bob
Reporter b 15.3.51 Durban, South Africa. Worked in South Africa for the Argus Group of newspapers before coming to England where he worked for the North Devon Journal and Herald and Sunday Independent before joining Westward TV/TSW in 1979. Works for the Scene South West programme. Education: Sutton Grammar School, Plymouth. m Carol, 2 s James, Rory. Address: c/o TSW, Plymouth. Starsign: Pisces. Hobby: sailing. Person he would most like to

meet: 'Bo Derek – for the obvious reasons.'

CRANHAM, Kenneth
Actor b 12.12.44
Dunfermline. Trained for the stage at RADA and the National Youth Theatre. Wide TV experience incl: Coronation Street; Danger UXB; Thérèse Raquin; Sound Of The Guns; Sergeant Cribb; Butterflies Don't Count; The Caretaker; 'Tis A Pity She's A Whore; The Bell; The Merchant of Venice; La Ronde; Shine on Harvey Moon. Education: Tulse Hill Comprehensive.
m Charlotte Cornwell, 1 d Nancy. Address: c/o Jeremy Conway, London W1. Starsign: Sagittarius. Hobbies: photography, music, walking. Person he would most like to meet: 'Willie Nelson, because of my interest in country music.'

CRAVEN, Gemma
Actress b 1.6.50 Dublin. Won a singing contest when she was three and decided on an acting and singing career immediately! Trained at the Bush Davies School in Romford, Essex. Made professional debut at the Palace Theatre, Westcliff-on-Sea 1968 as the maid in Let's Get a Divorce and then played Cinderella in the pantomime there. After summer season in Blackpool and pantomime in Watford, made her London West End debut in Fiddler on the Roof in 1970. Followed by extensive stage work in London incl: Audrey!; Trelawny; Dandy Dick; Black Comedy; Songbook; They're Playing Our Song. Also appeared at Bristol Old Vic and two seasons at Chichester Festival Theatre. Films incl: The Slipper and the Rose (Royal Film Performance 1976); Why Not Stay For Breakfast?; Wagner. TV incl: Hey Brian!; The Harry Secombe Show; BBC pantomime; The Late Late Show; The Russell Harty Show; Pebble Mill; So You Think You Know About Love?; Call My Bluff; Blankety Blank; Saturday Scene; The Des O'Connor Show; The Perry Como Christmas Special; The Val Doonican Show; The Good Old Days; Celebrity Squares; Whose Baby?; Rainbow; Gallery; Give Us a Clue; Parkinson; Song By Song By Alan Jay Lerner; Song By Song By Noël Coward; The Royal Variety Performance of 1979; Starburst; Emily; Must Wear Tights; Pennies From Heaven; She Loves Me; This Is Your Life (as subject); The Morecambe and Wise Show (three times); It's a Musical World; The Dick Emery Show; Enterprise. Her many awards incl: London Evening News Film Award for Most Promising New Actress 1976; Variety Club's Film Actress of the Year 1976; Society of West End Theatre's Award for Best Actress in a Musical 1980. Education: Loretto College, St Stephen's Green, Dublin; St Bernard's Convent, Westcliff-on-Sea, Essex.

actor Frazer Hines. Address: c/o Stella Richards Management, London SW6. Starsign: Gemini. Hobbies: crochet, eating out, attending horse races. Person she would most like to meet: 'Have already met (and married) him!'

CRAVEN, John
TV and radio journalist b 16th August Leeds. Started as trainee reporter in Leeds and after jobs on local papers in Yorkshire started on radio, first as a freelance, then as a full-time newsreader. Worked as a reporter on TV programme Look North and moved to Bristol in 1970 to work on Points West and as anchorman for a children's programme, Search. Has presented John Craven's Newsround, the first news programme in the world specially for children, since it started in April 1972. Has also presented Multi-Coloured Swop Shop; Breakthrough; Story Behind the Story; The Show Me Show, and a guest presenter on Start the Week on Radio 4. Author of six books. Education: Leeds Modern School. m Marilyn, 2 d Emma, Victoria. Address: c/o BBC, London. Starsign: Leo. Hobbies: aviation, wildlife. Person he would most like to meet: 'Too many to list but they include the Pope, Lech Walesa, the Queen Mother, etc.'

CRIBBINS, Bernard

Actor b 29.12.28 Oldham, Lancs. Widely experienced TV and stage actor who first appeared on the stage in Oldham Rep in 1942. Other rep work in Manchester and Hornchurch before coming to London where his recent stage work incl: Not Now, Darling; The Love Game; There Goes the Bride; Hiss and Boo. Films incl: Casino Royale; The Railway Children; Frenzy; The Water Babies. On TV he has done countless commercials and guest spots as well as two series of his own show, Cribbins. Other TV incl: Comedy Playhouse; Get the Drift; Children Singing; Jackanory; Call My Bluff; Looks Familiar; The Good Old Days; The Wombles; Feydeau Farce; You Must Be Joking; Junkin; Fawlty Towers; Star Turn (presenter); Dangerous Davies; Shillingbury Tales. Education: St Anne's Elementary School, Oldham. m Gillian McBarnet. Address: c/o Crouch Assocs, London W1. Starsign: Capricorn. Hobbies: golf, fly tying, bird watching.

CROWDEN, Graham

Actor b 30.11.22 Edinburgh. Started as trainee assistant stage manager at Stratford-upon-Avon followed by rep experience at Theatre Royal, Stratford; Dundee; Nottingham; Bristol Old Vic; Glasgow Citizen's Theatre. Has appeared in many productions at the

Royal Court London, and was a member of the National Theatre Company at the Old Vic, and the RSC. Large number of plays and series on TV incl: The Last of Mrs Cheyney; Twelfth Night; MacAdam and Eve; Nil Carborundum; The Enemy; The Soldier's Tale; Ten Commandments; Trelawney of the Wells; Long Lease of Summer; The British Hero; On the Highroad; Bellamira; Shades of Greene; Porridge; The Island; Raffles; The Camerons; Doctor Who; The Sun Trap; Beloved Enemy; The Professionals; The Brack Report. Education: Edinburgh Academy. m Phyllida Hewat, 3 d Lucy, Sarah, Kate, 1 s Harry. Address: c/o Peter Browne Management, London SW9. Starsign: Sagittarius. Hobbies: music, tennis, cooking.

CROWTHER, Leslie

Actor/comedian b 6.2.33 Nottingham. Originally intended for a musical career and studied piano seriously for a number of years. During this time he appeared in schools broadcasts for BBC Drama School, then rep at Regent's Park Open Air Theatre. Accent on Youth (radio) led to High Spirits in the West End and six seasons with the Fol-de-Rols. Other stage appearances incl: Let Sleeping Wives Lie; Palladium Pantomime; summer seasons; Royal Variety Performance. TV incl: High Summer; Crackerjack; The Black and White Minstrel Show; The Saturday Crowd; Crowther's in Town; My Good Woman; Big Boy Now; Hi Summer; Leslie Crowther's Scrap Book; Starburst; The Crowther Collection; Bud'n'Ches. Education: Nottingham High School; Thames Valley Grammar School; Arts Educational School, London. m Jean, 4 d Lindsay and Elizabeth (twins), Caroline, Charlotte, 1 s Nicholas. Address: Corston, Bath. Starsign: Aquarius. Hobbies: cricket (Lord's Taverners), collecting pot-lids. Person he would most like to meet: 'The anonymous gentleman who writes for the William Hickey column in the Daily Express! I'd like to know if he looks human!'

CRYER, Barry

Comedian/writer b 23.3.35 Leeds. Professional debut at Leeds City of Varieties when he was at Leeds University. Then the Windmill and stage musicals. Started writing in 1960 and has since written for most of Britain's top comedians – The Two Ronnies; Morecambe and

Wise; Tommy Cooper; Bruce Forsyth, and in recent years, Kenny Everett. Frequently appears on radio and TV incl: Blankety Blank; Give Us a Clue; Punchlines; I'm Sorry I Haven't a Clue; Just a Minute, and many more. Education: Leeds University (BA Eng Lit, failed). m singer Terry Donovan, 1 d, 3 s. Address: c/o Roger Hancock, London SW1. Starsign: Aries. Person he would most like to meet: 'Peter Ustinov, the complete writer/performer.'

CUFF, Susan

TV hostess b 21.7.53 Broxburn, Scotland. Became Mr & Mrs Hostess after a year as Miss Great Britain 1975, and a year's teaching at her old school in Manchester. Qualified teacher in dress design, still does some designing and at one time designed and made all the dresses she wore on the programme. Other TV incl: Happy Families; Innes Book of Records. Education: Moorclose Senior High, Manchester; Bath College of Home Economics. m TV journalist and presenter David Davies, 1 d Amanda Jane. Address: c/o Border TV, Carlisle. Starsign: cusp of Cancer and Leo. Hobbies: classical guitar. Person she would most like to meet: Rowan Atkinson.

CUKA, Frances

Actress b London. Trained for the stage at the Guildhall School of Music and Drama. Much stage experience incl:

the original production of Taste of Honey; Same Time Next Year; Waters of the Moon; Under Milk Wood. Films incl: Scrooge; Henry VIII and his Six Wives; The Watcher in the Woods. First TV in 1960 incl: The Old Wives Tale; Days in the Trees; Day of the Tortoise; Retreat; Point of Departure; Sense and Sensibility; Miss Nightingale; Within These Walls; The Boy Dominic; One Day at a Time; Crown Court (once as defending counsel and once as defendant); Tea on St Pancras Station; The Beggar's Opera; Member of the Wedding; Girl Talk; Charlie Boy. Has also been in Love Story five times. Education: Brighton and Hove High School. Address: c/o Miller Management, Teddington, Middx. Starsign: Leo. Hobbies: going to the theatre, opera and ballet, music in many forms, tennis, tap dancing. Person she would most like to meet: 'Jack Lemmon – as I can't meet Elizabeth I, I'll settle for him.'

CULLEN, Sarah

TV reporter b 6.10.49 Newcastle upon Tyne. Joined ITN 1972 as graduate trainee and has since covered many assignments, both at home and abroad, as TV reporter. Book: In Praise of Panic. Education: University College, London (BA Hons). Address: c/o ITN, London W1. Starsign: Libra. Hobbies: French cooking, politics, walking. Person she would most like to have met: 'My grandfather – one of the old school of Scottish journalists.'

CULLUM, Carolyne

Presenter/reporter b 9.10.47 Bryan, Texas. Journalistic training school and Kentish Express before joining Southern TV's Day By Day programme (1972-74). Then with BBC's news team and ITN. Presenter/reporter with TVS since Dec 1981. Education: England and the United States. m Christopher St John Wilson, 2 d Laurel, Miranda. Address: c/o PVA Management Ltd, London W1. Starsign: Libra. Hobby: collecting, especially china. Person she would most like to have met: Charles II.

CULVER, Michael

Actor b 16.6.38 London. Studied for the stage at LAMDA and since entering the industry in 1958 has done extensive TV and film work. Films incl: Goodbye Mr Chips; Conduct Unbecoming. TV incl: The Villains; The Adventures of Black Beauty; Philby, Burgess and Maclean; both series of Secret Army; Fanny

By Gaslight; Diamonds. Education: Gresham's School, Holt, Norfolk. m Lucinda, 2 s Roderic, Justin. Address: c/o John Redway and Assocs, London W1. Starsign: Gemini. Hobbies: go, golf. Person he would most like to meet: 'Fujisawa Shuko, probably the greatest living go player.'

CURRIE, Tony
Announcer/newsreader/presenter b 5.12.51 Ardrossan, Ayrshire. Started his own radio station at home when he was 11, and still runs it as a hobby. Presented first programme on Radio Clyde in 1973 and various other Radio Clyde programmes (incl: Homeward Bound; Through the Night) until 1976 when he joined Scottish TV as announcer/newsreader. Education: The Academy, Ardrossan. m radio presenter/producer Karin Spalter, 1 d Julia, 1 s Leo. Address: c/o STV, Glasgow. Starsign: Sagittarius. Hobbies: 'definitive' collection of Radio Times and TVTimes, going back to 1923, his radio station. Person he would most like to meet:

'Sylvia Peters – the first TV announcer I remember as a child.'

CURTHOYS, Ann
Actress b 16.2.42 Clevedon, Somerset. Dancing and drama school training before RADA and rep at Salisbury and Royal Shakespeare Company. Many TV plays and series incl: Return to Yesterday; You Can't Win; 1990; Public Eye; Rainbow; Rooms; Juliet Bravo; The Gentle Touch. Films incl: The Magnet; A Man For All Seasons. Education: Waterloo Secondary, Liverpool. m (1st) actor Tim Wylton (dis), (2nd) musician Roger Walker, 1 d Emma, 1 s Huw (both from 1st m). Address: c/o London Actors, Richmond, Surrey. Starsign: Aquarius. Hobbies: walking, cycling. Person she would most like to meet: 'Michael Wood, presenter of the TV series, The Dark Ages.'

CUTHBERTSON, Iain
Actor b 4.1.30 Glasgow. First break as an actor was on radio while studying at Aberdeen University. At one time aimed at a job in the Foreign Office. After two years' National Service in the Black Watch became a radio journalist with the BBC in Glasgow. Started acting at Glasgow Citizens' Theatre, of which he became General Manager and Director of Productions 1962; three years later he became Associate Director of London's Royal Court Theatre. Distinguished career both on the stage and in TV. TV incl: The Borderers; Diamond Crack Diamond; Budgie; The Onedin Line; Tom Brown's Schooldays; Scotch on the Rocks; Black Beauty; Sutherland's Law; The Ghosts of Motley Hall; Duchess of Duke Street; The Mourning Brooch; Z Cars; Doctor Who; Danger UXB; Casting the Runes; Charlie Endell; McPhee the Mother and Me; Vice Versa. Films incl: The Railway Children; Up the Chastity Belt. Education: Glasgow Academy; Aberdeen Grammar; University of Aberdeen (MA Hons French and Spanish). m actress Anne Kirsten. Address: c/o French's, London W1. Starsign: Capricorn. Hobbies: sailing, fishing.

D

throat surgery in the past couple of years. Education: convent school, Londonderry m hotelier Damien Scallon, 1 d Grace. Address: c/o Clifford Elson (Publicity) Ltd, London W1. Starsign: Virgo. Hobbies: sketching, reading, embroidery, flower arranging.

DANEMAN, Paul

Actor b 26.10.25 London. Studied for the stage at RADA and after some time in rep joined the Old Vic. First appearance on stage was as the front legs of a horse in Alice in Wonderland. Was the original Vladimir in Waiting For Godot at the Arts Theatre in London. Other stage work incl: Camelot; Hadrian VII; Don't Start Without Me; Who Do They Think They Are? (one-man show); Double Edge; Pygmalion; Shut Your Eyes and Think of England; The Jeweller's Shop. TV incl: Our Mutual Friend; Emma; Persuasion; An Age of Kings; Not in Front of the Children; Never a Cross Word; Spy Trap; Waste; Arnold; Partners; Stay With Me Till Morning; Tishoo. Education: Haberdashers' Aske's, London; Sir William Borlase's, Marlow; Reading University (Fine Arts). m (1st) Susan (dis), (2nd) Meredith, 2 d Sophie, Flora. Address: c/o Chatto and Linnit, London W1. Starsign: Scorpio. Hobby: painting. Person he would most like to have met: 'Jane Austen, because she'd be such wonderful company.'

DANA

Singer b 30.8.51 London. Wanted to be a music teacher, but while still at school won the Eurovision Song Contest 1970 in Amsterdam with All Kinds of Everything and became an overnight singing star. Other records since incl: Who Put the Lights Out; Please Tell Him That I Said Hello; It's Going to be a Cold, Cold Christmas; Fairytale; Something's Cooking in the Kitchen; The Girl is Back; Dream Lover; I Feel Love Coming On .Since the Eurovision Song Contest she has travelled the world, made a film (Flight of Doves), been in pantomime, cabaret, appeared with Frankie Vaughan in Canada and with Tom Jones at the London Palladium and appeared in countless TV programmes incl: Stars on Sunday; Golden Shot; When Irish Eyes Are Smiling; Celebrity Squares; They Sold a Million; A Day With Dana; Wake Up, Sunday; Starburst; Wednesday At Eight; Night Music. Has twice overcome

DANIEL, Jennifer
Actress b 23.5.38
Pontypool, Gwent. Trained at
Central School of Speech
and Drama, rep experience
at Dundee and Oxford.
Leading roles on West End
stage and in films. TV incl:
Hamlet; Great Expectations;
Coriolanus; Barnaby Rudge;
The Lie; The Vortex; General
Hospital; Public Eye; Rooms;
Van Der Valk; The Duchess of
Duke Street; People Like Us;
Young Merlin; Thomas and
Sarah; Suez; Barriers.
Education: Badminton
School. m actor Dinsdale
Landen. Address: c/o Jean
Drysdale Management,
London W8. Starsign:
Gemini. Hobbies: art,
antiques, reading, going to
the theatre and cinema.
Person she would most like to
have met: 'Dr Johnson, in a
good mood, just to listen.'

DANIELLE, Suzanne
Actress b 14.1.57 London.
Trained for 11 years at the
Bush Davies Stage School.
First professional stage
appearance was as a
member of the chorus of Billy
at London's Drury Lane. Has
also been in Monkey Walk.

Small parts in films incl: The
Stud; Carry On, Emmanuel;
The World is Full of Married
Men. But now she is known as
the girl who impersonates the
Princess of Wales opposite
Mike Yarwood. She was with
him in Mike Yarwood in
Persons, the Royal Variety
Show and in his 1981
Christmas show. She has
appeared in two Morecambe
and Wise shows and with
them also in their 1981
Christmas show. Other TV
incl: Carpathian Eagle; two
Tales of the Unexpected;
Jane. Education: school in
Romford. Address: c/o Fraser
and Dunlop, London W1.
Starsign: Capricorn.
Hobbies: tennis, golf,
swimming. Person she would
most like to meet: 'The person
giving the Academy Award
for Best Actress, 1982.'

DANIELS, Paul
Comedian/magician
b 6.4.38 Middlesbrough.
Became interested in magic
when he was 11. First job on
leaving school was junior
clerk in the treasurer's office,
Eston UDC. After a spell in the
army, returned to office work
but did part-time
entertaining. Ran a grocer's
shop before becoming an
entertainer full-time. His
father makes his apparatus.
TV debut on Opportunity
Knocks. TV incl: Be My
Guest; Wheeltappers and
Shunters Social Club; The
Paul Daniels Show; Fall In The
Stars; Blackpool Bonanza;
Paul Daniels Magic Show;
Odd One Out. Education:

grammar school. Divorced,
3 s Paul, Martin, Gary.
Address: c/o BBC TV,
London W12. Starsign: Aries.
Hobby: photography. Person
he would most like to have
met: 'Merlin, to get a few tips!'

DANTON, Graham
Writer/presenter b 29.5.31
Eltham, Kent. Merchant Navy
officer for 12 years. Master
Mariner and Extra-Master
Mariner. Two Royal Society of
Arts Silver Medals. New York
Film Festival gold medal for
documentary, Loss of the
SS Schiller. South-West TV
Personality of the Year
1968-73. Education:
grammar school; HMS
Worcester Training Ship.
m Ann, 1 d Susan,
2 s Clive, Brett. Address: c/o
TSW, Plymouth. Starsign:
Gemini. Hobbies: music,
modelling, shooting. Person
he would most like to meet:
'Burt Lancaster – my favourite
actor.'

DARRAN, John
Actor/newsreader
b 24.12.24 Mountain Ash,
Glamorgan. Joined BBC in
1946 and has worked as
actor, light entertainment,

newsreader, author. Written and read mid-morning stories on radio. Book: Counterspy. Education: Duffryn House Grammar School; Oriel College, Oxford (MA Hons History). m Joan, 2 d Andrea, Elizabeth, 1 s David. Address: Cardiff. Starsign: Capricorn. Hobbies: swimming, writing, food and wine. People he would most like to meet: 'Malcolm Muggeridge, because he's so obviously a happy man; Ludovic Kennedy, because of his ease of style on television and his total sincerity.'

DAVENPORT, Nigel
Actor b 23.5.28 Shelford, Cambridge. Decided to become an actor while reading English at Oxford University where he was a member of the Oxford University Dramatic Society. Military service in the RASC and after the war worked as an army radio disc jockey in Hamburg. First theatre job was understudy in a Noël Coward play. Seasons at Stratford, Chesterfield and Ipswich and one of the first members of the English Stage Company at London's Royal Court Theatre. First success in A Resounding Tinkle. Other stage incl: A Taste of Honey (and in USA); Notes on a Love Affair; Three Sisters. Film debut in 1952 in Peeping Tom. Other films incl: A Man For All Seasons; Sebastian; Sinful Davy; Play Dirty; The Royal Hunt of the Sun; The Virgin Soldiers; The

Mind of Mr Soames; Villain; Living Free; Mary Queen of Scots; Charlie One-Eye; The Island of Dr Moreau; Nighthawks; Chariots of Fire. TV incl: An Affair of Honour; Sharing the Honours; Goose With Pepper; The Apple Cart; South Riding; Oil Strike North; A Midsummer Night's Dream; Don't Rock the Boat; Bird of Prey. Education: St Peter's, Seaford; Cheltenham College; Oxford (MA). m (1st) Helena (dis), (2nd) actress Maria Aitken, 1 d Laura, 1 s. Address: c/o Leading Artists, London SW1. Starsign: Gemini. Person he would most like to have met: Sir Winston Churchill.

DAVID, Joanna
Actress b 17.1.47 Lancaster. Trained at Elmhurst Ballet School and Webber Douglas Academy of Dramatic Art. Rep at Ipswich, Canterbury, Guildford. Films incl: A Smashing Bird I Used to Know; All Neat In Black Stockings; The Mind of Mr Soames; One Plus One. TV incl: John Brown's Body; When Johnny Comes Marching Home; Sense and Sensibility; Last of the Mohicans; War and Peace; Colditz; Duchess of Duke Street; Softly, Softly; Ballet Shoes; Dancing Princesses; Jennie; Just William; Within These Walls; Two's Company; Affront; Lillie; Rebecca; Dear Brutus; South Bank Show; Charlotte; Fame is the Spur; Alexa; Red Signal. 1 d Emilia. Address:

c/o Peter Browne Management, London SW9. Starsign: Capricorn. Person she would most like to meet: 'Rudolph Nureyev, in admiration of.'

DAVIDSON, Jim
Comedian b 13.12.54 London. ITV's New Faces gave him his big chance after a variety of jobs, incl window cleaner, fork-lift truck driver. TV incl: What's On Next?; Night Out; Tiswas; Make 'em Laugh; The Jim Davidson Show. Education: secondary modern school. m Julie Gullick. Address: c/o Thames TV, London NW1. Starsign: Sagittarius. Hobbies: golf, fishing, football. Person he would most like to meet: 'Keith Emerson – the best keyboard player that ever walked the planet Earth!'

DAVIES, David
TV journalist/ presenter b 28.5.48 London. A reporter for BBC Wales and lobby correspondent for the London Broadcasting Company, before joining BBC in Manchester. A regular contributor to Look North West and Nationwide; Nine

O'Clock News; Grandstand;
BBC religious programmes
and sports programmes on
Radio 2. Is also a trained
teacher. Education: Royal
Masonic School; Sheffield
University (degree in
politics); St Peters College,
Oxford. m Mr & Mrs hostess
Susan Cuff, 1 d Amanda
Jane. Address: c/o BBC TV
News, Manchester. Starsign:
Gemini. Hobbies: tennis,
reading (mainly politics).
People he would most like to
meet: 'Andrew Lloyd Webber
and Tim Rice – Jesus Christ
Superstar, Evita, and Cats
are such achievements.'

DAVIES, Dickie
TV presenter b 30.4.33
Wallasey, Cheshire.
Entertainments purser on
Queen Mary and Queen
Elizabeth 1 before joining
Southern TV as
announcer/newscaster. Then
to World of Sport (1968).
Education: various
elementary and grammar
schools. m Liz, 2 s Daniel,
Peter (twins). Address: c/o
LWT, London SE1. Starsign:
Taurus. Hobbies: real family,
squash, cycling, golf. Person
he would most like to meet:
'Mother Teresa – anyone who
chooses her way of life must
have something to teach all of
us.'

DAVIES, Geraint Talfan
Journalist, now head of news
and current affairs, HTV
Wales b 30.12.43
Carmarthen. Newspaper
background incl 12 years in

newspapers in Cardiff,
Newcastle and The Times.
Was assistant editor, Western
Mail, Cardiff, before joining
HTV. Appears regularly in
Outlook. Education: Cardiff
High School for Boys; Jesus
College, Oxford.
m Elizabeth, 1 d Rhodri,
2 s Mathew, Edward.
Address: c/o HTV Wales,
Cardiff. Starsign: Capricorn.
Hobby: photography. Person
he would most like to meet:
'Lech Walesa – cometh the
deadline, cometh the man.'

DAVIES, Glynog
TV reporter b 2.11.50
Glanaman. Started in
commercial radio with
Swansea Sound. Joined HTV
Wales 1977 to report for Y
Dydd, Report Wales and Yr
Wythnos. Education:
University College Cardiff
(Hons degree Zoology and
Botany). m Eira, 1 s Iestyn.
Address: c/o HTV Wales,
Cardiff. Starsign: Scorpio.
Hobbies: music, folk
dancing, community work.
Person he would most like to
meet: 'Welsh playwright
Saunders Lewis – one of the
greatest Welshmen and the
doyen of Welsh literature.'

DAVIES, Marian
Presenter/reporter/singer
b 23rd November Neath,
South Wales. Was going to
study medicine but won a
scholarship which took her to
the Guildhall School of Music
and Drama, and so studied
opera instead. While at
school was given leave each
month for five years to appear
with the singing children in
Land of Song on TV. Later she
joined the Cliff Adams
Singers and The Granadiers
(her contemporaries were
Anita Harris and Jerry
Dorsey, before he became
Engelbert Humperdink). Until
recently she was also a
member of The Ladybirds
backing group. Other TV incl:
five years as one of the
presenters of How; guest
storyteller on Rainbow,
reading her own stories for
children; as a singer in 123
60; Sunday Best
presenter/reporter.
Education: Neath Grammar
School for Girls; London
University (B Mus). Address:
c/o Yorkshire TV, Leeds.
Starsign: Sagittarius.
Hobbies: swimming, walking,
macramé. Person she would
most like to meet again:
'Barbra Streisand – she's
fabulous.'

DAVIES, Windsor
Actor b 28.8.30 Canning
Town, London. Miner,
National Service, odd
jobbing, teacher, before
becoming an actor. On stage
he has been in pantomime at
the London Palladium,
Liverpool, and in Roll On Four

O'Clock at the Lyric, Hammersmith. But it is as Battery Sergeant Major Williams in the TV series It Ain't Half Hot Mum that he is best known. Other TV incl: A Little Bit of Wisdom (with Norman Wisdom); Billy Liar; Sam; The Heavy Mob; Celebrity Squares; Never the Twain. Education: Ogmore Grammar; Bangor Training College. m Lynne, 4 d Jane, Sarah, Nancy, Beth, 1 s Danny. Address: c/o Peter Prichard Ltd, London SW1. Starsign: Virgo. Hobbies: rugby football, reading, walking, bird-watching. Person he would most like to meet: 'Robert Mitchum – superb actor minus the "bull".'

DAVIS, Steve
Professional snooker player b 22.8.57 Plumstead, London. Wonder boy of snooker and World Professional Snooker Champion 1981. Began playing when he was 14, his father being his tutor. In addition to his Embassy World Title, between Dec 1980 and Jan 1982 he won the Coral UK Championship

(1980 and 1981), the Guinness Open, the Wilson's Classic, Yamaha Organs International Masters (and March 1982) and Jameson Whiskey titles and Benson and Hedges Masters. Pot Black Champion 1982. He also led the England State Express world team to victory and was the first player to score a maximum break of 147 on TV (in the Lada Cars Classic final which he lost to Terry Griffiths). Education: Abbey Wood Comprehensive. Address: c/o Steve Davis Ltd, Romford, Essex. Starsign: Leo. Hobbies: billiards, reading, music. People he would most like to meet: 'Bjorn Borg and Muhammad Ali – I admire professionalism.'

DAVISON, Peter
Actor b 13th April London. After school plays and amateur dramatics, trained at Central School of Speech and Drama. First job was season at Nottingham Playhouse. After appearing at Edinburgh Festival he went into TV series, The Tomorrow People. Big TV break was in Love for Lydia, followed by All Creatures Great and Small. Other TV incl: Print-Out; Once Upon a Time; Holding The Fort; Sink Or Swim; Doctor Who. Also writes songs, incl: the theme song for Mixed Blessings. Made his singing debut on Pebble Mill At One. m actress Sandra Dickinson. Address: c/o John Mahoney Management, London W1. Starsign: Aries.

Hobbies: driving, reading, cricket.

DAWSON, Les
Comedian b 2.2.34 Manchester. Began as jazz pianist with Manchester band, Cotton City Slickers. Worked in clubs and pubs as solo comic before successful appearance in Opportunity Knocks 1967. Appearances in such shows as Big Night Out; Sunday Night at the London Palladium, before his own series, Sez Les. Other TV incl: This is Your Life; Holiday With Strings; The Loner; also specials and his own series for ITV and BBC. Writer of comedy material and author of books; A Card for the Clubs; The Spy Who Came; Smallpiece Guide to Male Liberation; British Book of Humour. Education: elementary school and technical college. m Margaret, 2 d Julie, Pamela, 1 s Stuart. Address: c/o London Management, London W1. Starsign: Aquarius. Hobbies: golf, writing, gardening. People he would most like to meet: 'Leo McKern and Richard Burton, because I admire their individual styles of acting very much.'

DAY, Sir Robin
Interviewer/presenter b 24.10.23 London. Started career as barrister 1952. Served in the army during Second World War and after being called to the Bar served with British Information Services, ·

Washington, 1953-54. Freelance journalist 1954-55 and BBC radio talks producer before ITN newscaster and parliamentary correspondent 1955-59. Joined Panorama 1959 and introduced the programme 1967-72. Other TV incl: Roving Report; Tell the People; The Parliamentarians; Question Time; and many abrasive interviews. Radio: The World at One. Books: Television: A Personal Report; The Case of Televising Parliament; Day By Day; A Dose of My Own Hemlock. BAFTA Richard Dimbleby Award for Factual TV 1974. Education: Bembridge School; St Edmund Hall, Oxford University (BA). President of the Oxford Union Society 1951. m Katherine, 2 s Alexander, Daniel. Address: c/o BBC, London. Starsign: Scorpio. Hobbies: reading, talking, skiing.

DEACON, Brian

Actor b 13.2.49 Oxford. Window cleaner, butcher's van driver while member of the Oxford Youth Theatre. Webber Douglas School

training in London. Rep seasons at Bristol, Coventry (Belgrade), Leicester, Soho Poly, Leeds, Edinburgh, Exeter, Ludlow Festival. Other stage incl: Curse of the Starving Class. Films incl: Triple Echo; Il Bacio; Vampyres; Jesus. TV incl: First Sight; The Guardians; Public Eye; Love and Mr Lewisham; Ghosts; The Emigrants; Lillie; Watching Me, Watching You; BBC Shakespeare (Henry VI Parts I, II, III; Richard III). Education: primary and secondary modern until 17. m actress Rula Lenska, 1 d Lara. Address: c/o Leading Artists, London SW1. Starsign: Aquarius. Hobbies: tennis, squash, football, bridge, reading, cinema, gardening, entertaining friends. Person he would most like to have met: 'William Shakespeare – from his writing he seems to have possessed a most extraordinary mind, capable of seeing and understanding the most fundamental and universal problems facing mankind. An evening in his company would have surely been delightful.'

DEBENS, Mike

Presenter b 21.3.49 London. Brought up in the Midlands. Joined TVS 1982 from BBC, for whom he covered Sussex for Nationwide's regional section, South Today, as well as national news. Presenter of TVS news magazine programme Coast to Coast and is one of two reporters

based in Brighton. Education: Boldmere School, Birmingham. m Carmen, 2 s James, Timothy. Address: c/o TVS, Southampton. Starsign: Aries. Hobbies: flying, restoring old cars. Person he would most like to meet: 'The TVS cashier.'

DeCOURCEY, Roger

Ventriloquist b 10.12.44 London. Went into the Stock Exchange on leaving school but studied opera in the evenings. After a season as holiday camp sports organiser, he turned professional. Was with the Fol-de-Rols at Worthing before going into Sweet Charity in London. TV programme New Faces turned him into overnight success after 10 years in show business. Education: Henry Thornton School, Clapham, London. m Cheryl, 1 s Jamie. Address: c/o International Artistes, London W1. Starsign: Sagittarius. Hobbies: golf, squash. Person he would most like to meet: Placido Domingo.

De FAYE, Guy

TV reporter/presenter b 7.8.55 Jersey, Channel Islands. Joined Channel TV in 1979, where he works on Channel Report. Education: Grouville Primary and Victoria College, Jersey; Kingston Polytechnic, Surrey (BA Hons Law). Address: c/o Channel TV, Jersey. Starsign: Leo. Hobbies: wind-surfing,

squash, water-skiing, travelling, rock music, mind-altering substances. Person he would most like to meet: 'Lord Lucan, to arrange the publishing rights.'

DEEKS, Michael
Actor b 18.4.56 Farnham Royal, Bucks. First part was Jim Hawkins in Treasure Island at the Crucible Theatre, Sheffield. Has also appeared at Birmingham Rep; Leicester Phoenix; Soho Poly; Royal Court, London; National Theatre. TV incl: Armchair Theatre; Champions; Dick Turpin; The Schoolmistress; Circe Complex; Juliet Bravo; Strangers. Education: Reading Blue Coat School, Sonning; Licensed Victuallers, Slough. Address: c/o Plant and Froggatt, London W1. Starsign: Aries. Hobby: being pampered. Person he would most like to meet: 'Old Father Time, because I've never met him.'

DELANEY, Pauline
Actress b 8th June Dublin. Trained at the Brendan Smith Academy of Acting, Dublin, and then rep in the North of

England and the Dublin Globe Theatre. Appeared in the 1962 O'Casey season at London's Mermaid Theatre and in the West End in The Poker Session and The Hostage. Recent theatre incl Richard III. Films incl: Nothing But the Best; The Young Cassidy; Percy; Brannigan (with John Wayne); Rooney; Trenchcoat. Her numerous TV appearances incl: Public Eye; The Dead; The Achurch Letters; Crime of Passion (in the Detective series); The Seagull; The Playboy of the Western World; The Expert; The Avengers; Z Cars; Fallen Hero; Mixed Blessings; Maybury; Touch of Evil; Shoestring; Dangerous Davies; various plays. Education: convent schools in Dublin. m Gerry Simpson, 1 d Sarah. Address: c/o Green and Underwood, London W3. Starsign: Gemini. Hobbies: reading, listening to music.

DEMPSTER, Caroline
Journalist b 25.5.55 Hayes, Kent. Experience with Radio Forth before joining Scottish TV in Dec 1979, working as a researcher on Report and reporter on Scotland Today. Education: Beckenham Girls Grammar; Edinburgh University (BSc Social Sciences). Address: c/o Scottish TV, Glasgow. Starsign: Gemini. Hobbies: cycling, amateur dramatics, reading science fiction, walking, decorating, dressmaking. Person she would most like to meet: 'B A Robertson – looks like he's got a good sense of humour.'

DENCH, Judi OBE
Actress b 9.12.34 York. Wanted to be a designer and attended art school for a year before training at the Central School of Speech and Drama. Made her professional debut as Ophelia in Hamlet at Liverpool in 1957 with the Old Vic; London saw her in the same part a week later. She has since played a wide variety of roles during four seasons at the Old Vic, several seasons with the RSC, rep at Oxford as well as Cabaret, The Good Companions and London Assurance, in which she played opposite the actor who was to become her husband. Her range has been equally wide on TV incl: Hilda Lessways; Village Wooing; On Giant's Shoulders; Langrishe; Go Down; Macbeth; Comedy of Errors; The Teachers; Z Cars; The Age of Kings; Love Story; The Funambulists; Parade's End; Talking to a Stranger; The Morecambe and Wise

Show; Love In A Cold Climate; Going Gently; The Cherry Orchard; A Fine Romance (series co-starring with her husband). Won BAFTA Award for Best Actress of the Year 1981. Votd Funniest Female on TV 1981-82 by TVTimes readers. Education: The Mount School, York. m actor Michael Williams, 1 d Tara. Address: c/o Julian Belfrage, London SW1. Starsign: Sagittarius. Hobbies: sewing, painting, tapestry.

DENHAM, Chris
Presenter/reporter b 7.12.48 Glasgow. Newspaper experience on the Southern Evening Echo and freelance journalism before working for Radio Brighton, BFBS Cyprus (three years), Radio Bristol and BFBS Gibraltar. In 1976 he joined BBC in Norwich and worked on Look East for a couple of years. Then he went back to Bristol as a freelance and in 1979 joined BBC TV, in Plymouth to co-present Spotlight. He has also had his own chat show and presented documentary, light entertainment and sailing programmes. Education: Price's Grammar School, Fareham, Hants. m Sally, 1 d Tessa, 1 s Andrew. Address: c/o BBC TV, Plymouth. Starsign: Sagittarius. Hobbies: sailing, the countryside. Person he would most like to meet: 'The Princess of Wales, because I think she would be a fascinating person to interview.'

DENISON, Michael
Actor b 1.11.15 Doncaster. Studied for the stage at the Webber Douglas Drama School and made his acting debut as Lord Fancourt Babberley in Charley's Aunt at Frinton-on-Sea 1938. Came to London the same year to appear in Troilus and Cressida. Has since had a distinguished acting career, incl rep at Edinburgh, Glasgow, Birmingham, Shakespeare Memorial Theatre Company at Stratford (1955), Open Air Theatre, Regent's Park, and on tour and abroad. Has played White Knight and Tweedledee three times in different productions of Alice Through the Looking Glass. Recent plays incl: The Tempest (Prospero); Twelfth Night (Malvolio); The Dragon Variation (playing six parts); At the End of the Day; The Sack Race; Captain Hook and Mr Darling in Peter Pan (1975); The Black Mikado (Pooh-Bah); A Coat of Varnish; The Kingfisher (tour). Films incl: Tilly of Bloomsbury; Hungry Hill; My Brother Jonathan; The Blind Goddess; The Glass Mountain; Landfall; The Franchise Affair; Angels One Five; The Importance of Being Earnest; There Was a Young Lady; Contraband Spain; The Truth About Women; Faces in the Dark. Numerous TV appearances incl more than 80 as Boyd QC between 1957-63. More recent TV incl: many Crown Court episodes; Generation Game; Private Schultz; Bedroom Farce; Blood Money; Agatha Christie Hour (Red Signal); The Critic; The Week of the Scorpion. Education: Harrow, Magdalen College, Oxford. m actress and novelist Dulcie Gray. Address: c/o ICM, London W1. Starsign: Scorpio. Hobbies: golf, gardening, painting, motoring.

DERBYSHIRE, Eileen
Actress b 6th October, Manchester. Trained at the Northern School of Music (now Royal Northern College), LRAM. Speech and drama teaching before rep and radio work. Emily in Coronation Street since 1961. Education: Manchester High. m Thomas Holt, 1 s Oliver. Address: c/o Granada TV, Manchester. Starsign: Libra. Hobbies: concerning the Arts, the countryside and the home. Person she would most like to meet: 'William Shakespeare – what personality encased that superb mind?'

DICKINSON, Sandra
Actress b 20th October

Washington DC. After studying at the University of Wisconsin and Boston University, trained at the Central School of Speech and Drama in London. Became known in numerous TV commercials, but has done much theatre work, incl Legend, in which she played Marilyn Monroe. Her impressive list of TV credits incl: The Tomorrow People; What's On Next?; Cover; Hitch-hikers' Guide to the Galaxy; Triangle. m actor Peter Davison. Address: c/o Howes and Prior Ltd, London W1. Starsign: Libra.

DIMBLEBY, David

Interviewer/TV presenter b 28.10.38 London. First job was with BBC in Bristol as news reporter 1961, reporting for Enquiry 1964, but left TV (1965) to concentrate on family newspapers when his father Richard Dimbleby died. After six months in America for CBS, he joined Panorama 1967 as a freelance, then 24 Hours (1969); Yesterday's Men; Reporter at Large; Dimbleby Talk-in; Panorama 1975-77; General Election Results programme; The White Tribe of Africa; Person To Person. Now presenter of Panorama once more. Education: Glengorse; Charterhouse; Paris Sorbonne; University of Perugia; Oxford University. m Josceline, 2 d Liza, Kate, 1 s Henry. Address: c/o BBC TV, London. Starsign: Scorpio. Hobby: sailing.

Person he would most like to have met: 'Michael de Montaigne, a French writer who showed how to stay sane in troubled times.'

DIMBLEBY, Jonathan

Broadcaster/journalist/writer b 31.7.44 London. Thought of becoming a farmer, but discovered journalism while at University. Younger brother of David Dimbleby. Joined BBC in Bristol (1969) reporting for Points West, then World at One. Switched to ITV's This Week 1972. To Yorkshire TV for own series, Jonathan Dimbleby in Evidence, 1979. BAFTA's Richard Dimbleby Award 1974; coverage of Middle East, Southern Africa and British politics. Books: Richard Dimbleby; The Palestinians. Education: Charterhouse; London University (Philosophy). m journalist Bel Mooney, 1 d Katharine, 1 s Daniel. Address: c/o David Higham Assocs Ltd, London W1. Starsign: Leo. Hobbies: reading, music, sailing. Person he would most like to have met: 'Mahatma Gandhi – he believed in the peaceful power of the people.'

DINENAGE, Fred

Presenter b 8.6.42 Birmingham. Senior sports presenter TVS. Originally wanted to be a journalist, but after spells with the Birmingham Mail and Evening Argus, Brighton, joined Southern TV 1964 to

help introduce Three Go Round. Since then his TV appearances incl: Day By Day; Afloat; Weekend; Miss Southern TV; Calendar Sport; Sunday Sport; World of Sport; Bank Holiday Sport; Gambit; How; Miss Great Britain; Southsport; Pro-Celebrity Snooker; Pro-Celebrity Darts; Miss Anglia TV; Reflections; Cuckoo in the Nest; All Kinds of Everything; Showjumping; senior presenter Moscow Olympics 1980. Education: Birmingham. m Beryl, 1 d Caroline, twins Sarah and Christopher. Address: c/o TVS, Southampton. Starsign: Gemini. Hobbies: sport, family, reading, running a badge-making business in conjunction with his wife. Person he would most like to meet: 'The Pope – an inspirational man in a world that has too few.'

DOBIE, Alan

Actor b 2.6.32 Wombwell, Yorks. Trained at Barnsley School of Art and the Old Vic Theatre School. Began his career at the Old Vic in Sept 1952 as Paris' Page in Romeo and Juliet. Joined Bristol Old Vic the following year where he was The Tramp in the original production of Salad Days. Has since played every kind of part from a pantomime cat to Macbeth. His films incl: The Charge of the Light Brigade; Doctor Syn; White Bird. Radio work incl: My Cousin Rachel; Morning Departure; Love on the Dole; Look Back in Anger. More recently, An Inspector Calls; Dial a Poem; What's Your Pleasure; Hello, Hello, Hello, Here We Are Again. First impact on TV was in The Planemakers. Other TV incl: Dance of Death; The Corsican Brothers; The Siege of Manchester; Why Aren't You Famous?; Conquest; Resurrection; Danton; Diamond Crack Diamond; The Troubleshooters; War and Peace; Double Dare; Our Young Mr Wignal; Hard Times; The Dick Emery Show; Waxwork; The Death of Ivan Ilyich; Wobble to Death; The Detective Wore Silk Drawers; Mad Hatter's Holiday; Invitation to a Dynamite Party; Abra Cadaver; Sergeant Cribb in a series of plays from the novels of Peter Lovesey; Kessler; Nanny. m (1st) actress Rachel Roberts (dis), (2nd) singer Maureen Scott, 2 d Millie, Natasha, 1 s Casey. Address: c/o Vernon Conway Ltd, London SW11. Starsign: Gemini. Hobbies: farming, painting.

DODD, Ken OBE
Actor/comedian b 8.11.27 Liverpool. Always wanted to go on the stage; Christmas presents of a Punch and Judy set and a ventriloquist's doll helped him in his decision. Professional comedian since 1954. Inventor of the Diddymen. Many summer and variety shows and his own TV and radio programmes. TV incl: Ken Dodd Show; Doddy's Music Box; The Good Old Days; Thank Your Lucky Stars; Funny You Should Say That; Look Who's Talking; Ken Dodd's World of Laughter; Seaside Special; Stars On Sunday; Parkinson; Ken Dodd's Showbiz; Doddy's Music Show. Theatre; Malvolio in Twelfth Night; Ha Ha – A Celebration of Laughter (both in Liverpool); Ken Dodd's Laughter Show (London Palladium and provinces). Records incl: Love is Like a Violin; More Than Love; Let Me Cry On Your Shoulder; Tears; Tears Won't Wash Away My Heartache; Happiness; When Love Comes Round Again; This Is Our Dance; Just Out of Reach. Education: Holt High, Liverpool. Address: Knotty Ash, Liverpool. Starsign: Scorpio. Hobbies: watching racing, reading science fiction and psychology.

DONALD, Margaret
Freelance broadcaster b 25.6.38 Applecross, Ross-shire, Scotland. Began career as a primary teacher, later becoming lecturer in primary education and as such made seven working visits to the University of San Jose, California, as guest lecturer on Early Childhood. During teaching career published a book of 24 songs for the under-sevens. Broadcasting career began after she had been made redundant from her lectureship in 1977. Did documentaries and news reporting for BBC Radio Aberdeen, Radio Scotland and features for the World Service of the BBC, Radio 4 and Radio Highland before joining Grampian TV as relief announcer in 1980 and for whom she has written and presented a series of story and song programmes for children. Education: Inverness Royal Academy; Aberdeen College of Education (Diploma in Primary Education). m theatre manager, Peter Donald, 1 s Peter. Address: c/o Grampian TV, Aberdeen. Starsign: Cancer. Hobbies: piano, guitar, organ, autoharp, singing, jogging (two miles daily – in all weathers!). Person she would most like to meet: 'Paul Tournier – the profound wisdom in his books has been my unfailing solace.'

DOODY, Pat
Announcer b 11.11.38 Birmingham. After short service commission in the Royal Signals, went into British Forces Broadcasting Service and BBC Radio before joining Tyne Tees and Border TV. Managing director Videoforce Ltd, broadcast facility. Education:

Fernden, Haslemere, Surrey; King Alfred's, Wantage, Berks. m Jill, 2 d Pippa, Helenne. Address: Wetheral, Cumbria. Starsign: Scorpio. Person he would most like to have met: 'King Charles II, who achieved far more than is generally credited.'

DOONICAN, Val
Singer b 3.2.29 Waterford, Ireland. Originally worked in a steel foundry and orange-box factory before his first professional engagement in 1946. Radio work in Ireland, joined The Four Ramblers 1951 in Riders of the Range. Later went solo. First radio show, Your Date With Val, 1959. The famous chair and sweaters arrived with TV show in 1964. Will be in 20th own TV series 1982. Many variety shows and own series incl: The Val Doonican Show; The Val Doonican Music Show; Sunday Night at the London Palladium; Stars on Sunday. Hit records incl: Walk Tall; Elusive Butterfly; Paddy McGinty's Goat; No Charge; Rafferty's Motor Car; Special Years; Morning; If the Whole World Stopped Lovin'; What Would I Be? Education: De La Salle College, Waterford. m former cabaret and revue star Lynette Rae, 2 d Sarah, Fiona. Address: c/o Bernard Lee Management Ltd, Caterham, Surrey. Starsign: Aquarius. Hobbies: golf, oil painting, archery. People he would most like to have met: 'Nat King Cole and Maurice Chevalier. I admired their

performances and would love to have had a chat with them.'

DORAN, Veronica
Actress b 17.5.48 Carlisle. Trained as a dancer and for two years was a member of the Blackpool Tower children's ballet. Spent three years in rep. Films incl: For the Love of Ada; The Dream House; The Haunted House of Horrors; The Adventures of a Private Detective; The Pirates of Penzance. Plenty of TV experience before going into Coronation Street as Eddie Yates' 'intended', Marion Willis. Other TV incl: It's Dark Outside; Tickets Please; Village Hall; Crown Court; The Lady Killers; A Day in a Life; London is Burning; Upstairs, Downstairs; Funny Man; The Virtuoso; Fanny and Annie; Man About the House; In Loving Memory; Fancy Wanders; The Liver Birds. Education: St Margaret Marys and St Patricks, Carlisle; The Sacred Heart, Blackpool. Address: c/o Barry Brown, London SE11. Starsign: Taurus. Hobby: horse-riding. Person she would most like to meet: 'Bette Davis – a great star with a lot of guts.'

DORNING, Robert
Actor b 13th May St Helens, Lancs. Studied music in Liverpool but stage fright so marred his professional debut that he decided to take up dancing. Studied ballet and joined the Dolin/Markova company. The war ended

that career and after five years in the RAF, chose musical comedy for his return to the stage. That career was curtailed by an attack of synovitis in both knees, so he settled on an acting career in rep at Leatherhead and late night revues in London. Two years in Canada with the London Theatre Company and he returned to parts in films, They Came By Night and The One That Got Away. Other films incl: Live Now, Pay Later; The Human Factor; Ragtime; Evil Under the Sun. Stage incl: The Great Waltz; Something's Afoot; No Sex Please, We're British. He is also a TV comedy veteran from the days of Hancock's Half Hour; Tommy Cooper and Spike Milligan shows; The Army Game; Bootsie and Snudge; Pardon the Expression; and more recently, No Appointment Necessary; Big Deal at New York City; Clubs; Hogg's Back; P G Wodehouse; Can We Get On Now, Please. Education: Cowley, St Helens. m actress Honor Shepherd, 2 d actresses Stacy Dorning and Kate Dorning. Address: c/o Crouch Assocs, London W1. Starsign: Taurus. Hobby: golf. Person he would most like to meet: 'Katherine Helmond – she's absolutely fantastic.'

DORS, Diana
Actress b 23.10.31 Swindon. Studied at RADA and at 16 was under contract to the Rank Organisation.

Many films incl: Shop at Sly Corner; Good Time Girl; Here Come the Huggetts; Worm's Eye View; A Kid for Two Farthings; Yield to the Night and, more recently, The Amazing Mr Blunden; Steptoe and Son Ride Again. Stage incl: Man of the World; Three Months Gone. TV incl: The Lovely Place; A Nice Little Business; Queenie's Castle; Just William; Celebrity Squares; The Two Ronnies; Hammer House of Horror; Timon of Athens; Shoestring; many chat shows incl Russell Harty. Also hosted her own chat show, The Diana Dors Show – the first and only woman to do so in England. Books incl: Behind Closed Dors; For Adults Only. Education: Colville House, Swindon. m (1st) Dennis Hamilton (dec), (2nd) comedian Dickie Dawson (dis), (3rd) actor Alan Lake, 3 s Mark, Gary (from 2nd m), Jason (from 3rd m). Address: Sunningdale, Berks. Starsign: Scorpio. No time for hobbies. Person she would most like to have met: Mary Queen of Scots.

DOUGLAS, Alton

Comedian b 22.1.40 Birmingham. Began career as leader of own jazz band. Progressed to comedy and as a solo comic has appeared in summer shows and pantomimes. Sophisticated cabaret, hotel and theatre comedian. Writes comedy material and scripts. TV: has appeared as a warm-up comic on over 800 shows. Appearances in: Crossroads; A Soft Touch; The Golden Shot. Own BBC show The Original Alton Douglas. Recent TV appearances incl: Nights at the Swan; Seconds Out; Know Your Place; Muck and Brass. Radio incl: You and Yours, and more than 1000 commercials. Education: Saltley Grammar. m Jo. Address: c/o George Bartram Enterprises, Birmingham. Starsign: Aquarius. Hobbies: pet dog, Groucho Marx (Old English Sheepdog), jazz records, books on the theatre and comedy, paintings, models, all information on clowns, keep fit. Person he would most like to meet: 'George Burns – I have always had a great admiration for the man and his style of humour.'

DOUGLAS, Colin

Actor b 28.7.12 Newcastle. Emigrated to New Zealand when 16 but came back after five years and went to RADA. Spell in rep then Catterick and Sandhurst, became Captain and Adjutant in the Border Regiment and served in First Airborne Division. Was appearing in Alan Plater's mining play, Close the Coalhouse Door when he was chosen for part of Edward Ashton in A Family at War. Other TV incl: Dick Barton – Special Agent; Follyfoot; The Seventh Juror; Love Story; The Flockton Flyer; The Sweeney; Headmaster; The Greenhill Pals; Thicker Than Water; Even Solomon; The Night People; Omega Factor; Telford's Change; Eleanor; T'is Pity She's A Whore; Nanny. Education: Durham School; Farm School, Cumberland. m actress Gina Cachia, 1 d Amanda (dec), 4 s Timothy, Angus, Blaise, Piers. Address: c/o NEMS Management, London SW3. Starsign: Leo. Hobbies: fishing, golf, cooking. Person he would most like to meet: 'Curt Jurgens – he's a great actor.'

DOUGLAS, Jack

Comedian/actor b 26.4.27 Newcastle-upon-Tyne. Pantomime producer at 14 before joining small combo playing drums. Acting debut at 21 in Dick Whittington. Partnered Joe Baker for nine years, then went solo, created Alf Ippititimus and was with Des O'Connor for five years on stage and TV. Pantomimes, summer seasons, farces, musicals and films. Stage incl: Sting in the Tail. Hosted TV shows in Britain, America, Canada and Australia and appeared on Ed Sullivan Show. TV acting debut in The Reluctant

Juggler. Own cookery/chat show for Channel TV. Also for ITV, Red Saturday; The Shillingbury Blowers; The Alan Stewart Show. Established member of the Carry On team. Writer of cook books. Education: St Joseph's College, Beulah Hill, London. m Susan, 2 d Deborah, Sarah. 1 s Craig. Address: c/o Richard Stone, London WC2. Starsign: Taurus. Hobbies: painting, antiques, photography, cooking, shooting, driving.

radio's Living World. Has written 14 books on natural history, dogs and country topics. Education: Bromsgrove School; London University. m. Address: Abbots Bromley, Rugeley, Staffs. Starsign: Taurus. Hobbies: natural history and working dogs. People he would most like to meet: 'Producers with interesting series!'

Dawn Breakers; Mondo Candido; Queen Kong; Joseph Andrews; The Shout. TV incl: Public Eye; Bill Brand; Softly, Softly; The Sweeney; Raffles; Sam (third series); Bouquet of Barbed Wire (two series); All Creatures Great and Small (three series) for which she shared 1979 Variety Club Award for BBC TV Personality; The Lady Killers; Tales of the Unexpected; Take the Stage. Education: Holy Trinity Convent, Bromley, Kent. Address: c/o Chatto & Linnit, London W1. Starsign: Taurus. Hobbies: scuba diving, swimming, writing, music, travelling, walking, horse-riding, skiing. Person she would most like to have met: Harpo Marx.

DOYLE, John
News reporter b 9.8.34 Coventry. Started as reporter in Sevenoaks, Kent, and Exeter. TV with TWW in Cardiff and Bristol 1961-67, then Westward TV freelance till Nov 81 when he joined TVS. Winner of Royal Television Society News Award 1980. Education: private and grammar schools; Exeter University (Law). m Suzi, 3 d Sarah, Penelope, Melanie, 1 s Guy. Address: c/o TSW, Plymouth. Starsign: Leo. Hobbies: model railways, riding, flying, Romano/British archaeology. Person he would most like to meet: 'Walter Cronkite – he's the best there is!'

DRABBLE, Phil
Countryman b 14.5.41 Staffs. Has spent 22 years in writing, radio and TV. Mainly known as presenter of sheep dog series One Man and His Dog and In the Country series, and contributing to

DRINKWATER, Carol
Actress b 22.4.48 London. Three years' training at the Drama Centre, London, then wide experience in rep. Stage appearances incl: Stoke, Bristol Old Vic, Glasgow Citizens' Theatre, Open Space, Hampstead Theatre Club, Birmingham and Leeds reps, National Theatre, Dublin, Edinburgh and Malvern Festivals. Also appeared at Northern Italian Theatre Festival and toured South East Asia. In 1981 appeared in the first professional production of Cavalcade since the original at Drury Lane in 1931. Spent five weeks at Stockholm English Theatre. Films incl: Clockwork Orange; The

DRUETT, Geoffrey
Reporter/interviewer b 8.5.44 Wendover, Bucks. Graduate trainee with Tyne Tees TV 1966, political correspondent Anglia TV, 1974-77, presenter of Yorkshire TV's Calendar since 1977. Education: Taunton School, Somerset; Exeter College, Oxford. m Judith Brook, 1 d Vanessa, twins Jonathan and Hannah. Address: c/o Yorkshire TV, Leeds. Starsign: Taurus. Hobbies: music, theatre, caravanning. Person he would most like to meet: 'Lord Lucan – because I could do with a good "exclusive".'

DUDLEY, Peter
Actor b 21.6.35 Manchester.
Trained in rep before TV
work, but regularly appears
at Manchester Library
Theatre. Five previous parts
in Coronation Street before
becoming Bert Tilsley. TV
incl: Strangers; Siege of
Golden Hill; Against the
Crowd; Shabby Tiger; A
Raging Calm; Crown Court;
various TV plays and films.
Education: secondary
school. Address: c/o Peter
Campbell, London W1.
Starsign: cusp of
Gemini/Cancer. Hobbies:
painting, cooking. People he
would most like to meet:
'Anthony Wedgwood Benn
and Eartha Kitt, to discuss
comedy.'

DUFFY, Patrick
Actor b 17.3.49 Townsend,
Montana. Moved to Seattle
when he was 12 and his high
school drama teacher
recommended him for a
drama course at the
University of Washington in
Seattle, where he later joined
the Washington State Theatre
Company as their first 'actor
in residence' performing with
touring groups. He also met

his future wife who was a
dancer. Experience with the
Seattle Rep Co and on
Broadway before going to
Hollywood where his first job
was driving a truck. Small
parts in TV films before acting
with the San Diego Old Globe
Shakespeare Company.
More TV appearances then,
in 1976, he won the title role in
Man From Atlantis and
subsequently Bobby Ewing
in Dallas. Member of Nichiren
Shocshu Academy, a
Buddhist organisation.
m dancer Carlyn Rosser, 1 s
Padriac Terence. Address:
Santa Monica, California.
Starsign: Pisces. Hobbies:
collecting children's books,
antique toys.

DULUX Dog
Canine TV star b 28.6.75
Hemel Hempstead. Real
name Jenards Likely Lad of
Lardams but known to his
friends as The Duke (in
memory of John Wayne). The
latest in a long line of Dulux
dogs which have been the
symbol of Dulux Paints for 19
years. The Duke has been in
promotional work for the past
two years and was trained for
his 1981 commercials by
Barbara Woodhouse, to
whom he responded so well
that the final filming was done
with a tape recording of her
commands. Has appeared
on a Granada TV chat show,
opens shops and appears at
charity fetes and sales
conventions. Before going in
for promotion work he was a
qualifier at Crufts and in 1977
won a Reserve Challenge

Certificate. Address:
Shepperton, Middx, where he
lives with his wife, two of his
100 offspring and eight
grandchildren. Weighs
between 90 and 100 lbs and
when at home expects the
star treatment. Loves
children, especially his
owners' four children, and
has a passion for Polo Mints.
Starsign: Cancer.

DUNCAN, Peter
Actor b 3.5.54 London. Blue
Peter's daredevil have-a-go
action man since mid-1980.
As such his exploits have incl:
sailing a Chinese junk up the
Thames; a day on the Royal
Marines' assault course;
cleaning the face of Big Ben;
a parachute jump; two
London marathons; and,
while in Japan in 1981, was a
Samauri warrior for a day and
a Sumo wrestler. As an actor,
his films incl: Mr Quilp;
Lifetaker; Stardust; Flash
Gordon. In addition to Blue
Peter, his TV credits incl:
Sam; Warship; Fallen Hero;
Family Affair; Sons and
Lovers. Address: c/o Plant
and Froggatt, London W1.
Starsign: Taurus. Hobbies:
DIY, music. Person he would
most like to meet: 'The
attractive blonde lady two
doors down.'

DUNCANSON, John
Reporter/interviewer
b 14.4.40 Prestwick,
Ayrshire. After a BBC course
in broadcasting, spent four
years as presenter on BBC
TV and 14 years as
newsreader/ announcer with

various TV companies. Also producer/ presenter of radio shows. TV incl: About Women (Anglia TV); Reporting Scotland (BBC); Grampian Today (Grampian TV). Education: Barlborough Hall; Waid Academy; Royal High School, Edinburgh. m Norma, 1 d Eilidh, 1 s John. Address: c/o Grampian TV, Aberdeen. Starsign: Aries. Hobbies: sailing, boat building, learning Gaelic, folklore, music, cooking. Person he would most like to have met: 'Belgian gypsy guitarist Django Reinhardt – his long and fruitful association with Stephane Grappelli produced vibrant and innovative music which has influenced guitarists and jazz fans all over the world.'

DUNN, Clive OBE
Actor b 9.1.22 London. Third generation of his family in the theatre. Trained at Italia Conti School and first professional debut in Where the Rainbow Ends. Best known for his old men roles on TV, especially in Bootsie and Snudge and Dad's Army (also on stage).

Other TV incl: It's a Square World; The World of Beachcomber; Ooh, La La; Jokers Wild; My Old Man; The Good Old Days; Grandad. Record: Grandad. Appeared with the English National Opera Company as Frosch in Die Fledermaus. Education: Sevenoaks, Kent. m actress Priscilla Morgan, 2 d Polly, Jessica. Address: c/o BBC, London. Starsign: Capricorn. Hobbies: painting, water-skiing.

DURDEN-SMITH, Neil
Commentator/presenter b 18.8.33 Richmond, Surrey. Served in the Royal Navy 1952-62, and BBC producer 1963-66. Films incl: The Games. Radio: Test Match; World Cup; County Championship and Gillette Cup. Resident panellist Treble Chance; Forces Chance and Sporting Chance. Presenter: Champion's Choice; Sports Special; Review of the Sporting Press. Reporter for Today; World at One; Outlook; Movie-Go-Round; The World Today; Rugby Union; Badminton, hockey, etc; Trooping the Colour. TV incl: cricket; hockey; Rugby Union; International polo; sailing; bowls; rowing and county shows; Mexico and Munich Olympics. Reporter for ITN; World of Sport and Grandstand; chairman Tournament and Money Matters. Education: Aldenham; Royal Naval College. m TV presenter Judith Chalmers, 1 d Emma,

1 s Mark. Address: c/o 20 Conduit Place, London W2. Starsign: Leo. Hobbies: theatre and films, playing all forms of sport, reading newspapers. Person he would most like to meet: 'Fred Astaire – because I would like to find out how he has done it all.'

DUTTINE, John
Actor b 15.3.49 Barnsley, Yorks. After training at the Drama Centre, London, rep at Glasgow Citizens' Theatre, Watford and Nottingham. Films incl: Who Dares Wins. TV incl: Armchair Theatre; Pin to See the Peepshow; Z Cars; Holding On; Warship; Lord Peter Wimsey; Rooms; Coronation Street; Spend, Spend, Spend; Jesus of Nazareth; Beryl's Lot; Angels; Law Centre; Saturday, Sunday, Monday; Devil's Crown; People Like Us; Wuthering Heights; Strangers; The Mallens; To Serve Them All My Days; PS7-Warriors; The Day of the Triffids; The Outsider. Voted Best Actor 1980 by TVTimes readers. Address: c/o Peter Browne Management, London SW9. Starsign: Pisces. Hobbies: making wine/beer and drinking it, gardening, walking. Person he would most like to meet: 'Graham Greene, to thank him for the books and the Abbot Ale.'

DYDDGEN-JONES, Terry
Announcer/writer/performer b 3.7.50 Carmarthen. Trained as a teacher and

taught at St Joseph's RC School, Newport, for five years, before turning to acting and writing. Joined HTV Wales 1979 as continuity announcer. Education: Gwewdraeth Valley Grammar School; Caerleon College of Education. m Judith, 2 d Leah, Elen. Address: c/o HTV Wales, Cardiff. Starsign: Cancer. Hobbies: food, photography, spending time in the south of France. Person he would most like to meet: 'Joanna Lumley, to discuss a programme idea.'

TV incl: Joan and Leslie; Coronation Street (Ida Barlow); Emergency– Ward 10; Z Cars; Potter; The Secret Orchards; Nanny in Father, Dear Father; The School Mistress; Virginia Fly is Drowning. Education: Roedean; finishing school, Paris. m (1st) Kenneth Edwards (dec), (2nd) Harry Judge, 1 step-d Jennifer, 2 step-s Michael, David. Address: c/o Jimmy Garrod, Shepperton, Middx. Starsign: Capricorn. Hobbies: gardening, foreign travel, collecting things. Person she would most like to meet: 'The famous gardener, Gertrude Jeckell.'

DYSON, Noël
Actress b 23.12.16 Newton Heath, Manchester. Trained at RADA followed by rep at Oxford, Birmingham and Windsor. Other stage work incl: musicals; Dear Miss Phoebe; A Girl Called Jo; Watergate Theatre Club revue; Book of the Month; Playbill; Restoration of Arnold Middleton; Sisters (Royal Exchange Theatre, Manchester). First TV appearance in The Guinea Pig for the BBC 1948. Has since become one of TV's most in-demand actresses.

E

EASTWOOD, Clint
Actor b 31.5.30 San Francisco. Had several jobs – lumberjack, steel worker, garage hand, lifeguard – before being drafted into the army in 1951, where part of his duties were as swimming instructor. A film being shot at his army camp gave him an interest in acting and when he left the army he studied drama at Los Angeles City College. Got a film contract in 1955 and after several small parts in pictures (Francis in the Navy; Tarantula; Never Say Goodbye), was picked for the Rawhide TV series in 1959 – a role that not only lasted for seven years, but brought him fame and a fortune from his subsequent film performances. After Rawhide he went to Italy to star in A Fistful of Dollars; A Few Dollars More; The Good, The Bad and The Ugly. Since then his films incl: Hang 'Em High; Coogan's Bluff; Paint Your Wagon; Kelly's Heroes; The Beguiled; Play Misty For Me (also directed); Dirty Harry; Joe Kidd; Breezy (directed); High Plains Drifter (also directed); Magnum Force; The Eiger Sanction;
The Outlaw: Josey Wales; The Enforcer; The Gauntlet (also directed); Every Which Way But Loose; Alcatraz; Bronco Billy; Any Which Way You Can; Firefox. Came to England in 1969 to make Where Eagles Dare. Education: public school in Oakland; Oakland Technical High School. m former model Maggie Johnson, 1 d Allison, 1 s Kyle.

EDDINGTON, Paul
Actor b 18.6.27 London. First stage appearance with ENSA in Colchester Garrison Theatre 1944. Rep at Birmingham and Sheffield before training at RADA 1951. Then rep at Ipswich and TV (incl The Adventures of Robin Hood); London stage debut 1961. Joined Bristol Old Vic following year, leaving in 1963 to appear in A Severed Head in America. Returned to Bristol Old Vic 1965 and has since appeared in many plays there and in London's West End, incl: Absurd Person Singular; Donkey's Years; Ten Times Table; Middle-age Spread; Who's Afraid of Virginia Woolf; Noises Off. Wide TV experience incl: Special Branch; The Good Life; Yes, Minister; Let There Be Love. A governor of the Old Vic Theatre Trust since 1975. Education: The Friends' School, Sibford Ferris, Oxon. m actress Patricia Scott, 1 d Gemma, 3 s Toby, Hugo, Dominic. Address: c/o ICM, London W1. Starsign: Gemini.

Hobbies: music, reading, art. Person he would most like to have met: 'Richard III, to find out if he really was as grotesque as Shakespeare painted him – I suspect not.'

EDEN, Mark
Actor b 14.2.28 London. Fairground worker at Margate and Ramsgate before joining Swansea rep as assistant stage manager 1958. Further rep experience at Llandudno, Richmond, Windsor, Royal Court and Royal Shakespeare Company. Films incl: Dr Zhivago; The L-Shaped Room; The Password is Courage; Attack on the Iron Coast; Seance on a Wet Afternoon; Local Affairs. TV incl: many plays; The Saint; The Avengers; Catchhand; Crime Buster; Lord Peter Wimsey; The Top Secret Life of Edgar Briggs; Jesus of Nazareth; Wilde Alliance; General Hospital; Crown Court; London Belongs to Me; Sam; Law Centre; Coronation Street. Education: London state schools. m Diana, 1 d Polly, 2 s David, Saul. Address: c/o Richard Stone, London WC2. Starsign: Aquarius. Hobbies: playing piano, doing crosswords, writing, decorating, talking to the kids. Person he would most like to have met: 'Groucho Marx – I have seen all the Marx Brothers films dozens of times and he *still* makes me laugh. He was a genius'.

EDMONDS, Noel
Disc jockey b 22.12.48
Ilford, Essex. While a student
teacher chose to become a
Radio Luxembourg DJ (1968)
in preference to a place at
Surrey University. Went to
BBC 1969 and a year later
was given his own show on
Saturday afternoons. In 1973
he took over the Radio One
Breakfast Show from Kenny
Everett until 1978. On TV
introduced Top of the Pops,
pioneered a new phone-in
show for children, Z-Shed,
followed by Multi-coloured
Swop Shop (1976-82). Other
TV incl: Come Dancing; Top
Gear; Taking the Strain, a
series about stress;
Illusionists, a series on
magic; Lucky Numbers; Juke
Box Jury; a programme about
helicopters. Appeared on the
London stage Christmas
1981 in Captain Beaky's
Musical Christmas.
Education: Brentwood
School. m Gill. Address: c/o
Manor House Consultants,
Frome, Somerset. Starsign:
Capricorn. Hobby:
helicopters.

EDWARDS, Cenwyn
Producer b 27.10.45

Llangennech, Wales. Trained
with HTV and has since been
closely associated with Y
Dydd; Yr Wythnos (in which
he regularly appears); Report
Wales; Outlook; National
Eisteddfod OB; Too Low For
Comfort?; Albert Jenkins.
Education: Llanelli Boys
Grammar School; University
College, Bangor. m Eluned,
2 s Lowri, Gruffudd.
Address: c/o HTV Wales,
Cardiff. Starsign: Scorpio.
Hobbies: rugby, cricket,
drama. Person he would most
like to meet: 'Paul Simon – the
prophet of my generation.'

EDWARDS, Glynn
Actor b 2.2.31 Malaya.
Trained at Joan Littlewood's
Theatre Workshop and since
entering show business in
1963 has worked extensively
in films, all the top TV series
and dozens of plays, incl: The
Newcomers; Spindo; The
Main Chance; Man About the
House; Dixon of Dock Green;
Paper Lads; Target; The Rise
and Fall of Reginald Perrin;
Minder; History of Mr Polly;
You're Only Young Twice.
Other TV incl: Shadow of a
Gunman; The Lucky Feller;
Dick Emery Show; Les
Dawson Show; Crown Court;
Harry Worth Show.
Education: Salisbury
Cathedral School;
Clayermore. m (1st) actress
Yootha Joyce (dis), (2nd)
Christine Pilgrim (dis),
1 s Tom. Address: c/o Green
& Underwood Ltd, London
W8. Starsign: Aquarius.
Hobby: messing about in
boats. Person he would most

like to meet: 'Bob Hope – to
be a stand-up comedian is
the most difficult; he must be
the best.'

EDWARDS, Ian
Sports correspondent
b 23.5.42 Barmouth, Wales.
Editor of university
newspaper 1963-64.
Newspaper training as
general reporter specialising
in arts and music with
Western Mail 1966-69. News
assistant, BBC Wales in
Cardiff 1969-71; sports
correspondent, Tyne Tees TV
1971-75 when he became
ITN's sports correspondent.
Education: Friars Grammar,
Bangor; University College of
Wales, Cardiff (BA Hons
Modern Languages).
m Mari, 1 d Catrin,
1 s Steffan. Address: c/o
ITN, London W1. Starsign:
Gemini. Hobbies: listening to
music, running marathons.
Person he would most like to
have met: 'Chopin, for
musical inspiration.'

EDWARDS, Jimmy
Actor/comedian b 23.3.20
Barnes, Surrey. Served in the
RAF (decorated DFC) during
the war and made his stage

debut at London's Windmill Theatre 1946 and radio debut the same year. Starred in such long-running radio series as Take It From Here; My Wildest Dream; Does The Team Think? (which he devised). Many stage shows incl: pantomimes; Maid of the Mountains revival; Big Bad Mouse; Doctor in the House; Oh! Sir James! (which he wrote). TV incl: Whack-O!; Seven Faces of Jim; Bold as Brass; I Object; John Jorrocks Esq; The Auction Game; The Fossett Saga; Jokers Wild; Sir Yellow; Charley's Aunt; The Glums; Does The Team Think? Has toured extensively in Australia. Education: St Paul's Cathedral Choir School; St John's College, Cambridge (MA). m Valerie (dis). Address: c/o Peter Charlesworth Ltd, London SW7. Starsign: Aries. Hobbies: hunting, shooting, polo.

EDWARDS, Meredith
Actor b 10.6.17 Rhosllannerchrugog, Nr Wrexham, Clwyd. A member of the Circle of Bards and Honorary Life President of Equity (Wales). Son of a miner, he went into rep at Liverpool Playhouse and the Old Vic and during the war was a member of the touring Pilgrim Players and the Army Topical Theatre. Has considerable TV and film experience, incl: The Magnet; The Blue Lamp; The Cruel Sea; A Run For Your Money; Dunkirk. More recent films incl: Gulliver's Travels. TV incl: Father, Dear Father; Bless This House; General Hospital; Quiller; Coronation Street; My Good Woman; The Protestors; Hawkmoor; Off to Philadelphia in the Morning; Country Matters; The Boy Merlin; Lloyd George; Great Preachers of Britain (Christmas Evans); Medico; Fame is the Spur. Education: Rhos Junior School; Ruabon Grammar. m Daisy, 1 d Lisa, 2 s Ioan, Peter. Address: Mold, Clwyd. Starsign: Gemini. Hobbies: reading, walking. Person he would most like to meet: 'Mother Teresa, because I would like to meet a saint.'

EGAN, Peter
Actor b 28.9.46 London. Wanted to be an artist, but studied for the stage at RADA and while still a student there was invited by Sir John Clements to join the Chichester Festival Theatre company. This was followed by work with the Royal Shakespeare Company and the National Theatre. Other stage incl: Journey's End; What Every Woman Knows; Engaged; Rolls Hyphen Royce; You Never Can Tell (to re-open the Lyric Theatre, Hammersmith); Arms and the Man; also directed Rattle of a Simple Man and Landmarks. Films incl: One Brief Summer; The Hireling (BAFTA Award for Most Promising Newcomer 1974); Callan; Hennessy; Chariots of Fire. TV break came with Big Breadwinner Hog. Other TV incl: Mother Love; The Inheritors; The Organisation; The Love School; The Deep Blue Sea; Lillie; The Kitchen; Prince Regent; Dear Brutus; Tales of the Unexpected; Thriller. Education: St George's Secondary Modern School, Maida Vale, London. m actress Myra Francis, 1 d Rebecca. Address: c/o Fraser and Dunlop Ltd, London W1. Starsign: Libra. Hobbies: travel, swimming, poker, working, good wine. Person he would most like to meet: 'Jesus Christ, as He was the man whose teachings influenced and dictated my thinking in the most formative years of my life. My education was strictly Roman Catholic and I would like to have met the souce of this belief.'

ELLIOTT, Denholm
Actor b 31.5.22 London. Studied at RADA. Joined RAF at 18 as radio operator/gunner, was shot down in 1942 and it was while in a POW camp, through a group called The No Name Players, that his acting career really began. First stage appearance in England was in 1945 at the Amersham Playhouse and first London West End appearance the following year in The Guinea Pig. Many plays since in London, Manchester, Malvern Festival, Shakespeare Memorial Theatre, Stratford-upon-Avon (1960 season) and the Royal Shakespeare Company in London, as well

as tours and several visits to America. Films incl: The Sound Barrier; The Holly and the Ivy; The Cruel Sea; Nothing But the Best; King Rat; Alfie; The Seagull; Too Late the Hero; Percy; Madame Sin; Russian Roulette; The Doll's House; A Bridge Too Far; Zulu Dawn; Sweeney; Rising Damp; Sunday Lovers; The Missionary. Many TV appearances incl: In Hiding; You're All Right, How Am I?; Gentle Folk; School Play; Donkeys Years; Sextet; Clayhanger; Blade on the Feather; Marco Polo. BAFTA Award for best actor of the year 1980. Education: Malvern College. m Susan Robinson, 1 d Jennifer, 1 s Mark. Address: c/o London Management, London W1. Starsign: Gemini. Hobbies: golf, gardening, skiing, motorbikes.

ELPHICK, Michael
Actor b 19.9.46 Chichester. Trained at Central School of Speech and Drama and then worked extensively in rep, toured in Tony Richardson's production of Hamlet and was in The Winter's Tale at the Ludlow Festival. Other theatre incl: The Cherry Orchard; The London Cuckolds; Measure For Measure; Hamlet (Royal Court); Ticket of Leave Man (National Theatre). Films incl: Fraulein Doctor; Cry of the Banshee; Blind Terror; The Great Train Robbery; Black

Island; Quadrophenia; Elephant Man; The Curse of the Pink Panther; Privates on Parade. Over the past few years he has played some important roles on TV incl: Holding Forth (in which he played a character who aged from 21 to 65); The Nearly Man; Blue Remembered Hills; The Sweeney; The Knowledge; Wobble to Death; Private Schultz; Pocketful of Dreams; Don't Write to Mother; Chains; Bloomfield; Andy Robson; All the World's a Stage; Crown Court. m Julia, 1 d. Address: c/o Crouch Assocs, London W1. Starsign: Virgo.

ELSMORE, Philip
Actor/announcer b 16.11.37 Stourport- on- Severn, Worcs. After training at Webber Douglas School of Drama spent a year with the Old Vic Company 1958-59 and rep incl Birmingham, Oldham and Newcastle. Since 1964 has been in succession an announcer with Tyne Tees TV, Southern TV, and ABC TV. Joined Thames TV 1968. Has done many radio commercials. TV incl: Rainbow; Whodunnit?; Pauline's People; Armchair Thriller; Kenny Everett Video Show; Astronauts. Education: Pitman's College, Birmingham. m actress Joan Scott. Address: c/o Thames TV, London NW1. Starsign: Scorpio. Hobby: golf. Person he would most like to meet: 'On behalf of everyone living

in London, I would like to meet the inventor of an aircraft that makes hardly any noise; or, at least, much less noise than at present.'

EMERY, Dick
Comedian/singer b 19.2.17 London. Started in amateur shows, then chorus work and pantomime; Gang Shows in RAF, Windmill 1948. Radio incl: Happy Holiday; Educating Archie; Emery at Large. Films. TV incl: Two's Company; It's a Square World; The Army Game; Ooh, You Are Awful; Find The Lady (with Mickey Rooney); The Dick Emery Show; Emery – A Legacy of Murder. Pantomimes. Extensive tours of Australia and New Zealand. 1973 BBC Personality of the Year Award. Royal Command Performance. m dancer Josephine Blake. Address: c/o Tony Lewis, London W10. Starsign: Aquarius. Person he would most like to meet: 'Peter Ustinov – because I admire him and all his work tremendously.'

ENGLISH, Arthur
Actor b 9.5.19 Aldershot. Ex-sergeant instructor in the RAC and former painter and decorator who was 30 before he went into show business. Became famous by parodying the Spiv, but went 'straight' 20 years later. Stage incl: London's Windmill Theatre; Royal Variety (twice); revues; pantomimes;

summer season; On The Rocks. TV incl: Follyfoot; Copper's End; How's Your Father; Dixon of Dock Green; Crown Court; Doctor in the House; The Ghosts of Motley Hall; Are You Being Served?; Funny Man; many plays; Pygmalion. Education: 'Very little', he claims. m (1st) Ivy (dec), (2nd) dancer Teresa Mann, 1 d Ann, 1 s Anthony (both from 1st m), 1 d Clare (from 2nd m). Address: c/o Patrick Freeman Management, London W6. Starsign: Taurus. Person he would most like to meet: 'The Princess of Wales – I am a great royalist and have had the pleasure of meeting most of the Royal Family.'

Letch (documentary on the life of a disabled teacher, which won the Asian Broadcasting Award 1979); Pietro Annigoni; Y Ddwy Ddinas (Welsh language documentary to mark the Pope's visit to Britain). Appointed HTV's chief executive in North Wales, based in Mold, in 1980, and since 1982 responsible for the station's Welsh documentaries, features and religious programmes. Education: Llanfaircaereinon County School, Powys; University of Wales, Aberystwyth. m Elizabeth, 4 d Gwenno, Eleri, Gwerfyl, Angharad. Address: c/o HTV Wales, Clwyd. Starsign: Gemini. Hobbies: music, travel, people, ideas, writing, sport, food and wine. Person he would most like to meet: 'Having worked in TV for almost 20 years, I have learned that one comes across the unexpected, and I am sure that somewhere, unknown, unheralded, there is a person who hasn't made TV history, but when we meet them will make our lives richer.'

Midsummer Night's Dream; Vivat! Vivat! Regina!; Twelfth Night; Arms and the Man; Same Time Next Year; The Importance of Being Earnest; Heartbreak House; The Round Dance. Has appeared in many TV plays and series incl: Randall and Hopkirk (Deceased); Parkin's Patch; Bouncing Boy; Vienna 1900; The Onedin Line; The Skin Game; Wingate; Warship; The Duchess of Duke Street; I Claudius; Supernatural; Secret Army; 1990; Justice; Thriller; The Strength of Gemini; Man About the House; Mother Makes Five; Return of the Saint; The Sweeney; George and Mildred; The Professionals; The Outsider. Education: Bristol Grammar. m (1st) actress/singer Millicent Martin (dis), (2nd) Lynette Braid. Address: c/o Saraband Assocs, London N1. Starsign: Gemini. Hobbies: football, cricket, archaeology, horse-racing.

ERFYL, Gwyn
Executive producer/ presenter b 9.6.24 Llanerfyl, Powys. Originally a lecturer in philosophy and Welsh minister. Started in TV on a freelance basis and joined TWW/HTV 1963. Has since been associated with many documentaries and studio programmes incl: Sylw; Bywyd; The World of Frank

ESHLEY, Norman
Actor b 30.5.45 Bristol. Started work in a bank but left to join Bristol Old Vic School. First professional appearance was in Orson Welles' film The Immortal Story. Other films incl: Blind Terror; The Disappearance; Yanks. Stage incl: Romeo and Juliet; Measure for Measure; Hamlet; A

EVANS, Barry
Actor/director b 18.6.43 Guildford, Surrey. Trained at Central School of Speech and Drama. TV incl: Doctor in the House; Crossroads; Armchair Theatre; Love Story; Mind Your Language; Emery – A Legacy of Murder. Address: c/o Hazel Malone Management, London SW13. Starsign: Gemini. Hobbies: photography, gardening, animals, ecology. Person he would most like to have met: Marilyn Monroe.

EVANS, Bob
Reporter/interviewer
b 9.7.36 Birmingham. Was
freelance contributor to
magazines before joining
Channel TV in 1974. TV incl:
interviews with show
business and top sports
stars; writing, narrating and
directing documentaries;
specialist work with
children's programmes.
Education: Loughborough
College. m June, 2 d Gina,
Karen. Address: c/o Channel
TV, Jersey. Starsign: Cancer.
Hobbies: sport (particularly
golf), travel. Person he would
most like to meet: 'Walter
Cronkite – hopefully some of
his know-how would rub off.'

EVANS, Clifford
Actor/writer b 17.2.12
Senghenydd, South Wales.
Celebrated 50 years as actor
on stage, films and TV in April
1981, his first stage
appearance being at the
Embassy Theatre, London, in
April 1931 as Don Juan in The
Romantic Young Lady.
Studied for the stage at RADA
receiving Northcliffe and
Academy scholarships. First
appearance in London's
West End was in 1933. Has

since played in and directed
many plays in Britain and
America. Was appointed
Director of Productions by
Cardiff City Council for the
Festival of Britain 1952 and in
1957 founded the St David's
Theatre Trust to establish a
National Theatre for Wales.
Films incl: Love on the Dole;
The Foreman Went to France;
A Run for Your Money (which
he wrote). On TV he is still
remembered for his powerful
performance as Caswell
Bligh in The Power Game.
Other TV incl: Kilverts' Diary;
Dylan Thomas; Ten Years On;
the Sunday evening series
Sing to the Lord. Education:
Llanelly County School.
m Hermione. Address: c/o
London Management,
London W1. Starsign:
Aquarius. Hobby: chess.
Person he would most like to
meet: 'Mother Teresa – if she
isn't a saint, who is?'

EVANS, John
Sports reporter b 7.9.42
Tregaron. Trained as a
school teacher and taught in
Penarth for five years before
joining the BBC in 1968, first
as a staff announcer and then
freelance, presenting
gardening and sports
programmes. Re-joined the
staff in 1978. Gave the first
commentary in Welsh on an
international rugby match –
Wales v New Zealand – in
1972 and has commentated
on Welsh rugby internationals
ever since. m Marian,
1 d Sara, 1 s Iolo. Address:
c/o BBC TV, Cardiff. Starsign:
Virgo. Hobby: gardening.

Person he would most like to
meet: 'The perfect
commentator'.

EVANS, Linda
Actress b 18.11.44 Hartford,
Connecticut. First attracted
attention in a soft drink TV
commercial which led to her
part of Audra Barkley in the
TV series The Big Valley, and
now Krystle, the heroine of
Dynasty. Her films incl:
Twilight of Honour; The
Klansman; Avalanche
Express; Those Crazy
Calloways; Tom Horn. TV
appearances incl: Bachelor
Father; Ozzie and Harriet;
The Untouchables; The
Eleventh Hour. Education:
Hollywood High School.
m (1st) film director John
Derek (dis), (2nd) Stan
Herman (dis). Starsign:
Scorpio. Hobbies:
numerology, clothes,
horse-riding, dancing, good
literature.

EVANS, Robin
Sports reporter b 1.2.54
Bangor. Joined HTV in
February 1979 after three
years with Y Cymro and North
Wales newspapers.
Education: Ysgol

Glan-y-Mor, Pwllheli;
University College of Wales,
Aberystwyth (BA Hons
Welsh). m Heulwen.
Address: c/o HTV, Cardiff.
Starsign: Aquarius. Hobbies:
any sport, folk singing.
Person he would most like to
meet: 'The swine who stole
my wife's handbag
containing all our cash and
travellers' cheques while we
were on holiday in France.'

EVANS, Su
Actress/announcer
b 16.11.51 Cardiff. Trained
at the Guildhall School of
Music and Drama (AGSM)
and the Royal Academy of
Music (LRAM). Rep
experience at the Thorndike
Theatre, Leatherhead, and in
plays at Watford, Norwich
and Belfast. She has been in
BBC Radio 4 afternoon
theatre productions and read
morning stories. She has
presented programmes on
Ulster TV and has been
announcer and newsreader
on Southern TV. Now an
announcer with Central TV.
Education: Dowsett High
School, Southend-on-sea.
Address: c/o Central TV,
Birmingham. Starsign:
Scorpio. Hobbies: theatre,
table tennis, dog-walking.
Person she would most like to
meet: 'Edna O'Brien – I
admire her serenity and
insight.'

EVERAGE, Dame Edna
Actress, birthdate not
available, Wagga Wagga,
Australia. From household
duties and invalid

management has become a
megastar in the
entertainment world. First
appearance on stage was as
Mary Magdalen in Moonee
Ponds Passion Play circa
1950. Then came
monologues with Barry
Humphries in Melbourne
1957 and 1958 which were so
successful she was engaged
as supporting artist in Barry
Humphries' shows: A Nice
Night's Entertainment (1962);
Excuse I (1965); Just a Show
(1968); A Load of Olde Stuffe
(1971); At Least You Can Say
You've Seen It (1974). She
achieved stardom in 1976 in
Housewife Superstar
followed by other starring
roles in A Night with Dame
Edna (1979); Last Night of the
Poms (1981); An Evening's
Intercourse (1982). Films incl:
Adventures of Barry
McKenzie; Barry McKenzie
Holds His Own. On TV she
has had numerous interviews
with Michael Parkinson and
Russell Harty; appeared in
BBC 2's The Late Show (with
Eleanor Bron, John Bird and
Malcolm Muggeridge); Barry
Humphries' Scandals; An
Audience with Dame Edna.
Education: Moonee Ponds
Ladies College. m Norman
Stoddart Everage,
1 d Valmai, 2 s Bruce,
Kenneth. Address: c/o
Dennis Smith Promotions,
Victoria, Australia. Hobbies:
caring and sharing. People
she would most like to meet:
Virginia Woolf, Pearl S Buck,
Radclyffe Hall, Rosa
Luxembourg.

EVERETT, Kenny
Disc jockey/presenter
b 25.12.44 Liverpool.
Wanted to become a priest.
Jobs in a bakery, advertising
agency and newspaper
office before making a name
as a DJ with Radio
Luxembourg. Subsequently
with Capital Radio and BBC
Radio and on TV for BBC and
ITV. TV incl: Nice Time; The
Kenny Everett Explosion;
Making Whoopee; Ev; The
Kenny Everett Video Show;
The Kenny Everett Television
Show. Created the fabulous
Capt Kremmen. Education:
Peter Clavier School for junior
African missionaries.
m ex-singer Audrey
Middleton. Address: c/o BBC
TV, London W12. Starsign:
Capricorn. Hobby: squash.
Person he would most like to
meet: Princess Anne.

F

FALK, Bernard
TV reporter/broadcaster/film producer b 16.2.43 Southport. Experienced Fleet Street journalist and with Scottish TV before appearing regularly on BBC current affairs programmes incl: 24 Hours; Midweek; Nationwide; Tonight; Newsnight. TV also incl. documentaries: The Silicon Factor; Uncle Sam's Backyard; The Four Seasons; Now Get Out of That. Presenter of Breakaway and Start the Week on Radio 4. Education: minimal (he says). m Linda, 1 d Samantha, 2 s Andrew, Keiran. Address: c/o BBC, London W1. Starsign: Aquarius. Hobbies: golf, work, model soldiers. Person he would most like to meet: 'Jesus Christ – to ask if it was true and really happened.'

Daughter; The Expert; Love Story; Kipling; Z Cars; Softly, Softly; The Tomorrow People; Coronation Street (in which he appears intermittently as Annie Walker's son, in order to do stage work); Danger UXB; New Girl In Town; General Hospital; Crown Court; Tycoon; Play for Today. Stage incl: The Outcry; Edward II; Nil Carborundum; The Little Hut; Saturday, Sunday, Monday; The Lion In Winter; Da; Getting On; A Man For All Seasons; This Story of Yours; Blithe Spirit; The Odd Couple; The Taming of the Shrew; The Norman Conquests; tour of India with School for Scandal and Educating Rita. Films incl: One Way Pendulum; Submarine XI; The Knack. Education: Alleyn's. m actress Patricia Heneghan (dis), 1 d Theresa, 2 s James, Mark. Address: c/o London Management, London W1. Starsign: Aries. Hobbies: home-made wine and beer, photography, playing soccer, squash. Person he would most like to meet: 'The bloke who stole my son's Lambretta – I hate petty theft.'

FAIRCHILD, Morgan
Actress and Kung Fu expert b 3.2.50 Dallas, Texas. Real name Patsy McClummy. Moved to New York in 1971 after graduating from Lake Highlands High School and achieved some success as a model and actress. She was in the film Bonnie and Clyde and her TV credits incl: The Memory of Eva Parker; Dallas; Mork and Mindy; Young Maverick; Happy Days; Kojak; Barnaby Jones; Spiderman. Specialises in playing bitchy characters, and more recently has been in Search For Tomorrow, The Dream Merchants and Flamingo Road. m (dis) Starsign: Aquarius.

FARRINGTON, Kenneth
Actor b 18.4.36 Peckham, London. Originally wanted to study languages but after acting at school became a founder member of the National Youth Theatre and later went to RADA. TV incl: The Splendid Spur; An Age of Kings; The Prime Minister's

FEAR, Chris
Sports presenter 12.5.43 Gatleigh, Cheshire. Journalist experience with Maidenhead Advertiser and North Devon Journal and Herald before joining the BBC as a regional journalist in 1971. Later joined Westward TV/TSW where he presented a schools quiz for the

network, On Your Marks. Also developed and presented a new sport Target Bowls and since 1974 presented Westward Sport, now Sportsweek. Education: Peter Symonds School, Winchester. m Josephine, 1 d Sally, 1 s Robin. Address: c/o TSW, Plymouth. Starsign: Taurus. Hobbies: golf, motor-cycling. Person he would most like to meet: 'Leonid Brezhnev – to ask him what Russia is trying to do.'

FEAST, Fred
Actor/playwright b 5.10.29 Scarborough. Originally a variety artist. Has appeared in 70 TV plays incl: award-winning Soldier and Me; Another Sunday and Sweet F A; Ready When You Are Mr McGill. TV also incl: Days of Hope; Bill Brand; Country Matters; Fred Gee in Coronation Street as a regular character since 1976. Education: Graham School, Scarborough. m Kathleen, 3 d Julia, Andrea, Helen. Address: c/o Granada TV, Manchester. Starsign: Libra. Hobbies: gardening, fishing. Person he would most like to meet: Muhammad Ali.

FERRIGNO, Lou
Muscleman b 9.11.51 Brooklyn, New York. The Hulk in The Incredible Hulk, which is also his favourite cartoon character. Former sheet metal worker. Began body-building when he was 16 and won Mr Teenage America contest 1971 and Mr America title 1973. Following

year won Mr World and Mr Universe titles. Appeared in the body-building documentary film Pumping Iron, followed by TV documentaries Superstars and The World's Strongest Men. Then came overnight stardom in The Incredible Hulk. m former psychology student Sue. Starsign: Scorpio. Hobbies: carpentry.

FISH, Michael
Weatherman b 27.4.44 Eastbourne, East Sussex. Has been with the Meteorological Office for 20 years and has made appearances as a TV weatherman for nine years. Also appeared on various BBC TV programmes where a 'scientific expert' was needed, and written and narrated several schools radio programmes. Scripted and appeared with Patrick Moore on Sky At Night on meteorological satellites. Brief appearances on TV incl: Basil Brush; Generation Game. General PR for Meteorological Office. Education: Eastbourne College; The City University. m Susan. 2 d Alison, Nicola. Address:

c/o BBC, London. Starsign: Taurus. Hobbies: philately, travel, gardening, do-it-yourself, genealogy. Person he would most like to meet: 'Margaret Thatcher, to discuss Civil Service pay!'

FISHER, Ian
Broadcaster b 16.8.53 Edinburgh. Experience with BBC in Edinburgh and Radio Tees in Stockton-on-Tees before joining Border TV as a reporter/presenter in Sept 1979. Nominated for an award for co-production and co-presentation of Elvis Presley, a programme of world-wide reaction to Presley's death; also nominated for award for production of So You Think It's Crazy, a 30-part series highlighting the problems of unemployed school-leavers. Education: James Gillespie's School and Royal High School, Edinburgh. m Sheila. Address: c/o Border TV, Carlisle. Starsign: Leo. Hobbies: reading, listening to music, cooking, walking the dog, flying. Person he would most like to meet: 'Jimmy Webb – to find out what MacArthur Park is about.'

FISK, Martin
Actor b 28.4.46 London. A lorry driver before he became an actor, so it is perhaps appropriate that he is probably best known as the original Yorkie chocolate bar eating lorry driver of the TV commercial. Yet he trained at RADA and has been in many plays and TV series incl:

Brand; Poldark; The Sweeney; Rumpole of the Bailey; A Horseman Riding By; Coronation Street; Shoestring; Angels; Elizabeth Alone; On the Line. Stage incl: The Long and the Short and the Tall; One Flew Over the Cuckoo's Nest. Education: Highgate School. m Diane, 2 s Asa, Liam. Address: c/o Bill Horne Personal Management, London WC2. Starsign: Taurus. Hobbies: golf, football, gardening, reading.

FLAX, Fogwell
Comedy entertainer b 9.3.51 Liverpool. No training for show business. Held various jobs after leaving school then four years as a physiological measurement technician (cardiology) at the Royal Liverpool Children's Hospital. Turned professional in 1975 as half of Union Jack duo, being New Faces winners. Went solo in 1979 and won TV's Search For a Star competition in Dec 1980. TV since incl: Punchlines; 3-2-1; Live From Two; After All That, This; Clubland; Northern Life; Tiswas. Education: county

infant, junior and secondary modern schools in Liverpool; Kirkby College of Further Education. m Andrea, 1 d Deborah, 1 s Neil. Address: c/o BDA, Leigh, Lancs. Starsign: Pisces. Hobbies: Roman archaeology in Britain, model railways, music. Person he would most like to meet: 'Paul McCartney – his music and subsequent career have influenced my own considerably.'

FLEMYNG, Robert OBE
Actor/director b 3.1.12 Liverpool. Formerly a medical student, he first appeared on the stage in Truro in 1931 and was in his first London part in 1935 after three seasons at Liverpool Playhouse. Was appearing on Broadway when the Second World War was declared and he returned to England to join the RAMC. Rose to the rank of Lieutenant-Colonel, was awarded the Military Cross and other decorations. Returned to the stage in 1945. Wide theatre experience in London, on tour and abroad. Stage incl: French Without Tears; The Cocktail Party; The Guinea Pig (also the film) and many others. Films incl: The Blue Lamp; The Man Who Never Was; Medusa Trap; Four Feathers; The Thirty Nine Steps. Has been in TV since 1949 and between 1961 and 1964 had leading parts in two long-running series, Family Solicitor and Compact. Other TV incl: Probation Officer;

Spy Trap; Enemy at the Door; Rebecca; Edward and Mrs Simpson; The Lady Killers; Crown Court; Fame Is The Spur; Play For Today. Education: Haileybury College. m Carmen, 1 d Caroline. Address: c/o ICM, London W1. Starsign: Capricorn. Hobby: work. Person he would most like to have met: 'Sir Henry Irving, to try to define the magnetism.'

FLETCHER, Cyril
Comedian b 25.6.13 Watford. Formerly an insurance clerk. Famous for his odd odes which he began writing about his schoolmasters and his first boss. Became a comedian in 1936, studied at the Guildhall School of Music and Drama and soon had his own radio programme, Dreaming of Thee. Has been on radio, TV, in cabaret, summer season and pantomime ever since. First televised in 1936. Many series on TV incl: What's My Line?; That's Life; Gardening Today. m actress partner Betty Astell, 1 d actress Jill. Address: c/o Central TV, Birmingham. Starsign: Cancer. Hobbies: gardening, the countryside. Person he would most like to have met: 'Dan Leno, the first great pantomime dame.'

FORD, Anna
Newscaster b 2.10.43 Tewkesbury, but brought up in Wigton, Cumbria. Taught for Open University in Belfast for two years before Granada's Reports Action.

Has also been a researcher and presented schools programmes. Reporter with Man Alive 1977; later same year presented Tomorrow's World. Joined ITN as newscaster 1978. Voted Most Popular TV Personality (Female) by TVTimes readers 1978-79. Education: Manchester University (Economics graduate). m (1st) Dr Alan Brittles (dis), (2nd) cartoonist Mark Boxer, 1 d Claire. Address: c/o Anthony Sheil Assocs, London WC1. Starsign: Libra. Hobby: gardening.

FORDE, Peter
Farming editor b 28.7.32 Manchester. Journalistic experience on provincial newspapers in Manchester and West Country. TV series incl: Farm and Country News; Acres For Profit; The Happiness Business for Westward TV: Farming News for TSW. South-West Regional Information Officer for NFU. Winner in 1981 of Guild of Agricultural Journalists Co-operation Award. Education: St Bede's College, Manchester. m Josephine, 2 d Amanda,

Emma, 1 s Simon. Address: c/o TSW, Plymouth. Starsign: Leo. Hobbies: playing cricket, swimming (for health), ruminating in rural Europe, good food, fine wines. Person he would most like to have met: 'Dr W G Grace, the founder of modern cricket, to discover if he was the first to practice gamesmanship.'

FORDYCE, Keith
Commentator/presenter b 15.10.28 Lincoln. Began with British Forces Network and has since done many shows and series of wide variety both for BBC and ITV. Radio incl: Housewives Choice and World-Wide Family Favourites. TV incl: Thank Your Lucky Stars; Juke Box Jury; Ready, Steady, Go; Come Dancing; Treasure Hunt; Miss Westward; Miss England; Miss UK; Miss World; Picture Parade; The Groucho Marx Show; Kitchen Garden. Education: Lincoln School; Emmanuel College, Cambridge (MA Hons Law). m Anne, 4 d Rebecca, Kim, Julie, Samantha. Address: Torbay Aircraft Museum, High Blagdon, Paignton, Devon (of which he is curator). Hobbies: gardening, aviation, food and drink, staying in the Isles of Scilly. Person he would most like to meet again: 'David Niven – because he made me laugh so much last time we met.'

FORREST, Steve
Actor b 29.9.28 Huntsville,

Texas. After graduating from high school, joined the army at 18 and served in Europe. On discharge studied psychology at University of California, found an interest in acting and appeared with his brother, Dana Andrews, in film The Ghost Ship. Preferred writing to acting but in 1950 went to La Jolla Playhouse near San Diego. Gregory Peck was connected with that theatre, and arranged an audition for him and small parts in TV and radio followed. Continued to write until a major role in So Big. More than 25 feature films incl: The Bad and the Beautiful; Battle Circus; The Clown; Dream Wife; The Phantom of the Rue Morgue; Rogue Cop; Bedevilled; It Happened to Jane; Heller in Pink Tights; Five Branded Women; The Yellow Canary; The Flaming Lance; The Second Time Around. More than 100 TV roles incl: Testimony of Two Men; The Baron and most recently, SWAT. m Chris, 3 s Michael, Forrest Alexander, Stephen William. Starsign: Libra. Hobbies: reading, watching sport on TV, raising bees, golf.

FORSYTH, Brigit
Actress b 28th July Edinburgh. Secretarial training before going to RADA. Then rep, incl Salisbury, Lincoln, Cheltenham, Edinburgh, Watford and Hornchurch. Other theatre incl: tour of My Fat Friend; London's West

End, in The Norman Conquests; Dusa, Fish, Stas and Vi. On radio she has been in many plays, while her films incl: The Road Builder; The Likely Lads. Her many TV appearances incl: The Sinners; Adam Smith; Holly; Glamour Girls; The Master of Ballantrae; The Likely Lads; Henry (Playhouse); Graham's Gang; Jackanory; Holding the Fort; Tom, Dick and Harriet. Educated in Edinburgh. m TV director Brian Mills, 1 d Zoe, 1 s Ben. Address: c/o Jeremy Conway Ltd, London W1. Starsign: Leo. Hobbies: walking, music, cello, guitar. Person she would most like to meet: 'John Cleese, because he makes me laugh a lot.'

incl: Windmill Theatre 1945-51 with a two-year break in the RAF; Little Me; Birds on the Wing; The Bruce Forsyth Show; one-man show at London Palladium; The Travelling Music Show; Bruce Forsyth on Broadway. Films incl: Star; Heironymous Merkin; Bedknobs and Broomsticks; Seven Deadly Sins. TV incl: Music Hall; The Bruce Forsyth Show; The Canterville Ghost; The Mating Game; The Generation Game; Bring on the Girls; Bruce and More Girls; The Entertainers; Bruce's Big Night; Play Your Cards Right; Sammy and Bruce. Education: Latimer School, Edmonton. m (1st) former partner Penny Calvert (dis), (2nd) Anthea Redfern, 5 d Deborah, Julie, Laura (from 1st m), Charlotte, Louisa (from 2nd m). Address: c/o London Management, London W1. Starsign: Pisces. Hobby: golf. Person he would most like to meet: 'Fred Astaire – for style and elegance, he has no equal.'

Widely experienced in theatre, films and TV. Stage work incl: Mr Roberts; All My Sons; Teahouse of the August Moon. Films incl: Captive City; It Happens Every Thursday; The Glass Web; Escape from Fort Bravo; Trouble with Harry; Ambassador's Daughter; Everything But the Truth; Kitten with a Whip; Madame X; In Cold Blood; The Happy Ending; Topaz; And Justice For All; Sizzle. On TV he is probably best known for his Bachelor Father series. m former actress Julie Warren, 3 children. Address: Bel-Air, Beverley Hills. Starsign: Aquarius. Hobbies: sports fanatic, horses, tennis, antiques.

FOSTER, Barry
Actor b 21st August Beeston, Notts. After training at Central School of Speech and Drama joined Anew McMaster's company touring Eire in classical repertoire. London debut in Fairy Tales of New York at the Comedy Theatre where he has also appeared in My Place; Let's Get a Divorce; Getting Away With Murder. Stage also incl: Next Time I'll Sing to You; The Private Ear and the Public Eye (New York); Nottingham Playhouse; The Basement; Tea Party; After Haggerty; Scribes; Rear Column; Master Builder; Born in the Gardens. Films incl: King and Country; The Family Way; Twisted Nerve; Battle of Britain; Ryan's Daughter; Frenzy; Sweeney; Wild

FORSYTH, Bruce
Entertainer/comedian/singer/ actor b 22.2.28 Edmonton, London. Left school at 14 and started his working life as Boy Bruce, The Mighty Atom. But not 'discovered' until 1958 when, while in summer season at Babbacombe, he was asked to compère Sunday Night at the London Palladium. Since then he hasn't looked back. Stage

FORSYTHE, John
Actor b 29.1.18 Penn's Grove, New Jersey. Distinguished-looking American actor now heading the cast of Dynasty as Blake Carrington, but whose voice is already familiar to British viewers as that of Charlie Townsend in Charlie's Angels. He also introduces World of Survival, the American version of Anglia TV's Survival programmes.

Geese; A Woman Called Golda; Heat and Dust. TV incl: Hamlet; Mogul; Taste of Honey; Van Der Valk; Divorce His, Divorce Hers; Fall of Eagles; Old Times; Wingate; Three Hostages; A Family Affair; How Many Miles to Babylon. Education: Southall County Grammar. m singer Judith Shergold, 2 d Joanna, Miranda, 1 s Jason. Address: c/o Al Parker Ltd, London W1. Starsign: Leo. Hobbies: music, golf. Person he would most like to have met: 'James Joyce, to hear him talk.'

FOSTER, Marian
Journalist/broadcaster b 19.3.48 Newcastle-upon-Tyne. Wide experience of radio and TV on various talk programmes, news, etc. Own music programmes, Our Choirs; Songbook on BBC's Radio 4. TV incl: Newsview; Today at 6; Newsquest; Late Look (Tyne Tees); Swedish TV and Norddeutsche Rundfunk; About Women (Anglia); Pebble Mill at One; South East Journey; The Other Side of Ulster; Sunday Worship at Pebble Mill; Young Musician of the Year; NHK (Japan) Summit Conference Special; BBC Birdwatch 1981; 6:55 Special. Voted Points of View BBC Viewers' Favourite presenter 1980. Education: grammar school; Newcastle University (BA Hons and Dip Ed). Address: c/o BBC, Birmingham. Starsign: Pisces. Hobbies: music, piano playing and choral

singing (with London Symphony Chorus), gardening, cycling. Person she would most like to have met: 'Christina Grant Fraser – nurse and suffragette. Her story of courage inspires still a generation that never knew her.'

FOWLDS, Derek
Actor b 2.9.37 Balham, London. Trained for the stage at RADA (1958-60) where he gained an honours diploma. Has since worked mainly in TV incl: Francis Durbridge's The Doll; After That This; Miss Jones and Son; Clayhanger; Edward the Seventh; Robin's Nest; Cribb; Give Us a Clue; Strangers; Triangle. He was also in the The Basil Brush Show from 1969-73 and in each series of Yes, Minister. Education: Ashlyns School, Berkhamsted, Herts. m (dis), 1 s James. Address: c/o Barry Burnett, London W1. Starsign: Virgo. Hobbies: all sports, decorating, reading. Person he would most like to meet: Jane Fonda.

FOWLER, Harry MBE
Actor b 10.12.26 Lambeth Walk, London. Started

fending for himself when he was 13 after his grandmother was killed in the Blitz. One of his jobs was selling newspapers, and after being interviewed on In Town Tonight, he was always being asked to play Cockney parts in British films. Went into TV as Corporal Flogger Hoskins in The Army Game in 1957 and is still remembered for the part although the series ended in the early 60s. In addition to guest appearances on various shows, his TV credits incl: Our Man At St Mark's; The Name Game; Don't Say a Word; Get This!; Going A Bundle; more recently Stalingrad; World's End; The Little World of Don Camillo; Minder; Dead Ernest. Has been in more than 100 films since 1942 incl: Hue and Cry; Went The Day Well; Champagne Charlie; Lucky Jim; Lawrence of Arabia; The Longest Day; Flight from Singapore; Ladies Who Do; Two by Two; The Prince and the Pauper. Awarded MBE in 1970 Birthday Honours. Education: Central School. m Catherine. Address: c/o Essanay Ltd, London W14. Starsign: Sagittarius. Hobbies: tennis, stamp collecting, railway modelling. Person he would most like to meet: 'Fidel Castro – to brush up my Spanish!'

FOXWORTH, Robert
Actor b Houston, Texas. Has been acting since he was 10, starting at Houston Alley Theatre and remaining there

on a part-time basis until he completed his formal education. After graduating, he became a full-time actor, and his theatre credits incl PS Your Cat is Dead. He made his film debut in Treasure of Matecumbe and other films incl: The Astral Factor; Airport; Airport 77; Damien-Omen II. TV debut in Sadbird 1969. Has since been in The Storefront Lawyers series; Mrs Sundance; Hogan's Goat; and now in Falcon Crest as Chase Gioberti. Education: Mellon University.

FRANCIS, Derek
Actor b 7.11.23 Brighton. Went into acting when he came out of the army in 1947. TV incl: Oh, Brother!; Justice; Dickens of London; The New Avengers; Nicholas Nickleby; The Provincial Lady; The Strange Affair of Adelaide Harris; The Professionals; Great Expectations. Films incl: several Carry On films; Say Hello To Yesterday; To The Devil A Daughter. Stage incl: with Old Vic 1955-59; Laughter (Royal Court); Charley's Aunt (Adelphi). Education: Varndean School, Brighton; Brighton School of Art. m Penny, 2 d Tessa, Julia. Address: c/o Marina Martin Ltd, London W1. Starsign: Scorpio. Hobbies: puppetry, period costume research. Person he would most like to have met: 'Arthur Rackham – because I have always thought he was the greatest book illustrator of all time.'

FRANCIS, Jan
Actress b 5.8.51 London. Trained as a dancer and worked with Royal Ballet before deciding to become an actress. First stage part was in The Farmer's Wife at Cheltenham. Films incl: Dracula. Most experience in TV which incl: Hawkeye the Pathfinder; Ann of Green Gables; Lonely Man's Lover; Sutherland's Law; Village Hall; Looking for Clancy; The Launderette; Love's Labours Lost; Rooms; London Assurance; The Duchess of Duke Street; Raffles; Secret Army; The Party of the First Part; The Racing Game; Ripping Yarns; Target; Casting the Runes; Good Companions; Tales of the Unexpected; A Chance to Sit Down. m Martin C Thurley. Address: c/o Peter Browne Management, London SW9. Starsign: Leo.

FRANCIS, Raymond
Actor b 6.10.11 London. Did his training the hard way – in rep. Played Dr Watson in a Sherlock Holmes series for BBC at Alexandra Palace in 1950 but since 1955 has appeared almost exclusively in ITV programmes, incl 10 years as Lockhart in Murder Bag, Crime Sheet and No Hiding Place. More recently has played Dr Fuller in Together. Education: he claims 'nil'. m Margaret, 2 d Caroline, Frances, 1 s Clive. Address: c/o Fraser and Dunlop, London W1. Starsign: Libra. Hobbies: cooking, cricket-watching, gardening. Person he would most like to meet: 'Myself – we never argue, so there's no hassle.'

FRANCIS, Stu
Comedian b 30.1.48 Bolton, Lancs. Began as holiday camp entertainer (singer) when a teenager. Ran out of songs one night and began telling gags! Now an experienced club and theatre entertainer and has worked in summer seasons and pantomime. Own series and guest spots in radio and TV programmes, incl: host of Crackerjack since 1980. Education: Brownlow Fold Junior School and Smithills Base School, Bolton. m Wendy, 1 d Zoe, 1 s Andrew. Address: c/o Kennedy Street Artistes Ltd, Altrincham. Starsign: Aquarius. Hobbies: marathon running. Person he would most like to meet: George Burns – because of his terrific warmth and unique delivery.'

FRANCIS, Tony
Reporter b 17.11.46 Leicester. Journalist experience, then BBC

Midlands; Nationwide; ITN; Central TV. Education: Gateway Grammar School, Leicester; St John's College, Cambridge (MA Modern Languages). m (dec), 3 s Benjamin, Barnaby, Alexander. Address: Berkhamsted, Herts. Starsign: Scorpio. Hobbies: football, cricket, tennis, squash, painting, travel, learning more languages. Person he would most like to meet: 'Myself in ten years' time, so that I wouldn't have to say "If I knew then what I know now".'

FRANKLYN, Sabina
Actress b 15th September London. Training in weekly rep in Southwold and five years in rep all over the country. Tours of Charley's Aunt; The Man Most Likely To . . . ; Move Over Mrs Markham. TV incl: Jane Bennett in all episodes of Pride and Prejudice; Fawlty Towers; and with Kelly Monteith, Dave Allen, Mike Yarwood and Jim Davidson. Other TV incl: Keep It in the Family; When the Boat Comes In; Byron; Happy Ever After; Return of the Saint;

Blake's Seven. Education: Glendower School, Queen's Gate School. Address: c/o June Epstein Assocs, London W1. Starsign: Virgo. Hobbies: antiques, decorating, films, travelling, children. Person she would most like to meet: 'Jane Fonda – she's my favourite actress, has a super face and interesting views on life.'

FRANKLYN, William
Actor b 22.9.26 Kensington, London. Spent 10 years in Australia where his father, actor Leo Franklyn, was working. On returning to England appeared in My Sister Eileen when he was 15. Wartime service with paratroops until 1946. Post-war career started in Arsenic and Old Lace on Southsea Pier followed by rep at Ryde and Margate (with Brian Rix). First West End break in The Love of Four Colonels. One of the first stars of ITV, appearing in the first ITV play, Mid-Level. Other TV incl: The Makepeace Story; The Last Flight. Many early ITV series leading to Top Secret and BBC serials incl: No Wreath for the General; No Cloak, No Dagger. Latterly: Paradise Island; What's On Next; Masterspy; The Purple Twilight. Did Schweppes commercials for nine years and has been in more than 50 films. Education: Haileybury, Melbourne. m (1st) actress Margot Johns (dis), (2nd) actress Suzanna Carroll, 3 d Sabina (from

1st m), Francesca, Melissa (from 2nd m). Address: c/o Barry Burnett, London W1. Starsign: Virgo/Libra cusp. Hobbies: cricket, philately, photography.

FRASER, Bill
Actor b 5.6.08 Perth, Scotland. Began his working life in a bank, but the theatre lights beckoned and he joined a touring rep company. Since then he has played everything from Dame in pantomime to Shakespeare, incl performances with the National Theatre Company. Now one of our best character actors, his training, he says, has been '55 years in the business'. Before the war, in which he served in the RAF, he ran the Connaught Theatre, Worthing. Most recent theatre incl: Uncle Vanya. Made his name on TV as Snudge in The Army Game and Bootsie and Snudge. Other TV incl: Foreign Affairs; That's Your Funeral; The Corn is Green; Doctor's Daughters; K9 & Co; A Girl's Best Friend; Flesh and Blood. Films incl: Doctor At Large; All The Way Up; Up Pompeii; Up the Chastity Belt; Up the Front; Last Tribute; The Corn is Green; Wagner. Education: Strathallan School. m Pamela Cundell. Address: c/o Peter Crouch Assocs, London W1. Starsign: Gemini. Hobby: working.

FROST, David OBE
Author/interviewer/pre-senter/tycoon b 7.4.39

Tenterden, Kent. First TV as reporter for This Week, but achieved overnight success when picked to host That Was the Week That Was. This was followed by A Degree of Frost; Not So Much a Programme, More a Way of Life; The Frost Report; The Frost Programme; Frost Over England; Frost Over America; We British; The Wilson Interviews; The Nixon Interviews; David Frost's Global Village; The Falklands: Where Will It End? Books: I Gave Them a Sword (Frost on Nixon); I Could Have Kicked Myself – David Frost's Book of the World's Worst Decisions. Vast business interests. Founder of London Weekend Television; founder and Director of TV-AM. Education: grammar schools; Caius College, Cambridge (Hons degree English) where he edited university magazine and ran Footlights. m actress Lynne Frederick. Address: c/o David Paradine Productions Ltd. Starsign: Aries. Hobbies: football, cricket. People he would most like to meet: 'Either Cyrus the Great, because he was the first world-leader to use his power to ennoble rather than degrade the human condition, or Nicholas Parsons.'

with Ulster TV. Education: Ballymena Secondary Intermediate. m Linda, 3 s Darren, Nicolas, Gareth. Address: c/o Ulster TV, Belfast. Starsign: Gemini. Hobbies: 'My work in sport, plus watching sporting occasions – particularly soccer'. People he would most like to meet: Perry Como and Pelé.

FULLERTON, Jackie
Sports presenter b 22.5.43 Ballymena, Co Antrim. Started in accountancy. Full-time journalist since 1976

G

GABLE, Christopher

Actor b 13.3.40 London.
Ended a 10-year career as an
international ballet dancer
(he was one of The Royal
Ballet's highest paid stars) to
become an actor. First
'straight' appearance was at
Watford Rep in The Picture of
Dorian Gray. Has since
appeared at Oxford,
Manchester, London fringe
theatres and a year with the
Royal Shakespeare
Company. His break came
with appearances in Ken
Russell films incl: The Music
Lovers; The Dance of the
Seven Veils; A Song of
Summer; The Boy Friend.
Other films incl: The Slipper
and the Rose; Wagner. TV
incl: Willy; The Devil's Crown;
Tycoon; The Jack Buchanan
Story. Education: Royal Ballet
Schools. m former soloist
with Royal Ballet Carole
Needham, 1 d Emma,
1 s Tomas. Address: c/o
Ken McReddie, London W1.
Starsign: Pisces. Hobbies:
cooking, gardening. Person
he would most like to meet:
'Patrick White, the Australian
author, because it would be
nice to know someone of that
perception, creativity and
imagination.'

GALL, Sandy

Newscaster/reporter
b 1.10.27 Penang, Malaya.
Started career on Aberdeen
Press and Journal. Was
reporter for Reuter's for 10
years and since 1963 for ITN
has travelled virtually all over
the world. Speaks fluent
French and German. Books:
Gold Scoop, a novel about
Africa, 1977; Chasing the
Dragon, a novel about the Far
East, 1981. Education:
Glenalmond and Aberdeen,
Bonn and Mainz Universities.
m Eleanor, 3 d Fiona,
Carlotta, Michaela,
1 s Alexander. Address: c/o
ITN, London W1. Starsign:
Libra. Hobbies: golf, writing
thrillers. Person he would
most like to have met: 'Lord
Byron – a dashing, romantic
poet and man of action too.'

GALWAY, James

Musician/entertainer
b 8.12.39 Belfast. Had
decided to become a
musician by the time he was
14 and on leaving school was
apprenticed to a piano tuner.
A scholarship enabled him to
pursue his studies at the
Royal College of Music in
London and the Guildhall

School of Music. His music
career began with the violin
but he soon discarded this for
the flute and is now regarded
as the greatest flute player of
his generation. When quite
young he won junior, senior
and open classes in a flute
competition on the same day!
First job was with the wind
band of the Royal
Shakespeare Company at
Stratford-upon-Avon, later
playing successively with the
Sadler's Wells Company, the
Royal Opera House
orchestra and the BBC
Symphony Orchestra before
being appointed Principal
Flute with the London
Symphony Orchestra and
then the Royal Philharmonia
Orchestra. This was followed
by six years as first solo flute
with the Berlin Philharmonic
Orchestra. He has made
more than 20 records, which
range from the complete
Bach flute sonatas to a
Country album in Nashville,
Tennessee. His record
successes also reflect his
versatility – from a Grand Prix
du Disque for his Mozart
concertos, to top spot in the
pop charts for his rendering
of Annie's Song. His film and
TV work incl: Music in Time
(for Channel 4); Brendon
Chase. Education: St Paul's,
and Mount Collyer
Secondary Modern, Belfast.
m Annie, 2 d Charlotte,
Jennifer (twins), 1 s Patrick.
Address: c/o London
Management, London W1.
Starsign: Sagittarius.
Hobbies: stamp collecting,
chess, backgammon.

GAMBON, Michael

Actor b 19.10.40 Dublin.
Started acting at Dublin's
Gate Theatre. Then went on
to the National Theatre,
Chichester Festival, Royal
Shakespeare Company and
rep at Birmingham, Coventry,
Liverpool and Regent's Park
Open Air Theatre. Stage incl:
Mother Courage; The

Recruiting Officer; Juno and the Paycock; Major Barbara; When Thou Art King; Not Drowning But Waving; Otherwise Engaged; The Norman Conquests; Just Between Ourselves; Zoo Story; Alice's Boys; Betrayal; Close of Play; title roles in Galileo (National Theatre), King Lear and Anthony and Cleopatra (Royal Shakespeare Company, Stratford). TV incl: The Challengers; The Borderers; The Other One; La Ronde; The Breadwinner. Education: St Aloysius School, London. 1 s. Address: c/o Larry Dalzell Assocs Ltd, London WC2. Hobby: collecting Victorian machinery. Person he would most like to meet: 'The Managing Director of James Purdeys (Royal gunmakers) – I'd like to be shown around their factory.'

GARDEN, Graeme
Actor/scriptwriter b 18.2.43 Aberdeen. Son of a doctor, he studied medicine at King's College Hospital in London. Chose to become involved in show business after writing for radio, incl: I'm Sorry, I'll Read That Again. With Bill

Oddie also wrote some of the Doctor TV series and Astronauts. Other TV incl: Twice a Fortnight; Broaden Your Mind; The Goodies; Charlie's Climbing Tree. Records incl: Funky Gibbon; The In-Betweenies. Education: Cambridge University, where he was a member of the Footlights Club. Address: c/o Roger Hancock Ltd, London SW1. Starsign: Aquarius. Person he would most like to have met: Leonardo da Vinci.

GARDNER, Andrew
Presenter b 25.9.32 Beaconsfield, Bucks. 6ft 5in tall, first newscaster of News at Ten with Alastair Burnet in July 1967. Started in radio journalism in Central African Fedn, reporting extensively in Africa. Returned to UK 1961; freelanced as reporter/newscaster for Roving Report and Dateline, then News at Ten. Presented first transatlantic Telstar programme 1962. Also covered State occasions for ITV network on Queen's Silver Wedding, Princess Anne's wedding and the wedding of Prince Charles to Lady Diana Spencer. Joined Thames TV to front nightly Thames News programme. Education: Dauntsey's School, Wilts. m Margaret, 4 s Mark, Adrian, Maxwell, Adam. Address: c/o Thames TV, London NW1. Starsign: Libra. Hobby: collecting Victorian microscopes. Person he would most like to have met: 'Richard II to find out if he was as bad as history makes out!'

GARNER, James
Actor b 7.4.28 Oklahoma. Had 50 jobs before he turned to acting; he called to see a producer friend who offered him a job in the stage production of The Caine Mutiny Court Martial, and he's been an actor ever since. A part in Cheyenne followed and then Maverick; The Rockford Files; Bret Maverick. Films incl: Darby's Rangers; Marlowe; Support Your Local Sheriff; Grand Prix; Victor, Victoria. Served in Korea with the US Army and was awarded the Purple Heart. m actress Lois Clarke, 2 d Greta, Kimberly (step-d). Address: Los Angeles. Starsign: Aries.

GASCOIGNE, Bamber
Much-travelled question-master b 24.1.35 London. National Service in Grenadier Guards. Scholarship to Yale School of Drama. Wrote Share My Lettuce, 1957. Later dramatic critic, The Spectator and The Observer. Chairman of University Challenge since 1962. Presenter of Cinema 1964. Devised The Auction Game and scripted The Four

Freedoms; The Trouble With Women; wrote and presented The Christians. Books: World Theatre; The Great Moghuls; Treasures and Dynasties of China; Murgatreud's Empire; The Heyday; The Christians. Education: Eton; Cambridge. m Christina Ditchburn. Address: c/o Granada TV, Manchester. Starsign: Aquarius. Person he would most like to have met: 'Albert Einstein – I like his puzzled look.'

GASCOINE, Jill
Actress b 11th April Lambeth. Trained at the Italia Conti Stage School, then rep at Nottingham, Dundee, Glasgow, Worthing, Hornchurch and Leicester. TV incl: Rooms; Plays for Britain; General Hospital; The Norman Wisdom Show; Three Kisses; Balzac; Z Cars; Softly, Softly; Dixon of Dock Green; Within These Walls; Holding On; Six Days of Justice; Justice; Raffles; Beryl's Lot; Peter Pan; Oranges and Lemons; The Onedin Line; The Gentle Touch. Education: Kingston Grammar School. 2 s Sean, Adam. Address: c/o Marina Martin Management, London W1. Starsign: Aries. Hobbies: gardening, writing bad scripts, cooking and dieting. Person she would most like to meet: 'Jesus Christ – who else? There are so many questions.'

GEORGE, Beti
Radio and TV journalist b 19.1.39 Coedybryn,

Dyfed, South Wales. Started in radio by preparing contributions to a daily current affairs programme Bore Da. Presenter of Heddiw, a daily TV news/current affairs programme for BBC Wales; presenter Cil-y-Drwg, a chat show on Radio Cymru. Also presenter of various radio and TV documentaries incl: Welsh National Opera Co; George Guest at Cambridge; A Nun's Story; Youth Unemployment; Nuclear Defence. Education: Llandysul Grammar; University of Wales. 1 s Lestyn. Address: c/o BBC, Cardiff. Starsign: Capricorn. Hobby: needling. Person she would most like to have met: Rodrigo Borgia.

GERARD, Gil
Actor b 23rd January Little Rock, Arkansas. Former industrial chemist who achieved instant fame by bringing to life the comic-strip character of Buck Rogers. Gave up a lucrative job in industry to become an actor. Went to New York for acting lessons by day; drove a cab at night. Several bit parts in films (incl Love Story), a

regular part in TV series, The Doctors, for two years and more than 400 TV commercials before being chosen for the title role in Buck Rogers in the 25th Century. He turned down the part twice before accepting it. Education: Arkansas State Teachers' College; American Musical and Dramatic Academy, New York. m three times, each wife having the first name Connie. Starsign: Aquarius. Hobbies: writing poetry, disabled Olympic and muscular dystrophy. (He is National Chairman of the Muscular Dystrophy Readathon).

GIANT HAYSTACKS
Wrestler b 10.10.47 London. Weighs 35st. m Rita, 3 s Martin, Steven, Noel. Address: c/o Joint Promotions Ltd, London SW9. Starsign: Libra. Hobbies: walking, swimming, boxing. Person he would most like to meet: 'James Cagney: to me he is a unique person – singer, dramatic actor supreme. His type of talent is sadly missed these days.'

GIELGUD, Sir John CH
Actor/director b 14.4.04 London. A great-nephew of Dame Ellen Terry, he studied for the stage at Lady Benson's school and RADA, winning scholarships at both. First appearance on the stage was at the Old Vic in 1921 as the Herald in Henry V. Since then, during a distinguished career

spanning more than 60 years as an actor, director and manager, he has established himself as one of the world's greatest actors, notably in Shakespearian roles; he has played Hamlet more than 500 times. During and since the Second World War he has further distinguished himself in his one-man show, Ages of Man, and in such plays as The Importance of Being Earnest; The Lady's Not For Burning; Nude With Violin; Home; 40 Years On; No Man's Land (also on TV). Has done a great deal of radio work and his films incl: The Good Companions (1932) and more recently Gold; Galileo; Murder on the Orient Express; Chariots of Fire; Arthur (for which he won an Oscar); Wagner; The Wicked Lady. TV debut was in A Day By The Sea (in the part he had played on stage) in 1959. Other TV incl: The Cherry Orchard; Ivanov; The Mayfly and the Frog; Deliver Us From Evil; Edward the Seventh; Roald Dahl's Tales of the Unexpected (Neck); Why Didn't They Ask Evans?; English Gardens; Brideshead Revisited; Parson's Pleasure. Books: Early Stages (autobiography); Stage Directions; Distinguished Company; An Actor and His Time. Chevalier of the Legion of Honour; hon degree of Doctor of Law (St Andrews University); hon degree D Litt (Oxford University); knighted in Coronation Birthday Honours, 1953; Companion of Honour, 1977. Education:

Westminster School. Address: c/o International Creative Management, London W1. Starsign: Aries.

GILLESPIE, Robert
Actor b 9.11.33 Lille, France. Mother Hungarian, father Canadian of Scottish descent. Arrived in Plymouth 1940 on last boat to leave France from St Jean de Luz unable to speak English, only French, German and some Hungarian. When he was nine he made his first stage appearance as Old Shepherd in a nativity play at Urban Road Primary School, Sale. Was also in plays at grammar school and joined an amateur group, The Altrincham Garrick Society. Appeared at Manchester's Library Theatre as a semi-professional in 1951. After RADA and two years at the Old Vic played in rep at Glasgow, Ipswich, The Royal Court, London, and Belgrade Theatre, Coventry, Mermaid Theatre, London. Considerable energy as actor and director. Since 1971 he has directed 50 plays, many of them touring and incl in 1980 a production of Fearless Frank on Broadway and the revival of Priestley's Dangerous Corner in London. He directed the latter play again in Tel-Aviv, Israel, in 1982. Also a writer of plays and was a contributor to the BBC's That Was The Week That Was, for which he received the Writer's Guild Award of Merit in 1963. Since July 1968 has appeared in 86

commercials in the UK and on the Continent. Films incl: A Severed Head; The Magnificent Seven Deadly Sins; The National Health; The Thirty Nine Steps; The Prisoner of Zenda. Radio incl: Whatever Happened to the Likely Lads?; Lord Peter Wimsey; Galbraith and the Midas Touch; Beyond the Book; Tony's. Since 1958 he has made an increasing number of appearances on TV, having been in more than 100 shows, incl: The Black Brigand; Miss Em; Hotel Paradiso; The Queen and the Rebels; Maigret; Kipling; Crane; Danger Island; The Gamblers; Romeo and Juliet; The Drinking Party; Hugh and I; Mr Digby, Darling; Whatever Happened to the Likely Lads?; Sadie, It's Cold Outside; The Good Life; Couples; Rising Damp; Warship; Rosie; Robin's Nest; It Ain't Half Hot Mum; George and Mildred; Angels; Butterflies; The Fall and Rise of Reginald Perrin; Agony; Secret Army; three series of Keep It In The Family; The Sweeney; The New Avengers; Van der Valk; The Professionals; Return of the Saint; Sherlock Holmes. Education: Sale County Grammar School. Address: c/o CCA, London SW6. Starsign: Scorpio. Hobbies: reading, cinema, travelling, archaeology. Person he would most like to have met: 'Charles Darwin – he started off so many things which we have still to face.'

GLASS, Katie
Presenter/announcer b 7.4.53 Lusaka, Zambia. Training as a disc jockey and afternoon chat show hostess with Radio Orwell before joining Anglia TV in Sept 1977. Co-presenter children's programme, The Next Week Show, and presenter of programme for unemployed, Jobline.

Education: Mayfield School, St Leonard's, Sussex. m Jon Tremain. Address: c/o Anglia TV, Norwich. Starsign: Aries. Hobbies: music, films, theatre. Person she would most like to meet: 'Woody Allen – to say thanks for all those movies.'

GLOVER, Brian
Actor/writer b 2.4.34 Sheffield. Before becoming an actor was in turn a schoolmaster and professional wrestler. Entered show business 1968 when he played the schoolmaster in the film Kes. Films since incl: Brannigan; O Lucky Man; Quilp; Trial By Combat; The Great Train Robbery; An American Werewolf in London. On stage he has been in Much Ado About Nothing and played God in The Passion for the National Theatre. On TV he gives voice to the Tetley Tea Folk commercial. Other TV incl: Rank and File; The Frighteners; A Day Out; Speech Day; The Regiment; Porridge; The Wild Bunch; Secret Army; Return of the Saint; Sounding Brass; Minder. Is also a playwright. Education: Barnsley

Grammar; Sheffield University. m (dis), 1 d Maxine. Address: c/o Felix de Wolfe, London WC2. Starsign: Aries. Hobby: serendipity. Person he would most like to meet: 'Arthur Miller – I'd like to pick his brains.'

GODDARD, Liza
Actress b 20.1.50 Winchester. Started acting with Farnham Rep. Went to Australia with family 1965, acted on Australian TV 1969 returned to this country 1969 and has worked on stage, radio and TV. Stage incl: Sign of the Times; No Sex Please – We're British. Radio: The Victoria Line. TV incl: Take Three Girls; Yes, Honestly; The Brothers; The Upchat Line; The Greatest; Blankety Blank; Pig in the Middle; Murder At The Wedding. Films incl: Wagner. Education: Farnham Girls' Grammar, Arts Educational Trust. m (dis), 1 s Tom. Address: c/o Barry Burnett, London W1. Starsign: Aquarius. Hobbies: tapestry, horse-riding, health foods, reading. Person she would most like to have met: 'George Eliot – she was such a remarkable woman.'

GODWIN, Christopher
Actor b 5.8.43 Loughborough, Leics. Started in stage management with no drama school training. Played the leading parts in Alan Ayckbourne's plays at Scarborough for seven years until he came to London to star in

Ayckbourne's Ten Times Table. This led to his appearance in the TV play Don't Be Silly. Other TV since incl: Nice Work; Holding The Fort; Astronauts; The Other 'Arf; Nearly a Happy Ending; A Foggy Outlook. Education: Alleyn's College of God's Gift. m Christine, 2 s Ben, Tom. Address: c/o ICM, London W1. Starsign: Leo. Hobbies: cycling, cricket, roller-skating.

GOLDING, Rob
Reporter/presenter b 13.10.49 Ashford, Kent. Weekly and evening newspaper experience (on Leicester Mercury) and with BRMB commercial radio before joining ATV/Central TV 1979. Education: Kent South Secondary and East Kent Technical College, Ashford. m Jennifer, 1 d Mary-Jane. Address: c/o Central TV, Birmingham. Starsign: Libra. Hobbies: making and drinking beer, badminton, squash, do-it-yourself. Person he would most like to have met: 'Adolf Hitler – no one had a more profound effect on the structure of the world today.'

GOODWIN, Harold
Actor b 22.10.17 Wombwell,
Yorks. Trained at RADA and
was three years at Liverpool
rep. First stage appearance
in London's West End in
Venus Observed. Many
theatre productions since
plus 150 films incl: Dam
Busters; Bridge on the River
Kwai; The Longest Day; All
Creatures Great and Small.
Over 500 TV appearances,
most recent incl: Love Story;
The Crucible; That's My Boy.
Education: 'very little' (he
says). m Beatrice. Address:
c/o Joan Gray,
Sunbury-on-Thames.
Starsign: Libra. Hobbies:
reading, cricket. Person he
would most like to meet:
'Jimmy Cagney – he's of my
era and was a hero of mine as
a boy. I'd ask him about the
early Hollywood days.'

GORDON, Hannah
Actress b 9.4.41 Edinburgh.
Trained at Glasgow College
of Dramatic Art then rep at
Dundee, Glasgow, Coventry,
Windsor and Leatherhead.
Wide radio and TV
experience incl: What Every
Woman Knows; David
Copperfield; Middlemarch;
Love Story; The Rat Catchers;

Dr Finlay's Casebook; The
Exiles; Heloise and Abelard;
Great Expectations; Scobie
in September; Allergy; My
Wife Next Door; Dear
Octopus; Upstairs,
Downstairs; Telford's
Change; Waste; Miss
Morison's Ghosts; Goodbye,
Mr Kent. Films incl: Spring
and Port Wine; The Elephant
Man. Stage incl: What Every
Woman Knows; Othello;
Baggage; Can You Hear Me
At The Back?; The Killing
Game; The Jeweller's Shop.
Book: Woman at the Wheel.
Education: Trinity Academy;
St Denis School, Edinburgh.
m lighting cameraman
Norman Warwick, 1 s Ben.
Address: c/o David White
Assocs, London SW3.
Starsign: Aries. Person she
would most like to meet: The
Pope.

GORDON, Noele
Actress b 25th December
East Ham, London. Trained at
RADA, then rep in Edinburgh,
Birmingham and London
before such stage successes
as Black Velvet; Let's Face It;
The Lisbon Story (also the
film); Big Ben; Diamond Lil
(with Mae West); Brigadoon;
pantomimes; Call Me
Madam; Grayson's
Scandals; Royal Variety
Performance. Went to
America to study TV and
returned to join ATV 1955 as
advisor on women's
programmes. TV incl:
Week-End; Fancy That; Tea
with Noele Gordon; Lunch
Box; Midland Profile; Hi-T!;
Crossroads (for 17 years);

Noele Gordon Takes The Air.
Returned to stage 1981 to
appear in Gypsy at Leicester.
Chosen by John Logie Baird
for his early experiments in
colour TV. Eight times Top
Female TV Personality in
TVTimes Top Ten Awards poll
and first member of the TV
Hall of Fame. Four times
winner of Female TV
Personality of The Year Sun
Award. Education: Ilford
Convent. Address: c/o
Michael Summerton, London
W1. Starsign: Capricorn.
Hobbies: gardening, theatre.
Person she would most like to
have met: 'Elizabeth I, as I've
always wanted to play her
role.'

GORING, Marius
Actor b 23.5.12 Newport,
Isle of Wight. Studied for the
stage under Harcourt
Williams before joining the
Old Vic School in 1921. Has
since become one of our
most outstanding character
actors. Speaks French and
German and has made
frequent visits to the
continent acting in French
and German. Recent theatre
incl: Woe To The Sparrows;
Lloyd George Knew My
Father; Zaide; Peer Gynt.
Entered films in 1936,
specialising in Grand
Guignol roles. Films incl: Spy
in Black; A Matter of Life and
Death; The Red Shoes;
Odette; Circle of Danger; The
Barefoot Contessa; Quentin
Durward; Ill Met by
Moonlight; The Moonraker
(1958); Charlie Boy. TV incl:
The Adventures of the Scarlet

Pimpernel; The Expert;
Edward and Mrs Simpson;
William and Mary; Girl In A
Yellow Dress; The Leukas
Man. Education: Perse
School, Cambridge;
Universities of Frankfurt,
Munich, Vienna and Paris.
m (1st) Mary Westward Steel
(dis), (2nd) actress Lucie
Mannheim (dec),
1 d Phyllida (by 1st m).
Address: c/o Film Rights Ltd,
London W1. Starsign:
Gemini.

GORMAN, John
Writer/performer/composer
b 4.1.36 Birkenhead,
Cheshire. Started as a
telecommunications
engineer. Also a member of
The Scaffold group, and as
such made numerous TV,
stage and cabaret
appearances and won
international record success.
Worked on Tiswas for three
and a half years, originally as
a performer and then on
production. Creative
consultant to OTT as well as
performing and writing for the
show. Education: grammar
school; first-class
intermediate City and Guilds
Certificate in
Telecommunications.
1 d Persephone,
2 s Andrew, Crispin.
Address: c/o Central TV,
Birmingham. Starsign:
Capricorn. Hobbies: writing,
walking, chess, travel.
Person he would most like to
meet: 'Frank Sinatra – I
admire his sheer
professionalism.'

GOWING, Nik
ITN reporter b 13.1.51
London. Started freelance for
Radio Bristol while studying
at Bristol University, then
worked in Newcastle under
the Thompson Journalist
Training Scheme 1973-74
when he joined Granada TV,
first as a researcher and for
three years as a reporter on
Granada Reports and
Reports Extra. He moved to
ITN in 1978 and the following
year was their correspondent
in Rome for six months. He
has also reported on events
in Cuba, Libya and Papal
visits incl America and
Britain. In 1980 he was
appointed ITN's Eastern
European correspondent,
which involved reporting the
Polish crisis, for which he and
the ITN production team
received the BAFTA Award
for Best Actuality Coverage
1981. Education: Latymer
Upper School; Simon
Langton Grammar,
Canterbury; Bristol University
(BSc Geography). Address:
c/o ITN, London W1.
Starsign: Capricorn. Hobby:
skiing.

GRAHAM, Denys
Actor b 29th June Newport,
Gwent. Has worked in every
show business medium
except on ice! Studied at
RADA and joined Sir John
Gielgud's company at
Phoenix Theatre for two years
and then spent a year at
Stratford-upon-Avon.
Appeared in numerous plays
in London's West End incl:
The Thurber Carnival; The

Keep; Next Time I'll Sing To
You; The Old Boys. Was also
in the original West End
production of Under Milk
Wood. His films incl: The Dam
Busters; Dunkirk; Modesty
Blaise; Zulu; the remake of All
Quiet on the Western Front in
which he plays the Kaiser.
Has appeared extensively on
TV in plays, comedy shows
with Frankie Howerd and
Spike Milligan and major
series incl: Dixon of Dock
Green; No Hiding Place;
Kate; Coronation Street;
Angels; On The Line.
Education: Newport High
School; New College, Oxford
(MA Chemistry and Higher
Mathematics). Address: c/o
Ellison Combe Assocs,
Richmond, Surrey. Starsign:
Cancer. Hobbies: playing the
piano, singing, going to
concerts with a special liking
for the music of Handel.
Person he would most like to
meet: 'Bette Davis, because
she started it all'.

GRAND, Elaine
Interviewer b 8.6.28 Canada
(of British parents). Worked
for BBC in Canada before
making her home in Britain in
1958. Joined Associated
Rediffusion and

subsequently worked for BBC, and Granada, TWW and Southern TV companies. Also produced programmes for Granada and ATV. Joined Thames TV 1973 and is now a regular interviewer on After Noon Plus. Education: Winnipeg, Canada; Richmond, Surrey. Widow, 3 step-d Rebecca, Trudi, Jessica, 1 s David. Address: c/o Thames TV, London NW1. Starsign: Gemini.

GRANT, Russell
TV astrologer b 5.2.52 Hillingdon, Middx. Had first psychic experience when he was 12 and still at school. Started studying astrology seriously while appearing in stage shows, and it has now taken over his life, with radio and TV shows and his Starcast column in TVTimes Magazine. Founder president of the British Astrological-Psychic Society. Radio incl: Late, Late Show. TV incl: Royal Wedding Day broadcast; Rippon Reports; Star Signs; Horizon; Pebble Mill At One; Nationwide; Friday Live; Thames News; Extraordinary; Calendar; Granada Reports Extra; Central Today; his own series, Believe It Or Not. He is also resident astrologer on Granada's Live From Two; LWT's 6 o'clock Show; BBC Radio's Woman's Hour; BBC Wales; Friday night shows from TVS and TSW. Also presenter All Kinds of Everything; The Russell Grant Show. Education:

Abbotsfield School, Hillingdon. Address: c/o MAM (Agency) Ltd, London W1. Starsign: Aquarius Sun and Moon, Libra rising. Hobbies: maps and gazetteers of the British Isles. Person he would most like to have met: 'Sir Henry Irving, as he's my great-grandfather and we were born on the same day.'

GRAY, Charles
Actor b 29.8.28 Bournemouth. First professional appearance was at Regent's Park Open Air Theatre. Subsequently joined the Royal Shakespeare Company at Stratford-upon-Avon Memorial Theatre and, later, The Old Vic Company. Stage also incl: Expresso Bongo; Everything in the Garden (London West End debut); Kean (New York); Poor Bitos (Clarence Derwent Award for Best Supporting Performance, 1964); The Right Honourable Gentleman (New York); Ardele; Cause Célèbre; The Philanthropist (also on TV); The Man Who Came To Dinner. Films incl: The Night of the Generals; You Only Live Twice; The Man Outside; The Secret War of Private Frigg; The Devil Rides Out; Mosquito Squadron; The File of the Golden Goose; The Lord High Executioner; Oliver Cromwell; The Rocky Horror Picture Show; The Mirror Crack'd; Shock Treatment; The Jigsaw Man. Wide TV experience dating back to

1966 when he appeared in an American colour production of Anastasia. Other TV incl: The Moon and Sixpence; Hay Fever; Ross; Menace; The Cherry Orchard; The Merchant of Venice; Lady Windermere's Fan; The Millionairess; Upstairs, Downstairs; Song of Songs; The Upper Crusts; Twelfth Night; Fall of Eagles; The Ventures; Churchill's People; London Assurance; Cheers; Richard II; Hazell; Julius Caesar; Heartland; We, The Accused; The Schoolmistress; Troilus and Cressida. Address: c/o London Management, London W1. Starsign: Virgo.

GRAY, Linda
Actress b 12.9.41 Santa Monica. Has played the part of Sue Ellen in Dallas since the series started in the late 70s. Born and brought up only a short distance from the studios where the series is made. Was a top fashion model but gave up modelling in 1970 to become an actress and appeared in such TV series as Marcus Welby, McCloud and All That Glitters. Since Dallas she has also appeared in the film The Wild and the Free. Education: Notre Dame, West Los Angeles. m art director Ed Thrasher, 1 d Kelly, 1 s Jeff. Starsign: Virgo. Hobbies: keep-fit, cooking.

GRAYSON, Larry
Comedian b 31.8.30 Banbury. Never anything else

Starsign: Sagittarius. Hobbies: films, football-writing, putting up bookshelves that don't fall down. Person he would most like to meet: 'Mike Scott, Granada Programmes' Controller, because he decides my salary.'

but an entertainer, he learned his trade in summer shows and touring revues. Unknown till a spot on Saturday Variety 1972. Shut That Door!! series followed and subsequently The Good Old Days; Celebrity Squares; his own shows; The Generation Game. Education: Nuneaton. Address: c/o PVA Management, London W1. Starsign: Virgo. Person he would most like to meet: 'God – one day.'

GREAVES, Bob
Presenter b 28.11.34 Sale, Cheshire. Journalist on Sale and Stretford Guardian, Nottingham Evening News and Daily Mail, Manchester, first as reporter, then assistant news editor and news editor 1963-71. TV: Granada TV presenter; Granada Reports (since 1968); Reports Action and miscellaneous regional programmes. Education: Sale Grammar School. m (1st) Maureen Ashbrooke (dis), (2nd) Susan Woodford (dis), (3rd) Eugenie Verney, 1 d Cathy, 2 s Mark, Chris (from 1st m). Address: c/o Granada TV, Manchester.

GREEN, Michael
Industrial journalist b 8.10.43 York. Newspaper training, beginning on Somerset County Gazette and taking in Bristol Evening Post, Daily Mail and Daily Telegraph before joining ITN August 1973. Fronted much of ITN coverage of the 1974 miners' strike, and the fall of the Heath government, the Court Line collapse; the state rescues of Chrysler and British Leyland; the Callaghan government's attempts to persuade trade unions to limit pay rises voluntarily. Education: Wellington School, Somerset. m Judy, 1 d Xanthe, 2 s Oliver, Freddie. Address: c/o ITN, London W1. Starsign: Libra. Hobbies: would-be guitarist and pianist, squash (occasional), cricket (rare), enjoyer of theatre and concerts, collector of books (of which too few are read), lover of countryside and outdoor pursuits. Person he would most like to meet: 'Richmal Crompton, as I spent so many hours of my misspent youth engrossed in her William books.'

GREENAWAY, Jeremy
Reporter b 14.9.42 London. Reporter on weekly papers in West and North of England. Daily Express 1964-70. The Sun 1970-73. Freelance radio broadcaster 1974-77 (BBC, LBC, IRN, ILR Plymouth Sound). Joined Westward/TSW 1977. Radio incl: reports on BBC on cod war from Iceland; investigative programme on Concorde; mackerel fishery boom. TV incl: reporter/ researcher/ scriptwriter Westward Report; networked fishing documentary The Last Hunters; researcher Mighty Hunter; writer/commentator documentary on RAF Nimrod Squadron. Also various regional and regional networked current affairs programmes. Education: Norfolk House prep school, North London; Ashburton College, Devon; Newton Abbot College of Art. m Margaret (dis), 2 d Louise, Isobel, 1 s James. Address: c/o TSW, Plymouth. Starsign: Virgo. Hobbies: sailing, (owns offshore cruiser/racer and skippers other boats), playing (bass guitar) and listening to jazz. Person he would most like to have met: 'Ernest Hemingway – an author/journalist type who seems to have put so much of his experience into his writing.'

GREENE, Sarah
Actress b 24th October London. Worked in the

theatre in Birmingham and Manchester. On TV she has been in Together and Swish of the Curtain, before joining Blue Peter in May 1980. Voted Top Lady on TV in Swop Shop Awards 1982. Education: Gospel Oak Primary School and Grey Coat School, London; Hull University. Address: c/o Michael Ladkin, London WC2. Starsign: Libra/Scorpio cusp. Hobbies: dancing, scuba diving, crosswords, Scrabble. Person she most likes to meet: 'Mike Smith, every day, because he's my best friend.'

GREENWOOD, Paul
Actor b 2.8.43
Stockton-on-Tees. Trained at Guildhall School of Music and Drama then rep at Chesterfield, Harrogate and Birmingham and TV parts in Coronation Street and Z Cars. Big TV break came when he played Lulu's boy-friend in It's Lulu. Other TV incl: musical version of No Trams to Lime Street; The Growing Pains of P C Penrose; Rosie; Heartland. Wrote and sang the Rosie signature tune.

Stage incl: Goose Pimples; Cinderella. Education: Stockton and in any part of the world where his father was serving in the RAF. Address: c/o Saraband Assocs, London N1. Starsign: Leo. Hobbies: rambling, reading, music from Mozart to Bowie.

GREENWOOD, Roger
Journalist b 29.5.48 Manchester. Journalistic training, Bolton Evening News. TV: Channel TV, Jersey; Yorkshire TV, presenter/reporter Calendar, Calendar Sport, producer/reporter sports features, documentaries. m Susan Linda, 2 s Andrew, Jonathan. Address: c/o Yorkshire TV, Leeds. Starsign: Gemini. Hobbies: playing most sports, the clarinet, wining and dining, travelling. Person he would most like to have met: 'William Shakespeare: they say a little bit of everybody you meet rubs off on you, and I could certainly do with a bit of the Bard!'

GRIFFITHS, Derek
Actor b 15.7.46 Woking.

Acting since he was 11. Once a teacher, but started in show business as a jazz musician. Has appeared with the Young Vic and theatre work incl: Sing a Rude Song; the musical version of Two Gentlemen of Verona; The Black Mikado; The Travelling Music Show. His first appearance on TV was in Mind Your Own Business and subsequent TV incl: Don't Drink the Water; Don't Ask Me; The Rather Reassuring Programme; Hi! Summer; The Marti Caine Show; Secombe With Music; Showtime; Heads and Tails; Cabbages and Kings; Film Fun. Has also presented Playschool (for a decade), Playaway and Insight. Education: comprehensive school. Address: c/o Aza Artistes, London NW11. Starsign: Cancer. Hobbies: photography, flying light aircraft, aerobatics.

GRIFFITHS, Terry
Professional snooker player b 16.10.47 Llanelli, Wales. Playing snooker since he was 14. Turned professional Sept 1978 and became World Professional Champion 1979. Welsh World Team 1979, 1980; Benson and Hedges Masters 1980; Benson and Hedges Irish Masters 1980, 1981; Lada Classic 1982. Education: Coleshill Secondary Modern. m Annette, 2 s Wayne, Darren. Address: c/o CSS Promotions Ltd, London WC2. Starsign: Libra. Hobbies: gardening, family.

Person he would most like to meet: Robert Redford.

GRIFFITHS, Tweli
Reporter b 18.2.54
Pencader, Carms. Joined
HTV Wales in May 1977
straight from university where
he studied politics.
Education: Llandysul
Grammar; University College
of Wales, Aberystwyth
(BSc Econ). m Mair.
Address: c/o HTV, Cardiff.
Starsign: Aquarius. Hobbies:
fishing, home brewing.
Person he would most like to
have met: 'Einstein – so he
could tell me what Carl Sagan
was on about.'

GROUT, James
Actor b 22.10.27 London.
Trained for the stage at RADA
and made his first
professional appearance at
the Old Vic 1950 in Twelfth
Night. Wide stage
experience since incl: three
seasons at Stratford
Memorial Theatre. Other
stage incl: The Mousetrap;
Ross; Half a Sixpence (and
on Broadway); Flint; Straight
Up; Lloyd George Knew My
Father; 13 Rue de l'Amour;

Make and Break;
Quartermaine's Terms. Has
also directed for reps incl:
Coventry, Hornchurch,
Leatherhead, Leeds and
Oxford. Many TV
appearances incl: The First
Lady; Turtle's Progress; Diary
of a Nobody; Born and Bred;
All Creatures Great and
Small; Z Cars; Sister Dora;
The Marriage Counsellor;
Hymn for Jim; Jenny Can't
Work Any Faster; Microbes
and Men; Juliet Bravo.
Education: Trinity Grammar
School. m Noreen. Address:
c/o Crouch Assocs, London
W1. Starsign: Libra. Hobbies:
music, friends, Wiltshire.
Person he would most like to
have met: 'Whoever built
Stonehenge, to find out why.'

GUILLAUME, Robert
Actor b 30.11.30 St Louis,
Missouri. Raised by his
grandparents. From choirboy
at his local church he went on
to study classical singing at
Washington University. Sang
in shows and festivals before
appearing in Porgy and Bess
and Guys and Dolls on
Broadway. On TV playing the
wise-cracking butler in Soap
led to his own spin-off series
Benson. m (dis), 3 children.
Starsign: Sagittarius.

**GUINNESS, Sir Alec CBE
D/Litt (Oxon)**
Actor b 2.4.14 London.
Formerly a copy-writer in an
advertising agency until
winning a scholarship to the
Fay Compton School of
Dramatic Art. First appeared

walking on in Libel in 1934.
Joined John Gielgud's
company the same year and
later the Old Vic where he
played Hamlet in modern
dress in its entirety. In 1941
joined the Royal Navy and
was commissioned a year
later. Returned to the stage in
1946 in his own adaptation of
The Brothers Karamazov.
Other stage incl: The
Prisoner; Hotel Paradiso;
Ross; Wise Child; Habeas
Corpus; A Voyage Round My
Father; A Family and a
Fortune; Yahoo; The Old
Country. Entered films in
1947 in Great Expectations.
Other films incl: Oliver Twist;
Kind Hearts and Coronets;
The Lavender Hill Mob
(Academy Award
nomination); The Man in the
White Suit; The Captain's
Paradise; The Lady Killers;
The Horse's Mouth (Venice
Award as actor and Academy
Oscar nomination for his
script); The Bridge on the
River Kwai (British Film
Academy and Academy
Oscar awards); Our Man in
Havana; Tunes of Glory; A
Majority of One; Lawrence of
Arabia; Doctor Zhivago; The
Quiller Memorandum; The
Comedians; Scrooge;
Brother Sun, Sister Moon;
Murder by Death; Star Wars
(Academy Oscar
nomination). Special
Academy Award for services
to cinema 1979. TV incl: The
Wicked Scheme of Jebel
Jacks (USA); Conversation at
Night; Caesar and Cleopatra;
Gift of Friendship; Tinker,
Tailor, Soldier, Spy; Smiley's

People. Education:
Pembroke Lodge,
Southbourne; Roborough,
Eastbourne. m Merula
Salaman, 1 s actor Matthew
Guinness. Address: c/o
London Management,
London W1. Starsign: Aries.
Person he would most like to
meet: 'The next person I
meet.'

GUTTERIDGE, Lucy
Actress b 28.11.56 London.
Trained at the Central School
of Speech and Drama.
Theatre incl: rep at Norwich
and the Royal Shakespeare
Company (Nicholas Nickleby
and in New York). Films incl:
The Greek Tycoon; Little
Gloria. TV incl: The Devil's
Crown; The Marrying Kind;
End of Season; Betzy; Renoir
My Father; Tales of the
Unexpected (Skin); Sweet
Wine of Youth; Love in a Cold
Climate; Seven Dials
Mystery; Nicholas Nickleby.
Education: Garden House
(private school); Holland Park
Comprehensive; The Marist
Convent; Walbrook College
for Further Education.
m actor Andrew Hawkins,
1 d Isabella. Address: c/o
Jeremy Conway, London W1.
Starsign: Sagittarius.
Hobbies: reading, physical
activity – dancing,
movement, interest in people,
drawing.

GUYLER, Deryck
Actor b 29.4.14 Wallasey,
Cheshire. Started acting with
Liverpool Rep Company, but
it was his creation of Frisby

Dyke (the first time an actor
had used the Liverpool
accent on the air) in Tommy
Handley's wartime show
ITMA, that brought him
recognition. Other radio incl:
Just Fancy; Men From the
Ministry. Has since appeared
in numerous productions in
all entertainment media,
notably on TV in Please Sir!
and the Eric Sykes shows.
Other TV incl: Three Live
Wires; That's My Boy!; Best of
Enemies. Has been a
fanatical devotee of
washboard playing since his
schooldays. Education:
Liverpool College. m former
singer Paddy Lennox,
2 s Peter, Christopher.
Address: c/o Felix de Wolfe,
London WC2. Starsign:
Taurus. Hobbies: toy soldiers
(he has a collection running
into thousands), traditional
jazz records, his washboard.
Person he would most like to
meet: Pope John Paul II.

GWILYM, Mike
Actor b 5.3.49 Neath, South
Wales. Widely experienced
stage actor equally at home
in Shakespeare or modern
drama. Has appeared at
Glasgow Citizens' Theatre;

Edinburgh Festival;
Hampstead Theatre; Royal
Exchange, Manchester; The
Roundhouse, London; The
Royal Shakespeare
Company. Films incl: The
Priest of Love; Venom. TV
incl: How Green Was My
Valley; The Racing Game; Ice
Age. Education: Wycliffe
College, Gloucester;
Davidson College, North
Carolina; Lincoln College,
Oxford. Address: c/o Ken
McReddie, London W1.
Starsign: Pisces.

H

HALL, Bob

Presenter/reporter b 29th
October Ilkley, Yorks. Local
and national newspaper and
radio experience before
joining BBC TV as
presenter/reporter. Also on
Pebble Mill At One. Border TV
chat show, current affairs,
parliamentary programme
chairman; World of Sport film
and match reporter.
Freelance for ATV, Yorkshire
TV and Granada. Has been
with ATV/Central TV since
1980. Education: Prince
Henry's Grammar School,
Otley, Yorks. m Janet (dis),
1 d Sara, 1 s Matthew.
Address: c/o PVA
Management Ltd, London
W1. Starsign: Scorpio.
Hobbies: relaxing, reading,
photography. Person he
would most like to meet:
Frank Sinatra.

HALL, Robert

Reporter/presenter
b 14.8.54 London. Went into
TV on leaving university,
joining Channel TV 1977 as a
reporter/presenter. Moved to
Yorkshire TV 1980.
Education: Radley College;
Leeds University (BA Eng).
Address: c/o Yorkshire TV,

HAGMAN, Larry

Actor b 21st September,
Texas, where he was also
brought up. No formal
training for the theatre but his
apprenticeship was served
under distinguished direction
of Margaret Webster at the
Woodstock Rep Theatre, the
Margo Jones Company in
Dallas and musical
productions of St John
Terrell. Came to London to
appear in South Pacific with
his mother, Mary Martin.
While there was called up
and met and married his wife,
Maj. By the time he was 20
had appeared in more than
50 plays and some 100 TV
shows. Best known on TV for
his part in I Dream of Jeannie
and more recently as JR in
Dallas. m Swedish designer
Maj, 1 d Heidi, 1 s Preston.
Starsign: Virgo.

Leeds. Starsign: Leo.
Hobbies: walking,
photography. Person he
would most like to have met:
'John Logie Baird, because
without him I might be out of a
job.'

HALL, Sam

TV reporter/announcer
b 5.9.36 Stockport,
Cheshire. Widely
experienced in news
gathering. Before joining ITN
as a scriptwriter in 1973 had
been Reuter correspondent
in Scandinavia, Miami, and
Lagos, Nigeria. He was also
an announcer on Radio
Sweden, news editor of
Europa Magazine and had
worked for Visnews.
Reporting for ITN since 1980.
Stories he has covered incl:
Nigerian-Biafran war; Turkish
invasion of Cyprus; the
Jeremy Thorpe trial; Northern
Ireland; American hostages
in Iran; Alexander Kjelland oil
rig disaster; Brixton riots.
Education: Westminster
Abbey Choir School;
Chorlton Grammar School,
Manchester. m Susanna,
1 d Helen, 2 s Jonas,
Benedict. Address: c/o ITN,
London W1. Starsign: Virgo.
Hobbies: photography,
gardening, travel, music,
antiques, bonsai trees.
Person he would most like to
meet: 'Walter Cronkite –
formerly the world's most
experienced (and genuine)
newscaster.'

HALL, Terry

Ventriloquist b 20.11.26
Oldham. Self-taught

ventriloquist and with Lenny the Lion has appeared in most major theatres, summer seasons, pantomimes, in his own shows and in many radio and TV series. Also devised and wrote educational books on reading and arithmetic and scripted and presented TV series based on his reading books, Reading With Lenny. Education: St Patrick's School, Oldham; De La Salle College, Salford. m (1st) Kathleen (dec), (2nd) Dee Francis, 2 d Beverley, Melanie (from 1st m). Address: c/o George Bartram Enterprises, Birmingham. Starsign: Scorpio. Hobbies: walking, table tennis, theatre shows (musicals). Person he would most like to meet: 'Malcolm Muggeridge – I find his views and theories fascinating.'

HAMILL, Desmond
TV reporter b .2.11.36 Dublin. After service in the army (the Devonshire Regiment) and the 5th Battn the King's African Rifles in Kenya 1955-59, joined the Kenya Broadcasting Service 1960-64 and Rhodesian TV 1964-66. Was with the BBC

1966-67 when he joined ITN. ITN political correspondent, European/Common Market correspondent, and crime correspondent. Education: English School, Heliolopolis, Egypt; Exeter School, Devon. m Brigid, 1 s Sean, 1 d Sara. Address: c/o ITN, London W1. Starsign: Scorpio.

HAMMOND-HILL, Juliet
Actress b 13.11.53 London. Trained at the Webber Douglas Academy of Dramatic Art. Played Olivia in Arts Council tour of Twelfth Night and was in Royal Shakespeare Company's original production of Nicholas Nickleby. On TV she was in all three series of Secret Army as well as the spin-off, Kessler. Other TV incl: Blake's Seven; House of Carradus; Blood Money; Baal. Education: Lycèe Français de Londres. 1 d Sophie. Address: c/o Marina Martin Management, London W1. Starsign: Scorpio. Person she would most like to meet: 'Yves Montand – because he epitomises class and great acting talent.'

HAMMOND-WILLIAMS, David
TV reporter b 2.8.49 Eastbourne, East Sussex. Journalistic experience with the Evening Advertiser, Swindon, and the Western Mail, Cardiff, before joining HTV in Nov 1976. Presenter/reporter/North Wales news editor of Report

Wales; presenter/reporter of Outlook; presenter/ editor/reporter of Jobline Wales. Education: Eastbourne College Preparatory School: Bembridge School, Isle of Wight; Brighton Technical College; University College of North Wales, Bangor. m Shirley, 1 d Caroline. Address: c/o HTV Wales, Mold. Starsign: Leo. Hobbies: work, philately, squash, golf, snooker. Person he would most like to meet: 'Lord Lucan – who wouldn't?'

HANBY, Roz
Presenter b 2.10.51 London. Former British Airways hostess and the airline's poster girl for seven years. First job was as a sales assistant in a cake shop in Switzerland, but on her return to England in 1970 worked as a model. Joined BOAC in 1972 and trained as a stewardess on DC10 jets. Chosen from hundreds of applicants as their poster girl. Presenter of TVS's Watch This Space . . . That Monday Evening Feeling since April 1982. Spends most of her

holidays in France – she speaks French fluently and has a good knowledge of Spanish. Education: Lycèe Français. Address: c/o TVS, Southampton. Starsign: Libra. Hobbies: conservation and the environment, ancient cultures of Mexico and Indonesia. Person she would most like to have met: Queen Victoria.

HANDL, Irene
Actress/author b 26.12.02 London. Trained at Embassy School of Acting and went straight into West End play, George and Margaret. Many other plays, incl: Goodnight Mrs Puffin; Freeway; The Importance of Being Earnest; Blithe Spirit. Radio incl: Hancock's Half-Hour; Educating Archie. Films incl: the Carry On films; I'm All Right Jack; Brief Encounter; The Rebel; The Italian Job; On a Clear Day; Last Remake of Beau Geste; Hound of the Baskervilles; Very Heavy Metal; Hedda Gabler. Most recent TV incl: For the Love of Ada; Maggie and Her; A Legacy; Come Spy With Me; The Light Princesses; Metal Mickey. Appears with Peter Sellers on two of his albums in numbers she wrote – Shadows on the Grass, on Songs For Swinging Sellers, and Whispering Giant, on Seller's Market. Books: The Sioux; The Gold Tip Pfitzer. Education: Maida Vale High School for Girls. Address: c/o London Management, London W1. Starsign: Capricorn. Hobbies:

cooking, gardening, going to films, art, dogs, having fun. Person she would most like to have met: 'Napoleon – private and public images interest me equally.'

HANDS, Jeremy
Reporter/presenter b 4.4.51 Torquay, Devon. Journalistic apprenticeship with Hendon and Finchley Times group, then reporter for Herald Express, Torquay. Researcher with Westward TV, reporter with Border TV and with ITN since Sept 1978. Education: St Marylebone Grammar, London. m Julia, 1 d Lucy, 1 s Thomas. Address: c/o ITN, London W1. Starsign: Aries. Hobbies: sailing, writing, football, cricket, maritime history. Person he would most like to have met: 'Lord Nelson, because of his positive way of dealing with the French.'

HANLEY, Jenny
Actress b 15.8.47 Gerrards Cross. Trained as a nanny and children's nurse, but became a model and had been in most branches of show business before becoming presenter of

Magpie in 1974. Stage incl: Sabrina Fair; How To Ruin Your Health; Not Now, Darling (on tour). Films incl: The Private Life of Sherlock Holmes; On Her Majesty's Secret Service; Tam-Lin; Joanna; Scars of Dracula; A Victory for Danny Jones. Radio: Capital Radio drama. TV incl: The Persuaders; Shirley's World; The Golden Shot; Softly, Softly; Task Force (for five years); And Mother Makes Five; Robert's Robots; Man About the House; Warship; Emmerdale Farm; And Maisy Too (which she also wrote); The Return of the Saint; co-presented one series of Saturday Night At the Mill. Education: all over the Southern Counties and in Switzerland. m licensee Herby Clark. Address: c/o John Mahoney Management, London NW1. Starsign: Leo. Hobbies: driving, cooking, fishing, tapestry. Person she would most like to meet: 'Mel Blanc – the man of a million voices.'

HANN, Judith
Reporter/presenter b 8.9.42 Littleover, Derby. Journalistic training with Westminster Press. Freelance for BBC TV incl: Tomorrow's World. Books: But What About the Children?; Family Scientist; The Perfect Baby?. Twice winner of the Glaxo Award for science writers. Education: Parkfield Cedars, Derby; Durham University (BSc in Zoology) where she edited the university paper. m TV news editor John Exelby. 2 s

Jake, Daniel. Address: c/o
BBC TV, London W12.
Starsign: Virgo. Hobby:
cooking. Person she would
most like to meet: Alan Price.

HANSON, Susan
Actress b 2.2.43 Preston,
Lancs. Worked as a
singer/dancer before going
into rep at Edinburgh, Bristol
Old Vic, The Mermaid in
London and Newcastle. Also
worked in films (incl Catch Us
If You Can) before joining
Crossroads in 1965. Other TV
incl: Nearest and Dearest;
Going For a Song. Stage:
Cinderella. m singer Carl
Wayne. Address: c/o Central
TV, Birmingham. Starsign:
Aquarius. Hobbies:
collecting Victorian dolls,
travel.

HARCOURT, Reg
Political editor b 6.3.33
London. Newspaper
experience in the provinces
and Fleet Street before
joining ATV 18 years ago as a
reporter. Editor of Left, Right
and Centre; presenter ATV
Today; Platform for Today;
Midland Member. Education:
grammar school.

m (2nd) Anne,
1 s Nicholas. Address: c/o
Central TV, Birmingham.
Starsign: Pisces. Hobby:
listening to all kinds of music.
Person he would most like to
meet: 'Walter Cronkite,
because he was the best TV
newscaster of them all – a
natural in an artificial world.'

HARDWICK, Alan
Reporter/presenter
b 20.8.49 Staveley,
Derbyshire. On leaving
school he trained in
journalism with local
newspapers. Gained wide
journalistic experience as
general reporter, sports
reporter, sub-editor, news
editor and editor, on daily and
weekly newspapers
throughout Britain. Joined the
Calendar team at Yorkshire
TV 1973. Education:
secondary school and since
then as a journalist. m Julie,
1 d Clare. Address: c/o
Yorkshire TV, Leeds.
Starsign: Leo. Hobbies:
reading, trying to renovate
old houses, cycling, driving
'hairy' cars, trying to get into
the national sunbathing team.
Person he would most like to
meet: 'The "average" viewer.
His/her comments on
television would be
invaluable. And it would be
comforting to know that we're
putting out the right kind of
programmes at the right
time.'

HARDY, Robert CBE
Actor b 29.10.25
Cheltenham. Began his

career with Royal
Shakespeare Company at
Stratford-upon-Avon. First
caught the viewer's eye as
David Copperfield, Prince
Hal and in The
Troubleshooters. Other TV
incl: Age of Kings; Henry V;
Coriolanus; Mogul; Manhunt;
Elizabeth R; Daniel Deronda;
Edward the Seventh;
Mussolini in Caesar and
Claretta; Upstairs,
Downstairs; Hannah; The
Duchess of Duke Street;
Picardy Affair; Chronicle–
History of the Longbow;
Horses In Our Blood; All
Creatures Great and Small;
Twelfth Night; Speed King;
Fothergill; Winston Churchill
The Wilderness Years
(nominated Best Actor on
Television 1981 by BAFTA for
the latter two roles). Stage
incl: Dear Liar. Films incl: The
Spy Who Came In From the
Cold; How I Won The War;
Ten Rillington Place; Young
Winston; Blood Will Have
Blood; Yellow Dog; Frog; Le
Silencieux; Le Gifle. A
Liveryman of the Worshipful
Company of Bowyers, he
claims to be the only one who
makes bows. Book:
Longbow: A Social and
Military History. Education:
Rugby; Oxford (degree in
English). m (1st) (dis),
(2nd) actress Sally Cooper,
2 d Emma, Justine,
1 s Paul. Address: c/o
Chatto and Linnit, London
W1. Starsign: Scorpio.
Hobbies: horses, archery.
Person he would most like to
have met: Sir Winston
Churchill.

HARE, Doris MBE
Actress b 1.3.05 Bargoed, South Wales. Claims to have been born in the theatre, made her first stage appearance when she was three and has virtually been appearing in all sorts of entertainment ever since – music hall, the chorus, fit-ups, revue, Principal Boy in pantomime, touring at home and abroad, Royal Shakespeare Company, Chichester Festival, National Theatre Company and was in No Sex Please, We're British for a year in 1974. During the Second World War she broadcast regularly as Commère of Shipmates Ashore and was awarded the MBE for services to the Merchant Navy. On TV she has been in On the Buses and more recently Diamonds. Received Variety Club Special Award for her contribution to British show business 1982. Education: none (she says). m Dr Fraser Roberts (dis), 2 d Susan, Catherine. Address: c/o Brunskill Management Ltd, London SW7. Starsign: Pisces. Hobbies: gardening, cooking. Person she would most like to meet: Gene Kelly.

HARGREAVES, Allan
Presenter/reporter/interviewer b 2.5.35 Hong Kong. Joined the army 1952 and was posted to Cyprus as 2nd Lieut in The Royal Berkshire Regiment. After leaving the army joined the Cyprus Mail and was a regular broadcaster on Cyprus Radio

1959-60. Until 1968, when he and his family returned to Britain, he was attached to the British Forces Broadcasting Service in Tripoli, Tobruk and Malta where he was Station Controller. From 1968-77 he was reporter/presenter on Thames TV's Today. Also presented many documentaries and outside broadcasts. When Capital Radio started in 1973 he presented their first 90-minute Open Line phone-in and for a year continued to do so five nights a week. Also devised and presented other programmes. Deputy Editor Thames At 6, 1978-79 when he joined the reporting team of Thames Report, then Reporting London. Education: King's School, Parramatta, Australia; Junior King's School, Canterbury, Kent; St Martin's School of Art (graphic design), London. m Rosemary, 2 d Philippa, Johanna. Address: c/o Isobel Davie Ltd, London W1. Starsign: Taurus. Hobbies: painting, reading, gardening.

HARRIS, Anita
Singer/actress b 3.6.42 Midsomer Norton, Somerset. Won talent contest when three years old at Chippenham. Moved with her family to Bournemouth when she was seven; then ice-skating, learning the piano and dancing lessons. Charley Ballet in Italy, sang in Las Vegas 1959 then joined the Granadiers and later the

Cliff Adams Singers. London shows incl: two seasons at the London Palladium (Way out in Piccadilly; Singular Sensation) and three smash award-winning seasons at the Talk of the Town, pantomime and Peter Pan. TV incl: series with Bernard Braden; Tommy Cooper; Morecambe and Wise, David Nixon; The Saturday Crowd; West Country Tales; her own Anita in Jumbleland, Jumbleland and Anita. She has also made many records. In 1978 she was made Britain's Ambassador of the Performing Arts. In 1982 Variety Club named her as Concert Cabaret Performer of the Year; also won the Performer of the Year Award in the Lanson Champagne Awards. Education: Convent of the Cross, Bournemouth; Hampshire School of Drama, Boscombe. m manager Mike Margolis. Address: c/o London Management, London W1. Starsign: Gemini. Hobbies: golf, fencing, yoga, skating, cooking, water-skiing. Person she would most like to have met: 'Vesta Tilley – to research her life and times.'

HARRIS, Keith
Ventriloquist b 21.9.47 Lyndhurst, Hants. Self-taught, he made his debut at 14 and began designing and making own 'characters'; now has a family of more than 100. TV debut in Let's Laugh. First appeared in summer season at Rhyl in 1964 and has since

appeared in numerous summer shows, pantomimes, as well as radio, cabaret and overseas tours. TV incl: Cuddles and Co, guest spots on major variety shows and host of Black and White Minstrel Show 1977 and 1978. Education: St John's Junior and Chester Secondary Modern. Address: c/o Billy Marsh, London. Starsign: Virgo. Hobbies: do-it-yourself, eating good food. Person he would most like to meet: 'Eammon Andrews – with a red book under his arm!'

HARRIS, Rolf OBE

Entertainer/singer/ songwriter/ musician/ artist/ cartoonist b 30.3.30 Perth, Western Australia. Parents Cardiff-born but emigrated to Australia. Expert swimmer at 10 and junior backstroke champion of Australia at 15. Started career by winning Australian radio talent contest 1949. Came to Britain as art student 1952. First break on stage was One Under the Eight, followed by TV programmes Showcase (with Benny Hill) and It's a Great Life. Exhibited at Royal

Academy 1954, 1955. Returned to Australia 1959 to produce and star in children's series and own show. Came back to Britain via Canada and US as a success. Talk of the Town; Royal Variety Performance. TV incl: own series; many programmes for children; Hey Presto; It's Rolf; The Rolf Harris Show; Rolf On Saturday, OK?. Records incl: Tie Me Kangaroo Down, Sport; Sun Arise; Two Little Boys; Jake the Peg. Education: Perth Modern; Perth University and Teachers' Training College. m sculptress Alwen Hughes, 1 d Bindi. Address: c/o International Artistes, London W1. Starsign: Aries. Hobbies: painting, making jewellery, collecting rocks, fixing old chairs, anything to do with working wood, photography. Person he would most like to have met: 'Claude Monet – I admire his approach to painting so much.'

HARRIS, Steve

Reporter/presenter b 24.4.48 Wanstead, London. Journalistic experience on Northern Echo, Telegraph, Argus and Pennine Radio before joining Southern TV/TVS to report for and present Day By Day and, since TVS opened, Coast To Coast. Education: Forest School, Walthamstow; Durham University. m Patricia Moynehan. Address: c/o TVS, Southampton. Starsign: Taurus. Hobbies: cooking,

music, astrology, gardening, watching soccer and cricket, films, theatre. Person he would most like to meet again: 'Jo Grimmond, my boyhood hero.'

HARROW, Lisa

Actress b 25.8.43 Auckland, New Zealand. Trained at RADA 1966-68 and then joined BBC Radio rep company. With the Royal Shakespeare Company at Stratford 1969-71 and in London the following year. Other stage work incl: Romeo and Juliet (as Juliet); Six Characters in Search of an Author; Pygmalion; Wild Oats; Merchant of Venice. In 1976 she went on a Californian teaching trip for the RSC, and in 1979 a Californian lecture tour, also for the RSC. Films incl: All Creatures Great and Small; Star Maidens; It Shouldn't Happen to a Vet; The Final Conflict; A Man from a Far Country. Latest TV in the title role in the Nancy Astor series. Other TV incl: Rivals of Sherlock Holmes; Owen MD; The Water Maiden; The Great Caper; Churchill's People; The Expert; Miss Julie; Space 1990; The Professionals; Marya; The Look; Dr Jekyll and Mr Hyde; The Waterfall. Education: Auckland University. Address: c/o MLR Ltd, London SW5. Starsign: Virgo. Hobbies: opera, theatre.

HART, Tony

Artist b 15.10.25 Maidstone, Kent. Joined the 1st Gurkha

Rifles in India 1945 and, discovering his talent for art, spent his off-duty time at Art School in Madras. Returning to England he took a job as a display designer in London. Has been doing freelance graphics for cinema, TV and the press since 1952. Resident artist on Vision On since 1955. Current series Take Hart is seen throughout the world. Education: All Saints Choir School, London; Clayesmore, Dorset; The Indian Military Academy, Dehra Dun. m Jean, 1 d Carolyn. Address: c/o BBC TV, London W12. Starsign: Libra. Hobbies: cooking, garden stonework. Person he would most like to have met: 'My late grandfather. I never knew the man whose lifestyle and interests seem to have been so like my own.'

HARTY, Russell
TV journalist b 5.9.34 Blackburn, Lancs. Came to TV through lecturing in America and Britain, being a housemaster at Giggleswick and answering an advertisement for an arts producer which led to his work on Aquarius and his own chat show Eleven Plus. Has been a talk show host since 1971, incl: Russell Harty Plus; Saturday Night People; Russell Harty. Winner of International Emmy for his Dali programme, Hello Dali, and a Golden Harp award for another documentary, Finnian Games. Education: Queen Elizabeth School, Blackburn; Exeter College, Oxford. Address: c/o BBC TV, London W14. Starsign: Virgo. Hobby: sitting down and looking at the wall. Person he would most like to meet: 'Eileen Baverstock – she is very elusive and I have met everyone else.'

HATFIELD, Keith
Reporter b 18.1.43 Sutton Coldfield. Joined Birmingham Post 1963, Anglia TV 1964 and ITN 1967 Travelled widely on various assignments. Education: Bishop Veseys Grammar School. m (1st) Jane (dis), (2nd) Linette, 1 s Alexander, 1 step-s Michael. Address: c/o ITN, London W1. Starsign: Capricorn. Hobbies: antiques, clocks, glassware, furniture.

HAVERS, Nigel
Actor b 6.11.49 London. Broke the family tradition of going into Law (his father is Attorney General) by becoming an actor. Trained at the Arts Educational Trust. Spent a couple of years as Billy Owen in the radio serial, The Dales, and chief researcher for the Jimmy

Young Show before his first TV part in Comet Among The Stars. His acting career really took off when he played the title role in Nicholas Nickleby. Other TV incl: A Raging Calm; Upstairs, Downstairs; The Glittering Prizes; Pennies From Heaven; A Horseman Riding By; An Englishman's Castle; Coming Out; Goodbye Darling; Unity; Winston Churchill The Wilderness Years; Nancy Astor; After the Party. Theatre incl: Richard II; Edward II; Conduct Unbecoming; George and Margaret; Man and Superman; Season's Greetings. Films incl: Chariots of Fire (for which he was nominated Best Supporting Artist by BAFTA 1981). Education: Newton Court; Leicester University. m Carolyn, 1 d Katharine. Address: c/o Leading Artists, London SW1. Starsign: Scorpio. Hobbies: golf, sport in general, reading, acting. Person he would most like to have met: 'Sir Winston Churchill – the greatest man of the 20th century.'

HAWKINS, Carol
Actress b 31.1.49 Barnet, Herts. Trained as shorthand typist at a secretarial college but first came to the fore as an actress in the TV series, Please Sir!, The Fenn Street Gang and Mr Big. Other TV incl: The Two Ronnies; Whodunnit?; Blake's Seven; Porridge; Les Dawson Show; Together; Leap in the Dark; Robin's Nest; Time of My Life; Rings on their Fingers;

Bloomfield. In the theatre she has appeared in Bedroom Farce; The Undertaking; Sextet; Time and Time Again; and in pantomime. Films incl: Please Sir!; Bless This House; Not Now Conrad and a number of the Carry On films. Education: Whitings Hill Jnr School, Barnet; Southaw Girls' School, Whetstone. Address: c/o Barry Burnett, London W1. Starsign: Aquarius. Hobby: searching various beliefs for the truth. Person she would most like to meet: 'Satya Sai Baba, for his teachings about life which incorporates all religions.'

HAWTHORNE, Nigel
Actor b 5.4.29 Coventry. First professional appearance was in Cape Town in 1950 and in London the following year. Has since had wide stage experience ranging from revue (Nymphs and Satires), rep (Sheffield 1970), Young Vic (1972), toured North America with National Theatre (1974). Films incl: The Sailor's Return; Gandhi; Tale of Two Cities; History of the World Part One; Memoirs of a Survivor; Operation

Shakespeare. TV incl: Edward and Mrs Simpson (as Walter Monkton); Destiny; The Knowledge; Jessie; The Schoolmistress: Rod of Iron; Marie Curie (as Pierre Curie); Yes, Minister (as Sir Humphrey); The World Cup – A Captain's Tale. Education: Christian Brothers' College; University of Cape Town. BAFTA Award for Best Light Entertainment Performance 1981 for Yes, Minister. Address: c/o Ken McReddie, London W1. Starsign: Aries. Hobbies: writing, painting, gardening, photography, sport, swimming. People he would most like to meet: Doris (Annie Walker) Speed and Sir John Betjeman.

HAYCOCK, Gerald
TV reporter b 13.1.51 London. Started in radio as BBC graduate news trainee. Experience with Radio Solent, BBC national news, Westward TV, and ITN before joining HTV West in 1981. Education: Wellington College, Berks; Stirling University, Scotland (BA Hons); Macalester College, Minnesota. m Judy. Address: c/o HTV West, Bristol. Starsign: Capricorn. Hobby: politics – especially other people's. Person he would most like to meet: Mother Teresa.

HAYES, Geoffrey
Actor/presenter b 13.3.42 Stockport, Cheshire. Left school at 15 and tried a variety of jobs (testing dyes in

a cotton mill, British Rail booking clerk, etc) before joining Oldham Rep, first as a scene shifter, then as an actor. Student at Royal Northern School of Music and Drama, Manchester. Rep incl: Liverpool, Dundee and Manchester. Became presenter of Rainbow in 1973. Other TV incl: Z Cars; Softly, Softly; Dixon of Dock Green. Education: Cheadle, Cheshire. Address: c/o Felix de Wolfe, London WC2. Starsign: Pisces. Hobby: listening to all kinds of music. People he would most like to meet: 'Goldie Hawn – she's so beautiful, and Mozart, whose music I could listen to forever. Hope they play it in the afterlife!'

HAYES, Melvyn
Actor b 11.1.35 London. Learned the business with the famous juvenile troupe, Terry's Juveniles. Rep at Chesterfield, Guildford, Leatherhead, Midland Theatre, a number of tours in such plays as Play It Again Sam, Absurd Person Singular and One for the Pot. London stage appearances incl: Maskelyne's Mysteries;

Apples of Eve; South; Change for the Angel; The Fantastics; The Witch of Edmonton; Spring and Port Wine; Toad of Toad Hall; Dick Whittington pantomime at London Palladium. Films incl: The Curse of Frankenstein; Violent Playground; No Trees in the Street; The Young Ones; Summer Holiday; Wonderful Life. TV incl: Oliver Twist; Billy Bunter; The Unloved; The Silver Sword; Jo's Boys; Sir Yellow; Potter's Picture Palace; It Ain't Half Hot Mum. Education: Sir Walter St John's, Battersea. m actress Wendy Padbury, 3 d Talla, Joanna, Charlotte, 2 s Sacha, Damian. Address: c/o Richard Stone, London WC2. Starsign: Capricorn. Hobbies: breathing, meeting people in the street who ask questions like 'Didn't you used to be Melvyn Hayes?' Person he would most like to meet: 'The producer who says "We've only got a large budget".'

HAYES, Patricia
Actress b 22nd December London. Stage training at RADA (where she won the Gold Medal). Went to Stratford to appear in Shakespeare and returned there in 1974 to play Maria in Twelfth Night. In between she has done a great deal of rep and other stage work, radio and TV. Made her name as the maid in Priestley's When We Are Married and first became known on radio in Ted Ray's Ray's a Laugh. Probably has since worked

with more comics than any other actress, incl: Benny Hill; Ken Dodd; Arthur Askey; Spike Milligan; Terry Scott; Bruce Forsyth; Frankie Howerd; Norman Vaughan; Arthur Haynes; Tony Hancock. Recent stage incl: Habeas Corpus; Liza of Lambeth; Filumena; True West, at the National Theatre. TV gave her her first tragic role in Edna, The Inebriate Woman, for which she won BAFTA's and the Sun's Best TV Actress Awards in 1971. Other TV incl: Last of the Baskets; The Trouble With You, Lilian; On the Move; The Portland Millions; London Belongs to Me; Tea Ladies; Till Death Us Do Part; Spooner's Patch. Films incl: Goodbye Mr Chips; Carry On Again Doctor; Fragment of Fear; Love Thy Neighbour. Education: Sacred Heart Convent, London SW18. m actor Valentine Brooke (dis), 2 d Teresa, Gemma, 1 s actor Richard O'Callaghan. Address: c/o Herbert de Leon, London W1. Starsign: Sagittarius. Hobbies: housework, gardening, any sort of work. Person she would most like to have met: 'William Shakespeare (or whoever wrote the plays) – I'd ask him to write a good part for me.'

HAYGARTH, Tony
Actor b 4.2.45 Liverpool. Many jobs before he took up amateur drama while psychiatric nursing and liked it so much he decided to become an actor. This led to

rep, London's West End stage (Royal Shakespeare Company and National Theatre), films and TV. Stage incl: Don Quixote (National Theatre). Films incl: Percy; Let's Get Laid; Dracula; Dick Turpin; SOS Titanic; The Human Factor; Caleb Williams; Britt; Ivanhoe. TV incl: Last of the Summer Wine; Warrior Queen; Holocaust; The Beau Stratagem; I Claudius; Rosie; Z Cars; Shoestring; Kinvig; The Borgias; Dead Ernest; Lucky Jim; The Black Stuff. Education: Liverpool College. Address: c/o Richard Jackson, London W1. Starsign: Aquarius. Hobbies: photography, astronomy, collecting Edgar Allan Poe. Person he would most like to meet: 'Nobody – meetings often result in disappointment.'

HEINEY, Paul
Presenter b 20.4.49 Sheffield. Training at Birmingham Rep and the Mermaid Theatre, London, before becoming an assistant film recordist with BBC TV. Also worked for BBC Radio Humberside, Radio 1 and Radio 4. Latest TV: That's Life. Education: High Storrs Grammar, Sheffield. m TV presenter Libby Purves. Address: c/o BBC TV, London W1. Starsign: Aries. Hobby: yachting. Person he would most like to have met: Admiral Lord Nelson.

HELM, John
Sports presenter/
commentator b 8.7.42
Baildon, West Yorks. Entered
journalism on leaving school.
Sports Editor, Shipley Times
and Express, Air
Correspondent, Yorkshire
Evening Post before moving
into radio as Sports Editor,
BBC Radio Leeds and
network football producer for
BBC Radio. Presenter Sport
On 2 and golf commentator.
Education: Salt Grammar
School, Shipley; Bradford
Technical College.
m Hildred, 2 s Stephen,
Nicholas. Address: c/o BBC
TV, London W12. Starsign:
Cancer. Hobbies: playing
golf, having a good pint of
Northern beer. Person he
would most like to meet: 'My
wife – she says I'm never at
home and the children think
I'm dead!'

HELMOND, Katherine
Actress b 5.7.33 Galveston,
Texas. No formal acting
training but once ran her own
rep theatre in the Catskill
Mountains. More than 20
years in the theatre before
going to Hollywood and
appearing in such series as
The Six Million Dollar Man,
Bionic Woman and
best-seller Pearl. Best known
in Britain as the dizzy Jessica
Tate in Soap. m sculptor
David Christian. Starsign:
Cancer.

HENDERSON, Dickie OBE
Comedian/actor b 30.10.22
London. Played in Hollywood
version of Cavalcade when
10. Toured music-halls with
famous father, Dick
Henderson. Served in the
army during the war. London
revues and pantomimes after
demob; first TV 1953, Face
the Music followed by Arthur
Askey series, Before Your
Very Eyes; compèred
Sunday Night at the London
Palladium. Then 120 Dickie
Henderson Shows; a series,
A Present for Dickie; BBC
spectaculars; I'm Bob, He's
Dickie and I'm Dickie – That's
Show Business. Also many
stage appearances: a year in
Wish You Were Here; 20
months in Teahouse of the
August Moon; also When in
Rome; Stand by Your
Bedouin; Come Live With Me;
And the Bridge Makes Three.
Now makes many working
trips abroad, incl: USA,
Australia, Canada, South
Africa, Hong Kong, Holland.
Eight Royal Command
Performances. Education:
privately in Hollywood; St
Joseph's College, Beulah
Hill, London. m (1st) Dixie
Ross (dec), (2nd) Gwynneth,
1 d Linda, 1 s Matthew
(both from 1st m). Address:
c/o London Management,
London W1. Starsign:
Scorpio. Hobbies: golf, most
sports. Person he would most
like to meet: 'Woody Allen,
because he has the most
inventive comedy mind of
today.'

HENDERSON, Don
Actor/author b 10.11.32
London. As an untrained
actor auditioned for Royal
Shakespeare Company for a
'dare', was accepted and
remained with them for six
years. He has since had wide
experience in the theatre,
films and TV. Films incl: A
Midsummer Night's Dream;
Callan; The Ghoul;
Brannigan; Escape from the
Dark; The Voyage; The Prince
and the Pauper; Star Wars;
The Big Sleep; The Island. TV
incl: The Sweeney; The
Protectors; Frost Over
England; Crown Court;
Warship; Poldark; New
Scotland Yard; Softly, Softly;
Task Force; Dixon of Dock
Green; The XYY Man; Van
Der Valk; Crossroads; Get
Some In; Angels; Strangers;
The Saturday Party; Play for
Today; Dick Turpin; Parole;
Easterman; Scorpio Tales;
Thriller; Across the Andes by
Frog; Ripping Yarns; Bull
Week; Enigma Files; The
Kamikaze Pilots' Renunion
Dinner; The Onedin Line.
Education: several schools
during the war. m (1st) Hilary
(dec), (2nd) actress Shirley
Stelfox, 1 d Louise, 1 s Ian
(from 1st m), 1 step-d
Helena. Address: c/o
Essanay Ltd, London W14.
Starsign: Scorpio. Hobbies:
writing, painting, lazing,

sleeping late, thinking hard. Person he would most like to meet: 'Jesus Christ – He would be able to tell me if He was a space traveller, the Son of God, or both, and in any event, would be able to unravel so many mysteries about life, this world and what we are doing here.'

HENRY, Lenny
Comedy impressionist b 29.8.58 Dudley, Worcs. Schoolboy winner of talent contests. TV debut in New Faces 1975 when he was 16. Has since appeared in cabaret, theatre seasons, pantomimes and summer seasons. Also made several records. TV incl: The Fosters; Celebrity Squares; Blankety Blank; several series of Tiswas; Three of a Kind; OTT; many TV commercials. First coloured entertainer to appear on Black and White Minstrel Show (stage and TV). Was in 1980 Royal Variety Show with Tiswas team and guest star in Royal Variety Show 1981. Education: Blue Coat Secondary Modern, Dudley. Address: c/o Mike Hollis, Bridgnorth, Salop. Starsign: Virgo. Hobbies: football, music (particularly soul), reading, dancing. People he would most like to meet: 'Bill Cosby, Richard Pryor and Steve Martin, and to spend an entire afternoon in their company.'

HENRY, Paul
Actor b 1947 Birmingham. Trained at the Birmingham

School of Speech and Drama and took the part of Benny in Crossroads in 1975 after eight years at Birmingham Rep. For a time he was also Peter Stevens in The Archers. Stage work incl: Funny Peculiar (Westcliff-on-Sea); 1979 pantomime at Norwich. Record: Benny's Theme. TV also incl: Roads to Freedom; A Midsummer Night's Dream; The Recruiting Officer; Ten Torry Canyons; Romeo and Juliet; The Sweeney; OTT. m Sheila, 1 d Justine, 1 s Anthony. Address: c/o Richard Stone, London WC2.

HENSON, Nicky
Actor b 12.5.45 London. Trained at RADA as a stage manager, but made his stage debut as a guitarist. First London appearance was in a revue, All Square, followed by Camelot at Drury Lane in which he played Mordred. Since played a variety of parts in revue, musicals, as a member of the Young Vic company (where he played Pozzo, his favourite part, in Waiting for Godot), Toad in Toad of Toad Hall 1969, and Buttons in Cinderella

pantomime in London 1974. Other theatre incl: She Stoops To Conquer; Measure For Measure; Romeo and Juliet; Look Back In Anger; Rosencrantz and Guildernstern Are Dead; Hamlet; A Midsummer Night's Dream; The Taming of the Shrew; Man and Superman; Noises Off. Films incl: Witchfinder General; There's a Girl in My Soup; The Bawdy Adventures of Tom Jones. TV incl: Prometheus series; Seagull Island; A Midsummer Night's Dream; Chains. Education: St Bede's, Eastbourne; Charterhouse. m actress Una Stubbs (dis), 2 s Christian, Joe. Address: c/o Richard Stone, London WC2. Starsign: Taurus. Hobby: motorcycling. Person he would most like to meet: Samuel Beckett.

HEPWORTH, David
TV presenter and music journalist b 27.7.50 Dewsbury, Yorks. Worked in record shops and for an American record company before becoming a freelance journalist in 1978. He joined pop music magazine Smash Hits in 1979 and has been co-presenter of Old Grey Whistle Test since 1980. Education: Queen Elizabeth School, Wakefield; Trent Park College of Education, Barnet, Herts. m Alyson. Address: c/o Smash Hits, London W1. Starsign: Leo. Hobbies: reading magazines, buying leather jackets, worrying. Person he would most like to

meet: 'John Arlott, in order to steal a few anecdotes.'

HILL, Benny
Comedian b 21.1.25 Southampton. Various jobs – weighbridge operator, milkman, army driver, drummer – before stage debut in Stars in Battledress 1941. Stage shows: Paris By Night; Fine Fettle. Films: The Italian Job; Chitty Chitty Bang Bang; Those Magnificent Men in Their Flying Machines. TV: own shows for which he writes all his own scripts and music. Elected to TV Hall of Fame, TVTimes 1978-79. Voted Funniest Man On TV 1981-82 by TVTimes readers. Education: Shirley School; Western School; Taunton Secondary, Southampton. Address: c/o Richard Stone, London WC2. Starsign: Aquarius. Hobbies: work, travel. Person he would most like to have met: 'Charlie Chaplin – he brought so much joy to so many.'

HILL, Jimmy
Presenter b 22.7.28 Balham, London. Began career in football, first as an amateur for Reading 1949. Turned professional and joined Brentford the same year. Went to Fulham 1952; chairman of the Professional Footballers' Assn 1957; worked as TV commentator and interviewer; manager of Coventry City 1961; became head of London Weekend's sports unit 1967; Deputy Controller of Programmes 1971; joined BBC 1973. Wide business interests. TV: World of Sport; The Big Match; Grandstand; Match of the Day. Education: grammar school. m (1st) Gloria (dis), (2nd) Heather, 2 d (one from each m), 3 s (2 from 1st m, 1 from 2nd m). Address: c/o Jimmy Hill Ltd, London W2. Starsign: Leo/Cancer. Hobbies: golf, riding, tennis, bridge. Person he would most like to meet: Barbra Streisand.

HILL, Peter
Actor b 9.3.32 London. Trained at RADA 1952-54 followed by provincial rep (Library Theatre, Manchester, Oldham, Colchester) until 1972 when he went into TV with brief appearances in many BBC and ITV programmes. Break came in 1975 with his part in General Hospital. Other big parts in The Cedar Tree and Crossroads. Education: Whitgift Middle School, Croydon. m (dis), 1 d Joanna, 1 s Christopher. Address: c/o Jim Thompson, London SE1. Starsign: Pisces. Hobbies: walking, reading, watching cricket. Person he would most like to meet: 'Phil Drabble, because of his concern for nature and the countryside.'

HILL, Vince
Singer b 16.4.37 Coventry. Started entertaining in local pubs and clubs. Became vocalist for Band of the Royal Signals, then Teddy Foster Band. Helped form vocal groups Four Others and The Raindrops before going solo with recording The River's Run Dry. First big record hit Eidelweiss; others incl: Roses of Picardy; Look Around. Many singles and albums. Long association with Parade of the Pops (radio) and Stars and Garters (ITV). Appeared in almost every top TV variety show; starred in Roy Castle TV series and They Sold a Million; The Musical Time Machine. Hosted 26-week TV series in Canada. Also international tours; Talk of the Town and wrote score for TV musical Tolpuddle. Education: Whitemoor School, Coventry. m Anne, 1 s Athol. Address: c/o London Management, London W1. Starsign: Aries. Hobbies: photography, gardening, travelling, cooking, painting. People he would most like to have met: 'Either Hitler or Charlie Chaplin as we all share the same birthdate and I would like to see if there were any similarities!'

HINES, Frazer
Actor b 22.9.44 Horsforth, Yorks. Been in the 'business' since he was eight. By the time he was 15 he had appeared in half-a-dozen films and served apprenticeship in the theatre. Stage incl: Norman; Good Woman of Setzuan; Heirs and Graces; No Trams; Happy Birthday. Films incl: Zeppelin; Last Valley; The Weapon. Has played Joe Sugden in Emmerdale Farm since its start 1972. Other TV incl: Doctor Who. Also had a request programme on Pennine Radio. Education: Norwood College, Harrogate; Corona Stage School. m actress Gemma Craven. Address: c/o Al Mitchell Assocs, London WC2. Starsign: Virgo/Libra cusp. Hobbies: all sport, amateur jockey. Person he would most like to have met: 'John Wayne – I would just love to have been with him in She Wore A Yellow Ribbon, in the Ben Johnson part.'

HINES, Ronald
Actor b 20.6.29 London. Trained at RADA followed by rep, then signed up for films

incl: Robin Hood; The Buccaneers; Tell It to the Marines. Other films incl: Whistle Down the Wind; The Angry Silence; Two-headed Spy; Sink the Bismarck; Rough Cut. TV incl: The Long Wait; Strictly for the Sparrows; The Boy Next Door; Parole; Elizabeth R; Not in Front of the Children; The Square on the Hypotenuse; The Dreaming Bandsman; The Rivals of Sherlock Holmes; Jackanory; Sutherland's Law; This Year, Next Year; Gossip from the Forest; Deep Concern; Shadows; The Professionals; Shoestring; We'll Meet Again. Education: London Technical College. m Sheila, 2 d Deborah, Stephanie, 1 s Rupert. Address: c/o Leading Artists, London W1. Starsign: Gemini. Hobbies: oil and watercolour painting, antiques. Person he would most like to have met: 'Spencer Tracy – my boyhood and adulthood favourite performer.'

HINGE (Dr Evadne) and BRACKET (Dame Hilda)
A partnership of two female impersonators which came about by accident in 1972 when Dr Evadne was engaged as Dame Hilda's accompanist at a concert. The partnership has developed since that meeting and first came to prominence when their 'fringe' show, An Evening With Hinge and Bracket, took the Edinburgh Festival by storm in 1974. Within hours of their Edinburgh season

ending they opened at London's Royal Court Theatre Upstairs and after a two-week sell-out run, moved to the Mayfair Theatre in London's West End for a 17-week run. This was followed by a further 17 weeks in Sixty Glorious Minutes, at the Ambassadors Theatre. Since then their unique humour in stage performances of two middle-aged spinsters indulging in an anthology of songs and reminiscences has taken them throughout Britain, Australia and the Far East. They have also appeared in concert with the Grenadier Guards and have appeared before many members of the Royal Family, incl the Royal Command Performance in 1979. On radio their weekly show, The Enchanting World of Hinge and Bracket, started its fifth season in April 1982, while on TV, guest appearances on many top shows have led to an annual 'special' for the BBC and, also in 1982, their new series, Dear Ladies. Other TV incl: The Good Old Days; What's On Next?; At Home with Dr Evadne Hinge and Dame Hilda Bracket; Celebrity Squares; Hinge and Bracket. Their records incl: Hinge and Bracket Vol 1; Hinge and Bracket Vol 2; Hinge and Bracket in Concert; Hinge and Bracket at Abbey Road. Book: Dame Hilda's memoirs, One Little Maid.

Patrick Fyffe (Dame Hilda)
b 23rd January Stafford.

Hairdresser before trying his luck in show business. At one time as an amateur he was working or rehearsing day and night seven days a week with various companies. Has always been a fan of Gilbert and Sullivan, whose songs at one time figured largely in the Hinge and Bracket act. Education: secondary school. Starsign: Aquarius. Hobbies: gardening, cooking, antiques, music, old houses. Person he would most like to have met: 'Queen Elizabeth I – far more of a character than we have been led to believe.'

George Logan (Dr Evadne)
b 7th July Glasgow. Formerly a computer programmer. After grammar school and Glasgow University, studied at the Royal Academy of Music, Glasgow. Address: c/o Noel Gay Organisation, London WC2. Starsign: Cancer. Hobbies: electronic music, computers, reading. Person he would most like to have met: 'Maria Callas – I admire her enormously as a performer.'

1944. Has since appeared in hundreds of plays, films and radio and TV programmes. Stage roles range from the Nurse in Romeo and Juliet to the comedy maid in No, No, Nanette. Films incl: The Entertainer; Over the Odds; A Kind of Loving; Term of Trial; Rattle of a Simple Man; Some Will, Some Won't; The Nightcomers. Perhaps best known on TV for her series Meet the Wife; The First Lady; Ours is a Nice House and more recently, In Loving Memory (four series) and Flesh and Blood. Other TV incl: The Hard Case; Albert Hope; The Bed; She Stoops to Conquer; Your Songs of Praise Choice; Thomas and Sarah and four Alan Bennett plays, incl Me, I'm Afraid of Virginia Woolf, Afternoon Off and Intensive Care. Education: private school. m James Scott, 1 d actress Janette Scott. Address: c/o Felix de Wolfe, London WC2. Starsign: Gemini. Hobbies: travel, reading. Person she would most like to have met: 'Zero Mostel – I thought his comedy timing was perfect.'

Unsolved. Film documentaries: Longest River; Sweetest Salmon; Serenade in the City; Next Patient, Please; Yes, More About the Disabled. Education: Bideford Grammar. m Caroline, 1 d Georgiana, 1 s Giles. Address: c/o HTV, Bristol. Starsign: Gemini. Hobbies: walking, golf. Person he would most like to meet: 'Nana Mouskouri – she has been in the business as long as I have.'.

HODGE, Patricia
Actress b 29.9.46 Cleethorpes, Lincs. Brought up in Grimsby where her parents ran a hotel. Trained as a teacher and taught for a year before going to LAMDA (where she won the major award, the Eveline Evans Award as best actress). First appearance on London's West End stage was in a musical version of Rookery Nook. On TV has played a wide variety of roles in such programmes as The Naked Civil Servant; Quiller; The Girls of Slender Means; Target; Rumpole of the Bailey; Edward and Mrs Simpson; Nanny; Winston Churchill The Wilderness Years; Holding the Fort. Education: Wintringham Grammar School, Grimsby; St Helen's School, Northwood, Middx. m musician Peter Owen. Address: c/o ICM, London W1. Starsign: Libra. Hobbies: decorating, sewing, painting, music. Person she would

HIRD, Thora
Actress b 28.5.13 Morecambe, Lancs. Classic start to show business: born of theatrical parents and carried on stage when a few weeks old. At 16 she was making her mark in rep and was 'discovered' and given a film contract. She was an overnight success with her first London appearance in Flowers For the Living in

HOCKIN, Bruce
Reporter/interviewer/ current affairs editor b 23.5.36 Exmouth, Devon. Trainee journalist on Bideford and North Devon Gazette; reporter, feature writer, assistant news editor on Western Mail. Since 1968 regular presenter of HTV's Report West; Now It's Your Say; Press Call; Focus; Report Extra; Murder

most like to meet: 'Paul
Newman – he brings great
humour to his performances.'

HOGG, Sarah
Journalist b 14.5.46 London.
After studying politics,
philosophy and economics at
Oxford, joined the Economist
in 1967, was appointed
Literary Editor 1970,
Assistant Editor 1973 and
Economics Editor 1977. In
1981 she took a similar
position with the Sunday
Times and late 1982 became
co-presenter, with Peter
Sissons, of Channel Four's
news and analysis
programme. She is also the
station's Economics Editor.
Has played the Prime
Minister in reconstructions of
Cabinet and EEC debates
staged by Granada TV.
Education: Oxford University
(First Class Hons degree).
m Douglas Hogg (Tory MP
for Grantham), 1 d Charlotte,
1 s Quintin. Address: c/o
ITN, London W1. Starsign:
Taurus. Hobbies: skiing, her
children.

HOLDEN, Jan
Actress b 9.5.31 Southport.
Trained at the Old Vic Theatre
School and later joined the
company. Toured in rep for
two years. London stage incl:
Speaking of Murder; Tunnel
of Love and, more recently,
Banana Ridge; Shut Your
Eyes and Think of England.
Her many TV appearances
incl: The Odd Man;
Emergency – Ward 10;
Knight Errant; Harper's West
One; Agony; The Saint;

Casanova 73; Are You Being
Served?; Rt Hon Mrs;
Goodbye, Mr Kent.
Education: Lowther College,
North Wales. Twin d Belinda
and Arabella, 1 s Simon.
Address: c/o David White
Assocs, London W1.
Starsign: Taurus. Hobbies:
gardening, interior
decoration.

HOLLOWAY, Alison
Reporter/interviewer/actress
b 2.2.61 London. Drama
trained at Italia Conti Stage
School and took teacher's
diploma. But chose TV as her
career, joining Westward TV
when she was 14 to introduce
a children's programme.
Joined HTV West in 1981.
Education: Italia Conti Stage
School. Address: c/o HTV
West, Bristol. Starsign:
Aquarius. Hobbies: cooking,
piano, interior decoration.
Person she would most like to
meet: Prince Andrew.

HOLLOWAY, Julian
Actor b 24.6.44 Watlington,
Oxford. Trained at RADA and
made his London West End
debut in 1963 in a revue, All
Square. For the next six years
he appeared regularly in the

West End and then
concentrated almost
exclusively on TV, his many
appearances incl leading
roles in Helen – A Woman of
Today; The Importance of
Being Earnest; Snooker; An
Adventure in Bed; The New
Avengers; The Sweeney;
Rebecca; Minder; and more
than 30 single plays. In 1975
he succeeded Michael
Gambon in Alan Ayckbourn's
trilogy The Norman
Conquests on the London
stage, and the following year
played Professor Higgins in
Pygmalion at the Cambridge
Arts Festival. Has since been
dividing his time acting,
directing in the theatre and
producing films incl:
Loophole, starring Albert
Finney. Education: Harrow.
m actress Zena Walker (dis).
Address: c/o Norman
Boyack, London W1.
Starsign: Cancer.

HOLNESS, Bob
Radio and TV presenter
b 12th November Vryheid,
Natal. Stage and radio acting
in South Africa before coming
to England where he was
presenting TV programmes,
and announcing and

interviewing both on TV and radio. After another spell in South Africa for variety shows, radio acting, panel games and news, he returned to Britian where he presented a word game, Take a Letter, for two and a half years. Other TV incl: World in Action; Junior Criss Cross Quiz; What the Papers Say; Today (which he co-presented with Eamonn Andrews); TV commercials. On radio he presented Late Night Extra for eight years, as well as Top of the Form; record programmes (for 16 years on BBC World Service); LBC's AM Show, which he has co-presented with Douglas Cameron since 1974. Education: Ashford Grammar School; Kent; Maidstone College of Art. m Mary Rose, 2 d Carol Ann, Rosalind, 1 s Jonathan. Address: c/o Spotlight Ltd, London WC2. Starsign: Scorpio. Hobbies: music of every kind, gardening. Person he would most like to meet: 'No one in particular – everyone has a story to tell, as I find out every day on the AM Show.'

HONEYCOMBE, Gordon
Presenter/writer b 27.9.36 Karachi, British India. Is 6ft 4 ins tall. Started as a radio announcer 1956, acted with the Royal Shakespeare Company for a couple of years and joined ITN as scriptwriter and newscaster 1965. Left to freelance 1977. Is also a writer of some accomplishment, having

written several plays and dramatisations for the stage and TV and is the author of a number of best-selling books. Stage incl: The Redemption; Paradise Lost (also radio); God Save The Queen; A King Shall Have a Kingdom (also radio). Radio: Lancelot and Guinevere. TV incl: The Golden Vision; Time and Time Again (Silver Medal, New York Film and TV Festival, 1975); Something Special (series); The Late, Late Show; Family History (series about how he traced his ancestry back to 1318); narrated Arthur C Clarke's Mysterious World. Books incl: Neither the Sea Nor the Sand (also the screenplay); Dragon Under the Hill; Adam's Tale; Red Watch; Nagasaki 1945; The Edge of Heaven; Royal Wedding; The Murders of the Black Museum; The Year of the Princess. Education: Edinburgh Academy; University College, Oxford (MA English Language and Literature). Address: c/o Isobel Davie Ltd, London W1. Starsign: Libra. Hobbies: brass-rubbing, genealogy, bridge, crosswords, curry, pigs. Person he would most like to have met: Matthew Honeycombe (1660).

HOPKINS, Bo
Actor b Greenwood, South Carolina. Michael Blaisdel in Dynasty. Studied drama with Uta Hagen in New York before going to California with Desilu Playhouse training school in Hollywood.

First film role was in The Wild Bunch. Films since incl: The Man Who Loved Cat Dancing; American Graffiti; The Nickel Ride; The Day of the Locust; Posse; The Killer Elite; A Small Town in Texas; Midnight Express. In addition to Dynasty, his TV appearances incl: Doc Elliott series; Beggarman, Thief series.

HORDERN, Michael CBE
Actor b 3.10.11 Berkhamsted, Herts. Grew up on Dartmoor. Was once a schoolmaster, then sold school textbooks and dabbled in amateur dramatics which gave him a taste for the stage. No professional training before becoming assistant stage manager and understudy and making his professional debut in London in Othello in 1937. Two years in rep at Bristol's Little Theatre where he met the girl who was to become his wife. Served in the Royal Navy 1940-45 and rose to the rank of Lieut-Commander. Returned to the stage 1946, the year in which he made his TV debut in the title role of Noah. Now one of Britain's leading character actors, he has appeared in many plays, films and TV productions. Stage incl: King Lear (also on TV); Flint; Richard II and Jumpers (National Theatre); The Tempest (RSC and on TV); The Ordeal of Gilbert Pinfold. Many films incl: Alexander the Great; Cleopatra; The VIPs; The Spy

Who Came in from the Cold; The Taming of the Shrew; Where Eagles Dare; Anne of the Thousand Days; El Cid; Khartoum; Theatre of Blood; Alice's Adventures in Wonderland; Quilp; Royal Flush; The Slipper and the Rose. TV incl: The Dock Brief; What Shall We Tell Caroline?; The Browning Version; The Magistrate; Edward the Seventh; Chester Mystery Plays; Romeo and Juliet; Roald Dahl's Tales of the Unexpected; All's Well That Ends Well; You're Alright How Am I?; The History Man. Education: Brighton College. m former actress Eve Mortimer, 1 d Joanna. Address: c/o ICM, London W1. Starsign: Libra. Hobbies: fishing (he has devised a trout fly named Hordern's Nymph), gardening. Person he would most like to have met: 'Isaac Walton, because I could teach him a thing or two about fishing.'

HOROVITCH, David
Actor b 11.8.45 London. Trained at the Central School of Speech and Drama then rep at Cheltenham, Newcastle, Manchester, Farnham and Nottingham. Other theatre incl: Crucifer of Blood (Dr Watson); Julius Caesar; The Nurd; and a tour of India in She Stoops to Conquer. Many TV appearances incl: The Expert; The Shadow of the Tower; Target; Prince Regent; Intimate Strangers; Bouquet of Barbed Wire; Sandbaggers; Bognor (title

role); The Cleopatras. Education: St Christopher School, Letchworth. m Jane Roberts, 2 s. Address: c/o French's, London W1. Starsign: Leo.

HORSFALL, Bernard
Actor b Bishops Stortford, Herts, but raised in Sussex. Became interested in drama while at school but spent a year in Canada supposedly studying agriculture. On his return he taught at a prep school in Surrey and in 1950 enrolled at the Webber Douglas Academy of Dramatic Art to train to become an actor. Left to join a tour with Dundee Rep Company and the Old Vic. Recent stage incl: Who's Afraid of Virginia Woolf?; Jumpers; Clouds; Master Builder; To Kill A King. Films incl: Shout at the Devil; Gold; On Her Majesty's Secret Service; Gandhi; Brass Target; Inside The Third Reich. TV incl: Dancers in Mourning; Death of a Ghost; Family Solicitor; Suspicion; Beasts; General Hospital; Big Boy Now; This Year, Next Year; Enemy at the Door; Our Little Town; Minder; Badger By Owl-light; The Lady Killers; When The Boat Comes In. Education: Rugby School. m Jane, 2 d Hannah, Rebecca, 1 s Christian. Address: c/o Brian Wheeler Personal Management, London W4. Person he would most like to have met: 'George Leigh Mallory, to find out what happened.'

HOUSEGO, Fred
Presenter and TV personality b 25.10.44 Dundee. Former taxi driver and winner of Mastermind in 1980. First job was in an advertising agency as a messenger. Other jobs incl stacking shelves at Marks and Spencer and designing brochures, before becoming a postman for six years. During a strike he turned to taxi-driving in 1972 and as such he applied to be a contestant on Mastermind, having been a fan of the programme for many years. Since winning the title he has been in demand for radio (Start the Week; Just the Ticket) and TV (History on Your Doorstep; Blankety Blank; The Pyramid Game; This is Your Life; The 6 o'clock Show), as a speaker (Oxford Union and Cambridge Union) and has written many articles for periodicals. Pye TV Personality of 1981 and is a registered LTB guide. Book: Fred Housego's London. Education: Kynaston Comprehensive. m Pat, 2 d Kate, Abigail. Address: c/o Peter Charlesworth, London SW7. Starsign: Scorpio. Hobbies: photography, reading history, food and drink, collecting old rock 'n' roll records. People he would most like to meet: Actress Katharine Hepburn and Spanish poet Garcia Lorca.

HOUSTON, Robin
Newsreader/announcer b January 1947 London. Trained at RADA and has

been newsreader for Thames News for four years. Has also been a continuity announcer for London Weekend TV, a presenter for London Broadcasting/Independent Radio News, and a newsreader for Capital Radio. Address: c/o Jon Roseman Assocs, London W1. Starsign: Capricorn.

HOWARD, Trevor
Actor b 29.9.16 Cliftonville, Kent. Taken to Sri Lanka at an early age by his parents, then to America and Canada before returning to Britain. Trained at RADA and after a spell with RSC at Stratford, went into the army, taking part in the invasions of Norway and Sicily and returned to civvie street with a Military Cross. Old Vic 1947-48. First big lead was in Brief Encounter. Films since incl: Odette; The Clouded Yellow; Outcast of the Islands; Gift Horse; The Third Man; The Heart of the Matter; Cockleshell Heroes; The Key; Sons and Lovers; Mutiny on the Bounty; Von Ryan's Express; The Charge of the Light Brigade; Ryan's Daughter; Mary Queen of

Scots; Conduct Unbecoming; The Count of Monte Cristo; The Last Remake of Beau Geste; Light Years Away; Sir Henry At Rawlinson End; Windwalker; Gandhi; The Taming of the Shrew. Plays incl: The Devil's General; The Cherry Orchard; The Father; Two Stars for Comfort; Waltz of the Toreadors; Scenario; The Invincible Mr Disraeli; Napoleon at St Helena. Most recent TV: Catholics; Stars on Sunday; Scorpion Tales; Nightflight; Staying On; Exile of Jonathan Swift; Inside The Third Reich; A Dangerous Game. Education: schools in Sri Lanka, Los Angeles, Canada; Clifton College, Bristol. m actress Helen Cherry. Address: c/o Marina Martin Management, London W1. Starsign: Libra. Hobbies: cricket, travel. Person he would most like to meet: 'Elizabeth David, to thank her. When I met my wife she couldn't boil an egg: now I'd rather eat at home than anywhere else.'

HOWARTH, Jack
Actor b 19.2.1896 Rochdale. More than 60 years in the theatrical profession, starting at the age of 12 playing children's parts with Churchill's Minstrels in The Happy Valley, Llandudno. Stage director for the original productions of Dracula and Frankenstein in this country. Many years with Leslie Henson's company and was in 18 films and 100 TV programmes (incl the first

play from Granada), before becoming Albert Tatlock in Coronation Street from the first programme, on 9th December 1960. Education: Board School in Rochdale. m Betty, 1 s John. Address: c/o International Artistes Representation, London W1. Starsign: Pisces. Hobbies: watching cricket, circuses. Person he would most like to meet: 'Mrs Thatcher, because I admire her fighting spirit and for sticking to her guns. Also I agree with her tactics.'

HOWERD, Frankie OBE
Comedian b 6.3.22 York. Stage debut at 13. Camp concerts during the war. Revue and stage shows: Out of This World; Pardon My French; Way Out in Piccadilly; Charley's Aunt; Hotel Paradiso; A Midsummer Night's Dream; Alice in Wonderland; A Funny Thing Happened on the Way to the Forum; Palladium pantomimes 1968 and 1973; Die Fledermaus. Films incl: The Ladykillers; Runaway Bus; Touch of the Sun; Jumping For Joy; Further Up The Creek; Carry On Doctor; Carry On Up the Jungle; Up Pompeii; Up The Chastity Belt; Up The Front; The House In Nightmare Park; Sergeant Pepper's Lonely Hearts Club Band. TV incl: Fine Goings On; Up Pompeii; The Frankie Howerd Show; Frankie Howerd Strikes Again; HMS Pinafore; Then Churchill Said To Me. Many Royal Variety performances.

Book: Trumps. Education: Shooters Hill School, Woolwich. Address: c/o RSO Management Ltd, London W1. Starsign: Pisces. Hobbies: tennis, swimming, music, reading. Person he would most like to have met: 'Assuming the idea of meeting Jesus Christ would be presumptious, the person I would next most like to meet would be Judas Iscariot, for obvious reasons.'

HUDD, Roy

Comedian b 16.5.36 Croydon, Surrey. Claims he 'trained in the University of Life, variety, concert party and pantomime'. But he began in boys' clubs 1957 followed by holiday camp and summer shows. TV debut 1964 as a regular in Not So Much a Programme, More a Way of Life. Other TV incl: Hudd; The Illustrated Weekly Hudd; The Roy Hudd Show; Pebble Mill at One; The 607080 Show; Looks Familiar; Quick on the Draw; Blankety Blank; The Good Old Days; Look Who's Talking; Sooty; Movie Memories; various chat and variety shows. Radio incl: The News Huddlines; 'udds 'our an' 'arf. On stage as Fagin in the revival of Oliver! Bud Flanagan in Underneath the Arches and his permanently touring show, Roy Hudd's Very Own Music Hall. Education: School of Hard Knocks (he says). m Ann, 1 s Max. Address: c/o Aza Artistes, London NW11. Starsign: Taurus. Hobbies:

walking, sleeping, talking, music-hall (history and songs). Person he would most like to meet: 'The man who told me show business was easier than working!'

HUDSON-EVANS, Richard

TV/radio reporter b 3.12.42 Heswall, Cheshire. Training with BBC local radio, Thames TV outside broadcasts and BBC radio motoring, travel and transport units. Joined ATV/Central TV Dec 1978 as reporter and newsreader. Still a frequent contributor to BBC Radio 4 Going Places and Breakaway programmes. Author of books on motoring, motor-cycling, motor sport, and travel. Education: Mostyn House, Parkgate, Cheshire; Warwick School. m Sugunya. Address: c/o Bagenal Harvey Organisation, London W1. Starsign: Sagittarius. Hobbies: private flying, gliding, inland waterways, railways, motor-cycling. Person he would most like to meet: 'John le Carré – to solve the secret of creating the perfect read.'

HUGHES, Geoffrey

Actor b 2.2.44 Liverpool. Training at Stoke-on-Trent Rep, films and TV for the past 21 years. London stage incl: Maggie May; Say Good-night to Grandma. Films incl: Virgin Soldiers; Adolf Hitler, My Part in His Downfall; The Bofors Gun. TV: many plays and series; currently Eddie Yeats in Coronation Street. Education: Abbotsford

School, Yorks. m Susan. Address: c/o Richard Stone, London WC2. Starsign: Aquarius. Hobbies: natural history, music. Person he would most like to have met: 'Turlough O'Carolan, the 17th-century blind harper. An evening in his company must have been a joyful experience.'

HUGHES, Nerys

Actress b 8.11.41 Rhyl. Trained as a teacher at Rose Bruford Training College. Soon made a name for herself on TV in The Liver Birds followed by The Merchant of Venice; High Summer; Seasons; Diary of a Young Man; How Green Was My Valley; Doctor Who; Jackanory; Play Away; Third Time Lucky. Education: Howell's School, Denbigh. m Patrick Turley, 1 d Mari-Claire, 1 s Benjamin. Address: c/o Richard Stone, London WC2. Starsign: Scorpio. Hobbies: playing with the children, gardening. Person she would most like to have met: 'Young Lloyd George – energy, charming and some pretty good ideas for running a country. (But I wouldn't have liked to be married to him!).'

HUGHES, Vaughan
Journalist b 16.11.47 Anglesey. Weekly newspaper experience but since 1970 has worked on HTV Wales nightly Welsh language news programme Y Dydd as reporter, presenter and editor. Has also edited and presented documentaries in the Yr Wythnos series, is translator and narrator of foreign documentaries, and presenter of Eisteddfod and election specials. Education: Llangefni Comprehensive School. m Angharad, 1 d Heled. Address: c/o HTV Wales, Cardiff. Starsign: Scorpio. Hobbies: books, cars, hi-fi. Person he would most like to meet: 'The last of the non Welsh-speaking English.'

HULL, Rod
Entertainer/writer b 13.8.35 Isle of Sheppey. Inseparable from Emu, which was hatched in Australia after Rod had emigrated there when he was young and was running a breakfast-time chat show.

Someone sent him an emu's egg which he placed on a radiator and Emu was the eventual result of this action. Back in England he has made numerous guest appearances in various TV shows as well as his own shows, especially at Christmas and Easter. Other TV incl: EBC; Emu's World; the famous appearance on the Michael Parkinson Show; This is Your Life. Has also been on Desert Island Discs. His pantomime, Emu in Pantoland, has played all over the country for many years. He also created, wrote and hosted the first Children's Royal Command Performance in aid of charity in 1981. Education: Delemark Road School and County Tech, Sheerness. m (1st) dis, (2nd) Cheryl, 3 d Danielle, Debbie (from 1st m), Amelia (from 2nd m), step-d Katrina, 2 s Toby, Oliver (from 2nd m). Address: c/o International Artists, London W1. Starsign: Leo. Hobbies: bee-keeping, golf, keeping his family life private.

HUMPHRIES, Barry
Art historian b 17.2.34 Melbourne. Stage experience was gained at Union Theatre, Melbourne and Philip Street Theatre. Subsequently developed his one-man shows, starting with A Nice Night's Entertainment in 1962. Others incl: Excuse I; Just a Show; A Load of Olde Stuffe; At Least You Can Say You've Seen It; Housewife Superstar; A Night With

Dame Edna; Last Night of the Poms; An Evening's Intercourse with the Widely Liked Barry Humphries. Has appeared on many TV chat shows. Films incl: Adventures of Barry McKenzie; Barry McKenzie Holds His Own; The Getting of Wisdom; Shock Treatment. Education: Melbourne Grammar School, Melbourne University. m Diane Millstead, 2 d Tessa, Emily, 1 s Oscar. Address: c/o Dennis Smith Promotions, Victoria, Australia. Starsign: Aquarius. Hobby: travelling. Person he would most like to meet: Dame Edna Everage.

HUNNIFORD, Gloria
TV and radio presenter/interviewer b 10.4.40 Portadown, Co Armagh. Had her own radio programme in Canada 1959. In Northern Ireland she was involved in another radio series, Up Country, for the BBC and a two-and-a-half-hour daily progamme, A Taste of Hunni. For BBC World Service she did A Taste of Hunni – Irish Style which has been replaced by a programme titled simply Gloria Hunniford. Before her daily Radio 2 programme, which started at the beginning of 1982, she was a presenter for three years of Good Evening Ulster, a local news and magazine programme for Ulster TV, for whom she still does a regular programme, Gloria Plus. Other TV incl: The Six o'clock Show (for LWT); The Val

Doonican Show. Her records incl: Good Evening Gloria (LP). Education: Portadown College. m Don Keating, 1 d Caron, 2 s Paul, Michael. Address: c/o BBC, London W1. Starsign: Aries. Hobbies: antique collecting, tennis. Person she would most like to meet again: 'The Duke of Edinburgh – I enjoyed talking to him when I interviewed him.'

HUNT, Gareth
Actor b 7.2.43 London. Served in the Merchant Navy for six years after which he had a variety of jobs before training at Webber Douglas Academy of Dramatic Art. Rep at Ipswich, Bristol Old Vic, Coventry, Royal Court in London, and Watford before the Royal Shakespeare Company and the National Theatre. Stage incl: Conduct Unbecoming; Alpha Beta; Deathtrap. Films incl: Licensed to Love and Kill; The House on Garibaldi Street; The World is Full of Married Men. Made impact on TV as the handsome footman in Upstairs, Downstairs and as Gambit in The New Avengers; That Beryl Marston . . .! Education: Singlegate School for Boys. m (1st) Carol (dis), (2nd) Anette, 1 s Gareth (from 1st m). Address: c/o ICM, London W1. Starsign: Aquarius. Hobbies: golf, keep-fit, cricket, squash. Person he would most like to have met: 'Thomas Paine, to sit and listen.'

HUNT, Dr Garry
Science presenter b 23.5.42 London. ITN Science Consultant and presenter of Worlds Apart. Trained as a scientist in mathematics, physics, astronomy and meteorology. Holds a NASA Award for Space Studies and is also BSc, PhD, DSc, FIMA, FRAS, FRMetS, MBCS. Education: Wimbledon; Epsom; University of London. m Wendy, 2 d Sarah-Jane, Susannah. Address: c/o Dept of Physics and Astronomy, University College, London. Starsign: Gemini. Hobbies: travel, photography, music. Person he would most like to meet: 'David Attenborough – space explorer meets Earth explorer (the modern version of Stanley and Livingstone!).'

HUNT, Michael
Meteorologist b 8.10.20 Ebbw Vale, Gwent. Trained as a physicist. After war service in the RAF went to the Air Ministry Meteorological Office until 1961 when he joined Anglia TV and where he has been ever since. Author of articles on food and wine and environmental science. Fellow of the Royal

Meteorological Society and Associate Member of the Institute of Environmental Science. Education: Ebbw Vale Grammar School. m Lynette, 2 d Judith, Jessica. Address: c/o Anglia TV, Norwich. Starsign: Libra. Hobbies: food, wine, medieval architecture, heritage preservation. Person he would most like to meet: 'Arthur Koestler – the unique commentator on the events of my lifetime.'

HUNTER, Russell
Actor b 18.2.25 Glasgow. A former shipyard worker, he began acting as an amateur while still at the shipyard. His professional debut was with the Glasgow Unity Theatre at the first Edinburgh Festival in 1947. His many stage roles have ranged from concert party comic and panto dame to Shakespeare at the Old Vic, the Open Air Theatre at Regent's Park, Bristol Old Vic and the Royal Shakespeare Company. Has appeared all over Scotland in his famous one-man show, Jock, while in London he was in Hochhuth's Soldiers and the musical Lock Up Your Daughters during the Mermaid Theatre's 10th anniversary. On TV he is probably best known for his performance as Lonely which he played more than 50 times, in the Callan series. Other TV incl: Mackenzie; The Standard; Five Red Herrings; Mind Your Language; Dickens of London; Rule Britannia; The Gaffer; Play For Tomorrow.

Education: 'Minimal' he says.
Address: c/o Margery Abel
Ltd, London W1. Starsign:
Aquarius. Hobbies: smoking
cigars, collecting modern
paintings. Person he would
most like to meet: 'Dame
Peggy Ashcroft, because she
has remained the most
fascinating actress in this
country for over 50 years.'

Berridge (dis), (2nd) Ivy
Carlton (dec), (3rd) Margaret
Ward, 1 d (dec). Address:
c/o Essanay, London W14.
Starsign: Scorpio. Hobbies:
genealogy, bridge, walking.
Person he would most like to
have met: 'As a genealogist, I
would like to meet my
ancestors – notably my
eleventh great-grandfather,
1480-1542.'

HURNDALL, Richard
Actor b 3.11.10 Darlington,
Co Durham. Studied music in
Paris before switching to
acting. Trained at RADA and
made stage debut 1930. First
broadcast in 1933, since
when he has been in many
reps, incl
Stratford-upon-Avon
Memorial Theatre, and toured
in plays. West End shows
incl: The Affair; The New Men;
The Masters; Hostile Witness;
Justice is a Woman; Highly
Confidential. Former member
of BBC drama rep company,
has also appeared frequently
on TV since 1946 incl: Z Cars;
Softly, Softly; Dr Finlay's
Casebook; Callan;
Codename; The Avengers;
The Power Game; It's Murder,
But Is It Art?; The Inheritors;
The Regiment; The Onedin
Line; Van Der Valk; War and
Peace; Public Eye; Hadleigh;
The Protectors; Enemy At The
Door; Philby, Burgess and
Maclean; Running Blind;
Ripping Yarns; The Sound of
the Guns; Love In A Cold
Climate; Dark Secret;
Bognor; Blake's Seven.
Education: Clarement;
Darlington; Scarborough
College. m (1st) Mona

HYETT, Trevor
Presenter/interviewer
b 14.11.43 Wigan, Lancs.
Journalistic background (incl
TVTimes) before joining
Granada TV in 1974 as
frontman for local magazine,
current affairs and schools
programmes. Also network
pre-school and adult
education programmes.
Joined Thames TV as one of
the presenters and
interviewers for After Noon
Plus. Education:
Chorlton-cum-Hardy
Grammar School,
Manchester; Kingsbury
County Grammar.
1 d Corrina, 1 s Michael.
Address: c/o Thames TV,
London NW1. Starsign:
Scorpio. Hobbies: skiffle,
photography. Person he
would most like to meet:
'Lech Walesa for proving that
establishments and
conventions can be very,
very wrong.'

IFANS, Caryl
Presenter/singer/actress
b 16.4.58 St Asaph, Clwyd.
Started in a school group and
is still a member of a pop
group band. Co-presents
HTV's children's programme
Ser. Education: Ysgol
Gynradd Mornant,
Ffynnongroyw; Ysgol Dewi
Sant, Rhyl; Ysgol Glan Clwyd,
St Asaph; University College
of North Wales, Bangor.
m Rhys Ifans. Address: c/o
HTV Wales, Cardiff. Starsign:
Aries. Hobby: music. Person
she would most like to meet:
'Pamela Stephenson – she is
what I want to be.'

INMAN, John
Actor b 28.6.36 Preston.
One of his first jobs was as a
window dresser in a London
store. When 21 became an
actor at Crewe Rep. London
West End debut was in Anne
Veronica; stage work since
has incl: Salad Days; Let's
Get Laid; Charley's Aunt;
summer shows; pantomime
at Wimbledon, Bristol,
Nottingham, Victoria Palace,
London (Mother Goose).
Achieved overnight success
in TV series Are You Being
Served? Other TV incl: Odd

Man Out; Celebrity Squares;
The Good Old Days; Take A
Letter Mr Jones. Education:
Claremont School,
Blackpool. Address: c/o
London Management,
London W1. Starsign:
Cancer. Hobby: work. Person
he would most like to have
met: 'Frank Randall – he was
a well-known North Country
comedian and a brilliantly
funny man.'

INNES, Neil
Comedian/musician
b 9.12.44 Danbury, Essex.
Originally pianist and lead
musician with the Bonzo Dog
Doo Dah Band and
composer of I'm an Urban
Spaceman. Went on to join
Eric Idle's Rutland Weekend
TV and wrote and appeared
in the spoof Beatles group,
The Rutles. Also starred in
his own show series The
Innes Book of Records. Has
also appeared in the Monty
Python Live film and The
Secret Policeman's Other
Ball. Education: grammar
school. m Yvonne,
3 s Miles, Luke, Barnaby.
Address: c/o Roger Hancock
Ltd, London SW1. Starsign:
Sagittarius. Hobby: Belgium.
Person he would most like to
meet: 'Lobby Lud – he owes
me a fiver.'

IRONS, Jeremy
Actor b 19.9.48 Cowes, Isle
of Wight. Trained at the Bristol
Old Vic Theatre School.
Joined the Old Vic Company
in Bristol 1971 and toured
South America in The Taming
of the Shrew. In 1973 he

ICKE, David
Presenter/reporter/
interviewer b 29.4.52
Leicester. Formerly with
Coventry City and Hereford
United Football Clubs, but a
football injury put paid to his
soccer career and he went
into journalism, first with BBC
Radio Leicester and BRMB,
and then BBC TV. Member of
their sports team 1978-80
when he went freelance. TV
incl: Grandstand; The World
at One; PM; The World
Tonight; Newsnight.
Education: Crown Hills
Secondary School. m Linda,
1 d Kerry. Address: c/o PVA
Management Ltd, London
W1. Starsign: Taurus.
Hobbies: soccer, motor
racing, reading biographies.
People he would most like to
meet: 'My next door
neighbours – I have not had
time to meet them yet.'

played John the Baptist in Godspell in London. Other theatre appearances incl: Diary of a Madman (solo performance); The Caretaker; Much Ado About Nothing (both at the Young Vic); An Inspector Calls; The Taming of the Shrew (both for the New Shakespeare Company); Wild Oats (for the Royal Shakespeare Company); The Rear Column (for which he won the Clarence Derwent Award); An Audience Called Eduard. Films incl: Nijinsky; The French Lieutenant's Woman (for which he was nominated Best Actor 1981 by BAFTA); Moonlighting; Blackout. TV incl: The Voysey Inheritance; Langrishe Go Down; Love for Lydia; Notorious Woman; Churchill's People; Playaway; Brideshead Revisited (for which he was nominated Best Actor 1981 by BAFTA). Voted Best Actor by TVTimes readers 1981-82. Education: Sherborne School, Dorset. m actress Sinead Cusack, 1 s Samuel. Address: c/o Hutton Management, London SW5. Starsign: Virgo. Hobbies: walking, sailing, skiing, horse-riding.

ISAAC, Russell
Journalist b 28.9.55 Llwynypia, Cwm Rhondda. Before joining HTV in 1980 was doing research for an MA degree in Argentina, and returned there during the Falkland Islands crisis for HTV. Education: Ysgol Gyfun Rhydfelen; University

College of North Wales (BA Hons Social Theory; MA research Class and Ethnicity). Address: c/o HTV Wales, Cardiff. Starsign: Libra. Hobbies: rugby, most ball sports. Person he would most like to have met: 'Owain Glyndwr – to understand where we went wrong.'

J

JACKSON, Gordon OBE
Actor b 19.12.23 Glasgow. Trained as a draughtsman but playing parts in radio plays on Children's Hour brought him to the notice of Ealing Studios. The Foreman Went to France was the first of more than 50 films, incl: Whisky Galore; Mutiny on the Bounty; Those Magnificent Men in Their Flying Machines; The Prime of Miss Jean Brodie; Night of the Generals and stage appearances in Macbeth; Hamlet; Hedda Gabler; What Every Woman Knows; Noah; Twelfth Night; Cards On The Table. TV incl: Ghost Squad; Dr Finlay's Casebook; The Soldier's Tale; The Professionals; but best known for the part of Hudson in Upstairs, Downstairs. Education: Hillhead High School, Glasgow. m actress Rona Anderson, 2 s Graham, Roddy. Address: c/o ICM, London W1. Starsign: Sagittarius. Hobbies: music, gardening. Person he would most like to have met: 'Mozart, to thank him for the joy he brought to the world.'

JACOBS, David
Compère/interviewer b 19.5.26 London. First broadcast as an impressionist in Navy Mixture while still in the Royal Navy. Later became an announcer with the Forces Broadcasting Service in London. Chief announcer, Radio SEAC, Ceylon 1945-47. Joined BBC in 1947 as radio newscaster but shortly after went freelance and became one of the busiest men on the air as compère, disc jockey and actor (he played 23 parts in the Journey Into Space radio serial). Other radio incl: Pick of the Pops; The David Jacobs Show; Any Questions?; Any Answers?; Melodies For You. TV incl: Juke Box Jury; The David Jacobs Show; Miss World; Eurovision Song Contest; Frank Sinatra Show; Wednesday Magazine; Tell The Truth; Make Up Your Mind; David Jacobs' Words and Music; It's Sunday Night With David Jacobs; Now Who Do You Do?; Where Are They Now?; Blankety Blank; Punchlines; The Janet Brown Show; The Pyramid Game; Looks Familiar. Many business interests. Books: Jacobs Ladder (autobiography); Caroline. Education: Belmont College; Strand School. m (1st) actress Patricia Bradlaw (dis), (2nd) Caroline (dec), (3rd) model Lindsay Stuart-Hutcheson, 3 d Carol, Joanna, Emma, 1 s Jeremy (dec) (all by 1st m). Address: c/o Lewis Joelle, London SW1. Starsign: Taurus. Hobbies: talking, listening, hotels.

JAEGER, Frederick
Actor/director b 1928 Berlin. Came to England 1939 and took up acting at the suggestion of his English headmaster. Guildhall School of Music and Drama 1946-48 and started stage career at Preston Rep 1949. Many rep seasons in provinces before West End appearances such as The Comedy of Errors; Lock Up Your Daughters; The Potsdam Quartet; Big Fish, Little Fish; For Adults Only; A Patriot For Me; Mrs Gibson's Boys; Salad Days. Went into films 1956 which incl: The Black Tents; The War Lovers; The Iron Petticoat; Song of Norway; Ice Cold in Alex; Farewell Performance; The One That Got Away; Scorpio; One of Those Things; The Situation; 7% Solution; The Voyage; Nijinsky. Started TV 1955 in The Grove Family; appearances since incl: The Inside Man; The Pretenders; Special Branch; Warship; Z Cars; Department S; Ryan International; Little Women; Man at the Top; Persuaders; Paul Temple; Doctor Who; Dixon of Dock Green; Jason King; Me Mammy; The Sweeney; Hadleigh; The Main Chance; Protectors; Oneupmanship; Nuts; The Dick Emery Show; Shelley; Home Movies; Doombolt Chase; New Avengers; The Professionals; Some Mothers Do 'Ave 'Em; Omega Factor;

The Fall and Rise of Reginald Perrin; The Potsdam Quartet; Minder; Churchill; QED; The Onedin Line; Kelly Monteith Show; Take The High Road; Jim Davidson Show; Shoestring; Yes, Minister. Education: Germany, France, England. m (1st) painter Hazel Penwarden (dis), (2nd) Elizabeth, 2 step-d Caroline, Sarah. Address: c/o Joan Gray, Sunbury on Thames. Starsign: Taurus. Hobbies: squash, gardening. Person he would most like to meet: 'Anthony Wedgwood Benn, though I couldn't possibly explain why.'

JAMES, Keith
Actor b 10.12.37 Southend-on-Sea, Essex. Trained at the Guildhall School of Music and Drama, then rep at Dundee and York before London's West End, Royal Shakespeare Company and Edinburgh Festival. Many films, documentaries, TV programmes and more than 100 commercials. Films incl: Operation Snatch; Dutchman; A Challenge for Robin Hood; The Ruins Within. TV incl: Softly, Softly; Hugh and I; The Mind of Mr J G Reeder; Champion House; Coronation Street; Gazette; Doctor Who; Counter Strike; Castle Haven; Target; Public Eye; Keep It in the Family. For many years was a 'regular' in the Dick Emery Shows; has also been in Bernie Winters, Frankie Howerd and Mike Yarwood shows. Education:

Wentworth High School for Boys, Southend. m health visitor Betty, 2 d Natalie, Alison, 1 s Jonathan. Address: c/o Beryl Seton Agency, London WC2. Starsign: Sagittarius. Hobby: photography. Person he would most like to have met: 'TS Eliot – to say thank you.'

JARVIS, Martin
Actor b 4th August Cheltenham. Started in Manchester after training at RADA (silver medal and Vanbrugh Award). Soon came to London where his stage work incl: Cockade; Poor Bitos; Man and Superman; The Spoils of Poynton; The Bandwagon; The Prodigal Daughter; The Rivals (and in America); Hamlet. Played Edward VIII in The Woman I Love at Bromley and scored personal success in She Stoops to Conquer in Canada and at Hong Kong Arts Festival. His films incl: The Last Escape; Ike (in which he played George VI); The Circle; Caught In The Act. Many radio performances incl: War and Peace; Great Expectations; also readings and the author of several short stories for radio. TV incl: The Forsyte Saga; Nicholas Nickleby; The Pallisers; Ross; After Liverpool; The Samaritan; Zigger Zagger; True Patriot; David Copperfield; Killers; Charades; Enemy at the Door; Rings On Their Fingers; Breakaway; The Business of Murder; Jackanory; The

Bunker. Education: Whitgift School, Croydon; London University. m actress Rosalind Ayres, 2 s Toby, Oliver. Address: c/o London Management, London W1. Starsign: Leo. Hobbies: music, Indian food, movies, work, interior design. Person he would most like to have met: 'William Shakespeare – who was the Dark Lady?'

JASON, David
Actor b 2.2.40 Edmonton, London. Became an electrician on leaving school but all his spare time was devoted to amateur theatricals. His actor brother, Arthur, helped to get him his first professional part in South Sea Bubble at Bromley. More rep then Peter Pan. A Dick Emery season at Bournemouth led to the part of Captain Fantastic in Do Not Adjust Your Set, which established him on TV incl: Hark at Barker; Six Dates With Barker; Doctor in the House; Doctor at Large; Doctor at Sea. Other major TV series incl: The Top Secret Life of Edgar Briggs; Lucky Fella; A Sharp Intake of Breath; Open All Hours; Only Fools and Horses. Films incl: The Odd Job. Recent radio: Week Ending; Jason Explanation. Recently toured Middle and Far East in Not Now, Darling. Education: 'Some education', he says. Address: c/o Richard Stone, London WC2. Starsign: Aquarius. Hobbies: gliding, skin diving. Person he would most like to meet: 'The President of the United

States sitting next to the leader of the Soviet Union.'

JAY, Susan
Journalist b 16.2.47 Wolverhampton. Four years on newspapers (Sunday Mercury, Leicester Mercury) and 12 years in TV news reporting. Joined ATV as first woman reporter in news department 1968 and TVS 1982 as co-presenter The Real World, a popular science programme. Has won awards at San Francisco Film Festival for two of her Jaywalking programmes for ATV – On the Road to Nowhere (1974) and God Speed the Plough (1975). Education: Regis Comprehensive, Wolverhampton. Address: c/o PVA Management Ltd, London W1. Starsign: Aquarius. Hobbies: gardening, walking. Person she would most like to have met: Mrs Sylvia Pankhurst.

JAYNE, Keith
Actor b 10.12.60 Ruislip, Middx. After leaving drama school went into Henry V at Ludlow Festival and has since worked almost non-stop in all media. His

stage appearances incl: Carry On London; Peter Pan; The Innocents; Class Enemy; Ticket-of-Leave Man (National Theatre); pantomime. Films incl: Robin Hood Junior; The Unbroken Hour; The Prisoner of Zenda. On TV he has been seen in Churchill's People; Upstairs, Downstairs; Jubilee; Secret Army; Angels; Watch This Space; Rumpole of the Bailey; How's Your Father?; Kids; Goodbye Darling; The Dancing Years; The Onedin Line; Jack on the Box; Sink or Swim; Scarf Jack; Stig of the Dump; Last Summer's Child; Murphy's Mob; Wayne and Albert. Education: Downer Grammar School; Barbara Speake Stage School. Address: c/o CSM Artistes, London W3. Starsign: Sagittarius. Hobbies: driving, playing squash. Person he would most like to meet: 'The Queen – for an OBE.'

JEAVONS, Colin
Actor b 20.10.29 Newport, Monmouthshire. First stage appearance was at the Old Vic in 1951 after studying at Old Vic School. First TV appearance was in 1956 and his first film in 1962. Has since been in many TV series incl: Lucky Jim; Terry Scott On . . .; Billy Liar; The Fuzz; Kinvig. Since 1980 he has appeared in Shoestring; Great Expectations; Jackanory; Lady Killers; Hitch-hiker's Guide To The Galaxy; Dear Heart. Films incl: Caleb Williams; French Lieutenant's Woman. Education: church school and art school.

m Rosie, 2 s Barney, Saul. Address: c/o London Management, London W1. Starsign: Libra. Hobby: collecting 78 rpm records of opera and music-hall. Person he would most like to meet: 'Michael Bentine – because I like his work and because his friends enjoy being his friends so much.'

JEFFREY, Peter
Actor b 18.4.29 Bristol. No training for the stage but had 12 years of varied theatrical work, mainly with Bristol Old Vic and the Royal Shakespeare Company, before working in TV. Recent stage incl: Donkey's Years and (for the National Theatre) For Services Rendered. Films incl: Becket; The Fixer; If . . .; Ring of Bright Water; Anne of the Thousand Days; The Horsemen; The Odessa File; Midnight Express. TV incl: The Planemakers; Triangle; Villette; Elizabeth R; Boys and Girls Come Out to Play; Cakes and Ale; The Common; Destiny; London Belongs to Me; Porridge; Mr and Ms Bureaucrat; The Old Crowd; The Atom Spies; Rifleman; For Services Rendered; Minder; All's Well That Ends Well; Nanny; Britannia Hospital. Education: Harrow; Pembroke College, Cambridge. Address: c/o London Management, London W1. Starsign: Aries. Hobby: golf. Person he would most like to meet: 'The Pope – he may help us all to survive.'

JEFFRIES, Lionel
Actor/film-director/producer/
screen-writer b 10.6.26
London. After training at
RADA went into weekly rep
for two years at David Garrick
Theatre, Lichfield. Career has
been mainly in films (over 100
feature films since 1950) but
he was also in the first TV play
on ITV on the opening night of
Rediffusion, Facts of Life; part
of A Quick Double with Peter
Sellers. Also starred in TV
series, Room at the Bottom
(circa 1960). Recently has
returned to TV in Cream in My
Coffee; Shillingbury Tales;
Father Charlie; Tom, Dick and
Harriet. Films incl: The Colditz
Story; Windfall; Bhowani
Junction; The Baby and the
Battleship; The High Terrace;
Barnacle Bill; Blue Murder at
St Trinian's; Idle On Parade;
Two-Way Stretch; The Trials
of Oscar Wilde; The Hellions;
The Wrong Arm of the Law;
First Men in the Moon; You
Must Be Joking!; The Spy
with a Cold Nose; Camelot;
Chitty Chitty Bang Bang;
Eyewitness; What Changed
Charley Farthing?; The
Prisoner of Zenda; Ménage à
Trois; wrote and directed the
Railway Children; The
Amazing Mr Blunden;
directed Baxter; The Water
Babies; Wombling Free.
Education: Queen Elizabeth
Grammar School, Wimborne.
m Eileen, 2 d Elizabeth,
Martha, 1 s Timothy.
Address: c/o ICM, London
W1. Starsign: Gemini. Hobby:
looking at the garden ('not
gardening – Eileen does
that'). Person he would most

like to meet: 'A gardener – so
that Eileen doesn't have to do
it.'

JENKINS, Megs
Actress b 21.4.17
Birkenhead, Cheshire.
Started career at Playhouse,
Liverpool, 1933. London
debut, 1937. Plays incl: The
Light of Heart; View From the
Bridge; The Winslow Boy.
Films incl: Green For Danger;
Indiscreet. Radio: plays and
series. TV, many plays and
series, incl: Weaver's Green;
The Newcomers; The
Befrienders; Worzel
Gummidge; Young At Heart.
Education: Claughton
College, Cheshire. Address:
c/o Joseph and Wagg,
London W1. Starsign: Taurus.

JENKINS, Tina
TV journalist b 25.5.58
Chiswick, London. Started as
a trainee reporter with the
Dimbleby Newspaper Group
1977-79. Became a freelance
reporter with Radio Bristol
1979-80 and was a
researcher/reporter with
Nationwide 1981-82 when
she joined BBC Points West
in Bristol as a journalist.
Education: Chiswick

Comprehensive; Chiswick
Polytechnic. Address: c/o
BBC, Bristol. Starsign:
Gemini. Hobbies: walking,
cinema, theatre, bargain
hunting, dancing, swimming.
Thing she would most like to
meet: 'The Loch Ness
monster – with a cameraman!
A world scoop!'

JENSEN, David 'Kid'
Disc jockey b 4th July
Victoria, Canada. Became a
disc jockey at 16 and worked
for radio stations in Canada
before joining Radio
Luxembourg in 1968. After
six years moved to Radio
Trent and in 1975 switched to
the BBC where he has been
ever since. Has his own show
Mon-Thurs on Radio 1 and
formerly presented Quiz Kid.
TV incl: Top of the Pops; Pop
Quest; Pop 45; Nationwide;
Coast to Coast; hosted British
Rock and Pop Awards. In
America 1980-81 presenting
news and hosting a
successful coast-to-coast
chat show, Night People.
Travels thousands of miles a
year to present his live disco
shows. Education: Canada.
m former Icelandic air
hostess Gudrun,
1 d Anna-Lisa, 1 s David.
Address: c/o John Miles
Organisation, Bristol.
Starsign: Cancer. Hobbies:
cooking, most sports,
including football (he is a
QPR supporter). Person he
would most like to meet:
Frank Sinatra.

JEWEL, Jimmy
Actor/comedian b 4.12.12

Sheffield. First appeared on stage in Huddersfield when he was 10; in London when he was 16. Worked as a solo act until teamed up with cousin Ben Warriss 1934 – a partnership that continued until 1966. Radio series Up the Pole 1947 shot them to fame; TV debut 1948 followed by The Jewel and Warriss Show; Sunday Night at the London Palladium; It's a Living. Stage incl: The Sunshine Boys; Comedians; Clown Jewels. TV since 1966: Nearest and Dearest; Thicker Than Water; Spring and Autumn; Funny Man; A Spanner in the Works. Education: left school at 14 to work with father (comedian, same name). First went into scenic studio with father, making scenery, props. Worked in father's sketches and revues as stage manager, feed to father, juvenile lead, acrobat, dancer, etc. m Belle, 1 d Piper (adopted), 1 s Kerry. Address: c/o Jill Foster, London SW3. Starsign: Sagittarius. Hobby: golf.

JOHN, Peter
Actor b 6.4.43 Liverpool. Trained at RADA then National Theatre (1963-64) and rep incl Royal Court, Crewe, Chester, Watford, and Leeds. Has written five pantomimes for Palace Theatre, Watford and writes his own material for his music-hall act. TV incl: Agony; Don't Believe a Word of It; The Brain of Trevor;

Metal Mickey; The Pink Medicine Show; That Beryl Marston . . .! Education: Calday Grange Grammar, Cheshire; Urmston Grammar, Lancs. Address: c/o Evans and Reiss, London SW3. Starsign: Aries. Hobbies: writing, music-hall. Person he would most like to meet: 'Marlene Dietricn – a fascinating lady I should imagine.'

JOICE, Dick
Producer/presenter
b 30.1.21 Great Ryburgh, Norfolk. With a farming background he presented Anglia TV's Farming Diary from 1959 until the following year when he presented About Anglia which he did for four years. He was head of local programmes from 1963 to 1977 and since 1966 has produced and presented Anglia's Bygones programmes. Education: Culford School, Bury St Edmunds. Address: c/o Anglia TV, Norwich. Starsign: Aquarius. Hobby: engineering. Person he would most like to meet: 'The next viewer to come along.'

JONES, Elinor
Presenter/interviewer
b 16.4.46 Llanwrda, Dyfed, South Wales. Trained as an infant-junior teacher and taught for a few years at Heol Llanishan Fach, Cardiff before joining HTV Wales 1971 to present news and some programmes for women. Education: Llandeilo Grammar School; Swansea College of Education. m (dis), 1 d Heledd. Address: c/o HTV Wales, Cardiff. Starsign: Aries. Hobbies: crosswords, fashion, meeting people. Person she would most like to meet: 'Mavis Nicholson – because, to date, I haven't seen her conduct a dull interview.'

JONES, Freddie
Actor b 12.9.27 Stoke-on-Trent. Started as a laboratory assistant but a drama course at Tamworth and a scholarship to the Rose Bruford College of Speech and Drama set him on an acting career. Rep and Royal Shakespeare Company. London stage incl: Marat Sade (and film); Mister. Films incl: Deadfall; The Bliss of

Mrs Blossom; Far from the Madding Crowd; Otley; Goodbye Gemini; The Man Who Haunted Himself; The Elephant Man; Firefox; Krull. TV incl: Sword of Honour; Treasure Island; Cold Comfort Farm; Uncle Vanya; The Caesars; Germinal; Nana; Secret Orchards; Sweeney Todd; The Ghosts of Motley Hall; In Loving Memory; Tiny Revolutions. Named world's best TV actor at Monte Carlo International TV Festival 1969 for his performance in The Caesars. Education: Grammar School, Longton. m actress Jennifer Heslewood, 3 s Toby, Rupert, Casper. Address: c/o Norman Boyack, London W1. Starsign: Virgo. Hobbies: cooking, pottering around dreaming in the garden, watching seeds grow that he has planted, talking to locals in the pub.

JONES, Gemma
Actress b 4.12.42 London. Wanted to be a nurse, but after learning French in France went to RADA where, like her father Griffith Jones before her, she was a gold medallist. After 'resting', a period of rep and TV parts, stage roles incl: There'll Be Some Changes Made; Baal; The Marriage of Figaro; Alfie; Ashes; Getting On; Cabaret (Sheffield); The Homecoming; Henry IV Parts I and II. Films incl: Ken Russell's The Devils. TV incl: The Typewriter; The Spoils of Poynton; The Lie; Forget-Me-Not Lane; The

Duchess of Duke Street; The Merchant of Venice.
1 s Luke. Address: c/o Larry Dalzell Assocs Ltd, London WC2. Starsign: Sagittarius. Person she would most like to meet: Mr Right.

JONES, Griff Rhys
Comedy actor b 16.11.53 Cardiff but brought up in Sussex. Before becoming one of the Not The Nine O'clock News foursome was a BBC radio producer. While studying English at Cambridge University was a member of the Cambridge Footlights Company with thoughts of becoming a director. Stage appearances incl Not in Front of the Audience and films incl: The Secret Policeman's Other Ball. Education: Brentwood Grammar School, Essex. m designer Jo Harris. Address: c/o Talkback Management, London W1. Starsign: Scorpio. Hobbies: sailing, good food. Person he would most like to meet: 'My manager – he owes me four and a half grand!'

JONES, Ken
Actor b 20.2.30 Liverpool. Sign writer and amateur actor

before training at RADA and joining Joan Littlewood's Theatre Workshop in London in The Hostage. Considerable stage and TV work since. TV incl: Z Cars (first episode); Hunter's Walk; Go For Gold; Germinal; Her Majesty's Pleasure; Last of the Baskets; The Wackers; The Squirrels; First Class Friend; Dead Ernest; Seconds Out. Films incl: SWALK; File of the Golden Goose; Sherlock Holmes. Education: secondary modern. m actress/writer Sheila Fay. Address: c/o David White Assocs, London W1. Starsign: Pisces. Person he would most like to have met: 'Harry H Corbett, just to say "Thanks".'

JONES, Lewis
Actor b 21.3.24 Tredegar, Mon. Trained at RADA and toured in rep incl Edinburgh, London and Leatherhead. Left acting for nearly a decade and became a salesman. Made his comeback at National Theatre and a variety of TV work culminating in General Hospital; Bergerac. Also rep at Bromley, Coventry and Crewe. Stage incl: Almost Free; Who Killed Agatha Christie? Education: Hereford Cathedral School. m (1st) actress Mary Thornton (dec), (2nd) actress Paddy Frost, 2 d Elizabeth, Catherine, 1 s Robert (all from 1st m). Address: c/o Gardiner, Skemp, Quick Management, London SW3. Starsign: Aries.

JONES, Maggie
Actress b 21st June London.
After training at RADA played
with rep companies all over
the country. London stage
incl: Kean; Blithe Spirit; Cure
For Love. TV incl: The Forsyte
Saga; Nearest and Dearest;
Sam; Coronation Street;
Lovely Couple; Rosie; A
Sharp Intake of Breath; The
Nesbitts Are Coming; Happy
Endings; In Loving Memory;
The Barchester Chronicles.
m lawyer J O Stansfield.
Address: c/o NEMS
Management Ltd, London
SW3. Starsign: Gemini.
Hobbies: history, decorating.

JONES, Marty
Professional wrestler
b 13.12.53 Oldham. Started
training in Billy Robinson's
gym when he was six years
old and gained experience
as an amateur wrestler until
turning professional when he
was 17. As an amateur won
several schoolboy, northern
and Lancashire titles,
eventually the British
Intermediate Middleweight
amateur title. As a
professional he has
represented Great Britain in
Japan, Germany, Saudi
Arabia, Mexico, Canada and

Korea. Highlight of his career,
so far, is holding the British
Light Heavyweight title. Now
aiming for the world title.
Education: Failsworth
Secondary School.
m Pamela, 1 s Matthew.
Address: c/o Dale Martin
Promotions, London SW9.
Starsign: Sagittarius.
Hobbies: keeping fit, raising
money for charity. Person he
would most like to meet:
'Jimmy Savile (one-time
wrestler) in a contest at the
Royal Albert Hall.'

JONES, Nicholas
Actor b 3.4.46 London.
Trained at RADA and Bristol
Old Vic Theatre School.
Appeared with the Old Vic
and at the National Theatre.
Films incl: Cromwell; Daisy
Miller; The Block House. TV
incl: Our Mutual Friend;
Hamlet; Anna Karenina;
Kilvert's Diary; Husband to
Mrs Fitzherbert; Lillie;
Candide; Twelfth Night;
Wings; Cover; Flame Trees of
Thika. Education:
Westminster School.
1 d India. Address c/o
Hutton Management, London
SW5. Starsign: Aries.

JONES, Peter
Actor/author b 12.6.20
Wem, Salop. Rep experience
and many plays and revues in
London's West End incl Pass
The Butler, and films. Radio
incl: In All Directions; Just a
Minute; Hitch-hiker's Guide to
the Galaxy. TV incl:
Oneupmanship; Mr Big; Mr
Digby Darling; The Rag
Trade; M'lords, Ladies and

Gentlemen (chairman);
Cabbages and Kings;
Blankety Blank; Celebrity
Squares; Give Us a Clue;
Whoops Apocalypse.
Education: Wem Grammar
School; Ellesmere College.
m American actress Jeri
Sauvinet, 1 d Selena
Carey-Jones, 2 s Charlie,
Willie. Address: c/o Spotlight,
London WC2. Starsign:
Gemini. Hobbies: drawing,
cooking, reading, making
plans. Person he would most
like to meet: 'It would be
interesting to meet anyone
from the next world.'

JONES, Richard Morris
Director/journalist b 8.3.43
Newcastle-upon-Tyne.
Trained as a teacher but in
1963 became a freelance
researcher for TWW.
Progressed, via studio
management, to reporter and
in 1968 was appointed HTV's
staff reporter in North Wales.
Joined the BBC in 1973 as
regional journalist based in
Bangor, mainly to contribute
to Welsh language
programmes. Went freelance
May 1982 to make
documentaries for Channel
Four. Education: Talysarn
Primary School, Caernarvon;

Ysgol Dyffryn Nantlle, Penygroes; Glamorgan College of Education, Barry. m Manon, 1 d Lilo, 1 s Owain. Address: c/o Channel Four, Caernarvon. Starsign: Pisces. Hobbies: watching/playing/talking soccer, reading Welsh poetry. Person he would most like to have met: 'Owain Glyndwr – in order to hear at first hand about his successful campaigns against the English.'

JONES, Ron

Sports reporter/commentator b 29.11.42 Bedlinog, Wales. Trained as a teacher of physical education and began broadcasting with the Jamaican Broadcasting Corp in 1969 as cricket and football commentator. Joined BBC in similar capacity 1979. Commentator Welsh Professional Snooker Championship 1982. Is fully qualified soccer, cricket and athletics coach. Education: Lewis School, Pengam; Physical Education Dept, Cardiff College of Education; University of Wales, Aberystwyth. m Wendy Ann, 1 d Samantha, 2 s Timothy, Dean (twins). Address: c/o BBC TV, Cardiff. Starsign: Sagittarius. Hobbies: squash, music, reading. Person he would most like to meet: Frank Sinatra.

JONES, Sally

TV reporter b 3.1.55 Coventry, Warwicks. Trained under the BBC Journalist Training Scheme before

joining Westward TV in 1979 as reporter on Westward Diary. Scripted Cornish series Beyond The Tamar. Joined HTV Wales 1981 as first woman reporter on nightly news programme, Report Wales. Books: Legends of Devon; Legends of Cornwall (a best-seller). Education: Coleshill Grammar School; King Edward VI High School for Girls, Edgbaston; St Hugh's College, Oxford (MA English). Address: c/o HTV Wales, Cardiff. Starsign: Capricorn. Hobbies: writing, squash, tennis, horse-riding. Person she would most like to meet: 'George Melly – he has the most suggestive leer I ever saw.'

JONES, Simon

Actor b 27.7.50 Charlton Park, Wilts. Rep experience at Bradford, Crewe and Derby before appearing in Bloomsbury in London's West End in 1974. Since then his theatre credits incl: Seven Days to Doomsday; The Carnation Gang; The Clandestine Marriage; The Browning Version; Wild Oats; Privates on Parade (both for

Royal Shakespeare Company); Candida; The Millionairess; Design For Living. His films incl: Savage Messiah; The Romantic Englishman; Sir Henry at Rawlinson End; Reds; Gyro City. On TV he is probably best known for his appearances as Brideshead in Brideshead Revisited and as Arthur Dent in The Hitch-hikers' Guide to the Galaxy (which he also played on radio). Other TV incl: Rock Follies; Victorian Scandals; Fothergill; The Kindness of Mrs Radcliffe; No Visible Scar; Muck and Brass. Education: King's, Taunton; Trinity Hall, Cambridge (MA Hons Cantab). Address: c/o Kate Feast Management, London NW1. Starsign: Leo. Hobbies: novels of the 30s, contemporary sugar lump wrappings, archaeology, 19th-century watercolours, comics of the 50s, pipes. Person he would most like to meet: 'Orson Welles – to talk about the films he hasn't made and why.'

JONES, Steve

TV/radio presenter b 7.6.45 Crewe, Cheshire. Musician, teacher, ice-cream salesman before becoming a radio DJ in 1972. DJ on Radio Clyde 1973-78. Since 1979 LBC and currently regular Radio 2 presenter. Voted Scottish Radio Personality of the Year 1977. TV incl: Battle of the Comics; The Jones Boy; It's Friday; I'm Steve Jones; Sneak Preview; Steve Jones Illustrated; Watch This

Space; Edinburgh Festival Show; Bruce's Big Night; Saturday Morning Show; Steve Jones Game Show; Search For a Star; The Pyramid Game. Education: Crewe Grammar; College of St Mark and St John, Chelsea. m Lolita, 3 s Marc, Jason, Oliver. Address: c/o MAM, London W1. Starsign: Gemini. Hobbies: golf, swimming, tennis, current affairs. Person he would most like to have met: 'John Lennon – a big musical influence on me. In a way, leader of my generation.'

crosswords, reading, quizzes, Scrabble, plotting to overthrow Willy Rushton. Person he would most like to meet: 'Alan Alda – a superb actor, a brilliant comedian and he might give me a part in M*A*S*H.'

JUNKIN, John
Actor/writer b 29.1.30 Ealing, Middx. Started as a schoolmaster, but turned to script-writing after various jobs, incl liftman and labourer. Joined Joan Littlewood's Theatre Workshop in 1960. Stage incl: Sparrers Can't Sing; Maggie May; The Four Musketeers. Films incl: Hard Day's Night; Kaleidoscope; The Brass Target. Radio incl: five series of Hello Cheeky. Has written, co-written and appeared in hundreds of TV shows incl: Junkin (four series); Looking For Clancy; Out; Dick Turpin; Penmarric; Blankety Blank; The Professionals; Play of the Week (Dancing Country); Coronation Street. Has also written many songs with Denis King. Education: council and grammar schools. m Jennie, 1 d Annabel. Address: c/o Richard Stone, London WC2. Starsign: Aquarius. Hobbies:

K

KEE, Robert
Journalist/presenter
b 5.10.19 Calcutta, India.
Started as journalist on
Picture Post, 1948-51; was
Observer correspondent on
Suez Crisis; contributor to
Sunday Times. Bomber pilot
during the war; three years
prisoner of war. Entered TV
as a reporter for Panorama
1958-62; Television
Reporters International
1963-64, and made
Rebellion; This Year in
Jerusalem, etc; This Week
1964-70; Looking For an
Answer 1967; Robert Kee
Reports 1968; Kee Interview
1971. First presenter of ITN's
one o'clock news, First
Report 1972-76; General
Election and Referendum
programmes 1974; General
Strike Report; documentaries
– France; East Germany;
Jubilee; Spain 1976-77;
Faces of Communism
1977-78; BBC 1979; Ireland:
a TV History, 1981. Books
incl: A Crowd is Not
Company; The Impossible
Shore: A Sign of the Times;
Broadstrop in Season;
Refugee World; The Green
Flag; A History of Irish
Nationalism; Ireland: A
History. Education: Stowe;
Magdalen College, Oxford
(History Exhibition). m (1st)
Janetta (dis), (2nd) Cynthia,
2 d Georgiana, Sarah,
2 s Alexander, Benjamin
(dec). Address: Kew Green,
Surrey. Starsign: Libra.
Hobbies: Irish history,
swimming, cycling, listening
to music, writing.

KEEL, Howard
Actor b 13.4.17 Gillespie,
Illinois. Was once an aircraft
sales rep. Began his acting
career after winning a singing
scholarship and has since
appeared on stage and
screen in most of the big
singing roles in musicals, his
first being Billy Bigelow in
Carousel in 1945. This was
followed by the part of Curly
in Oklahoma!, in which he
made his London debut at
Drury Lane in 1947 when he
was unknown. Other theatre
incl: No Strings; Camelot;
South Pacific; On a Clear Day
You Can See Forever; Plaza
Suite; Ambassador (in
London); Man of La Mancha; I
Do, I Do; Salute to Broadway;
Kismet; Mr Roberts; Sunrise
at Campobello; Kiss Me,
Kate; The Rainmaker. Has
also appeared in variety with
Kathryn Grayson and at
London Palladium. His first
film was The Small Voice,
made in England in 1948.
Films also incl: Annie Get
Your Gun; Pagan Love Song;
Three Guys Named Mike;
Showboat; Texas Carnival;
Lovely to Look At; Kiss
Me,Kate: Calamity Jane;
Rose Marie; Seven Brides for
Seven Brothers; Deep in My
Heart; Kismet; Floods of Fear;
Big Fisherman; Armoured
Command; The Day of the
Triffids. TV incl: Tomorrow
and, more recently, Dallas, in
which he plays Clayton.
Education: Fallbrook High
School, California. Address:
c/o Actors Equity Assoc, New
York. Starsign: Aries.

KAY, Charles
Actor b 31.8.30 Coventry.
Trained at RADA and has
been a member of the Royal
Shakespeare Company and
with the National Theatre at
the Old Vic. Since 1972 has
made many TV appearances
incl: The Duchess of Malfi;
The Merchant of Venice;
Microbe Hunters; Fall of
Eagles; Loyalties; I Claudius;
Target; The Devil's Crown;
Lady Killers; To Serve Them
All My Days; Bergerac. Films
incl: Hennessey; Nijinsky.
Education: Warwick School;
Birmingham University.
Address: c/o Larry Dalzell
Assocs Ltd, London WC2.
Starsign: Virgo. Hobbies:
reading, listening to music,
bridge. Person he would
most like to have met: 'William
Shakespeare – for a hundred
reasons.'

KEEN, Diane
Actress b 29.7.46 London.
Brought up in Kenya, didn't
settle in England until she
was 19. Unknown until
chosen for The Cuckoo
Waltz. Other TV incl:
Crossroads; Fall of Eagles;
Softly, Softly; Public Eye; The
Legend of Robin Hood; The
Sweeney; The Feathered
Serpent; Country Matters;
Crown Court; The
Sandbaggers; Rings On
Their Fingers; The
Shillingbury Blowers; The
Shillingbury Tales; The
Reunion; The Morecambe
and Wise Show; Bruce Meets
The Girls. Education: several
schools in Kenya and
privately tutored. m (dis),
1 d Melissa. Address: c/o
Barry Burnett, London W1.
Starsign: Leo. Hobbies:
Egyptology, antiques.
Person she would most like to
meet: 'Mother Teresa,
because of my admiration for
someone who has sacrificed
their life in order to dedicate
themself entirely to relieving
the suffering of fellow human
beings.'

KEEN, Geoffrey
Actor b 21.8.18 London.
Joined Bristol Old Vic Theatre
School when 15. Left to work
in a paint factory, then won a
scholarship to RADA and has
scarcely stopped working
since. In the army during the
war, then Stars in Battledress.
Numerous plays (Alice's
Boys), films (more than 100
incl: The Angry Silence;
Cromwell; Dr Zhivago; Born
Free; Living Free; Moonraker;

The Rise and Fall of Idi Amin;
For Your Eyes Only) and TV.
Best known for The Trouble-
shooters. Other TV incl: The
Venturers; Justice; Mr Rolls
and Mr Royce; The Atom
Spies; Purple Twilight;
Churchill and the Generals;
Crown Court; The Lady
Killers; Cribb; Strangers.
m (1st) actress Hazel Terry,
(2nd) actress Doris Groves,
1 d Mary (from 2nd m).
Address: c/o London
Management, London W1.
Starsign: Leo. Hobby:
gardening.

KEITH, Penelope
b 2nd April Sutton, Surrey.
Trained at Webber Douglas
Academy of Dramatic Art,
then rep at Chesterfield,
Lincoln and Manchester.
After a time with the Royal
Shakespeare Company
('carrying a spear', she says),
she returned to rep in
Cheltenham. Stage incl:
Plaza Suite; How the Other
Half Loves; Fallen Angels;
The Norman Conquests (and
TV); Donkeys Years (and TV);
The Apple Cart; The
Millionairess; Moving;
Hobson's Choice; Captain
Brassbound's Conversion.

Most recent films: The Hound
of the Baskervilles; The Priest
of Love. Early TV was in Six
Shades of Black. Other TV
incl: Kate; The Pallisers;
Two's Company; Jackanory;
Saving It For Albie; Private
Lives; The Good Life;
Morecambe and Wise
Christmas Show 1977; To the
Manor Born; On Approval.
Awards incl: Variety Club
Show Business Personality of
the Year, Society of West End
Managers Award for Best
Comedy Performance
(Donkey's Years), BAFTA
Award for Best Light
Entertainment Performance
(The Good Life), all in 1977;
BAFTA Award for Best TV
Actress (Saving It For Albie
and The Norman Conquests)
and Radio Industries Club
Celebrity Award as BBC TV
Personality of the Year, both
in 1978 and 1979; TVTimes
Top Ten Award 1976, 1977,
1978, 1979, 1980; Variety
Club Award for BBC TV
Personality 1979. Education:
private school. m Rodney
Timson. Address: c/o Howes
and Prior Ltd, London W1.
Starsign: Aries. Person she
would most like to have met:
Noël Coward.

KEITH, Sheila
Actress b 9.6.20. A Scot.
Trained for the stage at
Webber Douglas Academy of
Dramatic Art. Stage work incl:
Present Laughter; Mame
(with Ginger Rogers);
Banana Ridge; Deathtrap;
appearances at Liverpool
Rep, Coventry, Bristol Old Vic
and Leatherhead. Films incl:

Ooh You Are Awful; House of Whipcord; Frightmare; The Comeback. TV incl: David Copperfield; Ballet Shoes; Within These Walls; Angels; The Cedar Tree; Jubilee; Roof Over My Head; Working Arrangements; Heartland; Racing Game; Rings on Their Fingers; Swing, Swing Together; Agony; Bless Me Father. Education: Aberdeen High School. Address: c/o NEMS Management Ltd, London SW3. Starsign: Gemini. Hobbies: browsing in book shops, nature study, antique furniture. Person she would most like to meet: 'Yehudi Menuhin – his autograph started my childhood collection. It would be fun to collect another now'.

KELLY, Chris
Producer/writer/presenter b 24.4.40 Cuddington, Cheshire. Taught French and Spanish for nearly two years before joining Anglia TV as announcer and newsreader in 1963. Other TV incl: quiz-master of Sixth Form Challenge; Zoo Time; Anything You Can Do; Clapperboard; Wish You Were Here; Friday Live; World in Action; The Royal Film Performance; Folio; Fit For Living. Education: Downside School; Clare College, Cambridge, where he was drama critic of Varsity, the university newspaper. m Vivien, 1 d Rebecca, 1 s Nicholas. Address c/o Granada TV, London W1. Starsign: Taurus. Hobbies:

collecting, cooking, sport. Person he would most like to have met: 'Samuel Johnson, because he was funny, brilliant and brave.'

KELLY, David
Actor b 11.7.29 Dublin. Wide theatre experience incl Abbey Theatre, Dublin, but better known on TV as one-armed washer-up in Robin's Nest. Also TV plays and series incl: Cowboys; The Gentle Touch; Strumpet City; Whoops Apocalypse. Education: Christian Brothers School, Dublin; National College of Art, Dublin. m actress Laurie, 1 d Miriam, 1 s David. Address: c/o Joy Jameson Ltd, London SW1. Starsign: Cancer. Hobby: painting. Person he would most like to have met: 'Graham Sutherland, the artist – he might have helped me improve my painting.'

KELLY, Gerry
TV journalist b 20.9.48 Ballymena, Co Antrim, Northern Ireland. Originally an English teacher and journalist. Started with Ulster TV 1975 as a reporter on local

sports programme. Joined evening magazine programme Good Evening Ulster in 1978. Editor of a summer programme Family Matters. Education: Manchester University (BA Education). m Helena, 2 d Sarah, Claire. Address: c/o Ulster TV, Belfast. Starsign: Virgo. Hobbies: golf, other less active sports, music. Person he would most like to meet: 'Jack Nicklaus – to find out how to back spin on a two iron.'

KELLY, Henry
Reporter/presenter b 17.4.46 Dublin. Trained in daily journalism on the Irish Times, where he worked for eight years, travelling over most of the world as a reporter. Joined Radio 4 in 1976, and has since done much radio work, incl: The World Tonight; Profile; Woman's Hour; Midweek. Has co-presented Game For a Laugh since the programme began in 1981. Book: How Stormont Fell ('a political Mickey Spillane'). Education: Belvedere College; University College, Dublin (BA Hons English Language and Literature). m Marjorie, 1 d Siobhan. Address: c/o LWT, London SE1. Starsign: Aries. Hobbies: golf, reading. Person he would most like to meet: 'God – we've a lot to discuss.'

KELLY, Matthew
Actor b 9.5.50 Urmston,

Manchester. Learned his craft in variety theatres, spending 10 years in variety, rep and London's West End stage. Five years in TV incl: The Bonus; Play for Today; Pickesgill People; The Critic; Ned Sherrin Show; Room Service; Holding the Fort (three series); Game for a Laugh; Madabout. Education: Urmston Grammar. m Sarah, 1 d Ruth, 1 s Matthew. Address: c/o Regan Assocs, London NW3. Starsign: Taurus. Hobbies: travelling, swimming, dancing, talking, laughing. Person he would most like to have met: 'Mae West, because she had the right idea!'

KEMPSON, Rachel
Actress b 28.5.10 Dartmouth, Devon. Trained for the stage at RADA and made her first stage appearance at Stratford-upon-Avon 1933. Appeared in rep at Oxford, Liverpool and with the Royal Shakespeare Company, the English Stage Company and the National Theatre Company at the Old Vic. Many distinguished roles, her most recent incl: A Family and a Fortune; The Old Country. Films incl: The Captive Heart; Georgy Girl; The Jokers; Tom Jones; Charge of the Light Brigade; The Virgin Soldiers; Jane Eyre; The Jewel in the Crown. TV incl: Jane; Jennie; Elizabeth R; Love For Lydia; Winter Ladies; Sweet Wine of Youth; Kate the Good Neighbour; Bosom Friends; The Bell. Education: St Agnes School, East Grinstead; Oaklea, Buckhurst Hill. m actor Sir Michael Redgrave CBE, 2 d actresses Vanessa and Lynn, 1 s actor Corin. Address: c/o Hutton Management, London SW5. Starsign: Gemini. Hobby: gardening.

KENDAL, Felicity
Actress b 25.9.46 Birmingham. Taken to India when three months old by her parents who were travelling actors. Grew up learning her art as a strolling player, eventually playing leading roles. Returned to Birmingham to live with an aunt. Her break came with a TV play with John Gielgud, The Mayfly and the Frog. Stage work incl: Regent's Park Open Air Theatre; Kean; The Norman Conquests; Clouds; Amadeus; On The Razzle; The Second Mrs Tanqueray (both for the National Theatre). TV incl: Crime of Passion; The Woodlanders; The Dolly Dialogues; Love Story; Edward the Seventh; The Good Life; Solo. Films incl: Shakespeare Wallah (about her parents' life in India); Valentino. Education: various convents while on tour.1 s Charley. Address: c/o Chatto and Linnit, London W1. Starsign: Libra.

KENDALL, Kenneth
Former BBC TV newsreader b 7.8.24 South India but brought up in Cornwall. Former schoolmaster and wartime Captain in the Coldstream Guards. Joined BBC in 1948, was a newsreader 1955-61 when he left to freelance, but returned to BBC in 1969. Voted best dressed newsreader by Style International and No 1 newscaster by Daily Mirror readers 1979. Retired from the BBC 1981 and now presents The South West Week, TSW's round-up of the week's news for the deaf and hard of hearing. Other TV incl: Songs of Praise; Doctor Who; Adam Adamant. Education: Felsted School, Essex; Oxford University (MA). Address: c/o Lewis Joelle, London SW1. Starsign: Leo. Hobbies: racing, theatre, gardening, dogs.

KENNA, Jenny
Presenter b 13.8.44 Farnham, Surrey. Started writing and illustrating children's books 1978 and her hobby led to two appearances on The Generation Game as a demonstrator. Has since

found a new style in her work which gives greater attention to country awareness and has led her to devise and develop the Windfalls series for TV. Has also appeared on the Rudi Carrol Show on German TV. Education: Fern Hill Secondary School. m Brian Lidstone. Address: c/o Windfall Marketing Ltd, London W1. Starsign: Leo. Hobbies: nature study, gardening, illustrating, cookery. Person she would most like to meet: 'David Bellamy: he shares my enthusiasm and dedication to wildlife.'

KENNEDY, Cheryl
Actress b 29.4.47 Enfield, Middx. Trained for the stage at the Corona Stage School. Has since appeared in Half A Sixpence (with Tommy Steele); The Boyfriend; 1776; Time and Time Again (with Tom Courtenay); Absent Friends (with Richard Briers); Flowers for Algernon (with Michael Crawford); My Fair Lady (in America with Rex Harrison); Time and the Conways (at the Old Vic); three plays at Oxford Playhouse. TV incl: Cliff

Richard and Mike Yarwood shows; That's Life; Omnibus; Play for Today; Play of the Month; Give Us a Clue; Celebrity Squares; The Sweeney; Target; The Professionals. Education: Holy Family Convent College, Enfield. m (dis), 1 d Samantha. Address: c/o Larry Dalzell, London WC2. Starsign: Taurus. Hobbies: stamp collecting, tennis, swimming. Person she would most like to meet: 'Singer James Taylor – for the lyrics of his songs.'

KENNEDY, Ludovic
Writer/broadcaster
b 3.11.19 Edinburgh. War service in Royal Navy (Midshipman to Lieutenant RNVR) 1939-46. Started writing as freelance journalist. Widely experienced TV broadcaster. Introduced Profile 1955-56; ITN newscaster 1956-58; introduced This Week 1958-60; commentator Panorama 1960-63; producer/reporter Television Reporters International 1963-64. Other TV incl: Time Out; World at One; The Middle Years; The Nature of Prejudice; Face the Press; 24 Hours; Ad Lib; Midweek; Newsday; Tonight; Did You See . . .?; obituary of Lord Mountbatten; Great Railway Journeys of the World. Films incl: The Singers and the Songs; Scapa Flow; The Sleeping Ballerina; Battleship Bismarck; Life and Death of the Scharnhorst; U-Boat War; The Rise of the

Red Navy; Lord Haw-Law. Books incl: Sub-Lieutenant; Nelson's Band of Brothers; One Man's Meat; Murder Story; Ten Rillington Place; The Trial of Stephen Ward; Pursuit; The Chase and Sinking of the Bismarck; A Presumption of Innocence; The Amazing Case of Patrick Meehan; The Portland Spy Case; The British at War (general editor); Menace; The Life and Death of the Tirpitz; Wicked Beyond Belief. Education: Eton; Christ Church, Oxford (MA). m former ballerina Moira Shearer, 3 d Ailsa, Rachel, Fiona, 1 s Alastair. Address: c/o AD Peters, London WC2. Starsign: Scorpio.

KENNEDY, Sarah
Reporter/presenter b 8.7.50 East Grinstead, Surrey. Worked in radio in Singapore and Germany before joining BBC Radio in London and still presents String Sound programme on Radio 2 and takes part in Start the Week With Richard Baker on Radio 4. Joined Southern TV 1978 and London Weekend TV 1981. TV incl: Royale Progress; Chipperfield Safari; Game For a Laugh. Education: Notre Dame Convent, Lingfield. Address: c/o PVA Management Ltd, London W1. Starsign: Cancer. Hobbies: squash, walking, theatre, cooking. Person she would most like to meet: 'Alan Boyd who produces Game For a Laugh.'

KERMAN, Jill
Actress b 4.7.46 Mill Hill,
London. Trained at RADA
then rep in Coventry before a
long run in Spring and Port
Wine in London's West End,
in which she played John
Alderton's sister. Later, on
TV, she was to play his
fiancee in Please, Sir! Other
TV incl: Bangelstein's Boys;
Judge Dee; Thicker Than
Water; Crown Court;
Strangers; Now and Then;
The Other One; Coronation
Street. Education: Copthall
School, London. m heating
engineer Nicholas Dance,
1 d Kira. Address: c/o
Essanay Ltd, London W14.
Starsign: Cancer. Hobbies:
sailing, drawing. Person she
would most like to meet: Clare
Francis.

KERSHAW, Richard
Presenter b 16.4.34 London.
Presenter BBC TV's
Newsweek. Previously with
Newsday and Nationwide
and 10 years as member of
Panorama reporting team.
Other TV incl: Platform One;
Tonight; 24 Hours; This
Week. Education: University
of Virginia Graduate School;
Cambridge University (BA

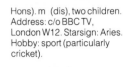

Hons). m (dis), two children.
Address: c/o BBC TV,
London W12. Starsign: Aries.
Hobby: sport (particularly
cricket).

KILBY, Alan
Professional wrestler
b 21.12.43 Sheffield. Deaf
and dumb. British heavy
middleweight champion,
1981 and winner of 25 years
Anniversary Cup title.
Education: Maud Maxfield
School for the Deaf. 2 d
Tracey, Stella, 1 s Adam.
Address: c/o Dale Martin
Promotions, London SW9.
Starsign: Sagittarius/
Capricorn. Hobbies:
weight-lifting, keep-fit.
Person he would most like to
meet: Jimmy Savile.

KINNEAR, Roy
Actor b 8.1.34 Wigan.
Trained for the theatre at
RADA. After rep at
Nottingham, Glasgow,
Edinburgh and Perth joined
Joan Littlewood's Theatre
Workshop in London.
Subsequently in Palladium
pantomime and with Royal
Shakespeare Company. First
came to the fore through That
Was The Week That Was.

Followed by A World of His
Own; A Slight Case Of . . .;
Inside George Webley; and
appearances in many plays
and series. Many films incl:
Juggernaut; The Last
Remake of Beau Geste;
Hammett. Education:
Heriots, Edinburgh; National
Service, which he claims is
the University of Life.
m actress Carmel Cryan,
2 d Kirsty, Karina, 1 s Rory.
Address: c/o Richard Stone,
London WC2. Starsign:
Capricorn. Hobby:
answering questionnaires
sent by Who's Who On
Television. Person he would
most like to meet: 'Alastair
Cooke – the greatest
broadcaster.'

KIRKBRIDE, Anne
Actress b 21.6.54 Oldham,
Lancs. Trained at Oldham
Rep. TV: Another Sunday;
Sweet F A; Deirdre in
Coronation Street since 1972.
Education: Counthill
Grammar School, Oldham.
Address: c/o Granada TV,
Manchester. Starsign:
Cancer. Hobbies:
embroidery, photography.
Person she would most like to
meet: 'Someone who's been
to the Moon. I don't want to go
just yet, but I'd like to meet
someone who has.

KITCHEN, Michael
Actor b 31.10.48 Leicester.
Worked with the National
Youth Theatre while still at
school and spent a year at the
Belgrade Theatre, Coventry
as assistant stage manager

before going to RADA. Subsequently worked at London's Royal Court Theatre, at Greenwich, the Young Vic and the National Theatre where his plays have incl: On the Razzle; The Provok'd Wife; No Man's Land; State of the Revolution; Bedroom Farce; Spring Awakening; Romeo and Juliet. Other plays incl: Othello; Macbeth; Charley's Aunt; The Picture of Dorian Gray; Big Wolf; Magnificence. Films incl: Unman Wittering and Zigo; Dracula Today; Breaking Glass; The Bunker. Much experience in TV incl: King Lear; The Brontës of Howarth; The Reporters; Country Matters; The Monkey's Paw; Savages; Young Stephen Hind; Churchill's People; Fall of Eagles; Brimstone and Treacle; No Man's Land; Bedroom Farce; The Misanthrope; The Long and the Short and the Tall; School Play; Caught on a Train; A Room for the Winter; Maybury; Lady Killers; The Best of Everything. Education: City of Leicester Boys Grammar. Address: c/o Plant and Froggatt Ltd, London W1. Starsign: Scorpio. Hobbies: music, photography, sport.

KLUGMAN, Jack

Actor b 27.4.22 Philadelphia. After war service made a living as a house painter and post office employee before studying

dramatics with American Theatre Wing in New York. First breaks with Kim Stanley in St Joan and Rod Steiger in Stevedore. Spent 10 years in summer stock companies before a part in Mr Roberts in New York and opposite Ethel Merman in Gypsy, after which he moved to Hollywood. Also appeared in The Odd Couple both in America and London and on TV which earned him two Emmys. Now has more than 400 TV credits to his name incl: The Defenders; The Virginian; The Fugitive; Harris Against the World. Since 1976 has played the unorthodox pathologist in Quincey. m actress Brett Somers, 2 s. Starsign: Taurus.

KNUTT, Bobby

Actor b 25.11.45 Sheffield. Started in show business as a one-time member of The Whirlwinds group and in working men's clubs. On TV has had his own chat show on Yorkshire TV and a keep-fit series, Inta Shape. Other TV incl: Print Out; Price of Coal; Coronation Street; Paul Squire series; Marti Caine series; Blankety Blank. Address: c/o Johnnie Peller

Enterprises Ltd, Sheffield. Starsign: Sagittarius. Hobby: body-building. Person he would most like to meet: Raquel Welch.

THE KRANKIES

Husband and wife comedy team that began when they met during a Christmas show in Glasgow in the mid-1960s. He was a backstage electrician and she was in a junior chorus line. By the time the show ended they had worked out a routine and they have been working together ever since, playing the northern clubs and for four years they were at the Pavilion Theatre, Glasgow. For two years they were the stars of Crackerjack and were the Club Comedy Act of the Year 1977-78. They were in the Royal Variety Show at the London Palladium 1978, in the Royal Show, Jersey, the following year, and in 1981 were in the first Children's Royal Variety Show at the London Palladium and in the same year at the Royal Show at Windsor. Real names are Ian and Janet Tough.
Ian Tough b 26.3.47 Glasgow. Education:

Braidfield Junior Secondary, Clydebank. Address: c/o International Artistes, London WC1. Starsign: Aries. Hobbies: golf, fishing. Person he would most like to meet: 'Eamonn Andrews, on a Wednesday night.'

Janet Tough b 16.5.47 Queenzieburn, Stirlingshire. Education: Kilfyth Academy. Starsign: Taurus. Hobbies: golf, swimming in the sea, American Express. Person she would most like to meet: 'The careers officer who strongly advised me against show business.'

KWOUK, Burt
Actor b 18.7.30 Manchester. Grew up in Shanghai, went to America and returned to England 1953. Has been here ever since establishing himself, after a variety of jobs, as TV's best-known oriental face. First acting break came in a Charlie Drake Show and in the Ingrid Bergman film The Inn of the Sixth Happiness. Also known as Peter Sellers' karate-mad houseboy in the Pink Panther films. Films incl: A Shot in the Dark; Madam Sin; Deep End; The Most Dangerous Man in the World; The Shoes of the Fisherman; Nobody Runs Forever; Goldfinger; You Only Live Twice; The Return of the Pink Panther; Rollerball; This Time With Feeling; The Pink Panther Strikes Again; The Last Remake of Beau Geste; The Revenge of the Pink Panther; The Strange Case of the End of Civilisation As We Know It;

The Fiendish Plot of Dr Fu Manchu; The Trail of the Pink Panther. Has been in all the top TV series incl: Tomorrow's People; It Ain't Half Hot Mum; The Return of the Saint; Robin's Nest; Les Dawson Show; Keep It In the Family; Speak for Yourself; Minder; Spearhead; Shoestring; Tenko. Education: school in Shanghai; read Law and Economics at Maine University (BA degree). Address: c/o London Management, London W1. Starsign: Cancer. Person he would most like to meet: 'My next employer – for obvious reasons.'

L

LACEY, Ronald
Actor/drama teacher/director
b 28.9.35 Harrow, Middx.
After National Service went to
drama school. Acting debut
in TV play The Secret Agent.
Then rep. Stage incl: St Joan.
Other TV incl: Harsh World;
Search Party; Pigs Ear With
Flowers; My Flesh, My Blood;
Blackmail; Hands With a
Magic Touch; The
Adventures of Don Quixote;
Dylan; Colditz; Churchill's
People; Porridge; Mayor of
Casterbridge; Tropic; Tiny
Revolutions; Aubrey
Beardsley; Day of the Janitor;
Lady Killers; Rothko. Films
incl: How I Won The War; The
Likely Lads; Charleston;
Nijinsky; Betrayal; Raiders of
the Lost Ark; Firefox; Zulu
Dawn. Education: Harrow
Weald Grammar School.
m (1st) Mela (dis), (2nd)
Joann, 1 d Rebecca,
2 s David (both from 1st m),
Matthew (from 2nd m).
Address: c/o Joyce Edwards
Representation, London SE1.
Starsign: Libra. Hobby:
collecting Victoriana. Person
he would most like to meet:
'Anyone who has achieved
anything worthwhile, or tried
to achieve anything.'

LAINE, Cleo OBE
Singer/actress b 28.10.27
Southall, Middx. Started as
hairdresser's apprentice,
then librarian, salesgirl, and
pawnbroker's valuer, before
being introduced to John
Dankworth after singing at
Southall British Legion Hall in
1951. Signed up to sing with
the Dankworth band. Has
appeared solo in cabaret,
jazz and other festivals in
Britain and abroad and sung
with London Philharmonic,
Royal Philharmonic, Halle,
Scottish National Orchestras.
Stage incl: Flesh to a Tiger;
Under the Sun; The Trojan
Women; A Midsummer
Night's Dream; her own
one-woman show, Talk of the
Town; Showboat; Colette.
Many TV appearances incl:
Cleo and John; Parkinson.
She and John Dankworth
were awarded Honorary
Music Degrees from Berkeley
College of Music, Boston,
Massachussetts 1982.
Education: state schools.
m (1st) George (dis), (2nd)
John Dankworth,
1 d Jacqueline (from 1st m),
2 s Stuart (from 1st m), Alex
(from 2nd m). Address: c/o
International Artistes, London
W1. Starsign: Scorpio.
Hobby: cooking.

LANDEN, Dinsdale
Actor b 4.9.32 Margate,
Kent. Spent a time at the
Florence Moore Drama
School before National
Service in the RAF and while
in the RAF formed a drama
group. Joined Worthing Rep
when he returned to civilian
life. Stage incl: The
Housemaster; Play on Love;
The Philanthropist;
Alphabetical Order; Plunder;
The Merchant of Venice;
Bodies; On The Razzle;
Uncle Vanya. Films incl: The
Valiant; We Joined the Navy;
Mosquito Squadron; Every
Home Should Have One.
Radio incl: The Family Film;
The Joke About Hilary Spite.
TV incl: Great Expectations;
Canterbury Tales; The Mask
of Janus; The Spies; Mickey
Dunne; London Assurance;
Devenish; Fathers and
Families; Glittering Prizes;
Pig in the Middle. Education:
King's School, Rochester.
m actress Jennifer Daniel.
Address: c/o Leading Artists,
London W1. Starsign: Virgo.
Hobbies: golf, walking.

LANDER, Jon
Journalist/broadcaster
b 18.2.29 London. Started
as a copy boy at the Press
Association. Worked on
newspapers until 1963 when
he joined ITN where, in turn
he was scriptwriter,
programme editor, political
correspondent, European
political correspondent and
occasional newscaster. Left

in 1979 to return to journalism. Returned to TV in 1981 to present ATV/Central TV's political programme, Left, Right and Centre. Education: George Dixon's, Birmingham; Tiffin's, Kingston-upon-Thames. m Helen, 2 d Jane, Ruth, 1 s Richard. Address c/o Central TV, Birmingham. Starsign: Aquarius. Hobbies: reading, walking, bird-watching, gardening. Person he would most like to meet: 'Helmut Schmidt – a very impressive man with enormous discipline and strength.'

LANDON, Michael
Actor b 31.10.36 Forest Hills, New York. Trained at Warner Bros acting school after career as athlete cut short by an arm injury. First big part in I Was a Teenage Werewolf; other roles in films and TV series. Part in Western series, Restless Gun, got him the part of Little Joe in Bonanza and later his own show, Little House on the Prairie. Education: University of Southern California. m (1st) Dodie, (2nd) actress Lynn Noe, 3 d Shawna Leigh, Cheryl, Leslie Ann (step-ds), (from 2nd m), 3 s Mark, Josh (from 1st m), Michael (from 2nd m). Address: Beverly Hills, California. Starsign: Scorpio. Hobbies: golf, swimming.

LANG, Robert
Actor/director b 24.9.34 Bristol. Former weatherman, joined Bristol Old Vic Theatre

School after the war then moved to the Old Vic in London. Much experience in theatre and TV. Among the many plays in which he has appeared, his favourites incl: The Cherry on the Top; Uncle Vanya; Last Day in Dreamland; Rivals of Sherlock Holmes; Flea in her Ear; Mistress Mouse Are You Within; Edward 'G' – Like the Film Star; Don't Feed the Fish; Death Ray; Bargain Hunters; Dial M For Murder; Donkey's Years; The Double Dealer; Semelweiss – the Microbe Hunter; Waste; The Medusa Touch; Rumpole and the Fascist Beast. TV series incl: An Age of Kings; Emergency – Ward 10; That Was the Week That Was; Not So Much a Programme, More a Way of Life; For Maddy With Love; 1990; The Brack Report. Education: Fairfield Grammar School, Bristol. m actress Ann Bell, 1 d Rebecca, 1 s John. Address: c/o Leading Artists, London SW1. Starsign: Libra. Hobbies: photography, gardening, pisciculture. Person he would most like to have met: 'Spencer Tracy – I've always liked his acting and the stories about him.'

LANGLEY, Bob
Writer/broadcaster b 28.8.39 Newcastle-upon-Tyne. Scriptwriter and programme presenter at Tyne Tees TV for five years before joining BBC as newsreader. Worked as reporter, presenter and interviewer on sundry

programmes incl: 24 Hours; Panorama; Nationwide; Pebble Mill; Saturday Night at the Mill; Langley South. Also wrote and appeared in BBC film series, The Pennine Way; The Border Line; Lakeland Summer. Education: 'Very little', he claims. m Patricia. Address: c/o BBC, Pebble Mill, Birmingham. Starsign: Virgo. Hobbies: writing, mountaineering, Americana, playing the guitar (badly), swimming, squash, history, the cinema. Person he would most like to have met: Fletcher Christian.

LARGE, Eddie
Impressionist/comedian b 25.6.42 Glasgow. Moved to Manchester as a child. First ambition was to be a footballer and was associate schoolboy with Manchester City FC before accident ended that career. Met Syd Little in a Manchester pub and teamed up as singing duo. Turned to comedy in northern clubs before winning appearance on Opportunity Knocks 1971. TV since incl: Crackerjack; Who Do You Do?; Now Who Do You Do?; David Nixon Show;

Seaside Special;
Wheeltappers and Shunters
Social Club; Wednesday at
Eight; Little and Large
Tellyshow; Little and Large
Show; Disneytime. Stage incl:
seasons at London
Palladium, pantomimes and
summer seasons and
cabaret. Education:
grammar school. 2 d Alison,
Samantha. Address: c/o
London Management,
London W1. Starsign:
Cancer. Hobbies: golf,
keep-fit, supporting
Manchester City FC. Person
he would most like to meet:
'Jack Nicklaus, so that I could
ask him why I can't play golf
as well as he does!'

LATHAM, Philip
Actor b 17th January
Leigh-on-Sea, Essex.
Trained at RADA after
National Service and went
into rep at Farnham. Most
recent stage work incl tours of
The Letter; The Winslow Boy.
Films incl: Spy Story; Force
Ten from Navarrone; Man
from a Far Country. TV incl:
Mogul; The Troubleshooters;
Maigret; Whose Life Is It
Anyway?; No Exit; Time-Lock;
Good at Games; The
Pallisers; The Cedar Tree;
The Professionals; The
Killers; Hammer House of
Horror; Name for the Day;
Nanny; No 10 (Wellington);
The Fourth Arm. He is also in
demand for his religious
readings. Education: Felsted
School. m Eve,
1 d Amanda, 1 s Andrew.
Address: c/o Bryan Drew Ltd,
London W1. Starsign:

Capricorn. Hobby: golf.
Person he would most like to
have met: 'Spencer Tracy – a
brilliant actor.'

LAVENDER, Ian
Actor b 16.2.46
Birmingham. Trained at
Bristol Old Vic School,
followed by rep at
Canterbury. While there he
joined Dad's Army team and
continued throughout the
series. Other TV incl: Mr Big;
Come Back, Mrs Noah; The
Glums; Have I Got You Where
You Want Me? Recent theatre
incl: French Dressing;
Getting Married. m actress
Suzanne Kerchiss (dis), 2 s
Daniel, Sam. Address: c/o
Richard Stone, London WC2.
Starsign: Aquarius.

LAWLEY, Sue
Broadcaster/journalist
b 14.7.46 Dudley, Worcs.
Journalistic training with
Thomson Regional
Newspapers before joining
BBC in Plymouth. Associated
with Nationwide 1972-75 and
since 1977 and Tonight
1975-76. Also involved with
General Election and Budget
programmes and presenter
of British Academy of Film

and Television Arts
programme. Education:
Dudley Girls High School;
Bristol University. m David
Ashby, 1 d Harriet, 1 s Tom.
Address: c/o BBC TV,
London W12. Starsign:
Cancer. Hobbies: family,
cooking, bridge, tennis.

LAWRENCE, Patricia
Actress b 19th November
Andover, Hants. Trained at
RADA (where she won the
Bancroft Gold Medal). After
many parts in rep, retired to
raise her family. Returned to
stage at Leatherhead.
London West End credits
incl: Funny Sunday/
Sometime Never; West of
Suez; Five Finger Exercise
(National Theatre tour). Films
incl: Tom Jones; The Hireling.
Many TV credits incl: Intimate
Strangers; Anna Karenina;
Our Mutual Friend; Love
Story; Telford's Change; To
Serve Them All My Days;
Seven Faces of Woman;
Barriers; Staying On;
Brimstone and Treacle
(Dennis Potter's banned
play); St Martin's Summer;
Tenko. Education: St
Swithin's School, Winchester.
m Greville Poke
(vice-chairman English
Stage Co; chairman LAMDA
and Thorndike Theatre),
2 s Christopher, James.
Address: c/o David White
Assocs, London SW1.
Starsign: Scorpio. Hobbies:
pen and ink drawing,
needlepoint. Person she
would most like to meet: 'Paul
Newman – I have been in love
with him for years.'

LAYTON, George
Actor/writer b 2.3.43
Bradford, Yorks. Trained at
RADA (where he won the
Emile Littler Award). Leading
parts at Coventry and
Nottingham; appeared on
Broadway in Chips With
Everything and starred in an
Australian production of
Funny Peculiar. His films incl:
Stand Up Virgin Soldiers, for
which he was nominated
Most Promising Newcomer in
the 1977 Evening News Film
Awards. Has starred in many
TV series incl: the Doctor
series; It Ain't Half Hot, Mum;
My Brother's Keeper; The
Sweeney; Murder; Robin's
Nest; Minder. Also narrates
Pigeon Street. Has co-written
(with Jonathan Lynn) more
than 60 TV shows incl: the
Doctor series; My Brother's
Keeper; My Name is Harry
Worth and half of one series
of Robin's Nest. Books incl:
The Balaclava Story; The Fib.
Education: Belle Vue
Grammar, Bradford.
m publicity executive,
1 d Claudie, 2 s Tristan,
Daniel. Address: c/o William
Morris Agency, London W1.
Starsign: Pisces. Hobbies:
soccer, tennis (no real
hobbies). Person he would
most like to meet: 'The person
in Wardour Street who
bashed in my car.'

LAYZELL, Alastair
Reporter/newscaster
b 28.6.58 Jersey, Channel
Islands. Joined Channel TV in
1977 and is anchorman of the
station's Channel Report.
Also presents Encore;

Talkback (discussion series);
election coverage; specialist
documentaries. Education:
Hautlieu Grammar, Jersey.
m Anne. Address: c/o
Channel TV, Jersey. Starsign:
Cancer. Hobbies: flying,
music, reading. Person he
would most like to meet: The
Pope.

LE MESURIER, John
Actor b 5.4.12 Bedford, but
brought up in Bury St
Edmunds and London.
Studied for the stage at Fay
Compton's Drama School,
followed by rep, pantomime,
cabaret, variety and
London's West End. Served
in the army during the war.
Many films and much TV.
Films incl: Those Dangerous
Years; Private's Progress; I'm
All Right, Jack; Punch and
Judy Man; We Joined the
Navy; Wrong Arm of the Law;
Carlton-Browne of the FO; Mr
Topaze; Mouse on the Moon;
Pink Panther; Never Take No
For an Answer; Casino
Royale; Salt and Pepper;
Magic Christian; Brief
Encounter; Confessions of a
Window Cleaner;
Jabberwocky; Stand Up
Virgin Soldiers; Spaceman

and King Arthur; The Fiendish
Plot of Dr Fu Manchu. On TV
was in Dad's Army (and the
film) from 1969. Other TV incl:
The Traitor (Best TV Actor
1971 Award); The Goodies;
Doctor at Large; Anywhere
But England; A Class By
Himself; Rust; Mr Loveday's
Little Outing; Silver Wedding;
High Ground; Flint; A
Christmas Carol; 3-2-1; The
Dick Emery Show; Worzel
Gummidge; Brideshead
Revisited; Bognor. Records
incl: What is Going to
Become of Us All? Education:
Sherborne. m (1st) actress
Hattie Jacques (dis), (2nd)
Joan, 2 s Robin, Kim.
Address: c/o Leading Artists,
London SW1. Starsign: Aries.
Person he would most like to
have met: 'Picasso, if only to
find out when he was joking
and when he was not.'

LEACH, Rosemary
Actress b 18.12.25 Much
Wenlock, Shropshire.
Trained at RADA and wide
rep experience incl:
Amersham, Coventry,
Birmingham, Liverpool,
Bristol Old Vic. Recent
theatre incl: Beggars Opera;
84 Charing Cross Road. First
appeared on TV in 1960. Has
since been in many Armchair
Theatre plays; two series of
The Power Game; three
series with Ronnie Corbett
(No That's Me Over Here);
Sadie It's Cold Outside; Life
Begins at Forty; Rumpole of
the Bailey; Germinal; Roads
to Freedom; On the Move
(educational series);
Jackanory; The Office Line;

plays incl: Cider With Rosie;
Birthday; Don Quixote;
Disraeli; Hindle Wakes; Just
Between Ourselves; Tiptoe
Through the Tulips; Hands;
Tolstoy; The Critic; also
presenter of The English in
Love. Films incl: That'll Be the
Day; S O S Titanic.
Education: grammar school.
m (dis). Address: c/o William
Morris, London W1. Starsign:
Sagittarius. Hobbies:
gardening, cooking.

LEEMING, Jan
Newsreader/interviewer
b 5.1.42 Kent. Fifteen years'
experience in theatre, radio
and TV in New Zealand and
Australia before spending six
years with HTV on news and
women's programmes,
followed by two years with
Pebble Mill and a year with
BBC's Radio 2. BBC TV
newsreader since 1980.
Radio and TV Industries Club
Newsreader of the Year
Award 1981. Education: St
Joseph's Convent Grammar
School, Abbey Wood, Kent;
Ewell Technical College.
m Patrick Lunt (BBC Radio 2
presenter), 1 s Jonathan.
Address: c/o BBC TV,
London W12. Starsign:
Capricorn. Hobby: work.
Person she would most like to
meet: 'Prince Philip – he
appears to have strength of
character, humour and kind
eyes.'

LEES, Michael
Actor b 5.9.27 Bury, Lancs.
Trained at RADA. TV incl:
People Like Us; Coronation
Street; Emmerdale Farm;

Pride and Prejudice; Stay
With Me Till Morning; Ferry
Ride Away; Spoils of War;
Nanny. Films incl: Cuba.
Education: De La Salle
College, Salford. Address:
c/o Roger Storey Ltd, London
W1. Starsign: Virgo. Hobbies:
walking, trees, Wagner,
observing other people.
Person he would most like to
have met: 'Brillat Savarin, to
eat and drink with him in the
grand manner.'

LEIGH-HUNT, Ronald
Actor b 5th October London.
Theatrical family
background. Trained at the
Italia Conti Stage School after
leaving the army. Played
many parts but is probably
still best remembered for first
starring role on TV in 1956 as
King Arthur in Adventures of
Sir Lancelot. First show in
London's West End was first
production of The King and I
in 1953. Stage also incl:
Funny Girl (with Barbra
Streisand) in London 1966;
most recent, touring with
Sleuth. Also Sir Peter in
School For Scandal; touring
with Black Coffee. Played in
more than 30 films incl: Le
Mans (with Steve McQueen).
TV incl: Rogue Herries; The

Freewheelers; Crossroads;
countless plays, serials and
comedy shows (with Dick
Emery, Norman Wisdom and
many others); Crime of
Passion; Doctor Who; On The
Green; Blake's Seven;
Pebble Mill At One; Enigma
Files; Diary of a Nobody;
Emmerdale Farm; Airline;
Minder; The Professionals.
Also a compère, presenter
and teacher of public
speaking and case
presentations. Education:
Tiffins. Widower, 1 d Laura.
Address: c/o NEMS
Management Ltd, London
SW3. Starsign: Libra.
Hobbies: motor-racing,
tennis, golf. Person he would
most like to meet: 'Sir Freddie
Laker, because he is the
prime example of positive
thought and action against all
odds. A few more like him and
we would not be in the state
we are now!'

LENNIE, Angus
Actor b 18.4.30 Glasgow.
Well-known to viewers as the
Crossroads chef but is a very
experienced film and TV
actor. Films incl: The Great
Escape; 633 Squadron;
Tunes of Glory; Oh What a
Lovely War; One of Our
Dinosaurs Is Missing; Great;
The Valiant; Petticoat Pirates.
TV incl: Sir Yellow; Bowler;
Justice; The Onedin Line; Z
Cars; Doctor Who; Clay,
Smeddum and Greenden;
The Dancing Princess;
Kidnapped; The Saint; Para
Handy; Softly, Softly; The
Danny La Rue Show; Send in
the Girls; The Bagthorpe

Saga; The House with the Green Shutters; The Taming of the Shrew; Stanley Baxter Series; Doom Castle. Education: Eastbank Secondary, Glasgow. Address: c/o Jean Drysdale Management, London W8. Starsign: Aries. Hobby: collecting theatre prints and posters. Person he would most like to meet: 'My next director!'

LENSKA, Rula
Actress b 30.9.47 St Neots, Herts. Trained as a secretary, but chose the stage as a career and studied at Webber Douglas Academy of Dramatic Art. Made a hit in Rock Follies, but other TV incl: Dixon of Dock Green; The Doctors; The Brothers; Edward the Seventh; Special Branch; The Saint; Private Schultz; Minder; Design For Living; Watching Me, Watching You; Aubrey Beardsley; To the Manor Born; Take a Letter Mr Jones; Seven Dials Mystery; Battle of the Bands and 'virtually every quiz show there is'. Theatre incl: Suddenly at Home; Flare Path; Forget Me Not Lane; A Midsummer Night's Dream; Secretary Bird; Candle in the Wind; Abel – Where is your Brother; Aladdin pantomime (Richmond); Mr Fothergill's Murder. Films incl: Soft Beds Hard Battles; Alfie Darling; Royal Flash. Education: Ursuline Convent, Westgate-on-Sea; Pitman's Secretarial College. m actor Brian Deacon, 1 d Lara. Address: c/o Vernon

Conway, London W2. Starsign: Libra. Hobbies: cooking, music, singing, handiwork. Person she would most like to meet: 'The Pope or my favourite actress, Jeanne Moreau – both wonderful.'

LEUCHARS, Anne
TV journalist b 2.8.53 Kampala, Uganda. Four years as newspaper reporter, feature writer and theatre critic and two years on regional TV news magazine programmes – Points West (BBC Bristol), Report West and Report Extra (both HTV West), Lookaround (Border TV). Also presented Mary Chipperfield and Friends, for Border. Reporting for Central TV (East Midlands) since 1981. Education: Farnham Girls Grammar School; Liverpool University (BA Hons Geography). Address: c/o Central TV, Birmingham. Starsign: Leo. Hobbies: newspaper and magazine addict, theatre, hill walking, natural history and wildlife, wind-surfing, parachuting, planning documentaries. Person she would most like to meet: 'Ben Nevis – because I love his relatives Carl Wark, Simon Fell and Ringing Roger.'

LEWIS, Emlyn
Reporter b 11.10.50 Bangor, Gwynedd. Started on North Wales Chronicle, Bangor, before joining HTV in 1976 to work on the station's nightly Welsh news programme, Y Dydd. Education: Llangefni

Comprehensive; Gwynedd Technical College. m Lyn. Address: c/o HTV, Mold, Clwyd. Starsign: Libra. Hobbies: farming, working in television. Person he would most like to meet: 'Prince Charles, because he seems to have everything going for him.'

LEWIS, Martyn
Newscaster/reporter b 7.4.45 Swansea. Father a Company Sergeant Major in Royal Engineers; mother a SRN who took part in the evacuation from Dunkirk. During university holidays worked as a docker in Iceland, as a ranch-hand in Canada and a lifeguard in the Rockies. Also made a 14,000-mile trip round America by Greyhound bus. Started working as a freelance journalist, mostly for the BBC in Belfast, in 1967, but 10 months later joined HTV (where he met the girl who was to become his wife). During the next two years provided daily reports for local news programme, made documentaries and presented regular weekly current affairs programme, Welsh Scene. Joined ITN

1970 and was their northern correspondent for seven years before returning to London where he is now a senior correspondent and, since Easter 1981, a regular News at Ten newscaster. Has reported for ITN from more than 30 countries, his assignments incl the development of the North Sea oilfields, the Cyprus war, the fall of the Shah of Iran, the Moscow Olympics and the attempted assassination of Pope John Paul II. Was a member of the first Western TV crew to enter Afghanistan after the Russian invasion (for a time he was under arrest by Russian troops). Was also a member of the ITN team covering the wedding of the Prince and Princess of Wales. On the studio team for 1979 General Election and a studio interviewer on 1981 Budget programme. Also co-presented first-ever video cassette News Review of 1980 and again in 1981. Education: co-educational Dalriada School, Co Antrim; Trinity College, Dublin (BA Economics, Philosophy and Geography) where he was actively involved with the rugby club, rifle club (captain), debating society and University Players (as actor, producer and writer). m Liz (daughter of Duncan Carse), 2 d Sylvie, Kate. Address: c/o ITN, London W1. Starsign: Aries. Hobbies: photography, tennis, jogging.

LEWIS, Peter
Broadcaster/actor/producer b 13.9.46 Welsh, but born just outside the land of his fathers. At one time was probably the youngest full-time professional broadcaster in the country. In addition to news and sport and current affairs commentating, presented network film programme, Movie Magazine, when he

was 17. Eighteen years of daily newscasting, fronting news and magazine programmes, children's programmes, sport, adult education, quiz shows, plays, commercials and interviews. Other TV incl: presenting Home and Design; London Weekend senior announcer; co-presenting HTV West's news magazine, Report West. Has worked for most of the ITV companies as well as BBC Radio and TV. Is on the Boards of several companies. Education: Cardiff Arms Park; agricultural college. m Rita, 3 s Benjamin, Toby, Daniel. Address: c/o Jim Thompson, London SE1. Starsign: Virgo. Hobbies: sailing, rugby, karate, motorsport and any physical activity for which he isn't too old. Person he would most like to have met: 'Oscar Wilde – what a pleasure to be insulted by such a wordsmith!'

LEWIS, Rhoda
Actress b 25.6.33 Moseley, Birmingham. Trained at the Birmingham School of Speech and Drama. Then rep at Kidderminster, Bristol,

Belgrade, Coventry, Nottingham and Bristol Old Vic. Considerable TV experience since 1960 in plays, series and serials. Plays incl: No 10; The Sea; Dylan; Possessions; Tigers Are Better Looking; The New Word; Pinnochio; Warm Feet, Warm Hands; Milton, Paradise Regained; The Wild West Show. TV incl: Taff Acre; Coronation Street; Emergency – Ward 10; Perils of Pendragon; Kilvert's Diary; Lorna Doone; Maybury; Edward the Seventh; The War of Darkie Pilbeam; Troubleshooters; Callan; Wings; Crown Court; The Avengers; Public Eye; The Likely Lads; The Onedin Line; Dixon of Dock Green; Z Cars; Softly, Softly; Hunter's Walk; Adam Smith; The Man at the Top; Doomwatch; Justice; Rooms; Beryl's Lot; Sadie It's Cold Outside; The Nearly Man; Mr H. Education: Malvern Hall High School for Girls, Solihull. m Norman Florence, 1 s Peter. Address: c/o Peter Browne, London SW9. Starsign: Cancer. Hobbies: collecting records and recipes, gardening, watching rugby. Person she would most like to meet: 'Peter Ustinov, whose humour and unique ability to entertain and delight is unfailing.'

LEWIS, Tony
Sports presenter/cricket commentator b 6.7.38 Swansea. Former captain, Glamorgan County Cricket Club and England captain in

148

eight Tests 1972-73. Ten years with HTV (Sports Arena, music programme Impromptu, etc) until 1981; BBC (Sport on 4, Saturday Night at the Mill, cricket commentaries). Education: Neath Grammar School; Christ's College, Cambridge (MA History). m Joan, 2 d Joanna, Anabel. Address: c/o Bagenal Harvey Organisation, London W1. Starsign: Cancer. Hobbies: music. Person he would most like to meet: 'Lord Lucan – there is a certain mystique about him.'

LEYTON, John
Actor b 17.2.39 Frinton-on-Sea, Essex. Trained at the Actors' Workshop and York Rep. Went from rep into Biggles TV series and then appeared in Harper's West One as a pop singer, Johnny Sincere, singing Johnny Remember Me which was issued as a single and reached No 1 in the hit parade. This took him into the pop scene for three or four years. Went to America 1964-71 where he was acting in films and TV series (Jericho). He still returns there periodically to work in films for TV. Also writes scripts. Films incl: The Great Escape; Guns at Batasi; Von Ryan's Express; The Idol; Krakatoa; East of Java. TV incl: Biggles; Harper's West One; The Nearly Man; Square Leopard. Education: Highate School. m Diana, 1 d Lara, 1 s Dominic. Address: c/o CCA, London SW6. Starsign:

Aquarius. Hobby: golf. Person he would most like to meet: 'The owner of next year's Derby so I could spend from now till next June backing it.'

LILL, Denis
Actor b 22.4.42 Hamilton, Waikato, New Zealand. Royal New Zealand Air Force 1958-65, trained as an airframe mechanic. Toured NZ with NZ Players and came to UK 1967. In rep and with the National Theatre before TV. Theatre incl: The Crucifer of Blood; The Cherry Orchard; The Devil's Disciple; Dandy Dick. TV plays and series incl: The Regiment; Fall of Eagles; The Case of Eliza Armstrong; Madame Bovary; Survivors; Lillie (as Bertie); Hedda Gabler; Bad Blood. Education: Hamilton Boys' High School. m Joan, 1 d Charlotte, 1 s Edward. Address: c/o St James's Management, London SW1. Starsign: Aries/Taurus cusp. Hobby: model aeroplanes. Person he would most like to meet: 'A benevolent multi-millionaire.'

LILLICRAP, Christopher
Actor/writer/musician b 14.2.49 Plymouth. Former teacher of drama and English in Mansfield. Extensive experience in rep incl Nottingham, Canterbury, Cheltenham and Theatre in Education. A self-taught musician, he and his wife have a cabaret act which they stage in top hotels and in

Denmark. Also the author, with his wife, of Stop the Rot, a musical for children which was premièred at the Palace Theatre, Westcliff, Oct 1981. First TV was Playboard in 1976. TV since incl: Rose of Puddle Fratrum; The Bands Played On (in which he played Harry Roy); Canned Laughter; two plays on Keats; Love Story (Wilfred and Eileen); Follow the Star; King Robert of Sicily; Jackanory Playhouse; Chopsticks; Rainbow. Presenter of several series incl: Playboard (five series); We'll Tell You a Story (fourth series 1982); Clock On. Education: Plympton Grammar, Plymouth; Rolle College of Education, Exmouth. m actress Jeanette Ranger. Address: c/o Aza Artistes, London NW11. Starsign: Aquarius. Hobbies: golf, gardening, Plymouth Argyle. Person he would most like to meet: 'Jane Fonda, a beautiful actress in every sense of the word.'

LINDEN, Hal
Actor/singer b 20.3.31 New York City. Began as a saxophonist and singer and

149

while in the US Army was in revues for Special Services. Enrolled at American Theatre Wing when he left the army and made professional stage debut in chorus of Mr Wonderful 1955. Understudied Sydney Chaplin in Bells Are Ringing in New York the following year and took over the role in 1958. (He was also in the film version.) Numerous other Broadway shows incl: Anything Goes; The Pyjama Game. Came into TV through being a guest on chat shows and variety programmes. He was also host or announcer on others. Now a regular in Barney Miller series. Education: City High School of Music and Art; Queens College; City College of New York. Starsign: Pisces.

LINDEN, Jennie
Actress b 8.12.40 Worthing, Sussex. Won a scholarship to Central School of Speech and Drama and graduated with a Central School Diploma and is an International Phonetic Associate. Stage incl: Never Too Late; Thark; My Fat Friend; On Approval; Hedda Gabler; also her own one-woman shows of verse, prose and song, Sounds Entertaining and Twice Brightly. Films incl: Doctor Who and the Daleks; Women in Love; A Severed Head (for which she was nominated for an Academy Award for Best Performance of a Newcomer). TV incl: The Trouble with England; You

Can't Win; For King and Country; Present Laughter; Return of Favours; Seasons of the Year; Lady Windermere's Fan; The Persuaders; Sister Mary; Little Lord Fauntleroy; Lillie; Charlie Muffins; Dick Turpin; Breadwinner; Degree of Uncertainty. Several radio plays. Education: private school, West Preston Manor, Sussex. m antique dealer Christopher Mann,
1 s Rupert. Address: c/o Roger Carey, London WC2. Starsign: Sagittarius. Hobbies: endless, but include music (piano), gardening, restoring antique furniture, collecting antiques, building onto cottages, reading, philosophy, UFO research, spiritualism, etc. Person she would most like to meet: 'Jesus Christ, whose advanced spirituality must have been the most extraordinary and wonderful presence ever witnessed by man on this planet.'

LINDSAY, Robert
Actor b 13.12.49 Ilkeston, Derbyshire. Studied at RADA then rep at Manchester before coming to London, where he took over from David Essex in Godspell. Other theatre work incl: The Old Vic and Hampstead Theatre Club. Considerable amount of TV incl: Letter from a Soldier; Get Some In (two series); Citizen Smith (four series: for which he also sings the opening song); Seconds Out; All's Well That Ends Well; A Midsummer Night's Dream;

Twelfth Night; King Lear. Education: Gladstone School for Boys, Ilkeston; Clarendon College, Nottingham. Address: c/o Felix de Wolfe, London WC2. Starsign: Sagittarius. Hobbies: reading, sport. People he would most like to meet: 'Jane Fonda and Shirley Williams — for different reasons.'

LIPMAN, Maureen
Actress b 10.5.46 Hull. Always wanted to act and trained at LAMDA. Much stage experience incl: London's Royal Court Theatre; Old Vic (The Front Page; The Good Natured Man); Candida; The Ball Game; Tira Tells Everything There is to Know About Her; Royal Shakespeare Company (As You Like It); the Stables Theatre, Manchester, On Your Way Riley. Films incl: Up the Junction; Gumshoe. Radio incl: Delivery; Special Co-respondent; Mother Figure; Over the Rainbow; Patterson; Just a Minute. Now well known for her role in Agony, but other TV incl: Couples; Doctor at Large; The Soft Touch; Don't Ask Us; The Lovers; The Evacuees; File It Under Fear (Thriller); Codename; The Knowledge; The Sporting Club Dinner; Rogue Male; Give Us a Clue; Crown Court; Blankety Blank; The Theatre Quiz; Jackanory Playhouse (The Witching Hour). Education: Newland High School, Hull.
m playwright Jack Rosenthal, 1 d Amy,

1 s Adam. Address: c/o Saraband Assocs, London N1. Starsign: Taurus. Hobby: finding time to think of one. Person she would most like to have met: 'Joyce Grenfell, because she was a "people-watcher" of brilliant precision. I wonder how she managed to observe and comment so accurately without ever resorting to malice?'

LISTON, Ian
Actor b 4.8.48 Crosby, Nr Liverpool. No formal acting training, but has more than 100 TV appearances to his credit incl: Doctor Who; Secret Army; The Onedin Line; Escape; The Professionals; Nelson; Within These Walls; Warship (Leading Seaman Lovell); Coronation Street (Danny Burrows); currently regularly in Crossroads as Ron Brownlow. Films incl: Scum; A Bridge Too Far; The Empire Strikes Back. Has written extensively for radio, produces and directs in the theatre and runs his own production company, Hiss and Boo Ltd. Education: Waterloo Grammar School; London University (BA Hons Business Studies). Address: c/o Jim Thompson, London SE1. Starsign: Leo. Hobbies: cricket, cooking and eating, listening to brass bands, music-hall, running his production company. Person he would most like to meet: 'The Queen Mother – a charming and gracious lady (and we share the same birthday!).'

LITTLE, Syd
Comedian b 19.12.42 Blackpool. Solo guitarist and singer in Manchester pubs before teaming up with Eddie Large as singing duo. Turned to comedy in northern clubs before winning appearance on Opportunity Knocks 1971. TV since incl: Crackerjack; Who Do You Do?; Now Who Do You Do?; David Nixon Show; Seaside Special; Wheeltappers and Shunters Social Club; Wednesday at Eight; Little and Large Tellyshow; Little and Large Show; Disneytime. Stage incl: seasons at London Palladium, pantomimes, summer shows and cabaret. Education: secondary school. m Sheree, 1 d Donna, 1 s Paul. Address: c/o London Management, London W1. Starsign: Sagittarius. Hobbies: making model boats, keep-fit. Person he would most like to have met: 'Lord Nelson, so that he could show me some of the marvellous ships of that era – most of which I have re-created in model form.'

LLEWELYN, Gwyn
Journalist b 6.3.42 Bangor, North Wales. Joined local newspaper (North Wales Chronicle) at 16 as junior reporter, then reporter and sub-editor Western Mail. Went to Wales (West and North) TV – the short-lived ITV station – 1962-63, followed by TWW as film reporter 1964-68 and HTV 1968-75 as presenter of nightly Welsh news magazine programme Y Dydd. Since 1975 freelance broadcaster/journalist but working exclusively for BBC, initially as morning radio programmes presenter but since 1979 as presenter of Heddiw, nightly news programme. Education: Sir Thomas Jones School, Amlwch, Anglesey. m Luned Margred, 2 d Siwan, Shari, 1 s Sion. Address: c/o BBC, Cardiff. Starsign: Pisces. Person he would most like to meet: The Pope.

LLOYD-ROBERTS, Sue
TV reporter b 27.10.51 London. Joined ITN as general news reporter 1976 straight from university. Has since covered many foreign assignments in France, Spain, Switzerland, Hong Kong, Singapore and India. Particular journalistic interest in environment and ecology. Has reported on Greenpeace campaigns, nuclear dumping in the Atlantic, whale hunts off the Spanish coast and seal culls off the Orkneys. Education: Cheltenham Ladies' College; St Hilda's College, Oxford (BA Hons History and Modern Languages). Address: c/o ITN, London

W1. Starsign: Scorpio. Hobbies: theatre, opera, skiing. Person she would most like to have met: Marco Polo.

LLOYD-WILLIAMS, Mike
Presenter/deputy news editor b 2.9.43 Aberdare, Glam. Journalistic training on various papers and Western Mail (where he was deputy news editor) before joining HTV Wales 1970. Concerned with news, arts, showbiz, farming, current affairs and other HTV programmes. Education: Porth County Grammar School; University College, Cardiff. Address: c/o HTV Wales, Cardiff. Starsign: Virgo. Hobbies: horses, poultry, tropical fish, amateur dramatics, boxing, ecology, cats, history, painting, sculpture, charities, gardening. Person he would most like to meet: 'No one – desperately trying to meet fewer.'

LOCKE, Philip
Actor b 29.3.28 St Marylebone, London. Trained at RADA. Has appeared in numerous productions at London's Royal Court Theatre, incl: The

Knack; with the Royal Shakespeare Company (Richard III, The Tempest, Julius Caesar, Antony and Cleopatra and in their TV production), and in Amadeus at the National Theatre. His first American appearance was in the Old Vic production of A Midsummer Night's Dream. His films incl: Escape to Athena and, more recently, Ivanhoe. TV incl: Doctor Who; Disappearance of Harry; Mill on the Floss; Dick Turpin; Omega Factor; Oliver Twist; Codename Icarus. Education: Central School. Address: c/o Jeremy Conway Ltd, London W1. Starsign: Aries. Hobby: painting. Person he would most like to meet: 'Garbo – reason obvious.'

LODGE, David
Actor b 19.8.21 Rochester, Kent. Began in Gang Shows and music-hall where he perfected his art. Has appeared in over 120 films (from Cockleshell Heroes to The Pink Panther). Also many series and appearances on TV, incl: Lovely Couple; Spike Milligan's Q8; Murder at the Wedding. Made a Freeman of the City of London 14th January 1982, for his charity work. Education: St Nicholas Church School; City Day Continuation School. m Lyn. Address: c/o Joan Gray, Personal Management, Sunbury-on-Thames, Middx. Starsign: Leo. Hobbies: Grand Order of Water Rats, the Variety Club of Great Britain. Person he would most

like to meet: 'The army Corporal whom I boxed against at the Royal Engineers HQ, Ripon, Yorkshire, in 1940 when I represented RAF Station Dishforth. (Incidentally, I lost) '

LOE, Judy
Actress b 6.3.47 Manchester. Worked in rep at Chester and Crewe after university. Stage incl: Hair; A Game Called Arthur; No Sex Please – We're British; Middle-Age Spread; Illuminations. TV incl: Ace of Wands; General Hospital; Edward the Seventh; Woodstock; Man of Straw; Z Cars; Miss Jones and Son; The Upchat Line; Couples; Ripping Yarns; Heartland; Visitors for Anderson; When The Boat Comes In; The Gentle Touch; Play For Today (Life After Death); Let There Be Love. Education: Urmston Grammar; University of Birmingham (BA Drama and English). m actor Richard Beckinsale (dec), 1 d Kate. Address: c/o Saraband Assocs, London N1. Starsign: Pisces. Person she would most like to meet: 'Too many and various.'

LONGFOOT, Merryn
Reporter b 29.10.53 Belfast. After reading English at London University's Bedford College, she became a trainee reporter at Bury St Edmunds, then moved to the Stamford Mercury and in 1980 was appointed local government editor at

Hereward Radio, the Peterborough local commercial radio station. Joined TSW as a reporter 1982. Education: Wicken Park Prep School, Bucks; Westonbirt School, Glos. m press photographer Len Longfoot. Address: c/o TSW, Plymouth. Starsign: Scorpio. Hobbies: riding, sailing, wind-surfing, motor-cycling, wine-making, do-it-yourself. Person she would most like to meet: 'Winnie the Pooh – I admire his philosophy and his knitted pullover.'

LONNEN, Ray
Actor b 19.5.40 Bournemouth. Started as an assistant stage manager in Belfast. Rep at York, Worthing, Farnham, Bromley and Coventry. Other stage work incl a tour of New Zealand and playing Guy Masterson in Guys and Dolls in Manchester. Came into TV 1965 in Emergency – Ward 10. Parts followed in The Power Game; Honey Lane; The Trouble Shooters; Pathfinders; General Hospital and more recently Z Cars; Hammer House of Horror; The Gentle Touch; Sandbaggers; Glamour

Girls; Harry's Game. His films incl: Zepplin; Lady Caroline Lamb. Education: 'Some – not much' he says. m actress Lyn Dalby, 1 d Amy. Address: c/o Caroline Dawson, London W1. Starsign: Taurus. Hobbies: cinema, criminology, tennis, music. Person he would most like to meet: 'James Stewart – to talk about all of his films'.

LONSDALE, Jennifer
Actress b 17th July Emsworth, Hants. Trained at the Arts Educational Trust. On stage she was in Two and Two Make Sex both in London and on a Canadian tour. TV incl: Come Back; Mrs Noah; XYY Man; House of Caradus; Lifelike (Play of the Week); Doctor Who; Love in a Cold Climate; Barriers; The Cedar Tree; That's My Boy. Education: state school and privately. Address: c/o Brunskill Management Ltd, London SW7. Starsign: Cancer. Hobbies: sailing, riding, writing. People she would most like to meet: 'Dame Rebecca West and Noël Coward, for the stories they could tell.'

LORD, Jack
Actor b 30.12.30 New York City, USA. Came into acting through making training films for the Navy. Before that he had been third mate in the Merchant Navy, studied fine art at New York University, organised his own art school in Greenwich Village (some of his work has been acquired by the Metropolitan Museum

of Art), took flying lessons and got a private pilot's licence. First acting break in TV series, Man Against Crime. Many roles in dozens of series, incl: Stoney Burke, but best known as Steve McGarrett in Hawaii Five-O. Films incl: God's Little Acre; Man of the West; Doctor No. Education: New York University. m 1st (dis), (2nd) fashion designer Marie de Narde. Address: Oahu, Hawaii. Starsign: Capricorn. Hobbies: painting, writing, collecting art.

LOVE, Geoff
Bandleader/composer/ arranger b 4th September Todmorden, Yorks. Started as a motor mechanic but interested in music since 11 when he joined a local amateur orchestra. Turned professional at 17 when he joined a stage band with which he tap-danced and sang. Spent six years in the army (King's Royal Rifle Corps) and learnt orchestration while in the band. After the war joined Harry Gold and His Pieces of Eight. Made first recordings 26 years ago; has since

received about 12 gold and numerous silver discs for the sale of his records. Also a platinum for his Western Movie Themes. Also records as Manuel and the Music of the Mountains and in 1980 celebrated 21 years under this title. Frequent radio and TV appearances, but probably best-known for his work with Max Bygraves on the Max Bygraves TV programmes. Education: Roomfield Boys' School, Todmorden. m Joy, 2 s BBC Radio broadcaster Adrian Love, computer lecturer Nigel Love. Address: c/o Noel Gay Organisation, London WC2. Starsign: Virgo. Hobbies: music, water-skiing. Person he would most like to meet: 'Frank Sinatra. If I could record with him I would die happy!'

LOVEJOY, Gary
Sports presenter/reporter b 25.7.55 Plymouth. After journalist training college and experience on evening newspapers, joined Westward TV in 1978, and TVS in 1982. Education: Plymouth College. m Sally, 1 s Ryan. Address: c/o TVS, Southampton. Starsign: Leo. . Hobby: sport. Person he would most like to meet: 'Alec Bedser, so he can explain why I am still uncapped!'

LUCAS, William
Actor b 14.4.25 Manchester. Trained at Bradford Theatre School after serving in the Royal Navy during the war.

Rep at Liverpool and other parts of the country. London stage incl: Amber for Anna; Ring of Jackals; Dual Marriageway. Films incl: Sons and Lovers; The Professionals; Payroll; Bitter Harvest. TV incl: Portrait of Alison; The Paragon; The Infamous John Friend; Rigoletto; A Flea off Pepe; Champion Road; Flower of Evil; Mogul; Warship; Black Beauty; The Spoils of War. Education: Manchester. 2 s Daniel, Thomas. Address: c/o Joy Jameson, London SW1. Starsign: Aries. Hobby: walking. Person he would most like to meet: 'Myself – to see who I am.'

LUCKHAM, Cyril
Character actor b 25.7.07 Salisbury, Wilts. One of TV's most distinguished actors. Originally wanted a career in the Royal Navy, but was invalided out 1931 as a Lieut. Trained for stage with Arthur Brough Players and Folkestone Dramatic School. First stage part was as footman in The Admirable Crichton at Folkestone. Since then has been in rep at Folkestone, Manchester,

Bristol, Liverpool, Coventry, Southport, and was a member of the Royal Shakespeare Company for three seasons. Has been in more stage, TV plays and series than he can remember. West End plays incl: The Family Reunion; Photo Finish; You Never Can Tell. Films incl: Anne of the Thousand Days; A Man for All Seasons; The Pumpkin Eater; The Naked Runner; Providence. TV incl: The Forsyte Saga; Public Eye; Jennie; The Cedar Tree; Wodehouse Playhouse; What Every Woman Knows; The Camerons; The Omega Factor; Murder at the Wedding; My Son, My Son; North and South; Donkey's Years; To Serve Them All My Days; The Winter's Tale; Tales of the Unexpected; The Brack Report; The Potting Shed; Jackanory. Education: RN Colleges, Osborne and Dartmouth. m actress Violet Lamb, 1 s opera singer Robert. Address: c/o Larry Dalzell Assocs Ltd, London WC2. Starsign: Leo. Hobbies: music, cricket, ornithology. Person he would most like to have met: 'William Shakespeare, to ask him direct if he did it all.'

LULU
Singer/actress b 3.11.48 Lennoxtown, Stirlingshire. Started singing in concert party when she was nine. First record, Shout, in 1963. Has been in many pop and variety shows since as well as twice playing the title role in

Peter Pan. In addition to being chosen for a Royal Variety Performance and joint winner of the Eurovision Song Contest (1969), she has also been voted the World's and Britain's Top Girl Singer and Britain's Top TV Performer. Her films incl To Sir With Love and her numerous TV appearances incl 10 TV series for the BBC. Education: Whitehall Senior Secondary, Dennistown, Glasgow. m (1st) Maurice Gibb of the Bee Gees (dis), (2nd) hairdresser John Frieda, 1 s Jordan (from 2nd m). Address: c/o Marion Massey, London W14. Starsign: Scorpio. Hobbies: water-skiing, buying clothes. Person she would most like to meet: 'Gloria Swanson, whom I have always greatly admired.'

LUMLEY, Joanna
Actress b 1.5.46 Srinagar, India. A brief period in a craft and furniture shop was followed by a move to London and a modelling course. After appearing in Queen magazine, her modelling career took off. Subsequently concentrated on acting. Stage incl: Don't Just Lie There, Say Something; Othello; Me Old Cigar. Films incl: Some Girls Do; On Her Majesty's Secret Service. Tam Lin; The Breaking of Bumbo; Games Lovers Play. TV incl: The Mark II Wife; Release; Two Girls; It's Awfully Bad For Your Eyes, Darling; Coronation Street; The Protectors; General

Hospital; The New Avengers; Steptoe and Son; Sapphire and Steel. Education: Mickledene Primary School; Army School, Kuala Lumpur; St Mary's Anglican Convent, Hastings. m Jeremy Lloyd (dis), 1 s James (born 1967). Address: c/o ICM, London W1. Starsign: Taurus. Hobbies: collecting junk, painting, drawing, reading. Person she would most like to have met: 'William Shakespeare, so I could pick his brains.'

LYNAM, Desmond
Journalist/broadcaster b 17.9.42 Ennis, Co Clare, Eire. Wide experience of local and network radio and TV. Radio incl: presenting Sport on 2; Sports Report; Today; various quiz programmes – Forces Chance, Treble Chance; Midweek; music programmes. Also commentates on tennis and boxing. TV incl: presenting Grandstand; Sportswide; Sunday Grandstand. Also commentates on boxing and football. Education: Sarndean Grammar School, Brighton; Brighton Polytechnic. m (dis), 1 s Patrick. Address: c/o BBC, London W12. Starsign: Virgo. Hobbies: all sports, theatre, poetry. Person he would most like to have met: 'George Bernard Shaw – I am a great admirer of his work and his philosophy. He said "The golden rule is that there are no golden rules" and I believe that.'

LYNDHURST, Nick
Actor b 20.4.61 Emsworth, Hants. Only left the Corona Academy in 1980 but has already appeared in many TV series, incl: Anne of Avonlea; Heidi; Prince and the Pauper; Going Straight; Butterflies; Only Fools and Horses; Spearhead; To Serve Them All My Days. Education: Corona Academy, London. Address: c/o Chatto & Linnit, London W1. Starsign: Aries. Hobbies: fishing, scuba diving. Person he would most like to meet: 'Brooke Shields – for purely selfish reasons.'

M

McCALLUM, David
Actor b 19.3.33 Glasgow. After training at RADA went into rep and, in 1957, was given a seven-year film contract with the Rank Organisation. Films incl: Billy Budd; Freud; The Great Escape; The Greatest Story Ever Told; Mosquito Squadron; Frankenstein; King Solomon's Treasure. While making The Greatest Story Ever Told was picked for TV series, The Man From UNCLE, in which he appeared for four years and won international fame. Other TV incl: Colditz; The Adventures of the Invisible Man; Kidnapped; Sapphire and Steel. Also directed an episode of Explorers. Education: University College School, London. m (1st) actress Jill Ireland (dis), (2nd) fashion model Katherine Carpenter, 1 d Sophie, 4 s Paul, Jason, Valentine, Peter. Address: c/o London Management, London W1. Starsign: Virgo. Hobby: cosmology.

of Scotland Agricultural College and holds Scottish and National Diplomas in Horticulture. Also awarded the Scottish Horticultural Medal for services to Scottish horticulture 1982. First broadcast on gardening topics for BBC in Scotland 1974 and since 1978 has been co-presenting with George Barron an annual TV series, Beechgrove Garden, for BBC in Scotland. Education: Kilmarnock Academy. m Billie, 1 d Jennifer, 1 s Douglas. Address: c/o BBC, Aberdeen. Starsign: Virgo. Hobbies: golf, curling, music. Person he would most like to meet: Annafrid Lyngstad of Abba.

MacARTHUR, James
Actor b 8.12.37 Los Angeles, California. Brought up in showbiz environment as adoptive parents were actress Helen Hayes and playwright Charles (Front Page) MacArthur. Acting debut at age of eight in the Corn is Green in summer theatre. Many plays (Life With Father; Invitation to a March) and films incl: Kidnapped; Third Man on the Mountain; Swiss Family Robinson; The Light In The Forest; The Interns; To Be a Man; Spencer's Mountain; The Truth About Spring; The Battle of the Bulge; The Love-Ins. Has played the part of Danny Williams in Hawaii Five-O since the series started. Education: Allen Stevenson School, New York; Solebury School, New Hope, Pennsylvania; Harvard University. m (1st) actress Joyce Bulifant (dis), (2nd) actress Melanie Patterson, 1 d Mary, 1 s Charles (both from 1st m). Address: Honolulu, Hawaii. Starsign: Sagittarius. Hobbies: surfing, shooting.

MacCORMICK, Donald
TV journalist b 16.4.39 Glasgow. Started with STV Glasgow, then moved to Grampian TV (Grampian Week and Points North) 1968-70 when he joined BBC Scotland (Current Account and Public Account). Since moving to BBC Current Affairs in London 1975 he has worked with Tonight; Newsweek; Platform One; Twentieth Century Remembered; Newsnight. Education: Kings Park Secondary School, Glasgow. m Liz, 1 d Anna; 1 d Sarah, 2 s Donald, Niall by previous marriage. Address: c/o BBC TV, London W12. Starsign: Aries. Hobbies: theatre, tennis, wine, current events in all media. Person he would most

McCOLL, Jim
Horticulturist b 19.9.35 Kilmarnock. Trained at West

like to meet: 'Saul Bellow, because he writes such terrific sentences.'

McDERMOTT, Helen
Announcer b 24.3.54 Bushey, Herts. Dancing/drama training and TV and stage appearances as actress/singer for several years before going into radio and TV. Made a record which went high in the Irish charts and singing engagements took her to Poland, Arabia, France and Italy. Became film critic for BBC Radio Plymouth and freelance announcer for Westward TV. Has worked for Anglia TV in Norwich since Nov 1979. Education: Arts Educational School, Tring and London. Address: c/o Anglia TV, Norwich. Starsign: Aries. Hobbies: singing, walking, wine-tasting, dinner parties (preferably other people's), swimming. Person she would most like to meet: 'Gene Kelly – he has everything.'

MACDONALD, Aimi
Actress b 27th February Glasgow. One-time child dancer who has established herself in show business as a dizzy blonde. She was spotted while appearing at the Embassy Club in London, which led to her appearing in At Last the 1948 Show on TV. TV since incl: Max Bygraves Shows; John Davidson series (in America); The Saint; Dixon of Dock Green; The Avengers: Les Dawson series; Rolf Harris Show; Man at the Top; Celebrity Squares; Blankety Blank; Give Us a Clue; Those Wonderful Scottish Girls; Do You Come Here Often?; Definition; Russell Harty. Has also appeared in pantomimes, at the Richmond Theatre in The Mating Game and Dead Easy, and in London's West End with Lionel Blair in Lady Be Good. Royal Variety Performance 1968. Education: Park School, Glasgow. m (dis), 1 d dancer Lisa Muldore. Address: c/o Eric Glass Ltd, London W1. Starsign: Pisces. Hobbies: skating, writing.

MACDONALD, Gus
Producer/presenter b 20.8.40 Larkhall, Scotland. Worked as an engineer before switching to journalism on The Scotsman. Went into TV by joining Granada TV 1967. Former editor of World in Action, he was successively Head of Current Affairs, Regional Programmes, and Features. Presented Camera, the series on the history of photography and early film. Also Devil's Advocate; Union World; editions of World in Action. Education: Allan Glen's School, Glasgow. m Teen, 2 d Jean, Tracy. Address: c/o Granada TV, London W1. Starsign: Leo. Hobbies: squash, films. Person he would most like to meet: 'Anatole Scheransky – now serving a long and brutal prison sentence for publicly criticising the Soviet regime.'

McDONALD, Trevor
Journalist/broadcaster b 16.8.39 San Fernando, Trinidad. At the age of 20 started reporting for local radio stations in Trinidad. Went on to become announcer, sports commentator and assistant programme manager. Joined Trinidad TV in 1962. Came to London in 1969 to join BBC World Service. Joined ITN as a reporter in 1971. Has reported on world events, incl Falkland Islands crisis, and has frequently been seen as a newscaster. Education: won a college scholarship. m Beryl, 1 d Joanne, 1 s Timothy. Address: c/o ITN, London W1. Starsign: Leo. Hobbies: collecting books (especially interested in political biographies), international politics, philosophy.

McDOWELL, Paul
Actor b 15.8.31 London. Has also been a painter, musician, singer-songwriter and satirist. Stage experience in Britain (The Establishment) and America (Second City) and was in the Royal Command Performance 1961 as the

singer with The Temperance Seven band. Films incl: It's Trad Dad; Take Me Over; The Thirty Nine Steps; Rough Cut; Porridge. TV incl: The Good Life; Porridge; The Two Ronnies; Play of the Week; Pasmore; Tales of the Unexpected; The Brack Report; Strangers. Education: Bolt Court School of Photo-engraving; Chelsea College of Art. m Trisha, 3 d Sidonie, Helena, Lola (from previous marriages), 1 s Taig. Address: c/o Carole James Management, Richmond. Starsign: Leo. Hobbies: other careers, writing, painting. Person he would most like to have met: 'Picasso, perhaps in another life.'

McGEE, Henry
Actor b 14.5.29 London. Trained at Italia Conti School. Several years in rep in England and then two years in Australia. On his return to England he started in TV. Appeared in the award-winning series of Feydeau farces, Paris 1900, and then The Worker with Charlie Drake. Next came the start of his association with

Benny Hill which still continues. Also enjoys working in the theatre and played the lead in Uproar in the House and The Man Most Likely To in London. Latest TV incl: Let There Be Love. Education: Stoneyhurst. Address: c/o Margery Armstrong, London SW1. Starsign: Taurus. Person he would most like to have met: 'John Liston (in his prime circa 1820) – the first comedy actor to earn more money than the leading tragedians. He must have known a thing or two.'

MacKAY, Fulton
Actor b 12th August Paisley. Trained to become a quantity surveyor but after serving in the Black Watch during the war decided to be an actor and went to RADA. Much theatre work incl: Citizens' Theatre, Glasgow; The Royal Lyceum, Edinburgh; The Old Vic; The National Theatre; The RSC; Manchester Royal Exchange. TV incl: Strife; The Blind Man; Special Branch; Porridge; Willie Rough; The Foundation; Clay, Smeddum and Greenden; Three Tales of Orkney; Choices; Ghosts; The Master of Ballantrae; Songs of a Sourdough; Going Gently. Films incl: The Brave Don't Cry; Laxdale Hall; Porridge; Gumshoe; Britannia Hospital; Local Hero. Has written several plays for TV under a pseudonym. Education: Clydebank High School. m Irish actress Sheila Manahan. Address: c/o

NEMS Enterprises, London SW3. Starsign: Leo. Hobby: oil painting.

McKENZIE, Julia
Actress b 17.2.42 Enfield, Middx. Trained at the Guildhall School of Music and Drama. Great deal of TV experience incl: musical specials of Jerome Kern, Gershwin, Sondheim and Sheldon Harnick; guest of The Two Ronnies, Stanley Baxter, Harry Secombe, David Frost, Russell Harty and Mike Douglas (coast-to-coast in America); appearances on all panel games from Call My Bluff to Give Us a Clue; own TV series Maggie and Her and That Beryl Marston . . .! Also drama series Fame Is The Spur. Theatre incl: Guys and Dolls. Education: Tottenham County School. m actor/director Jerry Harte. Address: c/o April Young, London WC2. Starsign: Aquarius. Hobbies: cooking, the theatre. Person she would most like to meet: Katharine Hepburn.

McKERN, Leo
Actor b 16.3.20 Sydney, Australia. Trained as an electrical engineer and commercial artist. Spent one and a half years in the army before coming to England in 1946 to follow the girl he eventually married. Three years with the Old Vic, two years with the Royal Shakespeare Company. Then sold his home and possessions and returned to

Australia after filming Ryan's Daughter. Came back to work here. Theatre incl: Rollo; Othello; A Man for All Seasons (London and New York); Crime and Punishment; Uncle Vanya; Volpone. TV incl: The Prisoner; The Sun is God; On the Eve of Publication; The Tea Party; Rumpole of the Bailey. Education: Sydney Technical High. m actress Jane Holland, 2 d Abigail, Harriet. Address: c/o ICM, London W1. Starsign: Pisces. Hobbies: sailing, swimming, ecology, environment preservation. Person he would most like to have met: 'Dr Johnson, not William Shakespeare. Johnson would talk, the Bard wouldn't.'

MACKESON, Vyvyan
Journalist b 6.11.53 Carlisle, Cumbria. Worked for Pennine Radio in Bradford, West Yorks, before joining Yorkshire TV as reporter/presenter. Joined TVS on 1st January 1982 as presenter of news magazine programme Coast To Coast. Education: Sussex University (BA Hons) where she gained

a year's scholarship to University of California at Berkeley; followed by a year at Centre for Journalism Studies, University College, Cardiff (Postgraduate Diploma in Journalism Studies). Address: c/o TVS, Maidstone. Starsign: Scorpio. Hobbies: riding, eating, lying on hot beaches. Person she would most like to have met: 'William Shakespeare – I'd like him to explain Hamlet.'

MACLEAN, Don
Comedian b 11.3.44 Birmingham. Began entertaining in clubs and pubs in Midlands area, then holiday camp entertainer. TV debut in Crossroads; also in Billy Cotton's Music Hall; Roy Castle Show; The Good Old Days; In All Directions; Jokers Wild; White Heather Club; Out For the Count; Crackerjack; The Black and White Minstrels; Celebrity Squares; The Cheapest Show On The TV; Supersavers. Radio incl: own series Maclean Up Britain; Wit's End; Keep It MacLean. Also comedy records. Education: St Philip's Grammar School, Birmingham. m Antoinette, 1 d Rachel, 1 s Rory. Address: c/o Morris Aza, London NW11. Starsign: Pisces. Hobbies: making models of First World War aeroplanes, squash. Person he would most like to meet: 'Jerry Lewis – he was the greatest comedy influence on me when I was young.'

MacLEOD, Donny
Presenter b 1.7.32 Stornoway, Isle of Lewis, Scotland. Former art student, sculptor, naval officer and town councillor, he started his TV career with Grampian TV and was former anchorman on Reporting Scotland. Worked with Nationwide and with Scottish Documentary Unit in Glasgow before joining Pebble Mill in 1973. Other TV incl: Macleod at Large; Saturday Night at the Mill; The Best of Scottish; 6.55 Special. Education: Royal College of Commerce, Glasgow; Gray's School of Art, Aberdeen. m Shirley, 1 d Catherine, 3 s David, Iain, Kevin. Address: c/o BBC, Pebble Mill, Birmingham. Starsign: Cancer. Hobbies: fishing, photography. People he would most like to meet: Lech Walesa or Alexander Dubcek.

MacLEOD, Kenneth
Presenter b 6.1.28 Scotland. Started in rep in Harrogate and Folkestone. TV debut was as the Duke of Montano in Othello for the BBC, televised from Alexandra

Palace in 1949. Joined Associated Rediffusion three months before the company opened and was the first person to be seen on ITV when transmission began in the UK. Presented such programmes as Teatime at the Embassy and Late Extra. Has been anchorman of Westward TV's nightly news magazine, Westward Diary (retitled Today South West), since the station opened in 1961. Education: King's School, Canterbury. Address: c/o TSW, Plymouth. Starsign: Capricorn. Hobbies: music, carpentry (rough), restoring antique woodwind instruments. Person he would most like to meet: 'Mstislav Rostropovich playing Bach on unaccompanied cello while I drink good single malt whisky.'

McMANUS, Mark
Actor b 1940 Hamilton, Lanarkshire. After leaving school had a number of jobs before going to Australia, 1960, where he drifted into acting and spent 10 years there as an actor. Returned to England and joined the Royal Court Theatre and the National Theatre. Stage incl: The Passion; Lark Rise and Candleford; The World Turned Upside Down; Herod; The Crucible (all with National Theatre). TV incl: Colditz; Crown Court; The Brothers; Sam; The Foundation; Target; The Albion Band; The Long, The Short and The Tall; Bull Week; Strangers; Union

Castle; Two Percent. m Paulette, 1 d Kate, 1 step-s Christopher. Address: c/o ICM, London W1.

McMANUS, Mick
Professional wrestler b 11th January London. Trained at John Ruskin Amateur Wrestling Club, London, and since then has literally fought his way to the top. The man viewers love to hate has been British Welterweight Champion. twice and was recently European Middleweight Champion. Collects antiques and, apart from the wrestling ring, recent TV has included Celebrity Squares. Retired from the ring 8th May 1982. Education: Wilson's Grammar School, London. m Barbara, 1 s Tony. Address: c/o Dale Martin Ltd, London SW9. Starsign: Capricorn. Hobby: golf. Person he would most like to have met: 'Michelangelo – just to sit and watch him at work.'

MACPHERSON, Archie
Sports commentator b 10.11.34 Glasgow. Was a

schoolteacher for 12 years, his last appointment being Head Master of Swinton Primary School, Lanarkshire. Got into radio and TV by writing short stories and scripts and broadcasting as an amateur player. Gave up teaching 1962 to write scripts and become an on-air reporter and presenter full-time. One of the World Cup commentators in 1974, 1978, 1982. Education: Coatbridge High School; Jordanhill College (BA degree). m Jess, 2 s Douglas, Stewart. Address: c/o BBC, Glasgow. Starsign: Scorpio. Hobbies: writing, golf. Person he would most like to meet: 'Woody Allen – witty, bright, civilised and loves New York as I do.'

McWHIRTER, Norris CBE
Author/editor/publisher b 12.8.25 London. Editor and compiler Guinness Book of Records since 1954 (160 editions in 22 languages and over 45 million sales) and, with Roy Castle, co-presenter of BBC TV's Record Breakers since 1972. Was athletics commentator for BBC TV 1951-72 (Olympic Games 1960-72 and on radio 1952-56) and other TV incl: What's in the Picture?; 400 radio and TV shows in American promotion tours 1963-76 (incl Johnny Carson, Merv Griffin, Art Linkletter, Orson Welles, Mike Wallace, Barbara Walters interviews); 57 TV and 58 radio shows in six countries during 1976 world tour; Desert Island

Discs; Any Questions. Served in submarines and minesweepers during the Second World War. Member of the Sports Council 1970-73. Books incl: Get to Your Marks (co-author); British Athletics Record Book (co-author); Ross: Story of a Shared Life. Education: Marlborough College; Trinity College, Oxford (BA International Relations, Economics), (MA Contract Law). m Carole, 1 d Jane, 1 s Alasdair. Address: c/o Guinness Superlatives, Enfield. Starsign: Leo. Hobbies: family, tennis, visiting small islands, researching in libraries. Person he would most like to have met: 'Raoul Wallenberg, who saved 80,000 Jews in 1944 – the 20th century's greatest hero'.

MADELEY, Richard
Presenter b 13.5.56 Romford, Essex. Started at 16 as reporter, Brentwood Argus. News editor, East London Advertiser when 19. Producer BBC Carlisle. Presenter/reporter Border TV. Joined Yorkshire TV 1980; presented Calendar; Calendar Sport; Calendar Goes Pop; Calendar At Your Service; Calendar Tuesday. Education: Coopers Company Grammar, Bow; Shenfield Technical, Brentwood, Essex. m Lynda Ruth. Address: c/o Yorkshire TV, Leeds. Starsign: Taurus. Hobbies: studying social/military aspects of World War Two, eating good food in hot countries, playing the guitar, cats. Person he would most like to meet: 'Laurie Lee, to tell him how much pleasure his books have given me.'

MADOC, Philip
Actor b 5.7.34 Merthyr Tydfil. First-rate linguist (seven languages), his studies took him to the University of Vienna where he was first foreigner to win the Diploma of Interpreters' Institute. After two years as interpreter, intended lecturing at Gothenburg University. Instead he went to RADA. Among many TV roles particularly remembered for Last of the Mohicans; Another Bouquet; The Life and Times of David Lloyd George. Education: Universities of Wales and Vienna. m actress Ruth Madoc (dis), 1 d Lowri, 1 s Rhys. Address: c/o Duncan Heath Assocs, London W1. Starsign: Cancer. Hobbies: languages, wind-surfing, squash. Person he would most like to meet: 'Willy Brandt – a remarkable combination of politics and humanity.'

MADOC, Ruth
Actress/comedienne b 16.4.43 Norwich. Love-sick Gladys Pugh in Hi-de-Hi. On leaving school went to Nottingham Repertory Theatre as assistant stage manager before going to RADA where she met her first husband. First professional

appearance was with him at Lyric Theatre, Hammersmith, in Under Milk Wood. (She was later in the film version with Richard Burton and Elizabeth Taylor.) For three years she was a member of the Black and White Minstrels but left to widen her experience which incl a singing role in Man From La Mancha (in London and South Africa), Fiddler on the Roof (stage and film versions), and pantomime. She was also in The Prince and the Pauper film. Her TV appearances before her rise to fame in Hi-de-Hi incl: Hunter's Walk; Leave It to Charlie; The Life and Times of David Lloyd George. Education: convent. m (1st) actor Philip Madoc (dis), (2nd) manager John Jackson, 1 d Lowri, 1 s Rhys (both from 1st m). Address: c/o Richard Stone, London EC2. Starsign: Aries. Hobbies: home, children. Person she would most like to meet: 'The Pope, because I find him very interesting'.

MAGILL, Ronald
Actor b 1922. First opportunity to tread a real stage came during the war in

which he served in the Royal Corps of Signals and toured with Stars in Battledress. On demob became a tyre salesman but after a year joined a travelling company, Arena, and has since played almost every theatre outside London. Also actor and director at Nottingham Playhouse for nine years. Some TV and a Charlton Heston film, Julius Caesar, before becoming licensee, Amos Brearly, in Emmerdale Farm. Education: Sir Josiah Mason Orphanage, Birmingham. Address: c/o Yorkshire TV, Leeds. Person he would most like to meet: 'William Shakespeare, so that he could explain some of those lines to me.'

MAGNUSSON, Magnus
Writer and presenter b 12.10.29 Reykjavik, Iceland. Family moved to Scotland when he was nine months old, and he has lived there ever since. Started as a reporter on Scottish Daily Express, moved to The Scotsman as chief features writer. Occasional TV engagements in Scotland led to invitation to join Cliff Michelmore as co-presenter of Tonight (1964-65). Thereafter Chronicle; Checkpoint; Cause For Concern; All Things Considered; Mainly Magnus; Personal Pursuits; Mastermind; BC – The Archaeology of the Bible Lands; Living Legends; Vikings! Books incl: Introducing Archaeology;

Viking Expansion Westwards; Landlord or Tenant? – A View of Irish History; BC – The Archaeology of the Bible Lands; Vikings!; Magnus on the Move; Treasures of Scotland. Education: Edinburgh Academy; Jesus College, Oxford. m journalist Mamie Baird, 3 d Sally, Margaret, Anna, 1 s Jon. Address: c/o BBC TV, London W1. Starsign: Libra. Hobby: translating Icelandic sagas and modern novels into English.

MAJORS, Lee
Actor b 23.4.40 Wyandotte, Michigan. Grew up in Kentucky being adopted by relatives on the death of his parents. A star athlete while at school, he might have had a football career, but a back injury during a game ended those hopes. He opted to follow the example of his teenage idol James Dean and went to California to try his hand at acting, and several jobs later he was signed for the Big Valley, which ran for four years. He was already established as a TV personality when offered the role of Steve Austin in The Six Million-Dollar Man. Other TV incl: The Men from Shiloh; The Ballad of Andy Crocker; The Fall Guy. Films incl: Will Penny; The Liberation of L B Jones; The Gary Francis Powers Story; The Norseman; The Naked Sun; Piranha. Education: Universities of Indiana and Eastern Kentucky. m (1st) childhood

sweetheart Kathy (dis), (2nd) actress Farrah Fawcett-Majors, 1 s Lee (from 1st m). Address: Bel Air, California. Starsign: Taurus. Hobbies: avid sportsman, fishing, hunting, golf.

MALCOLM, John
Actor b 26.3.36 Stirling. Trained at RADA, experience in rep touring and West End. Built Traverse Theatre, Edinburgh 1962-63, then two years with Royal Shakespeare Company. Built the Theatre Chipping Norton 1973-77. Recent theatre incl Loot. Films incl: Out of the Ice; Scrubbers. Since 1966 mainly TV, incl many TV documentaries such as Watergate; This Week 1844. Also Enemy at the Door; Nanny; Reid the Sheep Stealer; Coronation Street; Code Name Icarus; Seconds Out. Education: Archbishop Holgate's School For Boys, Barnsley. 1 d Aimée-Louise, 1 s Nathaniel. Address: c/o Barry Brown Management, London SE11. Starsign: Aries. Hobby: arguments.

MALONE, Roger
Sports compère/commentator/writer b 31.5.33 Alexandria, Egypt. Started on newspapers (Daily Express, Daily Herald) and Daily Telegraph sports man in the West since 1964. Launched Westward Sports Desk 1960. HTV Sports West compère and soccer outside broadcast commentator

since 1968. ITV World Cup commentator, Mexico 1970, West German 'guest' World Cup commentator 1974 and 1978. Education: grammar schools in Rugby, Hereford, Isle of Man and Bristol; Sandhurst. m (dis), 1 d Kate, 2 s Keith, Giles. Address: c/o HTV, Bristol. Starsign: Gemini. Hobbies: golf, watching cinema. Person he would most like to meet: 'Burt Lancaster, because he's starred in many of my favourite films.'

MALONEY, Ray
TV reporter b 19.11.27 London. Started in journalism on the Ironmongers' Gazette. Served on the BBC Radio Far East monitoring service and from 1964-72 was reporting abroad for ABC and for a time was bureau chief. He joined ITN 1972 and his assignments have incl the Northern Ireland troubles and the Vietnam and Cyprus wars. Education: Belmont Abbey. m Doreen. Address: c/o ITN, London W1. Starsign: Scorpio. Hobbies: history (he has 4000 books on history), current affairs.

MANNING, Bernard
Comedian b 13.8.30 Manchester. One-time singer in Oscar Rabin's band who now has his own club and drives a Rolls Royce. Worked in pubs and clubs, mainly in the north, until he was 'discovered' in the TV series The Comedians. TV since has incl: The Wheeltappers and Shunters Club; The Entertainers; Bernard Manning in Las Vegas; Bernard Manning; Under Manning. Royal Command Performance 1972 and Comic of the Year 1982. Education: elementary school. m Vera, 1 s Bernard. Address: c/o The Embassy Club, Manchester 9. Starsign: Leo. Hobbies: reading, TV. Person he would most like to meet: 'Enoch Powell – a great statesman'.

MANNING, Hugh
Actor b 19.8.20 Birmingham. Began working life as trainee accountant, but switched to acting and trained at Birmingham School of Speech Training and Dramatic Art. Birmingham Rep 1945, then Bristol Old Vic and London Old Vic. Probably best known for his part as Hunter in Kathleen Harrison's TV series Mrs Thursday. Other TV incl: Sergeant Cork; The Avengers; The Sullivan Brothers; The Venturers; Poldark; Emmerdale Farm. Many stage plays incl: Stalingrad; The Cherry Orchard; Paragraph for Mr Black; Uncle Vanya; A Woman Named Anne; one-man play Song of the Lion. Education: Moseley Grammar. Address: c/o Plunket Greene Ltd, London W1. Starsign: Leo. Hobbies: gardening, tennis, bridge, travel. Person he would most like to meet: 'Too many to choose one.'

MARKS, Alfred OBE
Comedy actor b 28.1.21 London. Formerly an engineer and auctioneer and had no formal training for the stage. First appeared on stage when he was nine in a Boys' Brigade concert and made his first professional appearance at the Kilburn Empire in 1946 in variety. Has since played a variety of parts on stage incl: Where the Rainbow Ends; A Day in the Life of . . .; Spring and Port Wine; The Young Visiters; Dead Silence; Don't Just Lie There, Say Something; The Entertainer; Twelfth Night; Zorba; The Sunshine Boys; Bus Stop. Has also appeared in many pantomimes. Films incl: Desert Mice; There Was a Crooked Man; Weekend With Lulu; Frightened City;

She'll Have to Go; Scream and Scream Again. First TV was Don't Look Now from Alexandra Palace in 1948, followed by Alfred Marks Time which ran for six years on ITV. Other TV incl: Paris 1900; Albert and Victoria; The Good Old Days; Looks Familiar; Blankety Blank; Opinions Unlimited; Funny Man; Does the Team Think?; Give Us a Clue; Maybury; Marti Caine Show; The Olympian Way; Theatre Quiz (compère); The Generation Game; Punchlines; Parkinson. He also compèred Sunday Night at the London Palladium. Education: Bell Lane School, London. m actress Paddie O'Neil. 1 d Danielle, 1 s Gareth. Address: c/o Barry Burnett Ltd, London W1. Starsign: Aquarius. Hobbies: target shooting, riding, stamp collecting, Beethoven. Person he would most like to meet: 'My income tax assessor to show him my threadbare suits.'

West 11; The Rebel: Saints Day; After the Rain; Awake and Sing; Night and Day; seasons at Dundee and the Welsh National. His films incl: Tunes of Glory; A Place to Go; The Killing Bottle; Royal Hunt of the Sun; Robbery; The Uncle; Love in Amsterdam; Poor Jack; Zeppelin; Nosy Dobson; Heroes of Telemark. In addition to The Gentle Touch, his most recent TV incl: Rooms; Romans in Britain; Breakaway. Education: elementary and further education RNAS. m (1st) Linda (dis), (2nd) actress Catherine Schell (dis), 1 s Benjamin (from 1st m). Address: c/o Rolf Kruger Management, London SE1. Starsign: Leo. Hobbies: dabbling, reading, writing, carving (wood), flying. Person he would most like to meet: 'The ape who reversed into the bonnet of my stationary MG.'

from London; Woman's Hour and Good Morning Scotland from Glasgow; series such as Talkabout, Open to Question, Encore (her classical record programme); First Person Singular (her long-running series of TV profiles). Has also presented networked symphony concerts and arts magazines from the Edinburgh Festival and is the anchor person of the news programme Reporting Scotland. Education: Dunoon Grammar School; Glasgow University. m Jack Anderson, 1 s David. Address: c/o BBC Scotland, Glasgow. Starsign: Pisces. Hobbies: opera, theatre, swimming, chess, cooking. Person she would like to have met: 'Sydney Smith (1771-1845), in order to laugh immoderately at stated intervals.'

MARSH, Reginald
Actor b 17.9.26 London. No formal training for the stage – 'just hard work', he says; in other words many years rep and touring. Has been in rep in all parts of the country as well as periods with the RSC and National Theatre. Recent stage incl: Thark. Has also written a number of plays incl: The Death is Announced, in which he appeared on the stage and in the TV version, The Man Who Came to Die. Since 1958 has largely concentrated on films and TV. Films incl: The Sicilians; Shadow of Fear; Jigsaw; The Young Winston; The Day the Earth Caught Fire; Sky Pirates. TV incl: Coronation

MARLOWE, William
Actor b 25.7.32 London. Formerly in the Fleet Air Arm. Wanted to be a writer but went to RADA and has since established himself as a very experienced stage, film and TV actor. On many occasions he has been cast in a villainous role, but his most recent TV puts him on the right side of the law, as Detective Chief Inspector Russell in The Gentle Touch. On stage he has appeared in Five Finger Exercise; Muse in

MARQUIS, Mary
Broadcaster b 11th March Argyll. Trained originally as an actress at the Royal Scottish Academy of Music and Drama and after a period in rep, joined Border TV to present current affairs and arts programmes and her own children's programme, Let's See. Then went to BBC Scotland as presenter/interviewer on nightly news magazine, Six-Ten. Since then she has had wide experience as presenter of current affairs and the arts in TV and radio incl: Today and Nationwide

Street; The Planemakers; Gazette; The Power Game; The Ratcatchers; Barlow; My Name is Harry Worth; Whodunnit?; Bless This House; The Sweeney; Crown Court; The Good Life; Terry and June; Help!; Crossroads; Richard Crossman in Nye; many plays. Book: Much More Than Murder. Education: 'Sufficient', he says. m former actress Rosemary Murray, twin d Rebecca, Alison, 2 s Adam, Alexander. Address: c/o NEMS Ltd, London SW3. Starsign: Virgo. Hobby: writing. Person he would most like to have met: Capability Brown.

Wildfell Hall; A Family at War; Special Branch; The Avengers; Strange Report; Softly, Softly; Z Cars; The Forsyte Saga; Country Matters; A Place to Die; Rooms; My Good Woman; Sam and the River; Warship; Spawn; Out; The Professionals; The Mourning Brooch; Murder at the Wedding; Buccaneer; Tales of the Unexpected. m Vicki, 3 s Sean, Paul, Joshua. Address: c/o Marina Martin Management, London W1. Starsign: Taurus. Hobby: football. Person he would most like to meet: 'Pelé – to complete my dream team of all-time football "greats".'

presenter weekend Late Show on Radio 2. Education: St Columb's College, Londonderry; St Joseph's Teachers' Training College, Belfast. Currently taking degree course with Open University. m Brenda, 1 d Ruth, 1 s Richard. Address: c/o Thames TV, London NW1. Starsign: Aries. Hobbies: cycling, swimming. Person he would most like to meet: 'Sir Harold Wilson – a very professional politician and a good schemer.'

MARTIN, Pamela Sue
Actress b 5.1.54 Westport, Connecticut. The superbitch of a daughter, Fallon Carrington, in Dynasty. Started as a photographic model in New York, specialising in teenage magazines and TV commercials. Made her first film, To Find a Man, while still at school. This led to her part in The Poseidon Adventure, followed by Buster and Bill; Time Out; Lady in Red. Previous to Dynasty her TV incl the title role in The Nancy Drew Mysteries. When not appearing before the cameras she is actively engaged in conservation as a member of the Greenpeace organisation fighting to save seals and whales. She lives in Los Angeles. Starsign: Capricorn. Hobbies: scuba-diving, tennis, skiing.

MARSHALL, Bryan
Actor b 19.5.38 London. Came to acting via an insurance office, service in the army, as a salesman, amateur dramatics and training at RADA. Rep at Bristol Old Vic, Chester, Scottish National Theatre before London West End debut in The Golden Rivet. Other stage incl: Season's Greetings. Films incl: Man in the Wilderness; Rasputin – the Mad Monk; Alfie; Quatermass and the Pit; Mosquito Squadron; Viking Queen; I Start Counting; Because of the Cat; The Tamarind Seed; The Tip Off; The Spy Who Loved Me; The Long Good Friday. First TV in 1963 and claims to have been in every type of production except a Western. TV incl: Persuasion; Vanity Fair; Villette; The Tenant of

MARSHALL, Peter
Presenter/interviewer b 11.4.45 Londonderry. After studying drama at the Arts Educational Trust and the Guildhall School of Music and Drama, became announcer/presenter with Ulster TV 1967-69. Moved to Anglia TV 1970-73 to work on About Anglia; About Women; Sports Desk; Police Call; newsreader and presenter of several special programmes, such as Christmas Concert in Brass. After a period of freelance work with various ITV companies, joined Southern TV 1974 and Thames TV as permanent announcer 1976. Also presenter/interviewer Reports West and Here Today for HTV. Compère Royal Film Première 1981, Miss World and Come Dancing (1981-82). Also

MARTIN, Phil
Reporter/announcer b 30.4.43 London. Started

with pirate radio stations, Radio England and Britain Radio 1966. Then went into newspaper journalism as staff reporter with Daily Express 1967-78. Became a presenter with Radio Newcastle 1978 and joined Tyne Tees TV 1979 as Northern Life reporter and announcer. Education: University College School, Hampstead; Bristol University. m Penny, 2 d Jennifer, Susi, 1 s Tom. Address: c/o Tyne Tees TV, Newcastle. Starsign: Taurus. Hobbies: country strolls, admiring others' gardens, collecting bric-a-brac. Person he would most like to meet: Mother Teresa.

MARTYN, Nicky
Comedian b 14.11.40
Warrington, Lancs. Began as a musician/singer in Warrington, later establishing himself as a comedy entertainer. Breakthrough came in the initial series of ATV's New Faces. He was the winner of his programme and went on to host all the Winners Shows incl the grand finale at the London Palladium. Other TV incl:

guest appearances in many other TV shows; The Summer Show; It's a Grand Life if You Don't Weaken. Education: Redhill Junior, Birmingham; Silver Street School, Warrington; Bewsy Secondary Modern, Warrington; Warrington Technical College. m Edwina, 1 d Philippa, 1 s David. Address: c/o The Neil Johnson Theatrical Agency, Warrington. Starsign: Scorpio. Hobbies: do-it-yourself, horse-riding. Person he would most like to meet: Bob Hope.

MASON, Hilary
Actress b 4.9.17
Birmingham. Won a scholarship to London School of Dramatic Art where she studied under Gertrude Pickersgill. Then rep (Preston, Southport, York, Guildford) and ENSA during the war. Films incl: Rockets on the Dunes; She'll Follow You Anywhere; Don't Look Now; I Don't Want to be Born; The Absolution. Many TV appearances incl: The Secret Garden; Z Cars; Dixon of Dock Green; Swizzlewick (serial); The Newcomers; The Doctors; The Six Wives of Henry VIII; Take Three Girls; Castors Away; Main Chance; Macbeth; Love and Mr Lewisham; Affairs of the Heart; Poldark; The Deep Blue Sea; United; The Phoenix and the Carpet; Ripping Yarns; Bess of Hardwick; Angels; Within These Walls; Early Struggles; Alice Dancing; Rooms; The

Case of Eliza Armstrong; Out of the Unknown; All Things Bright and Beautiful; The Fall and Rise of Reginald Perrin; My Brother's Keeper; Nicholas Nickleby; Duchess of Duke Street; Phyllis Dixey; The Three Hostages; Wilde Alliance; Thomas and Sarah; Just William; Worzel Gummidge; The Other One; The Indian Summer of Mr Brown; The House of Bernarda Alba; Penmarric; King Arthur; The Trial of Lady Chatterley's Lover; Minder; Deep Concern; The Last Visitor for Hugh Peter; Brendon Chase; Sink or Swim; England, Their England; That Beryl Marston . . . !; Tales of the Unexpected; Days; City. Education: secondary school, Birmingham, and 'lots of night school'. m Roger Ostime. Address: c/o Jimmy Garrod Management, Shepperton, Middx. Starsign: Virgo. Hobbies: writing, history, gardening. Person she would most like to meet: 'Caruso – to hear his real voice, not just a record.'

MASSEY, Anna
Actress b 11.8.37
Thakeham, Surrey. Always wanted to be an actress. Became a star overnight when 17, in her first part in The Reluctant Debutante. Other theatre incl: Dear Delinquent; The School for Scandal; The Right Honourable Gentleman; The Flip Side; The Elder Statesman; The Miracle Worker; The Prime of Miss

Jean Brodie; Donkey's Years; Heartbreak House; Jingo; The Importance of Being Earnest; Alaska; Family Voices (the last three all with National Theatre). Films incl: Vault of Horror; Frenzy. Many TV plays and series incl: The Green of the Year; The Pallisers; Couples; Rebecca; The Potting Shed; Behind the Scenes; Virginia Fly Is Drowning; A Little Romance; Maiden, Maiden. Education: mainly private school in London, but also in America and Switzerland and with private families in Paris and Rome. m actor Jeremy Brett (dis), 1 s David. Address: c/o Jeremy Conway Ltd, London W1. Starsign: Leo.

MATHIAS, Glyn
ITN Political Editor b 19.2.45 South Wales. Started as a reporter on South Wales Echo before joining BBC at Southampton. Political correspondent for ITN 1973 and Home Affairs correspondent 1979. Political editor 1981. Education: Llandovery College; Jesus College, Oxford; Southampton University. m Sian, 1 d Megan, 1 s Mathew. Address: c/o ITN, London W1. Starsign: Pisces. Hobbies: squash, walking, reading, talking.

MATTHEWS, Francis
Actor b 2.9.31 York. Started his career at Leeds Rep when he was 17. Service in the Royal Navy then more rep incl Oxford and Bromley. From

the latter he was chosen for a leading role in No Escape, with Flora Robson, and subsequently in Bhowani Junction with Ava Gardner. Radio incl: Not in Front of the Children; Local Time; Stop the World; Double Trouble. First TV of note was in Francis Durbridge series, My Friend Charles; has since been in many films and over 200 TV plays or series. Probably best known as TV's Paul Temple. Other TV incl: A Little Big Business; My Man Joe; Trinity Tales; Middlemen; Roof Over My Head; Don't Forget to Write; Morecambe and Wise Christmas Shows 1971 and 1978; Leslie Crowther Scrapbook; Crowther Collection. Has also sung on Saturday Night At The Mill and Marti Caine Show. Education: St Michael's Jesuit College, Leeds. m actress Angela Browne, 3 s Paul, Dominic, Damien. Address: c/o Richard Stone, London WC2. Starsign: Virgo. Hobbies: writing, tennis, cricket. Person he would most like to have met: 'William Shakespeare, to see if he really could write, or was just a semi-literate corn-merchant!'

MAYNARD, Bill
Actor b 8.10.28 Farnham, Surrey. Always wanted to be an actor, but started in Variety. A season at Skegness Butlin's with Terry Scott led to the TV series Great Scott–It's Maynard for which they were teamed and made stars. But Bill wanted to

act so was off TV for 10 years. First play was a thriller, You Too Can Have a Body, at Worthing. Also acted at Nottingham and with other reps and pantomime. First film: Till Death Us Do Part. Other films incl: Hitler: My Part in His Downfall; Confessions of a Pop Performer. Best known for his TV work which incl: Coronation Street; The Life of Riley; Paper Roses; Kisses at Fifty; Oh, No, It's Selwyn Frogitt; Paradise Island; Bill Maynard in Person; The Gaffer. Books incl: The Yo-Yo Man (autobiography). Education: Kibworth Beauchamps Grammar School. m Muriel, 1 d Jane, 1 s Martin. Address: c/o Richard Stone, London WC2. Starsign: Libra. Hobbies: snooker, golf, watching other people (ie his friends) work!

MEDWIN, Michael
Actor b 18.7.29 London. Made stage debut in 1940 and film debut six years later in The Root of All Evil. Many films both as actor and producer incl: (as actor) For Them That Trespass; Queen of Spades; The Lady Craved

Excitement; Shadows of the Past; Boys in Brown; Curtain Up; Street Corner; Hindle Wakes; The Oracle; The Techman Mystery; Above Us the Waves; A Hill in Korea; Checkpoint; I Only Arsked; Carry On Nurse; Heart of a Man; Crooks Anonymous; It's All Happening; Night Must Fall; I've Gotta Horse; Scrooge; The Jigsaw Man; and as producer, Charlie Bubbles; Gumshoe; O Lucky Man!; Law and Disorder. Also co-produced many London West End plays incl: If . . .; Spring and Port Wine. Acted with the National Theatre 1977-78. On TV probably best remembered for his role in The Army Game series, but also starred in own TV series For the Love of Mike, and Three Live Wires, and has recently returned to TV in Shoestring. Education: Canford and Institute Fischer, Montreux, Switzerland. m (dis). Address: c/o Leading Artists, London W1. Starsign: Cancer. Hobby: golf. Person he would most like to meet: 'My mother – I was adopted at the age of three months.'

MELVILLE, Alan
Writer/broadcaster b 9.4.10 Berwick-upon-Tweed. Formerly worked in his father's timber business but from 1936-40 was engaged with the BBC broadcasting and producing feature programmes. After serving with the RAF 1941-46, wrote sketches and lyrics for numerous London revues and was also co-author or author of many others. Has also written a number of plays and is the author of novels and two autobiographies, Myself When Young and Merely Melville. TV appearances incl: The Brains Trust; What's My Line; Spring in Park Lane; Melvillaining; Call My Bluff; Merely Melville; The Very Merry Widow; Before the Fringe; Raise Your Glasses. Education: Edinburgh Academy. Address: c/o PVA Management Ltd, London W1. Starsign: Aries. Hobbies: tennis, gardening, cooking, theatre/ opera. Person he would most like to meet: 'Adam – he was the first to do a great many things.'

MERCIER, Sheila
Actress b 1.1.19 Hull. Started stage career with Sir Donald Wolfit's company as did her brother, Brian Rix. Was WAAF adjutant during the war. Joined Brian's Whitehall Theatre company 1955 and was with him 11 years. Has played Annie Sugden in Emmerdale Farm since the programme started in 1972. Education: French Covent, Hull; Hunmanby Hall, Yorks. m theatrical manager Peter Mercier, 1 s Nigel. Address: c/o Yorkshire TV, Leeds. Starsign: Capricorn. Hobbies: reading, entertaining. Person she would most like to meet: 'Sir Laurence Olivier, because he is still the greatest actor in the world.'

METCALFE, Adrian
Producer/commentator b 2.3.42 Bradford, Yorks. Sports Editor Channel Four. Former Sunday Express news reporter, and a founder member of the World of Sport team since the programme started in 1964. Producer of Sports Arena and has worked for all American TV networks as a producer and commentator on 20 sports. Covered the Olympics for ITV from 1972-80 and is currently senior athletics commentator. In 1961 was the fastest runner in the world over 400 metres (45.7 secs), a record that stood for 10 years. Member of the British 4 by 400 metres relay team that won silver medals at the Tokyo Olympics in 1964. In 1963 he won a double gold in the World Student Games. Has produced over 100 documentaries and over 300 outside broadcasts. Education: Roundhay School, Leeds; Brunt's Grammar, Mansfield; Magdalen College, Oxford. m TV production assistant Anne Summerton, 1 d Hannah, 1 s Daniel. Address: c/o Channel Four, London W1. Starsign: Pisces. Hobbies: physical self-rehabilitation, food and drink.

MICHELL, Keith
Actor b 1.12.28 Adelaide, Australia. Trained as an art teacher – painting is still one of his main activities – and while teaching made his first acting appearance in Lover's

Leap in Adelaide in 1947. He also did radio work and gained admission to the Old Vic Theatre School in 1949, and from 1950-51 was a member of the Young Vic Theatre Co. His first London appearance was as King Charles II in the musical version of And So To Bed. From 1952-56 he was with the Shakespeare Memorial Theatre company, with whom he toured Australia 1952-53. He joined the Old Vic company in 1956 and from 1958-61 he starred in the musical Irma La Douce. Then followed many plays incl: The First Four Hundred Years (a programme in which he toured Australia as part of the Shakespeare 400th anniversary celebrations); Robert and Elizabeth; King's Mare; Man of La Mancha; Abelard and Heloise; The Apple Cart; Murder in the Cathedral (in Chichester Cathedral) and more recently, The Crucifer of Blood and On the Twentieth Century. In 1977 he compiled, directed and designed a Royal Review to music, In Order of Appearance, and in 1981 played Pete McGynty in Pete McGynty and the Dreamtime, his own adaptation of Peer Gynt with the Melbourne Theatre Company. Appeared in Captain Beaky's Christmas Show 1981. Films incl: Dangerous Exile; Hell Fire Club; Seven Seas to Calais; The Executioner; House of Cards; Prudence and the Pill; Henry VIII and His Six Wives;

Moments. No stranger to TV, his appearances incl many specials, as well as Pygmalion; Act of Violence; The Mayerling Affair; Wuthering Heights; The Ring Round the Moon; Julius Caesar; Antony and Cleopatra; Loyalties; An Ideal Husband; The Six Wives of Henry VIII: Captain Beaky and His Band; Captain Beaky, Vol 2; Ruddigore. His records incl: Ancient and Modern; At the Shows; Words, Words, Words; The Sonnets and the Prophet; Captain Beaky and His Band; Captain Beaky, Vol 2. He has held several one-man shows of his paintings and in 1975 illustrated a book of poems, Captain Beaky, which subsequently became a best seller, as did Captain Beaky, Vol 2. Education: Port Pirie High School; Adelaide Teachers' College; School of Arts and Crafts; Adelaide University. m Jeannette Sterke, 1 d Helena, 1 s Paul. Address: c/o Chatto and Linnit Ltd, London W1. Starsign: Sagittarius. Hobbies: jogging, swimming.

MICHELMORE, Cliff CBE
Commentator/presenter
b 11.12.19 Cowes, Isle of Wight. Service in RAF, then with British Forces Network in Germany 1947-49 when he joined BBC to produce, direct and write for children's TV. Sports commentaries from 1951 and a nightly interview programme 1955-57. Countless appearances on BBC and ITV programmes

incl: Tonight (1957-64); 24 Hours (1964-68); Our World (first world-linked satellite programme 1967); Holiday (since 1969); space programmes; general elections; Talkback; Wheelbase; Chance to Meet; Across the Great Divide; Opinions Unlimited; A Ripe Old Age; Let's Pretend; People's Choice; Fleet Air Arm; The Thynne Inheritance; Day By Day. Still remembered as presenter of Family Favourites from Hamburg on radio through which he met his wife who introduced the London side of the programme. Education: Cowes High; Loughborough College; Leicester College of Technology. m broadcaster Jean Metcalfe, 1 d Jenny, 1 s Guy. Address: Reigate, Surrey. Starsign: Sagittarius. Hobbies: golf, sitting around. Person he would most like to meet: 'Cleopatra, to see if it's true.'

MILLAR, Gavin
Film-maker/presenter
b 11.1.38 Clydebank, Scotland. Took a post-graduate course at the Slade School of Art before entering TV. Has been 18 years in TV 'picking it up' and amassing an impressive list of credits incl: documentaries on Norman McLaren, Sam Goldwyn, Busby Berkeley, Robert Louis Stevenson, and drama incl: The Three Girls; Two Gallants; An Imaginative Woman; Goodbye; Cream in My Coffee. Also produced

and presented Arena
Cinema. Education: King
Edward's School,
Birmingham; Oxford
University. m Sylvia,
2 d Kirstie, Isabel,
3 s James, Thomas,
Duncan. Address: c/o Judy
Daish Assocs, London W1.
Starsign: Capricorn.
Hobbies: trying to get home.
Person he would most like to
have met: 'Robert Louis
Stevenson – for his tolerance,
wit, good humour and prose.'

MILLER, Graham
Presenter/reporter
b 22.11.51 London.
Newspapers, BBC Radio and
Anglia TV before joining HTV.
Presenter/reporter of HTV's
Report West;
commentator/presenter
football, rugby, cricket and
darts outside broadcasts for
HTV; producer/presenter
various consumer
programmes and presenter
of occasional light
entertainment show for HTV.
Education: Luton Grammar
School; City of Birmingham
Polytechnic; 'University of
Life'. m Lesley. Address: c/o
HTV West, Bristol. Starsign:
Sagittarius. Hobbies: sport,
listening, watching old
English movies, more sport.
Person he would most like to
have met: W G Grace.

MILLIGAN, Spike
Actor/comedian/author
b 16.4.18 Ahmaddnagar,
India. Spent early life in India,
Burma and Ceylon where his
father was in the army. Came
to Britain 1933. Started as

singer and trumpeter
1936-39, later guitarist.
Professional debut in Naples
1945. Radio debut,
Opportunity Knocks 1949.
Since then radio incl: Crazy
People (which eventually
became the Goon Show and
brought him fame); The Last
Goon Show of All (written
specially for the 50th
anniversary of BBC
Broadcasting). TV incl: Idiot's
Weekly; A Show Called Fred;
Son of Fred; Milligan at Large;
Milligan's Wake; Muses With
Milligan; The World of
Beachcomber; Q5; Curry
And Chips; The Other Spike;
Comedy Machine; Q6; The
Muppets; Q7; The Best of
British; Q8; Q9; Q10. Theatre
incl: Treasure Island; The
Bed-Sitting Room (and film);
Son of Oblomov; For One
Week Only; his one-man
show. Films incl: The
Running, Jumping and
Standing Still Film; Watch
Your Stern; Suspect;
Postman's Knock; The Magic
Christian; The Great
McGonagall; The Adventures
of Barry McKenzie; The Last
Remake of Beau Geste; Life
of Brian; The Hound of the
Baskervilles; History of the
World, Part I. Records:
Russian Love Song; The Ying
Tong Song; I'm Walking
Backwards For Christmas;
The Goons; The Snow Goose.
Books incl: Puckoon; Adolf
Hitler: My Part in His Downfall;
The Goon Show Scripts;
Small Dream of a Scorpion;
Badjelly the Witch; Rommel?
Gunner Who?; The Spike
Milligan Letters; Monty – His

Part in my Victory; Mussolini –
His Part in My Downfall; Silly
Verse for Kids; The Bed
Sitting Room; The Goon Show
Script Book; More Goon
Show Scripts; The Book of
Goons; Milligan Book of
Records. Education:
Christian Brothers de la Salle,
Rangoon; London
Polytechnic. m (1st) June
(dis), (2nd) singer Patricia
Ridgway (dec), 3 d Laura,
Sile (from 1st m), Jane (from
2nd m), 1 s Sean (from
1st m). Address: c/o Spike
Milligan Productions, London
W2. Starsign: Aries. Hobbies:
painting, restoring antiques.
Person he would most like to
meet: Jesus Christ.

MILLS, Hayley
Actress b 18.4.46 London.
Trained at the Elmhurst Ballet
School and made her first
film, Tiger Bay, when she was
12 and had a five-year
contract with Walt Disney.
Since then she has made 22
films incl: Whistle Down the
Wind; The Chalk Garden; The
Family Way; Pretty Polly;
Truth About Spring, etc.
Made her stage debut in the
title role of Peter Pan 1970.
Other theatre appearances
incl: The Three Sisters; The
Wild Duck; Rebecca; A
Touch of Spring; The Summer
Party; My Fat Friend;
Trelawney of the Wells. TV
incl: Only a Scream Away;
Deadly Strangers; Flame
Trees of Thika. Education:
Elmhurst Ballet School; Swiss
finishing school. m (dis),
2 s Crispian, Jason.
Address: c/o ICM, London

W1. Starsign: Aries. Hobbies: gardening, travel.

MILLS, Sir John CBE
Actor b 22.2.08 Felixstowe, Suffolk. A star for nearly 50 years, started his career in musical comedy (Mr Cinders; Jill Darling; etc), then progressed to more serious roles. Stage incl: Charley's Aunt (twice); Cavalcade; Ross (New York); and more recently, Veterans; At the End of the Day; The Good Companions; Great Expectations; Separate Tables. First film The Midshipmaid with Jessie Matthews 1931, since when he has been in about 100 films incl: We Dive at Dawn; The Way to the Stars; Great Expectations; Scott of the Antarctic; The History of Mr Polly; Oh What a Lovely War; Hobson's Choice; The Colditz Story; Above Us the Waves; Dunkirk; Ice Cold In Alex; I Was Monty's Double; Tiger Bay; Tunes of Glory; Ryan's Daughter (for which he received an Oscar); Young Winston; Oklahoma Crude; The Human Factor; Trial by Combat; The Devil's Advocate; The Thirty Nine Steps; The Big Sleep; Zulu Dawn; Gandhi. TV incl: The Zoo Gang; Roald Dahl's Tales of the Unexpected (Galloping Foxley); Quatermass; Umbrella Man; Operation Safecrack; Young at Heart. Book: Up In the Clouds, Gentlemen Please! (autobiography). Education: Norwich. m (1st) Aileen Raymond (dis), (2nd)

playwright Mary Hayley Bell, 2 d actresses Juliet and Hayley, 1 s Jonathan. Address: c/o ICM, London W1. Starsign: Pisces. Hobbies: painting, reading, writing, staying at home.

MILLS, Royce
Actor b 12.5.42 Tetbury, Glos. Spent five years studying fine art, managing a summer rep and qualifying as a theatrical designer before starting to study at the Guildhall School, where he was the Major Open Scholar in drama, Shakespeare Prizeman and the Gold Medallist. He also won a BBC Sound Repertory Prize and has been a regular broadcaster ever since. After nearly three years with the Yvonne Arnaud Theatre he joined the Bristol Old Vic and has since appeared in theatres all over the country as well as America and Hong Kong. London West End debut in 1967 and more recently has appeared in The Bed Before Yesterday and The Streets of London. Also produces, directs and designs for the theatre and is a member of the Guildhall School's Board of Examiners. First film was Up Pompeii and most recent, History of the World Part One. First appeared on TV as a boy in 1954 but his TV career really started in 1969 with Oh Bother! TV since incl: Mike Yarwood, Dick Emery, Les Dawson, Marti Caine, Bernie Winters, Jim Davidson and Bing Crosby shows; Fraud

Squad; Play of the Month; Doctor in the House; Hark at Barker; Charley's Aunt; No, That's Me Over Here; Copper's End; Queenie's Castle; Inigo Pipkin; Dora; Armchair Theatre; Sir Yellow; A House in Regent Place; Kids from 47A; Shades of Green; The Tomorrow People; Rainbow; Pipkins; Masterspy; Bonkers; The Rather Reassuring Programme; Sykes; Sheppey; Rings on Their Fingers; Crossroads. Is also the voice behind many TV commercials. Education: Eastbourne College, East Sussex. m Una Morriss, 2 d Samantha, Miranda (both of whom have appeared in Crossroads). Address: c/o Roger Storey Ltd, London N12. Hobbies: painting, pondering, prevaricating. Person he would most like to meet: 'Lord Grade, to thank him for the many opportunities his companies have afforded me over the years.'

MOLLISON, Fiona
Actress b 9.1.54 Java. Brought up in England and trained for the stage at the Central School of Speech and Drama, followed by rep at Derby and Lincoln. Has also appeared at Oxford Playhouse and the Nuffield Theatre. Films incl: Sweeney Two. On TV she has been in three series of Strangers, and Spaghetti Two-Step. Education: Wimbledon High School. m David Gilmore. Address: c/o Hamper

Neafsey Assocs, London W1.
Starsign: Capricorn. Hobby:
cooking.

MONKHOUSE, Bob
Entertainer b 1.6.28
Beckenham, Kent. Freelance
cartoonist from age of 12,
drawing comic strips and
writing short stories. Sold first
jokes to Max Miller in 1944.
Trained as cartoon film
animator with Gaumont-
British when 17½.
Conscripted in RAF 1946.
First radio broadcast in
Works Wonders; first TV: New
To You, both in 1948.
Became BBC's first contract
comedian. With ex-Dulwich
schoolfriend Denis Goodwin
(dec 1975) formed a
script-writing team and
together they scripted
thousands of radio and TV
comedy shows for Arthur
Askey, Bob Hope, Jack
Benny, Jack Buchanan and
themselves. For a year they
wrote up to seven weekly
shows simultaneously.
London West End debut as
compère of Sauce Piquante,
1950. Stage also incl: Bob
Monkhouse startime
(Blackpool); pantomimes;
Boys from Syracuse; Come
Blow Your Horn. Films incl:
Carry On, Sergeant; Dentist
in the Chair; Dentist on the
Job; Weekend With Lulu;
She'll Have to Go. Recent
radio incl: Punchline. TV
series incl: What's My Line?;
Do You Trust Your Wife?; My
Pal Bob; The Big Noise;
Candid Camera; For Love or
Money; Sunday Night at the
London Palladium; Mad

Movies; The Golden Shot
(1967-74); Celebrity Squares
(1974-79); I'm Bob – He's
Dickie; Family Fortunes
(since 1980); Looks Familiar;
Starburst; Parkinson; Des
O'Connor Show. Works
principally as TV host and
cabaret attraction. Describes
himself as 'a standup
comedian'. Education:
Grange School, Beckenham;
Goring Hall, Goring-by-Sea;
Dulwich College. m (1st)
Elizabeth (dis), (2nd)
secretary Jacqueline,
1 d Abigail (adopted),
2 s Garry, Simon. Address:
c/o Peter Prichard Ltd,
London SW1. Starsign:
Gemini. Hobbies: collecting
vintage films (esp silent
comedies), collecting
original artwork by great
cartoonists, esp historic
characters (Popeye, Krazy
Kat, Pogo, etc). Person he
would most like to have met:
Charlie Chaplin.

MONTEITH, Kelly
Comedian b 17.10.42 St
Louis, Missouri. Trained for
the theatre at Pasadena
Playhouse and Pasadena
College of Theatre Arts,
California, since when he has
made regular appearances
in major nightclubs and
hotel/casinos in Las Vegas,
Reno, and Lake Tahoe,
Nevada. Other TV in America
incl: summer show on CBS;
The Kelly Monteith Show
(1976); a late night show, also
on CBS, No Holds Barred
(1980). For the past three
years he has appeared on
BBC 2 in his own show, Kelly

Monteith. Education: public
school and college. m (dis).
Address: c/o BBC, London.
Starsign: Libra. Hobbies:
reading, writing. Person he
would most like to have met:
'William Shakespeare – to
find out how he approached
the writing process.'

MONTGOMERY, James
Reporter b 16.9.45
Wimbledon, London. TV and
radio in Australia before
joining Southern TV and TVS.
Regular presenter/
interviewer Day By Day and
Coast To Coast; 18
documentaries; The Other
Side of Yesterday, a
programme of his songs and
music and sung by him;
presenter of regular Music In
Camera symphony orchestra
programmes. Education:
Marlborough House School;
Wellington College;
Magdalen College, Oxford;
The Sorbonne, Paris.
Address: c/o TVS,
Southampton. Starsign:
Virgo. Hobbies: swimming,
writing, music. Person he
would most like to have met:
Henry Purcell.

MOODY, Ron
Actor/singer/dancer/
writer/composer/
lyricist/cartoonist/
novelist/sociologist/
comedian etc b 9.1.24
Tottenham, London. Came
into acting almost by
accident: while studying for a
post-graduate degree he
was invited to take part in an
intimate revue at London's

New Lindsey Theatre. From there he went into the West End in Intimacy at 8.30, followed by For Amusement Only and For Adults Only. His first musical was Candide and then came Oliver!, his role as Fagin both on stage and in the film version making him an international star. (For his performance in the film made in 1967, he was nominated for an Oscar and won Hollywood Golden Globe, Variety Club Best Film Actor Award 1969, Moscow Golden Bear, and Premio San Jurge presented by Radio Nacional de Espana en Barcelona). His other stage appearances incl: Hamlet; The Clandestine Marriage; Richard III (in Canada). Has played Captain Hook in Peter Pan four times. Films incl: Summer Holiday; Mouse on the Moon; Ladies Who Do; Murder Most Foul; The Sandwich Man; David Copperfield; Twelve Chairs; The Flight of the Doves; Dogpound Shuffle; The Spaceman and King Arthur; Wrong is Right. Many TV appearances incl: Who's Moody?; Sunday Night at the London Palladium; The Good Old Days; Michael Parkinson Show; Saturday Night at the Mill; Who's a Good Boy Then?; Village Hall; Starsky and Hutch; Bing Crosby Christmas Show; Nobody's Perfect; Dial M for Murder; Hart to Hart; Hart of the Yard; Othello; Tales of a Brass Monkey. Books: The Devil You Don't; VVSI (and a third planned). Has also written four musicals (one-man show Move Along Sideways; Joey; Joey, Joey; Saturnalia). Education: London School of Economics, London University (BSc Economics). Address: c/o ICM, London W1. Starsign: Capricorn. Hobbies: driving his Bentley Continental, smoking Havana cigars. Person he would most like to meet: 'Me — I'm still looking for myself.'

MOORE, Brian
Commentator b 28.2.32 Benenden, Kent. Journalistic experience with World Sports, Exchange Telegraph, The Times, before joining BBC and then LWT. Compère of The Big Match and various ITV football programmes. Also major sporting documentaries for ITV. Education: local primary; Cranbrook. m Betty, 2 s Christopher, Simon. Address: c/o LWT, London SE1. Starsign: Pisces. Hobbies: family life, animals, all sport. Person he would most like to have met: 'The Rev John Russell of Devon, who died in 1883 but first bred Jack Russell terriers — dogs that have brought pleasure to millions of owners, including me, ever since.'

MOORE, Patrick OBE
Author/astronomer/TV presenter and personality b 4.3.23 Pinner, Middx. Was about to go to university when Second World War started. Rigged his RAF medical and

flew as a navigator. Passionately interested in astronomy since the age of six. Elected to the British Astronomical Association when he was 11. Has written many books, incl boys' novels, science fiction and science fact, incl: the best-selling Moon Flight Atlas and Atlas of the Universe. Is a regular contributor to magazines and journals. TV incl: BBC's longest-running programme, The Sky at Night, which celebrated 25 years in 1982. One Pair of Eyes; coverage of various space shots and many guest appearances on programmes such as The Morecambe and Wise Show; Face the Music; It's a Celebrity Knockout; Blankety Blank. Appeared as guest xylophonist in the Royal Command Performance, 1981. Address: c/o BBC TV, London W12. Starsign: Pisces. Hobbies: astronomy, cricket, music, tennis. Person he would most like to meet: 'Anyone who will get rid of income tax and VAT!'

MOORE, William
Actor b 19th April

Birmingham. Trained for the theatre at Birmingham Rep and started his acting career there in 1947. Has appeared at most rep theatres, incl Pitlochry and Swansea, where he met his future wife. For a time he taught at the Bristol Old Vic Theatre School. He appeared in the original production of When We Are Married in London's West End and has many radio credits. But he is best known on TV incl: Z Cars; Softly, Softly; Middlemarch; Dombey and Sons; Better Than the Movies; Dad's Army; Dick Emery Show; Charles Bravo; Terry Scott Show; Coronation Street; Rivals of Sherlock Holmes; South Riding; The Brontës; Sam; Love Story; The Cedar Tree; The Fenn Street Gang; No, Honestly; Dick Turpin; Sorry! m actress Mollie Sugden, 2 s Robin, Simon (twins). Address: c/o Joan Reddin Ltd, London W11. Starsign: Aries. Hobbies: painting, gardening, writing verse.

Lord John Sanger's Variety Circus. Radio breakthrough on Workers' Playtime and own radio series, You're Only Young Once. TV incl: Running Wild; variety; Sunday Night at the London Palladium; The Morecambe and Wise Show (BBC and ITV). Numerous variety, pantomimes, summer and royal shows, tours of Australia and Canada and Ed Sullivan Show in America. Films: The Intelligence Men; That Riviera Touch; The Magnificent Two. Freeman City of London 1976; Doctor of Literature, Lancaster University 1977. Education: Lancaster Road and Euston Road schools, Morecambe. m Joan, 1 d Gail, 2 s Gary, Steven. Address: c/o London Management, London W1. Starsign: Taurus. Hobbies: bird-watching, football, fishing, photography. Person he would most like to meet: 'Des O'Connor's singing teacher, because the poor chap needs some encouragement.'

Northcott Theatre 1976-78. Associate Director, Nottingham Playhouse 1978-80. Many plays and films incl: The Pumpkin Eater; The Story of Private Pooley; Perfect Friday. Entered TV in 1955 and has since made hundreds of appearances in such programmes as Softly, Softly; Spindoe; Judge Dee; Randall and Hopkirk (Deceased); Department S; Hadleigh; Dear Mother . . . Love Albert; The Sweeney. Education: 'negligible', he claims. m Dilys Laye (dis). Address: c/o NEMS Management, London SW3. Starsign: Aries. Hobbies: golf, photography, riding – showjumping and eventing.

MORGAN, Maria
Actress/vocalist b 26.6.55 Leamington Spa. Trained at the Central School of Speech and Drama (Gold Medallist). Since 1975 has presented A Handful of Songs on TV. Other TV incl: Get It Together; Rock On with 45. Has also recorded two LPs and three singles. On stage has appeared in Aladdin. pantomime with Little and Large at Liverpool and as Cinderella at Maidstone, Christmas 1981. m David Kassner, 1 s Alexander. Address: c/o President Records Ltd, London SW1. Starsign: Cancer. Hobbies: dancing, travelling, swimming, tennis and other sports, knitting, dining out. Person she would most like to meet: 'Sir Laurence Olivier – a brilliant and fascinating man.'

MORECAMBE, Eric OBE
Comedian b 14.5.26 Morecambe, Lancs. Child entertainer and winner of talent contests at Morecambe for three successive years. Booked for Bryan Michie's Youth Takes a Bow and met Ernie Wise 1941. Formed a double act but touring was interrupted by National Service as a Bevin Boy in the mines. Partnership resumed after the war when both booked for

MORGAN, Garfield
Actor b 19.4.31 Birmingham. Apprenticed as a dental mechanic before going to a Birmingham drama school. Started acting career with Arena Theatre, Birmingham. Besides acting also directs and was Director of Productions, Marlowe Theatre, Canterbury 1957-58, and at Manchester's Library Theatre 1959-60. Associate Director,

MORRIS, Beth
Actress b 19.7.49
Gorseinon, South Wales.
Trained at Cardiff College of
Music and Drama and rep
experience at Northampton,
Colchester, Bristol and
Birmingham before
appearing in London's West
End and with the Royal
Shakespeare Company.
Theatre incl: Man and
Superman; Banana Ridge;
Travesties (London and
Broadway); Passion of
Dracula; Mrs Grabofskies
Academy. TV incl: Play of the
Week; Play of the Month;
Jude The Obscure; Minder; Z
Cars; Softly, Softly; Armchair
Thriller; I Claudius; David
Copperfield. Education:
grammar school. m actor
Stephen Moore. Address: c/o
Ken McReddie, London W1.
Starsign: Cancer. Hobbies:
reading, my dog. Person she
would most like to meet:
Margaret Thatcher.

MORRIS, Colin
TV interviewer and producer
b 4.2.16 Liverpool. Man of
many parts – former
insurance agent, reluctant
actor, war correspondent
and author of the famous
Whitehall farce Reluctant
Heroes in which he acted in
the theatre and in the film
version. Former BBC
producer/writer, he came into
TV in 1954 when Reluctant
Heroes finished its four-year
run and became a BBC
trainee under Huw Weldon.
Retired from BBC in 1976
since when he has been
taking part in several
interview series incl: Heart to
Heart; My Way; Turning Point;
Women of Today. Has written
many plays for stage, film
scripts incl: Alexander the
Great; The Gathering Storm.
TV plays and series incl: The
Carnforth Practice; The
Newcomers. Holder of many
script awards from British
Academy (three), Writer's
Guild and Emerson College.
Education: Oldershaw
Grammar School. m Viera,
1 d Niki, 1 s Julian.
Address: London N6.
Starsign: Aquarius. Hobbies:
sailing; fell walking,
gardening. Person he would
most like to meet: 'Lao Tzu,
classical Chinese
philosopher who got it right'.

MORRIS, Desmond Dr
Zoologist b 24.1.28 Purton,
Wilts. Always interested in
animals (he kept a small
menagerie, incl hundreds of
mice, as a small boy), he
decided to study zoology
after military service, and in
1956 became head of the TV
and film unit set up by
Granada TV at London Zoo,
and presented a weekly TV
programme, Zoo Time, until
1967. In 1959 he became the
youngest-ever Curator of
Mammals at the zoo and
conducted experiments to try
to teach chimpanzees to
paint pictures. From 1965-67
he also presented a
fortnightly programme, Life in
the Animal World, on BBC 2.
He concentrated on his
writing until 1982, when he
returned to TV with the series
The Human Race. He has
also made a series for
Japanese TV, Manwatching
in Japan. Created new forms
of primitive gesture and
language for the film Quest
For Fire. A prolific writer, he is
equally famous for his
best-sellers incl: The Naked
Ape; The Human Zoo;
Intimate Behaviour;
Manwatching: A Field Guide
to Human Behaviour (for
which he visited 15
countries); Animal Days; The
Soccer Tribe. Director of
Oxford United FC; former
research Fellow, Wolfson
College, Oxford; former
Director of Institute of
Contemporary Arts.
Education: Dauntsey's
School, Wilts; Birmingham
University (BSc); Oxford
University (DPhil).
m Ramona, 1 s Jason.
Address: c/o Jonathan Cape,
London WC1. Starsign:
Aquarius. Hobbies: painting,
archaeology, lexicography,
football, racing. Person he
would most like to have met:
'The designer of Silbury Hill,
to ask why he built it.'

MORRIS, Johnathon
Actor b 20.7.60 Urmston,
Manchester. Trained for the

stage at Bristol Old Vic Theatre School but as a boy actor was in Oliver (title role) and South Pacific in amateur productions at Manchester Opera House. Was at Chichester Festival Theatre 1981. TV incl: Coronation Street; Crown Court; The Professionals; The Squad; That Beryl Marston . . .!; The Agatha Christie Hour (In a Glass Darkly). Education: Buglawton County Primary, Cheshire; Congleton Boys' Secondary. Address: c/o ICM, London W1. Starsign: Cancer. Hobbies: football, singing/guitar. Person he would most like to meet: 'An ancestor from medieval days.'

MORRIS, Johnny
Journalist/presenter/ entertainer b 20th June Newport, Mon. While still a farm manager in Wiltshire, auditioned for the BBC using a piece written by himself. Did both jobs then gave up farming in 1951 to work full-time in radio and TV in the West Region of the BBC. Numerous radio plays, news reports and roving reports incl: Pass the Salt; Journeyman Johnny; Around the World in 25 Years. TV incl: The Chestnut Man; Animal Magic; Johnny's Jaunt. Education: secondary school, Newport. m Eileen. Address: c/o BBC TV, London W12. Starsign: Gemini. Hobbies: music, gardening, watching people. Person he would most like to

have met: 'Hitler, to try to find out how he got that way.'

MORRISON, Fran
Reporter/presenter BBC TV current affairs group, presently on Nationwide b 27th January Glasgow. Former BBC news trainee. Considerable experience radio and TV producing, scriptwriting, reporting. Producer Radio 4's World at One, news scriptwriter radio and TV news, news reporter radio and TV. Former co-presenter BBC Scotland's current affairs programme Tuesday Night/Thursday Night; former reporter/ presenter BBC 2's Newsnight, then Newsnight's arts correspondent. Reporter on Tuesday Documentary on Westminster School; various freelance contributions to Radio 4's Midweek chat show; Miss World regional heats; presenter first night of the Proms BBC TV 1980; presenter brass band programmes also for BBC TV. Education: St Andrews University (MA Hons). m Robin Whyte. Address: c/o BBC, London W12. Starsign: Aquarius. Hobbies: her husband, theatre, films, parties, interesting people. Person she would most like to meet: 'Salvador Dali, because he's amusing and likes journalists, as well as being a genius.'

MOSLEY, Bryan
Actor b 25.8.31 Leeds. Served in the RAF (Air Traffic

Control) before training with Esme Church Northern Theatre School 1951-53. Rep St Andrews, Perth, Derby, Harrogate, York. Toured with New Pilgrim Players: York Mystery Plays 1957. Leading roles on TV in: Armchair Theatre (ABC); Play of the Week (Anglia); The Villains; The Planemakers. Other TV incl: Z Cars; Doctor Who; The Saint; The Avengers; No Hiding Place; Crossroads (in four different roles at various times). Many films incl: Get Carter; Charlie Bubbles; Far from the Madding Crowd; A Kind of Loving; This Sporting Life; Rattle of a Simple Man, Expert swordsman and arranges fights for stage, film and TV; founder member of Society of British Fight Arrangers. Was first actor to be given special citation as performer by American TV and Radio Commercials Festival (1969). First played Alf Roberts in Coronation Street 1961. Rejoined cast in 1969 and has since toured in and directed several stage plays and appeared as an Ugly Sister in pantomime 1978. Visited America and Canada in 1981 and was interviewed live on Canadian TV the first day Coronation Street was screened there coast-to-coast. Education: Leeds Central High; Leeds College of Art. m Norma, 3 d Jacqueline, Simone, Helen, 3 s Jonathan, Bernard, Leonard. Address: c/o Granada TV, Manchester. Starsign: Virgo. Hobbies: painting, drawing, fencing, swimming, making model soldiers, travel. Person he would most like to meet: 'My wife Norma, because she is like no one I have ever heard about and lovely with it!'

MOSS, Don
Presenter/compère/ producer/director b 27th April Peterborough. Announcer/producer with Forces Broadcasting Service 1953-56 in Austria, Middle East and Germany after which he went into rep until 1958 when he joined Radio Luxembourg as resident presenter/producer in Luxembourg. In 1961 he became a freelance producer/writer/presenter in radio and TV in Britain, presenting such BBC Radio shows as Housewives' and Family Choice; Pick of the Pops; Disc Jockey Derby (which he also devised); What's New; 12 O'Clock Spin; Pop Inn (for which he also wrote four pantomimes). For Radio Bristol: Morning West; Door to Door; Saturday Show. For Radio Victory, The Sunday Jaunt. On TV he has presented Thank Your Lucky Stars; Day By Day; As You Like It; Miss Southern TV; Your Say; Try For Ten; The Best in the West; Time Was; Three Little Words; Definition. He was also writer/producer of Bristol 600; deviser of Seven Year Flitch (and presenter) and Opinions Unlimited, and has compèred Come Dancing and International Dance Date. In addition he has

written and produced many radio and TV commercials and staged charity shows. Education: Peterborough Grammar School. m Jean, 1 d Susannah. Address: c/o MAM Agency, London W1. Starsign: Taurus. Hobbies: photography, travel. Person he would most like to meet: 'Lord Snowdon – he takes such marvellous pictures.'

MOUNT, Peggy
Actress b 2.5.18 Southend-on-Sea. Started as a secretary, but always wanted to be an actress. Many amateur shows before turning professional with Harry Hanson rep company. Many years in rep at Preston, Colchester, Wolverhampton, Liverpool. Big chance came with Sailor, Beware 1955 (stage and film). Probably best known for her TV roles in The Larkins. Other TV incl: George and the Dragon; Lollipop Loves Mr Mole; You're Only Young Twice. Stage incl: Romeo and Juliet; She Stoops to Conquer (both at the Old Vic); The Bandwagon; When We Are Married; The Rivals; There Goes The Bride; Il Campiello and Plunder; Lark Rise and Candleford (National Theatre); Mother Courage. Films incl: The Naked Truth; Hotel Paradiso; Inn For Trouble; One Way Pendulum; Ladies Who Do. Address: c/o Richard Stone, London WC2. Starsign: Taurus. Person she would most like to have met: Ivor Novello.

MOWER, Patrick
Actor b 12.9.40 Pontypridd. Formerly an apprentice engineering draughtsman, but decided to train as an actor and went to RADA. West End appearances since incl: House of Cards; Alfie; John Gabriel Borkman; A Boston Story; Night and Day. Films incl: The Devil Rides Out; Doctors Wear Scarlet; The Smashing Bird I Used to Know; The Cry of The Banshee; One Away; The Devil's Advocate. Many plays and series on TV incl: Catch Me a Spy; Haunted; Front Page Story; Callan; Special Branch; Target; Bergerac. Many plays and guest appearances in all top drama series. Played title role in Peer Gynt on BBC in 1980. Education: Oxford Grammar; Oxford Polytechnic. 1 d Claudia, 1 s Sam. Address: c/o London Management, London W1. Starsign: Virgo. Person he would most like to meet: 'Actor Michael Latimer – he owes me £500!'

MUIR, Frank
Scriptwriter/performer b 5.2.20 Broadstairs, Kent.

In the RAF 1940-46. Started writing seriously 1946 and following year teamed up with Denis Norden in Navy Mixture. Together for 17 years during which they wrote Take It From Here; Bedtime with Braden and TV series And So To Bentley; 'Whack-O!; The Seven Faces of Jim; Brothers-in-Law. Regular broadcaster on radio: My Word!; My Music; and on TV: Sound of Laughter; Call My Bluff; How to be an Alien; We Have Ways of Making You Laugh. BBC's Head of Comedy 1963; London Weekend's Head of Light Entertainment 1966-69. Books: You Can't Have Your Kyak and Heat It (with Denis Norden); The Frank Muir Book. Education: Chatham House, Ramsgate; Leyton County High. m Polly, 1 d Sarah, 1 s James. Address: Egham, Surrey. Starsign: Aquarius. Hobby: collecting books.

MULLIGAN, Grace
Cookery presenter b 23rd May, Dundee, Scotland. Succeeded Dorothy Sleightholme as presenter of Yorkshire TV's Farmhouse Kitchen in 1982. A former teacher, and a national judge for the Federation of Women's Institutes in bakery, meal cookery and preservation. Voluntary county organiser for the Federation. Is also a demonstrator and speaker on cookery subjects. Education: Lawside Academy, Dundee; Edinburgh College of

Domestic Science; Moray House Teacher Training College; Edinburgh College of Art. m Dr Brian Mulligan, 3 d Catriona, Grainne, Bronagh, 1 s Kevin. Address: c/o Yorkshire TV, Leeds. Starsign: Gemini. Hobbies: fine needlework, eating in good restaurants. Person she would most like to meet: Cookery writer Jane Grigson.

MURDOCH, Richard
Actor b 6.4.07 Keston, Kent. First professional appearance in chorus of The Blue Train 1927. Wide experience of stage, touring, summer season and pantomime. Best known on radio for Band Waggon; Much Binding in the Marsh; Men From the Ministry. TV incl: New Avengers; In the Looking Glass; Hazell; Owner Occupied; Warrior Queen; The Three Kisses; Rumpole of the Bailey; This is Your Life; The Disappearing Schoolgirls; The Professionals; Doctor's Daughters; The Old Boy Network; Winston Churchill The Wilderness Years. Education: Charterhouse; Pembroke College, Cambridge. m actress Peggy Rawlings, 2 d Belinda, Jane, 1 s Timothy. Address: c/o Essanay Ltd, London W14. Starsign: Aries. Hobbies: golf, sailing. Person he would most like to have met: 'Dan Leno, just because I wish I'd seen him.'

MURPHY, Brian
Actor b 1933 Ventnor, Isle of Wight. Always wanted to act and after National Service with the RAF trained at RADA. Became a stalwart of Joan Littlewood's Theatre Workshop, but fame only caught up with him after 20 years in the business with a Palladium pantomime 1976 and TV series, Man About the House, George and Mildred, The Incredible Mr Tanner. Stage incl: On Your Way Riley. m Carole, 2 s Trevor, Kevin. Address: Chalk Farm, London. Person he would most like to have met: 'Edmond Kean who, according to history, was the most exciting, terrifying, albeit erratic, actor of his time. What would TV have made of him?'

MURRAY, Pete OBE
Actor/compère b 19.9.25 London. Trained at RADA (bronze medallist) followed by rep at the Arts Theatre, Cambridge and appearances in London's West End and on Broadway. Disc jockey on Radio Luxembourg and BBC, latest show on Radio 2 being Pete

Murray's Late Show. Stage
incl: Say Who You Are; Sting
in the Tail. TV incl: Six-Five
Special; Thank Your Lucky
Stars; Juke Box Jury; Top of
the Pops; Open House; The
Last Enemy (play); Happily
Ever After (series); Mum's
Boys (series); Husband of the
Year; Pop at the Mill; Blankety
Blank; Give Us a Clue.
Education: St Paul's School,
London. m (1st) Germaine
(dis), (2nd) Tricia,
1 s Michael (by 1st m).
Address: c/o Tony Lewis
Enterprises Ltd, London W1.
Starsign: Virgo. Hobbies:
watching Arsenal, tennis,
riding, theatre.

NEDWELL, Robin
Actor b 27.9.46
Birmingham. Moved to
Cardiff at an early age and
while at school was
encouraged to become an
actor. Joined Welsh Theatre
Company, then Central
School of Speech and Drama
in London. Rep in
Birmingham, Liverpool,
Cheltenham, Bristol, Cardiff
and Sheffield. Toured in
Doctor in Love in Australia
1977, breaking all box-office
records. Appeared in
Polanski's film Macbeth, but
mainly worked on the fights—a
hobby, and one which he has
taught at drama schools.
Films incl: Stand Up Virgin
Soldiers; The Shillingbury
Blowers; A Slice of Life. On TV
well-known for the Doctor
series, incl Doctor Down
Under (made in Australia),
but has also appeared in The
Lovers; Wedding Bells; The
Upchat Connection; The
Pretenders; Romeo and
Juliet; The Government
Inspector; Shillingbury Tales;
West End Tales. Education:
Monkton and Canton High
Schools, Cardiff. Address:
c/o John Mahoney
Management, London NW1.

Starsign: Libra. Hobbies: collecting Japanese swords and prints, watching Llanelli Rugby Football Club, playing a 'mean game of darts', writing plays and TV series.

NELSON, Wendy
Presenter/broadcaster
b 30.1.50 Birmingham. Journalistic background, training under an IPC training scheme before working for the Oxford Mail, Banbury Mail and Birmingham Evening Mail. Joined BBC TV news 1974 and while with the BBC worked on Midlands Today, Pebble Mill At One, which took her to India and America, and a documentary, Daughters of Tradition. Moved to ATV in 1980 for ATV Today and Workout, a series on youth unemployment. Has been with Central TV News as programme presenter since 1981. Education: Banbury Grammar School. m John Nelson. Address: c/o PVA Management Ltd, London W1. Starsign: Aquarius. Hobbies: contemporary jazz ballet, swimming, gardening. Person she would most like to meet: Clint Eastwood.

NETTLES, John
Actor b 1948 St Austell, Cornwall. Became interested in acting while still at university, through taking part in dramatic society activities. Started serious acting at London's Royal Court Theatre. Member of the Royal Shakespeare Company 1976-79. Latest

theatre incl: American tour of The Hollow Crown; The Relapse; La Ronde. Latest TV is the title role in Bergerac. Before that his TV credits incl: four series of The Liver Birds; Family at War; The Merchant of Venice; Findings on a Late Afternoon (Play for Today). Education: Southampton University (History and Philosophy). m casting director Joyce Nettles, 1 d Emma. Address: c/o Saraband Assocs, London N1.

NETTLETON, John
Actor b 5.2.29 London. Trained at RADA. First stage appearance was 'walking-on' in Snow White and the Seven Dwarfs at the St James Theatre 1951. Joined Shakespeare Company following year touring with them and Elizabethan Theatre Company, rep at Nottingham and appearances in London's West End until 1961 when he joined the Royal Shakespeare Company until 1966. Further tours and plays in London before appearing at National Theatre in their first all-male production of As

You Like It. Films incl: A Man For All Seasons; And Soon the Darkness; Black Beauty. TV incl: One Fat Englishman; The Staff Room; A Pin to See the Peepshow; The Tempest; Sheppey; Crown Court; Yes, Minister; Tales of the Unexpected; Brideshead Revisited; The Flame Trees of Thika. Education: St Dunstan's College, Catford. m Deidre Doone, 3 d Sarah, Joanna, Jessica. Address: c/o Larry Dalzell Assocs Ltd, London WC2. Starsign: Aquarius. Hobbies: listening to music, gardening. Person he would most like to meet: 'Mr Smith (of BBC's Gardening World) for advice on my garden!'

NEWBON, Gary
Head of Sport, Central TV
b 13.3.45 Cambridge. Trained with Jaycock's News Agency, Cambridge (1964-67), Hayter's Sports Agency, London (1967-68) and Sunday Mirror, before joining Westward TV 1968. Joined ATV Network 1971 for ATV sports programmes – Star Soccer; Extra Time; ITV Munich Olympics 1972; ITV World Soccer Cup 1974; Moscow Olympics 1980; ITV World Cup Soccer 1982. Other TV incl: ATV Sport; Butlins Grand Masters Darts; State Express Grand Masters Snooker; Midlands Soccer Player of the Season; ATV Summer Sport; ITV greyhound host and ITV speedway host, World of Sport. Also contributor to World of Sport; Mid-week

Sports Special; Birmingham International Showjumping; ITN. Education: Cullford School, Bury St Edmunds. m Katie, 1 d Clair, 2 s Laurence, Neil (twins). Address: c/o PVA Management Ltd, London W1. Starsign: Pisces. Hobbies: squash, jazz, wine, Midlands Soccer Writers (past chairman). Person he would most like to meet: 'The man who invented Bollinger champagne.'

NEWELL, Patrick

Actor b 27.3.32 Hadley, Suffolk. Actor with a weight problem: the more he diets, the less work he seems to get. At one time weighed 23 st. Taste for acting stems from school dramatic productions. Trained at RADA and made stage debut with Harry Hanson's Company at Boscombe. Subsequently rep at Hornchurch, Bournemouth, Coventry. Plays in London's West End incl: The Boy Friend; Kismet; Trap for a Lonely Man; Hotel Paradiso. He also toured in The Country Wife. His films incl: Becket; The Gaunt Woman; The Long Duel; The Strange Affair; The Best House in London; The Alphabet Murder; The Boys; Sarah; Canterbury Tales. On TV he is still remembered as 'Mother' in The Avengers, but he has also been in Never Say Die; The Misfit; Elizabeth 1; Casanova; Murder Most English; Wilde Alliance; Coronation Street; Moll Flanders; Sherlock Holmes

and Dr Watson; Whizzkids Guide; Kinvig. Education: Taunton School. m former ballet dancer Derina, 1 d Holly, 1 s James. Address: c/o Tim Wilson Management, Richmond, Surrey. Starsign: Aries.

NICHOLAS, Paul

Actor/singer b 3.12.45 Peterborough. Former rock 'n' roll piano player, started his acting career in 1969 in the original London production of Hair. This was followed by parts in Jesus Christ Superstar and Grease. Invited to join the Young Vic and later worked for the Prospect Theatre Company and at London's Royal Court. Latest stage: Cats. Films incl: Tommy; Stardust; Lisztomania; Sergeant Pepper's Lonely Hearts Club Band; The World is Full of Married Men; Yesterday's Hero; Alice; The Jazz Singer; Nutcracker. TV incl: Season of the Witch; Two Up Two Down; Chips; The Lady Killers; The Boys from Ipanema; A LIttle Rococo. Tried pop singing in 1976 and was in the Top Ten four times. Education: Eton and Harrow. m Linzi, 1 d Natasha, 2 s Oscar, Alexander. Address: c/o Duncan Heath Assocs, London W1. Starsign: Sagittarius. Hobby: posing. Person he would most like to meet: 'My father – for obvious reasons.'

NICHOLLS, Sue

Actress b 23.11.43 Walsall, West Mids. Trained at RADA

followed by extensive theatre experience incl rep and cabaret in England and abroad. Appeared in London Assurance on Broadway and in North America. TV incl: Crossroads; The Fall and Rise of Reginald Perrin; Solo; The Professionals; Pipkins; Rentaghost; Tycoon; Not on Your Nellie; Heartlands; Coronation Street. Had a hit record with Where Will You Be. Education: Woodland Grange School and St Mary and St Ann, Abbots Bromley. Address: c/o Barry Brown Management, London SE11. Starsign: Sagittarius. Hobbies: music, singing, dancing, sauna, films, eating out. Person she would most like to meet: 'The fairy at the bottom of my garden – to ask him to pull his weight with the weeding!'

NICHOLSON, Mavis

TV interviewer b 19.10.30 Briton Ferry. Was first an advertising copywriter and when at 27, the first of her three sons was born, she decided that bringing up her children was a full-time job. Eventually took up freelance journalism and a chance appearance on a Today programme led to her breaking into TV at the age of 40. Her TV programmes incl: Mavis; Happy Returns; Mavis – Wanting to Know; Other People's Children; Volunteers; Medical Express; Good Afternoon; After Noon Plus; and for radio, Start the Week; Mid-week. Education: Cwrt Sart Mixed; Neath County School for Girls; University College of Swansea. m journalist Geoffrey Nicholson, 3 s Steve, Lewis, Harry. Address: c/o Thames TV, London NW1. Starsign: Libra. Hobbies: photography, cooking, the telephone. Person she would most like to have met: 'Colette, the French novelist, because she led life so energetically and didn't let age hinder her!'

NICHOLSON, Michael
Foreign correspondent b 9.1.37 Romford, Essex. One of British TV's most widely travelled newsmen. War correspondent since 1968 and in 11 years has covered as many wars – more than any other living newsman – latest being the Falklands crisis. Won American Emmy nominations for film reports from Vietnam, Biafra, Cambodia, Middle East. Major awards incl: Cannes Film Festival Silver Nymph Award for best newsfilm of 1975 with The Battle of Newport Bridge, the last battle in South Vietnam; British Newsfilm Award for filming of Turkish

paratroopers landing during their invasion of Cyprus 1975; Royal Television Society's Reporter of the Year Award 1978 for his reports during a four-month trek with UNITA guerillas in Angola. Books incl: The Partridge Kite; Red Joker. Education: University of Leicester (BA Hons Politics). m Diana, 2 s Tom, William. Address: c/o ITN, London W1. Starsign: Capricorn. Hobbies: writing novels, collecting cars. Person he would most like to have met: 'General Gordon of Khartoum, because I'd like to know why he stayed behind to face the Dervishes.'

NICOL, Megg
Presenter/singer/actress b 13.6.51 Toronto, Canada. Trained for the theatre at Edinburgh College of Speech and Drama for three years and then worked with most of the Scottish rep companies (Pitlochry, Perth, Dundee, Royal Lyceum in Edinburgh). Came to London and got a small part in Fire Angel followed by engagement to sing while John Curry skated in The John Curry Ice Spectacular at the London Palladium. Was also in I'm Getting My Act Together and Taking It on the Road in London. First presenter job was for Yorkshire TV's Pop Quest, then Best Disco in Town and Get It Together (combining presenting and singing). Education: many schools incl Rothesay Academy, Isle of Bute; Soeul Jnr High School, New Jersey,

America. Address: c/o Fraser and Dunlop, London W1. Starsign: Gemini. Hobbies: her work, herbal medicine, astrology and associated subjects, walking, swimming, music, writing, travelling. Person she would most like to meet: 'As a Gemini I have several and they seem to change daily.'

NIGHTINGALE, Anne
Presenter/disc jockey b 1st April Osterley, Middx. Newspaper background (Brighton Evening Argus, Daily Sketch, Daily Express, Cosmopolitan etc) and an expert on pop music. Introduced The Who to TV and was hostess of TV pop show That's For Me. Other TV incl: Sing a Song of Sixpence; Before the Event; London Scene; Pop Quest; The Old Grey Whistle Test. Was Radio 1's first girl disc jockey on Workshop. Other radio incl: What's New (also BBC World Service); Mailbag; Anne Nightingale's Request Show; Rock Around the World (for America). Education: St Catherine's Convent, Twickenham; Lady Eleanor Holles School, Hampton; Central London Polytechnic. m (1st) writer Gordon Thomas (dis), (2nd) pop musician Binky Baker, 1 d Lucy, 1 s Alexander (both from 1st m). Address: c/o MPC Artists, London W1. Starsign: Aries. No time for hobbies.

NOAKES, John
Actor/presenter b 6.3.34

Halifax, Yorks. Trained at the Guildhall School of Music and Drama. First job in the theatre was as a dog in a Cyril Fletcher pantomime. Other stage work incl rep at Bournemouth, Harrogate, York, Manchester, Sheffield, Worthing, summer show (with Cyril Fletcher), a Children's Theatre tour and Chips With Everything (on Broadway). On TV has been in plays and programmes for Granada, Thames and BBC but is probably best known for Go With Noakes (since 1974), Blue Peter and Country Calendar. Education: Rishworth School, London. m Victoria, 1 s Mark. Address: c/o Arlington Enterprises, London W1. Starsign: Pisces. Hobbies: sailing, collecting art nouveau pottery. Person he would most like to meet: 'Tristram Jones – a man after my own heart, but much braver.'

NORDEN, Denis
Scriptwriter/performer b 6.2.22 Hackney, London. Originally a theatre manager 1939-42. Wrote for troop shows in RAF 1942-45 after which he was a scriptwriter for variety shows. Teamed up with Frank Muir 1947-64 during which they wrote: Take It From Here; Bedtime With Braden for radio; for TV: And So To Bentley; Whack-O!; The Seven Faces of Jim; Brothers-in-Law; The Glums. Solo writer since 1964. Film scripts incl: Bueno Sera, Mrs Campbell; The Statue; Every Home Should Have One; The Water Babies. Regular broadcaster My Word!; My Music and on TV: The Name's The Same; How To Be an Alien; Looks Familiar; It'll Be Alright on the Night. Introduced 1982 BAFTA Awards. Education: Craven Park and City of London Schools. m Avril, 1 d TV producer Maggie, 1 s Nick. Address: c/o April Young, London WC2. Starsign: Aquarius. Hobbies: reading, loitering. Person he would most like to have met: 'The guy who side-swiped my parked car.'

NORMAN, Barry
Writer/presenter b 21.8.33 London. Journalistic background, mostly with the Daily Mail, before being made redundant, when he became a freelance TV reviewer and in 1972 was invited to join panel on BBC 2's Late Night Line-Up. This led to the Film series 1972-81 and The Hollywood Greats, 1977/8/9. Now presenting Omnibus on BBC 1. Books incl: End Product; A Series of Defeats; To Nick A Good Body; The Hollywood Greats; The Movie Greats; Have A Nice Day. Won BAFTA Richard Dimbleby Award 1981. Education: Highgate School, London. m Diana, 2 d Samantha, Emma. Address: c/o BBC, London W12. Starsign: Leo. Hobby: cricket. Person he would most like to have met: 'PG Wodehouse (too late now, alas) – the guru of all who try to write humour in English.'

NORTH, Roy
Actor/presenter b 16.3.41 Hull. Training at Rose Bruford College of Speech and Drama followed by rep at Hull, Harrogate and Leeds, and pantomimes and musicals in London's West End incl: Robert and Elizabeth; Canterbury Tales; Hullaballoo; Joseph and His Technicolour Dreamcoat. He was also in Hair in Amsterdam. He joined the Basil Brush Show in 1973 and remained with it until 1976. Other TV incl: The Boy from Nazareth; Seaside Special; Star Turn; Get It Together; Star Games; Shoestring; Music Round; The Brack Report; Celebrity Knockout; a schools documentary on craft design and technology. Education: Hull Grammar School. m Lesley. Address: c/o John Mahoney Management, London NW1. Starsign: Pisces. Hobbies: motorcycling, playing charity soccer for the Dennis Waterman XI, supporting Hull City FC, renovating his house, being a Lords Taverner. Person he would

most like to meet: 'Michael Parkinson – I'd like to receive and observe his interviewing technique, which I admire.'

OAKSEY, (Lord) John
Commentator/journalist
b 21.3.29 London. Trained to be a lawyer (his late father was senior judge at the Nuremburg Trials), but turned down a career in law to become a writer and amateur jockey. Has been a racing journalist (Daily and Sunday Telegraph and Horse and Hound) since 1956 and he rode as an amateur jockey from 1955-75, during which time he rode 200 winners and came second in the Grand National on Carrickbeg in 1963. Has been a member of the World of Sport racing team since 1970. Education: Horris Hill; Eton; New College, Oxford; Yale Law School. m Victoria, 1 d Sara, 1 s Patrick. Address: c/o LWT, London SW1. Starsign: Aries. Hobbies: skiing, riding.

O'CONNELL, Patrick
Actor b 29.1.34 Dublin.
Brought up in Birmingham
and worked in the publicity
dept of a big store, before
going to RADA and into rep.
Has appeared in many plays
in London and with the BBC.
Most recent theatre incl tours
of Philumena and Bodies.
Films incl: The McKenzie
Break; Cromwell; and more
recently Ragman's Daughter;
The Human Factor. On TV he
is probably best known as
Edward Hammond in The
Brothers (four series) and
more recently as Jack Blair in
We'll Meet Again. Other TV
incl: Redcap; Dixon of Dock
Green; North and South;
Frontier; Fraud Squad; Sling
Your Hook (Wednesday
Play); The Patriot Game;
England's Green and
Pleasant Land; Enemy At the
Door; Elizabeth R. m Patricia,
2 d Kate, Frances. Address:
c/o Green and Underwood,
London W3. Starsign:
Aquarius. Hobbies: drawing
and painting. Person he
would most like to have met:
'Beethoven – I could listen to
his music for ever and never
tire of it.'

O'CONNOR, Des
Entertainer b 12.1.32
Stepney, London. Started
career in RAF where he was
ordered to enter a talent
contest and won first prize.
Redcoat at Filey holiday
camp before making
professional show business
debut in Newcastle in 1953,
followed by numerous
seasons in variety shows up

and down the country and
developing into one of
Britain's premier
entertainers. Has had four
cabaret engagements at
London's Talk of the Town
and celebrated his 1000th
performance in 1972 during
one of his record-breaking
seasons there. Has made
many appearances in
America, Australia and
Canada. Summer shows at
Coventry, Eastbourne,
Jersey, Isle of Man and
Paignton. Compèred several
Royal Variety shows. TV incl:
compère of Spot the Tune
and Sunday Night at the
London Palladium; For Love
Or Money; own shows since
1963 incl Des O'Connor
Tonight. TVTimes Favourite
Male TV Personality on five
occasions (1969-73). Books
incl: Somebody Laughed
(autobiography). m (1st)
Phyllis (dis), (2nd) actress
Gillian Vaughan, 3 d Karen
(from 1st m), Tracey,
Samantha. Address: c/o
London Management,
London W1. Starsign:
Capricorn. Hobbies: show
business, all sports. Person
he would most like to have
met: 'Sir Winston Churchill – I
admire his determination,
leadership and inspirational
quality.'

O'CONNOR, Tom
Comedian b 31.10.40
Bootle, Lancs. Originally a
maths and music teacher at
St Joan of Arc School, Bootle;
also performed in working
men's clubs while still a
teacher. Appeared in the

second series of The
Comedians on TV and
became a full-time
entertainer 1974.
Opportunity Knocks and a
summer season at Blackpool
were followed by The Tom
O'Connor Show; Wednesday
at Eight; Royal Variety
Performance 1976; Tom
O'Connor at the Casino;
pantomimes at Southport,
Coventry and Liverpool;
summer seasons at
Yarmouth, Blackpool and
Eastbourne, Paignton and
Scarborough; eight TV series
of London Night Out.
Education: St James' Junior,
Bootle; St Mary's Grammar,
Crosby; St Mary's College,
Twickenham. m former
teacher Pat, 3 d Ann,
Frances, Helen,
1 s Stephen. Address: c/o
Clifford Elson (publicity) Ltd,
London W1. Starsign:
Scorpio. Hobbies: golf,
snooker, football. Person he
would most like to meet:
'Johnny Cash – my favourite
entertainer. I have all his
records.'

ODDIE, Bill
Writer/performer b 7.7.41
Rochdale, Lancs. Started

with Footlights while at Cambridge University. Wrote and appeared in I'm Sorry, I'll Read That Again on radio. Has also written episodes of Doctor in the House for TV. Other TV incl: That Was the Week That Was; Twice a Fortnight; The Goodies. Education: King Edward's School, Birmingham; Pembroke College, Cambridge. Address: c/o Roger Hancock Ltd, London SW1. Starsign: Cancer. Hobbies: bird-watching, sport, music, painting.

OGILVY, Ian
Actor b 30.9.43 Woking, Surrey. Started backstage at London's Royal Court Theatre before training at RADA. Then rep at Colchester, Canterbury and Northampton. Stage incl: The Waltz of the Toreadors; The Millionairess; Chichester Festival. Films incl: Stranger in the House; The Sorcerers; Witchfinder General; The Invincible Six; Waterloo; Wuthering Heights; Fengriffin; No Sex Please – We're British!; Design For Living. Extensive TV plays and series incl: The Liars; Upstairs, Downstairs; Catherine (Affairs of the Heart); A Walk With Destiny; before succeeding Roger Moore as Simon Templar in the Return of The Saint; Tom, Dick and Harriet. TV Times Award as Most Compulsive Character 1978/79. Education: Eton. m former model Diane,
1 step-d Emma, 1 s Titus.

Address: c/o Leading Artists, London SW1. Starsign: Libra. Person he would most like to have met: 'Dr John McKenzie – a Scottish ancestor who practised medicine in the Highlands in the middle of the last century.'

OLIVIER, Lord Laurence OM
Actor, director and manager b 22.5.07 Dorking. Founder Director of the National Theatre of Great Britain and probably our greatest actor. Studied under Elsie Fogerty and made his first stage appearance at the Shakespeare Festival Theatre, Stratford-upon-Avon, in 1922 when he played Katherine in a special boy's performance of The Taming of the Shrew. Has since had a distinguished career for nearly 60 years, presenting many plays under his own management. Appeared with the Birmingham Repertory Theatre 1926-28 playing leading and other parts both in Birmingham and London. Before joining the Old Vic in Jan 1937, appeared in a variety of roles in London and America incl Capt Stanhope in the original production of Journey's End and Victor Prynne in Private Lives. Was with the Old Vic Company until April 1938, during which he appeared in many Shakespearian roles incl Hamlet (in its entirety and at Elsinore). Served with the Fleet Air Arm during the war and in 1944 was appointed co-director of the Old Vic.

With the Shakespeare Company at Stratford during the 1955 season. Director of Chichester Festival 1961 season. Founder Director National Theatre 1963-73. Entered films 1927 in Too Many Crooks. Films since incl: Wuthering Heights; Rebecca; Pride and Prejudice; Lady Hamilton; Henry V; Hamlet (Oscar); The Beggar's Opera; Richard III (British Film Academy Award 1956); The Prince and the Showgirl; The Devil's Disciple; Spartacus; The Entertainer; Term of Trial; Othello; Khartoum; Oh What A Lovely War; The Battle of Britain; Dance of Death; Three Sisters; David Copperfield; Nicholas and Alexandra; Lady Caroline Lamb; Sleuth; Marathon Man; Wagner; The Jigsaw Man. First TV appearance 1958 in John Gabriel Borkman. Other TV incl: The Moon and Sixpence (Emmy); and more recently: Long Day's Journey Into Night (Emmy); The Merchant of Venice; Love Among the Ruins (Emmy); Cat on a Hot Tin Roof; The Collection (Emmy); Come Back, Little Sheba; Brideshead Revisited; A Voyage Round My Father. Knighted in Birthday Honours 1947 and created a Baron for services to the Theatre in Birthday Honours 1970. Created a Fellow of BAFTA 1974. Honoured with Order of Merit 1981. Many awards, honorary degrees and other honours incl: Legion d'Honeur; Commander of the Order of Dannebrog. Education: St Edward's School, Oxford. m (1st) Jill Esmond (dis), (2nd) Vivien Leigh (dis), (3rd) Joan Plowright, 2 d Tamsin, Julie-Kate, 2 s Richard (all from 3rd m), Tarquin (from 1st m). Address: c/o Temple, Gothard & Co, London WC2. Starsign: Gemini. Hobbies: swimming, gardening.

O'SULLEVAN, Peter OBE
TV commentator b 3.3.18
Ireland. Joined Press
Association as racing
correspondent 1945 and
Daily Express in similar
capacity 1950. Has been
race broadcasting since
1946, incl: Australia, South
Africa, Italy, France, USA.
Education: Hawtreys;
Charterhouse; College Alpin,
Switzerland. m Patricia.
Address: c/o BBC, London
W12. Starsign: Pisces.
Hobbies: horse racing, travel,
reading, art, food and wine.

O'SULLIVAN, Richard
Actor b 7.5.44 Chiswick,
London. Child star in films,
Stranger's Hand; Dangerous
Exile; Cleopatra; Cliff Richard
musicals. Stage incl: The
Government Inspector;
Boeing, Boeing; Palladium
pantomime. TV incl: Doctor at
Large; Doctor in Charge;
Father, Dear Father (and
film); Alcock and Gander;
Man About the House;
Robin's Nest; Dick Turpin.
Education: Corona Stage
School. 1 s James (by Tessa
Wyatt). Address: c/o Al
Mitchell Assocs, London
WC2. Starsign: Taurus.

Hobby: soccer (plays
regularly for charity teams).
Person he would most like to
meet: 'Marlon Brando – for
me, the finest screen actor.'

OULTON, Brian
Actor b 11.2.08 Liverpool.
After training at RADA began
in rep at Liverpool Playhouse.
Served in army during the
war. Wide experience in
theatre, rep and West End,
films, TV and radio. Stage
incl: His House in Order; The
Brontës; More Just William;
Hostile Witness; The National
Health; Forty Years On; debut
in pantomime 1981. King
Cole in Humpty Dumpty.
Films incl: several Carry On
films; Devil's Disciple; The
Thirty Nine Steps; I'm All
Right, Jack; Very Important
Person; The Iron Maiden; The
Intelligence Men; On the
Buses; Gandhi. TV incl: Hotel
Imperial; The Avengers;
Emergency – Ward 10; Softly,
Softly; The Troubleshooters;
George and the Dragon; The
Gamblers; Department S;
The Expert; Mr Digby,
Darling; The Main Chance;
Randall and Hopkirk
(Deceased); Codename;
Jason King; Father, Dear
Father; Adventures of Black
Beauty; Justice; Six Days of
Justice; Rule Britannia;
Crown Court; The Squirrels;
Emily; Headmaster; The XYY
Man; The Many Wives of
Patrick; Happy Ever After;
Just William; The Old
Curiosity Shop; Brideshead
Revisited. Education:
Wantage School. m actress
Peggy Thorpe-Bates,

1 d Jennifer, 1 s Nicholas.
Address: c/o Patrick
Freeman, London W6.
Starsign: Aquarius. Hobby:
writing plays and novels.
Person he would most like to
meet: 'Angela Rippon,
because she set the perfect
standard for newsreading,
and another standard of
perfection when she danced
with Morecambe and Wise. If
romance had not gone out of
fashion, she would have been
a perfect heroine in a musical
comedy.'

OWEN, Bill
Actor b 14.3.15 London. No
academic training before
going into rep at 19. Since
then he has been actor,
dancer, pop song writer,
playwright, panellist (in Tell
the Truth), and been in
pantomime. Stage incl: The
Threepenny Opera; more
recently, Pygmalion revival;
the National Theatre (The
Long Voyage Home). Has
been in countless films incl:
Perfect Strangers; The Way to
the Stars; Easy Money; My
Brother's Keeper; Holiday
Camp; Once a Jolly
Swagman; The Girl Who
Couldn't Quite; Hotel Sahara;
The Ship That Died of Shame;
Davy; Carve Her Name With
Pride; Carry On Cabby;
Georgy Girl; O Lucky Man; In
Celebration; The Comeback.
TV incl: Three Piece Suite;
The Challengers; The Quiet
Half-Hour; Treasure Island;
Last of the Summer Wine;
Brideshead Revisited; Tales
of the Unexpected.
m Kathie, 1 d Kathie,

1 s Tom. Address: c/o
Richard Stone, London WC2.
Starsign: Pisces. Hobby:
fishing. Person he would
most like to meet: 'Lillian
Hellman, a very fine, bold
playwright.'

P

OWEN, Nick
Presenter/reporter b 1.11.47
Berkhamsted, Herts.
Newspapers (Doncaster
Evening Post and
Birmingham Post) and local
radio (Radio Birmingham)
experience before joining
ATV/Central 1978 to present
news and sport programmes.
Education: Shrewsbury
School; Leeds University (BA
Hons Classics). m Jill,
2 s Andrew, Timothy.
Address: c/o Central TV,
Birmingham. Starsign:
Scorpio. Hobbies: playing
squash, watching cricket.
People he would most like to
meet: 'Dusty Springfield – my
schoolboy idol, and
Augustus Caesar – he helped
to change the course of
history.'

PALMER, Geoffrey
Actor b 4.6.27 London. No
acting training but went
straight into the theatre as
assistant stage manager at
London's Q Theatre. Now one
of the busiest actors on TV,
incl: The Fall and Rise of
Reginald Perrin; The
Houseboy; Butterflies; A
Midsummer Night's Dream;
The Last Song. Stage incl: St
Joan (Old Vic); Tishoo, Films
incl: O Lucky Man; The
Outsider; Retribution. Radio
incl: Little Secrets; Keys; The
Riddle of the Sands.
Education: Highgate School;
Royal Marines. m Sally,
1 d Harriet, 1 s Charles.
Address: c/o Larry Dalzell
Assocs, London WC2.
Starsign: Gemini. Hobbies:
squash, gardening. Person
he would most like to meet
again: 'Sydney Lotterby – I
want to work with him again.'

PARKIN, Leonard
Newscaster b 2.6.29
Thurnscoe, Yorks. Began as
a reporter on Wakefield
Express series of weekly
papers, then Yorkshire
Observer, Bradford
Telegraph and Argus and
Yorkshire Evening News.
Joined BBC Radio Newsreel
and TV news 1954;
correspondent in Canada
1960, Washington 1963-65;
Panorama and 24 Hours
1965-67. ITN roving reporter
(covering more than 50
countries) and News at Ten
newscaster since 1967. Was
first to report to Britain news
of President Kennedy's death
in 1963. Presenter of News at
One 1977; News at 5.45 since
1978; political interviewer ITN
election specials, the Nation
Decides and Europe Decides
1979. Education: Hemsworth
Grammar School, Yorks.
m Barbara, 1 s Jeremy.
Address: c/o ITN, London
W1. Starsign: Gemini.
Hobbies: fly fishing for trout,
collecting antiques.

PARKINSON, Mary
Interviewer/TV producer
b 16.7.39 Doncaster, Yorks.
Teacher of English and

sports until co-presenting
Tea Break with her husband
Michael 1972. Has since
been one of the presenters of
Good Afternoon; After Noon;
After Noon Plus. Education:
Notre Dame Collegiate,
Leeds; Endsleigh Sports
College, Hull. m TV
presenter Michael Parkinson,
3 s Andrew, Nicholas,
Michael. Address: c/o 58
Queen Anne St, London W1.
Starsign: Cancer. Hobbies:
golf, watching cricket,
reading. Person she would
most like to meet: 'The man
who pinched my husband's
bike in Barnsley in 1954.'

PARKINSON, Michael
Interviewer/TV presenter
b 28.3.35 Cudworth, Yorks.
Entered journalism on local
paper, then the Guardian;
Daily Express; columnist on
Sunday Times. Producer/
interviewer with Granada's
Scene; Granada in the North;
World in Action; What the
Papers Say; reporter on 24
Hours; executive producer
sporting documentaries with
LWT; presenter of Cinema;
presented Tea Break with his
wife before joining BBC in
1972, where he had his own
chat show. Also in Australia
1979, 1980, 1981. Much
radio work and author of
many books incl: Bats in the
Pavilion; Football Daft;
Cricket Mad; The Woofits;
Parkinson's Lore; Pictorial
History of the Western; Best:
An Intimate Biography.
Education: Barnsley
Grammar School. m TV
presenter Mary Parkinson,

3 s Andrew, Nicholas,
Michael. Address: c/o 58
Queen Anne St, London W1.
Starsign: Aries. Hobbies:
cricket, organised loafing,
cinema. Person he would
most like to meet: 'The man
who pinched my bike in
Barnsley in 1954.'

PARRY, Gwyn
Presenter b 13.4.46
Llanllechid, North Wales.
Spent three years with a
touring theatre company and
then presented children's
programmes and was
announcer for HTV 1976-80.
Now freelance presenter and
announcer. Education:
University College of North
Wales, Bangor.
1 d Branwen, 1 s Robin.
Address: Canton, Cardiff.
Starsign: Aries. Hobbies:
rock music, reading, squash.
Person he would most like to
meet: 'Dame Edna Everage –
I enjoy her irreverent humour
and bawdiness.'

PARRY, Ken
Actor b 20.6.30 Wigan,
Lancs. Weighs 19 st. Started
in rep at Wigan and other rep
at Warrington, Leigh,
Manchester, Coventry. In

London's West End he was in Wesker's The Kitchen. His films incl: Tom Jones; The Liquidators; The Taming of the Shrew; Two Times Two; A Whole Lot of Trouble. Many TV credits incl: Z Cars (in which he played 13 villains from time to time); A Midsummer Night's Dream (as Snout); The Merchant of Venice (as Old Gobbo); Coronation Street; Horne Aplenty; Never Say Die; Hazell; The Big Sleep; Vice Versa. Education: Spring View Secondary Boys School, Wigan. Address: c/o Roger Carey Management, London WC2. Starsign: Gemini. Hobbies: cooking, boxing, vintage films, clairvoyance. Person he would most like to meet: 'The Queen—she is so genuine in every way'.

freelance 1967. Sunday Mirror columnist; presenter Wales Today; match commentator for TV rugby with BBC Wales. Books incl: Number Eight (with Mervyn Davies); Boots, Balls and Banter. Education: Cardiff High School; Merton College, Oxford. Address: c/o BBC, Cardiff. Starsign: Libra. Hobbies: reading, music, squash. Person he would most like to have met: 'David Lloyd-George – for his gift of oratory.'

Award 1967 for Listen To This Space. TV incl: Eric Barker TV series (50s); 10 years straightman to Arthur Haynes (60s); guest appearances in many comedy shows, incl Benny Hill Show (70s); compère, Sale of the Century since 1971. Producer and director of short film Mad Dogs and Cricketers and A Fair Way To Play. Education: Colet Court; St Paul's School; Glasgow University. m actress Denise Bryer, 1 d Suzy, 1 s Justin. Address: c/o Richard Stone, London WC2. Starsign: Libra. Hobbies: photography, sport, gardening. Person he would most like to have met: 'Sir Winston Churchill, to talk to him about himself, history, and how he sees the future of mankind.'

PARRY, Roger
Reporter b 4.6.53 Surrey. An academic turned journalist, started as freelance with BBC Radio 1977 on Today, Newsbeat and Going Places before going to IRN and then Thames News. Education: Sutton Grammar School; Jesus College, Oxford (BSc Hons, M Litt Oxon). Address: c/o Thames TV, London W1. Starsign: Gemini. Hobby: squash.

PARRY-JONES, David
Presenter/commentator b 25.9.33 Pontypridd. Journalistic experience with Western Mail and Sunday Times and TV director with BBC Wales before going

PARSONS, Nicholas
Actor/compère b 10.10.28 Grantham, Lincs. Five years' engineering apprenticeship on Clydebank before acting and variety experience in Glasgow. Rep, cabaret and revues in London, incl six months resident comedian at Windmill Theatre. Stage incl: West End lead in Boeing Boeing (15 mths); Say Who You Are; Uproar in the House. Films incl: Don't Raise the Bridge, Lower the River; many British comedies in the 60s. Radio incl: BBC Drama Rep Company in 50s; Chairman Just A Minute (13 years); Radio Personality

PASCO, Richard CBE
Actor b 18.7.26 Barnes, London. Began as a student apprentice stage manager at the Q Theatre, London in 1943. Returned after war service to study at the Central School of Speech and Drama and won the Gold Medal. He walked-on at the Old Vic, spent three years with Sir Barry Jackson's Birmingham Repertory Company, and was a member of the Brook/Scofield Hamlet company 1955, which was the first British theatre company to visit Moscow since the Revolution. Subsequently joined George Devine's English Stage Company at the Royal Court and in 1964 went to Bristol

Old Vic for the quatercentenary Shakespeare season. He was also in Sixty Thousand Nights which celebrated the 200th anniversary of Bristol's Theatre Royal. In 1969 he joined the Royal Shakespeare Company, later appeared in Man and Superman for the Malvern Festival and went back to Bristol Old Vic in The Seagull 1978. In 1980 he returned to the RSC and more recently appeared with the London Symphony Orchestra Ensemble in The Soldier's Tale and Facade. He frequently appears at festivals in recital and anthology programmes, is a regular broadcaster and has recorded poetry and plays for record companies. An associate artist of the RSC, he received the CBE in New Year's Honours List 1977. No stranger to films or TV, his films incl: Room at the Top; Yesterday's Enemy; Sword of Sherwood Forest; The Gorgon; Rasputin; Hot Enough for June; A Watcher in the Woods; Wagner. He has appeared in dozens of TV plays and programmes incl: Dial M For Murder; Henry Irving; Ivanov; The Three Musketeers; As You Like It; Julius Caesar; The Chief Mourner; British in Love; Sweet Wine of Youth; The Poisoned Gift; Trouble With Gregory; Philby; The Houseboy; Timon of Athens. Education: King's College School, Wimbledon. m (1st) Greta Watson (dis), (2nd) actress Barbara Leigh-Hunt, 1 s William (from 1st m). Address: c/o MLR Ltd, London SW5. Starsign: Cancer. Hobbies: music, gardening, walking.

PEACOCK, Chris

TV reporter b 30.5.45 Cambridge. On leaving school went into journalism as a junior reporter on the

Wisbech Standard. After a couple of years he moved to Anglia TV, where he spent 18 months as a reporter before joining Southern TV/TVS in 1970, where he was a regular member of the Day By Day team. Since 1982 he has been a reporter/presenter for TVS's Coast to Coast. While with Day By Day, he was awarded the Royal Television Society Award 1980 for the best news feature of the year, on Vietnamese refugees in Britain. Was also a member of the team which won for Day By Day the Royal Television Society's 1979 Award for the best magazine programme. Education: Trent College, Nottingham. Address: c/o TVS, Southampton. Starsign: Gemini. Hobbies: the theatre, reading, old buildings, cultivating things, particularly prickly subjects such as cacti.

PEACOCK, Sue

Announcer/presenter b 30.5.52 Welling, Kent. Originally a drama tutor for Women's Institutes, who came into TV through BBC's The Big Time programme. Presented Did You See . . .?

quiz in the latter part of 1980 before becoming an announcer with LWT. Also a regular presenter with Radio City in Liverpool. Education: various private primary schools (with lots of ballet); Ware Grammar School; Herts and Essex High School. m Alan, 1 d Elizabeth, 2 s Antony, Douglas. Address: c/o Adza Vincent, London NW1. Starsign: Gemini. Hobby: theatre. Person she would most like to meet: 'Tom Conti, because I think he's a fabulous actor.'

PENHALIGON, Susan

Actress b 3.7.49 Manila, Philippines. Brought up in England and trained at the Webber Douglas Academy of Dramatic Art. Wide rep experience, having appeared in plays at Worthing (where she was the first nude Juliet in Romeo and Juliet), Manchester, Guildford, Brighton, Bromley and the Open Space Theatre in London. Films incl: No Sex Please, We're British, while on TV she has been seen in Public Eye; Country Matters; Bouquet of Barbed Wire; Fearless Frank; Call My Bluff; Give Us a Clue; The Taming of the Shrew; A Fine Romance; A Kind of Loving; Heather Ann. 1 s. Address: c/o Jeremy Conway Ltd, London W1. Starsign: Cancer.

PENTELOW, Arthur

Actor b 14.2.24 Rochdale. Originally a cadet clerk in the police, but amateur

dramatics was a spare-time interest. Served in Royal Navy for four years during the war and returned to Rochdale to become a student teacher. Joined Bradford Civic Theatre School to train as an actor and went into rep at Bristol Old Vic, Northampton and Birmingham. Was also in Orson Welles' production of Othello in London. Best known on TV as Henry Wilkes in Emmerdale Farm since the series started in 1972. Other TV incl: Z Cars; Armchair Theatre; The Troubleshooters; Coronation Street; Play For Today. Films incl: Privilege; Charlie Bubbles; United! Education: Rochdale Grammar. m pottery teacher Jacqueline, 2 s Nicholas, Simon. Address: c/o Green and Underwood Ltd, London WC2. Starsign: Aquarius. Hobbies: the countryside, gardening, tennis, music. Person he would most like to meet: 'Robert Benchley, for the laughs!'

PERKINS, Max
Reporter b 20.9.44 Bridgend, Glam. Reporter with the Free Press of

Monmouthshire, Pontypool, before joining HTV Wales in 1972. Has also presented documentary on low flying, Too Low For Comfort. Education: Winchester College; Jesus College, Oxford (BA English Lang and Lit). m Jennifer, 1 d Rachel, 1 s Matthew. Address: c/o HTV Wales, Cardiff. Starsign: Virgo. Hobbies: fishing, walking. Person he would most like to have met: 'King Arthur – to find out if he really existed.'

PERRIE, Lynne
Actress b 7.4.31 Rotherham. Trained in local rep. Films incl: Kes; Yanks. TV: Slatterly's Mounted Foot; Leeds United; Follyfoot; Mrs Petty; Queenie's Castle; The Intruders; It was a Good Story, Don't Knock It. Ivy Tilsley in Coronation Street since 1971. Education: Rotherham Grammar School for Girls. m Derrick Barksby, 1 s Stephen. Address: c/o Denman Variety Agency, Nottingham. Starsign: Aries. Hobbies: crochet, bulk freezing own garden produce, greyhound racing. Person she would most like to meet: 'The breeder of Mick the Miller, the greatest greyhound known.'

PERRY, Morris
Actor b 28.3.25 Penge. Turned down for the Foreign Office and worked in the City before studying for the stage at the Old Vic Theatre School. Rep at Exmouth, Swansea, Rochdale, Ludlow and

Edinburgh Festivals, London's Royal Court Theatre and the Royal Shakespeare Company 1977-78. Latest theatre King Lear at Lancaster Rep. A great deal of TV, starting with a small part in the original Avengers series. Since then TV has incl: City Beneath the Sea; Armchair Theatre; Count of Monte Cristo; The Troubleshooters; Rosmersholm; Special Branch; The Sweeney; Helen – A Woman of Today; Crown Court; Warship; Van Der Valk; General Hospital; Act of Rape; Thomas and Sarah; Secret Army; The Professionals; Escape Alfred Hinds; A Tale of Two Cities. Education: Penge Grammar School; Cambridge University. m actress Margaret Ashcroft, 4 s Frank, Matthew, William, Edmund. Address: c/o London Actors, Richmond, Surrey. Hobbies: piano, chess, reading Russian, standing on his head. Person he would most like to have met: 'Beethoven, a little to tap the wonder.'

PERTWEE, Jon
Actor/comedian b 7.7.19 London. Born into a theatrical family, it was inevitable that he eventually went on the stage. Trained at RADA, followed by rep incl Jersey and Brighton. War service in the Royal Navy after which he turned to radio in Waterlogged Spa; Up the Pole and The Navy Lark. Films incl: A Funny Thing

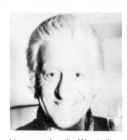

Happened on the Way to the Forum; The Ugly Duckling; Nearly a Nasty Accident; The House that Dripped Blood; Mr Drake's Duck; One of Our Dinosaurs is Missing; There's a Girl in My Soup; Oh Clarence. TV incl: Three of a Kind; Doctor Who; Whodunnit?; Worzel Gummidge. Noted for his range of accents and voices. Recent stage incl: Irene. Education: Wellington House; Sherborne; Frensham Heights. m (1st) actress Jean Marsh (dis), (2nd) Ingeborg Rhoesa, 1 d Dariel, 1 s Sean (both from 2nd m). Address: c/o Richard Stone, London WC2. Starsign: Cancer. Hobby: skin-diving. People he would most like to meet: 'The Queen Mother, because I think she is the greatest living English woman, and my dead father because there was so much left unsaid.'

PETERSON, Oscar
Concert jazz pianist
b 15.8.25 Montreal, Canada. Started musical career when he was six. First instrument was the organ, then the trumpet, but he gave this up

because of weak lungs and concentrated on the piano. He had a 15-minute spot on radio on a weekly basis when he was 15 and in 1944 he was featured for several years in Canada's most popular band, the Johnny Holmes Orchestra. He stayed in Canada until 1949 when an entrepreneur took him to New York. He stopped the show when he made his debut at Carnegie Hall in 1950 in Jazz at the Philharmonic. Began recording the same year and has since made almost annual tours of America, Europe, Great Britain and Japan. Has also toured Russia, Africa and the Far East. Taught jazz at the Advanced School of Contemporary Music in Toronto (which he founded with Ray Brown and Ed Thigpen) in the 1960s, but because he toured so much, the school had to close and he gave up teaching. Has toured extensively with Ella Fitzgerald. Recently he has been devoting more time to composing, in which field he is probably best known for his Canadiana Suite which depicts in music his favourite parts of Canada. Also composed the music for the film Silent Partner. His idol is fellow jazz pianist Art Tatum. Holder of numerous jazz and honorary awards. TV incl: Oscar Peterson Presents; Oscar Peterson's Piano Party; Oscar Peterson Invites; The Very Special Oscar Peterson; Parkinson; Jazz at the Gateway; Silent Partner. Education: Montreal High School and privately. m (1st) Lillian (dis), 3 d, 2 s; m (2nd) Charlotte, 1 s Joel. Address: Mississauga, Ontario, Canada. Starsign: Leo. Hobbies: audio, photography, sports, ham radio.

PETTIFER, Julian
Presenter/reporter b 21.7.35

Malmesbury, Wilts. Started with Southern TV 1958; joined Tonight 1962; war correspondent for 24 Hours 1965 and moved to Panorama 1969. As reporter for BBC his travels have taken him to Vietnam, Aden, Hong Kong, the Suez Canal zone and Northern Ireland. Documentary programmes incl: 90 South; War Without End; Millionaire; Vietnam – the Other World; and more recently The Regiment; The Country Game; World About Us; The China Programme; The History of Civil Aviation; Nature Watch. Education: Marlborough; St John's College, Cambridge. Address: c/o Curtis Brown Ltd, London W2. Starsign: Cancer. Hobby: travel. Person he would most like to have met: 'Charles Darwin, because there are a couple of things I'd like him to explain to me.'

PHILBIN, Maggie
Broadcaster b 23.6.55 Manchester. Came into TV straight from university through an advertisement which was for Multi-coloured Swop Shop – her first job.

Then The Show Me Show. Is also involved in the Tony Blackburn Show on radio. Book: The Maggie Philbin Good-looking Book. Education: Evington Hall Convent, Leicester; Manchester University (degree in Drama and English). Address: c/o Derek James Organisation, Frome, Somerset. Starsign: Cancer. Hobbies: riding, travelling, TV and cinema, eating. People she would most like to meet again: 'The friends I made at school—especially in the sixth form.'

PHILLIPS, Andrew
Presenter b 15.3.39 Long Melford, Suffolk. A solicitor with his own law firm in London, he formed, with others, in 1970, a legal action group (a sort of pressure group within the legal profession) which led to his being invited to become the legal eagle on Jimmy Young's radio show in 1979. He has been acting in that capacity ever since. In 1981 he also became the presenter of The London Programme for London Weekend TV. He has also made many one-off appearances on TV and radio. Education: Sudbury, Culford, Uppingham, Cambridge University (BA Economics and Law). m Penelope, 2 d Caitlin, Alice, 1 s Oliver. Address: c/o LWT, London SE1. Starsign: Pisces. Hobbies: local history, ecclesiastical architecture, golf, tennis, cricket, theatre-going, picture-viewing, politics. Person he would most like to have met: Oliver Cromwell.

PHILLIPS, Sian
Actress b 14.5.34 Carmarthenshire. Began broadcasting and televising in Wales, then joined BBC Repertory Company and Arts Council National Company (Welsh). Won an Arts Council bursary to RADA where she was a Meggie Albanezi scholar and gold medallist. Went into rep and appeared in the first London rep season of the Royal Shakespeare Company. London West End plays incl: Ride a Cock Horse; Night of the Iguana; Man and Superman; The Gay Lord Quex; Lizard on the Rock; The Burglar; Gentle Jack; Man of Destiny; You Never Can Tell (which opened the re-furbished Lyric, Hammersmith); Pal Joey; Dear Liar. Films incl: Becket; Laughter in the Dark; Goodbye Mr Chips; Murphy's War; Clash of the Titans. TV plays incl: Platonov; The Ideal Husband; Don Juan in Hell; Vessel of Wrath; Heartbreak House; The Achurch Letters. TV series incl: Shoulder to Shoulder; How Green Was My Valley; I Claudius; Tinker, Tailor, Soldier, Spy; Crime and Punishment; Winston Churchill The Wilderness Years. New York Critics and Hollywood Critics Awards for Goodbye Mr Chips. BAFTA Awards for How Green Was My Valley and I Claudius. Royal TV Society Award for I Claudius. Made Fellow of University of Wales 1981; made member of the Gorsedd of Bards for services to Welsh Drama. Education: grammar school; University of Wales (Hons degree English and Philosophy). m (1st) actor Peter O'Toole (dis), (2nd) Robin Sachs, 2 d Kate, Pat (both from 1st m). Address: c/o Saraband Assocs, London N1. Starsign: Taurus. Hobby: gardening. Person she would most like to have met: 'Eighteenth-century cleric Sydney Smith – he was the funniest man in England.'

PHOENIX, Patricia
Actress b 26.11.24 Portnum, County Galway, Ireland. Started career in radio play 1939, Children's Hour 1940. Stage: Manchester Arts Theatre Company, rep, variety shows. Stage incl: Suddenly Last Summer; The Miracle Worker; The L-Shaped Room. TV: Coronation Street (since first episode in 1960, apart from three-year break). Education: Fallowfield Central Shool, Manchester. m (1st) advertising executive (dis), (2nd) actor Alan Browning (dec). Address: c/o Saraband Assocs, Manchester. Starsign: Sagittarius. Hobbies: reading, dogs, gardening. Person she would most like to meet: 'Tom Paine – most admired.'

PIGOTT-SMITH, Tim
Actor b 13.5.46 Rugby,
Warwicks. Trained for the
stage at Bristol Old Vic
Theatre School and
appeared with the company.
Also in rep at Nottingham,
Birmingham and Cambridge
and with the Prospect
Company in London.
Member of the Royal
Shakespeare Company
1972-75. Films incl: Aces
High; Joseph Andrews;
Sweet William; The Day Christ
Died; Clash of the Titans;
Escape to Victory; Richard's
Things. TV incl: Eustace and
Hilda; Lost Boys; Measure
For Measure; Henry V; No,
Mama, No; Winston Churchill
The Wilderness Years (as
Brendan Bracken); Fame is
the Spur; I Remember Nelson
(Hardy); The Jewel in the
Crown. Education:
Wyggeston Boys' Grammar
School, Leicester; King's
Grammar School, Stratford
upon Avon; Bristol University.
m Pamela Miles, 1 s Tom.
Address: c/o Jeremy
Conway, London W1.
Starsign: Taurus. Hobbies:
reading, music, yoga. Person
he would most like to meet:
'Sir Laurence Olivier,
because he is the greatest.'

PIRRIE, Alastair
TV journalist/presenter
b 9.5.54 Stockton-on-Tees.
Started as journalist with BBC
Radio Cleveland, then
presenter with BBC TV and
radio and reporter on Radio
4. After a spell as a DJ with
Radio Tees joined Tyne Tees
TV as a reporter. Radio incl:

On the Move; Gospel Road;
Sunday; Pirrie PM; Trains and
Boats and Planes; Well – It's
Different. TV incl: Parents and
Children; See You Sunday;
Northern Life; Generation
Scene; Three's Company;
Saturday Shakeup;
Razzmatazz. Education:
grammar school to 'A' level.
Address: c/o Tyne Tees TV,
Newcastle. Starsign: Taurus.
Hobbies: collecting old
Hollywood movies, writing
(rock music and short
stories). Person he would
most like to meet: Jane
Fonda.

PITMAN, John
TV reporter b 18.11.40
Whitecroft, Glos. Newspaper
training on Gloucestershire
Echo, Brighton Argus and
Daily Mail. TV incl: Hyde Park;
Braden's Week; Man Alive;
Tonight; The Big Time; Times
Remembered; Let's Go
Naked; Decision; Sheena
Easton – The Making of a
Star; The Ritz; Fame.
Education: Bexhill and
Cirencester Grammar
Schools. Address: c/o BBC,
London W14. Starsign:
Scorpio. Hobbies: theatre,
cinema, tennis. Person he

would most like to have met:
'The late writer Dorothy
Parker, because she skilfully
combined humour and
pathos.'

PITTS, Valerie
Presenter b 19.8.40, Leeds,
Yorks. Trained at the Royal
Academy of Dramatic Art.
Wide experience as an
interviewer with Granada,
Tyne Tees and BBC,
particularly in South at Six,
Meeting Point and Animal
Magic. Has also been a BBC
announcer and a presenter of
Town and Around and
Playschool. Presenter
Gammon and Spinach and
writer and presenter for
Extraordinary (both for
Yorkshire TV). Has also been
a panellist on Call My Bluff
and Face the Music.
Education: Leeds Girls' High
School; Leeds College of
Music. m conductor Sir
Georg Solti KBE,
2 d Gabrielle, Claudia.
Address: c/o April Young Ltd,
London WC2. Starsign: Leo.
Hobbies: living, sailing,
windsurfing, swimming,
reading, music, looking at
paintings. Person she would
most like to have met:
'Wolfgang Amadeus Mozart –
to find out if he was really like
his portrayal in Peter Shaffer's
Amadeus.'

POLLARD, Su
Comedy actress/
comedienne/singer
b 7.11.49 Nottingham.
Started as a secretary with
the Nottingham Co-op and
first stage work was as an

amateur with the Co-operative Arts Theatre. First professional break came in the chorus in Desert Song and Rose Marie tours with John Hanson. Then came more musicals: a season in Godspell followed by Oh, Mr Porter; Big Sin City; Grease. Stage incl: Not Now, Darling; One of the Family; Philately Will Get You Nowhere and Christmas shows, incl Dame in a Goldilocks pantomime. In addition to appearing in cabaret and clubs, mostly in the North and Midlands, she has appeared with an all-girl group, Midnight News. TV incl: Summer Royal; The Comedians; a Silver Jubilee all-woman review; Clock-on; Two Up, Two Down; Crackerjack; We're Going Places; Get Set for Summer; Hi-De-Hi. Education: Peveril Bilateral School, Nottingham. Address: c/o Richard Stone, London WC2. Starsign: Scorpio. Hobbies: talking, walking, dancing, working – 'anything really'. Person she would most like to meet: 'Shirley Maclaine – she's got the lot!'

PORTER, Eric
Actor b 8.4.28 London. Started on the stage at Stratford-upon-Avon; subsequently worked with companies run by Lewis Casson, Donald Wolfit, Barry Jackson and John Gielgud before Bristol and London Old Vics. Has acted in nearly all Shakespeare's plays, played Captain Hook in Peter Pan in 1971 and been in

many films incl: The Fall of the Roman Empire; The Pumpkin Eater; The Heroes of Telemark; Kaleidoscope; The Lost Continent; Hands of the Ripper; Anthony and Cleopatra; Nicholas and Alexandra; The Day of the Jackal; Hitler – the Last 10 Days; The Belstone Fox; Hennessy; Callan; The Thirty Nine Steps; Little Lord Fauntleroy. Achieved fame at 40 as Soames Forsyte in the TV blockbuster The Forsyte Saga. Other TV incl: The Wars of the Roses; Cyrano de Bergerac; Man and Superman; Spilt Champagne; Separate Tables; Morecambe and Wise Show; Macbeth; When We Are Married; The Canal Children; The Winslow Boy; Anna Karenina; Harry Secombe Christmas Show; Why Didn't They Ask Evans?; Churchill and the Generals; Hamlet; The Crucible; The Sinbin; Winston Churchill The Wilderness Years; The Jewel in the Crown. TV Guild of Producers and Directors Actor of the Year Award 1967. Education: Tweeddale Elementary School, Carshalton, Surrey; Wimbledon Technical College. Address: c/o London Management, London W1. Starsign: Aries. Hobbies: woodwork, gardening. Person he would most like to have met: 'Leonardo da Vinci, the most complete intellectual and artistic man in history.'

POWELL, Peter
Disc jockey b 24.3.51 Stourbridge, West Mids. Started organising school concerts, appearing on local radio, running a mobile disco before joining Radio Luxembourg where he stayed for three and a half years. He left to join BBC Radio in 1977 and from time to time has been on TV presenting Top of the Pops. Also presents a children's holiday series Get Set For Summer. Education: Uppingham School, Rutland. Address: c/o BBC Radio 1, London W1. Starsign: Aries. Hobbies: driving power boats, water-skiing, squash, tennis, football, photography, driving a Porsche. Person he would most like to meet: 'The President of the USA because he is the most powerful man in the Western world.'

PRENDIVILLE, Kieran
Reporter b 25.12.47 Rochdale, Lancs. Started as copy boy in Oldham Press Agency and progressed to reporter (1968). Spent three and a half years in Fleet Street (1969-72) before becoming

researcher then a reporter for BBC TV incl: That's Life; Nationwide; Man Alive; Holiday Programme; Tomorrow's World; Risk Business; Summer Sunday. Also radio, incl: Archive series, Findings. Education: Cassock Nostra – Irish Jesuits. m Jan. Address: c/o BBC TV, London W14. Starsign: Capricorn. Hobbies: watching football, racing, playing cricket, Irish music. Person he would most like to meet: 'My first news editor, in a dark alley.'

PRESTON, Robert
Actor b 8.6.38 Newton Highlands, Massachusetts. Stage actor since 1932 but probably best known for his role of Harold Hill in The Music Man (one of his favourite parts) which he played in America 1957-60 and won a Tony and the New York Drama Critics Award for his performance. He was also in the film version. Other theatre incl: 20th Century (his first part in New York); The Male Animal; The Tender Trap; The Lion in Winter; (Tony and New York Drama Critics Award); Mack and Mabel (in which he played Mack Sennett). Films incl: Union Pacific; Typhoon; Northwest Mounted Police; Reap the Wild Wind; This Gun for Hire; Wake Island; Beau Geste; The Dark at the Top of the Stairs; The Macomber Affair; The Sundowners; All the Way Home; Child's Play; Mame. Has appeared in many TV programmes incl:

Playhouse 90; Omnibus; Chisholm. Education: Lincoln High School, Los Angeles. Starsign: Gemini. Hobby: acting.

PRICE, Bob
Gardening personality b 23.5.18 Port Talbot. Studied to become a landscape architect during the war, while in the army as a Captain in the Royal Engineers and answered his exam papers while serving in France. After the war he was giving gardening talks on BBC Radio and was invited by Noele Gordon to audition for a weekly gardening spot on her Lunch Box programme in 1956. Since then he has broadcast regularly on gardening matters. His TV appearances incl: High Tea; Citizen's Rights; Come Into the Garden; ATV Today and, since 1971, has appeared with Cyril Fletcher on ATV's Gardening Today (now Central TV's Gardening Time). Education: Wellington High School; Reading University. m Hilda, 1 d Judi, 1 s Michael. Address: c/o Central TV, Birmingham. Starsign: Gemini. Hobby: sport (all kinds, especially cricket, golf and tennis). Person he would most like to meet: 'Princess Anne. What a challenge an interview would be!'

PRICE, Tom
Actor b 28.5.59 Salford, Lancs. As a small boy all he ever wanted to be an

actor and to be in the cast of Coronation Street. His ambition came true in 1982 with his part of electrician Alec Hobson. Trained at RADA, then rep at Exeter and the Royal Exchange Theatre, Manchester. His first TV was as Brian in The Glamour Girls. Then, 'out of the blue', came his part in Coronation Street. Education: Salford Grammar School. Address: c/o Fraser and Dunlop, London W1. Starsign: Gemini. Hobbies: tennis, snooker. Person he would most like to meet: 'Albert Finney because he comes from the same background as myself.'

PRINCIPAL, Victoria
Actress b 3rd January Japan. Has played Pam Ewing in Dallas since the start of the series. Brought up in Ruislip, Middx, where her father was stationed at the US Air Force base, she is a former Miss Miami and in 1982 was voted the second most beautiful woman in America (first was Charlie's Angel Jaclyn Smith). Spent much of her late teens and student days in London and before getting to Hollywood

(where she attended law school) had been a stock-car driver, theatrical agent and model. Also a film actress but gave it up when she lost interest. Tempted to return to acting by small part in TV series Fantasy Island which led to her role in Dallas. Films incl: The Life and Times of Judge Roy Bean; The Naked Ape; Earthquake; I Will, I Will . . . for Now; Vigilante Force. Education: Miami Dade College, Florida. m actor Christopher Skinner (dis). Starsign: Capricorn. Hobbies: tennis, swimming, jogging, cooking, animals.

PRITCHARD, Margaret
Announcer/presenter
b 7.4.52 Bethesda, Gwynedd, North Wales. Trained at the Welsh College of Music and Drama and before joining HTV Wales had appeared in numerous radio and TV plays and in two theatre tours. Since joining HTV in 1972 she has been announcer/presenter/news-reader and for the past five years has been presenting children's programmes. Education: Ysgol Duffryn Ogwen, Bethesda, and is studying for an Open University part-time degree. m John, 1 d Angharad. Address: c/o HTV Wales, Cardiff. Starsign: Aries. Hobbies: current affairs. Person she would most like to meet: 'My husband – due to overtime I have not seen him for a week!'

PRYCE, Jonathan
Actor b 1.6.47 Holywell, North Wales. Trained at RADA and rep experience at the Everyman, Liverpool and Nottingham. Also with the Royal Shakespeare Company and as Hamlet at the Royal Court, London (for which he won a SWET Award as best actor in 1980). Also appeared in The Comedians in London and America where he won a Tony Award (1977). Films incl: Voyage of the Damned; Breaking Glass; Loophole; Something Wicked This Way Comes; Praying Mantis. Much TV incl: Daft as a Brush; Playthings; For Tea on Sunday; Glad Day; Partisans; The Comedians; The Caretaker; Timon of Athens; Roger Doesn't Live Here Any More. Education: Holywell Grammar; Flints School of Art; Edge Hill College. Address: c/o Fraser and Dunlop, London W1. Starsign: Gemini.

PURCHES, Graham
Journalist b 5.3.44 Portsmouth. Started as a cadet journalist in Australia then TV in Melbourne and

Hong Kong. Currently reporter/presenter Points West for BBC in Bristol. Education: Seaford College, Sussex. m Charlotte, 2 s Samuel, Oliver. Address: c/o BBC, Bristol. Starsign: Pisces. Hobbies: yoga, running, work. Person he would most like to meet: 'The policeman who gave me a parking ticket while I was interviewing the Chief Constable about rising crime figures – to discuss the theory of relativity!'

PURVES, Libby
Reporter/presenter b 2.2.50 London. Trained in studio management before going to Radio Oxford for five years. Returned to national radio working on Today and other Radio 4 programmes as reporter and presenter 1975-81. Became presenter of Choices early 1982. Other TV incl Southampton Boat Show (with her husband) 1981, 1982. Education: Sacred Heart Convent, Tunbridge Wells; Oxford University (1st class Hons English Lit). m Paul Heiney. Address: c/o BBC TV Choices, London. Starsign: Aquarius. Hobby: sailing. Person she would most like to meet: 'Bette Davis, my girlhood idol.'

PURVIS, Anne
Weather forecaster
b 11.10.52 Cardiff. Joined Met Office as a scientific officer 1974 and became interested in weather forecasting. Moved to

London Weather Centre 1979 and a member of the team of regular BBC forecasters since July 1981. Education: Cardiff High School for Girls; Cardiff University (Bsc Hons Mathematics). m George Purvis. Address: c/o London Weather Centre, London WC1. Starsign: Libra. Hobbies: jogging, reading, painting, walking. Person she would most like to meet: 'Sebastian Coe or Superman – or are they the same person?'

after his retirement on Don't Ask Me and Don't Just Sit There (1973-80). Other TV incl: guest appearances on many programmes; Enough Food on Our Plate; Multi-Coloured Swop Shop; Celebrity Squares; This Is Your Life; Parkinson. Holds a Doctor of Philosophy degree and Fellowships of the Royal Institute of Chemistry, Institute of Biology, Institute of Food Science and Technology, Royal Society of Edinburgh. Education; St Paul's; McGill University, Montreal; University College, London. m chartered accountant Dorothea, 1 d Elizabeth, 1 s John. Address: Hammersmith, London. Starsign: Capricorn. Hobbies: 'Living is for real, not hobbies'. Person he would most like to have met: 'Jane Austen – she wrote so well.'

PYKE, Dr Magnus OBE
Scientist and TV personality b 29.12.08 London. Expert in nutrition and populariser of science. Has held several important scientific and research appointments. Scientific adviser to the Ministry of Food 1941-45, President of the Institute of Food Science and Technology of the UK 1969-71, and secretary and chairman British Association for the Advancement of Science 1973-77. Travels the world lecturing on nutrition and is the author of many books on the subject. Became a TV personality

PYNE, Frederick
Actor b 30.12.36 London. Spent some time farming in Cheshire and Cambridgeshire. Signed on with the RAF and it was there he caught the theatre bug. Trained at RADA, then rep, followed by four years at the National Theatre at the Old Vic 1966-70. TV incl: Justice; Emmerdale Farm. Education: Holloway Grammar School, London. Address: c/o Yorkshire TV, Leeds. Starsign: Capricorn. Hobbies: music, foreign travel. Person he would most like to meet: 'An impossible question to answer!'

QUAYLE, Anna

Actress/writer b 6.10.37 Birmingham. Trained at RADA after touring for a number of years in Douglas Quayle's Company, (run by her actor/producer father) for whom she made her first stage appearance in East Lynn at the age of four. Accomplished performer on stage, film and TV. Stage incl: Stop the World I Want to Get Off; Full Circle (which she wrote); Out of Bounds (Bristol); Pal Joey; Kings and Clowns. Films incl: Chitty Chitty Bang Bang; SOS Titanic; The Seven Per Cent Solution; Towers of Babel. TV incl: The Georgian House; What's My Line?; Jackanory Playhouse; Aquarius; What a Performance; The Light Princess; Henry V; Brideshead Revisited; Sakharov The People From The Forest; Give Us a Clue; Father Charlie. Education: Convent of Jesus and Mary, Harlesden. m Donald Baker, 1 d Katy Nova. Address: c/o Elspeth Cochrane Agency, London SW4. Starsign: Libra. Hobbies: collecting books, exploring old buildings, churches, castles, etc,

Siamese cats (she has five). Person she would most like to have met: 'C G Jung, to spend a lot of the hereafter learning from him.'

QUAYLE, Lawrie

Reporter b 6.12.38 Douglas, Isle of Man. Legal practice in Manchester and Liverpool before becoming a DJ overnight with Manx Radio 1966. Transferred to Radio Caroline 1968 and later the same year joined Border TV as a reporter. Moved south to Westward/TSW 1971. TV incl: Westward Diary; Today South-West; Televiews; The South-West Week, the first regional round-up of the week's news for the deaf. Education: Manchester University (MA and LLB). Twice m, 1 d Sheron, 1 s Gary. Address: c/o TSW, Plymouth. Hobbies: reading, music, motor-cycling, walking, fireside conversation. Person he would most like to meet: 'Kenneth Griffith – I like the way he tackles documentary subjects which other people wouldn't touch with a barge-pole.'

QUICK, Diana

Actress b 23.11.46 Kent. Member of the National Youth Theatre when she was 16. Has since appeared at London's Royal Court Theatre, Bristol Old Vic, The Open Space, The Royal Exchange, Manchester. London's West End theatre has seen her in The Threepenny Opera and Billy.

For the National Theatre she has been in Phaedra Brittanica, Plunder, Troilus and Cressida and Tamburlaine, and for the Royal Shakespeare Company The Women Pirates and The Changeling. Films incl: Nicholas and Alexandra; The Duellists; The Big Sleep; The Odd Job. Many TV plays and serials for the BBC and ITV incl: The Playground and Sleeping Beauty (Wednesday Plays); Christ Recrucified; Complete and Utter History of Britain; At Last It's Friday; Napoleon and Love; Mr Garrick and Mrs Woffington; Hanging On; Brideshead Revisited; The Woman in White. Education: Lady Margaret Hall, Oxford. Address: c/o Fraser and Dunlop, London W1. Starsign: Scorpio. Hobbies: reading, writing, gardening, cooking, skiing, restoring furniture.

QUILLEY, Denis

Actor b 26.12.27. Trained at Birmingham Rep with whom he made his first professional stage appearance in 1945. After small parts in London and Nottingham and a British

Council tour of Italy, he appeared in the revue Airs on a Shoestring (700 performances) followed by his first leading West End part in Wild Thyme. Later he was to appear in Grab Me a Gondola (more than 600 performances) and in 1960 went into Irma La Douce. He left to make his first appearance in New York but returned to Irma La Douce and toured America in it. Many other leading roles followed incl: Regent's Park Open Air 1963 season; The Boys from Syracuse; High Spirits; and, in Australia, Robert and Elizabeth. Joined the National Theatre in 1971 to appear in Coriolanus; Tyger; Long Day's Journey Into Night; Richard II; The School for Scandal; Front Page; Macbeth; The Cherry Orchard; Saturday, Sunday, Monday; The Party. He also played Claudius in Hamlet and appeared in the same part in the opening production of the Lyttleton Theatre, 1976. His films incl: Life at the Top; Anne of the Thousand Days. On TV he has been in many plays and series incl: The Father; Pirandello's Henry IV; Murder in the Cathedral; Contrabandits (Australia); and more recently, The Crucible; Honky-Tonk Heroes; Sunday Thriller; Tales of the Unexpected; Gladstone in No 10. Education: Bancroft's School, Woodford Green, Essex. m Stella Chapman, 2 d Sarah, Joanna, 1 s David. Address: c/o NEMS Management, London SW3. Starsign: Capricorn. Hobbies: playing piano, flute, cello, walking. Person he would most like to meet: 'Placido Domingo – a great operatic tenor who is also a great actor.'

QUINTEN, Christopher
Actor b 12.7.57

Middlesbrough. Trained at Billingham Theatre School. Brian Tilsley in Coronation Street since Dec 1978. Other TV incl: Warship; Target; The Pink Medicine Show; The Little Big Show; Quatermass. Films incl: International Velvet. Education: Easterside Junior School; Brookside Secondary Modern. Address: c/o Bill Horne Personal Management, London WC2. Starsign: Cancer. Hobbies: gymnastics, keep-fit, photography. Person he would most like to meet: 'Harry Salzman, to discuss my contract.'

QUIRKE, Pauline
Actress b 8.7.59 London. While still at school was in Dixon of Dock Green; Kids About Town; Days of Hope and regular member of the teenage cast of You Must Be Joking. Turning point in her career was as the autistic child in Jenny Can't Work Any Faster. Other TV incl: Pauline's Quirkes; Pauline's People; Baby Talk; A Name For the Day; The Story of the Treasure Seekers. Education: Islington Green School, London. Drama training at Anna Scher Theatre. Address: c/o Anna Scher Theatre Management, London N1. Starsign: Cancer. Hobbies: reading autobiographies, watching plays, decorating, going to new places, eating out. People she would most like to have met: 'Judy Garland – she was a very talented lady and was used by people; and my nan, because I've heard so much about her.'

R

reporter and interviewer for a current affairs programme. Joined the Magpie team 1972. Returned to Scottish TV to present his own programme 1977. TV incl: World Worth Keeping; Edinburgh Festival Arts Programme 1974-81; Edinburgh Film Festival 1977-81; Sneak Preview; Two Plus Two; Today; Thames at Six; Encore for the Arts. Now producing The Real World and Seven Days. Education: Edinburgh Academy. Address: c/o Douglas J.Rae Assocs, London SW4. Starsign: Cancer. Hobbies: films, travel, sport. Person he would most like to have met: 'Vasco da Gama, one of the world's great explorers.'

RADCLIFFE, Nicholas
Reporter/newscaster
b 27.4.52 Wells, Somerset. Started as a cub reporter on Wells Journal, then went into local radio (Radio Forth) 1975, progressively as presenter, reporter and production. Joined STV 1976 reporting for Scottish TV news and presenting Scotland Today. Education: Wells Cathedral School; Edinburgh University. m Denise. Address: c/o STV, Glasgow. Starsign: Taurus. Hobbies: theatre, books, mediaeval music, golf, good food. People he would most like to meet: 'Sir Laurence Olivier or Sir John Gielgud, because I am fascinated by real talent in the theatre.'

RAE, Douglas
TV reporter/producer
b 22.6.47 Edinburgh. First job on leaving school was copy boy on the Scottish Daily Express. Had other newspaper jobs in Angus, Glasgow and Dundee before joining Scottish TV as

RAISON, Caroline
Newsreader/religious broadcaster b 21.9.43 Windsor. Trained at Lincoln Theological College on a general ordination course and has been a contributor to religious programmes since 1976. Joined Anglia TV as newsreader 1977. Education: St Mary's, Wantage; finishing school in Lausanne. m Nicholas,

1 d Miranda, 1 s Edward. Address: c/o Anglia TV, Norwich. Starsign: Virgo. Hobbies: music, reading to the children. Person she would most like to have met: 'Martin Luther King – a true disciple of Christ.'

RANDALL, Alan
Musical entertainer/singer
b 10.6.39 Bedworth, Warwicks. Started career as vibraphone player in Sonny Rose Band. Eventually went solo introducing George Formby songs and ukelele playing. Radio incl: Tony Brandon Show; John Dunne Show; Charlie Chester Show; Jimmy Young Show; I Remember George. TV incl: top variety shows such as Roy Castle Beats Time; Seaside Special; Wheeltappers and Shunters Social Club; The Good Old Days; Parkinson. Owns several George Formby ukeleles, records and personal possessions. Education: secondary school. m Mary, 1 d Susan, 1 s Martyn. Address: c/o International Artists, London W1. Starsign: Gemini. Hobbies: driving, playing golf, collecting records. Person he would most like to meet: 'The Queen – she is an inspiration to us all.'

RANTZEN, Esther
TV journalist b 22.6.40 Berkhamsted, Herts. After gaining an English degree at Oxford, joined the BBC as a radio effects girl before going into research. Became a

production assistant on Man Alive and in 1968 joined Braden's Week, researching and reporting on the show. Has been presenting That's Life, which she also produces, since 1973. Other TV incl: Big Time; That's Life – Having a Baby. Member of the Consumer Council 1981. Education: North London Collegiate, Edgware, Middx; Somerville College, Oxford. m independent producer, writer and reporter Desmond Wilcox, 2 d Emily, Rebecca, 1 s Joshua. Address: c/o Noel Gay Artists, London WC2. Starsign: Cancer.

RAWLE, Jeff
Actor/writer b 20.7.51 Birmingham. Worked at Sheffield Playhouse on leaving school until he went to LAMDA to train as an actor. A few weeks after leaving he was chosen to play the part of Billy Liar in the TV series of the same name. TV since incl: The Water Maiden; Death of a Young Young Man; Beryl's Lot; A Cost of Loving; Van Der Valk; Send in the Girls; Wilde Alliance; Leave it to Charlie; Singles; Juliet Bravo; Whose Child. Stage (West End) incl:

So Who Needs Men; Equus; Once a Catholic; Bent. Films incl: Life Story of a Man Called Baal; Correction Please; A Hitch in Time; Rating Notman; Crystal Gazing. Radio incl: Semi Detached; Daphne du Maurier Short Stories; Still Life; The Morning Story (several). Education: grammar schools in Birmingham and Sheffield. Address: c/o David White Assocs, London W1. Starsign: Cancer. Hobbies: playing various musical instruments, filling in VAT forms. Person he would most like to meet: Fred Astaire.

RAY, Robin
Writer/presenter b London. Studied at RADA. Extensive experience in radio and TV with both BBC and ITV. Radio series incl: Sounds Funny to Me, Sean; classical record programmes on Radio 3 and 4, such as A Touch of Genius; the first classical music programme on commercial radio, The Robin Ray Collection, for Capital. Still reviews classical records for Capital. TV (more than 400 shows for BBC) incl: Face the Music; The Movie Quiz; Music in Camera; Masters of the Keyboard; The Lively Arts; Robin Ray's Picture Gallery; Cabbages and Kings; Film Buff of the Year. Has also written and presented many documentaries. Stage work incl: Beyond the Fringe and, more recently, Side By Side By Sondheim; Tomfoolery;

which he compiled and starred in. He is an associate director of the Meadowbank Theatre, Detroit, USA. Books: Time for Lovers; Robin Ray's Music Quiz; Favourite Hymns and Carols. Education: Highgate School. m Susan Stranks, 1 s Rupert. Address: c/o Roger Hancock Ltd, London SW1. Starsign: Virgo. Hobbies: cinema, music, television.

REARDON, Ray
Professional snooker player b 8.10.32 Tredegar, Gwent. Started playing snooker when he was eight years old and turned professional 1969. World Champion 1970, 1973-74, 1975, 1976, 1978. Education: George Town Grammar, Tredegar. m Susan, 1 d Melanie, 1 s Darren. Address: c/o ISA, Bishopston, Bristol. Starsign: Libra. Hobbies: golf, music, collecting unusual seals. Person he would most like to meet: Jack Nicklaus.

REDFERN, Barrie
Broadcaster b 11th June Rotherham. Began as a student broadcaster

producing items for BBC Radio Stoke on Trent and working for BBC Humberside. Trained in TV with BBC in London and went freelance 1977, working for various radio (sometimes as producer) and TV stations (incl script writing and making trailers). Regional presenter BBC TV North in Leeds 1979 before going to Grampian TV as announcer 1980. Book: Local Radio. Education: Oakwood School, Rotherham; Alsager College of Education, Cheshire. Address: c/o Grampian TV, Aberdeen. Starsign: Gemini. Hobbies: skiing, rugby, film-making, driving an MG. Person he would most like to meet again: 'Alan Whicker — one of the most outstanding TV personalities.'

REED, Simon
Broadcaster b 5.8.47 Sutton, Surrey. Was with the Sutton and Cheam Herald and a BBC radio freelance before joining Thames TV in 1979 to become one of the presenters of After Noon Plus and Thames Sport. Education: King's College School, Wimbledon. m Janice. Address: c/o Thames TV, London NW1. Starsign: Leo. Hobbies: sport (watching and playing), work. Person he would most like to meet: 'Jeremy Isaacs — he might be able to get me some work.'

REES, Gwenda
Presenter/interviewer b 12.2.40 Clwyd, North

Wales. Formerly a teacher at Aberdare Girls Grammar School (1964-66) and Canton High School, Cardiff (1966-68), when she left to do part-time teaching and part-time TV. Has since been associated with such Welsh language programmes as Cofiwch Alw; Croeso Christine; Tins a Lei; Hamdden (1971-81). Now presenting Welsh documentaries for Channel Four. Education: Llanrwst Grammar School; University College of North Wales (Hons Welsh). m William, 2 s Alun, Dafydd. Address: c/o Glansevin Productions, Llangadog, South Wales. Starsign: Aquarius. Hobbies: food, wine, antiques, husband (not necessarily in that order). Person she would most like to meet: 'Katie Stewart — to thank her for inspiring my cooking.'

REES, Ken
TV reporter b 26.1.44 Cardiff. Regular contributor to ITV's News at 5.45 and News at Ten. TV career began 1968 as newscaster for HTV's news magazine, Reports West. Joined ITN

1978. Northern correspondent 1978-82. Assignments incl Falkland Islands crisis. Outside TV has produced documentaries for industry and education establishments. Education: Howardian High School, Cardiff. m Lynne, 1 d Samantha, 1 s Christian. Address: c/o Derek James Organisation, Frome, Somerset. Starsign: Aquarius. Hobbies: work, photography, clocks.

REES, Norman
Reporter b 2.3.39 Cardiff. Started with Western Mail, Cardiff and after seven years moved to TWW (now HTV) as reporter, scriptwriter and then news editor. He joined ITN as a news editor 1968 and became Washington correspondent in 1977. He returned to London 1981 as reporter. Many varied assignments incl coverage of the Falkland Islands crisis from Buenos Aires. Education: Canton High School, Cardiff. m Andrea, 1 d Nicola, 1 s Andrew. Address: c/o ITN, London W1. Starsign: Pisces. Hobbies: reading, squash.

REES, Roger
Actor b 5.5.44 Aberystwyth. Wanted to be a painter and studied at the Slade School of Fine Art in London until his father died and he turned to the stage to earn a living. Started painting scenery at Wimbledon rep, but later was given parts to play incl a

pantomime horse with Roy Castle. Went to Bath and Pitlochry reps before joining Royal Shakespeare Company 1967 to 'walk on', but culminating in 1981 in his marathon, eight-and-a-half-hour performance as Nicholas Nickleby in The Life and Adventures of Nicholas Nickleby (which won him the Society of West End Managers Award for best actor in a new play and a Tony Award for Best Actor 1981), which was recorded for Channel Four. Latest theatre: Masquerade. Education: Balham Secondary Modern; Camberwell Art School. Address: c/o ICM, London W1. Starsign: Taurus. Person he would most like to meet: 'St Paul: I like the way he writes.'

REID, Beryl
Actress b 17.6.20 Hereford. First appeared on stage in concert party Bridlington 1936. Made reputation as Monica in Educating Archie (radio). TV, radio, clubs, variety and revues (incl Half-past Eight in Edinburgh, in which she did 427

sketches in one season), before her first serious stage play, The Killing of Sister George (1965), followed some years later by Entertaining Mr Sloane. Appeared in film versions of both plays. Other stage work incl: Blithe Spirit; Romeo and Juliet; Spring Awakening and Il Campiello (for the National Theatre); The Way of the World (Royal Shakespeare Co). Has since largely concentrated on TV incl: The Rivals; Father, Dear Father; The Edward Woodward Hour; Harry Secombe Show; The Goodies; The Good Old Days; Alcock and Gander; Wink To Me Only; Smike; The Apple Cart; When We Are Married; Flint; Tinker, Tailor, Soldier, Spy; Does The Team Think?; Get Up and Go; Smiley's People; and her own programmes. Films incl: The Belles of St Trinians; Star; Inspector Clouseau; The Beast in the Cellar; No Sex Please – We're British; The Dock Brief. Education: Ladybarn House; Withington High; Levenshulme High, Manchester. m (1st) Bill Worsley (dis), (2nd) musician Derek Franklin (dis). Address: c/o Fraser and Dunlop, London W1. Starsign: Gemini. Hobbies: gardening, cooking, driving.

REID, George
Producer/presenter b 4.6.39 Tullibody, Clackmannanshire, Scotland. MP for Clackmannanshire 1974-79. Journalist on Daily Express

and worked for STV and Granada before joining BBC Scotland 1979. Has been associated with such programmes, mostly documentaries, as Scotland Now; Ship from the Clyde; Between the Lines; Beagan Ghaidlig; Scene; What the Papers Say; political party conferences; Current Account; African Odyssey; Agenda; The Pinch (drama). Education: Dollar Academy; St Andrews University. m Daphne, 2 d Caroline, Morag. Address: c/o BBC, Glasgow. Starsign: Gemini. Hobby: European ethnic minorities.

RHODES, Pam
Presenter b 22.9.50 Gillingham, Kent. Trained as a dancer but started in TV behind the scenes as programme organiser for Thames documentary programme This Week 1975-76. Joined Anglia TV and was presenter of live local news programme About Anglia for six years; also TV presenter British Forces Broadcasting Service for four years. Other TV incl: Merry-go-Round; The World About Us; Finding Out; Hurdy Gurdy; Star Games (interviewer); Wheels. Presentation announcer for LWT 1981. Holder of London Chamber of Commerce private secretary's certificate. Education: Gosport County Grammar School. m lighting film cameraman Paul Williams. Address: c/o Isobel Davie,

London W1. Starsign: Virgo/Libra cusp. Hobbies: teaching, dancing and drama, youth club work, piano, xylophone. Person she would most like to meet: 'Semprini – I've admired his choice and arrangement of music for years. I wish I could play like him.'

RICH, Craig

TV presenter b 3.3.38 Plymouth. A sailor by profession and a Master Mariner, he was 12 years in the Merchant Navy before becoming a lecturer in shipping subjects at London Polytechnic 1966-71, when he moved back to Plymouth where he is senior lecturer in maritime studies at Plymouth Polytechnic. Since 1978 he has been the BBC's weatherman in Plymouth. Also presents That's Rich, a mixture of chat show, documentary and entertainment. Education: Devonport High School. m Pat, 2 d Joanne, Sarah, 1 s Thomas. Address: c/o BBC, Plymouth. Hobbies: reading, most sports, especially squash, football and swimming. Person he would most like to meet: 'Joan Collins, because I have always admired her.'

RICHARD, Cliff

Singer/actor b 14.10.40 Lucknow, India. Came to England when he was seven. On leaving school worked as a clerk. First TV, Oh Boy! series in 1958 with The Shadows. Many TV, radio

and stage appearances and records, incl 100 hits. No 1 hit record, We Don't Talk Anymore, summer 1979. First record Move It in 1958. Gold discs (for selling over 500,000 copies each) for Living Doll; The Young Ones; The Next Time; Lucky Lips; Congratulations; Power To All Our Friends; Devil Woman; We Don't Talk Anymore; Daddy's Home. Also has 30 silver discs, each for sales of more than 250,000. Films incl: Serious Charge; Expresso Bongo; The Young Ones; Summer Holiday; Wonderful Life; Finders Keepers; Two a Penny; Take Me High; His Land. Education: Riversmead School, Cheshunt. Address: c/o Gormley Management, Esher, Surrey. Starsign: Libra. Hobbies: swimming, tennis, photography.

RICHARDS, Clare

Actress b 21.12.30 Edinburgh. Rep experience, incl Glasgow, Aberdeen and Perth, of 20 years and also much TV experience incl: Heather on Fire; Redgauntlet; Cesar Birotteau; Revenue Men; High Living; A Place of

Her Own; Toy Princess; Last Lane; Stanley Baxter series; That's My Boy. Education: Mallaig School, Mallaig, Inverness-shire. m Sonnie Whyatt-Parr. Address: c/o Joan Reddin, London W11.. Starsign: Sagittarius. Hobbies: reading, learning to sing. Person she would most like to have met: 'I always wanted to meet Sam Goldwyn, but when he heard about it, he died.'

RICHARDS, Gwyn

Presenter/reporter b 6.6.36 Burton-on-Trent, Staffs. Trained in textile manufacture and design. Rhodesian Mounted Police for four years before becoming radio producer/announcer and TV newscaster in Zambia. Returned to England as reporter for BBC's Midlands Today, then anchorman of ATV Today, followed by return to BBC to present Points West in Bristol. Regional reporter for Nationwide; presenter of BBC West feature programmes, Movie Magic; Sports Show and Day Out; many documentary films; presenter of BBC 2's Something in the Wind and In the Post; reporter Collecting Now. Education: Burton Grammar; Derby Polytechnic; Law, Police and Equitation, British South Africa Police, Salisbury, Rhodesia. m Helen. 1 d Phyllida, 1 s Simon. Address: c/o BBC TV, Bristol. Starsign: Gemini. Hobbies: squash, tennis, writing.

RICHARDSON, David
Presenter/reporter b 31.8.37 Norwich. With an agricultural background has presented many programmes on farming, food and the countryside and has contributed to Anglia TV, BBC TV and radio programmes for more than 21 years. Education: City of Norwich School. m Lorna, 1 d Fiona, 2 s Andrew, Rob. Address: c/o Anglia TV, Norwich. Starsign: Virgo. Hobbies: photography, agricultural history, collecting pigs. Person he would most like to have met: 'William Cobbett, of Cobbett's Rural Rides, to talk about what the countryside was like in his day.'

RIGG, Carl
Actor b Eton, Bucks. Trained at the Central School of Speech and Drama and the RSC Studio. TV incl: Doctor Who; The Sweeney; Marked Personal; General Hospital; Targets; Emmerdale Farm; Squadron. Education: grammar school. m actress Maggie Wells, 1 s Christian. Address: c/o Ken Mc Reddie, London W1.

Starsign: Taurus/Gemini. Hobbies: sailing, fishing, diving. Person he would most like to meet: 'Bernard Moitessier, one of the most experienced and brilliant lone navigators alive.'

RIPPON, Angela
Journalist/broadcaster b 12.10.44 Plymouth, Devon. On leaving school at 17 joined local daily newspaper working in the photographic department and after two and a half years joined the local Sunday newspaper, The Independent, as a junior reporter. In 1966 joined BBC Plymouth to report for and present Spotlight Southwest and Points West (Bristol). During this time she was a member of a team covering the Torrey Canyon disaster. Joined Westward TV to edit and introduce women's programme, Open House, 1969; also produced Westward Report and three documentaries. In 1974 rejoined BBC as a news reporter and in 1975 helped present News Extra. In 1976 introduced 'new look' Nine o'clock News. Appeared in the 1976 Morecambe and Wise Christmas show (in which she danced) and presented the Eurovision Song Contest 1977. Other TV incl: the Rippon Reports series; The Country Game; Antiques Roadshow; contributions to Newsday on BBC 2 and Top Gear. Newsreader of the Year 1977, 1978 and 1979. TV

Personality of the Year 1977. Books: Riding; Victoria Plumb (stories for children); Mark Phillips: The Man and His Horses (biography). Education: Plymouth secondary and grammar schools. m Christopher Dare. Address: c/o IMG, London W1. Starsign: Libra. Hobbies: riding, gardening, cooking. Person she would most like to meet: 'Shirley Maclaine – I have always admired her personality, dancing technique and wit.'

ROACHE, William
Actor b 25.4.32 Ilkeston, Derbyshire. After five years in the army, in which he received a commission in the Royal Welsh Fusiliers, he went into rep at Nottingham and Oldham. Films incl: Behind the Mask; His and Hers; Queens Guards. Has appeared regularly as Ken Barlow in Coronation Street since 1960. He and his wife run their own production company presenting plays and chat shows, in which they frequently appear. Education: Rydal School. m Sara, 1 d Verity. Address: c/o Spotlight, London WC2. Starsign: Taurus. Hobby: golf. Person he would most like to meet: 'Prince Charles – I feel he has a natural wisdom that transcends politics and could be a great service to this country and the world.'

ROBB, David
Actor b 23.8.47 London. Stage training at the Central

School of Speech and Drama. Theatre credits incl: Abelard and Heloise; Betzi; Cowardy Custard; An Audience Called Edouard; She Stoops To Conquer. Films incl: Conduct Unbecoming; The Four Feathers. TV incl: numerous Plays of the Week; Crown Court; The Glittering Prizes; I Claudius; French Without Tears; The Winslow Boy; Wings; Wuthering Heights; Hess; Romeo and Juliet; The Caledonian Cascade; Hamlet; The Legend of King Arthur; Forgive Our Foolish Ways; The Flame Trees of Thika; Fanny By Gaslight. Education: The Royal High School, Edinburgh. m Briony McRoberts. Address: c/o William Morris (UK) Ltd, London W1. Starsign: Leo/Virgo cusp. Hobbies: rugby (watching), riding, military history. Person he would most like to meet: 'God – but as late as possible!'

ROBERTS, Cefin
Actor/singer b 28.10.53 Bangor. Trained at Welsh College of Music and Drama and worked with the Welsh Theatre Company (for which

he has written two pantomimes) before presenting HTV Wales's Welsh language programmes for children. Played male lead in Welsh series Gwen Thomas, and took part in BBC 2 documentary play, The Extremist. Musician (guitar and piano) and composer (musical for the Welsh Youth Theatre and many songs and lyrics for TV), he has also written a 13-episode play for Welsh radio, worked on many fringe productions in Wales and is a member of a close harmony group Hapnod. Education: Ysgol Dyffryn, Nantlle; Trinity College, Carmarthen; Welsh College of Music and Drama. m Rhian, 1 d Mirain, 1 s Tirion. Address: c/o HTV Wales, Cardiff. Starsign: Soorpio. Person he would most like to meet: 'Shirley Bassey – her personality is something else! And she's Welsh!'

ROBERTS, Pernell
Actor b 18.5.28 Waycross, Georgia. Many jobs before he decided to become an actor while appearing in plays for the University of Maryland Theatre. Was a member of the Arena Stage in Washington from the end of 1950 to the middle of 1952. Then went to New York, appearing with a number of theatre companies, his big break coming in 1955 while with the Shakespeare-wrights, when he won the Drama Desk Award for the

Best Actor Off-Broadway for his performances in Macbeth and Romeo and Juliet. This led to Broadway and, in 1957, a film contract for Desire Under the Elms. Acted on Broadway for many years in classical plays and in such musicals as Kismet, The King and I and Guys and Dolls. Films incl: The Sheepman; Ride Lonesome; The Magic of Lassie. Numerous TV appearances incl: Gun Law; Have Gun, Will Travel; Cimarron City; Gunsmoke; Sugarfoot; Centennial; Hot Rod; Trapper John. Best known for his role as Adam Cartwright in Bonanza 1959-65. Education: Waycross High School; Georgia Institute of Technology; University of Maryland. Starsign: Taurus. Hobbies: swimming, tennis, riding, conversation.

ROBERTSON, Dale
Actor b 14.7.23 Oklahoma City, Oklahoma. A former schoolteacher and a one-time professional prizefighter, he made his first film, Fighting Man of the Plains, in 1949 after service in the US Army 1942-45. Well-known as a Western star, his other films incl: Caribou Trail; Two Flags West; Call Me Mister; Golden Girl; Return of the Texan; Outcasts of Poker Flat; Farmer Takes a Wife; Gambler from Natchez; Sitting Bull; Son of Sinbad; Day of Fury; Law of the Lawless; Blood on the Arrow; The Walking Mayor. On TV he

208

was probably best known as Jim Hardy in Wells Fargo, but other TV incl:The Iron Horse; Death Valley Days; Melvin Purvis; Kansas City Massacre. After devoting himself to his farm and business interests he returned to TV as Walter Lankershim in Dynasty. Education: Oklahoma Military College. Starsign: Cancer.

ROBERTSON, Mick
Presenter/reporter b 14.2.46 Petworth, West Sussex. Trained as a teacher and worked in London play scheme before joining Thames TV as a researcher. Presented Magpie from 1973-1981. During that time recorded two albums and three singles incl The Tango's Over. Recently played in pantomime. Currently presenting the children's out-of-school activities programme, Free Time. Education: Midhurst Grammar School. Address: c/o Thames TV, Teddington Lock, Middx. Starsign: Aquarius. Hobbies: playing cricket, walking in Dorset, the cinema, Portsmouth Football Club. Person he would most like to meet: 'Ry Cooder, whose music is ever cheerful.'

ROBINSON, Robert
Commentator b 17.12.27 Liverpool. Trained as a journalist after National Service in the West African Army Corps. First broadcast 1955. Radio: Today (1971-74); Stop the Week. TV

incl: Points of View; Ask the Family; All Our Yesterdays; Call My Bluff; Brain of Britain; Robinson's Travels; The Book Programme; Word for Word. Books: Conspiracy; Landscape with Dead Dons; Inside Robert Robinson. Education: Raynes Park Grammar School; Exeter College, Oxford (English language and literature). m Josephine, 2 d Lucy, Suzy, 1 s Nicholas. Address: c/o BBC TV, London W12. Starsign: Sagittarius. Person he would most like to have met: 'The man who invented the black pudding.'

ROCCO, Mark
Professional wrestler b 11.5.51 Manchester. Five years as amateur before turning professional in 1969. World Heavy Middleweight Champion. Education: grammar school. m Ann. Address: c/o Dale Martin Promotions, London SW9. Starsign: Taurus. Hobbies: horse-riding, yachting, squash. Person he would most like to have met: 'The American wrestler, Gorgeous George, who was probably

the biggest attraction wrestling has ever seen.'

RODD, Michael
Reporter/presenter b 29.11.43 North Shields. Joined Border TV 1965 and BBC Newcastle 1967. TV incl: Border News and · Lookaround; News at Ten; Look North; Nationwide; Screen Test; Science Session; 24 Hours; Tomorrow's World; The Risk Business; Tuesday Documentary. Education: Trinity College, Glenalmond; University of Newcastle. m Nita, 3 s Benjamin, Jonathan, Owen. Address: c/o Blackrod Ltd, London W1. Starsign: Sagittarius. Hobbies: music, building. Person he would most like to have met: 'Louis Armstrong – the greatest communicator of all.'

RODGERS, David
Presenter b 25.5.52 Yealmpton, Devon. After three years' training in film and TV production, joined BBC as presenter of morning radio show. Worked on American radio and TV before joining Westward TV

1971 as announcer. Presenter BBC Radio 4 1973-76, then returned Westward TV/TSW as presenter Treasure Hunt, Westward Diary, Westward Report, Preview West, Miss Westward. Also co-presenter TSW's What's Ahead. Education: Tavistock Comprehensive; Plymouth Art College. Address: c/o TSW, Plymouth. Starsign: Gemini. Hobbies: photography, films, swimming, food and wine. Person he would most like to meet: 'Johnny Carson, because he's the best in the business.'

ROËVES, Maurice
Actor/theatre director/writer b 19th March, Sunderland, Co Durham. Trained at the Royal College of Drama, Glasgow and has since had much experience both as actor and director. Stage incl: Macbeth; Romeo and Juliet; Othello; Tunes of Glory (world première); Carnegie; There Was a Man (one-man play at Edinburgh Festival 1977). Directed Little Foxes; Exit the King; City Sugar; Jacques Brel Is Alive and Well and Living in Paris; Doo Lally Tap (Edinburgh Festival 1979). Films incl: The Fighting Prince of Donegal; Ulysses; Oh What a Lovely War; Young Winston; A Day at the Beach; The Eagle Has Landed; Transfusion; When Eight Bells Toll; SOS Titanic; Escape to Victory. TV incl: many guest roles in series such as The Sweeney;

Target; Oil Strike North. Also Danger UXB; Twelfth Night; Journal of Bridgitt Hitler; On the Line; Inside the Third Reich; Heather Ann. Education: Church St Partick, Hyndland Secondary School, Glasgow. 1 d Sarah. Address: c/o ICM Ltd, London W1. Starsign: Pisces. Hobbies: five-mile early morning runs, seven-card stud poker, girls, writing. Person he would most like to meet: 'God, to ask Him "Was creation worth it?".'

ROGERS, Chris
Reporter/presenter b 1.4.50 Wellington, New Zealand. Political editor TSW since Jan 1982. Eight years' experience with BBC local radio in Oxford and Carlisle before joining Border TV where he presented the nightly programme Lookaround. Other TV incl two documentaries, Railway City (1981) and The Steam Horse (1982). Education: Salesian College, Cowley, Oxford; Lanchester Polytechnic, Coventry (BSc Hons Electrical Engineering). m Irene. Address: c/o TSW, Plymouth. Starsign: Aries. Hobbies: photography, hi-fi, motoring, classical music. Person he would most like to meet: 'God – to find out why He did it.'

ROGERS, Jean
Actress b 2.2.42 Perivale, Middx. Dolly Skilbeck in Emmerdale Farm since April 1980. Wide experience in radio, TV and theatre, incl rep

at Farnham, Coventry, plays at York, Westcliff and Hampstead Theatre Club, a year at the National Theatre and two seasons at Chichester Festival Theatre. She has made over 1500 radio broadcasts incl: Irene in The Three Sisters, Hermia in A Midsummer Night's Dream and David as a boy in David Copperfield. Is also a presenter and writer for Listen With Mother. Prior to Emmerdale Farm her TV appearances incl: George and Mildred; Callan; Comedy Playhouse; General Hospital; The Harry Worth Show; Charge. She was Nurse Rogers in Emergency – Ward 10, Julie Shepherd in Crossroads, and for three years presented Watch, a BBC Schools programme. Education: grammar school at Worthing; secretarial course at Worthing College of Further Education; two years at Guildhall School of Music and Drama where she gained her LGSM. m Terry Moakes, 1 d Justine, 1 s Jeremy. Address: c/o Margery Armstrong, London SW16. Starsign: Aquarius. Hobbies: cooking, wine-making, gardening, badminton, yoga. Person she would most like to meet: 'The Queen Mother – she's so radiant and full of life.'

ROGERS, Paul
Actor b 22.3.17 Plympton, Devon. Studied for the stage at the Michael Chekhov Theatre Studio, Dartington Hall, 1936-38, making his first

professional stage appearance in London 1938. He was at Stratford-upon-Avon in 1939 and also appeared in concert party at Colchester. In rep at Colchester 1940, where he returned after serving in the Royal Navy during the war. Joined Bristol Old Vic Company 1947 and the London Old Vic 1949, and was with them almost continuously (playing such parts as Malvolio, Iago, Bottom, Shylock, Henry VIII, Macbeth, Petruchio, Falstaff, John of Gaunt, Lear) until he joined the Royal Shakespeare Company in 1965. Made his first visit to New York with the Old Vic Company in 1956, appearing in The Homecoming, Timon of Athens and The Government Inspector. Other plays incl: Plaza Suite; The Happy Apple; Sleuth (and in New York); Othello (Bristol Old Vic); The Freeway; Grand Manoeuvres; Heartbreak House (National Theatre at the Old Vic); The Marrying of Ann Leete; The Return of AJ Raffles; The Zykovs. Films incl: Billy Budd; The Looking Glass War; The Home-coming. TV incl: The Three Sisters; The Skin Game; A Tragedy of Two Ambitions and, more recently, Butterflies Don't Count; The Executioner; Barriers. Education: Hooe, Plympton and Newton Abbot. m (1st) Jocelyn Wynne (dis), (2nd) Rosalind Boxall, 2 d Lucy, Emma (by 2nd m), 2 s Jan, Piers (by 1st m). Address: c/o London Management, London W1. Starsign: Aries. Hobbies: music, gardening, reading.

ROGERS, Ted
Comedian b 20.7.35 London. Started in bookshops and reached present status the hard way after touring, guest appearances, cabaret and one-night stands. Started by winning talent contest. After National Service in the RAF became a Butlin's Redcoat and in 1963, appeared in Billy Cotton's Band Show and had his own TV series, And So To Bed. Other TV incl: Sunday Night at the London Palladium; 3-2-1; a one-hour special, Ted on the Spot. On stage he has played the London Palladium 11 times and is the only British comedian to have worked with Bing Crosby both in Britain and America, being recommended to Crosby by Perry Como after meeting him during the Royal Variety Show in 1974. Has appeared on stage in Las Vegas, New York, Miami, and Toronto and in cabaret in Hong Kong and Sydney and 11 times at London's Savoy Hotel. Also entertained at the Prime Minister's Europe Rally. First radio series in 1979. Education: St Mary's Secondary, Kennington, London. m (1st) Margie (dis), (2nd) Marion, 2 d Dena, Fenella. Address: c/o Yorkshire TV, Leeds. Starsign: Cancer. Hobbies: polo, riding. Person he would most like to meet: 'Don Rickles, the American comedian who is so dynamic and creative on stage. I wonder if he's the same off!'

ROHDE, Shelley
Writer/interviewer b 17th May London. Experience on local, evening and national newspapers as feature writer and foreign correspondent. TV incl: reporting for Granada Reports; presenting Live From Two; Rohde Reports; A Private View. Book: A Private View of LS Lowry. Education: various girls' boarding schools. m (dis), 1 d Michele, 3 s Gavin, Christian, Daniel. Address: c/o Granada TV, Manchester. Starsign: Taurus. Hobbies: reading, listening to music, horse-riding, sitting in the sun (not all at the same time). Person she would most like to meet: 'Kermit – because he won't destroy my illusions.'

ROSE, Clifford
Actor b 24.10.29 Hamnish, Herefordshire. Started with Elizabethan Theatre Company, followed by rep at Ipswich, Nottingham, Bristol, Royal Shakespeare

Company before West End, films and TV. Films incl: The Marat/Sade; Work is a Four-Letter Word; The Wall. TV incl: Roads to Freedom; Callan; The Pallisers; How Green Was My Valley; The Lady From The Sea; The Devil's Crown; Richard II; Secret Army; Buccaneer; Kessler. Education: King's School, Worcester; King's College, London. m actress Celia Ryder, 1 d Alison, 1 s Jonathan. Address: c/o ICM Ltd, London W1. Starsign: Scorpio. Hobbies: music, travel, Russian. Person he would most like to have met: 'William Shakespeare – to discover the man behind those miraculous plays.'

ROSE, David
TV reporter b 11.2.41 London. Journalistic training on The Scotsman and then worked for Border TV on Lookaround; BBC Scotland and Current Account and Southern TV Day By Day. Joined ITN as a reporter 1972; has been their political correspondent since 1974. Education: Dalhousie School; Merchiston Castle School. m Rosalind, 1 d Isobel, 2 s Jeremy, Christopher. Address: c/o ITN, London W1. Starsign: Aquarius. Hobbies; sport, gardening. Person he would most like to have met: The Buddha.

ROSENTHAL, Jim
TV journalist b 6.11.47 Oxford. Journalistic

experience with Oxford Mail and Times before joining BBC Radio Birmingham 1968 and moving to BBC Sports Dept 1976. Joined London Weekend TV 1980. Education: Magdalen College School, Oxford. Address: c/o LWT, London SE1. Starsign: Scorpio. Hobby: football in the commentators' team. Person he would most like to have met: 'Charlie Chaplin – he was a very interesting fellow with a natural talent and wit.'

ROSSINGTON, Jane
Actress b 5.3.43 Derby. Amateur acting experience before joining The Archers as Monica Downs. Rep at Sheffield and York, various tours and TV work, then Nurse Ford in Emergency – Ward 10 and Jill Harvey in Crossroads since it started. Education: Sutton Coldfield Grammar; Rose Bruford College of Speech and Drama. m (1st) TV director Tim Jones (dis), (2nd) chartered surveyor David Dunger, 1 d Sorrel, 1 s Harry. Address: c/o NEMS, London SW3. Starsign: Pisces. Hobbies:

crochet, gardening. Person she would most like to meet: 'The Queen – I love royalty.'

ROSSINGTON, Norman
Actor b 24.12.28 Liverpool. Originally an office boy at Liverpool Docks, but started acting as an amateur and trained at Bristol Old Vic Theatre School. An original member of the cast of Salad Days. London plays incl: Tiger at the Gates; The Changeling; Progress to the Park; Royal Shakespeare Co; In the Red. Joined London Old Vic to tour USA in A Midsummer Night's Dream 1954. Supporting roles in scores of films and on TV. Films incl: Saturday Night and Sunday Morning; The Longest Day; A Hard Day's Night; Tobruk; Double Trouble; The Charge of the Light Brigade; Digby the Biggest Dog in the World; Man in the Wilderness; Young Winston. TV incl: Tracy and Me; The Army Game; Our House; Curry and Chips; The Misfit; Roads to Freedom; The Search for the Nile; Casanova; Hamlet; Lenin; Hunter's Walk; Crime of Passion; Comedy Playhouse; Armchair Theatre; Village Hall; Budgie; Follow That Dog; Spooner's Patch; Big Jim and the Figaro Club. Education: Sefton Park Elementary; Liverpool Technical College. Address: c/o Peter Charlesworth Ltd, London SW7. Starsign: Capricorn. Hobbies: woodwork, skiing, golf, languages.

ROSSITER, Leonard
Actor b 21.10.26 Liverpool.
Unable to afford to go to
university to study
languages, worked in an
insurance office for six years
before joining Preston Rep.
Became assistant stage
manager and then went to
Wolverhampton and
Salisbury. In Free As Air
1957-58 and a tour of The
Iceman Cometh. Joined
Bristol Old Vic 1959 and was
there two years. Followed by
great activity on stage, in
films and on TV. Stage incl:
Arturo Ui; The Strange Case
of Martin Richter; Disabled;
The Heretic; The Caretaker;
Semi-Detached (in New
York);Tartuffe; Make and
Break. Films incl: A Kind of
Loving; Billy Liar; This
Sporting Life; King Rat; 2001
– A Space Odyssey; Otley;
Deadlier Than The Male;
Oliver!; Luther; Barry Lyndon.
TV plays and series incl: Z
Cars; Thick as Thieves; Loch
Lomond; The Magistrate; The
Baby's Name Being
Kitchener; If There Weren't
Any Blacks, You'd Have To
Invent Them; Rising Damp
(he was also in The Banana
Box, the play on which the
series was based); The Fall
and Rise of Reginald Perrin;
The Loser. Education:
Liverpool Collegiate. m (1st)
actress Josephine Tewson
(dis), (2nd) actress Gillian
Raine, 1 d Camilla (from 2nd
m). Address: c/o ICM,
London W1. Starsign: Libra.
Hobbies: squash, football.

ROTHWELL, Alan
Actor b 9.2.37 Oldham,
Lancs. Trained at RADA and
is probably best known on TV
as David Barlow in
Coronation Street, a part he
played for eight years until
1968. Has also done much
stage work, mainly in rep.
Films incl: Linda; Zeppelin.
TV incl: Top Secret; Z Cars;
Hickory House; Daisy, Daisy;
Picture Box. Education:
Chadderton Grammar
School, Oldham.
m Maureen, 2 s Toby, Ben.
Address: c/o Elspeth
Cochrane Agency, London
SW4. Starsign: Aquarius.
Hobbies: music, literature,
cooking. Person he would
most like to meet: Sir Alec
Guinness.

ROWE, Brenda
Reporter b 18.12.50
Yorkshire. Training in
journalism with Bristol
Evening Post, was a
scriptwriter and newsreader
with the Swiss Broadcasting
Corp for 14 months before
spending five years as a TV
reporter in Bermuda. Joined
HTV West as a reporter in
1981. Education: Rose Green
High School, Bristol. m John,
1 d Rebecca. Address: c/o
HTV West, Bristol. Starsign:
Sagittarius. Hobbies: skiing,
sailing, wind-surfing. Person
she would most like to have
met: 'Peter Sellers, to see if he
was as funny as in his films.'

ROWLANDS, Patsy
Actress b 19.1.40. Always
wanted to be an actress and
after training at the Guildhall
School of Music and Drama,
made her first professional
appearance in the chorus line
of Annie Get Your Gun.
Toured and did a season with
the Fol-de-Rols before her
big break in Valmouth. Stage
incl: revue, plays and
recently, Shut Your Eyes and
Think of England; The Bed
Before Yesterday. Films incl:
Polanski's Tess; Little Lord
Fauntleroy. TV incl: The
Gamblers; In Loving Memory;
Public Eye; Bless This House;
The Squirrels; My Son, My
Son; Ladies; The History of Mr
Polly; Juliet Bravo; Kinvig.
Education: convent in
London. m (dis), 1 s Alan.
Address: c/o David White
Assocs, London SW1.
Starsign: Capricorn/
Aquarius. Hobbies:
gardening, cooking. Person
she would most like to meet:
'Fred Astaire, because to me
he is one of our greatest
entertainers and is part of the
real Hollywood magic as it
was in its heyday, and which I
find fascinating and
nostalgic.'

RUSHTON, William
Actor/writer/comedian
b 18.8.37 London. After

National Service in the army he joined a solicitor's office as an articled clerk, opted out to become a freelance cartoonist and helped to found and edit Private Eye. Came to the stage by joining Canterbury's Marlowe Theatre in The Bed-Sitting Room at the invitation of friends. Other stage incl: The Buxom Muse (at the Mermaid); Nights at the Comedy; The Private Eye Revue; Treasure Island; Gulliver's Travels; Pass The Butler. Films incl: Flight of the Doves; Those Magnificent Men in Their Flying Machines; The Bliss of Mrs Blossom; Adventures of a Private Eye. Came to fame with TV programmes That Was the Week That Was and Not So Much a Programme, More A Way of Life. Other TV incl: Don't Just Sit There; Up Sunday; Jackanory; Grubstreet; Any Questions; When Santa Rode the Prairie (which he wrote); Celebrity Squares; Dawson and Friends; You Can Make It; Those Wonderful TV Times; Ask a Silly Answer; Open House; Parkinson; Star Turn Challenge; Blankety Blank; I'm Sorry I Haven't a Clue; Wake Up Wizzy; The Day of the Grocer; Does the Team Think? Books: William Rushton's Dirty Book (!!!); Super Pig; Pig Sticking; The Reluctant Euro; The Filth Amendment; The Incredible Cottage (series for children). Education: Shrewsbury School. m actress Arlene Dorgan, 1 s Tobias, 2 step-s

Matthew, Sam. Address: c/o Roger Hancock Ltd, London SW1. Starsign: Leo. Hobbies: ping-pong, cricket, going to America. Person he would most like to meet: 'God, but only socially.'

RUSTAD, Alan
TV journalist b 20.12.52 Weybridge, Surrey. Experience on weekly papers in Surrey and BBC Radio before joining HTV in 1977. Presenter of HTV's current affairs programme, Outlook, and presenter/reporter of Report Wales, a nightly news programme. Education: Malvern College, Worcs. m Hilary, 1 d Joanna, 1 s Nicholas. Address: c/o HTV Wales, Cardiff. Starsign: Sagittarius. Hobbies: avoiding bankruptcy, pots, paint brushes. Person he would most like to meet: 'The man from Littlewoods who tells you you've won!'

RUTTER, Barrie
Actor b 12.12.46 Hull, Yorks. Started with the National Youth Theatre 1964 and became a leading player 1966 when he was voted the Most Promising Actor of the

Year by the London critics for his performance in Apprentices. Has since had seasons at Nottingham Playhouse, with the Royal Shakespeare Company and at the National Theatre. TV incl: Apprentices; Queenie's Castle; Our Kid; Bavarian Nights; Astronauts. Education: grammar school. m Carol. Address: c/o ICM, London W1. Starsign: Sagittarius. Hobbies: wine-making, rugby league, cricket. Person he would most like to have met: 'Lord Nelson – to resolve confusion: was it "Kismet" or "Kiss me"?'

S

meet: 'One of my, as yet unborn, grandchildren at the age of 35, to see how well he/she survived parental and grandparental love and conditioning.'

SACHS, Leonard
Actor b 26.9.09 Roodeport, Transvaal, South Africa. First appearance on the stage in South Africa 1926 and in London three years later. Has since had wide theatre experience as actor and director. With Peter Ridgeway founded the Players' Theatre 1936 and, except for army service, directed and produced at that theatre till 1947. Probably best known for his role as chairman of The Good Old Days (which started in 1953), but other TV incl: Family at War; Coronation Street; The Man From Haven; Crown Court; The Glittering Prizes. Education: Jeppe High School, Johannesburg; Witwatersrand University. m actress Eleanor Summerfield, 2 s Robin, Toby. Address: c/o Miller Management, Teddington, Middx. Starsign: Libra. Hobbies: walking, swimming. Person he would most like to have met: 'William Shakespeare – who else knew so much and said it so magnificently?'

SACHS, Andrew
Actor/writer b 7.4.30 Berlin, Germany. Came to England just before the war. Began working in the theatre after leaving school. Rep at Worthing and Liverpool and with Brian Rix on tour and London's West End. Other stage incl: A Voyage Round My Father; Habeas Corpus; No Sex Please – We're British; Not Now, Darling. Probably best known for his role as Manuel in Fawlty Towers (it won him the Variety Club Award as the Most Promising Artist in 1977), though he has many TV credits incl: James and the Giant Peach; Tommy Cooper Show; Ask Aspel; Strangers; Les Dawson Show; Rising Damp; The Tempest; The History of Mr Polly; This Is Your Life; Dead Ernest; Parkinson. Written several stage plays incl: Made in Heaven. Education: William Ellis School, Highgate, London. m actress Melody Lang, 1 d Kate, 2 s Bill, John. Address: c/o Richard Stone, London WC2. Starsign: Aries. Hobbies: wildlife, photography, art. Person he would most like to

SADLER, Brent
TV reporter/presenter b 29.11.50 Manchester. After training at the National Council for the Training of Journalists College in

Preston, had newspaper experience on the Harrow Observer and Reading Evening Post before going into TV. TV incl: reporter/news producer, Southern TV; reporter/presenter, Westward TV; reporter/ presenter HTV's Report West and Report Extra. Joined ITN as a reporter 1981. Education: Royal Masonic Boys' School, Bushey, Herts. Address: c/o ITN, London W1. Starsign: Sagittarius. Hobbies: water-skiing, snow-skiing, wind-surfing, sailing (he owns a motor sailer), riding, travel, the cinema. Person he would most like to meet: 'Any reigning Miss World – preferably without a chaperon – for a cosy dinner for two.'

SAINT, Johnny
Professional sportsman b 29.6.41 Manchester. Former amateur boxer. Spent two years as an amateur wrestler before turning professional on his 18th birthday. Former British Lightweight Champion, he has held the World Lightweight title since 1976.

Known as one of the 'cleanest' wrestlers in the business and is noted for his agility, and technique in escaping from wrestling holds. Education: comprehensive school. m Irene, 1 d Shelly. Address: c/o Dale Martin Promotions, London SW9. Starsign: Cancer. Hobby: physical training. Person he would most like to meet: 'Bob Hope, for his sense of humour on topical subjects.'

ST CLAIR, Isla
TV personality b 2.5.52 Buckie, Banffshire. Started singing with the Aberdeen Folk Singing Club when she was 10, was regularly on radio and TV while still at school and had her own radio series, Stories Are For Singing when she was 13. Has since travelled extensively throughout the world, incl Russia and America, performing folk concerts. Though well-known in Scotland, her big break came when she was chosen as hostess for The Generation Game in 1978. Other TV incl: Hoot 'n Nanny; Welcome to the Ceilidh; Isla's Island; Swop Shop; Celebrity Squares; Parkinson; Speak For Yourself; Disney Time; Saturday Night at the Mill. In 1980 presented a series for children, The Farm on the Hill, and the following year The Song and the Story, in which she sang songs and told the stories behind some of Britain's folk songs. Records incl: LPs – Isla St Clair Sings

Scottish Traditional Songs; Isla's Christmas Record; The Song and the Story; singles – Child in a Manger; Songbird; Christmas Dream. Voted Folk Singer of the Year 1971, Writers Guild of Great Britain Award as Best Newcomer 1979. Education: Aberdeen Academy; Buckie High School. m folk singer Hamish Bayne (dis). Address: c/o Peter Prichard Ltd, London SW1. Starsign: Taurus. Hobbies: riding, swimming, cats, dogs, good food. Person she would most like to have met: 'Robert Burns, because I find his work very moving.'

ST JOHN, Annie
Announcer/presenter b 8.9.54 Blackpool, Lancs. Trained at Rose Bruford Drama School and before joining HTV in 1981 as a continuity announcer, had worked at Blackpool Tower Circus (as an elephant rider), and in rep at Bolton, Salisbury and the Young Vic. Also appeared in Festival of Arabic Drama and worked in a variety of commercial and training films. TV incl: 3-2-1; Rainbow; Ask Oscar (as presenter). Education: Blackpool Collegiate Grammar School for Girls. m Michael. Address: c/o HTV West, Bristol. Starsign: Virgo. Hobbies: writing, classical music, winemaking, interior design, photography, working. Person she would most like to have met: 'John Logie Baird, just to let him know what he started.'

SALEM, Pamela
Actress b 22nd January
Bombay, India. Brought up in
England and trained for the
stage at the Central School of
Speech and Drama. Stage
experience incl rep at
Chesterfield, York and
Palmer's Green and touring
(Secretary Bird and Salad
Days). First important TV role
was in Jason King, since
when her TV credits incl: The
Onedin Line; Doctor Who;
Blake's Seven; Carnforth
Practice; Sons and
Daughters of Tomorrow; Into
the Labyrinth (three series);
Seagull Island; Bucaneer; All
Creatures Great and Small;
The Professionals; General
Hospital; Crown Court;
Strangers. Education:
schools in India and England;
Heidelburg University.
Address: c/o Marina Martin
Management, London W1.
Starsign: Aquarius. Hobbies:
tropical fish, shell collecting,
attempting to play the flute.
Person she would most like to
meet: 'Jane Fonda – she
combines woman, career
person and human being
magnificently.'

SALLIS, Peter
Actor b 1.2.21 Twickenham.
Formerly a bank clerk. Came
to acting through an amateur
group during war service in
the RAF. Studied at RADA;
first professional appearance
in London 1946. Rep and
touring for a number of years
before returning to London.
Recent stage incl: Zoo Story;
Cabaret; The Pay Off; Old
Heads and Young Hearts;

Sisterly Feelings. Films incl:
Sarah; Julie; The VIPs; The
Mouse on the Moon;
Anastasia; Full Circle;
Someone is Killing the Great
Chefs of Europe; The Divine
Sarah. Radio incl: End of
Term, a play he wrote himself.
Much TV, but perhaps best
known as Cleggy in The Last
of the Summer Wine. Other
TV incl: Into the Dark; How to
Murder Your Wife; The Big
Eat; Public Eye; Spyder's
Web; The Moonstone; The
Diary of Samuel Pepys;
Barlow; The Pallisers; Softly,
Softly: Task Force; The
Flaxborough Chronicles;
Yanks Go Home; A Crowded
Room; Leave it to Charlie;
Kamikaze Ground Staff's
Reunion Dinner; Tales of the
Unexpected; The Lady
Killers; You're Not Watching
Me, Mummy; She Loves Me.
Education: Minchenden
Grammar School, Southgate.
m actress Elaine Usher
(divorced and re-married),
1 s Crispian. Address: c/o
London Management,
London W1. Starsign:
Aquarius. Hobbies: painting,
gardening. Person he would
most like to meet: 'The
director most likely to employ
me in the South of France.'

SANDERS, Mal
Professional wrestler
b 28.3.58 Balham, London.
Started wrestling when he
was 14. Turned professional
at 17 after three years'
training with former World
Champion the late Mike
Marino. European
Middleweight Champion at

19. Education: Garth High
School, Morden. Address:
c/o Dale Martin Promotions,
London SW9. Starsign: Aries.
Hobbies: football, soul music.
People he would most like to
meet: Blondie singer Debbie
Harry and Roger Moore.

SANDERSON, Joan
Actress b 24th November
Bristol. Trained at RADA, first
professional appearance at
Stratford Memorial Theatre
where she returned in 1953 to
play leads. Rep career
started 1940; first West End
appearance in See How They
Run just after World War II.
Since appeared in numerous
plays (Habeas Corpus;
Popkiss; Banana Ridge;
Anyone For Denis); and many
TV appearances incl:
Upstairs, Downstairs;
Wodehouse Playhouse;
Please Sir!; Fawlty Towers;
Ripping Yarns. Holds LRAM
and LGSM (Elocution)
teaching diplomas.
Education: Northumberland
House, Bristol. m actor
Gregory Scott. Address: c/o
Bryan Drew Ltd, London W1.
Starsign: Sagittarius.
Hobbies: reading, cooking,
driving. Person she would

most like to meet: 'Actor Brian Wilde, because he makes me laugh more than anyone else on television.'

SAVILE, Jimmy OBE
Disc jockey/entertainer b 3.10.26 Leeds. Fitness fanatic and millionaire noted for his untiring efforts for charity, for which he claims to have raised more than £10,000,000. Left school at 14 years old. Began as a miner, also managed a dance hall. TV incl: Savile's Travels; Top of the Pops; safety-belt commercials, Clunk Click; Jim'll Fix It. Books: As It Happens (autobiography); Love is an Uphill Thing; God'll Fix It. Address: c/o Leeds General Infirmary. Starsign: Scorpio. Hobbies: cycling, walking. Person he would most like to meet: 'Miss Right (or Mrs Right, if her husband works away!).'

SCOTT, Brough
Sports presenter b 12.12.42 London. Was amateur and then professional National Hunt jockey 1962-71 riding exactly 100 winners before

giving up in an ambulance en route to Warwick Hospital. Had started racing TV and journalism during previous injury spells. Joined ITV commentary team 1977. On radio presented The Thoroughbred 1978. On TV produced Something to Brighten the Morning, a biography of Mill Reef 1973, and was presenter and writer of The Derby Stakes in 1979. Other TV incl: BBC racing commentaries July/August 1970; The Challenge of the Sexes (Southern TV); Sporting Chance (Tyne Tees); Thames Sport magazine, 1977-79. Sunday Times racing correspondent since 1974, Racing Journalist of the Year 1977, commended in IPC Press Awards 1980. Education: Radley; Oxford (History). m former British skier Susie McInnes, 1 d Sophie, 2 s Charlie, Jamie. Address: Ewhurst, Surrey. Starsign: Sagittarius. Hobby: making bonfires. Person he would most like to have met: 'My grandfather, lunatic war hero, friend of Churchill, knew Lloyd George but not me.'

SCOTT, Jack
Senior BBC weatherman b 9.11.23 Co Durham. Joined the weather service as meteorological assistant in 1941 straight from school. BBC weatherman since May 1969. Estimates he has televised over 3500 weather forecasts. Education: Spennymoor Grammar School, Co Durham;

Nottingham Technical College. m. Address: c/o London Weather Centre, London. Starsign: Scorpio. Hobbies: golf, collecting weather cartoons.

SCOTT, Selina
TV journalist b 13.5.51 Yorkshire. Journalistic training with DC Thomson Publications in Dundee before joining Grampian TV in Aberdeen as an announcer in 1978. While there she made a documentary Fall Out at Pentland. Became one of ITN's team of newscasters in London 1981, and was involved in ITN's coverage of the wedding of Prince Charles. Education: University of East Anglia. Address: c/o ITN, London W1. Starsign: Taurus. Hobby: antiques. Person she would most like to have met: 'Mary Queen of Scots – she has my sympathy as she lost her head when all around were keeping theirs.'

SCOTT, Terry
Comedian b 4.5.27 Watford. Was studying accountancy, but after war service in the Royal Navy, went into rep at

Grange-over-Sands. Then years of work in clubs, pubs, pantomime and summer shows before teaming up with Bill Maynard for Great Scott, It's Maynard. Stage incl: The Mating Game; A Bedful of Foreigners. Films incl: The Bridal Path; Carry On Up the Khyber; Carry On Camping; Carry On Henry; Carry on Up The Jungle; Carry On Loving. TV incl: Hugh and I; The Gnomes of Dulwich; The Scott On . . . series; Son of the Bride; Happy Ever After; Terry and June. Education: Watford Grammar School. m (1st) dis, (2nd) former ballet dancer Margaret Pollen, 4 d Sarah, Nicola, Lindsay, Alexandra. Address: c/o Richard Stone, London WC2. Starsign: Taurus. Hobbies: gardening, chickens. Person he would most like to meet: 'Katharine Hepburn, because she is a living legend.'

b 5.3.43 Bradford on Avon, Wilts. Gained his experience in regional TV with BBC in Plymouth and in radio in Bristol. Regional TV reporter 1963-68 and presenter 1968-78. Chairman of Talking About Antiques since 1969, presenter of Nationwide since 1978 and Antiques Roadshow since 1982. Education: Prior Park College, Bath. m Barbara, 2 s Charles, Oliver. Address: c/o BBC TV, London W12. Starsign: Pisces. Hobbies: music, 19th-century political cartoons.

SCOTT-WARREN, Tony
Announcer b 25.10.49 Moreton-in-Marsh, Glos. Joined Channel TV in 1978 after nine years in RAF Air Traffic Control. Education: Victoria College, Jersey. m Celia, 2 d Davina, Simone, 1 s Jason. Address: c/o Channel TV, Jersey. Starsign: Scorpio. Hobby: aviation history. Person he would most like to meet: Mrs Margaret Thatcher.

SCULLY, Hugh
TV journalist/presenter

SEABROOK, Peter
Horticulturist b 2.11.35 Chelmsford, Essex. Trained in commercial horticulture production and marketing. Joined BBC TV 1974, first to present Dig This! and, since 1975 on Pebble Mill At One. Author of several books, incl: Peter Seabrook's Complete Vegetable Gardener; Peter Seabrook's Book of the Garden. Also gardening correspondent to the Sun and Family Circle. Education: King Edward VI Grammar, Chelmsford; Essex

Agricultural College. m Margaret, 1 d Alison, 1 s Roger. Address: c/o BBC, Pebble Mill, Birmingham. Starsign: Scorpio. Hobby: gardening. Person he would most like to meet: 'In no hurry to meet anyone, except, perhaps, musicians like Chopin, to say "Thank you".'

SEATON, Stuart
TV presenter/journalist b 12.4.27 Caergwrle, North Wales. A journalist all his working life, specialising in agricultural journalism since leaving the RAF 34 years ago. Now managing editor Farmers Guardian. Presenter/commentator/ consultant The Other Man's Farm 1960-65; presenter/ script-writer Farming Comment 1961-65; presenter/script consultant Farming Outlook (Tyne Tees TV) 1965-67 and since 1970. Also contributor to BBC's radio farming programmes, commercial film script-writer and narrator. Education: grammar school. m Audrey, 1 d Val. Address: c/o Tyne Tees TV, Newcastle. Starsign: Aries. Hobbies: film-making, photography. Person he would most like to have met: 'Sir Winston Churchill – for reasons obvious to those privileged to be old enough.'

SECKER, Cathy
Announcer b 18.2.45 Bedlington, Northumberland. Originally worked in a bank. Became photographic and

fashion model and has also done TV commercials. Joined Tyne Tees as an announcer 1978. Education: The Gregg High School for Girls. m Wally Secker, 1 d Jayne, 1 s David. Address: c/o Tyne Tees TV, Newcastle. Starsign: Aquarius. Hobbies: photography, reading, gardening. Person she would most like to meet: 'Fred Astaire – I'm sure he's the only person who could teach my two left feet to dance!'

SECOMBE, Andrew
Actor b 26.4.53 Mumbles Head, South Wales. Trained at Central School of Speech and Drama, then rep at Frinton followed by rep at Chester, Bromley, Leatherhead and Cambridge. Was with the Prospect Theatre 1977-78 before going into Godspell for a national tour and in London's West End. After a season with BBC radio rep. played Puck in Britten's A Midsummer Night's Dream for Opera North. On TV he is known as one of the presenters of Play School. Other TV incl: Fox; Robin

Hood; Amnesty–Beausire; and most recently, Rover in Chip's Comic for Channel Four. Education: Girton House, Ewell. Address: c/o Eric L'Epine Smith, London W1. Starsign: Taurus. Hobbies: biking, gardening, spoon-playing. Person he would most like to meet: Professor Alan Gemmell.

SECOMBE, Sir Harry CBE
Actor/comedian/singer b 8.9.21 Swansea. Originally a clerk in a steel mill, but began entertaining at church socials when a child. Forces shows during wartime service in the army and the Windmill Theatre on demob 1946. First break on radio in Variety Bandbox, then Welsh Rarebit and Educating Archie before The Goon Show. Numerous variety shows; stage musicals (The Four Musketeers; Pickwick; The Plumber's Progress); TV and guest appearances worldwide. Books: Twice Brightly; Goon for Lunch; Katy and the Nurgla; Welsh Fargo. Knighted in Birthday Honours, 1981. Education: St Thomas Junior; Dynevor School, Swansea. m Myra, 2 d Jennifer, Katy, 2 s Andrew, David. Address: Cheam, Surrey. Starsign: Virgo. Hobbies: reading, photography, golf, cricket. Person he would most like to have met: Charles Dickens.

SELLECK, Tom
Actor b 29.1.45 Detroit. Family moved to California

when he was four. Played basketball at high school and won a scholarship to University of Southern California. TV debut in US Air Force Training film and worked as a male model before being discovered by Mae West and appearing in her film Myra Breckinridge. Other films incl: High Road to China. TV incl: Concrete Cowboys; The Rockford Files; The Sacketts; title role in Magnum P I. m model Jacki Ray. Starsign: Aquarius.

SERLE, Chris
Reporter b 13.7.43 Bristol. 6ft 5ins tall. Former actor (Bristol Old Vic), radio producer (Petticoat Line, Brain of Britain) and TV director. One of Esther Rantzen's 'boys' on That's Life. Also works on various other BBC programmes: Ticket to Ride; Medical Express; Jobs for the Boys; The Computer Programme; In At the Deep End. Education: Clifton College; Trinity College, Dublin. Address: c/o BBC, London W12. Starsign: Cancer. Hobbies: gliding, jazz

drumming. Person he would most like to have met: 'Mahatma Gandhi – to learn the secret of power without movement.'

SHACKLETON, Keith
Artist/naturalist b 16.1.23 Weybridge. Began travelling at an early age when his family moved to Australia. When they returned to England five years later he was already deeply interested in wildlife and painting. Spent five years in the RAF in Europe and the Far East during the war and at its end joined the family aviation business as a salesman and pilot for 15 years. Spare time devoted to painting and small-boat sailing. Represented Great Britain in international dinghy meetings several times and four times crewed the winning boat in the Prince of Wales Cup. Pressure of his own work forced him to give up aviation and as a full-time painter became involved in the TV series Animal Magic. Other TV incl Animals In Action. Has explored the world extensively as a naturalist – Antarctica, the Arctic, the Amazon, islands in the Atlantic, Pacific and Indian Oceans – and been busy with film commentaries. Has written and/or illustrated many books, incl Animals In Action. He is president of the Society of Wildlife Artists, chairman of the Artists' League of Great Britain, and a past president of the Royal Society of Marine Arists.

Education: Melbourne Grammar (Australia); Oundle. m Jacqueline, 1 d Sarah, 2 s Jason, Jasper. Address: c/o Anglia TV, Norwich. Starsign: Capricorn. Hobbies: sailing, field work. People he would most like to meet: Captain Cook, Charles Darwin, James Clark Ross, Captain Scott, The Queen Mother.

SHANE, Paul
Actor/comedian b 19.6.40 Rotherham. Originally a miner but was an amateur entertainer in his spare time. Worked for 20 years as a stand-up comic in northern clubs and playing small character parts on TV before he went into Hi-de-Hi. He had obtained a part in Coronation Street when he was spotted by one of the producers of the holiday camp programme and he has been playing the role of camp host Ted Bovis in Hi-de-Hi since the show started in 1979. Other TV incl: Sounding Brass; Turtle's Progress; Muck and Brass; The Generation Game; Punchlines; Swop Shop; Saturday Night at the Mill; Russell Harty; Tiswas; 3-2-1; This Is Your Life. Education: secondary modern. m Dorry, 3 d Janice, Andrea, Gillian. Address: c/o ATS City Varieties, Leeds. Starsign: Gemini. Hobbies: golf, fishing, gardening. Person he would most like to meet: 'Sammy Davis – I think he's the best all-round entertainer in the world.'

SHARROCK, Ken
Actor b 11.12.50 Liverpool. Various jobs – Merchant Navy, oil rigs – before training at Webber Douglas Academy of Dramatic Art. Was in the Mystery Plays at the Belgrade Theatre, Coventry and in rep at Westcliff. TV incl: The Muscle Market (Play for Today); Minder; Agony; Sunday Night Thriller; Angels. Education: Liverpool Institute Grammar School. m Lesley, 1 d Estelle. Address: c/o Pamela Simons, London WC2. Starsign: Sagittarius. Hobbies: horse-riding, fencing, walking. Person he would most like to meet: 'Sir Alec Guinness, because I admire his work so much.'

SHAW, Martin
Actor b 21.1.45 Birmingham. Became a sales clerk when he left school. Trained at LAMDA, rep at Hornchurch, Bromley and Bristol Old Vic. Then a leading part in TV play Travelling Light; a spell in the Doctor at Large series; Helen – A Woman of Today; Electra; The Professionals; Cream In My Coffee. Stage incl: Look

Back in Anger; The Contractor; Cancer; The Battle of Shrivings; National Theatre for The Baachae; Saturday, Sunday, Monday; A Streetcar Named Desire; Miss Julie; Teeth 'n' Smiles; They're Playing Our Song. Films incl: Polanski's Macbeth; Operation Daybreak. Education: Great Barr Comprehensive, Birmingham. m Jill, 1 d Sophie, 2 s Luke, Joseph. Address: c/o Hutton Management Ltd, London SW5. Starsign: Aquarius. Hobbies: walking, reading, strumming the guitar. Person he would most like to meet: God.

SHAW, Roger
Announcer/newscaster/ straightman b 8.9.31 Penzance, Cornwall. Variety of jobs before joining Westward TV in 1961 – lorry driver, barman, policeman (England and Malaya). Did his National Service in the RAF as a physical training instructor and for two years was the RAF's high jump champion. Education: Humphrey Davy School; Loughborough College. m Vivianne Mary, 1 d Karen Jane, 1 s Guy Conrad. Address: c/o TSW, Plymouth. Starsign: Virgo. Hobbies: old aircraft (Member Society WW1 Aero-Historian), ancient history, current affairs. Person he would most like to meet: 'Robert Stanford-Tuck – his great courage, determination and

acquired skills are an example in all walks of life.'

SHELTON, Joy
Actress b 3.6.22 London. Trained at RADA and has since become experienced in most entertainment fields. Radio incl: PC 49; Adventures of Julia. Films incl: Millions Like Us; Emergency Call; Greengage Summer; HMS Defiant; Waterloo Road. West End plays incl: Murder Without Crime; Other People's Houses; Three's A Family; Ever Since Paradise; The Chalk Garden; The Man Most Likely To . . . TV incl: Dangerous Corner; An Inspector Calls; Richard II; My Wife Jacqueline; Home With Joy Shelton; the comedy series Roots. Education: South Hampstead High School. m actor Sydney Tafler (dec), 1 d Jennifer, 2 s Jeremy, Jonathan. Address: c/o London Management, London W1. Starsign: Gemini. Hobbies: knitting, crochet. Person she would most like to meet: 'Ian Dury – he mentioned Sydney in a song and made him happy.'

SHENTON, Joan
Presenter b 16.3.43 Chile. Started as governess to ex-King of the Belgians' two daughers while on a vacation from Oxford, then became a waitress and went into radio on a programme for BBC World Service, Latin American Section. Moved to COI and did a weekly TV film

for Latin America. Joined Anglia TV as interviewer for About Anglia, then worked as a reporter on BBC's Nationwide for its first three years. Had her own show, Person to Person, on Capital Radio and works for Thames TV and has presented Money-Go-Round since 1977, and Help! 1977-80. Education: Santiago, Buenos Aires; Guatemala; Guildford, Surrey; St Anne's College, Oxford (Modern Languages). m TV producer Jack Crawshaw. Address c/o Thames TV, London NW1. Starsign: Pisces. Hobbies: Latin American folk singing, tennis. Person she would most like to have met: 'Paul Scott, author of the Raj Quartet. I found his portrayal of the women characters immensely sensitive and would like to have had a conversation with him. Sadly, he died several years ago.'

SILVERS, Phil
Actor and comedian b 11.5.11 Brooklyn, New York. In show business since 1922 when he first appeared as a boy tenor but later turned to comedy. Went into films in

1940 in Hit Parade of 1941 but returned to the stage in High Button Shoes in 1947. Other theatre incl: Top Banana (also the film); Do Re Mi; How the Other Half Loves; A Funny Thing Happened on the Way to the Forum (also the film) for which he received a Tony as the Best Actor in a Musical Comedy in 1972. His numerous films incl: You're in the Army Now; Roxie Hart; Cover Girl; Something for the Boys; It's a Mad Mad Mad Mad World; A Guide for the Married Man; Buona Sera, Mrs Campbell; The Strongest Man in the World; The Cheap Detective. Has appeared frequently on TV, notably as the fast-talking Sergeant Bilko in The Phil Silvers Show, for which he is probably best known and for which he received three Emmy Awards and, in 1956, the Television Showman Award. Book: The Laugh is on Me. Education: New Utrecht High School, Brooklyn. m (1st) Jo Carroll Dennison (dis), (2) TV hostess Evelyn Patrick (dis), 5 d Tracey, Nancy, Laurey and twins Cathy and Candy. Starsign: Taurus.

SINCLAIR, Belinda
Actress b 16.9.50 London. Trained at the Arts Educational Trust and appeared in Hair and The Rocky Horror Show and more recently in Guys and Dolls at the National Theatre. TV credits incl: Bright's Boffins; Hazell; The Dancing Years; Three Piece Suite; The Lady Killers; Shelley. m actor Paul

Geoffrey, 1 s Alexander. Address: c/o Jeremy Conway Ltd, London W1. Starsign: Virgo. Hobbies: playing with her baby, riding her horse. Person she would most like to meet: 'Paul Newman, 'cos he's a great actor and a nosh!'

SINDEN, Donald CBE
Actor b 9.10.23 Plymouth. Fellow of the Royal Society of Arts. Trained at Webber Douglas School of Dramatic Art and first appeared on TV in 1948 in Bullet in the Ballet. Wide stage and film experience, following his first appearance with Charles F Smith's company, MESA (Mobile Entertainments Southern Area) in 1941. First film The Cruel Sea (1953). Other films incl: Doctor In The House; Doctor At Large; Eyewitness; Twice Round The Daffodils; Decline and Fall; National Health; The Day of the Jackal. TV: numerous plays and guest appearances; The Organisation; Our Man From St Marks (three series); Two's Company (four series); Never the Twain (two series); Discovering Old Churches. Book: A Touch of the Memoirs (autobiography). m Diana Mahony, 2 s Jeremy, Marcus. Address: c/o John Cadell Ltd, London N6. Starsign: Libra. Hobbies: theatrical history, collecting theatricalia, ecclesiology, reading history, serendipity, London. Person he would most like to have met: 'Dr Johnson, because he was a

great man – a walking encyclopaedia, with a great sense of humour.'

SINDEN, Jeremy
Actor b 14.6.50 London. Trained for the stage at LAMDA. Stage incl: Chichester, Bristol Old Vic and Royal Shakespeare Company; The Mating Game (Bournemouth); The Chiltern Hundreds (tour); London West End – Journey's End; Lady Harry. Films incl: Star Wars; Chariots of Fire; Ascendancy. TV incl: The Sweeney; Bass Player and the Blonde; The Expert; Crossroads; Danger UXB; School Play; Soldiers Talking Cleanly; Have I Got You Where You Want Me?; Kelly Monteith Show; Fothergill; Dangerous Davies; Brideshead Revisited. Education: Lancing College. m actress Delia Lindsay, 1 d Kezia. Address: c/o Richard Stone, London WC2. Starsign: Gemini. Hobbies: walking, climbing, driving, travel, photography. Person he would most like to have met: 'Thomas Jefferson – he had the right ideas about most things.'

SINGLETON, Valerie
TV journalist b 9.4.37 Hitchin, Herts. Won a scholarship to RADA, went into rep and worked on TV advertising magazines before going to the BBC as an announcer. Joined Blue Peter 1962. Other TV incl: Blue Peter Special Assignments

series on capital cities, islands and homes; Blue Peter Royal Safari (Princess Anne's visit to Kenya, 1971); Val Meets the VIPs; Nationwide's consumer desk; Tonight; The Money Programme. Education: Arts Educational School. Address: c/o BBC TV, London W12. Starsign: Aries. Interests: looking at London, riding, skiing (snow and water), prowling round sale rooms, photography, travel, reading. Person she would most like to meet: 'Jesus Christ, to see what He was really like.'

SINSTADT, Gerald
Commentator b 19.2.30 Folkestone, Kent. Worked for the British Forces Broadcasting Service and the BBC before joining Anglia TV in 1966 as a commentator and presenter of the station's sports programme Eastern Sport. In 1969 he went to Granada TV as a commentator and presented their Kick Off programme until 1981. Soccer commentator for TVS 1982. On radio he covered the World Cup finals in

Switzerland (1954), Sweden (1958) and England (1966) and for TV the finals in Mexico (1970), West Germany (1974) and Argentina (1978). He was also one of the commentators for the Olympic Games in West Germany in 1972. Education: Harvey Grammar School, Folkestone. m Anne, 2 d Wendy, Philippa, 1 s Tarquin. Address: c/o International Management Group, London W1. Starsign: Pisces. Hobbies: opera, ballet, travel.

SISSONS, Peter
Newscaster b 17.7.42 Liverpool. Joined ITN as trainee 1964, reporting since 1967, covering Middle East War. Wounded during Nigerian civil war 1968. Industrial editor 1974. Presenter of News At One, April 1978. Late 1982, co-presenter, with Sarah Hogg, of Channel Four's news and analysis programme. Education: Oxford. m former teacher Sylvia, 1 d Kate, 2 s Michael, Jonathan. Address: c/o ITN, London W1. Starsign: Cancer. Hobbies: amusing the kids, giving spiritual support to Liverpool FC. Person he would most like to meet: 'The moron who dented my car.'

SKELLERN, Peter
Musician b 4.3.47 Bury, Lancs. Studied the piano at the Guildhall School of Music and Drama from the age of nine until he was 18. Was

member of two pop groups, March Hare and Harlam County and when the latter broke up worked as a hotel porter in Shaftesbury. Wrote the Number One hit You're a Lady in 1972 which marked the turning point in his career. Has been a guest on many TV programmes and in 1980 had his own series on BBC 2 and in 1981 another series, which he also wrote, Happy Endings. Has made 10 LPs, incl: You're a Lady; Astaire; Happy Endings. Education: The Derby School, Bury (when it was a grammar school). m Diana, 1 d Kathrine, 1 s Timothy. Address: c/o Pendulum Music, London W1. Starsign: Pisces. Hobby: sailing. Person he would most like to meet: 'Myself – in order to obtain an objective view of me.'

SMITH, David
TV reporter b 5.3.52 London. Reuter correspondent, Spain and Italy 1974-78 when he joined ITN. Commended in Royal Television Society Reporter of the Year Awards 1980 for his series of reports on famine in Uganda, Somalia and Ethiopia. Book:

Mugabe (a biography of Robert Mugabe). Education: Oxford University (BA English). m Pamela Reading. Address: c/o ITN, London W1. Starsign: Pisces. Hobbies: tennis, writing, decorating. Person he would most like to meet: 'Lord Lucan – then I could retire.'

SMITH, Giles
ITN industrial editor b 23.5.44 Beaconsfield, Bucks. Started in journalism on the Harrow Observer (at £8 a week). Specialising in industrial matters, he became industrial correspondent of the Western Mail, Cardiff, and later joined The Times as industrial reporter and then BBC in same capacity before moving to ITN 1974. Education: Merchant Taylors School, Northwood. m Gladwyn, 3 d Sian, Georgia, Alex. Address: c/o ITN, London W1. Hobbies: cricket, squash. Person he would most like to have met: Leon Trotsky.

SMITH, Mel
Comedy actor b 3.12.52 London. Totally devoted to drama while still at school and while at Oxford chose to produce The Tempest rather than take his degree. This production led to an invitation to join the Royal Court Theatre production team in London. From there he went to Bristol Old Vic, the Young Vic in London and for two years was associate director at Sheffield's Crucible Theatre. Recent theatre was Not in Front of the Audience at Drury Lane which he directed. On TV he is best known for Not The Nine O'clock News. Other TV incl: Muck and Brass; Smith and Goody. Education: Ealing Comprehensive; Oxford University. Address: c/o Talkback Management, London W1. Starsign: Sagittarius. Hobby: horses. Person he would most like to meet: 'My manager – he owes me five and a half grand!'

SMITH, Michael
TV cookery presenter/food advisor b 24.4.30 Yorkshire. Known throughout the world for his books, articles and lectures and on cookery and demonstrations. Was cookery adviser for Upstairs, Downstairs and The Duchess of Duke Street, and has made more than 70 appearances on BBC's Pebble Mill in his own spot Grace and Flavour. Also Posh Nosh series (1979); Mr Smith Goes to Market (1981); Just Desserts (1982). Designs restaurants, writes for English, Scottish and American publications and is food editor Homes and Gardens. Won Glenfiddich Top Cookery Writer's Award for Cooking With Michael Smith, 1982. Books incl: Fine English Cookery; The Best of British Cookware; The Duchess of Duke Street Entertains; Cooking With Michael Smith; Just Desserts. Education: minor public school; Ecole Hotelière, Lausanne Hotel School, Paris. m (dis), 1 d Mrs Rosanna-Marya Klouda, 1 s JF St John Smith. Address: Kingston-upon-Thames. Starsign: Taurus. Hobbies: opera, classical music in general, opera in particular. Person he would most like to meet: 'Shirley Williams – to put my views to her on the domestic scene of the woman.'

SMITH, Ray
Actor b 1.5.36 Trealaw, Rhondda, Glam. First job was as a building labourer, then National Service in the army before joining the London Players in Cardiff. Five years in rep in Channel Islands, Scotland and London before TV break in Shadows of Heroes. Other TV incl: Stella; Company of Five; Callan; A Family at War; Six Days of Justice; Public Eye; Sam; Country Matters; The Mill on the Floss; Second City Firsts; End of Season; The Beast; Warrior Queen; Target; Question of Guilt; The Atom Spies; Lloyd George; Juliet Bravo; Like I've Never Been Gone; We'll Meet Again. Films incl: Seven Men at Daybreak; Made; The

Painted Smile; Rogue Male; Masada. Stage incl: The Dresser; No Man's Land; What The Butler Saw. Radio incl: Some Trust in Chariots; Rape of the Fair Country; Story Time; Candida. Education: Trealaw Mixed Infants; Rhondda Technical College. m Gale, 1 d Branwen, 1 s Justin. Address: c/o Felix de Wolfe, London WC2. Starsign: Taurus. Hobbies: women, whippets, whisky, reading the occasional poem.

SMITH, Sally
Actress b 19.4.42 Godalming, Surrey. Modelling and acting since she was five. Trained at Aida Foster Stage School. Wide stage and TV experience. Played the lead in Marigold when she was 16. Since then has been in pantomimes (incl London Palladium) and stage work incl: Little Darlings; Roar of the Greasepaint, Smell of the Crowd (and on Broadway); Arms and the Man; Lock Up Your Daughters; Listen to the Wind; Honour Bright; Something Afoot; Company; An Evening With Ivor; No, No, Nanette. Films incl: The Trouble With Eve; She Always Gets Her Man; A Tale of Two Ships; Father Came Too. TV incl: The Human Jungle; The Avengers; No Hiding Place; The Subtle Man; Life of Bliss; The Beryl Reid Show. Education: Aida Foster Stage School. m musical writer Gordon Haskell. Address: c/o Tim Wilson Management,

Richmond, Surrey. Starsign: Aries. Hobbies: painting, breeding dogs, riding, swimming, badminton.

SNOW, Jon
Reporter b 28.9.47 Ardingly, Sussex. TV journalist of considerable experience and authority, and won the Royal Television Society's Journalist of the Year Award 1980-81 for his reports on Iran, Iraq and Afghanistan. Started as a radio reporter for LBC/IRN 1973-76. He then joined ITN, for whom he has reported most of the major news events from all parts of the world, the latest being the Falkland Islands crisis. Education: St Edward's School, Oxford; Scarborough Technical College; Liverpool University. Address: c/o ITN, London W1. Starsign: Libra.

SNOW, Peter
Reporter b 20.4.38 Dublin. 6ft 5ins tall. Joined ITN 1962 and was successively sub-editor, reporter, newscaster. Diplomatic correspondent 1966. Joined BBC's Newsnight as presenter and reporter Jan 1980. Book: Hussein

(biography). Education: Wellington College; Balliol College, Oxford (studying Classics). m (1st) Alison (dis), (2nd) Anne Macmillan (of Canadian TV), 2 d Shuna, Rebecca, 2 s Shane, David. Address: c/o BBC TV, London W12. Starsign: Aries. Hobbies: sailing, writing books, photography.

SOUBRY, Anna
Reporter/presenter b 7.12.56 Worksop, Notts. Journalistic training with Alloa and Hillfoots Advertiser before joining Grampian TV in 1981. Education: Hartland Comprehensive, Worksop; University of Birmingham; Inns of Court School of Law. Address: c/o Grampian TV, Aberdeen. Starsign: Sagittarius. Hobbies: squash, football (as a spectator), music. Person she would most like to have met: 'Queen Elizabeth 1 – a wonderful woman who created an era and led a nation.'

SPEAKE, Michael
Announcer/presenter b 1.10.43 Shrewsbury.

Experience in pirate radio and BBC and many voice-over commercials, educational and medical films. Also presented the BBC's Midland link for Family Favourites. Worked on BBC 1 and BBC 2. Joined Anglia TV as announcer 1975. Education: St Mary's School, Shrewsbury. Address: c/o Anglia TV, Norwich. Starsign: Libra. Hobbies: cars (own maintenance), hi-fi, cinema, watch and clock repairing, astronomy. Person he would most like to meet: 'Sir Michael Edwardes, so I can tell him about the doors on my TR7.'

training in rep. Annie Walker in Coronation Street since the first episode in 1960. Address: c/o Granada TV, Manchester. Starsign: Aquarius. Hobbies: walking, reading, bridge, foreign travel.

SPINETTI, Victor

Actor b 2.9.33 Cwm, South Wales. One-time waiter and factory worker. Trained for the stage at Cardiff College of Music and Drama. Career started in Welsh concert party. Stage since incl: Expresso Bongo; many plays at Theatre Royal, Stratford East incl: Make Me An Offer; Every Man in His Humour; The Hostage (and in America); Fings Ain't Wot They Used T'Be; Oh What A Lovely War (also film and in America); Jesus Christ Superstar; Windy City. Also a stage director, incl: Deja Revue; Let's Get Laid; Yes, We Have No Pyjamas; The Biograph Girl; In His Own Write (co-authored with John Lennon, National Theatre); London Palladium pantomime, King Rat. Films incl: all the Beatles' films (the only actor to be in them all); The Taming of the Shrew; The Pink Panther; The Voyage of the Damned. TV incl: Two in Clover; Take My Wife; The Sea; appearances ('enjoyable experiences' he calls them) with Tommy Cooper, Bernie Winters, Kelly Monteith, David Frost, Eamonn Andrews, Russell Harty and Mavis Nicholson; Jackanory Playhouse (The Magic Poltergeist); Give Us a Clue; Take the Stage. Education: Monmouth School. Address: c/o Howes and Prior Ltd, London W1. Starsign: Virgo. Hobbies: writing, reading, talking. Person he would most like to have met: 'Carole Lombard –

SPEAR, Bernard

Actor b 11.9.19 London. Came to acting via music-hall and concert party. Many TV appearances incl: Never Mind the Quality Feel the Width; The Night School; Mother Courage; Quatermass; Barmitzva Boy; The Paul Squire Show; The Olympian Way; My Son Reuben. Education: grammar school; CFS City of London. m ex-dancer Mary Logan, 1 s Julian. Address: c/o NEMS Ltd, London SW3. Starsign: Virgo. Hobbies: golf, do-it-yourself. Person he would most like to meet: 'Len Murray – to explain how to structure unions; one per trade.'

SPEED, Doris MBE

Actress b 3rd February Manchester. Spent childhood mainly on tour with parents, both musical comedy artists. Professional

SPENCER, Lyn

TV presenter b 24.10.51 Newcastle-upon-Tyne. Youth and community worker and also a teacher of English and drama before joining Tyne Tees TV 1975 as continuity announcer. Presented a Saturday morning children's show, Lyn's Look In, and a teenage magazine programme Check It Out. At present co-presents Razzmatazz. Education: Newcastle College of Further Education; Canley College of Education, Coventry. m Roger, 1 d Joanne. Address: c/o Tyne Tees TV, Newcastle-upon-Tyne. Starsign: Scorpio. Hobbies: ice-skating, modern dance, theatre, cinema, swimming. Person she would most like to meet: 'Superman, so he can take me away from all this.'

I discovered through TV she was a great actress. I would propose marriage.'

SPRIGGS, Elizabeth
Actress b 18.9.29 Buxton, Derbyshire. Trained for opera at the Royal School of Music but turned to straight acting and worked with the original Birmingham Repertory Co, before joining the Royal Shakespeare Company in 1962. She has since toured all over the world with the company and is an Associate Artist. Her leading roles with them incl: Gertrude (to David Warner's Hamlet); Mistress Quickly; Nurse (to Judi Dench's Juliet); Mistress Ford; Claire, in A Delicate Balance, which won her two drama awards; Lady Gay Spanker, in London Assurance, which transferred to London's West End and to New York. Joined National Theatre Company 1976, where she has appeared in Blithe Spirit (as Madame Arcati); Tales from the Vienna Woods; The Country Wife; Macbeth; Love Letters on Blue Paper (she originally created her part as Sonia, which won her the West End Managers Award for 1978, on TV). Other TV credits incl: Black and Blue; Village Hall; Victorian Scandals; The Glittering Prizes; Prometheus; The Expert; Abel's Will; Wings of a Dove; The Dybuk; Julius Caesar; Fox; Tales of the Unexpected; The Cause; We, The Accused; The Kindness of Mrs Radcliffe; Bognor;

Sergeant Cribb; Richard's Things; Shine on Harvey Moon; Frost in May; The Haunting of Cassie Palmer; two Alan Bennett plays. Her films incl: Work is a Four Letter Word; Lady Chatterley's Lover; An Unsuitable Job For a Woman. Education: Wheatley St Girls High School, Coventry. m musician Murry Manson, 1 d Wendy. Address: c/o Harbour and Coffey, London W1. Starsign: Virgo. Hobbies: people, animals. Person she would most like to meet: 'Julie Harris – my favourite American actress.'

SPURRIER, Paul
Actor/dancer b 23.5.67 Suffolk. Though young in years, considerably experienced. Has been acting since he was seven, when he was in Peter Pan at the London Palladium. Since then he has made three films – The Wild Geese; Lady Oscar; Black Boomerang. TV incl: Victorian Scandals; Anna Karenina; The Devil's Crown; The Lost Boys; Renoir My Father; Penmarric; Tales of the Unexpected (Galloping Foxley and The Boy Who Talked to Animals); Dark Secret; Vice Versa; The Boat. Education: Norwich School, Norwich. Address: c/o Sylvia Young Management, London E11. Starsign: Gemini. Hobbies: magic, tap dancing, cinematography. Person he would most like to meet: 'Fred Astaire – Richard Burton can't tap dance.'

SQUIRE, Paul
Entertainer b 11.7.50 Longton, Stoke on Trent. Started performing at the age of nine in a family trio with his brother and sister known as The Millionaires, well-known in northern clubs and cabaret for 18 years. Went solo in 1979 touring this country and working in Australia. TV incl: Search for a Star; Starburst; The Paul Squire Show; PS It's Paul Squire. Was in the Royal Variety Performance 1980. Education: secondary school. m Linda, 1 s Ben. Address: c/o Beverley Artists' Agency, South Shields, Tyne and Wear. Starsign: Cancer. Hobbies: golf, travel, 'my new son Ben'. Person he would most like to meet: 'Jose Feliciano – because I so admire his artistry.'

STAFF, Kathy
Actress b 12.7.28 Dukinfield, Cheshire. Started as a student with a touring theatre company in Scotland and then northern reps. On TV she is well-known as Doris Luke in Crossroads, Mrs Blewett in Open All Hours and Nora Batty in The Last of the Summer Wine. But she has

made numerous appearances in other TV programmes, incl: Castle Haven; Within These Walls; Hadleigh; Coronation Street; Les Dawson's Sez Les series. Films incl: A Kind of Loving; The Family Way. Education: St Mark's Church of England Primary School and The Lakes School, Dukinfield; Stamford Commercial College, Ashton-under-Lyne. m John, 2 d Katherine, Susan. Address: c/o EVM Mullings, Manchester 21. Starsign: Cancer. Hobbies: choral singing, church work. Person she would most like to meet: 'Sir Alec Guinness, a wonderful character actor.'

STANDER, Lionel
Actor b 11.1.08 New York Bronx. Colourful Hollywood character actor who found fame for the second time as Max, the Harts' butler in Hart to Hart. He was thinking of retiring from acting when he was offered the part. One-time newspaper reporter on the New York Daily News, he started acting in an off-Broadway play, since when he has appeared in more than 50 stage roles (he had been in 25 Broadway stage productions before his 26th birthday). Has appeared in over 1000 radio programmes. First film when he was 15: has since been in more than 200 films incl: The Scoundrel; Mr Deeds Goes to Town; the original A Star is Born; Kid From Brooklyn; Pal Joey; Call Northside 777; A Dandy in Aspic; The Gang

That Couldn't Shoot Straight; The Cassandra Crossing; New York, New York; The Loved One; Pulp. Though he denies he is a communist, he was prevented from working for many years during the McCarthy witch-hunt days and went to Italy where he made 21 films in eight years incl Polanski's Cul-de-Sac. Education: University of North Carolina. Married six times with five daughters by previous wives. Present m Stephana, 1 d Jennifer. Starsign: Capricorn.

STANDING, John
Actor b 16.8.39 London. Real name Sir John Leon, the fourth baronet. Acting in his family goes back seven generations (his mother was actress Kay Hammond), but he originally wanted to be an artist. After two years in the army with the 60th Rifles, studied at art school. Decided he was not good enough to become an artist and set out to become an actor. Began carrying a spear in Royal Shakespeare production of Titus Andronicus at Stratford; then rep at Birmingham and Bristol. London stage appearances incl: The Importance of Being Earnest; Ring Round The Moon; The Fighting Cock; The Irregular Verb to Love; Private Lives; Popkiss; A Sense of Detachment and, for the National Theatre, Plunder; The Philanderer; Tonight at 8.30. Films incl: Psychopath; King Rat; Walk, Don't Run; All

the Right Noises; The Legacy; The Eagle Has Landed; The Elephant Man; The Sea Wolves. TV incl: Arms and the Man; The First Churchills; Charley's Aunt; Love Story; Tartuffe, Rogue Male; Sinking of HMS Victoria; Home and Beauty; Ms or Jill and Jack; Tinker, Tailor, Soildier, Spy; The Other Arf; All the World's a Stage. Education: Eton; Millfield. m actress Jill Melford (dis), 1 s Alexander. Address: c/o William Morris Agency, London W1. Starsign: Leo. Hobbies: travelling, painting. People he would most like to meet: Rita Hayworth or Sir Garfield Sobers.

STEAFEL, Sheila
Actress b 26.5.35 Johannesburg, South Africa. Trained for the stage at Webber Douglas Academy of Dramatic Art then rep at Blackpool and the Players' Theatre, London. Stage incl: Billy Liar; Jump; How the Other Half Loves; Bristol Old Vic; Salad Days revival; Harpo in A Day in Hollywood, A Night in the Ukraine; her one-woman show, Steafel Solo. Films incl: Baby Love; Some Will, Some Won't; Otley; Goodbye Mr Chips; Tropic of Cancer; Percy; SWALK; The Waiting Room. Main TV credits incl: The Frost Report; Illustrated Weekly Hudd; Horne-a-Plenty; Beachcomber; How's Your Father?; The Good Old Days; Ghosts of Motley Hall; Diary of a Nobody. Also has a

regular weekly radio programme Week Ending. Education: Johannesburg Girls High School; Witwatersrand University. m (dis). Address: c/o Michael Ladkin, London WC1. Starsign: Gemini. Hobbies: cooking, dressmaking, drinking wine. Person she would most like to meet: Burt Lancaster.

STEEL, Bill
Broadcaster b 20.5.39 Newcastle-upon-Tyne. Wide experience as TV announcer with ABC, Thames, Border and Tyne Tees. Has also done voice-overs for thousands of TV commercials. On Metro Radio presented The Bill Steel Breakfast Show for three and a half years; on BBC's Radio Newcastle has his own show The Bill Steel Show. Presented Northern Life for three and a half years and currently senior announcer at Tyne Tees TV. Other TV incl: presenter Miss Tyne Tees TV; Songs for the Singing Sixties; name part in pantomime Dick Whittington. Starred with Mark Wynter and Sally Smith in stage production of Side By Side By Sondheim. Sings on LP Left To Write. Education: Pendower Boys School; Durham University. m Isabel, 1 s Christian. Address: c/o Tyne Tees TV, Newcastle. Starsign: Taurus. Hobbies: marathon running, sailing, squash, reading, hill walking. Person he would most like to meet: 'Frank

Sinatra – the world's most exciting entertainer.'

STEELE, Tommy
Actor b 17.12.36 Bermondsey, London. Started as bell-boy on a liner. Decided to go into show business and was 'discovered' while playing in the Two I's Coffee Bar in London. Within 10 weeks he was famous and a teenage idol. First stage appearance in variety, Empire Theatre, Sunderland 1956. London debut, Dominion 1957; panto in Liverpool same year. Buttons in Rodgers and Hammerstein's Cinderella at London Coliseum following year. Then She Stoops to Conquer (Old Vic); Half a Sixpence (London and New York); The Servant of Two Masters; Palladium panto Dick Whittington; Meet Me in London; Hans Andersen; An Evening with Tommy Steele. Films incl: Half A Sixpence. TV appearances incl: The Tommy Steele Show; Twelfth Night; In Search of Charlie Chaplin; A Special Tommy Steele; Tommy Steele and a Show; Quincy's Quest. Education: Bacon's School for Boys, Bermondsey. m former dancer Ann Donoghue, 1 d Emma. Address: c/o Talent Artists Ltd, London W1. Starsign: Sagittarius. Hobbies: squash, painting. Person he would most like to have met: 'John Logie Baird – I'd like to say to him "See what you've done!" '

STENNETT, Stan
Comedian b 30.7.27 Cardiff. Started singing and playing guitar at local concerts. Joined comedy act The Harmaniacs. First big break as resident comic on radio's Welsh Rarebit. Then resident comic with Cyril Stapleton's Show Band and resident comedy lead for seven years with The Black and White Minstrels on stage and TV. TV incl: Stan at Ease; Road Show; The Good Old Days; Those Wonderful TV Times; The Golden Shot; Celebrity Squares; Top Town. Appeared as a straight actor in Crossroads; Coronation Street. Stage: Leeds United; Scully's New Year's Eve; What a Performance; Cries From A Watchtower; trilogy of plays 1,2,3, written by his son Roger. Film: Possessions. Presents and appears in own summer shows and pantomimes. Starred in Cardiff's New Theatre panto for five consecutive seasons – a record for that theatre. Administrator for Roses Theatre, Tewkesbury. Education: secondary school. m Betty, 2 s Roger, Ceri. Address: c/o George Bartram Enterprises, Birmingham. Starsign: Leo. Hobbies: most sports, especially soccer (he's a director of Bridgend FC), flying (he pilots his own aircraft). Person he would most like to have met: 'Mack Sennett, because I am so often confused name-wise with the old Hollywood film mogul.'

STEPHENSON, Pamela
Comedienne b 4th
December Auckland, New
Zealand. Grew up in Australia
where she trained at the
National Institute of Dramatic
Art and became well-known
in classic roles. In Britain she
is best known for her
incredible impersonations in
Not the Nine O'clock News,
the satirical programme
which won an Emmy in
America and gained BAFTA's
award for the Best Light
Entertainment Programme in
1981. Came to England 1976,
having made part of the
journey overland. Within
months of her arrival she had
appeared on TV in Within
These Walls and Space 1999.
In addition to Not the Nine
O'clock News, other TV incl:
The New Avengers; Target;
Hazell; The Professionals;
Funny Man; Call My Bluff;
Behind the Scenes With . . .;
The Mike Yarwood Christmas
Show; The Michael Parkinson
Show. Her stage credits incl:
Crucible Theatre, Sheffield;
Charles Charming's
Challenges; Not in Front of
the Audience; The Pirates of
Penzance. Films incl: Stand
Up Virgin Soldiers; The
Comeback; History of the
World Part 1; The Secret
Policeman's Other Ball.
Education: Sydney Church of
England Girls' Grammar
School. m actor Nicholas
Ball. Address: c/o Harvey
Goldsmith, London W1.
Starsign: Sagittarius.

STEVENS, Julie
Actress b 20.12.36

Prestwich. Was a nurse
before going into TV. Spotted
in a TV talent show at Bury in
1957, singing and doing
impersonations: trained with
ABC TV as announcer,
hostess, commère and
personality girl. This led to
appearances on such shows
as Sunday Break; Family
Hour; For Love or Money;
Once Upon a Time. Made her
TV debut in The Avengers in
1962 (she claims to be 'the
Avengers girl, Venus Smith,
nobody ever remembers').
Other TV incl: Girls About
Town; Cabbages and Kings;
Play School (for 15 years);
several series of Play Away;
Look and Read; All Kinds of
Everything (live for HTV); a
presenter of TVS's Not For
Women Only. On stage she
has appeared at the
Manchester Library Theatre,
in rep at Ryde (Isle of Wight)
and has her own one-woman
show for children in theatres
and parks. Education: Stand
Grammar School,
Manchester. m (1st) actor
John White (dis), (2nd) actor
and theatre director Michael
Hucks, 1 d Rachel,
1 s Daniel (both from 1st m).
Address: c/o TVS,
Southampton. Starsign:
Sagittarius. Hobbies:
knitting, countryside, people.
People she would most like to
meet: 'The Pope and Barry
Manilow – they both have
tremendous rapport with
people.'

STEWART, Alastair
Industrial correspondent ITN
b 22.6.52 Emsworth, Hants.

Joined Southern TV's Day By
Day team as editorial
assistant 1976. Regular
contributor to Your Men At
Westminster and joint
presenter of People Rule.
Also reports in Southern
Report and Southerners.
Joined ITN 1980. Education:
St Augustine's Abbey School,
Ramsgate; Bristol University.
m Sally, 1 s Alexander.
Address: c/o ITN, London
W1. Starsign: Gemini/Cancer
cusp. Hobbies: riding,
swimming, writing,
aeroplanes.

STEWART, Ed (Stewpot)
Disc jockey/compère
b 23.4.41 Exmouth, Devon,
Started career as bass player
in Hong Kong jazz group.
Radio reporter/disc jockey in
Hong Kong 1961-65 when he
joined Radio London and
switched to the BBC two
years later for radio's Junior
Choice, on which he worked
for 12 years, before having
his own daily afternoon show
on Radio 2. TV incl: Anything
You Can Do; Stewpot;
Edanzed; Quizball; A
Question of Sport; Top of the
Pops; We Want to Sing; 2 G's
and the Pop People;

Crackerjack; Chipperfield's Circus; Play It Again Stewpot; Celebrity Squares; Runaround; Celebrity Golf; The Generation Game; Bruce's Big Night; Star Turn; Wish You Were Here. Education: St Edward's School, Oxford. m Chiara, 1 d Francesca, 1 s Mario. Address: c/o MAM Agency Ltd, London W1. Starsign: Taurus. Hobbies: football (Everton), cricket, cycling, golf. Person he would most like to meet: 'Pope John Paul II – he transcends all religions, especially the different forms of Christianity.'

STILGOE, Richard
Presenter/writer/performer b 28.3.43 Camberley, Surrey. A product of Cambridge Footlights revue, switched to music after starting out on an engineering course. Has since had wide experience of radio and TV incl: Pssst . . .; Just Watch It; The Thumb of Barnaby Locke; A Class by Himself; Don't Ask Us; Nationwide (Consumer Unit); And Now the Good News; That's Life; A Kick up the Eighties; Scoop. Plays 14 instruments, sings in opera and tours Britain with his own one-man stage show. Education: Liverpool College; Monkton Combe School; Cambridge University. m Annabel, 2 d Jemima, Holly, 3 s Rufus, Jack, Joe. Address: c/o Noel Gay Artists, London WC2.

Starsign: Aries. Hobbies: sailing, do-it-yourself. Person he would most like to have met: 'Guy Fawkes, to wish him better luck next time.'

STIRLING, Ian
Presenter b 28.10.41 Leven, Fifeshire. Originally a textile buyer, then a display artist before studying at the Royal Scottish Academy of Drama and Music, winning James Bridie Gold Medal 1967. Theatre and TV actor until joined Westward TV as a presenter 1974, and now TSW. Education: Glasgow High School. Address: c/o TSW. Starsign: Scorpio. Hobbies: gardening, do-it-yourself, listening to music. Person he would most like to meet: 'Bette Midler – my favourite entertainer.'

STOCK, Nigel
b 21.9.19 Malta. Wanted to be a doctor and has been haunted by this throughout his career by his doctor roles: a medical student in And No Birds Sing; Dr Watson many times; the title role in Owen MD; The Doctors. Discovered he liked acting by competing with his sister's party piece.

Studied at RADA and acted till the war, serving first with the London Irish Rifles and then the Assam Regiment, Indian Army in Burma. Major at 23. Many stage and TV appearances incl: Fall of Eagles; Churchill's People; On the Move; Wingate; London Assurance; Van Der Valk; Tinker, Tailor, Soldier, Spy; A Man Called Intrepid; Flesh and Blood; A Tale of Two Cities; Dear Brutus; The Union; Yes, Minister; Flesh and Blood. Between 40 and 50 films incl: The Lion in Winter; Cromwell. Education: St Paul's School, London. m Sonia Williams (dis), 2 d Penny, Polly, 1 s Robin. Address: c/o Derek Glynne Ltd, London SW1. Starsign: Virgo. Hobbies: ornithology, stamps. Person he would most like to meet: 'Soviet Foreign Minister Gromykov – to find out how he has managed to stay the course so long!'

STOPPARD, Miriam MB, BS, MD, MRCP
Doctor/medical reporter b 12.5.37 Newcastle-upon-Tyne. Worked for eight years in clinical medicine, mostly in teaching hospitals, specialising in dermatology. Joined pharmaceutical industry, became research director, then managing director for four years of UK subsidiary of a multinational. On TV she has appeared in Don't Ask Me; Don't Just Sit There; Where There's Life; The Health Show; So You Want to Stop Smoking.

Books: Miriam Stoppard's Book of Babycare; Miriam Stoppard's Book of Healthcare; The Face and Body Book; Marks and Spencer Book of Babycare; Marks and Spencer Book of Childcare. Also a regular contributor to magazines. Education: Universities of London, Durham, Newcastle and Bristol. m playwright Tom Stoppard, 2 step-s Oliver, Barnaby, 2 s William, Edmund. Address: c/o Yorkshire TV, Leeds, or BBC, London. Starsign: Taurus. Hobbies: family, gardening, photography. Person she would most like to meet: George Burns.

STRANKS, Susan
Presenter b 2.12.39 Trained at RADA, St Martin's School of Art in London, ballet, modelling and 10 years as an actress before becoming Magpie presenter for six years. Joined Nationwide 1974; also Hullabaloo on Capital Radio and her own TV programmes, Paperplay on ITV and On Location on BBC. Books incl: The Big Ideas Book; Are You Sitting Comfortably? Educated privately in London and Sussex. m actor/presenter Robin Ray, 1 s Rupert. Address: c/o Roger Hancock Ltd, London SW1. Starsign: Sagittarius. Hobbies: drawing, painting. Person she would most like to meet: 'Stephen Sondheim for his sense of humour and incredible way with words.'

STRATTON, John
Actor b 7.11.25 Clitheroe, Lancs. Rep in Dewsbury, Leeds, Hastings, service in Royal Navy during the war, more rep at Oxford and Dundee before West End. Films incl: The Cruel Sea; Man in the Sky. First TV 1948, much since incl: Letters from the Dead; When We Are Married; Forget Me Not; Backs To The Wall; Just William; Backs to the Land; Mill on the Floss: The Good Companions; Great Expectations; The Forgotten Story; The Tale of Beatrix Potter. Education: Royal Grammar School, Clitheroe. Address: c/o Larry Dalzell Assocs, London WC2. Starsign: Scorpio. Hobbies: Staffordshire pottery, tennis, travel.

STRAULI, Christopher
Actor b 13.4.46 Harpenden, Herts. Three-year stint at a teacher training college, qualifying as a maths and science teacher, before going to RADA. Went to the Bristol Old Vic 1970. Other reps, London's West End (incl: The Licentious Fly; Season's Greetings). Many TV appearances, but his break came with the part of Bunny in Raffles. Other TV incl: Harriet's Back in Town; Owen MD; Family at War; Warship; Angels; For Tea on Sunday; Gentle Folk; Measure for Measure; Romeo and Juliet; Only When I Laugh; Edward the Seventh; Eustace and Hilda. Education: Felixstowe Grammar School. m Lesley, 2 d Belinda, Hanneli, 1 s Barnaby. Address: c/o Joy Jameson Ltd, London SW1. Starsign: Aries. Hobbies: do-it-yourself, sports (tennis, badminton, squash), indoor games (board and otherwise), model-making, his family. Person he would most like to have met: William Shakespeare.

STREET-PORTER, Janet
Presenter/producer b 27.12.46 London. Wide journalistic experience on magazines and newspapers (Daily Mail, London Evening Standard, Observer) and commercial radio. Presented London Weekend Show, weekly current affairs programme for young people, for five years; presented Saturday Night People with Clive James and Russell Harty; produced two series of Twentieth Century Box (current affairs for young people); co-presenter of The 6 o'clock Show. Books: The British Teapot; Scandal! Education: grammar school, Fulham; The Architectural Association. m award-

winning TV director Frank Cvitanovich. Address: c/o LWT, London SE1. Starsign: Capricorn. Person she would most like to meet again: David Bowie.

STRIDE, John
Actor b 11.7.36 London. Trained at RADA, professional stage debut at Liverpool Rep 1957 before joining the army. On demob went to the Old Vic and within a year was playing leads. Five years with the National Theatre before TV's The Main Chance; Wilde Alliance; Love Among the Artists; Henry VIII; Diamonds. Films incl: Bitter Harvest; Brannigan; Macbeth; Juggernaut; The Omen; A Bridge Too Far. Education: Alleyn's School, Dulwich. m (1st) actress Virginia Stride (dis), (2nd) actress April Wilding, 3 d Philippa, Lindsay, Eleanor. Address: c/o William Morris Agency, London W1. Starsign: Cancer. Hobby: music. Person he would most like to meet: 'My Maker – most interesting.'

STUART, Jane
Announcer/newsreader b 19th January Jersey, Channel Islands. Trained to be a teacher and obtained a teaching certificate at Shoreditch College, Egham, before joining Channel TV in June 1978. Education: St John's Primary School, and Hautlieu Grammar School, Jersey. Address: c/o Channel TV, Jersey. Starsign:

Capricorn with Aquarian characteristics. Hobbies: singing, jogging, reading, music, summer, house painting, being an aunt. Person she would most like to meet: 'Peter Sissons, because he seems so relaxed, with a twinkling sense of humour.'

STUBBS, Una
Actress/dancer b 1.5.37 London. Trained as a dancer at La Roche Dancing School, Slough, and made her stage debut in A Midsummer Night's Dream at the Theatre Royal, Windsor. Subsequent stage work incl: a Norman Wisdom spectacular at the London Palladium and a Folies Bergere revue, also in London. Since then has successfully combined stage and TV work in comedy, straight drama and musicals. Other stage work incl: Grab Me a Gondola; On the Brighter Side; Young Vic Company (The Knack; The Soldier's Tale) 1970; since appeared in Cowardy Custard; Oh, Mr Porter; Irma la Douce; Baggage. TV started with Cool For Cats followed by Cliff Richard series; Till Death Us Do Part

(over 10 years); Fawlty Towers; Give Us a Clue; Worzel Gummidge. Films incl: Summer Holiday; Wonderful Life. m (1st) actor Peter Gilmore (dis), (2nd) actor Nicky Henson (dis), 3 s Jason, Christian, Joe. Address: c/o Richard Stone, London WC2. Starsign: Taurus. Hobbies: embroidery, needlework. Person she would most like to meet: The Princess of Wales.

SUCHET, John
ITN's Washington Correspondent b 29.3.44 London. Was with Reuters and BBC News before joining ITV in 1972. Has covered major news events since 1976, incl Iran revolution; Russian occupation of Afghanistan. Was an ITV newscaster before becoming Washington correspondent in 1981. Education: St Andrew's University (MA Hons). m Moya, 3 s Damian, Kieran, Rory. Address: c/o ITN, National Press Building, Washington DC. Starsign: Aries.

SUGDEN, Mollie
Actress b 21st July, Keighley, Yorks. Always wanted to be an actress. Eight years in rep and 'Mum' to a whole series of characters in successful comedy series on TV – Hugh and I; Please, Sir!; the Doctor series; For the Love of Ada; The Liver Birds – before her career really took off with Are You Being Served? Other TV incl: Coronation Street;

Whodunnit?; Come Back Mrs Noah; Tea Ladies; That's My Boy. Education: Keighley Girls Grammar School. m actor William Moore, 2 s Robin, Simon (twins). Address: c/o Joan Reddin Ltd, London W11. Starsign: Cancer. Hobby: gardening. Person she would most like to meet: 'Gertrude Jeckyll – to pick her brains about garden design.'

SWANN, Donald
Pianist/composer/entertainer b 30.9.23 Llanelli, South Wales. Studied Greek and Turkmenistan folk music at the Royal College of Music and contributed music to such legendary revues as Penny Plain; Airs on a Shoestring; Pay the Piper. Collaborated in writing musical play Wild Thyme and then with Michael Flanders in another revue, Fresh Airs, which led to their two-man entertainment At the Drop of a Hat, with which they subsequently toured America, Canada, Great Britain, Australia, New Zealand and Hong Kong. Returned to Eng.and with the same entertainment and later

At the Drop of Another Hat. Sets the work of a wide variety of poets and lyric writers to music and has devised a musical autobiography, Between the Bars. Much of his material is on records. Many TV appearances, the latest being Sunday Best. Education: Westminster School; Christ Church, Oxford. Address: c/o Intercity Entertainments, Croydon, Surrey. Starsign: Libra. Hobby: going to the launderette. Person he would like to meet: 'My late Uncle Mohamed, piano tuner in South Persia, to check his oriental intervals.'

SWIFT, Clive
Actor b 9.2.36 Liverpool. Was interested in drama societies while at Cambridge University and after a year in rep at Nottingham, joined the Royal Shakespeare Company (1960-68). Also directed at LAMDA and RADA and toured America for RSC in The Hollow Crown. Films incl: Catch Us If You Can; Hitchcock's Frenzy; Jack Gold's The National Health; The Sailor's Return; Excalibur. Many TV plays and series incl: Dombey and Son; Clayhanger; Roll on 4 o'clock; Goodbye America; Waugh on Crime; Romeo and Juliet; Home Movies; Edward Gibbon; South Riding; Christmas Ghost Stories; A Case of Spirits; Henry IV Part 1; A Family Affair; In Loving Memory; Winston Churchill The Wilderness Years. Books incl: The Job of Acting; The

Performing World of the Actor. Education: Clifton College, Bristol; Caius College, Cambridge (BA Hons Eng Lit). m writer Margaret Drabble (dis), 1 d Rebecca, 2 s Adam, Joseph. Address: c/o ICM, London W1. Starsign: Aquarius. Hobbies: music, cricket, The Actors' Centre (of which he is Hon Sec) 'son he would most like to have met: 'William Shakespeare – to resolve the endless speculation about whether he was someone else (Bacon or the Earl of Essex) and to have glimpsed "the man".'

SWINFIELD, John
Presenter/editor b 7.1.45 Staffordshire. Journalistic experience on weekly paper and Daily Mail in London, before working on BBC's Nationwide and The Money Programme. Joined Anglia TV Jan 1977, as presenter and editor of the station's business programme, Enterprise. Education: Shrubbery Co-educational Progressive School, Cambridge; Cambridge College of Art. m Bridgit, 1 d Anna, 1 s Dominic. Address: c/o Anglia TV, Norwich. Starsign: Capricorn. Hobbies: gardening, reading, squash, golf. Person he would most like to have met: Mahatma Gandhi.

SYKES, Eric
Comedian/writer b 4.5.23 Oldham, Lancs. Always wanted to be a comedian and

started as a gag writer. Is now the only TV comic who writes his own situation comedies and one of the few TV writers who works alone, which he has done for 20 years and claims is a record. Wrote radio scripts for Educating Archie, Variety Bandbox and many comedians. Apart from his own shows on radio and TV, other TV incl: Saturday Spectaculars; Curry and Chips; Charley's Aunt. On stage he has toured with Jimmy Edwards in Big Bad Mouse and his own show, A Hatful of Sykes, in Hong Kong, Canada, Australia, Rhodesia, South Africa and seasons and tours in the United Kingdom. His many films incl: The Bargee; One Way Pendulum; Those Magnificent Men in Their Flying Machines; Rotten to the Core; Spy With a Cold Nose; The Plank (which he scripted, directed and acted in and has remade); Shalako; Monte Carlo or Bust; Rhubarb; Theatre of Blood; Ghost in the Noonday Sun. Book: Sykes of Sebastopol Terrace. Education: Ward Street Central School, Oldham. m Edith Milbrandt, 3 d Catherine, Susan, Julie, 1 s David. Address: c/o Paul Elliott, London WC2. Person he would most like to have met: 'Sir Winston Churchill, because he was the greatest leader the world has ever known.'

TAMES, Roger
Football commentator and sports reporter/presenter b 21.9.51 London. Journalistic training with Essex and East London newspapers before joining Tyne Tees TV in 1976 as reporter/presenter Sportstime. Co-presenter Shoot 1977-78 and that programme's commentator 1979. Education: Brentwood School, Essex: University of Leicester (BA Hons English). m Tyne Tees TV presenter Lyn Spencer, 1 d Joanne. Address: c/o Tyne Tees TV, Newcastle. Starsign: Virgo. Hobbies: all sports, especially squash and football, music, cinema. Person he would most like to meet: Pam Ewing.

TARBUCK, Jimmy
Comedian b 6.2.40
Liverpool. Several jobs on
leaving school until some
friends pushed him into a
holiday camp talent contest
which he won. Compère for a
rock 'n' roll show, touring,
cabaret and clubs before
Comedy Bandbox; Sunday
Night At The London
Palladium; Royal Variety
Performance; his own TV
shows; summer seasons;
pantomime; records.
Education: Dovedale Road
and St Francis Xavier
Schools, Liverpool.
m Pauline, 2 d Cheryl, Lisa,
1 s Jimmy. Address:
Kingston, Surrey. Starsign:
Aquarius. Hobbies: football,
golf. Person he would most
like to meet: Ben Hogan, the
golfer.

TARRANT, Chris
Presenter b 10.10.46
Reading. One-time teacher of
English at a South London
comprehensive school.
Joined ATV/Central 1969 as
reporter on ATV Today. Other
TV incl: Show It Again;
Citizen's Rights; Tiswas; OTT;
The Pyramid Game; Live at
Two; Square One; Top of the

Pops; Children's Royal
Variety. Education: King's
School, Worcester.
m Sheila, 2 d Helen,
Jennifer. Address: c/o PVA
Management Ltd, London
W1. Starsign: Libra. Hobby:
fishing. Person he would
most like to meet: 'Bo Derek,
to show her my collection of
stuffed butterflies.'

TAYLFORTH, Gillian
Actress b 14.8.55 London.
Trained as secretary before
taking up acting after evening
classes at Anna Scher
Children's Theatre. First
professional part was in a
BBC Play For Today TV
production. Then Zigger
Zagger; The Rag Trade;
Phyllis Dixey; Thunder Cloud;
Little Girls Don't; Watch This
Space; Hi-de-Hi; Big Jim and
the Figaro Club; Sink or Swim;
On Safari. Education: William
Tyndale Junior School;
Barnsbury Secondary School
for Girls; Kingsway College of
Further Education. Address:
c/o Anna Scher Theatre
Management, London N1.
Starsign: Leo. Hobbies: any
sport, swimming, reading,
dancing, driving.

TAYLOR, George
Producer/presenter
b 25.12.25 Sunderland.
Former sports writer for Daily
Mirror, News Chronicle and
Daily Mail. Now presents
Tyne Tees TV's weekly
programme Sportstime and
since 1972 a darts series,
Double Top. Also presents
Shoot, Tyne Tees' football

programme and numerous
outside broadcasts on
cricket, speedway, snooker,
show-jumping, basketball
and boxing. Education: Bede
Collegiate School,
Sunderland. m Margaret.
Address: c/o Tyne Tees TV,
Newcastle. Starsign:
Capricorn. Hobbies:
snooker, golf. Person he
would most like to meet: 'The
Pools rep with a jackpot
cheque.'

TAYLOR, Shaw
Compère/presenter
b 26.10.24 London. RADA
after service in RAF. Then
stage tours and London's
West End. Two years in ice
shows. Relief announcer ATV
1957. Quizmaster on This is
Your Chance; Tell the Truth;
Dotto; Pencil and Paper;
Password; commentator on
Remembrance Day Services,
ice skating, water skiing.
Presenter Police Five (since
1962) and Drive-In. Also
well-known to bridge
enthusiasts for his TV series
on bridge. Education: council
school. m Jane,
1 s Richard. Address:
London W1. Starsign:
Scorpio. Hobby: sailing.

Person he would most like to meet: Sir Laurence Olivier.

TEWSON, Josephine
Actress b 26th February London. Trained at RADA followed by rep at Darlington, Salisbury, Bristol Old Vic. In London she has appeared at the Mermaid and at West End theatres, where her plays have incl: The Real Inspector Hound; Habeas Corpus; Rookery Nook. Her films incl: The Hound of the Baskervilles, while on TV she has been the foil for almost every British comedian, among them being Ronnie Barker, Ronnie Corbett, Dick Emery, Jimmy Tarbuck, Bruce Forsyth, Les Dawson, Frankie Howerd, Larry Grayson, Bernie Winters and Charlie Drake, who was responsible for her first big break on TV. Other TV incl: Lord Rustless Entertains; Son of the Bride; It's Tarbuck; Odd Man Out; Shelley. Education: grammar school. m (1st) actor Leonard Rossiter (dis), (2nd) dec. Address: c/o International Artists, London W1. Starsign: Pisces. Hobbies: watching cricket, music.

THIRKETTLE, Joan
Reporter b 14.9.47 Kent. Started with Associated-Rediffusion as a trainee researcher; left to work as a researcher for Radio Caroline. Later joined the Daily Mail, then Sunday Times. Next radio reporter for BBC and British Forces Broadcasting, and London

Broadcasting before joining ITN 1976. Education: at school in Kent till 18; took an external degree in English at London University. m publisher Jonathan Wallace (grandson of thriller writer Edgar Wallace), 1 d Daisy, 1 s Michael. Address: c/o ITN, London W1. Starsign: Virgo. Hobbies: reading, writing short stories, natural history, politics, foreign affairs. Person she would most like to meet: 'Too many to list!'

THOMAS, Elfyn
TV/radio journalist b 10.11.47 Porthyrhyd, Carmarthen. Journalistic experience on Carmarthen Journal, South Wales Evening Post and Herald of Wales before joining BBC Wales in 1969. Stationed in Bangor for 10 years as North Wales reporter for BBC TV news and a regular contributor to the Welsh programme Heddiw. Education: Gwendraeth Grammar School; Cardiff College of Commerce (Dip Journalism) Address: c/o BBC, Bangor. Starsign: Scorpio. Hobbies: sub aqua

diving, mountain and forest walking. Person he would most like to meet: 'The person who has not appeared on Heddiw'.

THOMAS, Gareth
Actor. Trained at RADA. Stage experience at Yvonne Arnaud Theatre, Guildford, Liverpool Playhouse, Derby Playhouse, Royal Shakespeare Company and Welsh Actors' Company. Most recently seen on stage at Theatre Royal, Newcastle. British TV credits incl: Parkin's Patch; Stocker's Copper; Sutherland's Law; Country Matters; How Green Was My Valley; Children of the Stones; Fathers and Families; Gotcha; Who Pays the Ferryman?; Blake's Seven; Hammer House of Horror; The Bell. Address: c/o Leading Artists Ltd, London SW1. Person he would most like to have met: 'Dr Jacob Bronowski, the Polish scientist, writer and broadcaster.'

THOMAS, Terry
Angling correspondent b 9.1.20 Cardiff. Has been in the fishing tackle industry

since leaving the army in 1946. Present consultant the Shakespeare Co, Redditch. Freelance contributor on angling matters to various journals; also broadcast on the subject on radio and TV before joining ATV/Central TV as angling correspondent 1967. Books incl: Casting. Education: Dulwich College; Frankfurt and Caen Universities. m Anne Veronica, 2 d Sybil, Cathryn. Address: c/o Central TV, Birmingham. Starsign: Capricorn. Hobby: music. Person he would most like to have met: 'William Shakespeare – to ask him how often he helped Bacon.'

THOMPSON, Derek
Sports presenter b 31.7.50 Stockton, Co Durham. The youngest-ever Grand National radio commentator when he was 22. Was also a member of the BBC's Olympic team in Moscow. Started as local radio sports correspondent 1970-71 before becoming a BBC radio network sports presenter 1971-80. Racing presenter for ITV 1981. Education: Guisborough Grammar School. m Janie (daughter of BBC's rugby commentator Bill McLaren). Address: c/o LWT, London SE1. Starsign: Leo. Hobbies: racing, golf, family.

THOMSON, Kennedy
Senior announcer at Grampian TV b 4.4.36 Glasgow. Training in theatre

and lecturing in speech and drama before joining Grampian TV in 1970. TV incl: Let's Do It; Hello There. Education: University of Glasgow; Royal Scottish Academy of Music and Drama. Address: c/o Grampian TV, Aberdeen. Starsign: Aries. Hobbies: theatre, films, TV, hospital radio broadcasting, swimming, cycling, reading, records. Person he would most like to meet: 'Sir Laurence Olivier because of his marvellous control of voice and inflection.'

THORBURN, Cliff
Sportsman b 16.1.48 Victoria, BC, Canada. Has been playing snooker for 18 years. Turned professional 1973, when he first came to England. Has won 10 Canadian championships, won the Australian Masters 1974 and was World Champion and Pot Black Champion in 1980. Education: high school. m Barbara, 1 s James. Address: c/o ISA, Bishopton, Bristol. Starsign: Capricorn. Hobbies: golf, chess, a good read. Person he would most

like to meet: 'Jack Nicklaus – a true champion and a man to learn from.'

THORNTON, Frank
Actor b 15.1.21 London. Stage-struck since boyhood. Started his career in Sir Donald Wolfit's company and in recent years has returned to Shakespeare on stage as well as being foil to almost every TV comedian. Now well known as Captain Peacock in Are You Being Served? Served as RAF officer during the war. Stage work incl: Aldeburgh; Royal Court; Royal Shakespeare Company (Twelfth Night); The Doctor's Dilemma; Play By Play; Shut Your Eyes and Think of England. TV incl: It's a Square World; The World of Beachcomber; Steptoe and Son; The Taming of the Shrew. Education: Alleyn's School, Dulwich. m actress Beryl Evans, 1 d Jane. Address: c/o Max Kester, Reigate, Surrey. Starsign: Capricorn. Hobbies: music, photography. Person he would most like to have met: 'William Shakespeare, to hear his comments on the claim that Francis Bacon wrote his plays.'

THORNTON, Graham
TV presenter b 5.4.57 Leeds. Joined Yorkshire TV as call boy when he left school at 16. Left after six years to join BRMB Radio as presenter. Went to Tyne Tees TV as presenter of regional children's programme, Saturday Shake-up; returned

to Yorkshire TV 1981 to present local teen pop series, Calendar Goes Pop, as well as Graham's Ark, networked children's pet programme, and, for Granada TV, Extraordinary People Show, networked children's chat show. Education: Cross Green Comprehensive School. m Jayne. Address: Nr Tadcaster, North Yorks. Starsign: Aries. Hobbies: badminton, learning to fly. Person he would most like to meet: Frank Sinatra.

THORPE-BATES, Peggy
Actress b 11.8.14 London. First professional engagement Croydon Rep 1934. Then in Shakespeare at Memorial Theatre, Stratford-upon-Avon and rep at Harrogate, Birmingham and Bristol. London West End debut in Country Wife 1938. Was with ENSA during the war. First TV, a leading part in Little Dry Thorn at Alexandra Palace. Countless radio performances and leading roles in most of London's West End theatres. Films incl: Georgy Girl; Mosquito Squadron; A Touch of Love. Leading roles in many TV

serials, series and plays incl: Oliver Twist; The Franchise Affair; Kipling; No Hiding Place; Riviera Police; Our Man at St Marks; Sanctuary (two series); Richard II; Timeslip; The Glittering Prizes; Two's Company; The Saint; Tales of the Unexpected; Rumpole of the Bailey (two series as Mrs Rumpole); Rumpole's Return (Christmas show). Education: Cone School of Dancing, Heathfield; RADA. m actor Brian Oulton, 1 d actress Jenny Oulton, 1 s Nicholas. Address: c/o Patrick Freeman, London W6. Starsign: Leo. Hobbies: architecture, re-planning houses. Person she would most like to meet: 'Jeremy Irons – to see if we could ever be mum and son on TV.'

THROWER, Percy
Horticulturist b 30.1.13 Winslow, Bucks. Started gardening straight from school when he was 14 at Horwood House, Bucks, where his father was head gardener. Then worked in the royal gardens at Windsor and public parks at Leeds, Derby and Shrewsbury. Has done 1300 gardening programmes on radio and 1200 programmes on TV. Awarded a National Diploma in Horticulture 1945; Royal Horticultural Society made him an Associate of Honour 1962 and awarded him the Victoria Medal of Honour 1974. Education: elementary school. m Constance, 3 d Margaret, Susan, Ann.

Address: Bomere Heath, Shrewsbury. Starsign: Aquarius. Hobby: shooting. Person he would most like to meet: 'Angela Rippon – I have always been full of admiration for her since the beginning of her career as a newsreader.'

TILBURY, Peter
Actor/scriptwriter b 20.10.45 Redruth, Cornwall. Started as assistant stage manager and acting at Chelmsford Rep. Later with Welsh Drama Company, Royal Shakespeare Company and the National Theatre. Known chiefly as writer of comedy programmes and series incl: Sprout (with Anthony Matheson); Shelley; Sorry, I'm a Stranger Here Myself (with David Firth); It Takes a Worried Man (in which he also played the lead). Education: Canton High School, Cardiff. Address: c/o Jill Foster, London SW3. Starsign: Libra. Person he would most like to have met: 'George Orwell – I like reading all his books.'

TIMOTHY, Christopher
Actor b 14.10.40 Bala, North

Wales. Trained at the Central School of Speech and Drama, then to New York with Chips With Everything. Then rep at Worthing, Leicester and Farnham and three years with the National Theatre, and a season with the Young Vic during which he went to Mexico with them in Macbeth. London West End theatre incl: Journey's End; Happy Birthday; Rosencrantz and Guildenstern Are Dead (as Rosencrantz). In 1980 he played Jesus in the York Mystery Plays. In 1981 was in the Chichester Festival, especially as Chesney Allen in Underneath the Arches, which transferred to London 1982. Films incl: Othello (Olivier's); Here We Go Round the Mulberry Bush; The Virgin Soldiers. TV incl: Some Mothers Do 'Ave 'Em; Fly on the Wall; Kate; Three Sisters; Twelfth Night; Julius Caesar; Murder Must Advertise; The Kitchen; Murder Most English (Flaxborough Chronicles); All Creatures Great and Small. Book: Vet Behind the Ears. Education: schools in Bala, London and Shrewsbury. m (dis), 2 d Tabitha, Kate, 4 s Simon, Nicholas, Robin, David. Address: c/o Plant & Froggatt Ltd, London W1. Starsign: Libra. Hobbies: reading, writing, swimming. Person he would most like to have met: 'Montgomery Clift – my favourite screen actor.'

TOBIAS, Oliver
Actor b 6.8.47 Zurich. Trained at E15 Drama School

and played with a rock group in Germany. Considerable experience in the theatre, films and TV. Stage work incl: Hair; Jesus Christ Superstar (as Judas). Films incl: 'Tis Pity She's A Whore (in Rome); Romance of a Horse Thief; The God King (in Ceylon); The Stud; Arabian Adventure; A Nightingale Sang in Berkeley Square. TV incl: title role in Arthur of the Britons; title role in Luke's Kingdom; Smuggler. Education: Michael Hall School, Sussex. Address: c/o Al Mitchell Assocs, London WC2. Starsign: Leo. Hobbies: interested in everything. Person he would most like to meet: 'Eisenstein, because he's the best director.'

TODD, Bob
Actor b 15.12.21 Faversham, Kent. Formerly a cattle breeder. Business failed overnight through no fault of his and at 42 turned his hand to acting. First on TV 1963 in Citizen James with Sid James. Has since been foil to Benny Hill, Dick Emery, Marty Feldman, Michael Bentine, Des O'Connor and has had his own series In For a Penny. Other TV incl: What's On Next?; Jim Davidson Show; Benny Hill Show; Alan Stewart Show; The Generation Game; Rhubarb; Give Us a Clue; Q9; Funny Man. Education: Kings, Canterbury. m Monica, 1 d Anne, 2 s John, Patrick. Address: c/o International Artists Representation, London W1.

Starsign: Sagittarius. Hobby: making people laugh.

TODD, Richard
Actor b 11.6.19 Dublin. Trained for the stage at the Italia Conti School and made his first professional appearance at the Open Air Theatre, Regent's Park in 1936 in Twelfth Night. Stage experience in rep at Dundee before and after the war, in which he served in the Parachute Regiment. From 1948-65 he was almost exclusively making films, incl: For Them That Trespass; The Hasty Heart; Stage Fright; Robin Hood; The Venetian Bird; Rob Roy; The Sword and the Rose; The Dam Busters; A Man Called Peter; The Virgin Queen; Yangtse Incident; Saint Joan; Chase a Crooked Shadow; Danger Within; The Long and the Short and the Tall; The Hellions; The Longest Day; Operation Crossbow. Subsequent films incl: Subterfuge; Dorian Gray; Asylum; Number One of the Secret Service; The Big Sleep; Double Edge. Since his return to the theatre in 1965 he has appeared in An Ideal Husband; Dear Octopus; The Marquise (Canada and US); Sleuth (Australia); The Hollow Crown (Canada and US); Equus (Australia); On Approval (South Africa); Quadrille; In Praise of Love; Nightfall; The Business of Murder. TV incl: The Boy Dominic; Stars on Sunday; Wuthering Heights; The Next Scream You'll Hear;

Celebrity Squares; Doctor Who. During his career he has received an Oscar (Best Actor) nomination for Hasty Heart; Hollywood Golden Globe Award; British National Film Award; Picturegoer Award; Daily Express Film Tribunal Award. Education: Shrewsbury and privately. m Virginia, 1 d Fiona, 3 s Peter, Andrew, Seumas. Address: c/o Richard Stone, London WC2. Starsign: Gemini. Hobbies: shooting, farming, gardening, working. Person he would most like to meet: 'Arthur Scargill, because I enjoy arguing.'

TONG, Jaqueline
Actress b 21.2.51 Bristol. Got her first part in Between the Wars while still at Rose Bruford Drama School and never went back. Has since appeared in many stage productions incl: The Winter's Tale at the Royal Exchange Theatre in London's West End. Has also made a horror movie, Tales From Beyond the Grave. TV incl: Voyage in the Dark; Upstairs, Downstairs; Hard Times; Phyllis Dixey; Spearhead; several Plays For Today, notably Out Of Step, written for her by Carol Bunyan; Coronation Street. Education: convent; primary school; girls grammar; technical college; art school. Address: c/o Jeremy Conway Ltd, London W1. Starsign: Pisces. Person she would most like to have met: 'Duke Ellington, naturally!'

TOPPING, Frank
Actor/writer/broadcaster b 30.3.37 Birkenhead. Trained at the North-West School of Speech and Drama followed by rep at Leatherhead and Wolverhampton and stage tours. Recently co-starred in Swann with Topping in London's West End. Was 10 years with the BBC as producer, writer and broadcaster. Won Grace Wyndham Goldie Award for writing and producing best radio play, 1975. TV incl: Coronation Street; Starburst; Sunday Best. Was University Chaplain at Sussex. Has written five books since 1977 Education: St Annes RC Junior School; St Anselm's College (RC Grammar School); Wesley College, Bristol (Theology). m June, 1 d Anne, 2 s Simon, Mark. Address: c/o Yorkshire TV, Leeds. Starsign: Aries. Hobbies: sailing, talking with friends late at night. Person he would most like to have met: 'John Donne – I'd like to talk to him about sailing with Raleigh.'

TOWNLEY, Toke
Actor b 6.11.12 Margaret Roding, Essex. Born in the vicarage, his father being the local vicar at the time. Started as a clerk with acting as a spare-time interest. Did not become professional until joined Birmingham Rep when 32. Has since appeared in numerous plays, films and TV programmes from the Alexandra Palace days. Has

played Sam Pearson in Emmerdale Farm since the programme started in 1972. Educated in many schools in various parts of the country. Address: c/o Margery Armstrong, London SW1. Starsign: Scorpio. Hobbies: music (flute and recorder), reading. Person he would most like to have met: 'Henry Irving – because of his complete dedication to the theatre.'

TROUGHTON, Michael
Actor b 2.3.55 Hampstead, London. Started his career at the Unicorn Theatre as assistant stage manager and played leads for a year. He then went to Watford, also as assistant stage manager and played small parts, followed by the Young Vic and Leeds Playhouse. Numerous TV appearances incl: several episodes of Backs to the Land (appearing with his brother, David); The Mill on the Floss; Love Story; A Moment in Time; three episodes of Testament of Youth; The Fatal Spring; Bless Me Father; The Member for Chelsea; The Grudge Fight; Nancy Astor.

Education: private school in
Harrow. m Caroline Rake.
Address: c/o Joseph and
Wagg, London W1. Starsign:
Pisces. Hobbies: collecting
old toys, model-making, golf,
gardening. Person he would
most like to meet: 'Lee
Travino, because my
handicap is too high.'

TROUGHTON, Patrick
Actor b 25.3.20 London.
Trained at the Embassy
School of Acting and won a
scholarship to Leighton
Rollin's Studio for Actors at
Long Island, New York. After
war service at sea joined the
Old Vic. Best known to
viewers as the actor who took
over from William Hartnell as
Doctor Who and played the
part for three years. Many TV
roles incl: The Six Wives of
Henry VIII; Family at War;
Little Women; Dr Finlay's
Casebook; Churchill's
People; Village Hall; Crown
Court; Love Letters on Blue
Paper; The Feathered
Serpent; The Survivors; Lorna
Doone; Angels; Space 1999;
The Sweeney; Treasure
Island; Yanks Go Home; The
Old Curiosity Shop; The Main
Chance; Colditz; Pathfinders;
Jennie; Coronation Street;
Edward and Mrs Simpson;
Bognor; 1001 Nights; Dick
Emery Show; Only When I
Laugh; All Creatures Great
and Small; Suez; Nanny;
King's Royal; John Diamond;
PQ17. Recent radio incl:
Bleak House. His films incl:
Frankenstein; The Protector;
Doomwatch; Scars of
Dracula; Viking Queen;

Sinbad and the Eye of the
Tiger; The Omen. Education:
Mill Hill Public School.
m Shelagh, 2 d Joanna,
Jane, 1 step-d Gill,
4 s David, Michael, Peter,
Mark, 1 step-s Graham.
Starsign: Aries. Hobbies:
golf, sailing. Person he would
most like to have met: 'Edith
Holden in 1906.'

TUCKERMAN, Ted
Angling reporter/presenter
b 25.11.30 Weymouth. A
lifetime angler; began as
freelance reporter for angling
press, local newspapers and
radio before moving into TV.
Catch '76, Catch '77 and
Catch '79 series for
Westward TV. Also weekly
angling inserts in Westward
Diary, short angling films and
documentary for Westward
Report on the decline of the
salmon; Fisheries News.
Education: commercial
college. m Gwynneth,
1 d Alison, 1 s Keith.
Address: c/o TSW, Plymouth.
Starsign: Sagittarius.
Hobbies: fishing,
photography, stamp
collecting. Person he would
most like to meet: 'The Queen
Mother – apart from her
charm and grace she is an
accomplished angler.'

TUOHY, Denis
TV journalist b 2.4.37
Belfast. Began career as
newscaster/reporter with the
BBC in Belfast 1960.
Presented Late Night
Line-Up on BBC 2 from
1964-67, when he took up an
Eisenhower Fellowship in

Communications to USA.
From 1967-72 he reported for
24 Hours and Man Alive, and
from 1972-74 he was
reporter/presenter on This
Week and People and
Politics. In 1974 he returned
to the BBC, again as
reporter/presenter, on
Panorama, Midweek and
Tonight. Since 1979 he has
been back on ITV, reporting
and presenting TV Eye and
Reporting London.
Education: Clongowes Wood
College, Naas, Co Kildare;
Queen's University, Belfast.
m Moya, 2 d Eleanor,
Catherine, 2 s Mark,
Christopher. Address: c/o
Thames TV, London NW1.
Starsign: Aries. Hobbies:
watching theatre, cricket,
rugby. Person he would most
like to meet: 'Graham
Greene, because I am a great
admirer of his work.'

TUSA, John
Reporter/presenter b 2.3.36
Czechoslovakia. Joined the
BBC as a general trainee
1960-62. Presented The
World Tonight on Radio 4
1970-78, then moved to TV as
presenter of Newsweek on
BBC 2 1978-79, since when

he has presented Newsnight. Also presented the TV series The Unsettled Peace. Education: Gresham's School, Holt; Trinity College, Cambridge. m Ann Hilary, 2 s John, Francis. Address: c/o BBC, London. Starsign: Pisces. Hobbies: playing squash, watching opera. Person he would most like to meet: The Pope.

would most like to meet: 'Greta Garbo, one of the most talented and stylish women in the entertainment world.'

TWIGGY

Actress b 19.9.49 London. Hairdresser's assistant turned model; became bored with the fashion scene at 20 and decided to become an actress. First screen role was in The Boy Friend. Other films incl: W; Shadow of Evil; There Goes The Bride; Blues Brothers. Stage debut in Cinderella pantomime at London Casino 1974. Other stage incl: Captain Beaky's Musical Christmas, concerts and cabaret. TV incl: Twiggs; Twiggy; The Frontiers of Science (Queen Victoria's Scandals); Bring On The Girls; Roller Coaster; The Muppet Show; The Val Doonican Music Show; Pygmalion. Records incl: The Boy Friend; Twiggy; Here I Go Again; Please Get My Name Right; A Woman In Love; Tomorrow Is Another Day. Books: Twiggy (autobiography). Voted World's Loveliest Woman 1977. Education: Kilburn High School for Girls. m actor Michael Witney, 1 d Carly. Address: c/o Neville Shulman, London W1. Starsign: Virgo. Person she

UNDERHILL, Terry

Horticulturist b 28.3.38 Leyton, London. On leaving school was apprenticed to the Birmingham Parks Dept, joined the staff of Liverpool University Botanic Gardens in 1960 and from 1964-80 was garden superintendent at Dartington Hall. Now passing on some of the knowledge he has gained in more than 26 years as a professional horticulturist in TSW's gardening programme, Gardens For All, which started in 1982. Education: Farmer Road Primary School, Leyton; Cranbourne Road Primary, Birmingham; Central Grammar School, Birmingham. m Dorothy, 3 s Philip, Richard, Duncan. Address: c/o TSW, Plymouth. Starsign: Aries. Hobbies: Morris dancing, natural history. Person he would most like to have met: 'One of the early plant collectors, such as George Forrest, who travelled the world, especially China, to find and bring back new plants.'

URICH, Robert

Actor b 19.12.48 Toronto, Ohio. Educated at Toronto High School and Florida State University. Obtained a degree in radio and TV communications and appeared in university productions. First job was as a radio account executive in Chicago but his acting interests took him into the theatre, where he was spotted and appeared in such TV series as The FBI; Gunsmoke; Kung Fu; Marcus Welby MD; Owen Marshall; Bob, Carol, Ted and Alice; SWAT; Soap; Tabitha; The Love Boat; more recently, detective Dan Tanna in Vegas. He appeared in the film of the same name which led to the series. Films incl: Magnum Force. m (1st) actress Barbara Rucker (dis), (2nd) actress Heather Menzies, 1 s Ryan (adop). Starsign: Sagittarius.

URQUHART, Robert

Actor b 16.10.22 Ullapool, Scotland. Originally in the Merchant Navy; studied at RADA for the stage then rep at Stratford-upon-Avon, Edinburgh and Glasgow Citizens' Theatre. London debut in The Second Mrs Tanquery and was Horatio to Alec Guinness's Hamlet 1951. Has made numerous appearances on stage, film and radio. Films incl: You're Only Young Twice; Knights of the Round Table; The Curse of Frankenstein; Yangste Incident; The Dunkirk Story. TV incl: Murder Stamp; Jango Smith; The Planemakers; The Pathfinders; The Simple Life; Country Matters; The Reporters; Helen – A Woman of Today; The Awful Mr Goodall; The Inheritors; The Button Man; Happy Returns; The Professionals; Man and Boy. Education: Heriot's School, Edinburgh. m (1st) actress Zena Walker (dis), (2nd) Jean, 2 d Alison, Rebecca, 1 s Jonathan. Address: c/o Boyack and Conway, London W1. Starsign: Libra. Hobby: messing about in boats. Person he would most like to have met: 'Thomas Merton – a man who saw things were wrong with the world and did something about it. His autobiography, poems and other writing continue to inspire one after many readings.'

USTINOV, Peter CBE

Actor/dramatist/director/raconteur b 16.4.21 London. Studied at the London Theatre Studio. Stage debut at the Barn Theatre, Shere 1938 and first London appearance following year at Players' Club in his own sketch, The Bishop of Limpopoland. Rep at Aylesbury, Richmond and world-wide film and stage appearances, many in his own plays which incl: The Love of Four Colonels; A Fiddle at the Wedding; Romanoff and Juliet; Photo Finish; Halfway Up the Tree; The Unknown Soldier and His Wife; Overheard. Films incl: The Goose Steps Out; One of Our Aircraft is Missing; The Way Ahead; Vice Versa; Private Angelo; Odette; Hotel Sahara; Beau Brummel; The Egyptian; We're No Angels; The Sundowners; Spartacus (Oscar); Topkapi (Oscar); Lady L; Hot Millions; Big Truck and Sister Clare; One of Our Dinosaurs is Missing; The Purple Taxi; Death On The Nile; Double Murder; Last Remake of Beau Geste; Evil Under the Sun. Many TV guest appearances: Parkinson; Imaginary Friends. Books incl: The Loser; Klop and the Ustinov Family; We Were Only Human; Dear Me (autobiography). Education: Westminster. Many honorary degrees; UNICEF golden statuette for his charity work; Benjamin Franklin Medal of Royal Society of Artists for his 'notable contribution to the Arts' – the first actor to receive it; CBE in Birthday Honours 1975. m (1st) Isolde Denham (dis), (2nd) Suzanne Cloutier (dis), (3rd) Helene de Lau d'Allermans, 3 d Tamara (by 1st m), Pavia, Andrea, 1 s Igor (all by 2nd m). Address: c/o William Morris Agency Ltd, London W1. Starsign: Aries. Hobbies: tennis, squash, music.

V

VALENTINE, Anthony
Actor b 17.8.39 Blackburn. Acting debut aged 10 in film No Way Back. Several years as child actor in BBC series, Vice Versa; Children of the New Forest; Whirligig; Billy Bunter. Adult career began in TV production of John Gabriel Borkman. Small parts in films and rep at Nottingham, Guildford, Leatherhead and Croydon before stage appearances in Two Stars for Comfort; The Platinum Cat; Half a Sixpence; No Sex Please – We're British; Hans Andersen. TV incl: An Age of Kings; Armchair Theatre; The Avengers; Callan; Codename; Colditz; Justice; Raffles; The Dancing Years. Education: Valerie Glynn School; Acton County Grammar. Address: c/o London Management, London W1. Starsign: Leo. Hobbies: squash, riding, guitar, skiing. Person he would most like to have met: 'Leonardo da Vinci – surely one of the most imaginative and creative minds the world has known.'

VAUGHAN, Frankie OBE
Entertainer b 3.2.28 Liverpool. Started career at Kingston Empire 1950. First TV appearance two years later. Has been topping the bill in theatres, cabaret and TV shows in Britain and America ever since. Many films incl: These Dangerous Years; The Lady is a Square (with Anna Neagle); Let's Make Love (with Marilyn Monroe); It's All Over Town. Education: Leeds College of Art. m Stella, 1 d Susan, 2 s David, Andrew. Address: c/o Alan Field (Promotions) Ltd, London N3. Starsign: Aquarius. Hobbies: charity work for boys clubs, fishing, painting. Person he would most like to have met: 'Al Jolson – one of the world's truly great entertainers.'

VAUGHAN, Norman
Entertainer b 10.4.27 Liverpool. Stage debut at 14 with a boys troupe in Leigh, Lancs. At 15 formed his own trio, The Dancing Aces, toured until military service at 18 and was in army shows with Harry Secombe, Spike Milligan and Ken Platt. Variety, a two-year stay in Australia and seasons with Twinkle at seaside resorts and Bath and Cheltenham. First TV 1954 followed by Saturday Showtime 1955, ITV's first light entertainment series. Compère of The Cliff Richard Show 1959 and 1960 and a season at Blackpool led to him taking over from Bruce Forsyth as compère of Sunday Night at the London Palladium 1962, and from Bob Monkhouse on The Golden Shot 1972. Other TV incl: Pebble Mill Showcase; Those Wonderful TV Times. Stage incl: Boeing Boeing; Play It Again Sam; The Happy Apple; The Tempest; No, No, Nanette; Once More Darling; There Goes the Bride; Wizard of Oz; Calamity Jane; Chichester Festival 1977; musical version of Not Now, Darling; A Bedful of Foreigners. m ex-dancer Bernice, 1 s David. Address: c/o Richard Stone, London WC2. Starsign: Aries. Hobbies: driving, reading, golf. Person he would most like to meet: 'Don Rickles, the American comedian and the funniest man I've ever seen.'

VAUGHAN, Peter
Actor b 4.4.24 Shropshire but brought up in Uttoxeter, Staffs. Joined Wolverhampton Rep on leaving school. Other reps all over the country and army service before West End plays: Entertaining Mr Sloane; Portrait of a Queen. Films incl: Twist of Sand; The Naked Runner; The Bofors Gun; Hammerhead; Alfred

the Great; Straw Dogs; The Man Outside; Eyewitness; The Pied Piper; Symptoms; The Blockhouse; Death in Rome; 11 Harrow House; The Mackintosh Man; The Savage Messiah; Valentine; Zulu Dawn; Porridge; Time Bandits; The French Lieutenant's Woman; The Missionary. Early TV role in Deadline Midnight he regards as landmark in his career. Other TV incl: The Gold Robbers; Treasure Island; Oliver Twist; Great Expectations; Citizen Smith; Fox; Winston Churchill The Wilderness Years. Many plays incl Season's Greetings. Education: Uttoxeter Grammar School. m (1st) actress Billie Whitelaw (dis), (2nd) actress Lillias Walker, 1 s David (from 2nd m). Address: c/o ICM, London W1. Starsign: Aries.

VERNON, Richard
Actor b 7.3.25 Reading, Berks. Trained at Central School of Speech and Drama. Much theatre experience incl: Peter Pan; A Friend Indeed (also on TV); Hay Fever; Saturday, Sunday, Monday; The Passion of Dracula. TV incl: Man in Room 17; Sextet; Sarah; Upstairs, Downstairs; Edward the Seventh; The Duchess of Duke Street; Aren't We All?; The Sandbaggers; Ripping Yarns; Suez; The Hitch-hiker's Guide to the Galaxy; Something in Disguise; Nanny. Latest films incl: The Human Factor;

Gandhi; Evil Under the Sun. Education: Leighton Park; Reading School. m actress Benedicta Leigh, 1 d Sarah, 1 s Tom. Address: c/o Leading Artists, London W1. Starsign: Pisces. Hobby: sailing.

VEZEY, Pamela
Actress b 19th September Bath. Trained at the Bristol Old Vic Theatre School and subsequently with the company and at various reps incl: Watford; Guildford; Farnham; Edinburgh; Exeter; Richmond; Coventry; Birmingham; Windsor. In London she was in The Pyjama Game and in The Ha-Ha at Hampstead Theatre Club. On TV she played Billy's mother in Billy Liar and is at present in Crossroads. Other TV incl: The Common (Play of the Month); Grange Hill; Sounding Brass. Education: High School, Bath. Address: c/o NEMS Management, London SW3. Starsign: Virgo. Hobbies: walking, gardening. Person she would most like to have met: 'Albert Schweitzer – refreshing to meet someone with no selfish ulterior motives and, I imagine, a restful personality.'

VILLIERS, James
Actor b 29.3.33 London. After training at RADA was at Stratford-upon-Avon for a season before making his first appearance in London's West End in Toad of Toad Hall in 1954. Subsequently he

worked with the Old Vic company in England and America and with the English Stage Company. His stage successes incl: Write Me a Murder; The Burglar; The Happy Apple; Private Lives (revival); The Little Hut; The Doctor's Dilemma; The White Devil; Henry IV (with Rex Harrison); Saint Joan; The Ghost Train (revival); The Passion of Dracula; Peter Pan (Captain Hook); The Last of Mrs Cheyney. Many films incl: King and Country; Half a Sixpence; Nothing But the Best; Otley; The Ruling Class; The Amazing Mr Blunden; Seven Nights in Japan; Joseph Andrews; St Jack; For Your Eyes Only. Also made numerous TV appearances incl: The First Churchills; Lady Windermere's Fan; The Millionairess; Pygmalion (Professor Higgins); The Other 'Arf. Education: Wellington College. Address: c/o ICM, London W1. Starsign: Libra. Hobbies: watching soccer and cricket.

VINE, David
Sports commentator/ interviewer/presenter b 3.1.36 Barnstaple, Devon.

Started on local weekly
newspaper; writer and news
and sport interviewer for
Westward TV 1962, BBC
1966. Specialises in
equestrian sport, winter
sports, bowls. The
Superstars. Commentaries
incl: Olympic Games (winter
and summer);
Commonwealth Games;
Horse of the Year Show;
World Ski Cup; Wimbledon
Championships. Education:
Barnstaple Grammar School.
Address: c/o BBC TV,
London W12. Starsign:
Capricorn. Person he would
most like to meet: 'The fan
who doesn't say "You're
better-looking on
television."!'

WAGNER, Robert
Actor b 10.2.30 Detroit,
Michigan. Family moved to
Hollywood when he was nine
and formed his acting
aspirations while still at
school. By the time he was 20
he had a film contract and in
order to gain experience did
50 film tests before his film
debut in The Halls of
Montezuma (1950). Many
films since incl: Titanic;
Beneath the 12-Mile Reef;
Broken Lance; The Mountain;
The Longest Day; Harper;
Madame Sin (which he also
produced); The Affair;
Towering Inferno; Concorde
– Airport 79. Well-known on
British TV for his Hart To Hart
series with Stefanie Powers
and Lionel Stander. Other TV
incl: It Takes a Thief; Colditz;
Cat on a Hot Tin Roof.
Education: Hollywood
Military Academy; Black Foxe
Military Academy; The
Harvard School; Santa
Monica High. TVTimes
Editor's Special Award
1981-82 for Hart To Hart.
m (1st) actress Natalie
Wood (dis), (2nd) Marion
Donen (dis), (3rd) remarried
Natalie Wood (who died 1981
in tragic drowning accident),

248

2 d Katherine (from 2nd m), Courtney (from 2nd m to Natalie Wood), 1 step-d Natasha. Hobbies: riding, hunting, water sports, tennis, golf.

WALDEN, Brian
Presenter b 8.7.32 West Bromwich, Staffs. University lecturer; MP for All Saints and Ladywood Division of Birmingham 1964-77, when took over presentation of Weekend World from Peter Jay. Education: West Bromwich Grammar School; Queens College, Oxford; Nuffield College, Oxford. m (3rd) Hazel, three children by former marriages. Address: c/o LWT, London SE1. Starsign: Cancer. Hobbies: chess, gardening. Person he would most like to have met: 'Napoleon Bonaparte, because he was an incomparable genius.'

WALKER, Nancy
Actress/director b 10.5.22 Philadelphia, Pa. Diminutive lady (4ft 11ins) of many talents, who comes from a vaudeville family and as a child toured Europe with her parents. Originally a dancer and singer, comedy came later when she made her Broadway debut in Best Foot Forward (also film). Other stage incl: Girl Crazy (also film); Broadway Rhythm (also film); Meet The People; On the Town; Fallen Angels; Pal Joey; Wonderful Town; Do Re Mi; A Funny Thing Happened on the Way to the Forum. Films incl: Lucky Me; Stand Up and Be Counted; The World's Greatest Athlete; Forty Carats; Murder By Death. Has appeared in nearly every major American TV show incl such series as McMillan and Wife (Emmy nomination for her role as the uninhibited maid, Mildred); Rhoda (as the Jewish mother); The Mary Tyler Moore Show. Has recently turned her attention to directing Broadway plays and a new film. Education: New York Professional Children's School. m music coach David Craig, 1 d Miranda. Starsign: Taurus. Hobby: work.

WALKER, Peter
Linkman/commentator b 17.2.36 Bristol. Professional cricket with Glamorgan CCC 1955-72; three caps for England (v South Africa 1960). Began broadcasting with BBC Wales on radio programme Good Morning Wales 1963. Also presented BBC Wales Sports Parade on TV at that time. Frontman for John Player Sunday League cricket; also linkman for Test matches, international table tennis, golf and bowls. Sports correspondent for Times newspaper in Wales. Books incl: Cricket Conversations; Winning Cricket; The All-rounder. Educated in South Africa. m (1st) dis, (2nd) Susan, 1 d Sarah, 2 s Justin, Daniel. Address: c/o BBC, Cardiff. Starsign: Aquarius. Hobbies: classical music, golf, squash, historical research. Person he would most like to meet: 'Sian Adey-Jones – to see if she's real.'

WALKER, Roger
Actor/musician b 22.12.44 Bristol but brought up in Derbyshire. Stage and teaching training at Rose Bruford School before going into rep at Coventry, followed by a year with the Royal Shakespeare Company. He was a teacher for six and a half years, mostly in Derbyshire, and after a spell as a busker in Leeds, became stage manager at Leeds Playhouse. More rep in Stoke and Manchester, and TV appearances for Granada and Yorkshire TV before coming to London, first at the Half Moon Theatre and then in ITV's Rainbow as a musician and performer. In the four years he was with the programme he made 350 appearances and wrote 75 songs. He left to return to straight acting and appeared in Shoestring, Sink or Swim and Playhouse before his roles in County Hall, Squadron and Goodbye Mr Kent. Has also appeared in

TV commercials and training films. Education: Derby Central School for Boys; Ilkeston College of Further Education. m (1st) (dis), (2nd) actress Ann Curthoys, 2 d Anna, Sarah (both from 1st m), 1 step-d Emma, 1 step-s Huw. Address: c/o Jim Thompson, London E1. Starsign: cusp of Sagittarius and Capricorn. Hobbies: motor-cycling, photography. Person he would most like to have met: 'My father, because I never met him.'

WALLACE, Eric
Reporter/presenter
b 16.7.38 Carlisle. Former management trainee and served in the Royal Navy before going to college to study film and TV techniques. Joined Border TV 1968. On TV he has been involved in such programmes as The Horse is the Hero; Rats of Tubruk; Triangle; The Life and Work of Ray Harryhausen; Bass Rock to Bamburgh; Travellers' Tales; The Book Programme; The Black and White Picture Show; a monthly sports programme. His films, all independently produced, incl: Strange Company; I Can Lick Any Girl in the House; Stimmung. Education: St Gabriel's; St Bede's; Creighton School; Austin Friars (all Carlisle); The College of the Venerable Bede, Durham. m Maureen, 1 d Deborah, 1 s Patrick. Address: c/o Border TV, Carlisle. Starsign: Cancer (Scorpio rising). Hobbies:

physical fitness, boxing, military history, biography, cinema, four cats. Person he would most like to meet and interview: 'The next British-born World Heavyweight boxing champion.'

WALLER, David
Actor b 27.11.20 Street, Somerset. Trained for the stage under Eileen Thorndike at the Embassy School of Acting. Various reps, incl Sunderland, York, Scarborough, Leatherhead, Ipswich and Coventry, between seasons with the Old Vic and the Royal Shakespeare Companies. Author of the play Happy Returns. Films incl: Work is a Four Letter Word; Perfect Friday. Many TV appearances incl: The Bankrupt; A Day Out; Parade; The Staff Room; The Piano Player; Two Tame Oats; A Song at Twilight; Helen – A Woman of Today; Madame Bovary; Crown Court; Hunter's Walk; Softly, Softly; Hadleigh; Dad; Heartbreak House; The Beaux Stratagem; Edward and Mrs Simpson (as Stanley Baldwin); Airport Chaplain; Waxwork; Enemy at the Door (as Major General Muller); The Tempest; Cribb (as Chief Insp Jowett); The Brack Report; PQ17 (as A V Alexander, First Lord of the Admiralty). Education: Friends' School, Ackworth and Bootham. m Elisabeth Vernon. Address: c/o Fraser and Dunlop Ltd, London W1.

Starsign: Sagittarius. Hobbies: cooking, gardening, painting.

WALTER, David
ITN political correspondent b 1.2.48 Newcastle-upon-Tyne. Joined BBC from university 1971 as a producer, first of Nationwide and then Newsweek. Moved to ITN 1980. Education: Charterhouse; Trinity College, Oxford (classics degree); Massachusetts Institute of Technology. m Pamela May, 1 d Natalie, 1 s Peter. Address: c/o ITN, London W1. Starsign: Aquarius. Hobbies: tennis, squash, gardening. Person he would most like to have met: 'W E Gladstone: somebody who could make speeches of that length must have had something.'

WALTERS, Julie
Actress b 22.2.50 Birmingham. Always wanted to be an actress. Started training as a nurse but left to study for teacher's certificate in English and Drama at Manchester Polytechnic School of Theatre. First stage role was at Liverpool's Everyman Theatre where she

was directed by Jonathan Pryce as Bianca in The Taming of the Shew. Came to London in Funny Peculiar 1976; also appeared at the Royal Court Theatre, Hampstead Theatre Club, Bristol Old Vic and in the Royal Shakespeare Company's production of Educating Rita, for which she won the Theatre Critics' Award as Most Promising New Actress and the Variety Club's Award as the Most Promising Artist 1980. Has been on TV in plays by Alan Bennett and her friend Victoria Wood, with whom she also appeared in the comedy series Wood and Walters. Other TV incl: Talent; Good Fun; Nearly a Happy Ending; Living Together; Happy Since I Met You; Say Something Happened; Intensive Care; The Boys from the Black Stuff; Monologue (one-woman show of Billy Bennett monologues). Education: Holly Lodge Grammar School, Smethwick. Address: c/o Saraband Assocs, London N1. Starsign: Pisces. Hobbies: travel, friends, champagne. Person she would most like to meet: 'Stevie Wonder – I think he's brill.'

WANLESS, Neville
Continuity announcer b 28.7.31 Wallsend-on-Tyne. Trained at LAMDA where he won the bronze, silver and gold medals for acting, verse-speaking and elocution. Was a radio newsreader for BBC in Newcastle 1961. Worked as a newsreader for 14 years. Joined Tyne Tees TV as announcer and in May 1982 became the station's longest-serving continuity announcer, having worked in that capacity for 11 years. Education: St Bees School, Cumbria. m Patricia, 1 d Melanie. Address: c/o Tyne Tees TV, Newcastle. Starsign: Leo. Hobbies: golf, amateur dramatics, hospital radio. Person he would most like to meet: 'Frank Sinatra, having seen him in concert, and followed his incredible career since the early 1950s.'

WARING, Derek
Actor b 26.4.30 London. Service in the Indian and British armies before training at RADA and five years in rep incl: Bath, Dundee and Amersham. On the London West End stage he has appeared with the Royal Shakespeare Company; as Prince Albert in Portrait of a Queen (with his wife as Queen Victoria); The World of Suzie Wong; Call It Love; Not to Worry; Cowardy Custard; Six of One; The Marquise; Cards on the Table. Films incl: Dunkirk; I Accuse; Last Days of Hitler; Battle of Britain. On TV he has played everything from a ringmaster to Sir Bernard Spilsbury (in The Killers). Other TV incl: Z Cars; Marked Personal; The Avengers; Carrington VC; Moody and Peg; Forget Me Not; She; Crown Court; An Unofficial Rose; Flaxborough Chronicles Hi-Summer; Wings; George and Mildred; Thundercloud; Doctor Who; The Professionals; Partners; Don't Rock the Boat. Brother of writer Richard Waring (Not in Front of the Children; Marriage Lines; My Wife Next Door; And Mother Makes Five); water diviner; expert chef. Education: Dulwich College. m actress Dorothy Tutin, 1 d Amanda, 1 s Nicholas. Address: c/o Barry Burnett, London W1. Starsign: Taurus. Hobbies: tennis, natural history, music, boats. Person he would most like to have met: 'Johann Sebastian Bach, whose music is sublime.'

WARING, George
Actor b 20.2.27 Eccles, Lancs. Joined the RAF when 18 and began acting with RAF Rep Company on the Continent. Back in this country, joined the Century Theatre after a variety of jobs and toured Lancashire, Cheshire and Staffordshire. Also worked in rep at Manchester, Sheffield, Richmond, Birmingham, Farnham, Cheltenham etc. West End plays incl: Emil and the Detectives; Alfie; The 4th of June; The Bells. Hundreds of TV appearances incl: Z Cars; Mrs Thursday; Doctor Who; Softly, Softly; Castle Haven; Crown Court; Armchair Thriller; Six Days of Justice; Arnold Swain in Coronation Street; Emmerdale Farm; Mixed Blessings. Education: Ducie High School, Manchester.

m (1st) (dis), (2nd) actress
Geraldine Gwyther,
1 d Georgina,
1 s Geoffrey. Address: c/o
Bernard Gillman Ltd,
Tolworth, Surrey. Starsign:
Pisces. Hobbies: listening to
good music, interior
decorating, cooking
interesting meals, tennis.
Person he would most like to
have met: 'Bertrand Russell,
because of his supreme
grasp of human affairs.'

WARMAN, Bob
Presenter b 11.10.46
Walsall, Staffs. Trained in
journalism and was a reporter
with Birmingham Evening
Mail. Went to BBC as a radio
producer 1972. Joined ATV
1973 and presented ATV
Today; Miss ATV and
compèred Nurse of the Year
competition 1973. Moved to
Yorkshire TV 1976 as
presenter of first British
breakfast TV programme;
also presented Calendar for
Yorkshire TV. Returned to
ATV/Central 1978 and
presenter of Central News
since 1982. Education:
Wrekin College; Wellington.
m Juliet Wood. Address: c/o
PVA Management Ltd,
London W1. Starsign: Libra.
Hobbies: photography,
gardening.

WARWICK, Richard
Actor b 24.4.45 Dartford,
Kent. Trained at RADA and
when he left was inundated
with stage, film and TV work.
Films incl: Romeo and Juliet;
If . . .; The Bedsitting Room;

First Love; The Breaking of
Bumbo; Alice in Wonderland;
Black Sun; International
Velvet. TV incl: The Vortex;
Please Sir!; The Last of the
Mohicans; Warship;
Brensham People; School
Play; A Fine Romance; It's My
Pleasure. Education: Dean
Close School, Cheltenham.
Address: c/o ICM, London
W1. Starsign: Taurus.
Hobbies: tennis, gymnastics.
Person he would most like to
meet: 'Bjorn Borg – my
number one hero.'

WATERMAN, Dennis
Actor b 24.2.48 London.
First acting appearance was
in Night Train to Inverness
when 11. By 16 he had been
in The Music Man, done a
season at Stratford-upon-
Avon, starred as the original
William in the first TV version
of Just William and been to
Hollywood to make the Fair
Exchange series. Films incl:
Up the Junction; The
Sweeney; Sweeney 2. TV incl:
The Sweeney; Give Us a Kiss;
Christabel; Dennis Waterman
– With a Little Help From His
Friends; Minder; The World
Cup – A Captain's Tale.
Stage incl: Windy City. Also
writes and sings songs and

has made several successful
records incl: Down Wind With
Angels; Waterman.
Education: Corona Stage
School. m (1st) Penny (dis),
2nd actress Patricia
Maynard, 2 d Hannah, Julia.
Address: c/o ICM, London
W1. Starsign: Pisces.
Hobbies: playing guitar,
writing songs.

WATERSTON, Sam
Actor b 15.11.40
Cambridge, Mass. Trained
for the stage at Yale, the
American Actors Workshop
in Paris, and at the Actors
Studio. First stage
appearance in 1947 as the
page in Anouilh's Antigone in
a production directed by his
father, George Waterston.
New York debut in 1962 and
has since had considerable
stage experience incl many
Shakespearean roles. First
film was The Plastic Dome of
Norma Jean in 1965 and films
since incl: Three; Generation;
The Great Gatsby; Rancho
de Luxe; Mahoney's Last
Stand; Capricorn One; Sweet
William; Eagle's Wing;
Hopscotch. TV incl: Dr
Kildare; The Glass
Menagerie; Much Ado About
Nothing; Oppenheimer;
QED. Best TV Actor
nomination BAFTA 1980.
Education: Groton School;
Yale University. m (1st)
Barbara (dis), (2nd) Lynn
Woodruff, 1 d, 1 s. Address:
c/o Creative Management
Assocs, New York. Hobbies:
skiing, guitar, poker.
Starsign: Scorpio.

WATFORD, Gwen
Actress b 10.9.27 London.
Started at Embassy, Swiss
Cottage. Rep at Buxton,
Croydon, Hornchurch,
Salisbury, Old Vic. Stage
plays incl: No Room at the
Inn; Daddy Longlegs; A Lady
Mislaid; Women of Twilight;
The Queen and the Rebels;
Time to Speak; The Woman
on the Stair; Singles; Bodies;
Present Laughter (for which
she won the SWET Award for
Actress of the Year in a
Supporting Role 1981); The
Jeweller's Shop. TV incl: Fate
and Mr Brown; Mr Brown
Comes Home; Till Time Shall
End; A Woman of No
Importance; Take Care of
Madam; Dangerous Corner;
The Waters of Babylon;
Second Time Around; The
Train Now Standing . . .; A Bit
of an Adventure; A Provincial
Lady; A Suitable Case For
Killing; Love Me to Death;
Don't Forget to Write; Aren't
We All?; The Shillingbury
Tales; The Case of The
Middle-Aged Wife; Present
Laughter. Films incl: Never
Take Sweets from a Stranger;
The Very Edge; Cleopatra.
Twice Actress of the Year.
Education: St Leonard's on
Sea. m actor Richard Bebb,
2 s Mark, Owen. Address:
c/o Miller Management,
Teddington, Middx. Starsign:
Virgo. Hobbies: playing the
piano, gardening. Person she
would most like to have met:
'Ellen Terry, because she
seems to have loved it all so
much!'

WATLING, Dilys
Actress b 5.5.46 Fulmer
Chase, Bucks. Studied art
until 17 then decided to join
the Italia Conti Stage School
and more training at the
Bristol Old Vic. Between
spells in rep incl Frinton and
Hornchurch, she made her
TV debut in Compact and
appeared in two films. Her
big stage break came in
Pickwick (with Harry
Secombe) followed by Our
Man Crichton; Promises,
Promises; Company; Fiddler
on the Roof; Kings and
Clowns; pantomime. On TV
she has appeared with
Tommy Cooper, Benny Hill,
Dickie Henderson,
Morecambe and Wise,
Frankie Howerd, Terry Scott,
The Two Ronnies and Mike
Yarwood. Other TV incl:
Coronation Street; United;
The Alchemist; Tonight;
Twice a Fortnight; The Likely
Lads; Going For a Song;
Celebrity Squares; Blankety
Blank; 3-2-1. Education: St
Mary's Convent, Woodford
Green, Essex. m (dis).
Address: c/o London
Management, London W1.
Starsign: Taurus. Hobby:
watching the ITV Seven with a
glass of Buck's Fizz. Person
she would most like to meet:
'Elizabeth Frink – I love
sculpture and bronzes, and I
particularly like hers.'

WATLING, Jack
Actor b 13.1.23 London.
First appearance on stage
was in Where the Rainbow
Ends at Holborn Empire,
1935. Apart from three years

in the RAF, has been
employed continuously in
stage, film and TV work ever
since. Films incl: The Winslow
Boy; Meet Mr Lucifer; The
Sea Shall Not Have Them;
The Admirable Crichton; A
Night to Remember; 11
Harrowhouse. Recent theatre
incl: Make a Break (tour); Two
and Two Make Sex. TV incl:
The Planemakers; The Power
Game; The Cedar Tree;
Doctors' Daughters;
Diamonds; Andy Robson.
m actress Patricia Hicks,
3 d Dilys, Deborah, Nicola,
1 s Giles. Address: c/o
Bryan Drew, London W1.
Starsign: Capricorn.

WATSON, Jack
Actor b 15th May London.
Started as stooge (Hubert) to
his father, comedian Nosmo
King, and was in variety for 15
years before becoming a
straight actor after a part in Z
Cars. Numerous film and TV
parts since. Films incl: The
Hill; The Idol; Tobruk; Grand
Prix; Red Gauntlet; Every
Home Should Have One;
Three Musketeers;
Juggernaut; Schizo; The
Purple Taxi; Wild Geese; The
Sea Wolves. TV incl:

Troubleshooters; Arthur of the Britons; Upstairs, Downstairs; The Hanged Man; The Charges; Sky; The Georgian House; Onedin Line; Killers; Goodbye America; Warship; Rob Roy; Who Pays the Ferryman?; Treasure Island; All Creatures Great and Small; The Cost of Loving; Kidnapped; A Horseman Riding By; The Camerons; Square Mile of Murder; Juliet Bravo; Into the Labyrinth; Kings Royal; Masada; Journeys of Marco Polo. m Betsy, 2 d Penelope, Fiona, 1 s Alastair. Address: c/o Joseph and Wagg, London W1. Starsign: Taurus. Hobbies: sailing, surfing, water skiing, golf, tennis. Person he would most like to have met: 'Louis Armstrong, for his uninhibited music and his radiant charm.'

WATSON, Moray
Actor b 25.6.30 Sunningdale, Berks. Trained at the Webber Douglas Academy of Dramatic Art, then rep at Leatherhead, Nottingham and Liverpool before London's West End and his first hit The Grass is Greener (also the film version with Cary Grant and Robert Mitchum). Other stage incl: The Public Eye and the Private Ear (Broadway); Don't Just Lie There, Say Something; On Approval; The Incomparable Max (his one-man show as Max Beerbohm). Films incl: Operation Crossbow; The Valiant; Every Home Should

Have One; The Sea Wolves. TV incl: Compact; The Borderers; On Approval; Quiller; Upstairs, Downstairs; A Place in the Sun; The Pallisers; Murder Most English; Rumpole of the Bailey; Company and Co; Pride and Prejudice; Winston Churchill The Wilderness Years; Doctor Who; Tales of the Unexpected; Nobody's Perfect; Union Castle. Education: Eton. m actress Pam Marmont, 1 d Emma, 1 s Robin. Address: c/o Leading Artists, London SW1. Starsign: Cancer. Hobby: gardening. Person he would most like to meet: 'Mary, the mother of Jesus, just to talk to her.'

WEBBER, Christine
Interviewer/presenter b 30th March Redhill, Surrey. Trained as a singer and has sung with Black and White Minstrels and in cabaret. Theatre work has also taken her on tours and into rep. On TV has been announcer for Southern TV and BFPO. Currently presenter of About Anglia for Anglia TV. Education: Lady Edridge Grammar, Croydon; Guildhall School of Music and Drama. m actor/writer Hugo Myatt. Address: c/o Jon Roseman Assocs, London W1. Starsign: Aries. Hobbies: conducting Breckband Brass Band, taking long walks with her yellow Labrador. Person she would most like to meet: 'Placido Domingo – I'd like to be sung to over a candlelit dinner.'

WEEKS, Alan
Sports commentator b 8.9.23 Bristol. First broadcast while serving in the Royal Navy (Midshipman to Lieutenant RNR) during the Second World War – over ship's radio in the corvette HMS Rushen Castle, giving nightly situation report to ship's company. Public address announcer, Brighton Sports Stadium 1946-65. First commentary for BBC TV on ice hockey in 1951. Has since presented Summer Grandstand (1959-62); Olympic Games (1960, 1964); World Cup (1962); Pot Black (since 1970). Commentated on soccer (1956-78); World Cup (1966-78); Winter Olympics (1964-80); Olympic Games (1968-80); Commonwealth Games (1970-78); ice skating (since 1958); gymnastics (since 1962); swimming (since 1970). Education: Brighton, Hove and Sussex Grammar. m Barbara Jane, 1 d Beverly, 2 s Nigel (dec), Roderick. Address: c/o The Bagenal Harvey Organisation, London W1. Starsign: Virgo. Hobbies: swimming, football. Person he would most like to meet: 'Frank Sinatra – I like a good song well sung.'

WEIR, Helen
Actress b 9.4.42 Oxfordshire. Trained at RADA and North West School of Speech and Drama, Southport. Currently appearing as Pat Merrick in Emmerdale Farm, but has

worked extensively in the theatre, starting with the Royal Shakespeare Company at Stratford. Has played a diversity of roles from Queen Elizabeth I in Dark Lady of the Sonnets in Regent's Park Open Air Theatre to leading lady in The Mousetrap. Other theatre work incl: Murder in the Cathedral (York Minster); The House of Bernarda Alba; The Importance of Being Earnest in London's West End. Has made one film, The Boy Who Turned Yellow (which received an Oscar). Apart from Emmerdale Farm, other TV incl: Rogue's Gallery; Armchair Theatre. m (dis), 1 s Daniel. Address: c/o MLR, London SW5. Starsign: Aries. Hobbies: preserving old properties (especially Victorian), eating. Person she would most like to meet: 'David Attenborough – if he can make animals superb performers, can he make me one?'

Manchester's Library Theatre. Briefly compère of BBC's North At Six and an appearance in The Verdict Is Yours before becoming PC Graham in Z Cars for three years. Took to writing and hasn't looked back since with awards both for acting and writing. TV plays incl: Bangelstein's Boys; Slattery's Mounted Foot; Roll On Four O'Clock; Say Goodnight to Grandma; Catherine Wheel; The Hallelujah Handshake; A Room Full of Holes; Leeds United; Kisses at Fifty; The Wild West Show; Your Man From Six Counties; Yanks (film script). TV appearances in addition to many of his own plays and Z Cars, incl: Man at the Top; Left; Passage to England; The Cost of Loving; Blue Remembered Hills; Jack Point; Cowboys. Also presenter of How To Stay Alive and sports commentator. Films incl: Kes; Villain; Straw Dogs; The Sweeney; Yanks; Chariots of Fire (film script, for which he won an Oscar). Education: Grammar School, Newton-le-Willows. m former teacher Pat, 3 d Genevieve, Catherine, Caroline, 1 adopt s Christie. Address: c/o Peter Charlesworth Ltd, London SW7. Starsign: Cancer. Hobbies: cricket, rugby, singing.

(1945-50) as his training before moving to London. Has since had wide experience in the theatre, films and TV. Subsequently joined the Royal Shakespeare Company and was in their Wars of the Roses 1964. Other stage incl: The Party; Look Back in Anger; Too True to be Good; Measure For Measure. Films incl: The Man Who Haunted Himself; Cromwell; The Pied Piper of Hamelin. Much TV incl: The Forsyte Saga; Mr Rose; Uncle Silas; Paper Dolls; Flower Dew; Raj; Trials of Marshall Petain; Oh, Brother; Footprints in the Jungle; Codename; Little Women and Good Wives; Last Wishes; Duchess of Duke Street; Affairs of the Heart; Diary of a Nobody; The Recruiting Officer; Timon of Athens; The Winter's Tale; Let There Be Love. Education: Christian Brothers, Wexford. m Audrey, 1 d Lucy, 2 s Simon, John. Address: c/o Joy Jameson Ltd, London SW1. Starsign: Scorpio. Hobbies: golf, music. Person he would most like to have met: 'William Saroyan (I once played in his The Time of Your Life) – I feel he was a great life-enhancer and a lovely man.'

WELLAND, Colin
Actor/writer b 4.7.44 Leigh, Lancs. Worked for five years as an art teacher before being taken on at

WELSH, John
Actor b 7.11.14 Wexford. Regards five years at the Gate Theatre, Dublin

WEST, Timothy
Actor b 2.10.34 Bradford. Studied modern languages at London Polytechnic 1951-53, but neglected studies to act Shakespeare in pubs with a group called The Taverners. Short spells as

furniture salesman and recording engineer before making the stage his career. Worked with various reps incl Northampton, Canterbury, Bath, Bristol and Salisbury, leaving there 1959 to make his London debut in Caught Napping. Stage work since incl leading roles in West End and with Royal Shakespeare and Prospect Companies, in UK and abroad. Films incl: Twisted Nerve; Looking Glass War; Nicholas and Alexandra; The Day of the Jackal; Joseph Andrews; The Devil's Advocate; News from Nowhere; Agatha; The Thirty Nine Steps; Rough Cut; The Antagonists. TV incl: Joy; Horatio Bottomley; Edward the Seventh; The After Dinner Game; Hard Times; Henry VIII; Crime and Punishment; Churchill and the Generals. Education: 13 schools (his actor father, Lockwood West, and mother were frequently on tour) incl: John Lyon School, Harrow. m (1st) Jacqueline Boyer (dis), (2nd) Prunella Scales, 1 d Juliet (from 1st m), 2 s Sam, Joe. Address: c/o Fraser and Dunlop, London W1. Starsign: Libra. Hobbies: listening to music, exploring old railway lines. People he would most like to meet: 'Dr Samuel Johnson, to discuss the human condition, and Goldie Hawn, for similar reasons.'

WESTCOTT, Simon
TV reporter b 23.8.49 Lagos, Nigeria. Raised in England. Member of the National Youth

Theatre in the 1960s. Joined Channel TV in 1972 where he trained as a reporter in Guernsey, before moving to Jersey. Joined Thames News in similar capacity 1978. Occasionally presents Thames News. Was reporter and writer of documentary on oil rig salvage: Orion, the Saving of Men and Steel. Education: Giggleswick School, Settle, Yorks (where he was taught English by Russell Harty). Address: c/o Thames TV, London NW1. Hobbies: writing, painting, sailing, travel, music. Person he would most like to have met: Mahatma Gandhi.

WESTON, Colin
Announcer/newsreader b 26.7.48 London. On leaving school started as a mailing clerk with ABC Television and spent four years with them at their Teddington studios. Announcer Granada 1968-70 and Anglia 1970-73 before going freelance. Has since worked for HTV, Westward, Border, BBC 1, BBC 2, London Weekend TV, Southern and, since 1979, Tyne Tees TV. Has also worked for Piccadilly Radio and Radio City. Education: Streatham Modern School. Address: c/o Tyne Tees TV, Newcastle. Starsign: Leo. Hobbies: collecting records, eating out, buying clothes, watching lawn tennis. Person he would most like to meet: 'The Queen Mother, because she always looks so genial and motherly.'

WESTWOOD, Barry
Presenter/interviewer/ producer b 7.9.27 Birmingham. Originally articled to a Birmingham firm of chartered accountants. After qualifying, moved to Southampton 1954 where he lectured in accountancy, taxation and company law, etc, and became Senior Lecturer in charge of Professional Studies at Southampton Technical College. Met Roy Rich, then Southern TV's Programme Controller, while presenting prize in best secretary competition 1959 and within 12 days was introducing his own TV programme. Has since produced/appeared in and/or introduced more than 4000 programmes, incl: Southern TV's award-winning Day By Day (1969-80); Sunday Break; Background; ABC Weekend; Your Point of View; Afloat; The Barry Westwood Talkabout; political and outside broadcasts and numerous adult education programme series. BISFA Gold Medallist; holder of Southern TV's Silver Merit Award. Owns and operates mobile CCTV studio. Education: Solihull School. Address: Fareham, Hants. Starsign: Virgo. Hobbies: caravanning, wine, music. Person he would most like to have met again: 'Lord Mountbatten, because I filmed a long interview with him just before his assassination and our conversation was unfinished.'

WHEELER, Charles
TV correspondent b 26.3.23
Bremen, Germany. Joined
the old Daily Sketch from
school and a year later was
doing war service in the Royal
Marines (1941-46). Then he
joined the BBC. Was
co-producer of Panorama
1956-58. Has become one of
the most respected foreign
correspondents on TV,
having been BBC
correspondent in India, Berlin
and Washington and chief
correspondent in America
and Europe, based in
Brussels. Became a
freelance broadcaster in
1976 since when he has
presented Newsday and
Panorama. Currently on
foreign film-reporting for
Newsnight. Education:
Cranbrook School, Kent.
m Dip Singh, 2 d Shirin,
Marina. Address: c/o BBC
TV, London W12. Starsign:
Aries. Person he would most
like to meet: Jacobo
Timerman.

WHICKER, Alan
Journalist b 2.8.25 Cairo,
Egypt. Mother from Suffolk,
father from Devon. After
service on Italian warfront as

Major commanding battle
cameramen, became foreign
correspondent in Fleet Street,
war correspondent in Korea.
Joined BBC in 1957 at start of
Tonight programme to
become TV's most travelled
man. Whicker's World began
in 1958 and is still turning.
Joined ITV in 1968 as
Yorkshire TV's largest private
shareholder. Numerous
international awards for
commentary writing,
documentaries,
Dumont/UCLA Award,
Personality of the Year,
Richard Dimbleby Award,
etc. Also TVTimes Special
Award. After 25 years as TV's
man around the world, wrote
best-seller Within Whicker's
World. Education:
Haberdashers' Aske's
School, Hampstead, London.
Address: Jersey, Channel
Islands. Starsign: Leo.
Person he would most like to
have met: 'Leonardo da Vinci,
to absorb that multi-faceted
brilliance.'

WHITE, Sheila
Singer/dancer b 18.10.50
Highgate, London. Started
with Terry's Juveniles when
she was 12 before training at
the Corona Stage School.
Early stage work incl: The
Sound of Music; Roar of the
Greasepaint, Smell of the
Crowd; On the Level; Dames
at Sea (also in France where it
was a huge success and
Sheila became the toast of
Paris); pantomimes and
Queen Daniella; tours. Films
incl: Here We Go Round the
Mulberry Bush; Ghost Goes

Gear; Stranger in the House;
Oliver!; Confessions of a
Window Cleaner;
Confessions of a Pop Star;
Confessions of a Driving
Instructor; Mrs Brown You've
Got a Lovely Daughter; The
Spaceman and King Arthur;
The Silver Dream Racer;
Biograph Girl; They're
Playing Our Song. Many TV
plays and series both here
and in France where, through
TV, films, cabaret and
records she was regarded as
a superstar. TV here incl:
appearances with Cliff
Richard and Billy Dainty;
such series as Z Cars;
Emergency – Ward 10;
Oranges and Lemons; Dear
Mother . . . Love, Albert;
Poldark; Love School; The
Songwriters. Also Alice in
Wonderland; I Claudius;
Ladies of Ridgemead;
Minder; Pickwick Papers;
Tiptoes; Jazz Age.
Education: Woodberry Down
Primary; Woodberry Down
Comprehensive; Campbell's
Private School, Muswell Hill.
Address: c/o Peter
Charlesworth Ltd, London
SW7. Starsign: Libra.
Hobbies: riding, tennis,
swimming, cooking, country
walks, singing, lisening to
records with headphones
very loud, driving, gardening.

WHITE, Stewart
Presenter b 18.4.47
Salisbury, Wilts. Experience
as BBC studio manager and
radio presenter before joining
ATV/Central as announcer
and presenter 1979.
Interviewer/presenter

Something Different; Now Come Close; Star Soccer. Narrator of documentary on Cardinal Newman. Has also been announcer on Southern TV. Education: Bishop Wordsworth School, Salisbury. m Jane, 1 s Edward. Address: c/o PVA Management Ltd, London W1. Starsign: Aries. Hobbies: sport, reading. Person he would most like to meet: 'Richard Nixon – on the assumption that nobody's all bad.'

WHITEHEAD, Geoffrey
Actor b 1.10.39 Sheffield. RADA trained, followed by work in Canterbury, Coventry and Sheffield Reps. TV incl: Bulldog Breed; Z Cars; Last of the Best Men; Robin's Nest; The Foundation; Sherlock Holmes; Inside the Third Reich. Education: Westbourne Road Prep; Trent College, Nottingham. m actress Mary Hanefey, 1 d Clare, 1 s Jonty. Address: c/o Bryan Drew Ltd, London W1. Starsign: Libra. Hobbies: football, cricket. Person he would most like to meet: 'Archbishop Hume – a very saintly man.'

WHITEHOUSE, Rob
Journalist b 8.9.52 Wolverhampton. After a post-graduate journalism course went into local radio (Beacon Radio) before joining ATV/Central TV as political reporter in 1979, where his work incl weekly political Midlands programme. Left, Right and

Centre, and daily news programme, ATV Today. Education: St Peter's Collegiate School, Wolverhampton; Wulfrun FE College; University of Warwick (BA Hons Sociology and Politics); University of Cardiff (Postgraduate course in Journalism). m Surrey Beddows. Address: c/o Central TV (West), Birmingham. Starsign: Virgo. Hobbies: photography, furniture renovation, jogging. Person he would most like to meet: 'Lord Lucan – we could swop some interesting stories.'

WHITELEY, Richard
Presenter b 28.12.43 Bradford, Yorkshire. TV trainee with ITN 1965, joined Yorkshire TV 1968. Presenter of Calendar and associated programmes, incl: Calendar Sunday; Calendar Tuesday; Calendar People; Calendar Forum; Election Calendar; Good Morning Calendar (breakfast programme); Goodnight Calendar; Calendar Profile; Country Calendar; Calendar Specials. Other TV incl: Enterprize 82; Past Masters;

Ferret Lovers' Weekly. Education: Giggleswick School, North Yorks; Christ's College, Cambridge, where he was editor of Varsity. Address: c/o Yorkshire TV, Leeds. Starsign: Capricorn. Hobbies; country pubs, walking. Person he would most like to have met: 'John Logie Baird, because I owe him a lot.'

WHITFIELD, June
Comedy actress b 11th November, London. After training at RADA and such stage shows as Love From Judy, came to the fore as Eth in the radio series Take It From Here (1953). More recently, Men of Property. On TV she has been foil to the best funny men in the business incl: Morecambe and Wise, Jimmy Edwards, Frankie Howerd, Terry Scott, Dick Emery, Stanley Baxter, Arthur Askey, Eric Sykes and Tony Hancock. Films incl: Carry On Abroad; Bless This House; The Spy With the Cold Nose. TV incl: Beggar My Neighbour; The Best Things In Life; Hancock's Half Hour; Scott On . . .; Happy Ever After; Terry and June. Education: Streatham High. m surveyor Tim Aitchison, 1 d Susan. Address: c/o April Young, London WC2. Starsign: Scorpio. Hobby: cooking. Person she would most like to meet again: 'My father, who died some years ago – there are so many conversations I would like to have with him.'

WHITMARSH, Michael
Broadcaster b 27.10.42
Plymouth. Experience in
weekly, evening and daily
newspapers (North Devon
Journal and Herald, Western
Morning News, Western Daily
Press) and a publishing
company in London before
joining BBC in Bristol and
Plymouth as a regional
journalist 1968. Joined
Westward TV/TSW 1980.
Education: Marlborough
College, Wilts. m Angela.
Address: c/o TSW, Exeter.
Starsign: Scorpio. Hobbies:
squash, sailing, old books,
painting. Person he would
most like to meet: 'Premier
Huo of China, to establish
China's aim in the world.'

WHITMORE, Richard
TV news presenter/ reporter
b 22.12.33 Hitchin, Herts.
On leaving school in 1951
became a junior reporter on
the Hertford Express,
returning there in 1954 (after
two years in the RAF). Left in
1959 to develop a freelance
agency in the Hertford-
shire-Bedfordshire area and
it was during this time that he
became interested in
broadcasting. First worked

for the BBC as a freelance
reporter for the South-East
regional radio and TV
programmes. Appointed
staff correspondent for BBC
Radio and TV News in 1964;
for the next eight years he
travelled extensively on news
stories in Great Britain,
Europe and the Middle East.
He also went on several
assignments to Northern
Ireland between 1969 and
1972, when he became a
regular newsreader on the
Nine O'Clock News. In Sept
1981 became presenter of
BBC TV's new lunch-time
news programme News After
Noon. Has also appeared as
a guest in such programmes
as Morecambe and Wise
Christmas Show (1977),
Saturday Night at the Mill and
Eric Sykes. During 1980 he
was chairman of the Radio 4
phone-in programme,
Person to Person. Author of
four books on Victorian
photography: Of Uncommon
Interest; Victorian and
Edwardian Hertfordshire
from Old Photographs;
Victorian and Edwardian
Crime and Punishment from
Old Photographs; Mad Lucas
(for publication at the end of
1982). Education: Hitchin
Boys' Grammar School.
m Wendy, 4 d Jane, Sarah,
Kate, Lucy. Address: c/o
BBC TV News, London W12.
Starsign: Capricorn. Hobby:
amateur dramatics. Member
for 30 years of leading
Hertfordshire amateur
dramatic society, The
Bancroft Players, of which he
is president. Is heading a
project to build a theatre in his
home town.

WHITTAKER, Roger
Singer/entertainer/song-
writer b 22.3.36 Nairobi,
Kenya. Called up at 18 into
the Kenya Regiment.
Afterwards became a
schoolmaster, singing in
clubs at night. Came to
Britain, got a biochemistry

degree but decided to try
showbusiness. By the end of
1963 he had a small late night
TV series. Has since
appeared in concerts,
cabaret and clubs all over the
world as well as his own TV
programmes, incl Night
Music. Prolific songwriter
incl: Durham Town; I Don't
Believe In If Anymore; New
World in the Morning; Why;
The Last Farewell. Has spent
the last two years mostly in
America. Has performed
about 160 concerts there and
appeared on all the major TV
shows, incl: Johnny Carson,
Diana Shaw, John Davidson,
Merv Griffin. Education:
Capetown and Bangor
Universities (BSc). m Natalie.
3 d Emily, Lauren, Jessica,
2 s Guy, Alexander.
Address: c/o Tempo
Entertainment Ltd, London
NW1. Starsign: Aries.
Hobbies: photography, flying
aeroplanes, collecting
antiques.

WILD, Jack
Actor b 30.9.52 Royston,
Lancs. Started acting career
as Artful Dodger in Lionel
Bart's stage show Oliver!
1964-67, followed by Big Sin

City. Has also appeared at the Hollywood Bowl in America. His stage success in Oliver! was repeated in the film version. Other films incl: HR Pufnstuff (and on TV); SWALK; Flight of the Doves; The Pied Piper; The 14; Alice. TV incl: Our Mutual Friend; The Ravelled Thread; Star Games; Everyday Maths; Jackanory Playhouse; The Government Inspector. Many guest appearances and variety in America. Education: Barbara Speake Stage School, London. Address: c/o Peter Charlesworth Ltd, London SW7. Starsign: Libra. Hobbies: football, snooker, bowling.

WILLIAMS, Kenneth
Actor b 22.2.26 London. Started as a lithographic draughtsman but began his acting career at Newquay Repertory Theatre 1948. Various other rep engagements before London debut as Slightly in Peter Pan 1952. Has since played in pantomime and many plays and revues. Has made more than 25 Carry On . . . films and other films incl: Raising the Wind; Twice Round the Daffodils; The Hound of the Baskervilles. In addition to chat shows and panel games, his TV credits incl: Hancock's Half Hour; What's My Line?; Password; International Cabaret; The Kenneth Williams Show; Meanwhile on BBC 2; Let's Make a Musical; Jackanory. Also broadcast regularly in

Round the Horne; Stop Messing About; Just a Minute, and other radio programmes. Book: Acid Drops. Education: Lyulph Stanley School; Bolt Court. Address: c/o ICM, London W1. Starsign: Pisces. Pastimes: reading, walking, doodling.

WILLIAMS, Michael
Actor b 9.7.35 Manchester. Trained at RADA, joined Nottingham Playhouse in 1959, appeared in Celebration at the Duchess Theatre, the revue Twists at the Arts Theatre, and some TV work. Joined Royal Shakespeare Company 1963, where he has been in Comedy of Errors; Taming of the Shrew; The Merchant of Venice; As You Like It; Troilus and Cressida; Marat Sade; The Jew of Malta; Tango; London Assurance; Jingo; Too Good To Be True; A Winter's Tale; King Lear; Schweyk in World War II. He was in the film version of Marat Sade. Other films incl: Eagle in a Cage; Dead Cert; Enigma. On TV his credits incl: Elizabeth R; A Raging Calm; The Hanged Man; Comedy of Errors; Ice Age; Turtle's Progress; Quest of Eagles; My Son, My Son; Love In A Cold Climate; Amnesty; A Fine Romance, in which he appeared with his wife Judi Dench. Education: St Edward's College, Liverpool. m actress Judi Dench, 1 d Tara. Address: c/o Leading Artists Ltd, London SW1. Starsign:

Cancer. Hobby: his family. Person he would most like to meet: 'My agent – he keeps on changing his hairstyle and I'm not sure I'd recognise him anymore.'

WILLIAMS, Simon
Actor b 16.6.46 Windsor, Berks. One of the tallest actors in the business (he stands 6ft 4in in his socks), he started in pantomime in 1965, followed by rep at Worthing, Birmingham and Croydon. London West End appearances incl: A Friend in Need; Hay Fever; His, Hers and Theirs; The Collector; No Sex Please – We're British; Gigi; The Last Mrs Cheyney. Films incl: Joanna; The Touchables; The Incredible Sarah; Jabberwocky; No Longer Alone; The Prisoner of Zenda; The Fiendish Plot of Dr Fu Manchu. TV breakthrough was as Captain Bellamy in Upstairs, Downstairs. Other TV incl: The Regiment; Man in a Suitcase; Romance; Wodehouse Playhouse; Mr Big; Liza; Agony; Company and Co; Strangers; Kinvig. Education: Harrow. m actress Belinda Carroll, 1 d Amy, 1 s Tamlyn. Address: c/o Leading Artists, London SW1. Starsign: Gemini. Hobbies: riding, reading, writing.

WILLIAMS, W I Cynwil
Presenter of religious programmes b 14.7.36 Lampeter, Dyfed. Trained for the Ministry in the

Presbyterian Church of Wales and as well as being religious adviser to HTV Wales, is minister of the Crwys Road Presbyterian Church of Wales where many BBC and HTV personalities are members. In the 1970s he appeared on many religious programmes, such as Llusern, was the presenter and scriptwriter of Duw a'i Awduron and is the joint presenter of Cynorth. Education: University College of Wales (BA, BD). m Frances, 3 d Catrin, Siriol, Lisa. Address: Penylan, Cardiff. Starsign: Cancer. Hobbies: reading, leading groups to Israel and Greece. Person he would most like to meet: 'Anthony Bloom – he combines charisma, integrity and Christian spirituality.'

WILLIS, Wincey
Presenter b 8.8.54 Gateshead. Formerly in the record business and a travel courier for five years. Came into TV through her hobby, animals. Sometimes she would be asked to bring an unusual animal to the studio by her record friends and on

one occasion was also asked to read the weather news. Has done so for Tyne Tees TV since Sept 1981, translating weather reports into layman's terms. Also on TV she has been in Graham's Ark and has her own series, Wincey's Pets. She is in the process of writing books for children on animal care. Education: The High School for Girls, Hartlepool. m Malcolm. Address: c/o Tyne Tees TV, Newcastle. Starsign: Leo. Hobby: everything to do with animals. Person she would most like to meet again: 'Gerald Durrell, who epitomises and has put into practice everything I believe in regarding animals.'

WILSON, Anthony
TV journalist b 20.2.50 Salford. After leaving Cambridge (Jesus College) with an Hons degree in English and having edited Varsity, received his training in TV journalism with ITN. Joined Granada TV and was involved with Granada Reports; Powerpoint; What's On; writer/presenter of So It Goes; Think Tank; World in Action 1980-81; now presenting Granada Reports again. Education: St Mary's Primary School, Marple, Cheshire; De La Salle College, Salford; Jesus College, Cambridge. m Lindsay. Address: c/o Granada TV, Manchester. Starsign: Pisces. Hobbies: music, reading, indoor gardening, films. Person he would most like to meet: Pol Pot.

WILSON, Bob
Sports presenter b 30.10.41 Chesterfield, Derby. Former Arsenal and Scotland goalkeeper. Joined the club 1963 from Loughborough College where he was a teacher of physical education. Joined BBC 1974 to present football spot Football Focus in Grandstand. Now co-presenter Match of the Day. Education: Chesterfield Grammar. m Margaret (Megs), 1 d Anna, 2 s John, Robert. Address: Brookman's Park, London. Starsign: Scorpio. Hobbies: squash, golf. Person he would most like to have met: 'Sir Winston Churchill – I admire his eloquence and leadership.'

WILSON, Francis
Weather presenter b 27.2.49 Irvine, Scotland. Trained at the RAF Farnborough with the Met Research Flight for three years. Thames TV's weather man since 1978. Books: Guide to Weather; Guide to Forecasting. Education: Dr Challoner's Grammar, Amersham; Imperial College, London University (BSc).

Associate, Royal College of Science, and Fellow, Royal Meteorological Society. m Eva. Address: c/o Thames TV, London NW1. Starsign: Pisces. Hobby: sitting in the sun. Person he would most like to meet: 'I don't mind meeting people, but I have no burning desire to meet anyone in particular.'

1 d Melanie (by 2nd m). Address: c/o NEMS Management, London SW3. Starsign: Taurus. Hobbies: collecting pictures, cooking. Person she would most like to have met: 'Noël Coward, because of his humanity, wit, insight and understanding of our profession.'

(Stables). Frequently seen on TV in a variety of roles and programmes incl: Dr Finlay's Casebook; The Revenue Men; My Good Woman; Crown Court; Big Boy Now; Cilla's World of Comedy; Pickersgill People; A Sharp Intake of Breath; Through the Night; Some Mothers Do 'Ave 'Em; In Loving Memory; Chalk and Cheese; Only When I Laugh; Virginia Fly Is Drowning; Shaping Up; Strangers. Directed Commitments (Play For Today). Also directs in the theatre, being an associate director at Oxford Playhouse and an assistant director at the Stables Theatre, Manchester. Most recently directed The House and Say Your Prayers for Joint Stock Company. Also at the Bush Theatre, Hampstead Theatre, and the Royal Court Theatre. Educated at Greenock. Address: c/o Green and Underwood Ltd, London WC2. Starsign: Cancer. Hobby: squash. Person he would most like to have met: 'Stan Laurel – he was a consummate artist who has given me so much pleasure year after year.'

WILSON, Jennifer

Actress b 25th April London. Wanted to be a dress designer but changed her mind when successfully auditioned for RADA. Rep, then Regent's Park Open Air Theatre, the Old Vic, a tour of America and Canada with them, Shakespearean tour of India. Two years in Spring and Port Wine in London's West End. Other stage incl: Lend Me Five Shillings; It Happened in Harrods; Pygmalion; Most Gracious Lady; Travesties; The Four Poster; Hong Kong Festival; Bedroom Farce; The Complaisant Lover; The Grass is Greener. Starred in dozens of TV plays and series but is probably best known as Jenny Hammond in The Brothers for six years. Other TV incl: Nicholas Nickleby; You Never Can Tell; Time and the Conways; The Widowing of Mrs Holroyd; Antigone; A Doll's House; Man of Our Times; The Second Mrs Tanqueray; The Befrienders; Cavalcade; You and Me. Educated in the Cotswolds and London College. m (1st) S Swain (dis), (2nd) actor/director Brian Peck,

WILSON, Malcolm

Newscaster/writer/ broadcaster b 25.7.50 Ayr, Scotland. Newspaper background with The Scotsman and in Edinburgh and Glasgow. Joined Scottish TV 1973 and moved to BBC Scotland 1976. TV incl: Scotland Today; Crimedesk (both for STV); Reporting Scotland; Sportscene (both for BBC); presented first experimental radiovision TV in Dec 1980; Nationwide Watchdog since 1979. Education: Ayr Academy; Edinburgh University. m Irene, 2 s Jamie, Louis. Address: c/o BBC TV, Glasgow. Starsign: Leo. Hobbies: crosswords, literature, losing charity football matches. Person he would most like to meet: 'The first Prime Minister of an Independent Scotland.'

WILSON, Richard

Actor/director b 9.7.36 Greenock, Renfrewshire. Originally a research scientist in Scotland but gave it up to study for the stage when he was 27. Trained at RADA, then rep at Glasgow, Edinburgh (Traverse) and Manchester

WINDING, Victor

Actor b 30.1.29 London. Trained as a draughtsman, but in evenings was acting in amateur dramatics and teaching drama in LCC night schools. At 29 he got a job with Farnham Rep and three years later went to London Old Vic. Then Malvern Festival and London's West

End incl: Next Time I'll Sing to You; Poor Bitos; Merchant of Venice. Films incl: The System; Medusa Touch; Sailor's Return. Much TV incl: Emergency – Ward 10; Probation Officer; No Hiding Place; The Informer; The Saint; Doctor Who; The Expert; The Flaxton Boys; Warship; Crossroads; Armchair Thriller; Bognor. Education: Westminster Technical Institute.
m Rosalind (dis), 3 d Celia, Kay, Jane, 1 s Julian. Address: c/o Richard Stone, London WC2. Starsign: Aquarius. Hobbies: music, travelling, gardening. People he would most like to meet again: 'All those I was billeted on, when evacuated during the war years 1939-43.'

WINDSOR, Frank
Actor b 12.7.27 Walsall, Staffs. Started in radio 1946 after RAF station shows. Founder member of the Oxford and Cambridge Players, later the Elizabethan Players and before going into TV was a classical actor. London stage incl: Androcles and the Lion; Brand; Travesties (with Royal Shakespeare Company); The Old Vic; Middle-age Spread; Mr Fothergill's Murder. Films incl: this Sporting Life; Spring and Port Wine; Sunday, Bloody Sunday; The Drop Out; Assassin; Someone is Killing the Great Chefs of Europe; Dangerous Davies; Coming Out of the Ice. Best known on TV for his roles as Sergeant Watt in Z Cars and in Softly, Softly. Other TV incl: An Age of Kings; A for Andromeda; Call My Bluff; Whodunnit?; Jack the Ripper; Headmaster; Crown Court; Kidnapped; The Union; Into the Labyrinth. Education: St Mary's School, Walsall. m former dancer Mary Corbett, 1 d Amanda, 1 s David. Address: c/o Jeremy Conway Ltd, London W1. Starsign: Cancer. Hobbies: tending his grapevine to make his own wine, dogs, working for World Wildlife Fund and Variety Club of Great Britain

WINKLER, Henry
Actor b 30.10.45 New York City. Alias Fonzie of Happy Days. Always wanted to be an actor. Gained a Master of Arts degree at Yale School of Drama where he appeared in more than 30 plays as a student. On graduation stayed on as professional actor. After a brief spell with the Arena Theatre in Washington (he was sacked after three weeks) found work in radio, TV commercials and acted with a children's group in New York. Started in Happy Days 1972. Films incl: Heroes; The One and Only. Education: McBurney Prep School; Emmetson College, Boston; Yale University.
m public relations executive Stacey Weitzman. Address: Beverly Hills, California. Starsign: Scorpio. Hobbies: listening to music, watching TV, reading, jogging.

WINTERS, Bernie
Comedian b 6.9.32 Islington, London. Went straight into show business on leaving school. Later formed a double act with his brother Mike, then joined the Merchant Navy to see the world. Resumed partnership with brother 1949 and appeared in numerous variety, musical and TV shows incl: Six-Five Special; Big Night Out; Blackpool Night Out. Went solo 1978 and his own series Bernie. Other TV incl: Mad About; Give Us a Clue; Starburst; Flanagan and Allen. Toured in stage show, Bud and Ches, with Leslie Crowther. Education: Crowland Rd School, Tottenham; Vartry Rd, Seven Sisters, London. m ex-dancer Siggi Heine, 1 s Ray. Address: c/o Joe Collins Ltd, London NW1. Starsign: Virgo. Hobbies: football, tennis.

WINTLE, Frank
Editor/presenter b 21.4.50 Cranleigh, Surrey. Journalistic experience on the Western Morning News, Plymouth, before joining the BBC, for whom he worked in Plymouth, Bristol and

London. Former Radio 4 producer. Joined Westward TV/TSW in 1980 where he became series editor of Westward Report and Western Approach. Presents Scene South West and A Day in the Life of . . . Book: The Plymouth Blitz. Education: Brighton College; Exeter School; Tavistock School; Exeter University. Address: c/o TSW, Plymouth. Starsign: cusp of Aries and Taurus. Hobbies: writing, walking, writing while walking. Person he would most like to meet: 'Ayatollah Khomeini, to discuss open marriages.'

WISE, Ernie OBE

Comedian b 27.11.25 Leeds. Child entertainer with his father in working men's clubs. Theatre debut at Bradford 1936; London debut in Band Waggon 1939 then toured in Bryan Michie's Youth Takes a Bow in which he met Eric Morecambe 1941. Formed a double act but touring was interrupted by National Service in Merchant Navy. After the war both booked for Lord John Sanger's Variety Circus and partnership resumed. Radio

breakthrough on Worker's Playtime and own radio series, You're Only Young Once. TV incl: Running Wild; Sunday Night at the London Palladium; The Morecambe and Wise Show (BBC and ITV). Numerous variety, pantomimes, summer and royal shows, tours of Australia and Canada and Ed Sullivan Show in America. Films: The Intelligence Men; That Riviera Touch; The Magnificent Two. Freeman City of London 1976. TVTimes Hall of Fame. Education: elementary schools. m Doreen. Address: c/o London Management, London W1. Starsign: Sagittarius. Hobbies: cricket, writing, boating, gardening, tennis, swimming. Person he would most like to have met: 'Queen Victoria, to find out why she was not amused.'

WITHERSPOON, Charles

Actor/playwright/presenter/announcer b 2nd September, Belfast. Varied career starting in insurance, then the stage and radio and now TV. Has written about 20 radio serials for children as well as two radio plays, innumerable documentaries and scripting and presenting a number of documentaries in the About Britain series on TV. Currently presenting a weekly Police Six programme on Ulster TV. Education: local primary school and college of technology. m (sep), 2 s Philip, Michael. Address: c/o Ulster TV, Belfast. Starsign: Virgo. Hobbies:

photography, motor-cycling, trout fishing. Person he would most like to meet: Malcolm Muggeridge.

WOGAN, Terry

Broadcaster b 3.8.38 Limerick, Ireland. Claims his training and background were 'bourgeois Irish'. Collected many awards for his radio work, incl: Radio Industries Club Award for Radio Personality of the Year 1974, 1976, 1978; TV Times Award for Most Popular TV Personality 1978-81; Variety Club Award (Radio Personality); Pye Radio Award 1980. Radio incl: Terry Wogan Show; Pop Score; Punchline; Twenty Questions; Quote, Unquote; Year In Question. TV incl: Lunchtime With Wogan; Come Dancing; Miss World; Eurovision Song Contest; Song for Europe; Variety Club Awards; Carl-Alan Awards; Disco; Startown; Blankety Blank; What's On Wogan; You Must Be Joking; Wogan. Education: Crescent College, Limerick; Belvedere, Dublin. m former model Helen Joyce, 1 d Katherine, 2 s Alan, Mark. Address: c/o Jo Gurnett Personal Management, London SW7. Starsign: Leo. Hobbies: family, reading, golf. Person he would most like to meet: Jimmy Young.

WOOD, Michael

Writer/presenter b 23.7.48 Manchester. Started in TV as a reporter for Yorkshire TV's

local programmes. He then joined BBC 2's current affairs team. TV incl: In Search Of . . .; Great Railway Journeys of the World; Now Showing; Shakespeare in Perspective; River Journeys. He also joined Angela Rippon for the BBC coverage of Prince Charles' wedding. Book: In Search of the Dark Ages. Education: Manchester Grammar School; Oriel College, Oxford (where he was an Open Scholar and gained a BA degree and did PhD research on medieval kingship). Address: c/o BBC, Manchester. Starsign: Leo. Hobby: music (playing loud R and B!). Person he would most like to have met: 'Genghis Khan – intellectual curiosity.'

WOOD, Victoria
Comedienne/writer
b 19.5.53 Prestwich, Lancs. Works in clubs, theatres and cabaret in the north and has been appearing, with her husband, in Funny Turns since 1977. Started writing TV plays 1978 – Talent; Nearly a Happy Ending; Happy Since I Met You. Also wrote the scripts for the Wood and

Walters series in which she appeared with Julie Walters, whom she first met at an audition. Other TV incl: New Faces; Thames Today; Pebble Mill at One; Call My Bluff; Take the Stage; Give Us a Clue; Cabbages and Kings; After Noon Plus; Live From Two; That's Life; Friday Night . . . Saturday Morning. Education: Bury Grammar School; Birmingham University (BA Drama and Theatre Arts). m magician Geoffrey Durham (The Great Soprendo). Address: c/o Richard Stone, London WC2. Starsign: Taurus. Person she would most like to meet: 'Ken Dodd, because he's our best comic.'

WOODHOUSE, Barbara
Author and expert in animal training b 9.5.10 Rathfarnham, Co Dublin. Established herself as a TV personality 1979 with her programmes on dogs and horses for which she won the Pye TV and Writers' Guild of Great Britain awards as TV Personality of the Year. Has trained more than 17,000 dogs which has earned her a place in the Guinness Book of Records. Trained in agriculture at Harper Adams Agricultural College where she was the only woman student. After college started a riding school in Oxford and spent three and a half years training horses in Argentina. First TV was as a subject on What's My Line?, when she beat the panel. Since 1980 her TV has incl: Training Dogs

the Woodhouse Way; Any Questions?; Woodhouse World of Animals; World of Horses and Ponies; Barbara Woodhouse Goes to Beverly Hills; Barbara Woodhouse's Problem Dogs. Has written many books incl: Talking to Animals (her autobiography and 17th book): Almost Human; No Bad Dogs; A-Z of Dogs and Puppies; Just Barbara; Barbara Woodhouse's Book of Ponies. Education: Headington School for Girls. m Dr Michael Woodhouse, 2 d Pamela, Judith, 1 s Patrick. Address: Rickmansworth, Herts. Starsign: Taurus.

WOODS, Peter
Freelance TV presenter
b 7.11.30 Essex. Started on local newspapers incl The Yorkshire Post before military service in the Royal Horse Guards in which he was commissioned. Spent 10 years in Fleet Street, first on the Daily Mail, then as special correspondent on the Daily Mirror. Was parachuted into Suez as a reporter for an exclusive on the 1956 attack. Joined BBC in 1959 as a reporter but left in 1963 to join ITN as their first American correspondent, based in New York. Rejoined BBC in 1967 as foreign correspondent. Also wrote for and presented Newsroom on BBC 2. Subsequently became a newsreader. Went freelance 1981. Since presented science programmes for BBC and

presenter of Newswatch UK for Central TV. Also voice-over on commercials. Education: Hull Grammar School; Imperial Services College, Windsor. m (1st) Kathleen (dis), (2nd) Esma, 1 d Susan, 1 s Guy (both by 1st m). Address: Montacute, Somerset. Starsign: Scorpio. Hobby: golf. Person he would most like to meet (and perhaps have a round of golf with): 'Jack Nicklaus, for whom I have a great admiration.'

WOODWARD, Edward OBE
Actor b 1.6.30 Croydon. Wanted to be a journalist but started work in a sanitary engineer's office. Trained at RADA, then years in rep before London debut in Where There's A Will. Other stage productions incl: Rattle of a Simple Man; A Tale of Two Cities; High Spirits (in America); The Wolf; Male of the Species; On Approval; The Dark Horse. Many radio plays. Films incl: Becket; File on the Golden Goose; A Fine and Private Place; Callan; Hunted; Young Winston; Wicker Man; Breaker Morant; Who Dares Wins. Over 500 TV appearances, incl: Emergency – Ward 10; Skyport; Sword of Honour; Au Pair Swedish Style; Entertaining Mr Sloane; Murders in the Rue Morgue; Night of Talavera; Julius Caesar; The Listener; Callan; Saturday, Sunday, Monday; The Bass Player and the Blonde; Trial of Lady Chatterley's Lover; Blunt

Instrument; Winston Churchill The Wilderness Years. Records (10 LPs and three gold discs) incl: Grains of Sand; This Man Alone; Love is the Key. Winner of eight national and international acting awards. Education: Eccleston Road and Sydenham Road Scools, Croydon; Elmwood School, Wallingford; Kingston Commercial School.
m actress Venetia, 1 d Sarah, 2 s Timothy, Peter. Address: c/o Eric Glass Ltd, London W1. Starsign: Gemini. Hobbies: collecting swords, gem polishing. Person he would most like to meet: 'Leonard Bernstein – a musician and composer of genius and such great passion.'

WOOLLARD, William
Presenter/producer b 20.8.39 London. Joined RAF after graduating from Oxford and was a fighter pilot based in Canada and America. Then worked for an oil company which took him all over the world. Taught the Dayaks and Chinese to play rugby and learnt Arabic at the Foreign Office language school. Back in England he worked in social science until he went to the BBC producing, directing and eventually presenting films for Tomorrow's World. Other TV incl: The Risk Business; The Secret War; The History of the Fighter; The History of Flight; Cross Channel; Top Gear; Connections; Policing the Eighties; 2001 and All

That. Education: grammar school; Oxford University; Tavistock Institute; Middle East Centre for Arabic Studies. m Isobel, 1 d Jessica, 2 s Alexander, Julian. Address: c/o Jon Roseman Assocs, London W1. Starsign: Leo. Hobbies: sailing, golf, riding.

WORSNIP, Glyn
Reporter b 2.9.38 Highnam, Gloucestershire. Trained as actor in rep and as writer/journalist in theatre, radio and TV. Photographic Intelligence Officer in RAF 1956-58. Stage incl: everything from farce with Frankie Howerd to Pirandello with Albert Finney and from revue to the Royal Shakespeare Company, incl: roles in London West End musicals Our Man Crichton; Oliver!; Canterbury Tales. TV incl: That's Life 1974-78; Nationwide (since 1976); Omnibus; Arena; Help Yourself; Joint Account. Education: Highnam C of E; Monmouth School; St John's College, Oxford (BA Hons English). m Jo Glanville, 1 d Elinor. Address: c/o Jeanne Griffiths Agency, London W1. Starsign: Virgo. Hobbies: walking, gardening, watching rugby and cricket. Person he would most like to meet: 'The perfect interviewee.'

WRIGHT, Billy CBE
Controller of Sport b 6.2.24 Ironbridge, Salop. Former captain of England football

team. Joined Wolverhampton Wanderers in 1938 when he was 14, leaving in 1959 when he retired. During those 21 years he made 472 first team appearances, and won three Division One Championship medals and a FA Cup Winners medal (against Leicester in 1949). Won his first International Cap against Belgium at Wembley in 1946 and went on to play for England 105 times. He captained England 90 times and when he retired he had the distinction of never having been booked. Awarded the CBE in 1959 for his services to football and became the first professional footballer to be made an honorary member of the Football Association. He joined the FA after his retirement as a coach and became England Youth Team manager and boss of the Under-21 side. He was appointed Manager of Arsenal FC in 1962, a position he held until 1966 when he joined ATV as sports producer and progressed to become Head of Sport and Outside Broadcasts until 1981 when he was made Sports Controller for both East and West Midlands. Education: Madeley Secondary Modern School, Salop. m Joy Beverley (of the Beverley Sisters), 2 d Vicky, Babette. Address: c/o Central TV, Birmingham. Starsign: Aquarius. Hobbies: golf, tennis, cricket, music. Person he would most like to meet: 'Perry Como – I've

been a fan of his for many years.'

WRIGHT, Jenny Lee
Actress b London. Left school at 16 to train with the Ballet Rambert. By 17 she was touring the world with a French cabaret group. On return to Britain joined Lionel Blair's group of dancers. She has played stooge to many comedians incl: Morecambe and Wise, Jimmy Tarbuck, Benny Hill, Frankie Howerd, Mike and Bernie Winters and Les Dawson. Other TV incl: The Protectors; The Golden Shot; Paul Temple; Public Eye; General Hospital; Beryl's Lot; The Generation Game; The Masterspy (in which she plays Miss Moneypacker); Search for a Star. Films incl: Husbands; The Triple Echo; The Revenge of Dr Death. Address: c/o Peter Charlesworth, London SW7. Hobbies: water-skiing, driving, antique hunting.

WYATT, Richard
Presenter b 25.7.49 Weston-super-Mare. Newspaper and radio

experience before joining HTV. Presenter weekly entertainment programme What's On. Also Country Crafts documentaries The Thatcher; Withies and Weavers; Forest of Dean Miners. Other TV incl: presenter HTV's programme for unemployed youngsters Jobline; I Think We'll Call Him Georgie Fame; The First Robin Cousins (Royal Television Society award); Bristol, Balloon City. Also presents HTV West's annual drama festival awards and the occasional disco show, plus the networked magazine programme Here Today. Education: 'still continuing' he says. Address: c/o HTV, Bristol. Starsign: Leo. Hobbies: people, music. People he would most like to meet: 'Bette Midler, and anyone who can get me a job in breakfast TV.'

WYATT, Tessa
Actress b 23.4.48 Woking, Surrey. Studied ballet and appeared in rep in school holidays. Rep at Cheltenham, Leatherhead, Bromley. TV debut at 14 in a Mr Pastry series. Stage incl: Minor Murder; The Philadelphia Story; The Crucible. Films: Wedding Night; I Think You'll Die Young Man; Spy Story; but mainly TV incl: The Tempest; The Black Tulip; Z Cars; Dixon of Dock Green; Sanctuary; Out of the Unknown; The Main Chance; Love Story; The Goodies; Within These Walls; Seaside Special; Celebrity Squares;

Robin's Nest. Education: Elmhurst Ballet School, Camberley. m disc jockey Tony Blackburn (dis), 2 s Simon (by 1st m), James (by actor Richard O'Sullivan). Address: c/o Miller Management, Teddington, Middx. Starsign: Taurus. Person she would most like to meet: 'Dame Margot Fonteyn, because she is incredible!'

WYMAN, Jane

Actress b 4.1.14 St Joseph, Missouri. Formerly married to President Reagan when he was Governor of California. First appeared on the stage when she was eight. Singing and dancing lessons, two unsuccessful trips to Hollywood and a short career as a blues singer before she started getting parts in the film city. Her break came in 1936 in My Man Godfrey. Later films incl: The Lost Weekend; Night and Day; Magic Town; The Yearling; Johnny Belinda (1948 Academy Award as best actress); Three Guys Named Mike; How to Commit Marriage. Retired in 1962 but has been persuaded out of retirement to appear as the formidable matriarch in TV's Falcon Crest. Education: Noyes Grammar School, St Joseph; Los Angeles High School. m (1st) Myron Futterman (dis), (2nd) Ronald Reagan (dis), (3rd) Fred Karger (dis), (4th) remarried Fred Karger (dis), 1 d Maureen, 1 s Michael (both from 2nd m). Starsign: Capricorn. Hobbies:

painting, sketching, interior decorating, designing.

WYNDHAM, Rene

Reporter/singer/ songwriter b 20.7.48 London. Joined the TSW news team in Feb 1982. Worked as a freelance reporter for BBC Radio Bristol for five years before moving to Plymouth in April 1979 to join BBC South West. Has also contributed to BBC Radios 2, 3 and 4 and for a short while was a researcher for Nationwide. Covered several foreign assignments (incl documentaries at Hanover and Bordeaux), worked for Network Africa in Rwanda and in 1981 spent four months working for French radio and TV in Rennes. A semi-professional singer/songwriter (she sings in nine languages but writes in English), she completed a 14-concert tour of Kenya, Mauritius, Madagascar, Djibuti and Tanzania in 1980 for the French Cultural Centre and Alliance Française. And in Jan 1982, prior to joining TSW, she gave concerts in Hong Kong and China. Education: Camden School for Girls; Exeter University (BA General Arts French, German and Philosophy, BA Hons degree in French, MA in French); Bristol University (postgraduate diploma in Radio, Film and Television). Address: c/o TSW, Plymouth. Starsign: Cancer. Hobbies: singing, song-writing, travel, languages, all-year-round swimming, yoga, modern dance, rough walking,

graphology, silvercraft. Person she would most like to meet: 'Miles Kington – to share in his humour, music and love of French.'

WYNTER, Mark

Actor b 29.1.43 Woking, Surrey. Former choirboy (at Downham, Kent) who sang in Canterbury Cathedral and Royal Albert Hall. After a variety of jobs became one of Britain's best known and highest paid singing stars with such hits as Image of a Girl; Venus in Blue Jeans and Go Away, Little Girl. Singing engagements took him seven times around the world, but he now concentrates on acting with leading rep companies and in London's West End (Conduct Unbecoming; Phil the Fluter; Charley's Aunt; On the 20th Century). Stage also incl: Side By Side By Sondheim (Britain and Canada). Films incl: The Haunted House of Horror; Red; Superman; The Jealous Mirror. Radio incl: It's Mark Time. TV incl: Call In On Wynter; Tale of Two Rivers; According to Dora; Tribute to Terence Rattigan; The Cedar Tree; Sally Ann; Once Upon A Time. Education: Forest Hills Comprehensive. Address: c/o Talent Artists Ltd, London W1. Starsign: Aquarius. Hobbies: squash, swimming, reading, theatre, running, cycling. Person he would most like to have met: 'Mark Twain, because his book gave me my first taste for adventure, and because he was a great raconteur.'

Y

YATES, Alastair
TV presenter/reporter
b 3.9.52 Burton-upon-Trent,
Staffs. Was with BBC local
radio before switching to
BBC Midlands TV where he
was newsreader and
presenter of Midlands Today
and Eureka. Joined
Grampian TV 1981 as
reporter/presenter of North
Tonight. Education: Manor
House Preparatory School,
Ashby-de-la-Zouch;
Burton-upon-Trent Grammar
School. m Penny,
1 s James. Address: c/o
Grampian TV, Aberdeen.
Starsign: Virgo. Hobbies:
gardening, horse-riding, golf.
Person he would most like to
meet: 'The person who
returns the world to its former
peace.'

YARWOOD, Mike OBE
Impressionist b 14.6.41
Stockport, Cheshire. Started
as entertainer by entering a
pub talent contest. Appeared
in pubs and clubs at night
while still a traveller. Warm-up
for Comedy Bandbox led to
engagements throughout the
country, the London
Palladium, Royal Variety
Performances and TV incl:
Will the Real Mike Yarwood
Stand Up?; Look – Mike
Yarwood; The Best of Mike
Yarwood; Mike Yarwood in
Persons; two Christmas
shows. Book: And This Is Me
(autobiography). Education:
secondary modern school.
m ex-dancer Sandra
Burville, 2 d Charlotte,
Clare. Address: c/o Derek
Block Artistes Agency,
London W1. Starsign:
Gemini. Hobby: football.
Person he would most like to
meet: 'Sir Laurence Olivier – I
greatly admire his dedication
and talent.'

YATES, Marjorie
Actress b 13.4.41
Birmingham. Trained at
Guildhall School of Music of
Drama then rep at Liverpool.
London stage incl: Royal
Court Theatre (Sea Anchor;
Small Change; Inadmissible
Evidence) and the National
Theatre (incl: A Fair Quarrel;
As You Like It). TV incl: Kisses
at Fifty; Connie; All Day on the

Sands; Lovely Day
Tomorrow; Marya; Couples;
The Sweeney. Films incl:
Black Panther. State school
education. m London
University official and local
councillor Michael Freeman,
1 d Polly, 1 s Carl. Address:
c/o Boyack and Conway,
London W1. Starsign: Aries.
Hobbies: birdwatching,
tennis. Person she would
most like to meet again: 'Jack
Nicholson, as I was
speechless the first time.'

YATES, Pauline
Actress b 16th June
Liverpool. No academic
training for the stage; went to
Oldham Rep straight from
school. Also experience at
Liverpool Rep but has
worked mainly on TV, incl:
Hancock; The Second
Interview; Harriet's Back in
Town; Nightingale's Boys;
Going, Going, Gone Free;
Rooms; My Honourable Mrs;
Crown Court; The Fall and
Rise of Reginald Perrin;
England's Green and
Pleasant Land; Keep It in the
Family. Film: The Four
Feathers. Education:
Childwall Valley High School
for Girls, Liverpool.
m actor/writer Donald
Churchill, 2 d Jemma, Polly.
Address: c/o Kate Feast
Management, London NW1.
Starsign: Gemini. Hobbies:
theatre, tapestry. Person she
would most like to meet:
'Don't like meeting new
people – like old friends.'

YIP, David
Actor b 4.6.51 Liverpool.

Trained at the E15 Acting
School and had rep
experience at Nottingham,
Chichester, Glasgow
Citizens' Theatre, and with
the Young Vic, Royal
Shakespeare Company,
Stomu Yamashta's Red
Buddha Theatre (London and
Europe) and the Unicorn
Theatre. Has come to the fore
on TV through his role in The
Chinese Detective, but he is
no stranger to TV, his credits
incl: Cuckoo Waltz; 3-2-1; It
Ain't Half Hot Mum; Going to
Work; Mystery of the
Disappearing Schoolgirls;
Doctor Who; Chelsea
Murders; Spies; Whodunnit;
Savages; Quatermass. Also
wrote and presented
documentary about the
Chinese community in
Liverpool for ATV's Here and
Now programme. Education:
Mount Pleasant Primary
School and Toxteth High
School, Liverpool. Address:
c/o Fraser and Dunlop,
London W1. Starsign:
Gemini. Hobbies: football,
tennis, swimming, reading,
writing. Person he would
most like to meet: 'Samuel
Becket, because his plays
helped me into the theatre.'

YORK, Susannah
Actress b 9.1.42 London.
Trained for the stage at RADA
where she was the most
promising actress in 1958.
After a spell at Worthing rep,
made her TV debut in
Armchair Theatre 1959. A
very experienced stage, film
and TV actress. Theatre incl:
Wings of a Dove; Mrs

Warren's Profession; A
Singular Man; A Cheap
Bunch of Nice Flowers; Man
and Superman; The
Importance of Being Earnest;
The Great Ban; The Maids;
Private Lives; Peter Pan
(1979-80); Singular Life of
Albert Nobbs; Appearances;
Hedda Gabler. Her films incl:
Tunes of Glory; There Was a
Crooked Man; Greengage
Summer; Freud; Tom Jones;
The Seventh Dawn; Scene
Nun – Act One; Sands of the
Kalahari; Scruggs;
Kaleidoscope; A Man For All
Seasons; Sebastian; The
Killing of Sister George;
Duffy; Oh What a Lovely War;
The Battle of Britain; Lock Up
Your Daughters; They Shoot
Horses, Don't They?; Country
Dance; Jane Eyre; Zee and
Co; Happy Birthday, Wanda
June; Images; The Maids;
Gold; Conduct Unbecoming;
That Lucky Touch; Skyriders;
Eliza Fraser; Silent Partner;
The Shout; Superman I and II;
Spectre; Falling in Love; The
Awakening; Alice in
Wonderland; Loophole. Her
TV appearances incl: The
Crucible; The Creditors; La
Grande Breteche; Fallen
Angels; Prince Regent;
Second Chance; We'll Meet
Again. Books: In Search of
Unicorns; Lark's Castle.
Education: Scotland State
School; Marr College, Troon;
English private school.
1 d Sasha, 1 s Orlando.
Address: c/o ICM, London
W1. Starsign: Capricorn.
Hobbies: living –
countryside, travelling,
books, horses, films, writing,

paintings. People she would most like to have met: Spencer Tracy and Albert Schweitzer.

YOUENS, Bernard
Actor b 28.12.14 Hove, Sussex. Acting training in fit-ups, reps and tours. Stan Ogden in Coronation Street since 1963. Education: Connaught Road School, Hove; Rutherford College, Newcastle-upon-Tyne.
m Edna, 2 d Ann, Diana, 3 s Brian, Peter, Michael. Address: c/o Granada TV, Manchester. Starsign: Capricorn. Hobbies: golf, bridge. Person he would most like to meet: 'Marlene Dietrich, my schoolboy crush.'

YOUNG, David
TV presenter specialising in architectural subjects
b 30.9.32 Yeovil, Somerset. Contributes weekly column to Yeovil Mail and regular weekly contributor to Westward Diary as Roving Architect visiting both modern and old buildings. Other TV incl: An Englishman's Home; series for About Britain on the architecture of the South Western Counties; presenter of Discovery series for BBC on architecture, archeology and past in SW England. Former chairman, Somerset County Council Education Committee; Associate Royal Institute of British Architects; member Society of Architectural Illustrators; Associate Chartered Institute of Arbitrators; Fellow of the Royal Society of Arts. Books: Cobblestones, Cottages and Castles; Devon villages section of AA Book of English Villages. Education: Yeovil Grammar School; Royal West of England School of Architecture, Bristol.
m Margot, 2 d Amanda, Belinda, 1 s Jeremy. Address: Yeovil, Somerset. Starsign: Libra. Hobby: collecting coins. Person he would most like to have met: 'Leonardo da Vinci, because he was the greatest designer of all time.'

Z

ZUBER, Marc
Actor b 5.5.44 Lucknow,
India, but brought up in
England. Trained at Webber
Douglas Academy of
Dramatic Art followed by
seasons at Chester, Bolton,
Richmond and The Shaw
Theatre in London and the
Royal Shakespeare
Company where he
appeared in Destiny; King
Lear; Troilus and Cressida.
His films incl: The Wind and
the Lion; Black and White in
Colour (which won an Oscar
as best foreign language film
1977); A Private Enterprise;
Penny Gold; Satanic Rites of
Dracula; Sweeney 2; The Sea
Wolves. His many TV credits
incl: The Black Pool; Hijack to
Mogadishu; Mr Singh My
Heart's Delight; The Pump;
Quiller; Blake's Seven;
Hadleigh; The Regiment;
Crown Court; A Little
Princess; Changes;
Accident; Something's
Wrong; Orson Welles' Great
Mysteries; Destiny; Softly,
Softly; The Sweeney; Angels;
Buccaneers; Enigma Files;
and most recently, The
Merchant of Venice and the
title role in Bloomfield.
Address: c/o Michael Ladkin
Personal Management Ltd,
London WC2. Starsign:
Taurus. Hobbies: sports,
reading. Person he would
most like to meet: Marlon
Brando.

ZAVARONI, Lena
Entertainer b 4.11.63 Isle of
Bute. Discovered singing
with her parents in a
Rothesay pub, but achieved
instant stardom as five times
Opportunity Knocks winner,
singing Ma, He's Making
Eyes At Me! Since toured the
world, appeared in a Royal
Variety Performance and
starred with her friend Bonny
Langford in their own TV
show, Lena and Bonny.
Topped the bill at the London
Palladium for one week in
October 1978 and recorded
her first BBC series, Lena
Zavaroni and Her Music
(screened May/June 1979).
Has now starred in her own
BBC TV series for three
consecutive years, and
recorded another series in
spring 1982. Education: local
school in Rothesay; Italia
Conti Stage School. Address:
c/o Dorothy Solomon,
London SW7. Starsign:
Scorpio. Hobbies: reading,
tennis. Person she would
most like to meet: Robert
Redford.